African American Children

A Self-Empowerment Approach to Modifying Behavior Problems and Preventing Academic Failure

Carolyn M. Tucker

University of Florida

Allyn and Bacon

Boston ▪ London ▪ Toronto ▪ Sydney ▪ Tokyo ▪ Singapore

Series Editorial Assistant: Susan Hutchinson
Editorial-Production Service: Omegatype Typography, Inc.
Manufacturing Buyer: Suzanne Lareau

Copyright © 1999 by Allyn & Bacon
A Viacom Company
160 Gould Street
Needham Heights, MA 02494

Internet: www.abacon.com

Library of Congress Cataloging-in-Publication Data

Tucker, Carolyn M.
    African American children : a self-empowerment approach to modifying
behavior problems and preventing academic failure / Carolyn M. Tucker.
        p.   cm.
    Includes bibliographical references and index.
    ISBN 0-205-29290-9
    1. Afro-American children—Education.   2. Behavior modification—
United States.   3. School failure—United States—Prevention.
I. Title.
LC2731.T83   1999
371.39′3–dc21   98-8571
                                                                           CIP

Printed in the United States of America
10   9   8   7   6   5   4   3   2   1   02   01   00   99   98

This book is dedicated to the memory of my father, Thomas Lee Tucker, who loved me unconditionally, taught me how to love, made me believe that I can fly, and lived long enough to sustain me through the writing of the last line of this book. For all of these gifts, I shall forever be grateful to him and will hold him close in my heart.

CONTENTS

PREFACE

There is increasing concern across the nation among individuals of all social classes and ethnic groups about the academic failure and behavior problems that occur among many African American children. This concern is reflective of the growing realization that when African American children fail, all other children in their classrooms and all Americans are negatively impacted. Efforts to reduce and prevent academic failure and behavior problems of African American children have not been very effective. This is likely because these efforts have been based on experiences and research with European American children and associated theories that are not culturally sensitive.

The major purpose of this book is to offer a new, culture-sensitive, socioeconomic-sensitive, research-based, practical approach to addressing academic and behavior problems of African American children. This approach is anchored in self-empowerment theory, which suggests that African American children must be taught to modify their own academic failure and behavior problems through self-motivation, self-control, self-praise, engagement in success behaviors, and development of adaptive skills (communication, socialization, and daily living skills) for academic and social success. This theory realizes that multiple environmental, social, economic, family, and other factors influence the academic and social behaviors of African American children. Yet, it also realizes that most of these factors are not likely to change in the school lifetime of a child.

Thus, a second purpose of this book is to clearly set forth specific behaviors, skills, and strategies that African American children can be taught to help themselves achieve academic and social success. These interventions are based on research with African American children and culture-sensitive theories that have relevance for understanding the behavior and achievement of these children. This research and these theories are reviewed in this book.

Third, this book was written to offer culture-sensitive ways of defining and assessing behavioral and academic problems, as such problems are often to some degree in the eye of the beholder. Additionally, culturally sensitive strategies for teaching and counseling African American children are presented. The importance of recognizing the individual and group differences among African American children in the teaching and learning process is emphasized.

Fourth, this book was written to reinforce the view that culturally sensitive education for African American children not only means understanding and accommodating their learning preferences, which often include preferences for oral learning, active learning, and spontaneous interactions in the classroom. It also means teaching African American children to master and appreciate learning that is passive, boring, structured, and transferred in written form. Indeed, it recognizes that African American children must be taught to write the songs they want to sing, to wait their turn to sing them well, and to praise themselves for the writing and the singing.

A major emphasis in this book is on teaching African American children to teach and manage themselves and expecting that they can and will do so. The goal of such teaching and expectations is the self-empowerment of these children for academic and social success, which in turn will positively impact all children and all Americans.

The achievement of academic and social success for African American children requires partnership efforts, commitment, and heart. It also requires reminding ourselves each day that African American children are like all children—they too are different and special.

Indeed, self-empowerment of African American children is not easy. However, "anything worth doing ain't easy!"

Acknowledgments

Much of the research in this book was conducted by graduate and undergraduate students at the University of Florida who constitute the Academic Achievement and Adaptive Functioning Research Team that I direct. The research methods and strategies and the self-empowerment theory on which these interventions are based were developed and tested in the Research-Based Model Partnership Education Program, which these students helped to develop and conduct. For the work and support of these students and the work and support of the teachers and community leaders who also help conduct the Model Program, I shall forever be grateful.

Special thanks to Cynthia Mingo and Priscilla Strickland for their comments in this book regarding what African American children need from their parents and teachers for academic success. I also thank the many parents and children who have been involved with the Model Program and, thus, have helped formulate my views about the need to self-empower African American children for academic and social success.

Sincere appreciation is extended to the following supporters of my research that has culminated in the ideas expressed in this book: the Jessie Ball duPont Fund (Sherry Magill, Executive Director); the Hitachi Foundation (Julie Banzhaf and Laurie Regelbrugge, Vice Presidents); Burger King (Chuck Gatton, owner); the *Gainesville Sun* (John Fitzwater, Editor); Edutek: Education Solutions, Inc. (Harry Slaughter, President); McGurn Investment Company (Kenneth McGurn, President); First Union Bank (C. B. Daniel and Sam Goforth, Presidents); Florida legislators (Bob Casey, Cynthia Chestnut, and George Kirkpatrick); Mt. Olive AME Church; the University of Florida (John Lombardi); and Florida's Department of Education (Frank Brogan, Commissioner of Education).

It is especially difficult to find the words to express my deep and sincere appreciation for the assistance provided by Jordan Vosmik in the preparation of this book. Her typing, editing, and consultation were invaluable, and her emotional support and friendship will forever be treasured. I also thank Ces Bibby, my secretary and friend, for her typing assistance in the final days of book preparation. Thank you to Vikki T. Gaskin-Butler, Texas A&M University; Sharon-ann Gopaul-McNicol, Howard University; and Robin Young Porter, Young-Rivers Associates in Louisville, Kentucky, for their helpful reviews.

To my husband, Theotis Callaway, I extend a warm and loving thank-you from the bottom of my heart for his steady support and encouragement throughout every phase of writing this book. To my cherished mother, Arethea Tucker, my godmother, Rena Brown, and my special auntie, Shirley Hardy, I also extend my deep appreciation for their interest in my academic work and for their unconditional love and support. I am also thankful to Reverend Thelma Shaw Young and Karen Holbrook for being sources of inspiration for my efforts to make positive differences in the lives of others, and to Mary and William Callaway for supporting these efforts.

Last but not least, I must thank my grandfather and hero, Roy Tucker, for inspiring me to strive for excellence and teaching me that "anything worth doing ain't easy."

1

Behavior Problems and Academic Failure by African American Children

A Topic in Need of Cautious Discussion

Any discussion of behavior problems and academic failure by African American children must be undertaken with caution to avoid promotion of the view that African American children simply do not measure up to the standards of behavior and academic performance that all Americans accept and value. It is important to realize that there are differences of opinion regarding what qualifies as a behavior problem or academic failure and regarding the process for assigning these often stigmatizing labels. The fact that these labels are often used in evaluations of African American children does not necessarily mean that they are valid descriptors.

Definition of Behavior Problems

Common Mistakes

Several common mistakes are often made by teachers, counselors, psychologists, and others when defining or discussing behavior problems among African American children. Some of these mistakes are as follows:

1. We accept the data and research results indicating that African American children behave worse than European American children on almost every academic and behavioral measure ever constructed without acknowledging or realizing that most of this research was conducted by European Americans using measures and theories based on research with European Americans.

2. We often quickly label many African American children as behavior problem children simply because they act differently than their European American peers in certain situations. The African American children assigned this label often experience the negative expectations and attention that come with it, internalize these experiences, and then act in accordance with the assigned label.

3. For ease of communication, we make statements about an African American child's behavior that unintentionally create a long-term negative image of the child—statements such as "She is a major behavior problem." Indeed, for the sake of convenience, we sometimes do not cautiously separate the child from the behavior so as to allow positive feelings and support for the child as well as corrective actions to modify problematic behavior.

4. We fail to realize that the term *behavior problem* does not have a universal meaning; its meaning varies and often reflects more the views of the person using the term than the behavior that is being described (Wicks-Nelson & Israel, 1997). Thus, labeling African American children as behavior problem children may be a reflection of the prejudices against and stereotypes of African American children held by those using the term.

5. We allow the term *behavior problem* to elicit a common set of negative images, which may or may not be descriptive of a particular child. Consequently, two different African American children may engage in very different behaviors and have their behaviors singularly described as behavior problems. When this occurs, the same behavior problem interventions tend to be used for both children, which turn out to be inappropriate for at least one of them.

A Culturally Sensitive Definition

Behavior problems among children are commonly called externalizing behaviors, conduct disorders, or delinquent behavior (Mason, Cauce, Gonzales, & Hiraga, 1994). These behaviors typically include fighting, hitting, stealing, lying, cheating, using drugs, arguing with teachers, and breaking classroom rules. Common disruptive behaviors in the classroom include out-of-chair behavior without permission, partially-out-of-chair behavior without permission, touching others' property without permission, vocalization, playing, orienting away from task or subject matter, noise other than vocalization, and aggressive behavior (O'Leary, Kaufman, Kass, & Drabman, 1970).

There is increasing popularity of the view that when defining or identifying behavior problems among a group of children, it is important to consider the influence of culture on the definition of and perception of behaviors. For example, when African American teen males aggressively argue with each other in an intimidating manner, teachers who do not understand African American culture may label their behavior as fighting when actually the teens are verbally "woofing" or relieving tension in lieu of fighting. Woofing is a common practice among African American teens. Without a rule against it and without an understanding of this behavior, it would be labeled fighting and invalidly considered a behavior problem.

A culturally sensitive definition of the term *behavior problem* is needed. To be culturally sensitive means having an awareness of differences among various cultures, refusing to consider any culture as superior to another, and refusing to characterize any differences among cultures as deficits based on the norms of the majority culture or some other unjustly considered superior culture.

It is indeed difficult to provide a culturally sensitive definition or description of the term *behavior problem* in light of the diverse use and often unintentional misuse of the term. Yet, it is important to define this term or label in a way that acknowledges the fact that behavior problems are, at least to some degree, defined differently by various cultural groups and that the label may or may not be appropriate depending on the setting in which the behavior occurs.

One culturally sensitive definition of the term *behavior problem* for consideration is as follows: A behavior problem is an action or inaction of an individual that (1) is inconsistent with the specified, understood, and culturally accepted behavioral rules for the setting in which the action or inaction occurred, and (2) has potentially negative consequences for the individual and/or others.

This definition recognizes the fact that behaviors considered problematic in one setting may not be problematic in other settings. For example, tapping one's feet and hands while reading, which is not unusual among African American children, is usually viewed as problematic in the classroom but is often not considered problematic in home settings.

The preceding definition also recognizes that the rules to which behaviors should ideally adhere must be specified and accepted by the cultural groups impacted by these rules. For example, school rules ideally should be known and accepted by African American children, their parents, and their teachers in order for behaviors inconsistent with these rules to be labeled behavior problems. Indeed, the rules may not be a part of the child's or child's parents' native culture; however, once the rules are accepted by them as a condition of the child's school attendance, behaviors inconsistent with these rules while at school can appropriately be labeled behavior problems.

It is the responsibility of principals, teachers, and parents or primary caregivers to be sure that children and their parents know and accept the school rules. This acceptance can be facilitated by specifying the immediate and future consequences for the child, classmates, and others of behaviors inconsistent with the school rules.

Prevalence of Behavior Problems

A paucity of research on the prevalence of behavior problems exists in any culture. This is perhaps because of the cultural differences in views regarding what are considered to be behavior problems. A behavior that is accepted or reinforced in one mini-culture may be disapproved of or punished in another. In the United States with its many different mini-cultures, children often are expected to adjust to cultural demands that are significantly different from those of their own mini-culture. These children should be expected to encounter greater behavior problems (Erickson, 1992). Because schools in the United States reflect the behavioral norms and standards of the majority European American culture, it is likely that children from nonmajority cultures, such as African American children, will have more behavior problems than European American children.

It is estimated from survey data that from one-third to one-half of all child referrals from parents and teachers concern the problems usually defined as behavior problems or conduct-disorder behaviors (Faulstitch, Moore, Roberts, & Collier, 1988). A significant percentage of referrals for school-age African American children are made for behavioral and academic problems, particularly hyperactivity (Allen & Majidi-Ahi, 1989). Referrals for behavior problems among African American preadolescents and adolescents are most commonly for problems such as defiance of authority, truancy, destruction of property, fighting, theft, and sexual aggression. The diagnoses commonly given these preadolescents and adolescents are adjustment reaction, conduct disorder, or personality disorder (Sykes, 1987). It has also been reported that, when compared to other cultural groups, African American youth are disproportionately represented among perpetrators and victims of aggressive or violent crimes (Hacker, 1992; Rosenberg & Mercy, 1991).

It appears that there is an inverse association between the prevalence of behavioral problems and income. It has been found that African American children from low-income families evidence more behavior problems than other African American children; furthermore, this was the case whether the children in the study lived with one parent or two parents (Patterson, Kupersmidt, & Vaden, 1990).

From the existing research, it cannot be concluded that the rate of behavior problems is higher among African American children than among European American children as some studies suggest (Gillum, Gomes-Marin, & Prineas, 1984). In fact, Achenbach and Edelbrock (1981) found in their normative sample for the Child Behavior Checklist that of 119 items analyzed for demographic differences, only five showed significant racial differences and these differences were small. It is indeed possible that the higher prevalence of behavior problems in any areas among African Americans as compared to European Americans is associated with the comparative lower income of African Americans rather than their ethnicity.

Given the paucity of research on the behavior problems of African American children and the limited attention to this group, it is senseless to invest a lot of time and energy on whether or not these youth are diagnosed as having more behavior problems than their European American peers. Simply comparing these two groups of children and validly or invalidly finding that African American children have more behavior problems contributes little to our understanding of behavior problems among African American youth and gives little or no insight as to what can be done to modify and prevent the occurrence of these problems.

Reasons for Focusing on Behavior Problems

The Paucity of Needed Research

Teachers across the United States are eager for information and intervention strategies for reducing behavior problems and increasing success behaviors among African American children. Whether this eagerness is a reflection of the teachers' general concern for African American students or a reflection of their desire to make their teaching jobs easier, the interventions and information that they desire will likely result in positive learning experiences for African American students. Yet, there is little systematic research with African American students that facilitates understanding of their behavior and from which interventions can be developed for reducing their behavior problems and for motivating and teaching them success behaviors (Hale-Benson, 1986). Without such research we shall continue to see problems that negatively impact the school life and learning of African American children and that negatively impact the quality and quantity of teaching that occurs in their classroom.

Based on interviews with African American school teachers ($N = 13$) in a pilot study by Tucker, Herman, Pedersen, and Vogle (in progress), the most common behavior problems in the classroom reported by the elementary school teachers ($n = 5$) and the percentage of the elementary school teachers reporting each problem are as follows: inattentive behavior and associated failure to follow instructions (29.4%), inappropriate talking and horseplay (23.5%), and talking back to teachers in a disrespectful way (11.8%). The most common behavior problems in the classroom reported by the high school teachers ($n = 8$) and the percentage of high school teachers reporting each problem are as follows: talking back to teachers in a disrespectful way, including an argumentative way (50%), and inappropriate talking and horseplay (37.5%). It is interesting to note that problems such as fighting and hitting, which are often associated with images of African American children with behavior problems, were not mentioned by the teachers in this pilot study. Clearly, culturally sensitive research studies with large numbers of participants are needed to validly identify behavior problems among African American children; such studies need to include African Americans as researchers.

Their "At Risk" Status

It is common knowledge that poverty is disproportionately higher among African American children than among European American children. The U.S. Congress estimated that because of poverty and minority status, 13.8 million children in the United States are at risk of developing mental health problems (Tuma, 1989). These mental health problems are often manifested as behavior problems, which are associated with a number of other problematic occurrences that impede academic and life success of African American youth. For example, behavior problems have been found to be significant predictors of teenage pregnancy among African American adolescents; furthermore, teenage pregnancy has been found to be significantly higher among African American adolescents referred for counseling than among European American adolescents referred for counseling (Kovacs, Krol, & Voti, 1994).

It has also been reported that African American children represent 70 percent of the children in out-of-home care (Tatara, 1992). Given the importance of family stability, rules, and support in the development of self-control and prosocial behaviors in children, these African American youth are at risk for behavior problems. Because many of these youth are poor, they are also at risk for using drugs and for engaging in other criminal behaviors (e.g., stealing). Without major success in preventing and modifying such problem behaviors among today's African American children, future generations of African American youth will be overrepresented in out-of-home care and will be at risk for behavior problems.

Underutilization of Professional Counseling

African American families tend not to voluntarily seek psychological or psychiatric help for their children's behavior problems. When the behavior problems of African American children become serious, these children often are referred to mental health professionals (e.g., psychologists, counselors, and psychiatrists) by their school, a juvenile court, or the social welfare system (Franklin, 1982). Many African American children with behavior problems, however, actually receive no clinical intervention at all and, at some time in their lives, end up in trouble with law enforcement. The underutilization of mental health professionals by African American children and their families likely occurs for both culture-related and economic reasons. Attention to these reasons is important; otherwise culturally sensitive interventions that have the potential for preventing or reducing behavior problems among African American children and adolescents will be useless.

Among the culture-related reasons for the tendency of African Americans not to seek help for behavior problems from mental health professionals is the tradition among African Americans to seek help for such problems from family physicians, ministers, and friends rather than from counselors, psychologists, support groups, or others with whom there has been no established relationship (Neighbors, 1985). Additionally, skepticism among African Americans about the ability of European American counseling professionals to understand and relate to the problems of their children, family, and community has been passed down from generation to generation. This skepticism is not unfounded given the differences and separation between the lives of most counseling professionals and the lives of most African Americans. These differences and separation have also reinforced the tendency among African Americans to keep family concerns in the family rather than discuss them with outsiders, especially those who do not live in the neighborhood (e.g., counselors, psychologists, teachers, etc.). Furthermore, for some African Americans, children's behavior problems are not the kinds of problems for which one should seek counseling (Hall & Tucker, 1985). Clearly, intervention strategies to modify behavior problems of African American children and the marketing of these strategies must address the cultural issues that deter utilization of counseling for these problems.

Many if not most African Americans also allow the perceived cost of counseling to keep them from seeking help for the behavior problems that their children manifest. Given the typically high cost of seeing a psychologist or counselor and given the fact that many African Americans cannot afford insurance that covers counseling for behavior problems, it is understandable that seeking counseling from a professional person or organization is usually not even explored. Therefore, attention must be devoted to developing and advertising culturally sensitive, low-cost interventions for behavior problems. This advertising must target African American families at high risk for having children with behavior problems (e.g., low-income families), and it ideally should feature African Americans with whom these target families can identify.

Definition of Academic Failure

Common Mistakes

Three noteworthy mistakes are commonly made when defining or using the term *academic failure*. One mistake is to use the term to describe school performance based on a few samples of school behavior (e.g., in-class written exams) or based on behavior at a few particular periods of time (e.g., at the middle of the semester). There are many reasons why a student may not perform well on an academic test on a particular day—perhaps the student is simply not feeling well, is hungry, has extreme test anxiety, or simply does not realize the significance of the test and does not put forth her or his best work effort to accurately answer the test questions. Consequently, students often make failing test grades that are not reflective of their academic learning or typical academic work and receive an evaluation or grade indicating academic failure.

A second mistake when using the term *academic failure* is in not specifying the academic performance, school behavior, or other variables that will result in an evaluation of academic failure and in not specifying what will result in an evaluation of academic success. It is common for African American parents and children not to have a clue as to why a failing grade or evaluation was given. The responsibility for this lack of knowledge belongs to all involved—teachers, parents, and children. It is the responsibility of the teachers to specify the criteria used for determining academic failure and academic success and to inform parents and students of these criteria and ways to meet the criteria for academic success. It is the responsibility of African American parents and their children to request this information and to engage in behaviors that will meet the criteria for academic success and avoid academic failure.

The third mistake made when using the term *academic failure* is in not clearly stating what the term means. It is important for children and their parents to be told that *academic failure* is a term for describing the children's academic performance for a specific time period in a particular area or areas, and that it does not describe their ability nor indicate what their academic performance will be in the future. Furthermore, it is important to use the term *academic failure* to describe behavior(s) or performance, not persons. It is a mistake to refer to an African American child or any child (or adult) as an academic failure; such descriptions are often internalized and thus impede self-confidence, self-motivation, and behaviors to overcome academic failure and to promote academic success.

A Culturally Sensitive Definition

Academic failure is a term that has several meanings, some of which have negative ramifications for evaluating the academic progress of African American children. Sometimes it means scoring below a certain number of points or grade on in-class, teacher-prepared, written or verbal tests, and sometimes it means scoring less than a certain score on standardized achievement tests that use norm test scores for European American children. The term *academic failure* is also sometimes used to describe the outcome of not having test scores because of being absent or because of dropping out of school. Additionally, it has often been used as a convenient label for describing lack of success in meeting the expectations of teachers regarding completion of academic work, attitudes toward learning, and classroom behaviors. Many educators view academic failure as a major cause and effect of behavior problems.

Clearly, use of the term *academic failure* by teachers is to some degree a reflection of the teachers' cultural values regarding academic performance. Given that most teachers in the United States are European Americans and are culturally different from most African Americans, it is not unusual for African American parents to disagree with teachers' views about their children's academic performance. African American parents and children often feel that European American teachers' limited understanding and negative stereotypes of African American children result in these children receiving evaluations of academic failure. Whether or not these feelings are anchored in truth, they indicate the need for a definition of academic failure that is culturally sensitive, clear, and as objective as possible. Such a definition would facilitate constructive parent–teacher communication and parent–child communication about what can be done to avoid academic failure and facilitate the academic success of African American children and other children as well.

One culturally sensitive definition of the term *academic failure* for consideration is as follows: *Academic failure* is a term for describing academic performance in which none of the culturally sensitive, multiple criteria for satisfactory school performance in a specific area or set of areas over a specified time period were met after having received understandable instructions for meeting the criteria.

Commonly used criteria for academic failure include grades, test scores, school and classroom behavior, school and classroom learning attitudes, and school attendance that are unsatisfactory. Culturally sensitive criteria are based on norms for the cultural group being evaluated and view culture-related differences in attitudes and behaviors as differences rather than deficits. Awareness of cultural norms and differences among children by their teachers is facilitated by the participation of teachers in multicultural educational training and by the efforts of teachers to nonjudgmentally get to know their students and the values, traditions, and socialization experiences that these students bring to the classroom setting.

Prevalence of Academic Failure

Given the multiple ways of defining and evaluating academic failure, it is difficult to determine its prevalence. However, there are several indications that academic failure as traditionally defined and evaluated is more prevalent among African American children than among European American children. These indications include the report that the high school completion rate for African Americans is only 81 percent, whereas it is 90 percent for European Americans (National Center for Education Statistics, 1992). It has also been reported that national dropout rates for European American students, Hispanic American students, and African American students were 4.48 percent, 9.1 percent, and 10.0 percent, respectively (National Center for Education Statistics, 1992).

In a survey of over 299 African American school counselors and psychologists, Gary, Beatty, and West (1982) found that poor academic achievement was the most frequently cited problem, followed closely by learning problems and excessive aggression. There is some indication that academic problems and academic failure are associated with low family income. National mathematics achievement data indicate that 30 percent of low-income children scored below basic levels of achievement (National Center for Education Statistics, 1992). More recently, it has been reported that youth from families with the lowest incomes are eight times more likely than youth from families with the highest incomes to discontinue school without receiving a high school certificate or diploma (National Center for Education Statistics, 1995). A comprehensive review of the data on the status of children in the United States that was published by the Children's Defense Fund in 1994 suggests that low-income children in the United States, among whom minority children are overly represented, have lifestyles and environments that are conducive to academic failure. It was also suggested in this review that the environments of low-income children are plagued with high rates of crime, racism, and violence and that the schools in these environments have inadequate resources for combating these problems and their negative impact on school performance.

Reasons for Focusing on Academic Failure

"At Risk" Status

Poverty, minority status, and residing in an urban area are conditions that characterize the lives of many African American children. These conditions increase the likelihood that students will have difficulty acquiring academic skills and making adequate school adjustment to avoid academic failure and school dropout and to experience academic success (Ascher, 1988; Winfield, 1991). Clearly, African American children are at risk of academic failure.

When African American children fail academically, all other children and all Americans are negatively impacted. The increased attention of teachers to the children who fail often takes away the attention of these teachers to facilitating the academic success of the children who are academically progressing well. School dropout that often comes with academic failure results in fewer and more poorly prepared future employees for American businesses. School dropout also results in an increased likelihood of unemployment, poverty, and crime, all of which have a negative impact on the lives of all Americans. Clearly, special attention by all to the negative educational plight of many African American children is indicated because we all are negatively impacted by this plight.

Evidence of Underachievement

It has been reported that as many as 20 percent of dropouts are gifted (National Commission on Excellence, 1983) and that poor African American students are overrepresented in this group of gifted dropouts (1992 in Ford, 1992). Research is needed to understand and modify the indicated underachievement of African American children.

There is also evidence of a decline over time in the academic achievement of African American children that often occurs around fourth grade. This seeming underachievement among African American students is especially evident among males. One of the few studies of the academic performance of African American children revealed that by fourth grade, the African American males in the study experienced a sharp decline on criterion-referenced math and reading tests and that between fourth and sixth grades the African American males in the top reading group dropped from 23 percent to 12 percent (Simmons & Grady, 1990). Furthermore, African American males are typically outscored by their female counterparts on National Assessment of Education Progress reading tests (Winfield, 1988; Winfield & Lee, 1990).

Expectation of Failure

Because of the link between poverty and academic failure and given that African American children are overly represented in the lowest socioeconomic classes, it has been concluded that these African American students should be expected to fail (Dornbusch, Ritter, & Steinberg, 1991). Such conclusions likely contribute to or exacerbate the problem of academic failure among African American students. Indeed, children and adolescents tend to live down to or up to the expectations people hold about them.

Conclusions

The meanings of the terms *behavior problems* and *academic failure* are not universal; rather, their definitions are often subjective and reflective of cultural values. Given that most teachers are culturally different from most African American families, it is understandable that some behaviors that teachers consider behavior problems are not considered as such by African American children and parents. It is also understandable that African American parents sometimes differ with teachers over the appropriate criteria for determining academic failure.

Culturally sensitive definitions and discussions of behavior problems and academic failure are needed. Such definitions and discussions at least reflect awareness of cultural differences in how these problems are viewed. Strategies for modifying these problems among African American children and for facilitating academic success among these children and adolescents are especially needed. This is because of the many indications that behavior problems and academic failure are linked to low socioeconomic status—the status level in which African Americans are overly-represented. Furthermore, existing research suggests that behavior problems and academic failure as construed by the majority culture are more prevalent among African American students than among European American students.

Future research is needed both to examine factors in behavior problems and academic failure of many African American children and to determine effective intervention strategies to modify these problems. It is important that this research avoids past mistakes such as using research measures developed and normalized on European American students and not including others who understand African American culture in the research planning. Research to simply examine differences in the occurrences of these problems among African American students versus European American students is not indicated, as results of such research typically do not provide implications for improving the academic and social success of African American students. Instead, these results simply promote or reinforce negative images and low expectations of African American students.

Given that there are culturally diverse views about behavior problems and academic failure and just concern about the use of these labels in evaluating the behavior and school performance of African American children, cautious discussions of these topics are indicated. In other words, the discussions should assume and respect the views and concerns of all involved, avoid conclusions based strictly on majority values and research, and include culturally diverse individuals. When discussing behavior problems and academic failure of African American children, African American parents and teachers ideally should be at the discussion table.

2 Eighteen Realities to Consider When Developing Interventions for Behavior and Academic Problems

There are many realities that African American families confront each day in their efforts to improve the quality of their lives and to prepare for future life success. These realities often include poverty, high crime neighborhoods, racism, and discrimination. African American families often survive these negative realities by recognizing and acknowledging them and by engaging in efforts to see them as challenges and motivators for life success rather than as obstacles and sources of hopelessness and despair.

Similarly, there are several realities that must be recognized, acknowledged, and considered when developing interventions to reduce or prevent behavior problems and academic failure by African American children. These realities have received little or no attention simply because promotion of African American children's academic and social success has not been among our nation's research or educational priorities. Following is a brief discussion of the realities that must be considered and addressed in efforts to reduce and prevent behavior problems and academic failure among African American children.

Realities

Reality 1. "Interventions must be based on culturally sensitive theories." It is appropriate and makes sense for theories about the causes of behavior problems and academic failure of African American children to provide the basis for interventions to modify these problems. In the past such interventions have typically been based on theories about the behavior problems and academic failure of European American children. Perhaps this is why it has been concluded that current theories about the achievement or underachievement of African American students are inadequate (Ford, 1994).

It is important that culturally sensitive theories provide the basis for interventions to be used with African American children (Garcia & Coll, 1990; Harrison, Wilson, Pine, & Chan, 1990; Spencer, 1990). Culturally sensitive theories are based on research with African American youth and families who are similar in values and socioeconomic status to the

African American youth and families to whom the theories are directed. These theories recognize and respect differences among various cultural groups. These theories also avoid portraying any culture as superior to any other culture, and avoid characterizing any differences among cultures as deficits on the basis of the norms of the majority culture or some other culture unjustly considered to be superior.

Culturally sensitive theories about the behavior and performance of African American youth take into consideration the diversity of this ethnic group and the social, economic, and environmental influences within and beyond their immediate families and communities that impact the behavior and performance of these youth. These theories recognize that social variables such as unemployment and job discrimination, which are disproportionately high among African Americans, have a tremendous impact on family life and on motivating children to achieve academic and social success (Boyd-Franklin, 1989). Culturally sensitive theories discourage the tendency to blame primarily African American parents in general and single parents in particular for the behavior problems and academic failure that occur among African American children.

Much of the research on underachievement and academic failure among African American children and among other nonmajority children has traditionally been anchored in cultural deficit theories. These theories basically view academic problems of African American children as due to the culture of poverty in which these youth have lived. This culture of poverty has been described as being fraught with cultural deprivation, inadequate socialization, antisocial cultural practices and behaviors, few or no male role models, crime, undisciplined home life, and so forth (Jencks, Smith, Acland, Bane, Cohen, Gintis, Heyns, & Michels, 1972; Monihan, 1965). Clearly, cultural deficit theories are inaccurate and culturally insensitive because they deny the heterogeneity of African American culture and disregard the fact that African American youth from the various African American communities and mini-cultures experience academic and social success (Ford, 1994).

A culturally sensitive theory that the present author offers for use in the development of interventions to reduce and prevent behavior problems and academic failure and facilitate social and academic success of African American children is self-empowerment theory (SET). This theory will be discussed in more detail in Chapter 3. SET postulates that academic and social success of African American children is significantly and directly influenced by several modifiable internal variables including levels of (1) self-motivation to achieve social and academic success, (2) perceived self-control over their behavior and academic success, (3) self-reinforcement for engaging in social and academic success behaviors, (4) adaptive skills (communication, socialization, and daily living skills) for life success, and (5) engagement in success behaviors. SET recognizes that multiple external factors including social, cultural, socioeconomic, political, neighborhood, physical, school, teacher, family, and parent factors also influence the academic and social performance of African American children. However, SET asserts that the influence of these variables is indirect and that these variables are difficult or impossible to modify in the school life of a child. Consequently, African Americans must be prepared through self-management attitudes, behaviors, and skills to achieve academic and social success under whatever external conditions exist.

Reality 2. "Self-empowerment for academic, social success, and economic success needs to be included among intervention goals."   Based on self-empowerment theory, prevention and modification of behavior problems and academic failure by African American children require teaching children and adolescents (1) to teach themselves through self-instruction-based learning, (2) to motivate themselves through establishing short-term and long-term goals and engaging in activities and behaviors for achieving these goals, (3) to self-manage their behaviors and feelings through the use of cognitive-behavioral strategies, (4) to praise themselves for engaging in academic and social success behaviors and, (5) to use adaptive skills and success behaviors required for classroom success, getting and keeping a job, and future economic and social success for themselves and for their family and community.

Indeed, God bless self-empowered children who have their own motivation, behavior management system, method of self-instruction, skills for success, command of success behaviors, and reinforcement strategies for academic and social success. These qualities self-empower children for life success; that is, they give children some significant control over their economic and social destinies whether or not they receive the desired support, praise, and encouragement from important others such as parents and teachers. Self-empowerment for academic, social, and economic success facilitates self-worth, self-esteem, and self-confidence as well as long-term maintenance of life success behaviors.

There has been much support for some of the different components involved in the self-empowerment of children. For example, autonomous, self-regulated learning has received attention as an important factor in academic achievement (Connell, 1991; Kanfer, 1990; Zimmerman & Martinez-Pons, 1988). Pintrich and De Groot (1990) defined autonomous, self-regulated learning as involving metacognitive planning and monitoring strategies, management and control of effort, and cognitive strategies for learning and remembering. Autonomous learning has been defined as learning that involves making personal choices about one's behavior and experiencing connectedness between one's actions and personal goals and values.

Bandura (1986) has emphasized the importance of developing competencies through self-directed experiences arranged to strengthen and generalize a sense of personal efficacy. In this type of learning, instructive aids and external assistance are reduced as students' competencies are expanded. The ultimate goal is to strengthen students' self-beliefs that they have what is needed to exercise control over their own learning, development, and behavior. Rosenbaum (1980) emphasized that in order to control one's own behavior, one must have the necessary skills and behaviors in one's own repertoire. Furthermore, it has been asserted that "a major goal of formal education should be to equip students with the intellectual tools, self-beliefs, and self-regulatory capabilities to educate themselves throughout their lifetime" (Bandura, 1993, p. 136).

Self-empowerment of African American children is particularly indicated given that many of these children and their families experience poverty, discrimination, and racism that impede goal attainment and foster a sense of powerlessness. It is reasonable that African American children in these life situations will think and believe that they cannot achieve academic and social success and, thus, they fail to do so. It is also likely that many African American children will not get the support and encouragement that they need from parents, family members, teachers, counselors, or psychologists to achieve against the many odds that they face. Consequently, interventions that facilitate self-motivation, self-control, self-instruction, self-reinforcement, and skills and behaviors for academic, social, and economic success are especially needed for use with many African American children.

Reality 3. "Interventions need to be based on Difference Model research that investigates why some African American children succeed and others do not." The research studies that have included adequate samples of African American children and European American children have typically been conducted to compare the functioning or performance of these two ethnic groups. According to Oyemade and Rosser (1980), such research adheres to the traditional Deficit Model research approach. This research approach, which was criticized by Oyemade and Rosser (1980), often identifies differences in performance between African Americans and European Americans and reports lower performance by African Americans as deficiencies, using European American middle-class standards. Such an approach incorrectly assumes that there are equal opportunities available to both groups, which typically is not the case. Results of Deficit Model research that compares African American children and European American children, which is analogous to comparing apples and oranges, often reinforce perceptions or stereotypes of African American children as being less intellectually and socially capable and competent than their European American peers.

If we are serious about modifying and preventing behavior problems and academic failure among African American children, it is clear that we need interventions based on the Difference Model research approach proposed by Oyemade and Rosser (1980). This approach advocates recognizing cultural and other significant differences when investigating the academic, cognitive, and social behavior of groups that differ culturally or socioeconomically. It supports separately examining factors in the behavior and performance of African American youth and factors in the behavior and performance of European American youth.

Indeed, because of cultural differences and associated experiences, African American youth often do not experience maximum achievement from the same experiences or influence factors that result in maximum achievement for European American youth (Tucker, Harris, Brady, & Herman, 1995). This view is supported by findings (Willig, Harnish, Hill, & Maehr, 1985) that, although motivation is an important determinant of school performance in African American children, Hispanic children, and Anglo American children, various motivational factors affect these ethnic groups differently. Furthermore, Kerckhoff and Campbell (1977) showed that the Wisconsin Model—a commonly used multivariate model for predicting educational and occupational status attainment—was significantly less powerful in explaining the educational and occupational attainment of African American children than it was in explaining the educational and occupational attainment of European American children. These researchers concluded that the attainment process is different for African Americans as compared to European Americans. This does not imply that the attainment process of one group is better than that of the other; the two processes are simply different.

The Difference Model research approach also supports focusing on African American children, their families, and their environments when conducting research to understand academic failure and behavior problems of African American youth. It is important to include in this research assessment the views of African American parents and children as to what can be done to overcome academic failure and behavior problems among African American youth. In the recent past, however, such research has been minimal; furthermore, this research has focused mostly on low-income children and their families. Indeed, there are other groups of African American families (e.g., urban middle-class African American families) that need research-based interventions to address academic failure and behavior problems of their children (Ford, 1994).

Because there are groups of African Americans who differ significantly in backgrounds, socioeconomic levels, lifestyles, values, and acculturation into the majority culture (Allen & Majidi-Ahi, 1989), it is important to study these groups separately as advocated by the Difference Model research approach. We will likely find that there are different determinants of academic and social success of, for example, urban middle-class African Americans in the North and rural low-income African Americans in the South. Clearly, academic and social success interventions for such different groups of African Americans will differ to some degree. It is important for researchers, teachers, counselors, and psychologists to identify and respect these differences.

Reality 4. "Behavior problems and academic failure are related."   Conversations with teachers about whether or not there is a relationship between behavior problems and academic failure usually suggest that the two problems often occur in pairs. In other words, children who have significant behavior problems often underachieve and make low or failing grades, and children who make low or failing grades often manifest behavior problems.

Research supports a relationship between academic failure and behavior problems among African American children. For example, a negative relationship was found for African American children (and European American children) between delinquency and school achievement; that is, as school achievement decreased, delinquency increased (Moffitt, 1993). In a study by Lochman and Sims (1981) involving African American children from low-income, single-parent families, a negative relationship was also found between aggressive behavior—a type of behavior problem—and paying attention in class—a behavior important in academic success. Furthermore, in the Lochman and Sims study, reduction in aggressive behavior through participation of the children in an anger-control intervention group was accompanied by an increase in attentiveness in class. Lochman and Sims concluded that there is a relationship between behavior problems and academic behaviors that determine academic failure or success.

We cannot conclude from the foregoing research that academic failure or low grades cause behavior problems or vice versa. However, it makes sense that African American children or any children who engage in problem behaviors are not focused on learning while so engaged and, thus, will miss learning information or concepts on which they will later be tested. It also makes sense that children who experience academic failure as assessed by their teachers may act out in response to this feedback, whether the failure assessment is fair or unjust. Furthermore, because determinations of academic failure and a behavior problem are usually influenced by culture-based and subjective judgments, it is not farfetched to think that the perceived existence of one of these problems will increase the likelihood of perceiving the existence of the other problem.

Because African American children from low-income backgrounds are often expected to manifest behavior problems and academic failure, this expectation may become a self-fulfilling prophecy for these children. African American youth and other youth in general tend to live up to or down to the expectations of teachers, parents, and other authority figures in their lives.

Given the empirical evidence and logic suggesting that behavior problems and academic failure are related among African American children, it makes sense to:

1. Focus on the development of interventions to address each of these problems.
2. Ask questions about the existence of both problems when feedback about the existence of one of these problems is provided.
3. Assess changes in both problems after implementing an intervention to address one of the problems.
4. Determine whether the existence of one problem has rendered a negatively distorted view of the level of existence of the other problem.
5. Explore whether the expectations of behavior problems and academic failure are the culprits in their existence.

Reality 5. "Boosting the self-esteem and knowledge of African American children may not decrease behavior problems or modify academic failure among these children." Clearly, it is important to create school, home, and community environments that help African American children develop positive feelings about themselves, their history, and their culture. This is especially important because of the unjust negative stereotypes and television images of African Americans that permeate our world. It is also important because schools have traditionally ignored the richness and beauty of African American culture and the many important contributions that African Americans have made to the world in all areas including medicine, physics, mathematics, architecture, agriculture, and the arts.

The common negative portrayals of African Americans and their culture likely have a negative impact on the self-esteem, self-acceptance, and school performance of African American children. Because of the difficulty in conducting empirical research to assess these negative consequences, they cannot be stated with certainty. However, it is logical to conclude that negative portrayals of African Americans increase the likelihood of academic failure and behavior problems among African American students or make their academic and social success more challenging.

Phinney (1992) found that ethnic identity is an important predictor of self-esteem among persons from nonmajority groups and among European Americans residing in settings in which they are minorities. Many African American parents, psychologists, and counselors believe that boosting African American children's self-esteem and increasing their knowledge of African American history and culture are needed interventions to help deter or neutralize the feared or actual negative impact on these children of racism (Hale-Benson, 1986; Peters, 1981). Lee (1982) asserted that tangible educational gains by African American children will not occur without positive self-acceptance and self-esteem, which are important for confidence to compete and for general psychosocial adjustment.

Yet, it must be realized that many African American children who experience academic failure and behavior problems have positive self-esteem. Furthermore, many African American students labeled delinquent or behavior problem children and many students with nothing but failing grades obtain high global self-esteem scores, think that they are "cool," and have much "black pride." In a study of elementary and high school African American students living in a small southern city, it was found that global self-esteem of males was positively associated with maladaptive behavior and negatively associated with adaptive skills (Gaskin-Butler & Tucker, 1995). In other words, high self-esteem was associated with both frequent maladaptive behavior (hitting, fighting, etc.) and low levels of adaptive skills (communication skills, etc.). The reverse was found for the African American females; high self-esteem was associated with both low maladaptive behavior and high adaptive skills. Further-more, self-esteem was not a significant predictor of academic achievement for the African American males and females in the Gaskin-Butler and Tucker study.

In a study involving 328 inner-city African American eighth graders, Jordan (1981) found that global self-concept was not significantly related to these students' academic achievement. Jordan concluded that this finding raised doubt about the usefulness of edu-cational intervention programs that seek to raise academic achievement levels of African American students by enhancing their global self-esteem.

There is no doubt that having positive self-esteem and knowledge and appreciation of African American history and culture are important goals for African American chil-dren and adolescents. Yet, achieving these goals alone may not significantly reduce behav-ior problems or academic behavior. Furthermore, there is a lack of convincing evidence to date that general self-esteem can be manipulated directly by schools. Self-esteem likely follows, not precedes, real accomplishment. The benefits of teaching racial pride and boosting self-esteem without also giving priority to facilitating academic learning and competence are likely short term, intangible, and deceptive (Frisby & Tucker, 1993).

Reality 6. "Reading, writing, and speaking standard English and following classroom rules are not "acting white" behaviors; they are necessary self-empowerment vehicles for future success." Many of the behaviors, attitudes, and values embraced by middle-class European Americans must also be embraced by African Americans in order for African American children to achieve academic and social success (Lee & Lindsey, 1985). African American students, like their European American peers, must engage in behaviors such as reading, writing, and speaking standard English and following classroom rules for upward mobility in U.S. society. Learning these behaviors ideally should occur in early childhood. Yet, some African Americans feel that accepting behaviors, attitudes, and values of middle-class European Americans that lead to their success in life is "acting white" and is a devaluation of African American culture (Fordham & Ogbu, 1986). Consequently, these African Americans reject these success vehicles. The fact is, however, that these behaviors, attitudes, and values that lead to success are not innate characteristics or possessions of European Americans. It is legitimate and wise to characterize them as success behaviors, attitudes, and values that anyone who wants to be successful can adopt without changing one's core identity or commitment to one's culture.

Indeed, many successful African American children, adolescents, and adults have adopted these success behaviors, attitudes, and values and simultaneously embraced and valued African American culture. Embracing and valuing both are not incompatible. In fact, reading, writing, and speaking standard English, valuing working and studying, and other so-called "white middle-class behaviors and values" were instrumental in helping the ancestors of African Americans to achieve freedom and success against all possible odds. Thus, adopt-ing these behaviors, attitudes, and values should be constructively and appropriately reframed for African American children as "acting African American" rather than be consid-ered as "acting white."

The specific behaviors, attitudes, and values that need to be encouraged among Afri-can American children need to be determined with input from various individuals who are knowledgeable about education and who really want to self-empower African American children for academic and social success. Among these various individuals should be African American parents, teachers and other educators, and psychologists and counselors. Furthermore, the decision-making process about the behaviors, attitudes, and values to teach African American students should be guided by the goal of preparing these students for academic, economic, and social success and moral lives in the twenty-first century. This decision-making process should not instead be guided by whether desirable attitudes, behaviors, and values belong to one culture or another. Clearly, reading, writing, and speaking standard English, becoming proficient in math, following rules, relating positively with teachers, self-managing one's behavior and emotions, and striving for excellence will be among the behaviors and values deemed important by any group genuinely concerned about facilitating the academic, social, and economic success of African American children now and in the future.

According to Chimezie (1988), when there is a conflict between the school and African American children's characteristics, such as a preference for oral versus written communication, it is not always the school or teacher that must change or adapt. Consideration must be given to each characteristic of African American children to determine whether it needs to be retained, modified, or discouraged. Chimezie labels this process selective adaptation and asserts that whether there should be some change in the characteristic should be based on the effect of the characteristic on the African American child's school learning and performance rather than on whether it is a product of African American culture. Chimezie went on to state that teachers should not accommodate African American children's preference for oral language over reading by trying to teach these children only using oral formats. Chimezie further stated that insistence on developing African American children's reading skills is not cultural genocide (Chimezie, 1988). African American children must learn to read and to write in standard English in order to compete nationally and internationally in the twenty-first century.

It is tremendously important to help African American children understand and take pride in the development of their culture-related characteristics. It is also important to help them understand the need to change some of these characteristics when it is clear that doing so will better enable them to obtain the skills and knowledge that they need for academic, social, and economic success. Furthermore, it is important for teachers to respect African American children's cultural differences in the learning and behavior change processes that are required to ready these children for success in the twenty-first century. Respecting cultural differences of African American children does not require that teachers and schools accommodate all of these children's behaviors, characteristics, and learning styles; rather, it requires that teachers be aware of and understand these children's culture-related behaviors, attitudes, values, and learning preferences. Additionally, it requires that teachers patiently and compassionately work with African American children to compassionately and gradually modify those characteristics that impede life success.

Teaching children to read, write, and speak standard English and learn through various learning modalities will enable them to become adults who can teach themselves and obtain and disseminate information for controlling their own destinies (e.g., for establishing their own businesses). Teaching children to adhere to and value classroom rules will shape and reinforce self-control, self-discipline, and patience, all of which facilitate self-empowerment for academic, economic, and social success.

Reality 7. "Interventions must not only seek to eliminate undesirable behaviors but also to teach desirable replacement behaviors."   Most parents, teachers, counselors, and psychologists are guilty of telling children and teens not to do something without going on to say what the children should do instead; in other words, replacement behaviors for the undesirable behaviors are not specified. Often these adults do not specify replacement behaviors simply because no particular ones are desired or because they do not know what replacement behaviors to suggest. The adults do know for certain that they want the children to stop the undesirable behaviors because the behaviors are potentially harmful, are irritating, or are simply unacceptable.

When children are not told what they might do or should do instead of what they are doing, they may in fact do some other behaviors that are also undesirable to the adults present. The consequences for both the adults and the children are often feelings of frustration and anger. Additionally, the adults (e.g., parents and teachers) often feel that the children are insensitive and rebellious, and the children often conclude that the adults are unfairly critical and controlling. Because these feelings are often not constructively expressed by parents or children due to lack of knowledge and skills needed to do so, emotional distance (i.e., a lack of perceived closeness and caring) often results. The consequences of emotional distance between children and their parents and teachers include spending less time together and communicating less, both of which impede teaching and learning that are needed to prevent behavior problems and academic failure and to facilitate the academic and social success of children.

Clearly, it is important for parents and teachers and for children themselves to suggest replacement behaviors when giving feedback to others about undesirable behaviors. It is also important to suggest calmly and respectfully the replacement behavior, to communicate how to do the replacement behavior, and to express calmly any negative or positive feelings that occur in relation to the request to engage in an alternative replacement behavior.

For example, if a parent desires for his daughter, Karen, to stop yelling at her younger brother, the following could be said:

> Karen, please stop yelling at Gerald now and whenever you are angry with him. It makes me feel upset when I see this happen. Instead of yelling, just walk away from him, take three deep breaths to calm down, and then calmly tell him why you are angry with him and what you want him to stop doing and to do instead. If there is something that you think that needs to be done to stop your need to yell, please discuss it with me. Are there any feelings that you want to share about what I just said? Thanks, sweetheart, for listening to me and for considering my request.

In order for parents and teachers to effectively eliminate inappropriate behaviors by African American children, it is important for adults to think about what they would like the youth to do instead. We cannot assume that children should know what is expected of them or what is appropriate. This is in part because adults differ in what they think is appropriate and children cannot read the minds of adults. Furthermore, when adults do communicate the behaviors that they expect from children, it is important not to assume that the children know how to do the desired behavior. In the example given earlier, Karen was given a suggestion for calming down. She may not have known an intervention for helping her to become calm. Indeed, children must be taught what it is we want and expect them to do; however, we first must know what it is we want and expect.

Reality 8. "Interventions need to involve African Americans who will consistently and actively encourage and help children to be the best that they can be."   African American children will especially benefit from interventions to modify and prevent behavior problems and academic failure that involve African Americans who consistently and actively encourage and help them to be the best that they can be. Even though parents love their children and want the best for them, often low-income African American parents cannot actively provide such encouragement and help for various reasons. Furthermore, many African American children are in living situations that are not conducive to receiving consistent encouragement and help. It has been reported that African American children represent 70 percent of the children in out-of-home care (Tatara, 1992); many of these children do not have significant relationships with individuals who consistently and actively encourage and help them. Furthermore, few of these children have fathers or father figures in their lives who could do this.

African American role models and mentors can play major roles in providing consistent help and encouragement to African American children who do not otherwise receive such support. However, finding African American role models and mentors in general and African American male role models and mentors in particular who meet the traditional defining standards of being at least employed and somewhat educated and successful is often problematic.

According to Ascher (1992), the flight of middle-class African Americans from inner-city neighborhoods and the high incidence of unemployment among the African Americans who remain have resulted in a lack of appropriate mainstream role models in inner-city homes, communities, and media. Furthermore, Ascher (1992) called attention to the fact that only 1.2 percent of all teachers are African American men. It must also be considered that many African American adults feel that they are too busy to be role models and mentors for African American children. These adults are too busy holding on to their middle-class status or fighting racism and discrimination via various projects and organizations.

The reality is that interventions to modify and prevent behavior problems and academic failure of African American children would more likely be successful with the involvement of individuals, especially males, who will consistently give them encouragement and help throughout the intervention period and beyond this period. It is not a requirement that these individuals speak perfect English, have prestigious jobs, have good incomes, or be successful as traditionally defined. It is also not necessary that role models and mentors for African American children be African American, although in some cases African American intervention support persons would be ideal. It is simply most important that intervention support persons be respected in their communities and be committed to helping children help themselves to reach their full potential.

Reality 9. "African American students need goals and need to see a direct relationship between doing well in school and achieving their goals."   Most parents, grandparents, and other adult family members of African American children passionately tell these youth how important it is for them "to be somebody." These adults also often indicate passionately what they do not want the children to be. For example, in interviews with African American grandmothers, Hale-Benson (1986) found that these women did not want their grandchildren to do hard, menial jobs or domestic work; yet, they did not have aspirations regarding the kinds of jobs or careers that they thought their grandchildren should pursue. Clearly, if African American parents and grandparents do not have acceptable careers or jobs in mind for their children, it is not likely that they will discuss these possibilities together. However, such discussions are needed to help children learn what the desire for them to be somebody really means; furthermore, these discussions serve as catalysts for the children to think about careers and jobs, including ones that may be very different from those identified by parents and other family members.

Many African American youth, especially those who are from low socioeconomic backgrounds, grow up feeling the need to be successful without having a destination or road map for reaching this destination. In other words, these children do not have short-term career goals (e.g., to successfully pass first grade, to graduate from junior high school) and long-term career goals (e.g., to become a civil rights lawyer). Those children who do have such goals often have not had experiences that will help direct them to these goals or help them establish more desirable goals. Goals are important for self-motivation that promotes and sustains behaviors such as studying, doing homework, and so on that lead to academic success.

Children will usually expend much time and energy doing something that they want to do or achieve when they perceive direct connections between what they want to achieve (i.e., their goals) and the time and energy that they expend. For example, it is important for children to be taught the connection between doing well in geometry and becoming a pilot. A pilot is likely the best person to help make this particular connection. It does not take an act of Congress to arrange for a pilot to visit a school and talk with the children about the importance of studying math, self-discipline, knowing how to speak standard English, and so forth to becoming a successful pilot. It also would not take a tremendous amount of time for a school principal, community leader, or parent to arrange for a child who wants to become a pilot to visit an airport, meet with pilots there, and take an airplane ride. Such learning experiences often motivate children to be academically engaged so as to reach their related short-term and long-term goals.

It is important that schools, parents, and community leaders work in partnership to make certain that the education of African American children include (1) identifying long-term career or job goals, (2) identifying short-term goals related to their long-term goals, (3) meeting many African American males and females in various jobs and careers, and (4) participating in school and field trip experiences that will provide information related to their career goals. These educational experiences are particularly important for African American children because there are so many exciting and lucrative careers to which many African American children will never be exposed without schools and community leaders providing this exposure. To help African American children achieve such careers, these children need to be assisted in seeing the relationship between school success and career success in an effort to facilitate their self-motivation to learn and achieve.

Reality 10. "It cannot be assumed that African American children know how to study but are simply choosing not to do so." "Child, you had better get in there and study. No television until you have finished studying for your test." These are familiar statements by

African American parents, as the overwhelming majority, if not all, of these parents want their children to make good grades in school and to graduate at least from high school. This indeed is a noble desire; however, its underlying assumption is that their children know how to study in order to make good grades.

Teachers, too, simply tell students to be sure to study. Seldom do they ask if students know how to study. Knowing how to study is not a skill with which children are born. Students need to be taught how to study and most of them need assistance in setting their own study schedule and environment. Because few schools have classes on how to study, many students do not have the opportunity to learn how to study. Consequently, these students study ineffectively or only pretend to study to satisfy parents and teachers who want them to study.

The consequence of poor study skills and habits is usually academic failure. Common reasons that children give for academic failure include not having had time to study and forgetting that there was a need to study (for a test). The first of the two reasons can be addressed by having daily structured routine study times when there are no social activities for any family members, including parents. Ideally, parents can use this time for quiet activities such as reading the paper or a novel, writing letters, and paying bills. Not knowing how to study can be addressed via study skills training classes, which are typically available at the college level through various academic support programs.

Study skills training is often provided to middle-class students by their parents or by tutors hired by parents. For most African American students these types of academic support are not available. Consequently, study skills training must be given high priority in their schools, after-school programs, and church school programs. Study skills training needs to begin for children in general and African American children in particular at the kindergarten level. Utilization of study skills learned must be consistently reinforced in children's homes and schools throughout their education journey.

Reality 11. "School will not or cannot teach African American students all of the adaptive skills and success behaviors they need for school and life success." Interventions for the modification and prevention of behavior problems and academic failure and interventions for the facilitation of academic and social success typically include teaching success behaviors (e.g., using good eye contact) and facilitating adaptive skills. Adaptive skills include communication skills (e.g., how to express feelings clearly and nonaggressively), socialization skills (e.g., how to effectively resolve interpersonal conflict), and daily living skills (e.g., how to plan and organize to complete a task). Training interventions to teach these skills and success behaviors to children typically require individualized instruction, modeling, practice, feedback, and praise.

Many adaptive skills and success behaviors are learned from parents and through life experiences such as working in a family business, traveling, holding offices in school organizations, and participating in summer camp. These kinds of experiences are typically not part of the life experiences of children from low socioeconomic environments; consequently, these children may have deficits in their adaptive skills and inadequate success behaviors as compared to their peers who do have these experiences.

Given that most teachers are already overworked and underpaid, it is not likely that teachers have the time and energy to provide all of the adaptive skills and success behavior training that many African American children from low-income families and other children need. Furthermore, at least some teachers may feel that it is not their responsibility to teach adaptive skills and success behaviors. Some of the teachers who feel this way may choose to reinforce quiet, passive behavior among African American students and low-ability students rather than try to teach these students needed adaptive skills. Indeed, quiet, passive behavior among African American students is satisfactory to some teachers whether or not these students are on-task with regard to assigned tasks (Cooper, 1979; Harvey, 1980; Massey, Scott, & Dornbusch, 1975).

Kaufman, Lloyd, and McGee (1989) found that among sixty-one special education teachers and regular school teachers (97 percent of whom were European American and all of whom were from a largely rural area in the Southeast), the greatest among their concerns were control and order in the classroom. The least among the teachers' concerns were students' conflict resolution skills, social skills, skills for giving feedback to others, ability to recognize their own and others' feelings, and level of voluntary participation in class. However, these adaptive skills and behaviors would deter peer conflicts and other behavior problems and would help prepare African American students for future job success and social success in most aspects of their lives.

Interestingly, 70 percent of the elementary school teachers in the Kaufman, Lloyd, and McGee (1989) study reported that adaptive skills such as how to express anger are critically important for a child in their classroom; 50 percent of these teachers felt that a child should not be placed in their classroom without having already mastered the anger management skill. Approximately 15 percent of all of the teachers felt that they should not have to deal with children who have not learned critical success behaviors. Yet, many African American children exposed to much crime, poverty, racism, and discrimination within and outside of their neighborhoods have not learned adequate adaptive skills and success behaviors and have justified underlying anger. Learning to constructively deal with this anger and learning adaptive skills and success behaviors are crucial for these African American children because such learning helps deter behavior problems and academic failure.

Many parents and teachers either do not have the knowledge and skills or do not make the time to teach African American students adaptive skills and success behaviors. How are these students supposed to learn them? Schools must find a way to help teach these skills and behaviors to African American students and other students, perhaps through after-school programs in which teachers can elect to participate and be paid to do so. Community-based schools and training programs must also provide some of this training with the support of local businesses. Additionally, African American churches can reassume their traditional, major role in providing children with success behavior and adaptive skills training. One thing is for certain, African American parents cannot depend on schools to provide their children with all of the training that they need to be academically and socially successful.

Reality 12. "Blaming African American parents' marital status for their children's behavior problems and academic failure is useless and often unjustified." There are countless very successful African Americans who have been reared in single-parent homes. Similarly, there are countless academically and socially successful African American children who are being raised in homes in which there is only one parent. In both instances the single parent is usually the mother. Yet, contemporary clinicians have indicated that deviations from having a mother and father family structure is detrimental to all family members, especially the children (Golombok, Spencer, & Rutter, 1983). Their view is supported by research studies with inadequate samples of African Americans or with no African Americans represented. These studies indicate that students from two-parent homes do better academically (Kurdek & Sinclair, 1988; McCartin & Meyer, 1988), have fewer behavior problems (Hammond, 1979; Kurdek & Sinclair, 1988), and evidence less susceptibility to peer pressure to engage in deviant activity (Steinberg, 1987). It is inappropriate, however, to make conclusions about African Americans based on studies in which they were not adequately represented or not represented at all.

Most African Americans would likely agree that having both parents actively involved in parenting their children is desired but that it is not marital status that is critical in whether African American children are academically and socially successful. Research with African American children provides support for this view. For example, in a study involving mostly low-income students that was conducted by Tucker, Brady, Harris, and Fraser (1992), no significant differences were found in grade point averages (GPAs) or in standardized Metropolitan Achievement Test (MAT) scores of the participating African American students from two-parent homes as compared to the African American students from one-parent homes. In this same study, it was found that the participating European American students with fathers living in their homes had higher GPAs and higher MAT scores than those European American students who did not have fathers living in their homes. It is noteworthy that some research with African Americans suggests that the father's presence in the home may have a significant impact on skills and behavior of African American children. Dunn and Tucker (1993) found that the low-income African American children in their study whose fathers resided in their homes evidenced higher overall adaptive functioning scores and lower maladaptive behavior (e.g., fighting, hitting) than did the African American children whose fathers did not reside in their homes.

Based on what we know today, we cannot conclude that not having a father in the home will necessarily lead to academic failure and behavior problems. This is particularly true given that in many African American families without fathers living in their homes, there are father figures and other primary caregivers living in their homes or in their neighborhoods. There are many African American children and adults from such homes who are model students and citizens. Thus, it is time for us to realize that what produces successful children and adults is not just marital status. Furthermore, blaming single parents for being single is nonproductive as well as unjust. Blaming African American parents for their children's academic failure and behavior problems does not instruct or engage these parents in being a part of the solutions to these problems.

Reality 13. "Interventions must involve partnership efforts and ideally should be based in the African American community."   Consistent with the old African American proverb that "it takes a village to raise a child" is the perspective offered here that "it takes a partnership to raise a child." Given the numerous and serious challenges that many African American children face, including poverty, racism, discrimination, limited academic resources, limited educational travel, and drug-infested neighborhoods, it is obvious that interventions to prevent behavior problems and academic failure among these youth need to be multidimensional. These interventions also need to involve individuals other than parents, for example, extended family members, teachers, counselors, psychologists, and community leaders who are interested in the success of African American children. Because what is seen as behavior problems and academic failure is often in the eyes of the beholders and given that these problems are often situational, it is important that the perspectives and observations of several different culturally sensitive individuals help shape interventions to modify the problems. The intervention team should include individuals from different settings in which the target children live, learn, and socialize.

Some of the intervention partners other than parents need to be African Americans from backgrounds similar to the backgrounds of the target children. This is because such African Americans may differ from European American teachers, counselors, and psychologists in their perceptions and understanding of African American children. Kaufman, Swan, and Wood (1980) found that in assessing behavior and other problems of children, the participating parents, teachers, psychologists, and educational diagnosticians significantly agreed in their ratings of 72 percent of the European American children in their research, but they significantly agreed in their ratings of only 42 percent of the African American children in their research. Through intervention partnerships parents, teachers, counselors, psychologists, and community leaders can work together to identify and agree on the problems of the target children and can develop appropriate intervention programs for these children (Tucker, Chennault, Brady, Fraser, Gaskin, Dunn, & Frisby, 1995).

Parents or primary caregivers need to be active partners in intervention programs for African American children. Existing research with low-income, minority families indicates that the most powerful interventions are those in which parents have an active role in the decision-making processes about their children (Ascher, 1988; Leler, 1983). Furthermore, most if not all African American parents very much want to facilitate the academic and social success of their children. Indeed, these parents understand that their own futures and advancement of African American communities depend on those African American children and adults who excel academically and economically (Hilliard, 1979; Nobles, 1988). History evidences that even in times of overt and hostile racism, African American parents sacrificed and struggled to provide a good education for their children (Corder & Quisenberry, 1987).

Ideally, partnership intervention programs for African American children would be most effective based in the African American community (e.g., in community centers or churches). Such locations would be accessible to the children, their families, and involved community leaders and would likely be comfortable, non-anxiety-producing intervention settings for these individuals. On the other hand, many African American students' schools may not be comfortable intervention settings for African American members of the intervention partnership. Indeed, many African Americans are very reluctant to even attend teacher conferences, PTA meetings, and other school activities at their children's schools in part because these schools do not seem like places that welcome African Americans; they instead seem like places for European Americans to be. For those African American parents, grandparents, and community members who have difficulty reading and speaking standard English, school environments, especially those outside of the African American neighborhood, can be very anxiety producing.

Community-based partnership intervention programs to prevent and modify the behavior problems and academic failure of African American children seem especially appropriate because such programs provide opportunities for African American communities to help "pull themselves up by their own bootstraps." Such self-help is empowering and thus facilitates long-term intervention program success. It is also helpful for psychologists, teachers, and counselors who are program partners to spend time working in the environments that influence the behaviors and attitudes of the African American children for whom they will help develop interventions. Such experiences foster cultural sensitivity among these professionals, facilitate their understanding of the complexity of the factors in the target children's behavior problems and academic failure, and increase the likelihood of their recommended interventions being culturally sensitive and effective. Indeed, such potential benefits make community-based partnership education programs win-win intervention strategies because they will likely have a positive impact on the lives of both program participants and program providers.

Reality 14. "All African American children are not the same and, thus, no intervention will be effective for all African American children." There is a general tendency among Americans, including African Americans, to see only the common aspects of African American mini-cultures and to overlook the cultural diversity among African Americans. Similarly, there is a tendency to ignore the fact that there is diversity among African Americans in various areas including values, characteristics, economic status, education, religious background and practices, family structures, lifestyles, and acculturation (Dillon, 1994). Indeed, African Americans are as different as day and night. Consequently, any intervention to prevent and modify behavior problems and academic failure among African American children must recognize and adjust for the foregoing specified differences in their life experiences. This view is consistent with that of Dillon (1994) who suggests that the diversity among African Americans must be considered in program development, policy making, and program implementation. This consideration, however, rarely occurs. Such consideration is especially important in selecting interventions for African American children with behavior problems or academic problems. Indeed, an intervention such as timeout might be effective for some middle-class African American children but not be very effective for some very low-income African American children. One reason as to why timeout may be ineffective for the latter group is the possible unavailability of a quiet place within their often crowded home environment for timeout to occur. Yet, consideration is often not given to such real-life, income-related issues.

It is also important to note that there are individual differences in learning styles among African American students (Cushner, 1992) just as there are differences in their learning experiences and learning environments. All African American children do not learn best from oral teaching modes. The different learning styles among these children must be recognized and accomodated when developing interventions to facilitate their academic and social success. This recognition requires rejection of traditional negative stereotypes and generalizations about African American children and increased emphasis on assessment of the individual strengths, weaknesses, and needs of these children toward the goal of preparing them for academic and social success. Additionally, emphasis needs to be given to the assessment of home, cultural, community, social, and other factors that contribute to these children's strengths, weaknesses, and needs. Interventions for African American children should be based on these assessments rather than on assumptions about and stereotypes of African American children and their families. Like Asian children, European American children, Hispanic children, and other children, African American children too are different and special.

Reality 15. "The outcomes of academic efforts and success often include peer rejection and later underachievement; this must change." Most of us have known children who were teased for making excellent grades and for being "bookworms." Some of us may have been involved in the group that did the teasing. Yet, it has only been in recent years that we have begun to recognize that for some African American children and adolescents, the consequences of studying and engaging in other success behaviors, being achievement motivated, and making good grades often include peer rejection and later underachievement.

There is some research support for this recognition. For example, Merchant (1991) found that urban African American elementary school students who had a preference for college and who were intrinsically motivated as compared to those who did not have these preferences and were not intrinsically motivated had higher self-perceptions of their scholastic ability and yet surprisingly perceived themselves as less socially accepted by their peers. The research of Fordham and Ogbu (1986) suggests that African American students who engage in success behaviors and make good grades experience some social rejection from their peers because their success behaviors are viewed as "acting white" behaviors. Fordham and Ogbu (1986) also found in interviews with African American students that some of these students chose to study less and underachieve rather than not have the acceptance of their peers or be teased by them. Some other success-oriented African American students reported engaging in clowning behavior to deflect attention from their success behaviors and high grades.

Given the potential negative consequences for African American students of making good grades and engaging in success behaviors (e.g., making complete sentences), it is critical that interventions to prevent and modify behavior problems and academic failure include ways to handle these potentially negative consequences. African American children need to be taught specific responses to use when they are accused of "acting white" or are called "nerds." These responses might include statements such as the following: "I am simply doing what I can to get into college," "I am simply being academically cool," or "I am paying the dues for being the millionaire who I plan to become." It is also important to help African American students adopt the view that engaging in success behaviors is really "acting African American" in an effort to make things better for the next generation of "black folks."

Reality 16. "African American parents must be treated as equals and must not be victimized in intervention processes to help their children." It is not uncommon for African American parents to complain that at meetings with teachers, counselors, psychologists, principals, and others to plan interventions to help their children in school their parenting skills have been questioned and criticized and their opinions have not been sought or respected when given. These parents report leaving such meetings feeling angry and distrusting of these professionals. Thus, it should not be surprising that after hearing this information "over the grapevine" or having such an experience, many African American parents choose not to attend meetings to discuss their children's academic or behavior problems.

It is likely that the teachers and other education professionals involved in intervention planning meetings where African American parents felt they were not respected were not aware of anything that was disrespectful. Cultural or socioeconomic-related differences in verbal and nonverbal language may be contributing factors to different perceptions by African American parents versus the education professionals at such meetings. However, regardless of the causes of African American parents' feelings that they are not respected in some meetings with education professionals, it is important to be proactive to make these parents feel respected and equal to other meeting participants.

Research supports treating parents as equal partners with teachers, psychologists, and other members of intervention teams who work with African American children. In a study involving low-income African American mothers of children with disabilities, it was found that the mothers who interacted with professionals who considered themselves "experts" did not enjoy these interactions and felt demeaned by them (Kalyanpur & Rao, 1991). The authors of this study reported that the mothers felt empowered, however, when they felt their input was valued. It was also reported by the authors that there was no understanding shown by the professionals involved that there are cultural differences in parenting styles.

Given that African American parents likely differ in what makes them feel respected and equal with education professionals, it is a good idea for teachers, psychologists, counselors, and other education professionals to be proactive in addressing this issue by making statements such as the following:

> It is our wish to show you the great deal of respect that you deserve as a parent as we work together as equal partners to help your child make better grades and have more positive experiences with his teachers and peers. With you as an equal partner with us, there is a good chance that these goals will be achieved. Is there anything that you would like to see us do or not do as we work together? Is anything that will make you feel more comfortable as a partner with us? Thank you for sharing that with us. Why don't we continue with you telling us what you and your child see as contributing to his less than satisfactory grades? Is it ok with you to begin there?

The basic idea in the foregoing set of statements is to simply communicate to African American parents the wish to respect them, and then solicit their input as to how to do this. Of course, it is especially important to empower parents by beginning the discussion component of the meeting with their input so as to be sure that their input does not get lost in the intervention discussion process.

Reality 17. "When African American students are successful, all students around them are positively impacted." It is understandable that given the limited dollars for education, some individuals and groups of individuals will complain about spending state and national dollars on intervention programs to modify and prevent behavior problems and academic failure among African American children. Yet, it must be realized that the underachievement, academic failure, and behavior problems of many African American children are in part due to many problems such as low socioeconomic status, racism, and discrimination that these children cannot control. It must also be realized that even if we could blame African American children and their parents for the academic failure and behavior problems that these children experience, there are some significant negative consequences of not trying to help modify and prevent these problems.

One of these negative consequences is a reduction in learning by the other children in the classrooms of African American children who are experiencing behavior problems or academic failure. The more time that teachers spend responding to these problems among African American children, the less time they spend teaching other children and the less all children will learn. Furthermore, given the influence that peers have on each other, we can be certain that behavior problems in one group will often be modeled by their peer group. Thus, when African American children experience problems in the classroom, the behavior of all children in their classrooms will likely be negatively impacted.

It is also important to note that when African American children fail, drop out of school, or are suspended from school, our neighborhoods are put at risk because these youth become vulnerable to engaging in crime and mischief. It is true that "an idle mind is the devil's workshop." For school dropouts of any ethnic group, our homes, vehicles, and neighborhoods become their workshop sites.

It is clear that the cost of intervention programs to address behavior problems and academic problems of African American children is less than the cost of not addressing these problems. It is also clear that these intervention programs indirectly serve all children, for when African American children achieve academic and social success, all children in their classrooms and all Americans are positively impacted.

Conclusions

Many realities must be faced in order to develop interventions to modify behavior problems and academic failure among African American children. Among these realities is that these interventions must be based on culturally sensitive theories and must recognize and respect the individual and cultural differences among African American children. Contrary to existing stereotypes, all African American children are not alike or similar.

Ideally, parents, families, and community members should be involved as active and equal partners in the planning and implementation of intervention programs for African American children. Basing these programs in African American communities will facilitate the involvement of parents in these partnerships and will facilitate the cultural sensitivity of the teachers, psychologists, counselors, and other education professionals who participate in these partnerships. The ultimate consequence will likely be culturally sensitive education and counseling for future generations of African American students.

Telling African American children what not to do and expending much energy just trying to keep them under control are not effective interventions for facilitating their academic and social success. The reality is that African American children need to learn communication skills, socialization skills, and daily living skills for academic and social success. They also need to be taught how to teach themselves. Additionally, it is important that they be provided with experiences at home, at school, and in the community that facilitate self-motivation, self-control, and self-praise—all of which help facilitate the self-empowerment of African American children to succeed regardless of environmental conditions.

African American children also must be taught success behaviors that include reading, writing, and speaking standard English. This is not a matter of "acting white"; it is a matter of "acting African American" for success. Most importantly, it is a matter of preparing African American children to compete nationally and internationally for the future economic and social empowerment of themselves and African American communities and, thus, all Americans. This is perhaps the greatest reality of all.

CHAPTER

3 Factors Underlying Behavior Problems of African American Children

There is general agreement that multiple factors underlie behavior problems of African American children and that these factors include and extend beyond family variables. Too often the discipline styles, family structure, level of family support, and lifestyles of African American families have been viewed as most responsible for the behavior problems of African American children. It is now recognized that several context factors including the family, low socioeconomic status, discrimination, racism, school and neighborhood environments, teacher behaviors and expectations, culture, and the many social problems in the communities and the nation in which African American children live often underlie the behavior problems of African American children (Barbarin, 1993; McAdoo, McAdoo, & Flanagan, 1990). It is also recognized that none of these context factors alone and no single combination of these variables adequately explains the behavior problems of all African American children.

There are many theories and theoretical models regarding the central underlying factors in behavior problems; few of these theories indicate recognition that many external and internal factors likely have a direct or indirect impact on the behavior of children. Even fewer of these theories specifically address the behavior problems of African American children. There is also limited research to identify at least some of the significant factors in behavior problems of African American youth. Yet, theories and research that address the behavior problems of African American youth are needed to provide direction for interventions to modify these problems.

This chapter will briefly review theories and theoretical models that attempt to explain behavior problems with some attention to the direct or indirect role of the multiple factors in these problems and with some cultural and socioeconomic sensitivity. Research on the factors in behavior problems that has at least included a focus on African American children will also be reviewed. Attention to these theories and research is important because they may provide directions for developing future theories and research that will provide added knowledge for developing interventions to modify behavior problems among the diverse groups of African American youth in the United States.

Ecological Theory

According to the ecological theoretical model (Bronfenbrenner, 1979; Garbarino, 1982), behavior problems and other behaviors of children and adolescents are not only influenced by factors in their immediate environment, such as the family, but also are indirectly influenced by aspects of the environment in which they are not participants such as their parents' workplaces and support network. In other words, factors such as a parent's workplace (e.g., a stressful job setting) can impact the parent's behaviors with her or his child (e.g., levels of parental control), which in turn impact the child's behavior (e.g., level of behavior problems).

Behavioral Theories and Postulates

Behavioral theories of conduct disorders or behavior problems emphasize that children learn these behaviors in experiences and interactions with aspects of their environment including their parents, family, community, and peers. These theories are at least somewhat culturally and socioeconomically sensitive in that they recognize that social-environmental factors influence the behaviors that children learn rather than primarily attribute behavior problems to factors within the child such as low intellectual and cognitive functioning.

There are several postulates that have been set forth to explain how this learning of behavior problems occurs. For example, Patterson (1976) and Patterson and Reid (1973) have postulated that negative behaviors are developed and sustained through negative reinforcement in interactions with others. An example of this negative reinforcement of inappropriate behaviors is the following common interaction:

MRS. JONES: Mary, come in here and help me with the dishes.

MARY: I don't feel like washing no dishes. Nobody can get any peace around here! It's do this and do that all the time, and I am sick of it!

MRS. JONES: Just forget it! If you feel like that after all that I do for you, just forget it!

In this example, Mary's defiant behavior is negatively reinforced; that is, it resulted in removal of a negative outcome for her (i.e., dishwashing) and, thus, her defiant behavior will likely occur again. Mrs. Jones's withdrawal response is also negatively reinforced because it resulted in termination of an aversive verbal interaction with Mary. Such interactions often develop and sustain both inappropriate behaviors in children and ineffective parenting behaviors for modifying the children's inappropriate behaviors.

It has also been postulated that behavioral problems occur because they are positively reinforced with verbal or physical attention (Wahler, 1976). For example, when a teacher or parent only talks with a child or does something with the child in an effort to discourage the child from engaging in the problem behavior, the child learns from this to act inappropriately to get something positive, that is, a teacher's or parent's time, attention, or expression of affection. In other words, the child's inappropriate behavior is positively reinforced by positive consequences (e.g., attention) and, thus, will likely continue to occur.

A third of the many behavioral postulates regarding behavior problems is that children engage in these behaviors when they have not learned the skills necessary to act appropriately in a given situation (Freedman, Rosenthal, Donahoe, et al., 1978). For example, Shirley, a nine-year-old, may express anger toward Martha, a ten-year-old, by starting a physical fight with Martha. Shirley may start the fight to express her anger because she has not learned how to express anger constructively. Shirley may have learned to express anger through fighting from individuals in her neighborhood, the peers with whom she associates, television, or through a host of other socioenvironmental influences.

Respondent conditioning (classical learning) and observation learning have also been postulated as ways by which behavior problems are learned. Respondent conditioning is the process by which anxiety-related behavior problems are learned. It involves pairing a non-anxiety-producing or neutral stimulus (e.g., quietly sharing a funny story in class with a peer) with a fear-evoking stimulus (e.g., a yell by the teacher) such that the neutral stimulus (sharing a story) becomes anxiety-producing. Such pairings of neutral and anxiety-producing stimuli are usually not intentional; they occur as part of human interactions. The result is often a behavior problem in a child (e.g., social withdrawal due to anxiety about talking in class) that baffles adults such as teachers and parents as to its cause. Yet, the cause, at least in part, is sometimes the innocent but anxiety-producing yell by a parent or teacher.

Observation learning or modeling is the process by which behavior problems and appropriate behaviors are learned from seeing someone else do the behavior. For example, a twelve-year-old child may use profane language after being around his thirteen-year-old friends who use such language and who are viewed by other teens in the neighborhood as "cool." Children learn from other children and from adults. The most powerful influential agents on youth are individuals most similar to themselves such as peers and individuals who in the eyes of these youth have popularity, power, and status. Thus, for children, peer gang members are powerful influential models.

It should be noted that behavioral theorists also acknowledge that behavior problems can occur in association with physical factors (e.g., the ingestion of poisons), genetic factors, environmental conditions (e.g., stimulus deprivation), and gender. However, current knowledge about the relationships between behavior problems and both genetic factors and physical factors occurring during the prenatal and perinatal periods is very limited (Erickson, 1992). Yet, because behavior problems can be the product of various factors, most contemporary behavioral theorists hold the view that each child with one or more behavior problems must be individually considered to determine the factors operant in her or his behavior problems. These theorists recognize that behavior problems and behavior are not influenced only by reinforcement contingencies and conditioning.

Behavioral Undercontrol Theory

According to behavioral undercontrol theory, difficulty with self-control is a central factor in the occurrence of behavior problems (Barber, 1992). It is postulated that self-control is a learned behavior and that it is learned and reinforced in the family context; however, it is suggested that the teaching and reinforcing of self-control by parents and other family members is facilitated or impeded by many various social and community factors that impact families (Forgatch & Stoolmiller, 1994).

Self-Empowerment Theory

The rationale for self-empowerment theory is that many of the social, socioeconomic, environmental, physical, school, teacher, family, and other variables that indirectly or directly influence the occurrence of behavior problems among African American children will likely not change over the duration of childhood and, thus, their impact on these youth and how these youth can constructively respond to this impact are of central importance in understanding and modifying their behavior problems.

Self-empowerment theory postulates that behavior problems and academic failure as well as prosocial behavior and academic success are significantly influenced by levels of (1) self-motivation to achieve academic and social success, (2) perceived self-control over one's behavior and academic success, (3) self-reinforcement for engaging in social and academic success behaviors, (4) adaptive skills for life success, and (5) engagement in success behaviors. It is these variables on which African American youth must depend when in situations where adults and others do not know how to or do not choose to motivate, state and enforce rules, or praise and encourage these youth.

Based on this theory, prevention and modification of behavior problems and academic failure require interventions such as teaching children (1) to teach themselves through self-instruction-based learning, (2) to motivate themselves through establishing short-term and long-term goals and engaging in activities and behaviors for achieving these goals, (3) to self-manage their behaviors and constructively express their feelings through cognitive-behavioral strategies, and (4) to praise themselves for learning adaptive skills and for engaging in success behaviors—behaviors required for classroom success, getting and keeping a job, and future economic and social success for themselves and for their families and communities. This teaching ideally should occur via a partnership educational effort involving parents, teachers, schools, educational policy makers at local, state, and national levels, community leaders, business leaders, the African American church, and African American children themselves.

Relevant Research

For too long research with European American youth has been used to understand the behaviors of African American youth. Much of this research has been Deficit Model research in which the behavior or performance of African American youth is compared with that of European American youth, with the behavior or performance of the European American youth being the standard by which the behavior or performance of the African American youth is judged or evaluated (Oyemade & Rosser, 1980). Research that is relevant to understanding behaviors of African American youth needs to at least include an adequate sample of these youth and needs to study them separately rather than compare them with European American youth.

Research that examines African American youth who are culturally and socioeconomically similar is considered Difference Model research (Oyemade & Rosser, 1980). This type of research recognizes and respects cultural and socioeconomic differences; in other words, groups that significantly differ on these variables are studied in separate models. When research with African Americans ignores or only statistically controls for cultural and socioeconomic differences, these differences should be acknowledged as possible confounding variables; furthermore, the results should be acknowledged as inconclusive, and the need for future similar research using a Difference Model research approach should be stated.

The research that will be presented here is Difference Model research that includes African American youth or research with African Americans that does not control for socioeconomic and cultural differences but has implications for future research for understanding, modifying, or presenting behavior problems among African American children. Given the paucity of research, especially empirical research, with African American children in general, it is indeed important to pay attention here to the very few studies with these young people that primarily focus on their behavior problems. The research studies that will be discussed appear to fall into two groups—studies that focus on external factors (e.g., family support and neighborhood learning resources) in behavior problems and studies that focus on internal or self factors (e.g., self-efficacy, self-regulation, self-control) in behavior problems.

Research on External Factors

One of the few studies with African American youth to examine factors in their behavior problems was conducted by Craig and Cauce (1994) using the ecological theory model. Participants in this study were mostly low-income African American families that included ninety-one girls and fifty-three boys. This study specifically investigated whether there was a significant relationship between the occurrence of behavior problems among African American children and environmental variables outside of the children's immediate environment. The specific environmental variables investigated were the primary parent's job autonomy, work satisfaction, social support satisfaction, number of social support persons, and neighborhood environment.

Results of the Craig, Cauce, Gonzales, and Hiraga (1994) study were as follows: (1) Low parental job autonomy was associated with high parental use of restrictive control, which in turn was associated with high levels of behavior problems by the children; (2) amount of perceived parental social support predicted (increased) parental warmth, which in turn predicted (decreased) behavior problems by the children; (3) parents who had high job satisfaction and who had high satisfaction with their perceived social support tended to have low family conflict, which in turn predicted (decreased) behavior problems by the children, and (4) high numbers of neighborhood risk factors were directly associated with high levels of behavior problems among the children. These results support the ecological theoretical model.

The foregoing findings suggest that behavior problems of African American children are at least in part the indirect result of the social problems in the United States (e.g., inequity in education and job discrimination) that contribute to African Americans being in low-income jobs with little power or control and living in problem-infested neighborhoods, both of which are beyond the control of African American children. The findings also suggest that the role of extended family members in providing support to African American parents is an important role in that it may help deter behavior problems among the children of these parents (Craig et al., 1994). These findings are consistent with the view of McAdoo and McAdoo (1990) that economic hardship, limited access to supportive services, and the psychological burden of oppression have all combined to contribute to psychological disturbances in African American youth.

In another study external variables in the immediate environment of African American children were investigated as factors in a common behavior problem—aggressive behavior. The study was conducted by DeRosier, Cillessen, Coie, and Dodge (1994) with 125 African

American boys in first grade or third grade from mostly lower-class families. This study examined the relationship between social characteristics of a group (i.e., affective quality and intensity, level of activity, and level of cohesiveness) and the level of aggressive behavior among group members. Aggressive behavior was defined as a verbal or physical act by one child with the intention to harm, threaten, or offend the target of the act. Among the findings from this study were that: (1) High levels of physical activity and competition resulted in more aggressive interactions among pairs of boys; (2) groups discouraged aggression when they had been engaged in playful competition; groups encouraged aggression when they had engaged in some aversive behavior; and (3) when the group sided with the victim of an aggressive act, group aggressive behavior rose.

According to DeRosier, Cillessen, Coie, and Dodge (1994), the foregoing findings suggest that there is a strong relationship between the nature of the behavior and activities of African American children's peer social group and the aggressive behavior of each child in the group. Additionally, according to the authors, the findings suggest that an African American child's social environment (e.g., school environment, peers, and friends) must be considered as a potential cause of aggressive behavior in these children. Of course, whether or not these findings actually hold for a group of African American girls similar in age, socioeconomic status, and culture to the African American males in this study will need to be determined in future research.

The influence of African American children's immediate environment, such as their peers and school environment, on perceptions of these children has also been demonstrated. Coie, Dodge, and Coppotelli (1982) found that being a racial minority (i.e., being the only one or among few African American children in a class of mostly European American children or being the only one or among few European American children in a class of mostly African American children) was associated with being perceived as an undesirable playmate by class members. Because in most schools in the United States, African American children as compared to European American children are in the minority, African American children are at higher risk of being considered undesirable playmates than European American children. Interestingly, Coie, Dodge, and Coppotelli (1982) also found that African American children were perceived by classroom peers as engaging in more aggressive and disruptive behaviors than European American children regardless of whether or not the majority in the class was African American or European American.

Another immediate environmental factor that research has shown to be linked to behavior problems of African American children is the existence of cultural differences between European American teachers and the African American children in these teachers' classrooms. This link was found in a recent study by Eaves (1997) conducted to determine whether the ratings of 458 fourth-grade and fifth-grade boys by their teachers varied systematically with teacher or student race. Results based on classroom observations were that the African American teachers in the study seldom were observed having difficulty maintaining control in their classrooms, whereas the European American teachers in the study frequently appeared hesitant to be directive and to follow through on consequences for not following directions. These observation-based findings were supported by informal discussions with the teachers who were observed. Eaves concluded from these findings that national, state, and local issues involving integration, busing, and civil rights may cause European American teachers to be reluctant to intervene to modify and prevent problem conduct among African American children.

It is also possible that simply not knowing how to relate to African American children and fear of being viewed as a racist in interactions with these youth may result in some European American teachers' reluctance to firmly discipline African American children for inappropriate behaviors. This reluctance may result in the actual occurrence of behavior problems among African American children in the classes of some European American teachers.

The behaviors of African American parents in interactions with their children have also been investigated as factors associated with behavior problems of children. In a study conducted by the present researcher and her associates (Tucker, Brady, Harris, & Fraser, 1993) the association between thirteen selected parent behaviors and both maladaptive behaviors (behavior problems) and adaptive functioning (i.e., communication skills, socialization skills, and daily living skills) of 266 African American children and 414 European American children was examined. The children in this study were in second, fourth, or eighth grade. The parent participants were the primary caregivers; over 97 percent of these participants in both ethnic groups were mothers. The African American participants were mostly from low-income families, whereas the European American participants were from various income-level families with over 62 percent having incomes of $35,000 or less. Both maladaptive behavior and adaptive behaviors of the children were assessed using the Survey Form of the Vineland Adaptive Behavior Scale. A Structured Interview Questionnaire for Parents (SIQP) was used to assess the self-reported level of occurrence of the parent behaviors.

Results indicated that two parent behaviors among the thirteen investigated parent behaviors were found to be significantly associated with maladaptive behavior in the African American children but not with maladaptive behavior in the European American children. Specifically, it was found that among the African American second graders and their parents, reported frequent praise by mothers and reported provision of most discipline by fathers were significantly associated with lower maladaptive behavior. It was also found that among both African American eighth graders and their parents and European American eighth graders and their parents, reported use of verbal reprimands by parents for unsatisfactory conduct or grades of their eighth graders was significantly associated with lower overall adaptive functioning by these eighth graders. Additionally, among both of the ethnic groups, reported use of encouragement by parents for unsatisfactory grades or conduct by their eighth graders was significantly associated with higher levels of communication skills, socialization skills, and overall adaptive functioning among these eighth graders.

The authors concluded from the foregoing findings that the associations of parent behaviors with children's adaptive functioning or maladaptive behaviors may or may not be similar for African Americans and European Americans. Thus, it cannot be assumed that parent behaviors shown in research with European Americans to have certain influences on children's maladaptive behaviors or adaptive functioning will similarly influence the maladaptive behavior or adaptive functioning of African American children.

Research on Self Factors

Research on behaviors and psychological characteristics of African American children (i.e., self factors) that impact their level of behavior problems has been very limited. Even though such self factors are likely influenced by family, social, environmental, socioeconomic, cultural, and other such variables, the resulting levels of these factors may in turn significantly influence the occurrence of behavior problems in African American children.

In a recent study by the present researcher and her colleagues (Tucker, Vogle, Reid, & Keefer, 1997), the associations between three self factors and maladaptive behaviors of African American children from low-income families were investigated. Sixty-nine children (thirty males and thirty-nine females) in grades ranging from first grade to twelfth grade and their primary caregivers (mostly mothers) participated in this study. The primary caregivers provided demographic and family income data and self-reported their perceived level of support given to their child or adolescent. The self factors investigated were the children's perceived level of parental support, level of achievement motivation, and level of self-control. These self factors were assessed via self-report instruments. Maladaptive behaviors were assessed using a Behavior Problem Checklist that was verbally administered to the participating children. Results revealed that self-reported perceived level of self-control was the only significant predictor of the children's self-reported maladaptive behaviors. In fact the self-control factor accounted for nearly 68 percent of the variance in level of maladaptive behaviors. No significant differences in the investigated variables were found in association with age, grade level, or gender of the child or in association with the presence or absence of the father in the home. There were also no differences found in the investigated variables in association with the primary caregiver's self-reported perceived level of involvement with her or his child or family income.

The researchers concluded that self factors such as self-control deserve increased attention in our efforts to understand the occurrence of behavior problems of African American children. They suggest that self-management-based theories and self-management research that address behavior problems of African American children may hold much potential for developing interventions to modify and prevent behavior problems among these children.

Lochman and Sims (1981) conducted a study to actually test the effects of twice weekly forty-minute group sessions that included self-management techniques on aggressive behavior of African American children. Participants in this study were twelve elementary school African American children from low-income, single-parent families among whom were eleven males and one female, all identified as most aggressive and disruptive in their classes. The group sessions included discussions of (1) a social problem-solving method, (2) situations that elicit anger and the physiological feelings that accompany anger, and (3) the use of positive self-statements to decrease one's anger arousal. The researchers concluded that although there was not a control group in this study, support was provided for further investigation of the effectiveness of self-management approaches with African American children.

Conclusions

There is little doubt that many factors underlie the occurrence of behavior problems among African American children. Some of these factors are external to these children and to a large degree beyond their control. The other factors are self factors such as behaviors (e.g., problem-solving behaviors) and psychological variables (e.g., perceived level of self-control), over which children have direct control and that are modifiable, but which are usually influenced by external factors.

Culturally and socioeconomically sensitive theories and research to understand, modify, and prevent behavior problems among African American children are desperately needed. Self-management-oriented theories and research, which have received very little attention in research with African American children with behavior problems, may hold potential for developing intervention approaches to address behavior problems of these children. These theories need to be based on research and clinical data from African American samples rather than on research findings from studies with European American children and families. It cannot be assumed that factors in behavior problems of African American children are the same as the factors in behavior problems of European American children.

Difference Model research approaches are needed because these approaches seek to examine separately factors in the behaviors of groups that differ culturally, socioeconomically, regionally, or in other significant ways. This research ideally should include qualitative as well as quantitative studies because quantitative research is often limited by the unavailability of culturally sensitive assessment instruments. Indeed such Difference Model research will likely be a constructive alternative to traditional Deficit Model research, which typically involves simply comparing African Americans and European Americans using performance measures standardized on European Americans, and then invalidly interpreting lower scores or performance by African Americans as inferior performance or behavior reflective of varying deficits.

4 Assessment of Behavior Problems among African American Children

As indicated in preceding chapters, cultural, socioeconomic, and religious backgrounds of observers (e.g., teachers, counselors, and psychologists) as well as stereotypes of African American children influence whether behaviors of these children are labeled as behavior problems. Consistent with this view is that of Hale-Benson (1986) that African American children's behaviors often are labeled as behavior problems because these children are expected to conform to a white behavioral model.

Many of the traditional strategies for assessing the existence of behavior problems neither adequately take into account the cultural and other differences between observers and African American youth nor do they take into account the differences among African American youth. Consequently, many African American children likely are unjustly labeled as having one or more behavior problems. The adults around these youth typically accept these labels without questioning their validity and expect the behaviors associated with the label. The labeled children often act in accordance with these expectations and thus in accordance with the labels given them. Clearly, culturally sensitive strategies for assessing behavior problems among African American children and adolescents are needed. Such strategies will likely decrease both the just and unjust reports of the incidence of behavior problems among African American children.

Assessment Process

The process of assessing behavior problems involves collecting information to determine (1) if behaviors of concern are consistent with the definition of a behavior problem; (2) when, how often, where, and under what conditions the behavior of concern occurs (i.e., its prevalence and severity); and (3) possible causes of the behavior of concern. Culturally and socioeconomically sensitive assessments of behavior problems are important and necessary for these assessments to be valid and reliable. Such assessments must be based on a culturally and socioeconomically sensitive definition of the term *behavior problem* and must use data collection procedures that are culturally and socioeconomically sensitive. Culturally and socioeconomically sensitive refers to reflecting or taking into account the existing values, traditions, beliefs, history, life experiences, and living conditions.

Being culturally and socioeconomically sensitive when assessing behavior problems of an African American child would involve getting information on the occurrence of the behaviors of concern not only from the child's teacher and an administered behavior problem checklist but also from the child, the child's parents and other primary caregivers, and one or more appropriate professionals, such as counselors and psychologists who are knowledgeable about and experienced in working with African American children similar to the child being assessed. The information obtained would include behavioral observation data and interview data that present information about the child's behaviors and attitudes at home, in the classroom, and on the playground. It would also include information about the child's family, the relationships of family members with the child, family rules and values, parenting strategies used, the child's physical and emotional health, the physical and psychological stressors and resources within the child's family, and the child's strengths and weaknesses. Respect for the views, intellect, communication style, requests, and traditions of family members would occur throughout the information gathering process, and parents and primary caregivers would be treated as partners with equal status to that of the professionals involved in the assessment process.

Culturally and Socioeconomically Sensitive Assessment

The growing discontent with the recognized behavior disorders and problems that appear in the *Diagnostic and Statistical Manual of Mental Disorders* (fourth edition) (DSM-IV; American Psychiatric Association, 1994) provides some evidence that the current system of identifying and labeling children's behaviors of concern is not satisfactory. This discontent centers around the less than adequate agreement regarding problem identification among professional psychologists, psychiatrists, and others who use the DSM-IV (Silverman, 1994). In other words, when such professionals observe or review data on the behavior of the same child, adolescent, or adult, they often come up with different DSM-IV labels for the same behaviors. Furthermore, behaviors of children and adolescents as well as adults often meet the criteria for more than one label or diagnosis. For example, in a study by Cohen et al. (1993), 365 youngsters who were found to have anxiety disorders also met the criteria for the disruptive behavior disorder.

Given the paucity of research to understand the behaviors of African American children, it is likely that the DSM-IV system for classifying behaviors is even more unsatisfactory for use with these children. Thus, rather than use DSM-IV to diagnose behaviors of African American children, it may be more useful to simply describe their behaviors, assess the socioeconomic, cultural, and other factors that provide the context for the occurrence of these behaviors, and help these children modify the behaviors that are directly or indirectly problematic for themselves and others around them. Doing this may avoid inaccurately diagnosing behavior problems among African American children and, thus, reduce the likelihood of their occurrence. Indeed, children often act in accordance with their diagnosis or label.

There is also continued discontent among nonmajority psychologists, psychiatrists, and counselors that the DSM-IV provides little to no guidance regarding factors to consider when making a behavior problem or conduct-disorder diagnosis as well as other diagnoses for nonmajority children. In fact, it is acknowledged in the DSM-IV that "concerns have been raised that the Conduct Disorder diagnosis may be misapplied to individuals in settings where patterns of undesirable behavior are sometimes viewed as protective (e.g., threatening, impoverished, high crime)" (p. 88). It is also stated in the DSM-IV that this diagnosis "should be applied only when the behavior in question is symptomatic of an underlying dysfunction within the individual and not simply a reaction to the immediate social context" (p. 88). Additionally, it is stated in the DSM-IV that "it may be helpful for the clinician to consider the social and economic context in which the undesirable behaviors have occurred" (p. 88).

Given that most psychologists, psychiatrists, and counselors often actually make the formal declaration that there is a behavior problem, often using the DSM-IV as their guide, and given that most of these professionals are European Americans, it is likely that decisions about the existence of a conduct disorder or behavior problem among African American children are not culturally sensitive. The fact that the DSM-IV only states that it *may be* helpful to consider the social and economic context of children's behaviors rather than state that it is indeed helpful to do so renders diagnoses for African American children suspect. In other words, there is uncertainty that culturally sensitive strategies are used in the identification of behavior problems among African American children. Fortunately, there is growing recognition and acknowledgment that such strategies are needed.

A study by Eaves (1975) provides direct empirical research support of the need for culturally sensitive strategies to identify behavior problems among African American youth. In this study race of teachers (African American or European American) and race of 458 fourth- and fifth-grade male students (African American or European American) were examined as factors in the identification of students' behavior problems by teachers. Findings generally showed that the European American teachers demonstrated a strong tendency to rate the African American male students as more deviant and the European American male students as less deviant when contrasted with the ratings of the African American teachers; to the contrary, the ratings of the African American male students did not vary by race. The specific findings from this study included the following:

1. The African American teachers saw no significant differences between conduct and behavior problems exhibited by the two different racial groups of male students; however, the European American teachers rated the African American male students as significantly more deviant and the European American male students as significantly less deviant.

2. The African American teachers saw no significant differences between the African American male students and the European American students on the variable of inadequacy or immaturity; however, the European American teachers rated the European American students as significantly more mature than did the African American teachers.

3. With regard to the variable of social delinquency, European American teachers attributed more extreme behavior to the African American male students than did African American teachers. African American teachers saw no differences in the socially delinquent behavior of the African American male students and the European American male students.

Clearly what are behavior problems may, at least in part, be in the eye of the observer. When teachers (observers) are from different cultural or socioeconomic backgrounds from the children they observe, the behaviors that the teachers see and the labels they use for these behaviors may be significantly influenced by the teachers' culture or socioeconomic background and the children's culture or socioeconomic background. Common stereotypes of African American children such as that they are lacking in self-control may negatively bias teachers' expectations and perceptions of the behaviors of these children.

Evidence of the need for culturally and socioeconomically sensitive strategies for identifying behavior problems also comes from other research findings. Rutter, Tizard, and Whitmore (1970) found that the reports of parents and teachers regarding the existence of behavior problems agreed only 7 percent of the time. It has also been found that lack of agreement between parents and teachers in their ratings of children's maladjustment increases with decreases in parents' social class (Glidewell & Swallow, 1968, cited in Gould, Wunsch-Hitzig, & Dohrenwend, 1981). This latter finding suggests that parents in the lowest socioeconomic classes are more likely to disagree with teachers about whether or not their children display behavior problems and about the severity of such problems. It has also been found that when rating adaptive and desirable adjusted behavior in children from lower middle-income families, African American mothers rated the behavior of these children as significantly better adjusted than did teachers (Wall & Paradise, 1981).

In sum, the research findings cited in this section suggest that because African American parents are disproportionately represented in the low socioeconomic classes, it is likely that many African American parents will differ with the teachers of their children about the level and type of behavior problems and the level of behavioral adjustment displayed by these children; teachers will likely perceive more behavior problems and parents will likely perceive better adjustment. Cultural and socioeconomic factors appear to play a role in the differences among and between parents and teachers in their perceptions of behavior problems and adjustment in African American children. Culturally and socioeconomically sensitive strategies for identifying behavior problems of African American children seem clearly indicated.

Assessment Guidelines

In Chapter 1, a culturally sensitive definition of behavior problems was offered. It was stated that behavior problems are actions or inactions of an individual that (1) are inconsistent with the specified, understood, and culturally accepted behavioral rules for the setting in which these actions or inactions occurred, and (2) have potentially negative consequences for the individual or others. This definition suggests using the following important guidelines for developing culturally sensitive strategies to identify behavior problems among African American children.

1. *Separate the children from their behavior problem.* Too often African American children are referred to as "behavior problem children" or "behavior problem teens." This shorthand description conveys the message that the behavior problems that some African American children manifest are aspects of their personalities and permeate their beings. Consequently, rejection of these behavior problems or refusal to tolerate them is experienced by the children as rejection of themselves as human beings. Teachers do not want "behavior problem children" in their classrooms, and many students do not want these

children in their academic or social groups. The unwanted children respond to this perceived rejection with hostile behaviors and with other negative behaviors that are consistent with their "behavior problem" label; this action–reaction cycle then repeats itself.

Examples of common shorthand statements that fail to separate children from their
behavior and, consequently, stigmatize and perpetuate behavior problems among these
youth are:

> "Gerald, you have gotten on my last nerve."
> "Mary, why are you such a loud person?"
> "John, you are a disturbance to the entire class."
> "Clarence is the class clown."
> "Jennifer, you are so rude; no one wants a rude person for a friend."

The following alternatives to the foregoing statements separate children from their
problem behaviors:

> "Gerald stop throwing balls of paper at your classmates. This behavior makes me
> feel angry and disappointed that you are not studying. Please study the word
> definitions that I have given you to learn."
>
> "Mary, why do you yell at your classmates?"
>
> "John, your dancing, singing, and making funny faces in class disturbs your class-
> mates and me."
>
> "Clarence does many clownlike behaviors in the class."
>
> "Jennifer, you choose to engage in a lot of rude behaviors such as cursing that will
> keep others from being your friend, though they would like to be your friend."

2. *Identify specific rather than vague or global behavior problems.* The preceding
alternate statements also state the specific behavior problems or give an example of the
behavior problems to which attention was being called. Limiting one's reference to specific behavior problems of a child connotes recognition that there are other aspects of the
child's behavior that are satisfactory and that the child as a person is not being rejected.
Consequently, the child will likely be more cooperative in efforts to modify the specified
problem behaviors.

However, the fact is that teachers, psychologists, counselors, parents, and others
often use vague or global terms to describe behavior problems of children—terms such as
hyperactive, withdrawn, angry, disruptive, rebellious, and *defiant.* Because these terms are
vague and have different meanings and associated behaviors among different groups and
individuals, these terms may be misleading in describing the behavior of a particular child.
Furthermore, commonly used vague terms such as *defiance* often lose their meaning without this being realized. Recently, the present author had the opportunity to ask teachers at
a school about the meaning of the term *defiance* given that defiance was one of the behaviors that resulted in school suspension. Interestingly, there was much variety in the definitions given by the teachers. Parents with children in the school generally did not know the
school's definition of the term *defiance.* Yet, some of their children had been suspended
from school for defiance. Clearly, such vague or global terms do little to facilitate identification of behavior problems among children.

Teachers, parents and primary caregivers, counselors, psychologists, and others involved with children and adolescents can contribute much to modification of behavior problems by African American children by specifically describing the behaviors that they observe and perceive to be problematic. For example, rather than simply saying that a child's aggressive behavior is a concern, it would be useful to add that the child verbally and physically threatens other peers who touch her or his possessions, makes demands of peers, and takes what is wanted (e.g., a pencil) from peers without asking. It is also useful to give an example of an occasion in which the behavior problem occurred. Such specific information facilitates clear identifications of behavior problems and provides clear implications for modifying and preventing their occurrence.

3. *Be aware that behaviors perceived as behavior problems by some may not be perceived as such by others.* Some behaviors of African American children that are deemed acceptable in certain African American mini-cultures (i.e., groups with many common values, traditions, and experiences but that differ in some significant way such as with regard to socioeconomic status) may be deemed unacceptable in majority mini-cultures and in some other African American mini-cultures. For example, it is acceptable among some African American mini-cultures for African American teens to use the term *nigger* in expressions of friendship, in playful interactions, or in jokes, whereas this verbal behavior is viewed as a behavior problem among most majority mini-cultures and among some African American mini-cultures.

It is indeed not unusual for teachers in various cultural groups to be extremely disturbed by the use of the term *nigger* by African American students and all other students. Some African American students feel *nigger* is a term that African Americans can use in a nonderogatory manner, but that it should not be used by European Americans because of its historical use by European Americans to degrade and subjugate African Americans. These cultural and socioeconomic differences in the perceptions of communications that involve the word *nigger* can lead to being punished by teachers and principals at school for such communications and to feelings of belonging and closeness with family at home and friends at home and at school.

Humming and rhythmic tapping on the desk while sitting in class are also examples of behaviors that some people would consider behavior problems and others would not. Whereas most teachers would consider these behaviors to be behavior problems, many African American parents would not consider these behaviors problematic because they are behaviors with rich histories in African American cultures. African American children often are not even aware that they are engaging in these behaviors until they are told to stop these behaviors. When most African American children engage in humming and rhythmic tapping at home while studying or doing homework, these behaviors are usually not even noticed and typically are not discouraged. For some children, not doing these behaviors becomes disruptive to their concentration. Thus, labeling African American children's humming and rhythmic tapping behaviors as behavior problems may be a major source of conflict between teachers and both the children who hum and tap and their parents. This problem, however, is one that can be overcome with culturally sensitive strategies for identifying behavior problems among African American children.

It is also important to note that some behaviors that most if not all teachers, other school staff, psychologists, and counselors consider behavior problems at school are in fact encouraged in some African American families. For example, many African American fathers and other members of African American families encourage children, especially their sons, to fight if threatened, hit, or humiliated and to fight if necessary to provide needed defense of siblings. Fighting skill and courage are viewed by these African American families as necessary among African American boys and men given that these boys and men continue to be common victims of racism and gang violence. Evidence of the existence of this view was provided in an interview study in which fifteen African American grandmothers and fifteen European American grandmothers from working-class backgrounds were asked about their views regarding fighting by children (Hale-Benson, 1986). The African American grandmothers in the study reported feeling that African American children need to know how to fight, whereas the European American grandmothers in the study disapproved of fighting.

It is important for teachers, psychologists, and other professionals who work with African American children to know that their parents may not accept the view that fighting by their children is a behavior problem simply because teachers and other professionals consider it a behavior problem. It is also important for these professionals to understand that African American youth will be resistant to and angry about having behaviors taught or sanctioned at home perceived as behavior problems at school.

4. *Realize that rules in a setting often determine whether or not some behaviors are considered behavior problems.* The rules in particular settings rather than the behaviors or perceptions of the behaviors are often determinants of whether or not the behaviors are labeled behavior problems. Unless African Americans know the rules of the setting that they are in, they may find their behaviors viewed as defiant, aggressive, rebellious, or otherwise problematic. For example, refusing to remove one's hat and laughing and talking loudly may be viewed as problematic behaviors in a performing arts theater; yet, for those African American children who have not visited a performing arts theater before, their behaviors are simply a reflection of not knowing the often unspoken rules of behavior in such settings. Ironically, it is often expected that African American children from low socioeconomic backgrounds should know what are and are not appropriate behaviors even in social settings that are not part of normal life experiences for them.

Clearly, it is important that when identifying behavior problems, behaviors that occur without an understanding of the behavioral rules of the setting should not be labeled behavior problems. Avoidance of this mislabeling will require sensitivity to the lack of knowledge that might underlie inappropriate behaviors in certain settings. This sensitivity is especially important given that problem behaviors often occur to mask such a lack of knowledge. For example, in a situation where each member of a group of peer adolescents is calculating the gratuity for their postbasketball game meal, an African American student (or any student) who has never had to calculate gratuity and does not know how to do so might avoid disclosure of this lack of knowledge by criticizing the food and loudly expressing this dissatisfaction as a reason for deciding not to leave a tip for the waiter.

5. *Consider that in order for behaviors of African American youth to be diagnosed as behavior problems the behaviors must have occurred after having learned alternative appropriate behaviors.* It is certainly not appropriate for teachers, parents, or others to label behaviors of African American children as problematic when these youth do not have alternative behaviors in their repertoire of behaviors to use instead of the problem behaviors. It is desirable for teachers, parents, and other educators to teach African American youth the behaviors that are appropriate in particular settings and to teach them why these behaviors are appropriate. Most important, teachers must role-play situations or ask questions to determine whether the children understand and can do what it is that they have been taught. It cannot be assumed that just because African American children have been taught appropriate behaviors that they have truly learned them.

Learning of desirable or appropriate behaviors for different settings, especially when those settings are very different from one's home environment, requires practice by the learner and patience by the person in the teacher role. The practice can be facilitated by playing a "What Would You Do If Game." In this game children are given several situations and asked what they would do in each situation. Examples of such situations are as follows:

> What would you do if your teacher asked you to take your hat off?
>
> What would you do if someone told your teacher that you cheated off of her paper and you did not do so?
>
> What would you do if someone slapped your sister for refusing to participate in a plan to play a practical joke on her teacher?

At a minimum weekly discussions of such questions at school, church, and at home will help teach African American youth desirable behaviors for a variety of settings. This teaching ideally should occur regularly and should involve having the children praise themselves, and having others (e.g., parents and teachers) praise them for decreases in inappropriate behaviors and increases in the use of alternative behaviors to the inappropriate behaviors.

Given that a definition of problem behaviors is not universally agreed on and depends on the situation in which such behavior occurs, it is particularly important that children are not ridiculed, degraded, and humiliated for inappropriate behaviors. Instead, children should be told when the inappropriate behaviors are at least acceptable (if ever), why they are not acceptable in a specified context, and what is appropriate in that context and why. Ridicule, degradation, and humiliation only draw the attention of others (e.g., peers); such attention serves as a reinforcer of the inappropriate or problem behavior(s). Ridicule, degradation, and humiliation of African American children by teachers, parents, and others also generate in these youth feelings of anger, hurt, and frustration that often result in physical, verbal, or displaced aggression by these youth. Because of their knowledge of slavery, African American children are especially likely to respond with inappropriate behaviors to perceived subjugation and humiliation by European Americans—the ethnic identity of most teachers in the United States.

Assessment Procedures

The perceived existence, severity, and prevalence of behavior problems in African American children are to some degree influenced by cultural and socioeconomic differences between these youth and some of those who have the responsibility of monitoring and shaping their behavior (e.g., teachers, principals, counselors, and psychologists). It is thus important that procedures for assessing the occurrence of a behavior problem in an African

American child reflect awareness of and respect for these differences. Such assessment procedures include the following: (1) involving the child's parents in the problem assessment process, (2) assessing the views of the child about the behavior of concern, (3) observing and interacting with the child in more than one setting, (4) getting the perspectives of culturally and socioeconomically sensitive professionals about the child's behavior, and (5) using a partnership approach with parents, the child, teachers of the child, principal of the child's school, and a psychologist or counselor working together as respected partners in the problem identification process.

Involving Parents

In order for the behavior problems of a child to be successfully modified, cooperation and support of the child's parents or primary caregiver will likely be needed. Furthermore, successful modification of behavior problems usually also requires agreement between parents, teachers, and others involved (e.g., principals, psychologists, and counselors) about the existence, severity, and prevalence of the behavior problems. This agreement about the occurrence of behavior problems is often central in providing justification for the use of time and resources to modify them.

There are several specific procedures for successfully involving African American parents in the assessment of behavior problems that their children may have. Some recommended specific procedures follow.

1. *Inform parents that they are needed experts.* The teacher and other professionals involved with the child (e.g., school counselor or psychologist) should meet with parents face-to-face versus via telephone to discuss the specific behaviors of their child that are of concern. Such meetings should occur when teachers first become concerned about the child's behaviors. In a telephone call or letter to arrange this meeting, it should be expressed how much the teacher and other professionals would appreciate this meeting and why. The point should be made that the parents really know their child better than the teacher and can share some insights that will likely be helpful to the teacher in establishing a better relationship with the child and in helping the child stop the behaviors that are interfering with the child's school success. It should also be explained to the parents that once at the school, they will be asked to observe in their child's class to possibly see their child's behaviors of concern and to get a sense of what could be done differently in the class to modify these behaviors.

2. *Initiate a discussion regarding transportation to the school.* Before contacting parents, options for arranging transportation for them should be considered so that provision of transportation to the school or assistance in arranging or paying for this transportation can be offered to the parents in the initial contact call or letter. It is important for teachers to initiate discussion of the transportation issue because parents who do not have and cannot afford transportation are often embarrassed to acknowledge this; instead, the parents may simply give some other reason as to why they cannot meet, or they may agree to meet and then later cancel the meeting. African American parents across the socioeconomic spectrum have their pride and do not want to come across as not having the basic necessities of life such as transportation.

3. *Meet with parents more than once, including in their own environment.* It is important to meet with parents about their child's behavior on more than one occasion. The first occasion might ideally be at the parents' home or at a location near the parents' home such as at a community center, a fast-food restaurant, or at a church. Meeting at public places near the parents' homes might address safety concerns about meeting in the parents' homes. The willingness of a teacher to meet with African American parents in their neighborhood communicates to parents that the teacher is genuinely interested in the child and in establishing a positive parent–teacher partnership that enables the child to be academically and socially successful. It is noteworthy that when schools were segregated, visits to the homes of African American children by teachers were common and served to build successful partnerships for education between teachers and parents and between teachers and their students.

When trying to arrange meetings with parents, the teacher should ask the parents what days, times, and places might be best for them to meet. Discussions of the best times for regular telephone meetings, parent–teacher meetings, and visits to observe in the child's class are also likely to be helpful in establishing a partnership with parents for promoting their child's academic and social success.

4. *Strive to gain the parents' trust.* Since the days of slavery in America, many African Americans have been taught not to completely trust European Americans, especially those in power. Indeed, during slavery times, if African Americans revealed too much personal information, they often suffered at the hands of cruel slave masters and other European Americans. Consequently, over the years, from parent to child, the message has been carried to tell European Americans very little about your business and your family. This heritage and the almost total lack of historical incidents where European Americans personally protected African Americans have resulted in today's generation of African Americans finding it very difficult to trust European Americans who even appear to have authority over them (Bynum, 1991).

Teacher behaviors that facilitate parents' trust include (a) honest communication with parents about wanting or needing more understanding of nonmajority children, (b) discussions with parents about what will and will not be confidential information before that information is shared, (c) asking parents' permission to involve a counselor, psychologist, or other professional in identifying or evaluating behavior problems their child might have, (d) asking parents' permission to disclose information from them to specified persons (e.g., a school counselor) involved in identifying behavior problems that their child might have, (e) listening to rather than lecturing parents, (f) expressing to parents the desire to establish a comfortable partnership with them, and (g) asking for recommendations from parents for establishing this partnership.

5. *Treat parents similarly to the way professionals are treated.* It is important that the efforts to welcome parents to meetings and to make them feel comfortable be as extensive as efforts executed for meetings with professionals such as superintendents of schools. Parents should be provided with clear directions, greeted with warm smiles and expressions of joy that they came to the meeting, escorted to the meeting place, given name tags, and offered coffee or other beverages just as is done with professionals who visit the school.

6. *Tell parents about their child's positive behaviors when discussing their child's behaviors of concern.* African American parents often have conditioned anger, irritation, or avoidance responses to contacts from teachers because these contacts are usually made to discuss problems with their children. Teachers understandably label these responses by parents as reflections of disinterest in their children's education. This is typically not the case. African American parents often simply get tired of only receiving "bad news" about their children. It is not uncommon for African American parents to ventilate this feeling in parent workshops. In addition, parents often say, "I know that my child does something well and is good sometimes." These perspectives of parents, however, typically do not get shared with teachers because of the conditioned responses to teachers giving them negative feedback about their children. Two strategies can decondition parental responses that block their communication with teachers: (a) Teachers and parents can initiate contact with each other only to discuss what the parents' children are doing well and appropriately that can be praised at home and school, and (b) teachers can include identification of children's academic strengths and success behaviors in parent–teacher meetings to discuss the children's behaviors that may be behavior problems.

Assessing the Views of the Child

It is indeed interesting that with all of the concern about behavior problems of children in general and African American children in particular, there are few reports of the involvement of the children in identifying the occurrence of and contributing factors to their behavior problems. Yet, support has been provided for such involvement. Specifically, it has been found that, when given the opportunity, students contributed novel thoughts and perspectives regarding school problems (Street, Kromrey, Reed, & Anton, 1993), solutions to address adolescent drug and alcohol abuse (Glassford, Ivanoff, Sinsky, & Pierce, 1991), and useful teacher motivational strategies (Thorkildsen, Nolen, & Fournier, 1994). It has also been found that students' and parents' perspectives are essential to ensure the success of innovative school programs (Byrnes, Shuster, & Jones, 1994).

When soliciting the perspectives of African American children regarding their own behavior, the following specific procedures are recommended.

1. *Assess the children's awareness of their behaviors of concern.* Ask the children if they are aware of engaging in the specific behaviors of concern. Many children are not aware of engaging in certain behaviors, such as kicking or hitting other children for fun during class time.

2. *Assess the children's awareness of the consequences of their behaviors of concern.* Ask the children what they think are the consequences of the behaviors in question to themselves and to others. Because behavior problems have negative consequences for the individual and others, whether or not children are aware of such consequences will help determine whether or not they see themselves as having behavior problems that need to be modified.

3. *Avoid using guilt or embarrassment-evoking tactics.* Avoid making comments to make the children feel guilty or embarrassed about the behaviors of concern. Embarrassing or making children feel guilty only negatively impacts their self-esteem and results in them being noncooperative in sharing their views about their behaviors. Furthermore, guilt and embarrassment strategies will not motivate children to participate in interventions to help them modify their behaviors.

4. *Use an empowerment approach that facilitates cooperation.* Empower the children in the discussion of their behaviors. This can be done by letting the children know that they can end the discussion when this is desired and that they are really helping you by talking with you. Additionally, let the children know that they are in control of their behavior and are very knowledgeable about when, where, and how often they engage in each of various behaviors.

5. *Find opportunities to give positive feedback.* Too often as a result of concern with the behavior problems and academic problems of African American children, we forget to notice and acknowledge their positive behaviors and strengths. Yet, African American children need positive attention and affection to facilitate self-esteem and self-confidence just as do other children. Furthermore, they can more comfortably and honestly acknowledge their problem behaviors when they feel that their positive behaviors are recognized and valued by individuals with status such as their teachers.

6. *Show interest in the children as well as in their views of their behaviors.* For various reasons many African American children are suspicious of questioning by European Americans and others who are culturally and socioeconomically different from themselves. Perhaps television is a major reason for this suspicion given that European Americans and other ethnic characters on television programs are often involved in questioning African Americans and then arresting them or killing them for one reason or another. In any case, it is particularly important to establish some rapport with African American children before soliciting information from them. Talking with them about such topics as their interests or hobbies, what they want to be in the future, and what they enjoy most and least about school are usually helpful in building rapport. It is, however, important to be honest with African American children about why you want to talk with them—to learn about their behaviors at school and home.

Observing and Interacting with the Child

Most African American children must live and learn in two different cultures—the one in which they are being raised (i.e., their home environment) and the one in which they spend much of their time preparing for future economic and social success (i.e., their school environment). Their behaviors that are accepted in one culture may be considered behavior problems in the other culture. Thus, it should be expected that some African American children will not be perfect in learning and remembering which behaviors are appropriate or inappropriate in each cultural environment. By observing and interacting with these children in both settings, we can determine the prevalence of the behaviors of concern, their severity and frequency, and whether they are culture-specific behavior problems. All of this information is important for developing appropriate interventions to modify the behaviors of concern or for deciding to allow the behaviors to occur but in ways that do not have negative consequences for the children or others.

When observing and interacting with African American children in their home environments, it is especially important to be culturally and socioeconomically sensitive. The following specific procedures will facilitate culturally and socioeconomically sensitive observations and interactions.

1. *Become knowledgeable about the children's living environments.* Most professionals (e.g., teachers and psychologists) involved with evaluating and addressing behavior problems of African American children are European Americans and most are from middle-class backgrounds that are very different from the home and community environments of these children. Consequently, these professionals are often not prepared for the poverty, crowded living conditions, substandard housing, and other living conditions that they may find where African American children live. As a result the professionals may be surprised and uncomfortable with these conditions. Children from such an environment who are being assessed for behavior problems will likely perceive this discomfort and, thus, limit their interactions with these professionals or reject these professionals altogether.

Thus, to minimize possible surprise and discomfort in response to the living environments of African American children whose behaviors are being assessed, it is important that the professionals involved with the assessments read about African American cultures, visit the children's neighborhood, and learn about the strengths and resources in the children's neighborhood. African American children will relate more comfortably and more honestly with professionals who perceive the strengths of their families and neighborhoods and who are knowledgeable about and comfortable with both.

2. *Attempt to minimize embarrassment about living conditions.* Many African American children and their parents in the low socioeconomic classes are embarrassed by their living conditions and resent or reject others who evidence feelings of superiority over them because of living comfortable, middle-class lives. To minimize this embarrassment, it is important that with parental approval children being assessed for a behavior problem help choose where they might interact with a psychologist or teacher in their living environments. For example, children might choose a community center, basketball court, or the backyard of their homes. It is also effective for the professionals to share their life experiences that are similar to that of the children's families with the children and their parents. Indeed, many middle-class Americans, especially those who are African Americans, have not always lived comfortable, middle-class lifestyles.

Embarrassment by African American children and their parents regarding visits to their home environments from professionals to assess the children can also be minimized by warm responses from the professionals to efforts from the children and their parents to welcome them. For example, if a parent took time off from work to be home or if extra clean-up efforts were made for a visit by professionals, the visiting professionals should express appreciation for these actions. Perhaps most importantly, professionals can tactfully communicate to the African American children being visited that "it is not where you come from that is really important; rather, it is where you are headed in life that is important."

Involving Culturally and Socioeconomically Sensitive Professionals

When identifying behavior problems among African American children, it is most appropriate to include the perspectives of one or more professionals other than teachers of these children. This is because teachers often do not have the time to focus on the prevalence and actual frequency and severity of behaviors of concern in any one child or group of children because teachers usually have a large group of students who need and deserve their attention. Furthermore, the teachers of African American children are often from cultural and socioeconomic backgrounds that are very different from the backgrounds of these children. Such teachers typically have not had training or experiences that promote awareness of and sensitivity to cultural and socioeconomic differences; consequently, these teachers may perceive, experience, and respond to the behaviors of African American children very differently from the parents of these children or from professionals who are aware of and sensitive to cultural and socioeconomic differences. It is thus wise to have involved in the problem assessment process a counselor, psychologist, or other teacher who is culturally and socioeconomically sensitive.

It is important that this team of culturally and socioeconomically sensitive professionals include one or more African American professionals. This is because children and their parents will likely feel more trusting of the team because it includes an African American—someone of their own ethnicity with whom they can at least physically identify. Indeed, most African American parents and professionals are skeptical of evaluations made by a team of European Americans who have or are perceived as having authority over them.

Where do you find African American professionals to help identify and modify behavior problems of African American children? Most school administrators and others typically do not know the answer to such a question. Indeed, African American counselors, psychologists, and teachers are not always readily available to consult on cases involving behavior problems of African American children. However, there are several strategies that can be used to identify and recruit these African American consultants. These strategies include advertising in the local newspaper, recruiting via the regional and state teachers' associations, psychologists' associations, and counselors' associations, and soliciting the help of African American parents and nearby universities in finding appropriate African American professionals. It is important that all team members selected be very interested in and care about promoting the academic and social success of African American children.

Using a Partnership Approach

Ideally the parents of the children whose behaviors are of concern should be partners with the teachers of the children and the counselors, psychologists, or other professionals who will help assess the occurrence of the behaviors of concern. It is important for these individuals to work together as equally respected partners in all aspects of the problem assessment process. There are several specific procedures that will facilitate such partnerships.

1. *Obtain parental approval of the team.* The parents of the children whose behaviors are of concern should ideally be informed and given the courtesy of approving those individuals who will be deciding whether or not their children have behavior problems and the nature of these problems. This procedure will facilitate parents' participation in and cooperation with the problem identification process. It will also facilitate parents' participation in and support of interventions to modify identified behavior problems or interventions to assure that if behaviors of concern occur, they will not have negative consequences for their children or the classmates of their children.

2. *Establish a team plan and team objectives.* It is very important for the team of partners to meet for the purpose of planning what will be done to assess the behaviors of concern. The specific objectives of the assessment and timeline for accomplishing them as well as procedures for handling team disagreements should be decided at the planning meeting. Furthermore, a team coordinator should be identified by an appropriate school administrator.

The objectives of the team when assessing children's behaviors of concern should include determining (a) whether the behaviors of concern meet the criteria of a culturally and socioeconomically sensitive definition of a behavior problem, (b) when, where, and under what conditions the behaviors of concern occur, and (c) what might be contributing factors to these behaviors. Once these objectives are met, formulation of a plan for addressing the behaviors of concern and for assessing the effectiveness of the plan should occur. The ultimate objective is, of course, to empower the children with replacement behaviors, skills, and knowledge to modify their own behaviors in ways that facilitate their academic and social success.

3. *Optimize the likelihood of parent participation in team meetings.* All efforts should be made to schedule team meetings in advance and to facilitate parents' attendance to these meetings. Facilitation of parents' participation often will involve placing phone calls to remind parents of the meetings, assisting them with transportation, having someone at the meeting site who can babysit their children while they are in the meetings, and holding the meeting in the community near the parents.

Assessment Methods

Among the traditional methods of assessing behavior problems in children are those that with some modification can be culturally and socioeconomically sensitive. Only these methods will be discussed next along with how each might be used in assessing behavior problems of African American children.

The Clinical Interview

Traditionally, clinical interviews are conducted with a child's parent and teachers to determine the frequency, duration, and prevalence of the behaviors of concern and to determine the conditions (e.g., thoughts, feelings, experiences, and activities) that cause or contribute to and maintain the behaviors of concern. There are structured interviews in which a list of questions is asked in an organized format and answers are recorded in a systematic manner. Such interviews are designed to minimize the role of the interviewer's subjective judgment. There are also unstructured interviews in which the interviewer is given great latitude in what is asked toward the goal of getting desired information. Additionally, there are semistructured interviews in which the interviewer is allowed some flexibility in what is asked, how questions are phrased, and how responses are recorded (Wicks-Nelson, 1997, p. 101).

According to Edelbrock, Costello, Dulcan, Kalas, and Conover (1985), research on the validity of interviews is needed. One of the few studies on this topic, which involved administration of the structured Diagnostic Interview of Children, found that structured interview test–retest reliability based on child reports were lower for younger children than for older children, whereas the reliability based on parent reports was higher for the younger children (Edelbrock et al., 1985). The authors of this study suggest that the found reliabilities of the parent reports may indicate that parents are less aware of their children's behaviors as they grow older and that the lower reliability of the younger children's reports relative to the reliability of the older children's reports may reflect the lower cognitive development of the younger children. This study is mentioned here because even though the study did not focus on African American children, it supports clinical judgment to ask simpler questions of younger children, regardless of ethnicity, and to perhaps rely less on the interview information from younger children as compared to the information from older children in the process of assessing behavior problems.

There are some clinical interviews that seem especially appropriate when assessing behavior problems of African American children. Adjustments in the interview process with African American children are indicated when interviewing younger versus older children.

The Semistructured Clinical Interview with the Younger Child.   Many of the problems of younger African American children include such problems as not paying attention, playing and talking when they should be doing schoolwork, not following instructions, getting out of their seats at inappropriate times, making disruptive noises, engaging in off-task behaviors to make classmates laugh, social withdrawal, refusal to follow rules, and refusal to cooperate with requests from teachers and parents. According to Hale-Benson (1986), these problems may be related to the schedule of classroom activities, the fatigue level of the children, the difficulty or monotony of classroom activities, the level of flexibility of class rules, and the nutrition or health of the children. Thus, when conducting a clinical interview with a child, it is important to assess these areas and other such areas that might be related to the behaviors of African American children that are of concern or that may be behavior problems.

Assessment of what was occurring before, during, and after the behavior of concern, as perceived by the child, is also important to get some sense of the reinforcement and other contingencies or factors that might be contributing to or sustaining the behavior. What the child has learned in the home, school, or community regarding the behavior and the child's perceptions regarding the occurrence and the consequences of the behavior are also important to know in determining whether the behavior is a problem and what might be factors in the occurrence of the behavior.

The child whose behavior is being assessed is truly the expert regarding the occurrence of the behaviors that are of concern to teachers, parents, and others. It is recommended that the African American child be asked about the behavior(s) of concern using a semistructured interview format—an interview in which questions need not be asked in a particular format and can be integrated among other questions and conversation to facilitate the comfort of the interviewee (the child). The child can be asked questions similar to the following, simplifying them to be age appropriate.

1. Does the behavior occur? If so when, where, and how often?
2. Why does the behavior occur?
3. Do you remember the last time the behavior occurred? If so, what were you thinking, feeling, and doing just before you did it? What were you thinking and feeling, and what else were you doing while you did the behavior? What did you think, feel, and do just after you did the behavior?
4. When is it okay for this behavior to occur? When is it not okay for this behavior to occur?

5. What have you been taught about this behavior at home? What have you been taught about it at school? What have you been taught about this behavior at church, if you attend church?

6. Do your friends do this behavior? Why do they do it?

7. Can you not do this behavior if you choose not to do it?

8. What has happened to you in the past when you have done this behavior at home? What has happened to you in the past when you have done this behavior at school? What has happened to a friend, classmate, or someone else because of doing this behavior at school?

9. What would it take for you not to do this behavior?

10. Do you get bored, tired, or hungry in class? What time of day does this usually occur? What do you do when you get bored, tired, or hungry in class?

11. Do you eat breakfast and lunch every day?

12. Do you ever just not feel well at school? When does this occur? What do you do when this occurs?

13. Do you want to stop doing this behavior? Why or why not?

14. How do you feel talking with me (the interviewer) about this behavior?

15. Are there any questions that you would like to ask me?

Other questions that will be asked will depend on the specific behaviors that are of concern. For example, if the child's behaviors include sexual acting out behaviors in class such as fondling another child's or one's own genitals and engaging in sex talk, then the questions in the interview would also address related issues such as self-esteem issues, family teachings regarding sexuality, sexual behaviors and discussions to which the child is exposed at home, the child's sexual experiences, possible sexual abuse, and so on.

With parental permission to do so, it is important that a semistructured interview with any child be conducted in a confidential and comfortable setting in which others will not distract the child or hear what the child has to say. Rapport should be established with the child by talking with the child about her or his interests, hobbies, aspirations, and so on. The child should be told that what is discussed in the interview may be shared with the child's parents, teachers, and other adults outside the child's family who are interested in helping the child be successful in school. Responses to questions asked should be written either during or immediately after the interview. If they are written during the interview, the child being interviewed should be told that notes will be taken so as not to forget the child's responses to questions asked because the child's thoughts and opinions are important. The child should also be told that she or he does not have to answer any question that makes the child feel uncomfortable or that she or he simply does not want to answer. Written parental consent for clinical interviews with the child should be obtained.

The Semistructured Clinical Interview with the Adolescent.   In addition to the just-mentioned behaviors in which younger African American children often engage, older African American children or adolescents often display behaviors such as alcohol use, use of other drugs, stealing, frequent use of profane language, and verbal and physical aggression. It is not uncommon for African American adolescents to be overtly uncommunicative, uncooperative, and unresponsive in interactions with adults, especially those who try to direct, supervise, and instruct them. These overt behaviors often mask underlying depression due to family problems, school failure, rejection by valued others, and destructive behaviors such as eating disorders and drug abuse (Franklin, 1982; Gibbs, 1981). Adolescent behavior problems also sometimes mask feelings of inadequacy because of poor grades, limited socialization experiences and communication styles, and living conditions that are different from those of their more economically advantaged peers. Indeed, African American adolescents often engage in problem behaviors because they do not know, or do not know how to engage in, the alternative appropriate behaviors sanctioned by the majority culture.

The anxiety often associated with community violence, physical punishment, fear of failure, and other problems is also associated with behaviors of African American adolescents that are often of concern to teachers, counselors, and parents. In younger adolescents anxiety-related problems include hyperactivity, acting out, and aggression, whereas in older adolescents the problems often include delinquent activity, substance abuse, and promiscuity (Franklin, 1982; Gibbs, 1982).

Peer pressure and the desire to be accepted by peers are especially strong in adolescence and, consequently, often result in group memberships (e.g., membership in gangs, tightly bonded groups of same-sex friends) that encourage engaging in behaviors that are illegal or inappropriate. Such behaviors are typically viewed by gangs and sometimes by other groups as shows of group loyalty that are necessary for the privilege of group identity and group protection (Mancini, 1980). Premarital sexual activity and low academic achievement among low-income African American adolescents have been linked to their high involvement in certain types of peer groups (Felner, Aber, Primavera, & Cauce, 1985). Among inner-city African American adolescents, not belonging to a gang or peer group has been linked to being excluded from activities, being negatively labeled, and being physically harassed (Viadero, 1988).

Level of social support (e.g., support from church and extended family), level of comfortableness, and level of perceived safety in schools and neighborhoods dominated by European Americans may also be factors in behavior problems of African American adolescents and, thus, assessment of this support is important when assessing the behavior problems of these adolescents. African American adolescents who do not feel supported and do not feel safe often respond with hostility, fear and anxiety, and other acting-out behaviors. Furthermore, when they see violence, illegal activities, and poverty in their families and neighborhoods, they often develop a sense of social isolation and hopelessness about their future, which increases their vulnerability to anger, involvement in self-destructive activities such as sexual acting out, and drug use (Gibbs, 1988; Hare, 1988). In a study of African American adolescents' perceptions of their family climate, it was found that those adolescents who perceived high levels of conflict in their families reported more psychological symptoms than those who perceived low levels of conflict (Dancy & Handal, 1984).

Given the many areas of the lives of African American adolescents that are often factors in their behavior problems, it is clearly important that clinical interviews to assess their behavior problems involve a multidimensional assessment. This type of assessment focuses on different aspects of the individual and on family, school, and community influences that may be factors in the behaviors of concern.

Some of the specific areas of assessment and questions in each area that are usually important in multidimensional interviews with African American adolescents with behaviors of concern are as follows:

1. The adolescent's feelings about self and perceptions about others' views of herself or himself

    a. What are your thoughts and feelings about yourself as a person? What are ten characteristics that you like about yourself and ten characteristics about yourself that you would change if you could?

    b. How do you feel about your physical self such as your skin color, weight, and hair? How do you think that your peers and family feel about your skin color, weight, and hair?

    c. What are ten characteristics that you like about your physical self and what are ten characteristics about your physical self that you would change if you could?

    d. Does how you feel about yourself as a person or about your physical self contribute to your _____ behavior (the behavior problem)?

2. Emotional well-being

    a. How often do you generally feel happy or at least not unhappy, if ever? What makes you feel happy? What do you do when you feel happy?

    b. How often do you feel unhappy, if ever? What kinds of experiences make you feel this way? Can you give an example of a time you felt really unhappy? What did you think about and do when you felt this way? What was the outcome of your action(s) for you and others involved?

    c. How often do you feel really down, if ever? What kinds of experiences make you feel this way? Can you give an example of a time that you felt really down? What did you think about and do in this situation? What was the outcome of your action(s) for you and others involved?

    d. Have you ever felt that life is not worth living? When did this happen? What were you thinking, feeling, and doing just before having this thought? Did you think of ending your life? What kept you from doing this? What was the outcome of this situation for you and others involved?

    e. Do you ever feel anxious or nervous? What causes you to feel this way? Can you give me an example of a situation recently when you felt anxious? What did you do and think about in this situation? What was the outcome of this situation for you and others involved? What helped you to get over your anxiety or nervousness?

    f. Do your emotions have anything to do with your doing the behavior (the problem behavior)? How are they related?

    g. When you feel anxious, unhappy, or really down, with whom do you talk to feel better? Why do you choose to talk with this particular person?

3. Interpersonal relationships

    a. Do you have a group of friends with whom you are really close? Would you call this group a gang? What do you get from this group? Does it influence your _____ behavior (the behavior problem)?

    b. What would happen if you chose not to be close with your friends or gang or not to do what they do?

    c. Do your friends do the _____ behavior (the problem behavior)? What are the consequences of the behavior for you and what are the consequences of the behavior for your friends?

  d. How do your family and community view hanging with a group or gang?

  e. Have you ever gotten in trouble because of your group or gang?

  f. What difficulties, if any, do you have getting along with adolescents who are not African American?

  g. Have you had any experiences in which you feel that you have been treated differently because you are African American? How did you handle these experiences? What was the outcome of your actions?

  h. Do you have difficulty trusting others? If so, why?

4. Views on sex in adolescence

  a. What are your views on sex in adolescence?

  b. What and who have influenced you to feel the way that you feel about having sex?

  c. What are your views as to the risks and consequences of sex in adolescence?

  d. What have you been taught about sex and birth control, and what has been the source of this information?

  e. Have you experienced peer pressure or pressures from your girlfriend (or boyfriend) to have sex, and if so, how has this pressure affected you and your behavior at school?

5. Perceived behavior management skills and communication skills

  a. How satisfied are you with how well you handle anger and frustration? Have you allowed your anger or frustration to get you in trouble? What was the trouble?

  b. Have you had any training in handling anger and frustration so that you do not get into trouble?

  c. How satisfied are you with your English when talking before your entire class? How satisfied are you with your English when talking with individuals whom you do not know?

  d. When you disagree with your parents or teachers, how do you express your disagreement? What do you do and say?

  e. What have you been taught at home and at school about handling disagreements? What have you been taught at home and at school about handling anger and frustration?

  f. Can you tell family members and friends the thoughts and feelings that you want to tell them? If not, why not?

  g. Does feeling angry or frustrated ever lead to your _____ behavior (the behavior problem)?

6. Family life

  a. If you could change anything about your family life, what would you change? Why?

  b. If you could change anything about your roles and responsibilities in your family, what would you change? Why?

  c. Are there rules in your home? Do you think that the rules are fair? What happens when rules are not followed by you or others?

  d. When there are conflicts and arguments in your home, how are they handled? How do conflicts and arguments at home affect you?

    e. Do you get the privacy and proper sleep that you need in your home? Do you feel that you eat enough of the food that you need for good health?

    f. In your family do you call each other harsh names or criticize each other to get a good laugh? How many siblings and others live in your home?

    g. Do you give praise, encouragement, and shows of affection (kisses, hugs, etc.) to family members or others living in your home? Do you receive praise, encouragement, and shows of affection from family members?

    h. What are your feelings about your relationship with your parents or guardians and your siblings? How would you change each of these relationships if you could?

    i. What is the attitude of your family toward European Americans? Does ethnicity or race of another person have any effect on your relationship with that person?

    j. Is your neighborhood desegregated? Are your neighbors mostly African Americans or European Americans?

    k. Does anything that happens at home have an effect on the occurrence of your _____ behavior (the behavior problem)?

7. School life

    a. If you could change anything about your life as a student at your school, what would you change? Why?

    b. If you could change your relationships with your teachers at school, what would you change? Why?

    c. Do you feel safe and relaxed at your school and in your classes? If not, why not?

    d. Do you feel like you are part of your school—that you belong there? If not, why not?

    e. Do you have any difficulty keeping up with your class work? Why? How does this make you feel?

    f. Is there anything about the students or teachers at your school that contributes to your _____ behavior (the behavior problem)?

All the preceding interview areas and interview questions will likely not need to be covered in an interview with an adolescent. The areas and questions addressed will depend on the nature of the behavior of concern, which may indeed be a behavior problem. It is usually a good idea to ask one or two questions from all interview areas to make sure that an area that is particularly related to the problem of concern is not overlooked.

    Because African American adolescents may feel particularly uncomfortable sharing personal information such as information about their thoughts and feelings and their family life, it is a good idea to emphasize to these adolescents that they are not obligated to answer any question. It is also a good idea to be clear regarding the level of confidentiality of their responses to the interview questions and to give these adolescents samples of the kinds of questions you will likely ask. A rationale for the interview should be presented. A rationale might be that talking with them about all aspects of their lives will give the interviewer the opportunity to get to know them and will generate some ideas for assisting them in being academically successful and in reaching their future goals.

    Given that a semistructured multidimensional interview often takes more than an hour, the interview should ideally be conducted in parts at different times. This is especially important for many African American youth whose cultures influence them to enjoy more lively activities than participation in a clinical interview. To make the interview as interesting as possible, the interviewer should ask questions with enthusiasm and show great interest in the responses received.

The Clinical Semistructured Interview with the Parent. Parents should be interviewed for several reasons, including to get their views regarding the occurrence of the behavior of concern, its possible causes, whether they view the behavior as problematic, their feelings about having their child's behavior assessed, and their feelings toward those involved in the assessment process. It is important that African American parents give written consent to be interviewed because doing so is another way of acknowledging and respecting their control in the assessment process. It is also important to address each parent with an appropriate title, such as Mr. or Mrs. For too long African American parents have been addressed by their first names and expected to address others such as psychologists by their professional titles. Such a double standard is not conducive to a partnership with parents in the assessment of behaviors of concern in their children.

Questions similar to the following questions ideally should be asked in interviews with African American parents to assess behaviors of concern in their children.

1. Are there any questions, comments, or concerns you would like to share regarding the concerns about your child's behavior or this meeting?
2. Do you feel that your child has a behavior problem? If so, what behavior do you consider a behavior problem? If not, why do you think that others (specify) have concerns about your child's behavior (specify the behavior of concern)?
3. What and who do you think contribute to the behavior (the behavior problem)?
4. Have you observed your child at school? Was there anything during your observation that concerned you about your child's behavior or the behaviors of others who interacted with your child (e.g., teacher)?
5. Have you observed the behavior (the behavior problem) at home or anywhere?
6. How do you feel about meeting to discuss your child's behavior?
7. Do you think it is possible that the behavior occurs at school but not at home? If so, why do you think that this is the case?
8. Have you had any reports of concern with your child's behavior in the past? What was the concern and who raised it? How was this situation resolved?
9. How would you like to see this concern with your child's behavior handled? How would you like future concerns about your child's behavior handled?
10. What have you found to be effective in disciplining your child? How does your child feel about such discipline?
11. What do you think is important for teachers and others who work to educate your child to know about your child and your family that will help them understand and work successfully with your child?
12. Are you willing to meet with your child's teacher and the school counselor or a psychologist as a team to help identify and understand any behavior of concern by your child and then help address the behavior in a way that the team agrees is satisfactory?
13. What will make meeting with us possible and most comfortable and convenient for you?

The semistructured clinical interview with African American parents should include opportunities throughout for their questions, comments, and concerns. It is important to make parents feel that their thoughts and feelings matter and that their parenting is not under investigation. It is also important to look for and give deserving praise for the parenting efforts and skills and for the parents' concern about their child's school and life success.

Behavioral Observation

Direct observation of the child in the classroom, on the playground, or at home is also a traditional assessment method; however, direct observation at the child's home often does not occur. This is because of the time, energy, and effort involved in scheduling and making a home visit to conduct the observation. Behavioral observation in an African American child's home is especially unlikely given that many of these children live in low-income, high-risk neighborhoods in which many teachers, counselors, and psychologists feel uncomfortable and afraid to enter. It is these professionals who typically conduct behavioral observations. Yet, behavioral observations across multiple settings including the home can provide valuable information for understanding what causes and sustains behaviors of concern or behavior problems.

Direct behavioral observations in the home may involve observing single discrete behaviors (e.g., yelling behavior) to observing family interactions (e.g., discipline strategies, alliances). Whatever is being observed should be clearly defined so that you know what to focus on and to record. Usually what is being observed will shed some light on the child's behavior. For example, yelling by the child may mirror the yelling by parents and siblings to get attention, to create fear, or just to have fun. The use and meaning of yelling in the home and the consequences it brings give some insight to why the child yells and what sustains this behavior.

Direct behavioral observations in more than one setting and at different times of the day for several days give some idea of how prevalent a behavior is and some indication of what conditions might be instrumental in its occurrence. For example, if a child distracts others by off-task talking or touching them a lot only in the late morning every day whether the child is involved in indoor tasks or outdoor tasks, attention is directed to determining what it is about the midmorning that could cause the off-task talking and touching behavior. Some good hypotheses to be examined can be generated at this point. It may be hypothesized that the child is hungry just before lunch because of no breakfast and, thus, finds it difficult to concentrate and learn at this time. Information to support or refute this hypothesis can be obtained. If the information suggests that the child is indeed hungry, then an intervention might be to work in partnership with the child's parents to make sure that the child receives breakfast each day or a midmorning snack. Behavioral observations would continue in order to see if the off-task touching and talking behavior decreased after providing the child with breakfast or a midmorning snack.

Conducting behavioral observations usually involves counting the frequency or duration of a behavior of concern within a short period of time (e.g., five minutes). The frequencies or durations should be systematically recorded on a behavioral observation sheet, which can be easily constructed by hand or computer. A teacher, teacher's aide, or designated other can observe and record the occurrence of the behavior(s) of interest. Any changes in the behavior with the implementation of an intervention or for some other reason such as a visit by a parent or other observer can be determined. Changes in the behavior due to an observer's presence likely show that the child knows that the behavior is inappropriate and can easily control it. These changes, often called reactivity changes, also are a weakness in behavioral observations in general because they interfere with getting a true baseline of how frequently and when the behavior being observed occurs. One solution to this problem is to have the observer present for long periods of time in the home or classroom before actually recording the occurrence of the behavior of concern; as a consequence, children and families (in the case of home observations) return to their normal behaviors and interactions before the formal observations and recording of data on the occurrence of the behavior of concern begin. Indeed, good behavior to impress an observer is usually temporary and, thus, after a while is not maintained in the presence of the observer.

Because most teachers, counselors, and psychologists are European Americans and given that these are the individuals who usually conduct behavioral observations of children, the African American child who is assessed for a behavior problem will likely be culturally and socioeconomically different from the observer. Thus, it is important to either recruit an African American observer who is socioeconomically and culturally sensitive, or use observers who are not African American but have this sensitivity and are knowledgeable about and comfortable with African American children and families. These children and families sense discomfort from others different from themselves. Such discomfort increases and sustains reactivity changes in behavior, rendering the behavioral observations invalid. Given the difficulties inherent in behavioral observations and their usefulness, it is recommended that they be used in combination with at least one other assessment method.

The Problem Checklists and Rating Scales

Traditional methods of assessing behavior problems also include use of one or more behavior problem checklists or rating scales. Such checklists include a broad range of behavior problems and usually can be used by a psychologist, teacher, parent, or other to indicate whether or not each behavior problem is characteristic of the child being evaluated and to what degree the behavior occurs. A checklist or scale can be used by a psychologist or counselor to gain a fuller understanding of the behaviors of the child assessed and provide some indication of the situational aspects of the child's behavior problems.

Examples of common behavior problem checklists are the Revised Behavior Problem Checklist (Quay & Peterson, 1983) and the Child Behavior Checklist (Achenbach, 1978; Achenbach & Edelbrock, 1981, 1983). A self-report version of the Child Behavior Checklist for youth is available (Achenbach & Edelbrock, 1983). A counselor or psychologist usually scores and interprets the completed behavior problem checklists.

Problem checklists and rating scales can be useful when assessing behaviors of concern among African American children but only when used with caution; that is, they must be used with the understanding that they are not culturally sensitive and may not be reliable or valid for children from certain cultural backgrounds. There is limited research in which problem checklists and rating scales have been used with large numbers of African American children; thus, the appropriateness of these instruments for these children remains questionable. Furthermore, because the behavior is sometimes in the eye of the beholder, the numbers and severity of behaviors indicated via a problem checklist or rating scale may vary depending on who completes the checklist or scale. The professional completing the checklist is often a psychologist or counselor who is usually not African American.

Problem checklists and rating scales may be useful when completed by professionals who are culturally and socioeconomically sensitive and when used as a source of information rather than as a reliable measure of behavior problems. As a source of information, they can serve as a useful component of a multimethod assessment package for assessing behaviors of concern or behavior problems of African American children and adolescents. Additionally, such packages ideally should include semistructured clinical interviews with the child and the child's parents and teachers and behavioral observations by teachers, parents, and a counselor or psychologist who is knowledgeable about African American cultures and experienced in working with children similar to the African American child being assessed.

Conclusions

Assessment of behaviors of concern and behavior problems of African American children ideally should involve the African American child being assessed as well as the child's parents and teachers and a counselor or psychologist who is culturally and socioeconomically sensitive. It is important that the assessment process be democratic in that the views of all involved are heard and respected, especially the views of African American children and their parents. Too often African American children are left out of the assessment process; yet, they are the true experts regarding the occurrence of behavior problems or behaviors of concern to others and the operational factors in these behaviors.

Culturally and socioeconomically sensitive assessment procedures are necessary for making it possible for African American children and their parents to participate in the assessment process and for keeping them engaged in this process. Important among these procedures is empowering these parents by actively seeking their input and giving them equal control with others involved in the assessment process. Also important to the assessment process is involving as many culturally and socioeconomically sensitive African American professionals as possible and using a partnership assessment approach. Furthermore, all involved in the assessment process must be keenly aware of the fact that behaviors that are of concern to teachers and schools may not meet the culturally sensitive definition of a behavior problem. The behaviors may be in need of modification for a particular setting but may indeed be a culturally sanctioned behavior for which the child should not be admonished.

Multimethod assessments that include semistructured interviews, direct behavioral observations, and problem checklists or rating scales for information rather than measurement purposes are also indicated for use with African American children. Use of these methods in combination deters stereotype-based views of African American children and gives a broader view of the factors and conditions that influence these children's behaviors. Interviews with African American adolescents in particular usually need to be multidimensional assessments. This type of assessment focuses on different aspects of the individual and on family, school, and community influences that may be factors in the behaviors of concern.

Through assessment partnerships that are culturally and socioeconomically sensitive, behaviors of African American children that are of concern and their behavior problems can be accurately identified and evaluated. Consequently, these concerns and behavior problems can be addressed in ways that focus less on simply changing the problematic behaviors of African American children and more on understanding these behaviors and modifying the environmental and social conditions instrumental in their occurrence. Culturally and socio-economically sensitive assessments ultimately seek to find ways to empower African American children and their families to facilitate the children's academic and social success.

5 Modifying Behavior

General Intervention Approaches

African American parents in particular are generally resistant to giving tangible rewards (e.g., money) to their children and pleading with their children to engage in appropriate rather than inappropriate behaviors. These parents typically feel that children should control their impulses to act out or break rules because they have been told how to behave and because they know right from wrong. Many of these parents are also resistant to allowing teachers, counselors, and others to use structured reinforcement programs such as token economy programs to modify the behavior of their children. Such programs are considered by these parents as bribery approaches designed to control and manipulate their children rather than to help their children learn ways to control their own behavior for academic and social success.

Because most educators as well as psychologists are European Americans, the lack of trust in European Americans in general by many African American parents often precludes support from these parents for strategies to simply control or "manipulate" their children. Most African American parents want their children to have the self-motivation and self-control needed to engage in positive behaviors for success rather than negative behaviors that deter success. In other words, African American parents want their children to be self-empowered for social and academic success.

Self-Empowerment Intervention Approach

Simply stated a self-empowerment intervention approach for modifying behavior problems among African American children is one in which the ultimate goal is to promote self-motivation, self-control, and self-praise as well as behaviors and skills that will help these youth modify their own problem behaviors. To achieve this ultimate goal, interventions must target internal influences or self variables (e.g., self-esteem and self-statements) and external influences (e.g., family, school, community, socioeconomic conditions, and racism) on the occurrence of the behavior problems of concern. However, many of the external negative influences on the behavior of African American children, such as racism and poverty, are resistant to change and will not change significantly within the school life time of today's children. In contrast, with persistence and appropriate interventions, most of the internal influences on the behavior of African American children can be significantly impacted within the school life time of these children. Consequently, it seems logical to give more attention to modifying internal influences or self variables than to modifying external influences associated with the occurrence of behavior problems of African American children. Furthermore, it is internal variables that ultimately self-empower African American children. However, modification of both internal influences and external influences of behavior problems when possible is ideal.

According to Bronfenbrenner (1979), it is prudent to empower African American youth to self-instruct, self-manage, self-control, self-evaluate, and self-reinforce their own behavior in the presence of systems over which we often have little control. Bronfenbrenner (1979) describes these systems as follows: (1) microsystems—systems that directly and regularly impact a child such as the family, school, and neighborhood; (2) mesosystems— systems that involve relationships between or among the microsystems such as the family-school relationship; (3) exosystems—systems that indirectly impact a child's microsystems such as parents' employers, and (4) macrosystems—the values and mores of the institutions of society. Regarding the latter, LaRue and Majidi (1989) identified discrimination against African Americans as a pervasive macrosystem value that has both direct and indirect effects on African American children. An example of discrimination having a direct impact is tolerance of quiet off-task behaviors and the academic failure of African American children in schools so that attention and resources can be devoted to the successful education of their European American peers. An example of discrimination having an indirect impact on African American children is the common situation in which parents do not get high-paying jobs for which they qualify because of discrimination and, consequently, experience monetary stress and having to live in a low-income neighborhood, both of which often contribute to behavior problems among their children.

A self-empowerment intervention approach for modifying behavior problems among African American children likely has much potential for developing interventions that are effective in reducing the occurrence of problem behaviors and increasing the occurrence of prosocial behaviors by African American children. This is because this intervention approach is culturally and socioeconomically sensitive; that is, its associated interventions (e.g., self-motivation, self-monitoring of behavior, and self-praise) are feasible and affordable for use with children and their families across the socioeconomic spectrum. The associated interventions do not require expensive external reinforcers or expensive long-term therapy by a psychologist or other mental health professional and they can easily be taught to most children and their parents. Additionally, these interventions take into consideration the existing values, norms, and traditions that influence children's behaviors and are valued so that one's dignity and self-esteem are maintained in the behavior change process.

Self-empowerment of African American children is also important because it is necessary for redirecting the negative plight of the masses of disadvantaged African Americans, especially given the recent movement toward abandoning welfare and other programs that provide help to the disadvantaged from others. Indeed, the only way that the masses of low-income African Americans will do more than barely survive is through their own efforts, knowledge, and skills for self-empowerment. Indeed, future generations of African Americans must establish and control their own businesses, create safe communities, and be actively engaged in the education of their children. The hope for making these accomplishments realities lies in partnership efforts (e.g., parent–school–community partnerships) to assist African American youth to be self-motivated, self-disciplined, and self-praising so that they can achieve against all of the many odds that their ethnicity typically brings.

Making Therapy Approaches More Sensitive

Psychodynamic Therapy

When using psychodynamic or insight therapy to modify children's behavior problems, it is typically important to uncover the underlying conflicts that are contributing to the problems and to deal with these conflicts directly. The therapist tries to show a child the relationship between present and past feelings and tries to interpret the child's verbal and nonverbal behaviors and the child's play behavior. Accomplishing these therapy goals with African American children requires an understanding of their language, ways of communicating, culture, and social environment. This understanding can be facilitated through readings on cross-cultural counseling, visiting various predominantly African American neighborhoods, and spending time with African American children through experiences such as volunteering at an after-school tutoring and skills training program for African American children and their parents.

Because many African American children enjoy activities that involve movement, music, and creative expression, the use of vehicles such as play, drawing, dance, and writing of poems and rap music will likely be effective in enabling these children to express and interpret their own feelings. It is indeed more culturally and socioeconomically sensitive to allow African American children to express and at least help interpret and explain their own feelings and conflicts than to have the therapist assume these responsibilities as the expert. It is also sensitive to communicate with African American children in ways that empower them when dealing with conflicts and emotions that are negatively impacting their behaviors and their lives. One empowerment strategy is to give these children the opportunity to teach the therapist about rap music, dance, their religion, and other aspects of their world that are important to them in the process of gaining insight into their own behaviors. This strategy gives children some control in the therapy process. Indeed, a culturally and socioeconomically sensitive psychodynamic approach may hold much potential for modifying the behavior problems of African American children.

Behavior Therapy

Behavior therapies view children's behavior problems as behaviors that are learned and intentionally or unintentionally reinforced in their social environments just as desirable behaviors are learned and reinforced. A major assessment focus is to determine the specific conditions and settings in which behavior problems are learned. This information is used to design and implement interventions to modify target behavior problems. Often interventions to modify behavior problems of children involve modifying their physical and social environments, rewarding appropriate behaviors, and extinguishing inappropriate behaviors by making every effort to not reinforce these behaviors. Parents typically are involved in implementing behavior change interventions.

There are several strategies for making behavior therapy approaches culturally and socioeconomically sensitive when used to help modify behavior problems of African American children. It is advisable to ask for parents' permission to use these approaches and to actively involve parents in planning and implementing behavior change interventions. It is also advisable to use no-cost humanistic rewards that provide support for the children involved and that facilitate the occurrence of positive family interactions rather than use material rewards. Examples of such humanistic rewards are shows of affection (e.g., hugs, kisses), praise, expressions of positive feelings, an invitation to go fishing with Dad, and an "I am proud of you" certificate. It is best to have the parents and the children jointly select the rewards and reinforcers that they value and would like to use in the process of increasing appropriate behaviors and decreasing inappropriate behaviors.

It is also advisable to teach African American children appropriate or adaptive behaviors to replace the inappropriate behaviors. Too often these children are told what is wrong with their behavior without being told about replacement behaviors—behaviors that should be done instead of the inappropriate behaviors. Furthermore, children are often not told how to do the replacement behavior. The following script of an African American adolescent introducing himself to his new teacher illustrates this point.

ADOLESCENT: Hey what's happening? I am Rick.

TEACHER: Don't say that when you introduce yourself to a teacher or any other adult. Introduce yourself appropriately.

Many African American students do not belong to clubs and organizations where they are likely to learn how to introduce themselves "appropriately." The term *appropriately* in the preceding script likely means in accordance with majority values regarding formal interactions with new acquaintances. Because many African American youth do not learn and adopt the values and norms of the majority culture through their life experiences, these youth need to be told and taught exactly what behaviors are appropriate in school environments and other settings in which the majority culture is dominant. This type of teaching often does not occur in schools because teachers do not have the time to do so. What African American children are taught at home as being appropriate behaviors may or may not be consistent with what is viewed as appropriate by members of the majority culture.

Behavior therapy approaches can be made culturally and socioeconomically sensitive when used to modify behavior problems of African American children through the interpersonal style of the therapists who use the approaches. It is important for behavior therapists to be warm, friendly, nonauthoritative, and knowledgeable about and respective of cultural differences between themselves and their clients. These therapist behaviors and the specified knowledge are especially important in therapy involving European American therapists and African American children and their parents, given that many African Americans are uncomfortable with European Americans being in positions of authority.

Cognitive Therapy

Cognitive therapy assumes that problem behaviors and the thoughts and emotions that are often associated with these behaviors can be changed by changing one's dysfunctional thoughts underlying the behaviors. The cognitive therapy approach to modifying behavior problems of African American children can be made at least somewhat culturally and socio-economically sensitive by having these children examine and question their dysfunctional thoughts and then generate replacement thoughts in a manner that utilizes their own communication styles and that is self-empowering. For example, when African American children feel angry and perhaps want to strike out at the persons who were instrumental in causing the anger, these children can tell themselves something such as: "I am going to slap this guy if he laughs at me again. Why is he doing this? He is trying to get me put out of school. I refuse to let this clown bend me out of shape and cause me to get in trouble and kicked out of school. I am too smart for that. I am just going to be cool. I am going to outsmart this turkey and make both my parents and myself proud of not getting into trouble today."

It is advisable to give African American children examples of cognitive interventions that involve giving attention to their dysfunctional thoughts, examining the meaning or implications of these thoughts, and generating new functional thoughts that avoid engaging in behaviors that are considered behavior problems. These children should then be challenged to practice independently going through these cognitive steps and coming up with more functional thoughts that deter behavior problems. Ideally, it should be explained to African American children that this cognitive activity allows them to take charge of their own behavior and behavior change to avoid behavior problems that get them into trouble.

Group Therapy

Group therapy approaches typically involve family and peers as units of intervention. Given that the family is very important in shaping the lives of most African American children, these approaches have much potential for the modification of behavior problems among these youth. Group therapy is particularly useful for children who have difficulty with interpersonal relationships in general and peer relationships in particular. This is because it provides opportunities for peers and family members to model and role-play the behaviors that these children need to learn for social and life success.

One way to make group therapy approaches culturally and socioeconomically sensitive is to encourage group members to generate problem situations that they experience in their everyday lives and to discuss how these situations might be handled most constructively in the future. It is also helpful to have at least one group leader who is a nonmajority person and is culturally and socioeconomically sensitive. This person can make sure that underlying issues in behavior problems, such as racism and discrimination that European American therapists are often uncomfortable addressing, are indeed addressed openly and honestly.

Group therapy approaches to modify behavior problems of African American children have great potential for facilitating self-empowerment of these youth. This is because these approaches allow these youth opportunities to figure out solutions to their own problems, to teach themselves through modeling and role-plays, and to receive immediate feedback including encouragement to praise themselves for actively participating in their own behavior change.

Family Therapy

Family therapies generally assume that behavior problems in children occur not because of particular characteristics of the children but because of disturbed family relationships

(French, 1977). Therefore, interventions to modify behavior problems of children target the family system and follow examination of family dynamics to determine how these dynamics affect the child with behavior problems (Allen & Majidi-Ahi, 1989).

Behavioral family therapy, which is among the more recently recognized family therapies, holds much potential for effectively working with African American families because of its emphasis on increasing positive interactions among family members. By calling family members' attention to routine patterns of behaviors that lead to conflict and behavior problems, behavior family therapists can assist families in identifying needed behavior changes for modifying the behavior problems. Family therapists can also encourage family members to look for and reinforce each other's desirable behaviors rather than their undesirable behaviors. The actual occurrence of reinforcement by family members rather quickly increases positive family interactions and decreases conflict and behavior problems. Such family involvement in therapy empowers these families.

Behavioral family therapy approaches can be made more culturally and socioeconomically sensitive for African Americans by giving great attention to assessing the dynamics of the family involved and avoiding any assumptions about their family dynamics based on common family dynamics in European American families. Additionally, therapy approaches used with African American families must be based on the assessed dynamics in these families rather than on what is assumed about these dynamics based on experiences of working with European American families. Consequently, the therapy approaches used will likely be more effective and result in shorter-term therapy and less costly therapy. Given that most African American families are not socialized to be comfortable with long-term therapy and cannot afford such therapy, approaches conducive to short-term therapy are important with these families.

Behavioral family therapy approaches used to address behavior problems of an African American child also can be made to be more culturally sensitive by basing them on and utilizing them with the individuals who are primary caregivers for the child and in essence are the child's family. A child's caregivers should not be viewed or treated as a dysfunctional family simply because it is not a traditional family and does not function like a traditional family. All members of nontraditional families should be encouraged to be actively involved in family therapy. Therapy approaches used should recognize the role of each nontraditional family member involved with the child client whether or not that family member actually participates in therapy sessions. These approaches should also respect family values and traditions such as not using tangible reinforcers with children and using physical punishment that is not physical abuse.

Structural family therapy has been reported to be especially effective in treating African American adolescents (Sykes, 1987). This type of therapy recognizes problematic behavior as adaptations to stressful environments and difficult life situations. Additionally, it fits well with the need to assess external as well as internal factors that may have helped weaken the family structure and thus contributed to behavior problems of adolescents in the family (Sykes, 1987). Structural family therapy tries to identify the problem within the structure of the family that is contributing to the presenting problem (e.g., behavior problems of a child or teen in the family). It specifically focuses on family alliances, triangulations, roles and responsibilities assumed and not assumed by family members, and how treatment interventions are received. Structural family therapy is also short term and goal directed, making it suitable for low-income families. Two other characteristics of this type of therapy are that it emphasizes activating the family's own resources for change and growth and it aids the family in developing needed external resources (e.g., day care). These characteristics are consistent with a self-empowerment approach to behavior change (Sykes, 1987).

Structural family therapists can make their therapy more culturally and socioeconomically sensitive for African American families by showing respect for the nontraditional family structures that often exist in such families and by acknowledging and praising the resourcefulness and strengths of family members that have facilitated family functioning in the face of many physical, social, and economic difficulties. When trying to address behavior problems of an African American adolescent in non-traditional families, significant family members might include a mother's boyfriend who is very involved in the adolescent's life and an aunt who regularly provides after-school care for the adolescent. Getting such individuals involved in family therapy might involve nontraditional strategies such as having the therapist call these family members to warmly encourage them to participate in family therapy.

Structural family therapists can also make therapy more culturally and socioeconomically sensitive by giving priority to empowering family members to obtain the external resources that they need. This empowerment may involve the assumption of nontraditional roles by the therapist such as assisting a parent with completing a job application and with finding out how to get free medical care for a child whose behavior problems are linked to a physical illness.

Family therapy to address behavior problems of African American children, regardless of the type of family therapy, is more culturally and socioeconomically sensitive than is typical when the therapist has had the experience of knowing and socially interacting with African American families, is knowledgeable about mainstream African American culture, is aware of potential family problems often associated with poverty (e.g., alcoholism, physical abuse, low self-esteem, and premarital sex), and includes intervention strategies that empower family members. Family empowerment strategies include providing family members with information, guidance, and encouragement to make the contacts necessary to get family assistance that is needed (e.g., food stamps, transportation to AA, etc.), and teaching children and parents methods and strategies that they can use to modify behavior problems. Another important family empowerment strategy is for the therapist to work in partnership with family members and appropriately attribute positive behavior changes to their own efforts.

General Intervention Strategies

There is no one intervention strategy and no one set of intervention strategies that will be effective in modifying behavior problems of all African American children. Thus, efforts are made to present in this chapter various general strategies for consideration in addressing any behavior problems among these children.

Given that many African American parents are very effective as behavior modifiers, general recommendations from a group of African American parents for addressing behavior problems of African American students are included in this chapter. Additionally, recommendations for modifying behavior problems of African American students from a group of African American elementary school students and a group of African American high school students are included. Indeed, it may well be African American students themselves who really know what might be helpful in modifying behavior problems of other students similar to themselves. Yet, researchers have rarely solicited such information from African American youth.

Given that the majority of African American children are in working-class families with incomes in the lower socioeconomic levels, it is important that the strategies used be cost-effective and practical. Because African American children are culturally different from their European American peers, the intervention strategies for African American children should reflect this difference or sensitivity to it. Given the importance of self-empowerment of African American youth for social and academic success, effort is made to include self-empowering intervention strategies and approaches.

Because most of the psychologists, counselors, and teachers who will be involved in modifying behavior problems of African American youth are European Americans, it is important that these professionals be as best prepared as possible to meet this challenge. Thus, important considerations and recommendations are provided for helping psychologists, counselors, and teachers understand the behavior of African American youth and for assisting these youth in discontinuing any existing behavior problems and in engaging in behaviors that will facilitate the social success of these youth.

Recommended Strategies

In an interview study the present author and her colleagues assessed the views of African American students and their primary caregiving parent (or primary caregiver) and the views of African American teachers regarding what African American students, parents, and teachers can do to reduce behavior problems when they occur in African American students (Tucker, Herman, Pederson, & Vogle, 1997). The student participants included elementary school students ($n = 24$) and high school students ($n = 19$) who were attending an after-school partnership educational program that provided academic tutoring, computer use training, and adaptive skills training. These students ranged in age from seven to eighteen and were fairly equally distributed across gender for each school level (elementary versus high school). They were from low-income families. The primary caregiving parent participants were all mothers or mother figures who ranged in age from twenty-seven to sixty-three. The teacher participants included elementary school teachers ($n = 5$) and high school teachers ($n = 8$) from among eight different desegregated schools. The mean years of teaching experience for the elementary school teachers and the high school teachers were 21.4 years and 16.3 years, respectively. Ninety-one percent of the teacher participants were females. All participants lived in a small city in the Southeast.

The recommendations of all participants in response to each of two questions were summarized by participant group (i.e., elementary school students, high school students, elementary school parents, high school parents, elementary school teachers, and high school teachers). Two additional questions were asked only to the participating African American students and were summarized separately for each of the two groups of student participants (i.e., elementary school students and high school students).

The first question asked of all participants in each participant group was: "What can parents do to stop/reduce behavior problems that are occurring among African American students?" The responses to this question and the percentage of times each response was given among all responses given within each participant group are as follows:

Elementary School Students
Parents can punish (mostly physically) their children or use restrictions (73.5%)

Parents can spend time talking and listening to their children (11.8%)

Various other recommendations (14.7%)

High School Students
Parents can punish their children or use restrictions (42.9%)

Parents can spend time talking and listening to their children (28.6%)

Parents can get involved with teachers and counselors at their children's school (9.5%)

Various other reasons (19.0%)

Elementary School Parents
Parents can spend time talking and listening to their children (30.8%)

Parents can punish their children or use restrictions (19.2%)

Parents can get involved with teachers and counselors at their children's school (19.2%)

Various other reasons (30.8%)

High School Parents
Parents can spend time talking with, listening to, and doing things with their children (34.9%)

Parents can specify rules and punish their children or use restrictions (26.1%)

Parents can show their children that they are loved and important (17.4%)

Various other reasons (21.6%)

Elementary School Teachers
Parents can get involved with teachers and counselors at their children's school (31.6%)

Parents can teach and model social skills and other appropriate behaviors for their children (21.1%)

Parents can specify rules and consequences for breaking them and use behavioral contracts (15.8%)

Various other reasons (31.5%)

High School Teachers
Parents can spend time listening to and talking with their children (40.0%)

Parents can get involved with teachers and counselors at their children's school (35.7%)

Parents can punish their children or use restrictions (14.3%)

Various other reasons (10.0%)

The second question asked of all participants in each participant group was: "What can teachers do to stop/reduce behavior problems that are occurring among African American students?" The responses to this question and the percentage of times each response was given among all responses given within each participant group are as follows:

Elementary School Students
Teachers can have more order in the classroom and use firmer discipline (48.4%)

Teachers can talk with the children about their behavior problems and teach appropriate behaviors (19.3%)

Teachers can stop yelling and being disrespectful to the children in their classes (12.9%)

Various other reasons (19.4%)

High School Students
Teachers can have more order in the classroom and use firmer discipline (44.8%)

Teachers can talk with the children about their behavior problems and try to help (27.6%)

Teachers can involve parents in stopping the behavior problem (13.8%)

Various other reasons (13.8%)

Elementary School Parents
Teachers can have more order in the classroom and use firmer discipline (40.0%)

Teachers can involve parents in stopping the behavior problems (33.3%)

Teachers can talk with the children about their behavior problems and try to help (14.8%)

Various other reasons (11.9%)

High School Parents
Teachers can talk with the children about their behavior problems and try to help (45.5%)

Teachers can involve parents and guidance counselors in stopping the behavior problems (9.1%)

Teachers can avoid shaming the children and labeling them (9.1%)

Various other reasons (36.3%)

Elementary School Teachers
Teachers can involve parents in stopping the behavior problems (37.4%)

Teachers can talk with the children about their behavior problems and try to help them (25.0%)

Teachers can be more encouraging and supportive of the children (18.8%)

Various other reasons (18.8%)

High School Teachers
Teachers can involve parents in stopping the behavior problems (50.0%)

Teachers can teach and model appropriate behaviors and values (20.0%)

Teachers can work individually with the children and be firm but caring in this process (20.0%)

Various other reasons (10.0%)

One of the two questions asked only to the participating students was: "What can African American children do to successfully manage or express their anger so as to keep it from getting them into trouble?" The responses to this question and the percentage of times each response was given among all responses given within each participant group are as follows:

Elementary School Students
Children can walk away, cool down, and think of the consequences of their actions before acting (33.3%)

Children can participate in positive activities and sports to release their anger (23.1%)

Children can express their feelings in a way that might help the situation rather than make it worse (15.4%)

Various other reasons (28.3%)

High School Students
Children can walk away, cool down, and think of the consequences of their actions before acting (48.0%)

Children can talk out their feelings with someone (24.0%)

Children can participate in positive activities and sports to release their anger (12.0%)

Various other reasons (16.0%)

The other of the two questions asked only to the participating students was: "What can African American children do to help themselves resist the temptation to do the wrong thing?" The responses to this question and the percentage of times each response was given among all responses given within each participant group are as follows:

Elementary School Students
Children can use self-control through using self-talk (35.7%)

Children can engage in positive activities and efforts to reach their goals (21.4%)

Children can think of the consequences of their actions and of what is right versus wrong (10.7%)

Various other reasons (32.2%)

High School Students
Children can think of the consequences of their actions and of what is right versus wrong (35.7%)

Children can be in the right kind of places and with friends that do not get them into trouble (29.1%)

Children can engage in positive activities and efforts to reach their goals (16.7%)

Various other responses (18.5%)

It is clear from the preceding interview results that there was much agreement among African American parents, children, and teachers as to what each of them can do to reduce or stop behavior problems when they occur among African American students. Among the most noteworthy findings are that there was much agreement among students and parents that parental use of punishment and restrictions and more parent–child, two-way communication may reduce or stop the occurrence of behavior problems among African American students. It was also particularly noteworthy that there was high agreement among and between the students and parents that teachers need to have more order in their classrooms and need to use firmer discipline in order to help modify behavior problems of African American students in their classrooms. Furthermore, the students thought that having teachers talk with rather than yell at African American students about their behavior problems and then teach these students alternative appropriate behaviors would be helpful in stopping or reducing the behavior problems. The teachers seem to agree that behavior problems of African American students would likely be modified by teachers and parents working together to bring about such modifications and by teachers spending time talking and listening to and encouraging African American students.

The interview data that were only obtained from the students and that were obtained in response to questions about what African American students could do to avoid getting in trouble or doing the wrong thing were surprising. There was high agreement among and between the group of elementary school students and the group of high school students that self-management strategies might be helpful in avoiding problem behaviors. Interestingly, the recommended self-management strategies were cognitive-behavioral approaches with the goal of acquiring self-control over one's behavior and emotions. Additionally, focusing on goals and engaging in positive activities with positive peers were identified as important ways that African American students can stop or reduce the occurrence of behavior problems. In sum these strategies generally support self-empowerment approaches for reducing or stopping behavior problems and for facilitating the social success of African American students.

Other General Intervention Strategies

Because behavior problems of African American children are often the product of many external and internal factors, multiple intervention strategies involving significant others in the children's lives such as teachers and parents are most appropriate. Thus, in this section intervention strategies that can be used by parents and teachers as well as intervention strategies (i.e., self-management strategies) that can be used by children who have behavior problems will be discussed. Because modification of some behavior problems requires or can be expedited by an available psychologist or counselor, general intervention strategies that these professionals can use to help African American children overcome behavior problems will also be discussed.

Because behavioral problems may be the product of physical problems such as malnutrition or abnormal hormonal levels, children with behavior problems should first be given a physical examination to determine whether such physical problems exist and are contributors to the behavior problems of concern. If medications such as neuroleptics, stimulants, and benzodiazepines are recommended by the examining physician, these medications should be used only after behavioral interventions have been tried. Given that the long-term effects of such medications are not known and given the many unpleasant and potentially serious side effects of such medications, they should indeed be an intervention alternative of last resort. Furthermore, when such medications as those just mentioned are recommended, a second opinion from a pediatrician or other appropriate medical professional should be sought.

One good way of getting physician referrals for first and second opinions concerning physical problems that might be contributing to behavior problems in children is to contact hospitals with good pediatric departments that are associated with reputable universities. Because most physicians today want to avoid increasingly common, costly malpractice suits and are practicing team health care, getting a second opinion is encouraged or at least accepted among most physicians. Thus, most physicians will in fact recommend someone to provide a second opinion about whether your child has a particular physical problem and about the need for any medication that has been recommended for your child.

Self-Management Strategies That Children Can Use.
These are strategies for directing one's own behavior and thoughts, especially in the presence of anxiety, pain, anger, or thoughts that disrupt desired and appropriate behaviors. Following is a brief discussion of three self-control strategies that African American children can use and that the present author has found to be effective in clinical experiences with numerous African American children across the socioeconomic spectrum.

Strategy 1.   African American children and adolescents can use silent thoughts and self-statements to control their behaviors and associated emotional and physiological responses. These thoughts and statements can empower these children; that is, they can make them feel in charge of what they do rather than feel that others make them do what they do. Children should be given examples of self-empowering self-statements or thoughts. Examples of self-statements and thoughts that children can use to resist peer pressure to do the wrong thing and to manage anger that could lead to fighting or other behavior problems follow.

Examples

I refuse to let John get me into trouble with the teacher; I am just too smart for that.

I am going to take three deep breaths to calm down. I am not going to let her push my buttons to make me fight and get put out of school.

I am too mature to be fighting.

I am getting really angry. Let me walk away now. I will tell him how I feel and why I am angry after I calm down.

I can handle this situation without yelling and screaming, acting like a clown.

Strategy 2.   Children can use problem solving to deal with disagreements and conflicts that often result in the use of profane language, fighting, or anger. Following are five practical problem-solving steps for deciding what to do in situations that could result in inappropriate behaviors.

Step 1. Write or clearly think through exactly what the problem is; that is, identify what it is that has you concerned or upset.

Example

I want to go to a basketball beach party with my friends, but my mother and daddy will not allow me to go.

Step 2. Think of all the possible actions you could take.

Examples

I could go without permission.

I could explore with my parents having a party at my house or my aunt's house.

I could plan another activity with my friends that my parents would allow.

Step 3. Think of the positive and negative consequences of each possible action identified in Step 2.

Example

I could go without permission.

Possible Positive Consequences
I could have a really good time.

I will impress my friends that I will hang with them no matter what.

Possible Negative Consequences
My parents could find out and be really upset and angry with me and ground me for a month.

I could really feel guilty about lying to my parents and doing what they told me not to do.

I could end up having to ride home with a drunk driver, risking an accident.

Step 4. Decide on one or a combination of the actions in Step 4 that have none or the least negative consequences.

Step 5. Discuss what you have decided with an adult whom you trust and whom you think that your parents respect. It is almost always helpful to check out your decisions with an adult.

Step 6. Praise yourself for having taken time to go through the preceding problem-solving steps, which is a very responsible and intelligent thing to do.

Strategy 3.   Children can use delay of gratification to help keep them on task and to responsibly rather than inappropriately or illegally satisfy their wants. Children must be taught through practice the merits of choosing something valuable that will be received in the future over something less valuable that will be received much sooner. For example, children must be taught to refuse an invitation to play their favorite sport until after studying for a test. Another example is that children must be taught the value of choosing to receive a $500 savings bond that can be cashed in six months versus choosing to receive $50 immediately. Parents, teachers, and community leaders can provide children with lessons and games to teach them delay of gratification. This learning will be especially helpful to children in resisting peer pressure to do what is fun but wrong rather than what is not fun but is the right thing to do.

Children can and should be taught the foregoing three self-management strategies by their parents, teachers, and others who are significant in their lives. These adults must convince children that the children can and must control their own behaviors to avoid getting into trouble. Indeed, self-control or self-management strategies will not likely be effective for children unless they believe that they control their own behavior (Bandura, 1977). It should be acknowledged to children that this type of behavioral self-management is not easy because there are always individuals (e.g., friends and relatives, including adults) who will attempt to influence them to behave inappropriately, disobey rules, and to put fun before work that is important for academic and social success. Given these life conditions, children should be prepared to deal with failure to use taught self-management strategies. Specifically, children should be told that such failure does not mean that they have failed or are weak and that with effort and determination they will be successful in self-managing their behavior in the future. Furthermore, children should be praised and encouraged to self-praise for their self-control efforts as well as for successful self-management outcomes.

Strategies Parents Can Use.   In addition to teaching children self-management strategies, parents can use various other strategies to assist children in reducing or stopping their problem behaviors. Following are some of these strategies.

Strategy 1.   Parents can initiate or volunteer their involvement in any assessment of or intervention to modify behaviors of their children that teachers or others view as problematic. Whether invited to do so or not, parents should input their perspectives on the behaviors of concern and on recommendations for addressing these behaviors. Parents' involvement in any intervention that teachers and parents agree is appropriate is critical for the intervention to be effective over the long term. Parents' roles ideally should include encouraging their children to self-praise and feel good about themselves for progress toward modifying their problem behaviors and for engaging in alternative behaviors to replace the problem behaviors. Parents can help teach and insist that teachers teach their children replacement behaviors. An example of a replacement behavior for fighting when angry is teaching children to use thoughts or self-statements to control their behavior and their emotional and physiological responses when they are angry.

Strategy 2.   Parents must help their children be aware of the specific behaviors that are problematic and why and when they are problematic. It is not fair to children to simply say to them that "you are disrespectful to the teacher." Instead, children must be told specifically what they have been doing that is viewed by their teachers as disrespectful. For example, children may be told that their behaviors with the teacher that are disrespectful include talking when the teacher is talking, ignoring the teacher's request to stop talking during an assigned task, and deliberately mispronouncing the teacher's name. Ideally, parents should discuss the occurrence of these behaviors with their children daily and with the children's teachers at least weekly to determine any change in the occurrence of the behaviors due to the intervention efforts. Desired changes in the children should be attributed to the children's efforts and should be accompanied by praise of the children and encouragement of the children to self-praise their modifications of the specified disrespectful behaviors.

Strategy 3.   Parents can cautiously use punishment to discourage their children's behavior problems. Caution needs to be emphasized because it is easy for punishment to turn into or be perceived as abuse. Punishment of children is designed to help them learn, whereas abuse is the use of aversive stimuli to purposely and unjustly mistreat them as a repercussion for an inappropriate behavior. Abuse involves using more severe levels of aversive stimuli than are necessary to correct a behavior (Grasha, 1995).

Avery and Ivancevic (1980) stated that when used with care and common sense, without anger, and in a nonabusive manner, punishment can be an effective means of reducing or stopping problem behaviors. Some helpful guidelines for effectively and humanely administering punishment to stop problem behaviors follows.

1. Inform children of the problem behaviors that will be punished and why. Especially with older children, it is advisable for parents to include their children in discussions regarding appropriate punishments for specific behaviors by the children; however, parents should let the children know that the parents will make the final decision about appropriate punishments in general and in a particular situation when the children and parents disagree about what is appropriate.

2. Punish children immediately following the behavior problem. For example, do not wait until the afternoon to punish a child for something done that morning. At the time of the punishment, always remind the children why they are being punished, and include in the reminder the specific rule that was broken (if one exists), which led to the punishment.

3. Punish the children for specific behavior problems such as lying, stealing, ignoring appropriate requests from adults, and so forth. Avoid punishing a child for some vague action like "having a bad attitude"; the child may not know what this means and will surely resent rather than learn from such punishment.

4. Make the severity of the punishment consistent with the seriousness of the behavior problem. Stealing a gun and taking it to school to threaten a peer indicates the need for a more severe punishment than using profane language in an angry verbal exchange with a peer at school.

5. Punish problem behaviors by a child every time they occur. Parents, teachers, the babysitter, and others who spend significant time with the child should be aware of the behaviors that are to be punished and how. Written consent by parents to punish their child in specified ways should be provided to these significant others. This written statement should also include identification of the types of punishment that parents do not want to be used with their child and a request to be informed about when, why, and how their child was punished.

6. Be sure that the physical and psychological well-being of the child is protected when administering punishment, including physical punishment. This will likely occur if the punishment is administered in a nonabusive manner when parents are calm and if the goal of the punishment is to teach a lesson rather than to ventilate frustration or to inflict pain as a repercussion for engaging in an inappropriate behavior. Some punishments that typically do not threaten the well-being of a child include taking away some of a child's privileges, having the child do extra household work, and having the child go to her or his room at home after removing all sources of enjoyment, for example, games and television (Grasha, 1995).

Strategy 4. Parents can overstep their pride and personal discomfort regarding seeking help for their children's behavior problems. Even given the tradition of reliance on extended family members, other non-blood-related kinships, and the African American church, many African American parents, as well as their children, feel uncomfortable asking for assistance in helping their children overcome behavior problems. This is in part because of the physical distance that now often separates children and their parents from family members, family kin, and home church. Furthermore, there are many African Americans who have never sought refuge in church or in their extended family. Indeed, not all African Americans are alike in their ties with family and church. Yet, these resources are often available to African American children and their parents.

African American male extended family members, in particular, can be asked to spend time with male children with behavior problems for the purpose of understanding the nature of these problems and teaching them alternative constructive behaviors for social and academic success. Other extended family members and kin as well as friends and local church leaders and members can also be invited to serve as positive role models who help children to be self-motivated to modify their behavior problems, develop adaptive skills, and engage in success behaviors. Those who agree to be role models should also help teach these children appropriate behaviors and skills for handling various life situations.

Strategies Teachers Can Use. Teachers spend a great deal of time with African American students; yet, because of cultural and socioeconomic differences between these students and their teachers, the two groups typically have very little understanding of each other. Consequently, teachers often do not know how to facilitate the modification of behavior problems among African American students. Following are some strategies that teachers can use in efforts to stop or reduce problem behaviors among African American students.

Strategy 1. Teachers can conduct very organized classes that include regular reviews of the behaviors expected during and outside of classes. Behaviors that are unacceptable inside and outside of the classroom should also be regularly reviewed along with the consequences for engaging in these unacceptable behaviors. It is especially important that teachers follow through in administering these consequences in response to unacceptable behaviors.

Strategy 2.   Teachers can remind students to avoid engaging in specific problem behaviors which they have engaged in before, and teachers can explain to students why engaging in these behaviors should be discontinued or avoided. Pointing out positive humanistic consequences of discontinuing or avoiding the problem behaviors will likely be more effective than pointing out negative consequences of engaging in the problem behaviors (Tucker & O'Leary, 1982). Often when students are told about the negative consequences of undesirable behaviors, the consequences given are exaggerated or unrealistic; consequently, the students perceive the reasons as scare tactics and dismiss them. Many times the students' perceptions are justified because teachers often threaten to implement negative consequences that they do not follow through in implementing. Failure of teachers to follow through with negative consequences for problem behaviors often increases the likelihood of these behaviors.

Strategy 3.   Teachers can help identify and then encourage prosocial behaviors and adaptive skills (i.e., communication skills, socialization skills, and daily living skills) in their students in general and in students with behavior problems in particular. Teachers must make a concentrated effort to focus on promoting adaptive skills in children with behavior problems given that teachers' attention is almost automatically drawn to these students' problem behaviors. This is because the problem behaviors by some students often endanger or disrupt the learning of other students as well as threaten teacher authority. These potential outcomes of problem behaviors and the often needed individual attention to students with behavior problems are of much concern to teachers (Preator, 1990). These outcomes and attention to behavior problems can be reduced by teaching all students in the classroom adaptive skills and prosocial behaviors because these skills and behaviors are antagonistic to behavior problems. Furthermore, the students will experience teacher attention in association with adaptive skills and prosocial behaviors, which over time will reduce the students' dependence on attention from teachers for engaging in problem behaviors.

Strategy 4.   Teachers can weekly or biweekly invite to their classrooms positive role models who can help facilitate in students with behavior problems the self-motivation to achieve social and academic success. These guests can talk about their jobs or careers and explain how self-discipline, behavioral control, constructive expression of anger, prosocial behaviors, and adaptive skills contributed to their job success. African American professionals with backgrounds similar to the African American students should be included among classroom guests, as African American students will likely be able to identify with such professionals. This type of teaching/learning experience will likely help empower all students for social, academic, and life success and help combat racist attitudes and behaviors among American youth—our nation's leaders in the twenty-first century.

Strategy 5.   Teachers can spend extra time getting to know the African American students in their classrooms with the particular goal of determining factors in their behavior problems and finding positive behaviors and attitudes of these students to praise. Such attention deters viewing African American students as behavior problems and negatively interacting with them in accordance with these views. African American students, like other students, tend to respond positively and appropriately in environments where they are genuinely valued, receive positive attention, and feel important and comfortable.

Strategy 6.   Teachers can provide learning experiences that are designed specifically to promote the self-empowerment of African American students and all other students in their classrooms. Self-empowerment experiences are experiences that facilitate self-motivation, self-control, self-praise, adaptive skills, and success behaviors (e.g., asking questions about what one does not understand and using good eye contact) for social, academic, and life success. Self-motivation can be facilitated through having students establish short-term and long-term goals and participating in field trips that create enthusiasm about these goals. Self-control can be facilitated through teaching students self-management strategies discussed earlier in the self-management interventions section of this chapter. Students can be encouraged to praise themselves for accomplishments that made them feel good, studying and completing in-class and homework assignments, engaging in success behaviors, using good eye contact, and so on by regularly giving them opportunities to share during class what they praised themselves for the preceding day. Adaptive skills can be facilitated through activities like role-plays of the inappropriate ways and the appropriate ways to respond to name calling, being hit by a bully, and being reprimanded by the teacher. Success behaviors can be posted in the classroom, reviewed daily as a class, and praised when they occur.

Strategy 7.   Teachers can pair a child with behavior problems with another child who engages in the appropriate behaviors that the teachers want the child with the behavior problems to learn. The child who engages in the appropriate behaviors would serve as a model for the child with the behavior problems. Models in general provide a definition of socially appropriate behavior, and observing a model is sometimes more effective than simply telling someone (e.g., a child with behavior problems) to engage in specific prosocial behaviors.

Support for the effectiveness of having children serve as models was provided in a large study involving 11,051 students from among 66 high schools (Sarason, Sarason, Pierce, Shearin, & Sayers, 1991). The procedure involved asking the student participants to donate blood. One group of students was shown an informational slide show about blood and its uses and then asked to donate blood. The second group viewed a slide show about blood that also showed a number of students (models) giving blood and indicated the popularity of high school blood drives. The group of students shown the slide with the models had 16.9 percent more donations to the blood bank than the group of students simply shown the informational slide show.

Strategies Parents and Teachers Can Use.   Teachers and parents can play major roles in reducing and stopping behavior problems among African American children. Some strategies that teachers and parents often find effective in helping children reduce or stop their behavior problems follow.

Strategy 1.   Teachers and parents can use step-by-step, self-instructional methods to teach African American children adaptive skills and success behaviors that are antagonistic to problem behaviors in that they reduce the need to engage in problem behaviors for attention.

The desired attention will be obtained from the use of their new skills and their engagement in success behaviors. Use of self-instruction learning guides to teach a child adaptive skills and success behaviors allows the child to successfully learn independently. This strategy is empowering in that it allows the child a sense of pride and accomplishment from having performed a behavior or skill without dependence on the teacher or others.

Use of self-instruction teaching and learning involves having the teacher or parent write the steps for a task, skill, or behavior on a sheet of paper, review the steps with the children, and model doing the steps. Then the children can practice doing the task, skill, or behavior independently using the written steps as a guide. The children should be encouraged to praise themselves as they successfully move through each step. The children should also be told to expect to make mistakes or get stuck at a step and, when this happens, to simply go back to an earlier step and start over from there. Children should also be encouraged to ask for help if they have difficulty following one or more of the steps. When using this self-instruction teaching approach, parents and teachers should praise the children for their efforts to learn rather than just praise a successful outcome (i.e., getting through all the steps and successfully performing the learned skill or behavior).

An example of a step-by-step guide is the one below for constructively expressing anger:

Step 1. Take three deep breaths to calm yourself.

Step 2. State why you are angry.

Step 3. State how what happened made you feel in addition to being angry.

Step 4. Invite the person with whom you are angry to share her or his feelings about what you have stated.

Step 5. Propose what you want to have happen to avoid in the future the situation that led to your anger.

Step 6. Agree on this proposal or some modification of it that is acceptable to you.

Step 7. Thank the person with whom you were angry for listening to and talking with you about your feelings.

Step 8. Praise yourself for sharing your feelings in a calm and organized or mature manner.

Strategy 2.   Teachers and parents should avoid using punishment procedures with African American children that interfere with their learning and with their establishment of positive interpersonal relationships that can facilitate life success. Such punishments often include timeout or contingent social isolation, response cost, overcorrection, and verbal reprimands. Timeout or contingent social isolation typically involves removing a child from a situation in which an undesired behavior occurred and placing the child in an isolated corner of the classroom or home for a specified period of time (Drabman & Spitalnik, 1973). Sometimes the child is required to engage in an appropriate behavior in order to return to the situation in which the undesirable behavior occurred (O'Leary, O'Leary, & Becker, 1967).

Timeout or contingent social isolation is less than ideal for use with African American children because of its association with the past humiliation and isolation of slaves as methods for subjugating and controlling them. Use of timeout or contingent social isolation also reinforces common feelings among African American children that they do not belong at their school. A sense of belonging at school and in the classroom is associated with academic and social success of African American children. The isolation that comes with timeout is not conducive to a sense of belonging in their school among African American children, many of whom already experience a sense of not belonging or fitting in at their schools and classrooms because of being culturally or socioeconomically different from the majority of their peers and school administrators.

Response cost is a common way of punishing children by taking away a previously given reinforcement (e.g., access to television) following an inappropriate behavior (Kazdin, 1972). This punishment method sometimes undermines trust of European American teachers, which for many African American children is particularly difficult to establish. This difficulty with establishing trust of European American teachers is likely associated with the past exploitation of African Americans by European Americans that has been a well-documented part of U.S. history.

Overcorrection is a punishment procedure in which children are required to repeat an appropriate behavior that is the opposite of or a replacement for a problem behavior (Foxx & Azrin, 1972). For example, if a child kicked and consequently damaged the paint on a trash can at school as an expression of anger, an overcorrection punishment for the child would be to require the child to paint that trash can and all trash cans throughout the school. Such a punishment is very humiliating for most African American children and for other children as well. Furthermore, when used at school, overcorrection interventions can take children away from academic learning for a significant amount of time.

Verbal reprimands are disapproving statements such as "I am so tired of telling you to stop talking; all you do is disrupt others and keep them from learning." Verbal reprimands are statements commonly used by teachers and parents toward children. These statements are typically made with strong emotionally negative tones that often elicit anxiety and embarrassment in children, both of which can negatively impact subsequent behavior. The present author and her colleagues found with parents of a group of African American eighth graders and parents of a group of European American eighth graders that reported parental use versus parental nonuse of verbal reprimands for inappropriate conduct or unsatisfactory grades was significantly associated with lower overall adaptive functioning among the eighth graders of both groups of parents (Tucker, Brady, Harris, Fraser, & Tribble, 1993). Madsen, Becker, Thomas, Koser, and Plager (1970) reported finding in their research that 77 percent of teachers' interactions with their students were negative, whereas only 23 percent of teachers' interactions with their students were positive.

The aforementioned punishments and any other punishment should be used after positive interventions such as teaching and encouraging alternative behaviors to problem behaviors have been unsuccessful. Punishments should also be used in conjunction with praise and for any appropriate behaviors observed (Jones, 1980). Furthermore, when deciding whether or not to use a punishment, consider that it may result in undesirable emotional effects, such as negative self-statements, negative generalizations, peer reactions, rebellion, and avoidance of the individual who administers the punishment (Jones, 1980). Additionally, consider whether the punishment will cause the child to miss valuable academic learning and, thus, will cause the child to fall behind academically, which in turn often results in more problem behaviors. Such consequences of punishments have the potential for long-term negative effects on the social and academic success of any child and, thus, should be used as last alternatives. Using timeout and other such punishments because they are convenient and have a short-term effect is not justifiable.

Strategy 3.   Parents and teachers can verbally reinforce the appropriate behaviors in which children are already engaging and can reinforce the new behaviors that they teach to replace the problem behaviors. Even more important, parents and teachers can teach children to reinforce themselves for social and academic success behaviors. It is advisable for parents, teachers, and children to use a variety of reinforcers to avoid having any one reinforcer lose its effectiveness. Some reinforcers that might be used include the following (Grasha, 1995, p. 180): (1) social reinforcers such as praise and compliments ("you really drew a beautiful picture"), attention ("tell me about what you enjoyed at school today"), and expressions of affection ("I really like the person that you are"); (2) physiological reinforcers (food and liquids); (3) environmental reinforcers (going to a museum); (4) mental image reinforcers (imagining oneself feeling good all over after having correctly answered a question asked in class by the teacher); (5) reinforcing fun activities (watching television after homework is done); and (6) verbal self-reinforcement ("I am very proud of myself for following all of my teachers' directions today").

Strategy 4.   Teachers and parents can talk with children in general and African American children in particular about stress and its common effects on behavior. These effects often include feeling tense and engaging in hostile behaviors, withdrawn behaviors, and other behaviors in response to any perceived negative event in their lives. Because children are impacted by their environments, it is reasonable to assume that African American children living in low-income environments in which there are typically many stressors will likely experience stress. Teachers and parents can talk with children about stress, its symptoms, how normal it is, and the importance of managing it for social and academic success. Teachers and parents can teach children simple deep breathing exercises, muscular and cognitive relaxation exercises, and meditation to reduce their stress. Most importantly, parents and teachers can encourage African American children to talk with them about their stress or symptoms of stress because talking about their stress and associated symptoms often lessens both. Furthermore, when children talk about their stress or stress symptoms, teachers and parents can better identify the specific stressors for the children and can develop strategies for removing or helping the children remove or cope with the stressors in their lives.

Partnership Strategies

Often parents, teachers, school administrators, psychologists, and counselors must work in partnership to implement strategies to modify behavior problems that are occurring among African American children and other children as well. Some specific partnership strategies for modifying behavior problems of African American children follow.

Strategy 1.   Teachers, parents, psychologists, and counselors can work together and strive to have a multicultural perspective in interacting with one another and when interacting with the children whose behaviors are of concern. Multiculturalism is the valuing and respecting of individual and group differences, realizing that equality does not mean sameness nor inferiority, and believing in the worth and dignity of all individuals (Asante, 1991).

Strategy 2.   Teachers and parents can work together to write a simple contract with the child who engages in behavior problems for the purpose of facilitating unified efforts to modify the child's problem behaviors. These contracts usually include the following information: (1) the general and specific target behavior, (2) the contract participants' names (i.e., the names of the teacher, parent, and child), (3) clear statements of what each participant agrees to do, (4) consequences for each participant for not doing what she or he agreed to do, (5) a schedule for discussing progress and needed changes in the contract, (6) signatures of the participants, and (7) the date that the contract will begin (Grasha, 1995, p. 184). Contracts can be used with most children except the very young (younger than age 8); they are especially appropriate for adolescents who typically want power sharing with their parents and often see parents and teachers as having their own behavior problems that the adolescents would like to see modified. Contracts are negotiated and give some power and responsibilities to all involved toward the goal of modifying the behavior problems of the child and the behaviors of teachers and parents in ways that support achievement of the behavior change goal.

It important to note that many African American parents may be reluctant to write contracts simply because they have difficulty reading or writing due to their educational level. Thus, it is important that the contract is simple, that it is read and discussed with the parent and the child repeatedly as it is being constructed, and that copies of it are sent home with the parent and child. A major advantage of a contract to facilitate modification of behavior problems is that it entails a working partnership for success that deters the common problem in which a child promotes verbal miscommunication between parents and teachers in ways that impede negative behavior change by the child.

Strategy 3.   To the degree possible, teachers and parents can model the success behaviors (e.g., good eye contact, ask questions about what is not understood, etc.) and use the adaptive skills (communication, socialization, and daily living skills) that they want their children to learn and use. Indeed, a well-known lesson is that children tend to do what they see parents and teachers do rather than what these adults tell them to do. Indeed, teachers who yell in their classrooms and parents who yell at home to tell children to be quiet unintentionally teach these children to yell when making requests.

Given that many African American parents have not had training to develop adaptive skills that their children need to learn for social, academic, and life success in the twenty-first century, these parents often will not be able to teach these skills to their children. However, these parents can stress the importance of these skills and arrange for their children to learn these skills through tutoring, after-school programs, and mentoring by family members and other members of their community. Additionally, African American parents can be taught adaptive skills along with their children and by their children at the parents' invitation. One of the greatest ways to learn and remember adaptive skills is through teaching them to someone else. This is a win-win strategy for African Americans that ultimately facilitates empowerment of African American families through their own efforts.

Strategy 4.   Teachers and the parents of an African American child with behavior problems can work together to find at least one person similar to the child who can and is willing to work one-on-one with the child after school hours to teach the child adaptive skills and success behaviors to replace the problem behaviors observed at school or home. This person should be an effective model for the child. Based on existing research, Grasha (1995) concluded that an effective teacher-model for a child or anyone is warm and friendly, worthy of respect, engages in the behaviors to be taught, can teach those behaviors to a child using a step-by-step approach, and is similar to the child with respect to gender, age, socioeconomic status, and physical characteristics. It is important for parents and teachers to work in partnership to involve such teacher-models in the education of African American children with behavior problems and those who are at risk for the occurrence of behavior problems. These teacher-models can be students in after-school programs or high school student volunteers who want to help other students. It may be necessary to provide a small monetary compensation (e.g., $15 per week) to the teacher-model (i.e., a student); yet, such an investment in the future of an African American child is indeed worthwhile.

Conclusions

Given that there are multiple external and internal factors that contribute to behavior problems of African American children, interventions to address these problems need to be multidimensional and usually need to involve all of the significant persons in the lives of these children. Many of the external factors in African American children's lives such as neighborhood violence and poverty are not easily modifiable or not modifiable at all during their childhood life span; consequently, emphasis needs to be given to modifying internal factors in their behavior problems—factors that children can be taught to control such as thoughts that influence behavior and emotions. Ideally, interventions to modify behavior problems of African American children should address both modifiable external factors and internal factors toward the goal of self-empowering these children for social and life success. Self-empowering African American children involves facilitating self-motivation, self-control, self-praise, adaptive skills, and success behaviors for social and life success.

Self-management strategies (e.g., control of one's thoughts, problem solving, delay of gratification behaviors, learning appropriate behaviors through self-instruction, and self-praise of appropriate behaviors) are most ideal for addressing behavior problems of African American children because they focus on enabling these children to stop or reduce problem behaviors even in the presence of environmental conditions and individuals that encourage the problem behaviors. Furthermore, self-management strategies respect the concern of African American parents about not having others, especially European Americans, in authority, controlling their children's behaviors through such strategies as manipulating tangible reinforcers. Additionally, these strategies are consistent with self-empowering African American children for social and life success.

Traditional therapy approaches must be modified to be culturally and socioeconomically sensitive in order to be effective in modifying behavior problems of African American children. This is because these approaches are based primarily on research and clinical experiences with European American children and their families. Yet, the culture and life experiences of African Americans are typically very different from those of European Americans and require interventions that adjust for these differences. Making traditional therapy approaches culturally and socioeconomically sensitive for working with African American children and their families involves respecting the family unit regardless of its structure, involving primary caregivers, teachers, and others who are involved in the children's lives as partners in the therapy process, and using interventions that will empower children and their parents for addressing the factors that are contributing to the children's problem behaviors.

African American children with behavior problems should be included in the process of deciding what must be done to help them modify their problem behaviors. Parents, teachers, and psychologists or counselors should also be involved in this behavior modification process. The involvement of parents and teachers typically includes changing their own behaviors in relation to the child with behavior problems. For example, teachers must avoid the use of easily implemented punishments with an African American child that humiliate the child, impede the child's trust of the teacher, and impede the child's feelings of belonging in the school environment.

Interventions to facilitate the modification of behavior problems of African American children should include providing these children with replacement behaviors for the problem behaviors. In other words, these children should be taught adaptive skills and success behaviors that will bring them positive attention and that will facilitate social success that will be sustained over time. Indeed, it is not enough to simply tell African American children what not to do; they must be taught what to do instead and taught the skills to engage in these alternative behaviors.

6 Modifying Specific Behaviors

Practical Intervention Strategies

The behavior problems that are discussed in this section are common among most African American children as well as among children in general. The conclusion that these problems are common is based on available research, reports of teachers in some of their continuing education workshops, and the present author's clinical experience with African American children and their parents. It is important to note that there has been very little published research on behavior problems among African American children. Such research is needed in order to identify the best possible interventions to modify and prevent these problems. Given the disproportionately high rates of school suspensions, school dropout, and juvenile delinquency among African American children, it is clear that such interventions are needed.

For each behavior discussed in this section, one or more culturally and socioeconomically sensitive strategies for addressing the problem are presented. The strategies recommended are consistent with an overall goal of self-empowering African American children. Self-empowering African American children involves teaching them to be self-motivated, self-controlled, and self-reinforcing and teaching them adaptive skills and success behaviors for academic, social, and life success.

Temper Tantrums

Most parents have experienced their children's temper tantrums. Temper tantrums usually involve children yelling, crying, and pleading for what they want or in retaliation for what they did not get that they wanted. Sometimes children will also hit, kick, and express negative feelings toward the parents. The underlying hope of the children is to disturb the parents enough or to show enough pain so that the parents will be motivated to give them whatever the children had initially desired. Some children frequently engage in temper tantrums and, consequently, cause their parents much stress, frustration, and embarrassment. Temper tantrums tend to occur more often in younger children than in older children such as teenagers.

Temper tantrum behavior serves to focus the attention of a parent (or other primary caregiver) on the child's wants and on the child's frustrations and other feelings that result because these wants have not been met. Most children and adults need and enjoy attention, at least periodically. When a parent pays attention to a child threatening or engaging in a temper tantrum by trying to calm the child to avoid the embarrassment of the child's behavior, the child learns to throw more temper tantrums to get the parent's or guardian's attention. Consequently, the temper tantrums generally increase over time.

Often parents get upset with children for embarrassing them. These feelings are typically shown by yelling at and jerking the child, which in turn bring more attention from observers of the temper tantrum situation and thus more embarrassment to the parents. Parents often report feeling like a clown in the situation or feeling concerned that they will appear to be child abusers. Children learn that by simply throwing a temper tantrum, they can upset parents and get them to throw a parent temper tantrum, which in turn draws sympathy for the children (positive attention) from observers of the temper tantrum interaction.

To modify temper tantrums, parents (and other adults) must tell their children that this behavior is unacceptable and will result in withdrawal of a privilege (e.g., no television for two hours after getting home). This discussion ideally should occur at a nontantrum time when both the parents and the children are calm. Additionally, parents must tell children what they should do instead of engaging in temper tantrum behavior when they want something that they are told they cannot have, or when they feel frustrated because their wants are not being met. For example, a parent might tell a child the following:

> When you yelled, screamed, and hit me because I did not give you the $10 that you requested, I felt disrespected by you and angry. Such behavior by you is not acceptable. I understand that you feel frustrated and upset when you do not get what you want. Instead of yelling, screaming, and hitting me when you have these feelings, I want you to take two or three deep breaths and say the following three times: "I am going to be calm; I am not going to yell, scream, or kick; I am going to be calm." Then calmly and quietly tell me your upset feelings using no more than two or three sentences. Later in the day or the next day after I tell you that you cannot have something or do something, we will talk about what you wanted and under what conditions you might get what you wanted in the future. If you do these things, I will feel very proud of you and will tell you so. If you instead yell, scream, or hit me or anyone else because you do not get what you want, you will not be allowed to watch television the remainder of the day. Are there any questions? I am very happy that we discussed this together. I love you.

When the temper tantrum behavior actually occurs, parents should do their best to ignore it. This withdraws the attention that the child desires—attention that reinforces or increases the temper tantrum behavior. When the child stops the temper tantrum behavior, the parent should give the child immediate attention by talking with the child about some positive topic, giving the child a hug or kiss in the process. When the child engages in some appropriate behavior of any kind following the tantrum behavior, the child should be praised for doing so.

Most parents agree that simply ignoring temper tantrums and then praising appropriate behaviors will sometimes result in the disappearance and then reappearance of the temper tantrums. This is why it is recommended that in addition to using the ignore and praise strategy, parents should give their child a negative consequence (e.g., withdrawal of a privilege) following each temper tantrum and discuss with their child an alternative or replacement behavior for the temper tantrum behavior. It should be noted, however, that regardless of the intervention used to successfully stop a child's temper tantrums, these tantrums often reappear in the future. When temper tantrums reappear, the intervention that was successfully used to stop them should simply be readministered; the intervention will likely be effective again.

Williams (1959) described a case study in which a 21-month-old boy engaged in a temper tantrum whenever his parent put him to bed and began leaving his room. To modify this problem behavior, the parent would put the child to bed and then leave the room despite the child's temper tantrum behavior. As a result, on each successive night, the length of the temper tantrums decreased from 45 minutes to no tantrums on the seventh night. It appears that the child's temper tantrums were being maintained by the reinforcement of having the parent remain in the room in response to the temper tantrum.

It is particularly difficult for African American mothers to ignore their children's temper tantrum behavior, especially because of their tendency to be very nurturing. It is especially difficult for some African American parents, especially those with low incomes, to ignore such behavior because of the high risk of the assumption by observers that they are neglectful, psychologically abusive parents. Furthermore, many low-income parents in general have many stressors in their lives and, consequently, have a low threshold for yelling and screaming by their children. Thus, these parents will almost automatically respond in some way to the child to stop the temper tantrum behavior rather than ignore the child and reattend to the child when the temper tantrum behavior has stopped. It is important for African American parents not to have their authority as parents undermined by the fear of what others will do or say as long as they are using a behavior change intervention that is nonabusive and implemented to teach rather than physically or psychologically hurt their child in the process of modifying the child's problem behavior.

Inattentive and Hyperactive Behaviors

When engagement in inattentive and hyperactive behaviors by a child is more severe and frequent than is typical for the child's social, academic, or job success, the child may have an attention deficit/hyperactivity disorder (ADHD). The specific types of behaviors that are considered inattentive and hyperactive behaviors and are used to make the diagnosis ADHD include the following: does not attend to details, makes careless mistakes in schoolwork or in other activities, has a short attention span, does not appear to listen when others are talking, loses things, fidgets and squirms, runs about or climbs excessively, talks a lot, is impulsive, and often blurts out answers to questions (American Psychiatric Association, 1994).

It is not known how prevalent these behaviors are or ADHD is among African American children. It is reported that approximately 3 percent to 5 percent of all school-age children have ADHD (American Psychiatric Association, 1994). However, population studies have indicated a prevalence of ADHD as high as 20 percent (Taylor, 1994). It has also been reported that among all children, ADHD is more prevalent among younger children than among adolescents (Schaughency, McGee, Raja, Feehan, & Silva, 1994) and occurs more frequently among males than females with the estimated male-to-female ratios ranging from 4:1 to 9:1 (American Psychiatric Association, 1994). These prevalence data specifically for African American children are not known.

No single cause of ADHD has been found (DuPaul, Guevrement, & Barkley, 1991). Researchers have linked several factors to ADHD, but these linked factors have not been conclusively identified as causes of ADHD. These linked factors as reported from the literature by Wicks-Nelson and Israel (1997) include the following: brain disease (Kessler, 1980); birth trauma and head injury (Barkley, 1990); brain structure and functioning problems (Semrud-Clikeman, Filipek, Biederman, Steingard, Kennedy, Renshaw, & Bekken, 1994); abnormalities in the central nervous system transmitters (Hechtman, 1991; Taylor, 1994); abnormal electrophysiological responding (Hechtman, 1991; Taylor, 1994); pregnancy and birth complications (Sprich-Buckminister, Biederman, Milberger, Faraone, & Lehman, 1993); prenatal maternal alcohol consumption (Streissguth, Barr, Sampson, Darby, & Martin, 1989); genetics (Gillis, Gilger, Pennington, & Defries, 1992); lead (Tesman & Hills, 1994); and psychosocial variables such as family adversity (McGee, Partridge, Williams, & Silva, 1991; Stormont-Spurgin & Zentall, 1995), parenting behaviors (Campbell, 1995); and negative parent–child interactions (Barkley, Anastopoulos, Guevremont, & Fletcher, 1992).

Researchers have also concluded that sugars, food additives, and sugar substitutes do not appear to play a significant role in hyperactivity (Erickson, 1992). Stevenson (1989) concluded that genetic effects accounted for about half of the explainable variance of hyperactivity and inattentiveness and that other psychosocial factors, such as social attention to these problems, may sustain or increase their occurrence. Regarding psychosocial factors, Wicks-Nelson and Israel (1997) concluded from the existing research that whether or not family variables cause ADHD, hyperactivity, or inattentiveness in children is not clear (Wicks-Nelson & Israel, 1997).

It is especially important to note that even the factors that have been linked to ADHD, hyperactive behavior, or inattentiveness in children may not be important links to the occurrence of these problems in African American children. Existing research to study factors in ADHD, hyperactive behavior, and inattentiveness has not been culturally and socioeconomically sensitive and has not included large samples of African American children with a specific focus on these youth. We cannot assume that factors in behavior problems or disorders of African American children are the same as those of European American children and adolescents. Difference Model research to examine factors in hyperactivity, inattentiveness, and other behavior problems of African American children is needed. This type of research separately investigates factors in the behavior or life experiences of groups that are different socioeconomically and culturally or any other significant way rather than simply compare the groups on the investigated variables (i.e., Deficit Model research).

Due to cultural differences between African American parents and European American professionals who teach and counsel children, these two groups often disagree on whether the occurrence of inattentive and hyperactive behaviors in African American children are problematic, and if so, whether these behaviors fit the diagnosis of ADHD. This disagreement is not surprising given research indicating that European American parents, European American teachers, and European American physicians often disagree as to whether a European American child's behavior indicates hyperactivity (Sandoval, Lambert, & Sassone, 1980). Furthermore, in a study in which clinicians from China, Indonesia, Japan, and the United States were asked to rate the behaviors of boys presented in video vignettes, ratings of hyperactivity and disruptive behaviors by the Chinese and Indonesian clinicians were found to be higher than the ratings by the Japanese and U.S. clinicians (Tao, 1992). These findings strongly suggest that cultural expectations and values play a role in interpreting what is deviant, abnormal, problematic, or is a disorder.

Given that the severity of behaviors such as those associated with ADHD (e.g., hyperactivity) are often influenced by the culture of the observer, it is important to avoid giving an African American child the diagnosis of ADHD. Instead of using this label, it is more reliable and appropriate to simply describe the behaviors of the child that appear problematic, identify what is contributing to the occurrence of these behaviors, and seek ways to modify the behaviors such that they do not impede the social, academic, and life success of the child. It is also important to involve the child and the child's parents and teacher as well as a culturally sensitive counselor or psychologist in this assessment and intervention process.

Indeed, a child who engages in hyperactive and inattentive behaviors needs individualized education and interventions for these behavior problems. If the child's teacher is not very knowledgeable about or comfortable with African American children, it is also helpful to involve a culturally sensitive teacher as a consultant to the child's teacher or as a partner with the partnership team to identify and address the child's behaviors of concern. It is important to note that a culturally sensitive teacher is usually needed to effectively address behavior problems of African American children and that such a teacher is not necessarily an African American teacher; indeed, all African American teachers are not culturally sensitive. European American teachers who are highly motivated to address behavior problems of African American children and who have thus taken time to learn about African American cultures, to interact socially with African Americans, and to learn about the immediate environments and the families of the African American children in their classrooms tend to be very culturally sensitive.

Traditional psychotherapy is typically not very helpful in treating inattention, hyperactivity, or ADHD (DuPaul, Guevrement, & Barkley, 1991). Following are several specific intervention recommendations for modifying attention difficulty and hyperactive or overactive behavior in an African American child.

Recommendations for Parents

1. Parents can reduce their own stress and anxiety in response to their child's inattentive and hyperactive behaviors. Specifically, parents can tell themselves that their child is not deviant but rather acts differently from the expectations of others, and that with patience, calmness, and help from others, their child's behavior can be modified to facilitate her or his social and academic success. Parents also need to take time out for themselves for rest, relaxation, exercise, and fun away from the child. Giving all of their attention to the child with the behavior problem will only be stressful and result in hostile and unpleasant interactions with the child that negatively impact the child, the parents, and the entire family.

2. Parents can choose not to blame themselves for their child's hyperactive and inattentive behaviors because the causes of these behaviors are not known for certain. When parents unfairly blame themselves for these behaviors by their child, they often have low expectations of the child and do not provide the child with needed discipline.

3. It is important for parents to arrange for their child to have a physical examination and possibly an Electroencephalogram (EEG) and neuropsychological evaluation to rule out a physical problem such as a tumor or hormone imbalance as a reason for the child's inattentive and hyperactive behavior. Even problems like not hearing well or seeing well may contribute to inattentive behavior by a child. If the examination reveals a physical factor in the hyperactive and inattentive behaviors of their child, parents must have the problem addressed without delay. If medication or surgery is indicated, then at least a second opinion should be sought from among medical professionals who are highly recommended by individuals that the parents trust and respect. Medication and surgery should be last alternatives given the risks of any surgery and given that the long-term effects of popular medications for treating ADHD, hyperactivity, and inattentiveness are not known.

4. Parents should not give their child commonly prescribed stimulant medications (or any other medications) to reduce hyperactive and impulsive behavior until after having given careful consideration to their effectiveness, frequency of needed use, and side effects. Parents should not give their children these medications simply because medical professionals recommend them and describe them as very popular and effective. Parents must think for themselves and carefully consider the positives and issues of concern associated with the use of stimulant medications (e.g., Ritalin) to reduce their child's hyperactive and impulsive behavior. The positives associated with the use of stimulant medications to reduce hyperactive and impulsive behaviors include the following:

 a. The use of stimulant medications is the most popular treatment in the United States for ADHD, hyperactivity, and impulsiveness (DuPaul & Barkley, 1993). [Methylphenidate (Ritalin), dextroamphetamine (Dexedrine), and pemoline (Cylert) are the most commonly used of these stimulant medications.]

 b. Research and clinical data suggest that 70 percent of medicated children show increased attention and reduced impulsivity and activity level (Murphy, Greenstein, & Pelham, 1993). Additionally, existing research and clinical data suggest that stimulant medications also reduce children's aggressive, noncompliant, and oppositional behaviors. In sum, the existing data suggest that stimulant medications are effective (Swanson, McBurnett, Christian, & Wigal, 1995).

The issues of concern associated with the use of stimulant medications to reduce hyperactive and stimulant behaviors include the following:

 a. The effects of most stimulants are rapid but wear off in a few hours and, thus, must be given two or three times a day.

 b. Children under age four may benefit the least and suffer more adverse side effects than children age four and older (Barkley, 1990).

 c. The side effects of stimulant medications for some children include difficulty sleeping, narexia, stomach pain, headaches, irritability, rashes, and involuntary muscle movement, all of which often but do not always diminish in two or three weeks or with reduction in medication dosage (Barkley, 1990; Biederman, 1991; Gadow & Pomeroy, 1991).

 d. Sometimes a child's growth is suppressed while taking the drugs but rebounds when the drug is stopped.

 e. Children worry about becoming drug addicts and about being teased because of changes in their behavior when the medication wears off.

f. National organizations that focus on children with ADHD (e.g., Attention Deficit Disorder Association and the Children with Attention Deficit Disorder) criticize the use of stimulant medications with children who appear to have ADHD. These organizations fear that these medications are given to children who are misdiagnosed (Wicks-Nelson & Israel, 1997). Given the little that is known by most physicians and psychiatrists in this country about the determinants of the behaviors of African American children who engage in hyperactive behavior, impulsive behavior, and inattentive behavior and appear to have ADHD, it is indeed likely that some of these children will be misdiagnosed and, thus, given medications that they do not need.

g. The long-term effects of stimulants on children in general and on African American children in particular are not known.

Recommendations for Parents and Teachers

1. Parents and teachers can make sure that the child has organized days at home and school and that these days include a mix of structured activities and unstructured activities. Physical activities such as group sports and group games that allow much physical movement should be included in that they help channel the child's energy, and they give the parents and teachers relaxation and fun-time opportunities with and away from the child. Again, having relaxed, pleasant parents and teachers who are not obsessed with parenting and teaching, respectively, and who give their own mental health some priority in their roles is very important for having the patience and energy to effectively parent and teach a child who often engages in inattentive and hyperactive behavior.

2. Parents, teachers, and significant others can tell the child the value of paying attention, listening to instructions, focusing on the child's assignments, and reading quietly. It should be explained how these behaviors are important in becoming a nurse or a musician or whatever the child wants to be.

3. Parents and teachers can playfully and creatively challenge the child to gradually increase periods of time of focused activity and have the child praise herself or himself for meeting the goal time of structured activity. Some of these activities should be activities that the child really enjoys such as drawing or listening to music. Parents, teachers, and significant others in the child's life should praise the child for engagement in calm, focused activity.

4. Parents and teachers can see to it that the child follows a schedule of activities for the day, which includes times for a nap, a highly physical activity, a mentally challenging activity, quiet relaxation, studying, nutritious meals three times a day, and a reasonable bedtime. Nutritious meals and a structured bedtime are especially important given that both hunger and fatigue are reported by teachers and parents to be associated with hyperactivity and other behavior problems in children.

5. Parents and teachers must find activities to challenge the child such as learning to use the computer and use of academic software that includes problem-solving challenges. Writing stories, involvement in science projects, and creation of a small business are other kinds of activities that might be challenging and interesting for the child and constructively channel the child's energy.

6. Parents, teachers, and significant others can avoid yelling at the child and criticizing the child's active and inattentive behaviors. As the result of such negative attention, the child will often experience hyperactivity and inattentiveness as ways of getting attention. Consequently, the child's hyperactivity and inattentiveness are reinforced.

7. The parents and teachers can choose to use short-term versus long-term punishments when disciplining the child who engages in severe inattentive and hyperactive behaviors. An example of a short-term punishment is having the child spend ten minutes writing the reasons why the behavior that he or she engaged in should not occur. Of course, it is important to tell the child what the child should do in the future instead of the inappropriate behavior.

8. Parents and teachers can give the child leadership roles and responsibilities to constructively channel the child's energy. Teachers can also seat the child away from other children who manifest behavior problems.

9. Teachers and parents can involve the child in activities or experiences that involve learning and experiencing the benefits of self-control and delay of gratification. It has been theorized (Sonuga-Barke, 1994) and many parents and teachers have observed that hyperactivity and inattentiveness in children are linked to difficulty delaying gratification and an impulsive style. Learning self-control and delay of gratification are important for social and academic success. Simple behaviors like saving one's money and watching it grow and following steps for doing a task can facilitate the development of self-control and delay of gratification. Both of these skills are important in self-empowering African American children for social, academic, and life success.

10. Teachers and parents can teach the child to observe and record the child's own behaviors toward the goals of increasing on-task behaviors and decreasing off-task behaviors through the child's own efforts; in other words, teachers and parents can teach the child to self-monitor the child's own behaviors for self-control. For example, a child can record how many minutes she or he spends working on each assignment without getting out of her or his chair or talking with any other child. The teacher and parent can make this record a big deal and really praise the child for any little progress or for maintaining any improvements made earlier in on-task behavior. Most importantly, the child can be encouraged to praise herself or himself and to feel really proud of her or his efforts to do assignments without getting off task and to keep the requested on-task time record. To help the child stay on task with assignments, teachers and parents can give the child written steps to follow to do the assignment and can teach the child self-statements to say quietly to help stay focused on the assignment. Some examples of such self-statements are as follows:

> I know I can do this assignment without getting up and talking; I simply need to follow the steps.

> > Step 1 is to record the time that I am starting.
> > Step 2 is to place my name on the assignment sheet.
> > Step 3 is to read the directions on the sheet.

> I am proud that I am following the steps.

> > Step 4 is to do what the directions state. I am to read each sentence and write *true* beside it if it is true and *false* beside it if it is false.

> I am doing a good job following directions.

11. Parents and teachers can remind themselves that the goal for the child who is engaging in inattentive and hyperactive behaviors is to modify her or his behaviors for social and academic success rather than to simply slow the child's activity level or get the child to sit quietly most of the day. Parents and teachers can also support each other by praising each other and publicly acknowledging each other's efforts in the process of providing the individualized attention needed to help the child engage in prosocial behaviors and other behaviors for academic success.

Understandably, most African American parents are tremendously concerned when their children are hyperactive and inattentive. They especially worry that these children will be maladjusted adults who will experience little or no success in their lives. Interestingly, many African American children and other youth as well who are labeled as having ADHD become reasonably adjusted and successful adults. Given that it is not known what determines whether or not African American children with behaviors associated with ADHD will be maladjusted adults, it is wise to use multiple intervention strategies such as the previously specified strategies to facilitate their success in school and life. The emphasis of such strategies must be to assist these children in self-managing their behavior, as they may not get the support and structure that they need from many who will be involved at some point in their education.

Aggressive/Disruptive Behaviors

Aggressive/disruptive behaviors include fighting, hitting, threatening to fight or hit, disobeying, using hostile and intimidating verbal voice tones, being demanding and defiant, being destructive of self-possessions and possessions of others, disturbing others, and expressing feelings in a loud, insulting, and often hostile manner. These behaviors are included in the summary list of aggressive behaviors adapted from Achenbach (1993) by Wicks-Nelson and Israel (1997). In some texts aggressive/disruptive behaviors are referred to as one of several types of conduct disorders. To parents and teachers they are typically referred to as aggressive/disruptive behaviors. Teachers commonly report these behaviors among the behavior problems of African American students in their classrooms. Thus, aggressive/disruptive behaviors are being considered here among the behavior problems of African American children that are being discussed in some detail in this book.

Aggressive/disruptive behaviors often occur among African American children from low-income families and among gifted students. They occur among the latter particularly at school. These behaviors are often the result of feeling alienated and unaccepted, especially among their peers (Ford, 1992). It has been suggested that children learn these behaviors from seeing others in their environment engage in these behaviors and that the behaviors are inadvertently reinforced by parents. Parents' attention and emotional reaction to the behaviors often serve to reassure children that they are loved and important. Parents, however, feel that they convey their love and the importance of their children by working hard to feed and clothe these youth and by giving them desired clothes and other material things. Children typically view the meeting of such physical needs and desires as among parents' responsibilities rather than as shows of parental love and of the children's importance to parents. What these youth often want in order to feel loved are their parents' time, encouragement, affection, praise, and attention.

There is some indication from a research study with African American adolescents that feelings and perceptions of the intentions of others may be factors in the aggressive/disruptive behaviors of some African American youth from low-income environments. In this study by Graham, Hudley, and Williams (1992) so-called "aggressive" African American students and Latino American students from a low income metropolitan community were compared with so-called "nonaggressive" African American students and Latino American students from the same community. Results included that the so-called aggressive students in both racial groups perceived peer-instigated negative outcomes as more intended than did their nonaggressive peers. Additionally, the aggressive adolescents as compared to the nonaggressive peers were more likely to state that they felt angry toward the peer who instigated the negative outcomes and were more likely to endorse hostile behavioral actions. The authors concluded that blaming others based on the perceived intent of their negative actions and the associated feelings as well as the seemingly low threshold for retaliatory behavior by the aggressive students might serve as genuine survival strategies for coping with the dangers and violence that are part of the daily lives of many African American youth and other youth living in low-income, high-risk environments.

It has also been asserted by Lochman and Sims (1981) that it is the perceptions of behaviors or the cognitive processing of behaviors by others rather than the behaviors themselves that provoke aggressive responses as well as other responses in a child. According to these authors, a child's cognitive processing or labeling and attribution given to a behavior of another person or stimulus event is influenced by the child's learning history, prior state of arousal, and the context of the behavior or stimulus event. Furthermore, if the label or attribution is that the behavior or stimulus event is a threat, then the child responds physiologically (e.g., muscles tighten, heart rate increases) and cognitively by planning to react. According to Camp (1977), so-called aggressive children spend very little time processing behavioral alternatives and instead react impulsively, in a reflexive manner, to perceived threats.

It is indeed possible that African American youth view many stimulus events and behaviors of others at their school and in their communities as potential threats. Many African American children are taught by their parents and their experiences with racist police and others not to trust the European American majority. Many of these youth are stressed because of the communities and home environments in which they live, and many are in school environments in which they are in the minority and, thus, feel vulnerable and the need to be guarded. Such life circumstances could indeed lead to impulsive, reflexive, hostile actions without much cognitive processing. Such aggressive responses could indeed be survival responses that are reflections of their learning experiences and their everyday lives.

The paucity of research to examine the factors in aggressive/disruptive behaviors of African American children render the existing explanations of these behaviors speculative. Therefore, the precise interventions for modifying aggressive/disruptive behaviors are not known. However, given that there are many environmental factors that are difficult to control or to modify, which common sense and clinical experiences with African American children suggest contribute to aggressive/disruptive behaviors by these youth, self-management intervention approaches realistically need to be emphasized in efforts to modify these behaviors. Parents, teachers, schools, and communities also can play important roles in providing learning experiences (e.g., problem-solving training, assertiveness skills training, and other adaptive skills training) and environments that facilitate this self-management and that foster, teach, and reinforce alternative behaviors to aggressive/disruptive behaviors among African American children.

Support for and emphasis on self-management in interventions to modify aggressive/disruptive behaviors come from one of the few existing research studies on modifying aggressive behaviors by African American children. In this study by Lochman and Sims (1981), the effects of forty-minute group sessions to reduce aggressive behaviors among a group of twelve African American elementary school children from low-income, single-parent families were tested. These children consisted of eleven males and one female who were identified as the most aggressive and disruptive in their classes. The group sessions occurred twice per week over a six-week period and focused on teaching these children self-management strategies to control the emotions underlying their aggressive behavior. Specifically, the group sessions included discussion of (1) situations that made the children angry, (2) the physiological feelings that occur with increases in anger, (3) a social problem-solving method for addressing problem situations such as those that elicit anger, and (4) positive self-statements to decrease one's anger arousal. The sessions also included modeling and practicing how to respond nonaggressively in various anger-producing and threat-producing situations. The goals of the training were to alter the children's physiological responses (e.g., reduce muscle tension via relaxation), cognitive processing of events, and response alternatives to perceived threats and anger. Results indicated that after the six-week intervention period, aggressiveness among the children had decreased significantly and on-task class behavior had increased.

A limitation of this research, however, is the absence of a control group. Yet, the results add to the growing support for teaching African American children self-management strategies such as a problem-solving technique and use of coping statements rather than having others provide structures to control their behavior and thus their future. The history of African Americans evidences the danger of such controls.

Following are some specific suggestions as to what can be done to assist African American children in reducing or eliminating their aggressive/disruptive behaviors and in learning alternative replacement behaviors that will facilitate their self-empowerment for social, academic, and life success.

Recommendations for Psychologists and Counselors

1. A group approach such as that reported by Lochman and Sims (1981), which was discussed earlier in this section, can be used by psychologists and counselors to teach African American youth alternative behaviors to aggressive behaviors. Given the oral tradition of African Americans and the enjoyment of activity and movement, the use of role-playing for active participation in social learning with a group of peers is a culturally sensitive intervention method. In group sessions, different interactions involving making requests, expressing anger, expressing frustration, giving negative feedback, expressing positive feelings, and so on can be modeled and demonstrated via role-playing by the children; then exactly what can be said and done in each type of interaction can be taught using the same methods. Peer group members can give each other constructive feedback. The group participants can also be videotaped and have the videotapes reviewed one-on-one so that children can see their verbal and nonverbal behaviors and receive constructive feedback about these behaviors without embarrassment. New behaviors taught ideally should be called success behaviors to deter or effectively respond to assertions that the behaviors taught in the group sessions are "acting white" behaviors.

Group participants can also discuss the importance of learning behaviors that are alternatives to their labeled aggressive behaviors or interpersonal styles. They can be taught that the power and strength that they aggressively project can be more effectively projected through self-empowerment, that is, self-motivation, self-control, self-praise, and communication skills, social skills, and daily living skills for job and life success. Inviting successful young college students, athletes, lawyers, businesspersons, and other professionals to group sessions to talk with the children in the group about self-managing their behavior is an effective strategy for motivating group participants to make positive behavior changes.

2. In group and individual sessions, psychologists and counselors can teach children to stop and think before responding to feelings including anger, frustration, anxiety, and sexual arousal. They should be taught to take at least one minute to think about what they want to say and do and how to say it in as positive, respectful, and calm a way as possible so as to not get themselves into trouble with teachers, parents, and others. The children should also be taught to think about the consequences of anticipated actions (i.e., what they plan to say and do) to help them decide what to actually say and do.

Recommendations for Teachers, Parents, Psychologists, and Counselors

1. Teachers, parents, counselors, psychologists, and any others involved in modifying aggressive behaviors by African American children must agree on behaviors that are aggressive. For example, some African Americans do not consider talking loudly to express an emotion aggressively given that such volume is often a habit developed from having to talk over loud music in the home and in the neighborhood. Some African American males are labeled aggressive just by the way they walk into the classroom or because they disagree with the opinion of an authority figure. It is especially important that the African American child who is labeled as aggressive/disruptive be included in the discussion of what behaviors are perceived as aggressive.

2. It is recommended that parents, teachers, psychologists, and counselors involved in addressing the behavior of an African American child avoid use of the term *aggressive/ disruptive* in describing the child given that this term has been used as a part of unjust negative stereotypes of African Americans and, thus, is resented by many of them.

3. It is important to encourage African American children to assertively express their negative and positive feelings rather than suppress these feelings. To assertively express feelings means to state them constructively and with confidence, clarity, and consideration for the feelings and values of others. For too long African American children have been told by parents, teachers, family members, and others to be quiet or shut up when expressing their opinions. African American parents and family members have done this for many reasons, including to help protect their children from saying something that will get them in trouble with the police. In many African American cultures children have been told that they are to be seen and not heard, that children are too young to have feelings, and that big boys and big girls do not cry. Some teachers often give priority to keeping African American children quiet who are behind academically so that they can attend to helping the other children in their classroom learn.

For all of the preceding reasons many African American children have a lot of feelings including anger, frustration, hurt, love, and affection that they have not learned to express effectively. The negative feelings as well as the positive feelings often get displaced through aggressive or disruptive ways. Ultimately, many African American children and adults do not know how to assertively express their feelings or how to receive these feelings from others. Yet, expressing negative feelings and frustrations is important in commanding the respect that one deserves, and expressing positive feelings is important in building positive relationships for productive, meaningful, and successful lives. Furthermore, people in general enjoy working with and supporting children and others who are positive in interactions with them.

4. When teaching African American children to assertively express negative feelings, it is useful to teach them to do the following to decrease the likelihood of listeners feeling disrespected and angry and responding in a defensive or violent manner:

a. Use statements that begin with "I" rather than "you." For example, rather than saying "you get on my nerves," one could say "I get really irritated and frustrated when you wear my clothes without asking."

b. Express a genuine positive feeling or compliment that is related to the topic of your negative feeling before expressing the negative feeling. For example, one could say, "I know that you are a good friend and that I can always count on you, but I felt really hung out to dry when you did not take my side in the argument with John."

c. Address the listener's behavior rather than the entire person. For example, rather than saying "I feel that you are a liar," one could say, "I feel that the excuse you gave me was a lie."

d. Be specific about the behavior that elicited negative feelings. For example, rather than saying "your silliness has to stop," one could say, "I just cannot handle it when you tease and annoy girls when we go to football games together like you did last night."

e. State your negative feelings about the listener's behavior after stating the behavior, and say what you would like to have happen to keep you from having similar negative feelings in the future. For example, one could say, "When you yelled at me, Mrs. Jones, it made me feel embarrassed, angry, and hurt. The next time I do something that is wrong, I would like for you to tell me softly or one-to-one after class rather than yelling at me in front of my peers." This way of expressing feelings is the feedback formula method, which is shown in Table 6.1.

5. When teaching African American children alternative behaviors, communication styles, and skills to modify aggressive/disruptive behaviors and when teaching these youth any constructive social or academic skills and behaviors, it is useful to use a self-empowering, step-by-step teaching method. This method allows an African American child to experience self-empowerment that can counteract feelings of powerlessness, which often accompany minority status and which often result in active or passive disengagement from the teaching and learning process.

TABLE 6.1 **Research-Based Model Partnership Education Program Feedback Formula**

First Part: When you _____ ,
                                              (be specific about the behavior)

Second Part: I feel _____ .

Third Part: In the future, I would appreciate it if _____

               _____ .

Optional: Remember, the rule at the education center is _____

               _____ .

- -

Example:

When you play with other students while I am trying to help you with your homework, I feel disrespected and hurt.

In the future, I would appreciate it if you would pay attention to me and your homework while I am helping you with your homework.

Remember, the rule at the education center is to stay in your seat and pay attention during homework and study times.

The step-by-step teaching method involves (a) breaking the skill or behavior to be learned into steps; (b) having the teacher model the skill or behavior using the steps and saying each step aloud (i.e., cognitive modeling); (c) having the student perform the same skill or behavior (as modeled by the teacher) while the teacher instructs the student using the steps; (d) instructing the student to perform the skill or behavior while using the steps to instruct himself or herself aloud and then silently (i.e., covert self-guidance); (e) having the student memorize the steps and practice the skill or behavior using the steps covertly; and (f) having the student self-praise his or her progress toward and attainment of the behavior or skill throughout the learning and practice processes. The detailed steps in the step-by-step method are presented in Table 6.2. An example of how this method is used in teaching children effective anger management is presented in Table 6.3.

Recommendations for Church and Community Leaders
1. Leaders of churches and community centers in African American communities can organize and conduct assertiveness training groups for children who are labeled aggressive and or engage in some aggressive/disruptive behaviors. Most African American children can benefit from participation in such training groups when these groups emphasize the constructive expression of negative and positive feelings, engagement in success behaviors (e.g., good eye contact, making complete sentences), and adaptive skills training (e.g., problem-solving skills), all of which deter and prevent the development of aggressive/disruptive

TABLE 6.2 The Step-by-Step Method for Teaching New Behaviors and Academic Tasks

1. The teacher figures out what steps are involved in doing the behavior or task by doing it himself or herself prior to meeting with the learner.
2. The teacher writes the steps on a large index card or sheet of paper using clear print and simple wording. (For example, "Step 1. Read instructions carefully.")
3. The teacher explains to the learner what will be taught using the steps on the sheet or index card.
4. The teacher shows the learner how to do the behavior or task by reading aloud and then doing each step (i.e., the teacher models for the learner). The learner is told to listen and observe the demonstration and to feel free to ask questions as the teacher demonstrates each step.
5. The teacher instructs the learner to read aloud and then do each step. The teacher assists the learner in getting a step correct when an error is made or when the learner has forgotten how to do a step. It is important to make sure that the learner does not skip any steps.
6. The teacher instructs the learner to read silently and then do each step.
7. The teacher instructs the learner to study the steps in an effort to memorize them.
8. The teacher instructs the learner to think and then do each step without looking at the card or paper on which the steps are written.

Notes

a. The teacher praises effort as well as successful accomplishment of each step.
b. When the learner has great difficulty with any step, the teacher directs the learner to an earlier step that can be done successfully and then instructs the learner to move down to the next step from there.
c. Give the learner a copy of the steps for use in practicing the behavior or task at a later time.
d. On a day soon after the training in doing the behavior or task, the teacher asks the learner to do it without the card or paper with the steps. If the learner is not able to successfully do this, then the teacher repeats the step-by-step method for doing the behavior task.

behaviors and other behavior problems. African American churches typically have educators and counselors in their congregations. Ministers can use their influence to mobilize these educators and counselors to donate their time to conducting or teaching others to conduct assertiveness training groups and other groups and activities for empowering African American children and adolescents for social, academic, and life success.

2. Leaders of churches and community centers in African American communities can conduct parent training to teach African American parents how to respond constructively to, modify, and prevent aggressive/disruptive behaviors by their children. Parents cannot leave it to schools to provide such training and activities. Most schools are finding it difficult to meet the academic needs of many African American students and, thus, providing needed adaptive skills training and self-empowerment training is out of the question. Yet, many African American parents often do not have the knowledge to provide their children with the self-empowerment training that they need in these times of elevating academic standards, growing divisions between the races and between the haves and have nots, decreasing social programs, and weakening of affirmative action. Church and community leaders can arrange for the provision of this training at neighborhood churches and com-

TABLE 6.3 A Step-by-Step Approach for Children to Use for Managing Anger

1. When you begin to feel angry, say STOP silently or imagine a big red stop sign with the STOP in white letters.

2. Quickly walk away from the person or situation that made you angry. Walk away without saying or doing anything to the person.

3. Take three deep breaths to help you get calm and relaxed.

4. Think about possible actions to take in response to the person or situation that made you feel angry.

5. Consider likely consequences of each possible action.

6. Decide on the action that will have more positive consequences and will not get you in trouble with your parents, teachers, or school officials. (It is usually a good idea to share your thoughts and decisions with an adult whom you respect, trust, and like before doing what you decided.)

7. When you are calm, do the action that you decided to do.

8. Calmly express your feelings to the person who made you angry. Say what the person did, how it made you feel, and what you would like the person to do in the future to keep this anger-producing situation from happening again. For example, you might say the following: "When you jumped in front of me in the lunch line, I felt angry and disrespected. In the future I would appreciate it if you would ask me if you may get in front of me."

munity centers. These leaders can solicit any needed financial support for this training from the local businesses patronized by African American families in their neighborhoods.

Noncompliance

The term *noncompliance* means failure to follow instructions or to respond appropriately to requests. Because parents and teachers are most typically in positions of authority in relation to children, these adults most often make requests of and give instructions to children. There is no reported research on how prevalent noncompliance is among African American children or any youth. However, parents and teachers experience this problem with some youth in all age groups. Noncompliance is usually first recognized or described as such in children between the ages of three and eight. It is perhaps most disturbing to adults when the noncompliance is perceived by them as an intentional show of disrespect to retaliate against them or to humiliate them. Such noncompliance occurs most often in the preteen to teen years when children are desiring more autonomy and less parental control and are being influenced greatly by their peers in directions that are often antagonistic to parents' instructions and requests.

Noncompliance by children is an indication that parents do not have adequate control over their children's behaviors (Erickson, 1992). From a self-empowerment perspective noncompliance by children can in fact be an indication that the children do not have adequate control or do not choose to exercise control over their own behavior, especially when faced with behavioral influences from peers or personal wants that compete with rules and instructions or requests of parents and teachers.

There are many factors that can influence children to choose not to control their behavior so as to comply with the rules, requests, and instructions of authority figures. One common factor in the noncompliance of children is learning that they do not have to comply. This learning occurs, for example, when parents withdraw their command or request to a child because the child expresses the lack of desire to do what is asked. Rather than listening to whining and complaining from the child in response to a request or instruction, a parent often tells the child to just forget the request. Next, the parent typically gets upset with the child and does the task that had been requested of the child. The child learns that all she or he has to do is whine and complain to avoid compliance and the noncompliance will be tolerated by the child's parent(s).

The negative attention from parents (e.g., the parents' verbalized frustration to the child) that children get for noncompliance is also often a factor in the continuation of the noncompliance. This negative attention is often experienced by the child as better than no attention at all. Indeed, some children are noncompliant to get attention from their parents. Many African American parents who are in the low socioeconomic groups in the United States are preoccupied with the survival of their families and many middle-class African American parents are working two jobs or over 60 hours per week to stay in the middle class. Consequently, there is often not a lot of time for parents to attend to their children's needs for focused time with them, conversation with them, and hugs and kisses from them.

African American children are also sometimes noncompliant to parents' and teachers' rules, requests, and instructions as a way of punishing these adults for various reasons. African American youth often punish parents because these youth perceive the parents as being unloving, too controlling, selfish in their decision to get a divorce, and so on. African American children punish teachers because they perceive them as uncaring, unfair, discriminatory, and so on. Whether or not these perceptions are anchored in reality, they must be recognized and addressed to modify the existence of the resulting noncompliance.

It is also important to note that African American children are often noncompliant because the rules for their behavior are not clear and have not been discussed with them. The rules for children are often not clear or explained because they are made following behaviors that upset the parent or teacher who made the rule. For example, many parents tell their sixteen-year-old teen to be home at a decent hour; then, when the adolescent returns home at 12:00 midnight, the parent is upset and consequently makes the rule that the teen should be home at 8:00 P.M.—a time that is unreasonable by most standards for sixteen-year-olds and that will elicit future curfew noncompliance.

Peer influences, environmental influences, the influence of drugs, noncompliance by children on television, and many other variables also contribute to noncompliance by children. These variables are difficult or even impossible to control. Thus, facilitation of compliance in children will require facilitation of self-motivation, self-control, self-reinforcement, and skills that promote appropriate compliance to rules, requests, and instructions of parents, teachers, and other authority figures. Furthermore, because requests and instructions from adults, including those from parents and teachers, can be inappropriate, it is important to instruct children as to what to do when they feel that requests and instructions from anyone are not appropriate (e.g., requests for sexual activity).

There are several strategies that African American parents (and other primary caregivers) and teachers of their children can use to reduce or extinguish inappropriate noncompliance by these children and to facilitate their compliance to appropriate requests, instructions, and rules. These strategies include the following:

1. Parents and teachers can clearly establish and regularly review their rules for and expectations of their children. This review should include an opportunity for these youth to ask questions about the rules and for parents to explain the importance of the rules and behaviors expected. The benefits of these rules and expected behaviors to the children's school and life success should ideally be taught to the children in an age-appropriate manner.

2. Parents and teachers should make it clear that noncompliance to rules and to requests and instructions from them will not be tolerated. Furthermore, the consequences for noncompliance to rules, requests, and instructions should be specified and ideally should be written. A copy of this information should be provided to children old enough to read. Indeed, too often parents and children forget what they said are the rules and the consequences.

Consequences for being noncompliant ideally should include withdrawal of privileges and engagement in activities that will teach the child appropriate compliant behaviors. For example, if a child calls another child a "bastard" and the rule at school (and at home) is to call peers only by their names, then the consequence for the action of calling another child a "bastard" could be a homework assignment to write a five-page essay on the meaning of the word *bastard* and why it should not be used to label or describe another person. For repeatedly coming home from a friend's house after curfew, a thirteen-year-old adolescent could lose the privilege of visiting friends for two nights.

It is important that consequences for noncompliance or any behavior problem be short term, reasonable, and easy for the parents to enforce. If a parent decides that the punishment for staying out beyond a curfew should be loss of the privilege of going out anywhere for two weeks, then the parent will likely also be punished because the parent may have to miss social events to be there with the adolescent and lose having relaxing time alone away from the adolescent. It is important to remember that the purpose of punishing children is not to humiliate or inflict psychological or physical pain but rather to call the children's attention to rules, to teach them that a certain behavior is inappropriate, and to promote engagement of appropriate replacement behaviors for the inappropriate behaviors.

3. Parents and teachers must respond calmly to noncompliance by children. In other words, rather than yelling, lecturing, and showing that they are upset in response to noncompliance, parents and teachers should simply state the rules that were broken or identify the request or instruction to which children did not comply and then state and enforce the consequences. When parents do not become upset because of their children's noncompliance, their children experience less control over their parents' and teachers' behaviors. Noncompliance by the children thus loses its reinforcing consequences (e.g., getting their parents and teachers to be upset) and becomes less likely to occur.

4. When parents or teachers are calm and have time to focus on children's noncompliant behaviors, the parents or teachers should remind the children of the specific noncompliant act, tell the children how their noncompliant behavior made the parents or teachers feel, and tell the children the compliant behavior that is expected in the future. The benefits of compliance to the appropriate requests, rules, and requests of parents and teachers should also be explained to the children. These benefits for children include positive feelings toward them and respect for them, which result in giving them encouragement, praise, help when needed, good recommendations for summer jobs, scholarships, athletic opportunities, and college.

5. It is important for parents and teachers to enthusiastically and immediately recognize, praise, and express positive feelings in response to children's compliant behaviors. It is also important for these adults to encourage children to praise themselves for their compliant behaviors. Often the compliant behaviors of children go unnoticed, but as soon as they do not comply, they are reprimanded. Given that this is usually the case, it is important for parents and teachers to make a conscious effort to notice children being compliant to a rule, request, or instruction. An example of what can be said in response to observed compliance by children is as follows:

> Henry, I noticed that you quickly and thoroughly cleared your desk to get ready for lunch just as I requested. You did a great job! Your behavior made me feel great. I hope that you will always immediately follow my instructions for getting ready for lunch and that you will always do a great job. You deserve praise from yourself for following instructions and for doing such a good job.

6. It is important for parents and other adults who spend time with children to respond respectfully and cooperatively to requests given to each other. It is also important for these adults to follow rules set for the home or school. For example, if a parent or teacher says that yelling is not acceptable at home or school, then these adults must not yell at each other. Compliant and cooperative behaviors by adults are important because children imitate or model what their parents, teachers, and other significant adults in their lives do.

7. It is important for parents and teachers to remember that use of requests rather than commands is more useful in facilitating compliant behaviors by children. An example of a request is "please bring me a glass of water." An example of a command is "bring me a glass of water and don't take all day to do it." When children follow through in responding to requests or commands, they immediately should be thanked. This appreciative response reinforces future compliance with requests and instructions.

8. To reduce noncompliance by children, parents and teachers can use a social learning theory approach developed by Forehand and McMahon (1981). This approach has been shown to be effective in reducing noncompliance (McMahon & Wells, 1989). This approach involves giving direct, concise commands, allowing the child sufficient time to comply, rewarding compliance with parental attention, and applying a negative consequence, such as withdrawal of a privilege, for noncompliance.

9. It is important for parents and teachers to release the anger and frustration that they justifiably feel in response to their children's noncompliant behaviors, but it is just as important to avoid directing this anger release toward the children. When angry and frustrated with a child, a parent or teacher can say the words "stop" and "be calm" to themselves, take a few slow, deep breaths, walk away from the child, calmly relax for a few minutes, and then speak to the child briefly about the child's noncompliant behavior. In talking with the child, the parent or teacher should identify the noncompliant behavior, her or his feelings about it, and the consequence for it. When sharing feelings with the child, the parent or teacher should be concise and use statements that begin with "I feel," rather than statements that begin with "you made me feel." As a way of deterring anger from occurring, parents can remind themselves that 100 percent immediate compliance from their children is not a realistic goal.

It is also important for parents and teachers to teach African American children how to recognize inappropriate requests and instructions and what to do when these occur. Inappropriate requests and instructions include those involving not telling their parents (or primary caregivers) something and those involving doing something illegal or immoral, including participating in activities of a sexual nature (e.g., allowing their genitals or other body parts to be touched, participating in pornographic picture taking). Children can generally be told that if an instruction or request involves keeping something secret, feels uncomfortable, or feels wrong, then it is likely an inappropriate request or instruction to which they should not comply.

Children should be told by parents and teachers that when they feel a request or instruction is inappropriate, they should (1) immediately leave the presence of the person who made the request or gave the instruction, (2) talk as soon as possible with an adult that they trust about the request or instruction, and (3) ask the trusted adult (if it is not a parent) to talk with their parents about what happened. Because children are sometimes abused by their parents and teachers, it is important that they are encouraged to first talk with a person whom they trust. It is a very good idea for parents, teachers, and church and community leaders to provide opportunities for children to role-play how to respond appropriately to inappropriate requests and instructions from adults and other children.

Oppositional Defiant Behaviors

Oppositional defiant behaviors of children convey very negative and often hostile and provocative opposition to authority figures. These behaviors occur even if the children clearly recognize that their defiant actions will cause or are causing negative consequences for them. In other words, the oppositional attitude is important, regardless of whether it makes sense and no matter what it costs the child or others.

Oppositional defiant behaviors usually include behaviors such as opposing the suggestions of others, actively refusing to comply with requests and rules, being spiteful, annoying, and vindictive, swearing and using obscene language, being argumentative with adults, being annoyed with and provocative to others; furthermore, these behaviors are more extreme than typical noncompliant behavior. Additionally, children who are labeled as having an oppositional defiant disorder are often described as passively resistant, negatively oriented, and as having a generally bad attitude (Erickson, 1992).

Oppositional defiant behaviors typically begin between ages three and eight. They are associated with family problems, low self-esteem, anger toward parents and their life situation. Oppositional defiant behaviors are often ways for children to achieve distinction within and outside of the family as significant persons not liked by themselves or others.

Anger typically underlies oppositional behaviors. This anger is often associated with blame that a child who manifests oppositional behaviors attributes to a parent for a divorce, an affair, perceived favoritism toward a sibling, or feeling not wanted by her or his parents (Erickson, 1992).

Modification of oppositional behaviors is not easy because the anger that underlies these behaviors is often justified; furthermore, the experiences leading to the anger are usually complex and cannot be changed. Helping children understand these experiences and view them in less anger-producing ways is also difficult, given that this process typically involves having parents talk about unpleasant past experiences, many of which they themselves do not understand. Furthermore, parents also often have hurt and angry feelings surrounding past experiences such as divorce or an affair that have impacted their children. Typically, parents have difficulty sharing these hurt and angry feelings; thus, their children often do not understand their parents' feelings and do not learn how to express their associated feelings of hurt and anger. Indeed, children usually do not learn to express their painful feelings or any feelings when they have parents who cannot or choose not to share their own feelings.

Difficulty with expressing painful feelings is particularly common among African Americans, especially African American men. Thus, African American children in general and male youth in particular often do not learn how to verbalize and explore their painful feelings. They often suppress these feelings and miss the opportunity for new information, thoughts, and perspectives as well as for support that sharing such feelings often brings. In fact being a strong male and a strong female who can keep these feelings on the inside traditionally has been admired in many African American mini-cultures.

Yet, when feelings and emotions are not verbally expressed, they get expressed in various other ways (e.g., through defiant behaviors), some of which are not appropriate. For example, a mother might rub her son's head in a playful gesture, and the son might respond with profane language to communicate that he does not want his head touched. The son might then say to a sibling who observed this interaction, "If you don't like what I said, we can step outside and I'll play piano on your head." Such responses by the son are defiant oppositional behaviors that are likely displaced anger or hurt.

Hurt and anger, which may originate in the family, are often exacerbated by frustrating, hurtful, and anger-producing life experiences associated with being African American in the United States, particularly in its poorest neighborhoods. These life experiences include experiencing racism and receiving a second-class education, both of which can elicit feelings of powerlessness and low self-esteem. Too often the response of African American youth to these feelings is acquisition of pseudo power through generating fear in others and appearing fearless and uncontrollable.

Counseling Intervention Considerations and Alternatives

Family therapy with a culturally and socioeconomically sensitive therapist is ideally needed to help African American youth express their angry and hurt feelings and emotional needs and to join with the family in changing family communication, alliances, and organization to facilitate psychosocial adjustment, emotional support, and overall quality of life of each family member. Given the realities of the lives of many African Americans including limited money for the cost of any therapy, money for family therapy as it is traditionally practiced simply will not be available to them. Furthermore, African American family members, particularly fathers and father figures often do not desire or are not available to enter family therapy. It is also the case that even if therapy is free, often African American family members do not have transportation to the therapist's office, which is typically located on the other side of town from the homes of most African American families. Additionally, they often cannot afford a babysitter to attend free counseling. Contrary to popular belief, these are not excuses, just realities.

One alternative to traditional family therapy is nontraditional family therapy in African American neighborhoods by volunteer therapists in easily accessible community centers and churches where babysitting services can be provided. This family therapy can involve any significant person in the child's life. Empty chairs can be provided for the significant family members who cannot be at the therapy session. The child who engages in oppositional defiant behaviors can express to the missing family members what she or he would like to say to them by directing her or his comments to the chairs representing those persons. The family therapy sessions will likely need to be longer than the traditional one-hour or one and a half-hour sessions. Because it often takes a while to build rapport and facilitate disclosure of feelings among African American children and the significant others in their lives, the family therapists should be prepared to give these clients the time, patience, and support that they need to identify and address factors in the oppositional defiant behaviors of concern.

Peer group counseling is also an effective therapy method with children who manifest oppositional defiant behaviors. This therapy is often a valuable supplement to family therapy with these youth. Because it is sometimes simply impossible to get African Americans to enter family counseling, peer counseling is also an effective alternative to family counseling. Peer group counseling offers a vehicle, a support system, and role models for helping African American youth identify and address their feelings, recognize the associations between their feelings and their behaviors, and empower themselves for academic and social success. Peer counseling also facilitates sharing of painful feelings by African American children enabling them to see that they are not alone in having angry and hurt feelings or in having experiences in their families, neighborhoods, and the outside world that help contribute to these feelings.

Peer group counseling and family counseling that involve African Americans work best in settings that are culturally and socioeconomically sensitive. Such settings ideally include the following: (1) warm, friendly, and respectful support staff (e.g., receptionists) among whom are African Americans, (2) reception area music by diverse music artists including African Americans, (3) magazines by African American publishers, (4) individuals who can verbally administer data collection forms, (5) access to a telephone for arranging transportation, and (6) a place where young children and siblings can play and be supervised while parents participate in or wait for an older child to participate in therapy.

Recommendations for Parents and Teachers

Parents and teachers can do much to help an African American child modify her or his oppositional defiant behaviors and replace these negative behaviors with more appropriate behaviors. Following are some recommendations for parents and teachers who desire to modify defiant behaviors by African American children.

1. Parents and teachers should avoid blaming themselves for the occurrence of defiant behaviors by African American children and avoid reacting with negative emotion and pleading with these children to stop being defiant, hostile, and so on. A child who is in fact acting the way that he or she is to punish or upset his or her parents or teachers and others certainly will not change this behavior given that it is accomplishing the desired intent. Furthermore, causing teachers and parents to become upset provides attention and negative control that the child wants, which reinforces the child's problem behaviors.

2. Active efforts can be made by parents and teachers to find a big brother or big sister for the child who can spend time with the child, earn the child's trust, listen to the child's feelings, help the child establish positive short-term and long-term goals, and encourage the child to get involved in constructive after-school activities. It is important that the big brother or sister is genuinely interested in the child and spends time with the child in person or by telephone on a daily or almost daily basis. If one big brother or sister does not work out, then efforts should be made to find another until a good match is found for the child.

3. Parents and teachers must provide the child who engages in defiant behaviors with clear rules and knowledge regarding the consequences for noncompliance with these rules. When the child fails to comply with a rule, it is important to state the rule that was broken and state the consequence for doing so in a matter-of-fact way while staying in control emotionally. When the child follows a rule or engages in other appropriate behaviors, the child should be praised and encouraged to feel good about herself or himself for engaging in these behaviors. In general, it is important to maintain and communicate to the child the expectation that the child will follow rules and respect others, whether or not the child meets these expectations.

4. Parents and teachers should avoid letting the child's defiant behaviors deter them from talking to the child about topics other than the child's behavior and doing fun and interesting activities with the child. Even a child who is unfortunately labeled as having an oppositional defiant disorder needs to be treated as a child whose personal and social development will be facilitated by positive and fun one-on-one activities like going to a nice restaurant for lunch with her or his dad, going with her or his parents to a basketball game, and sitting and talking with a parent or teacher about the child's aspirations for the future. Indeed, it is important to get to know and establish a positive relationship with the child being masked by the child's oppositional defiant behaviors.

5. Parents and teachers can arrange experiences for the child to feel good about herself or himself. For example, these adults can involve the child in starting a small business with the assistance of family members or a business or community leader. The child could make the product or deliver the service, do the marketing, and so forth and have fun, learn a lot, and experience elevated self-esteem in the process.

Social Withdrawal or Shy Behavior

Children who are described as socially withdrawn or shy tend to be quiet with an unfamiliar adult, play alone rather than with peers in a group situation, and are easily stressed by challenges or occasional failure (Kagan, Reznick, & Snidman, 1990). The prevalence of this particular behavior problem among African American children as well as among children in general is not known; however, social withdrawal is not uncommon among African American children.

It is not clear what causes social withdrawal in African American children or in other children. Given the nature of the problem and based on clinical experiences of the author, variables associated with social withdrawal in African American children vary across children. Furthermore, in any particular child, social withdrawal seems to be associated with more than one factor. Some of the factors that seem to be associated with social withdrawal in African American children include social skills that are not at a comparable level to those of their peers; lack of self-confidence; fear of failure; movement into a predominantly European American school from a predominantly African American school; peer rejection due to physical differences, language differences, and racism; and physical, psychological, or sexual abuse.

Empirical research on the causes of social withdrawal in African American children is particularly needed in order to identify ways to help self-empower these children for social and academic success. Regardless of their cultural backgrounds and differences from the majority children in the United States, African American children and adolescents must be empowered to compete successfully with all other children in social and academic arenas anchored in the majority culture and in cultures of other countries. In other words, African American children must learn social skills for later communicating with and forming relationships and partnerships with individuals from cultures throughout the world that are very different from their own. Research-based interventions to modify social withdrawal or shy behavior among African American children is needed.

Based on self-empowerment theory and clinical experiences of the author, there are several intervention strategies that help modify social withdrawal or shy behavior in an African American child. Following are some of these intervention strategies.

Intervention Strategies That Parents and Teachers Can Use

1. Teachers and parents can involve the child who is socially withdrawn in structured activities that involve working in pairs and later in small groups with peers who have great interpersonal skills. The goal of these working partnerships is to facilitate the social integration of the child with others who will model desirable social behavior for the child. Various peer-mediated interventions have been shown to improve the social behavior of withdrawn children (Odom & Strain, 1984).

2. The child or adolescent can participate in after-school programs at school or in the community that provide social skills training such as training in how to make friends, public speaking, building self-confidence, and so forth.

3. Given that a child's social withdrawal behavior could be a manifestation of very serious problems such as posttraumatic stress from abuse, it is important for parents and teachers to work in partnership to arrange for the child to talk with a culturally sensitive counselor, psychologist, pastoral counselor, or other mental health professional who can help determine the causes of the social withdrawal and specific interventions to modify it. A professional of the same gender as the child is recommended.

4. Parents and teachers can provide the child with positive reasons for interacting with her or his peers; this will help provide the self-motivation to do so.

5. Parents and teachers can help the child establish short-term and long-term goals, and then identify the social skills that will be important in successfully attaining these goals.

6. Parents and teachers can involve the child in organizations (e.g., Boy Scouts or Girl Scouts) where the child will have the opportunities to participate in programs that will build self-confidence and do so with much encouragement and support. For the African American child the church has also been the provider of many opportunities for social skill development.

7. If the child has just moved to a new school or community, parents and teachers can help the child establish new friendships by encouraging this activity and helping the child identify those qualities that make the child a desirable friend. Parents can meet the parents of other children in the neighborhood and in the child's class toward the goal of arranging social activities for the children of the families involved.

8. Parents and teachers can look for and praise social behaviors in the child, and most importantly encourage the child to praise herself or himself for these behaviors.

Because social withdrawal or shy behavior is not disruptive in the classroom or at home, it is often not given the important attention that it deserves. It is too often true that as long as African American children are quiet and not disrupting other children, their behavior is not a major problem. Yet, social withdrawal can inhibit the psychosocial development of these children as well as their communication skills, daily living skills, and socialization skills, all of which are important to their self-empowerment for social, academic, and life success. Clearly, high priority must be given to modifying social withdrawal behavior when it occurs in African American children.

Suicidal Behavior

Between 1980 and 1992 suicide greatly increased among African American children, especially males. The suicide rate for African American males in the ten to fourteen age range rose from 0.5 to 2.0 per 100,000, a 300 percent increase; and the suicide rate for African American males in the fifteen to nineteen age range rose from 5.6 to 14.8 per 100,000, a 164 percent increase. For females in the age range of ten to fourteen, the suicide rate rose from 0.2 to 0.4 per 100,000, an increase of 100 percent; and for females in the age range of fifteen to nineteen, the suicide rate rose from 1.6 to 1.9 per 100,000, an increase of 19 percent (Centers for Disease Control and Prevention, 1995).

Yet, suicidal attempts have not significantly increased. Perhaps what has at least in part caused the aforementioned tremendously high increase in suicide rates is use of more lethal methods to attempt suicide, thus resulting in more actual suicides. This is suggested by the fact that 81 percent of the increase in suicide rate among fifteen- to nineteen-year-olds from 1980 and 1992 has been attributed to the use of firearms in suicidal attempts that ended up being actual suicides (Wicks-Nelson & Israel, 1997).

Indeed, in many African American communities there is an infestation of guns and gun-related violence as well as stress, despair, depression, and hopelessness, all of which trigger suicidal behaviors. These behaviors include high-risk behaviors such as heavy alcohol and drug use, withdrawing emotionally and often physically from family and friends, and verbalizing thoughts of ending one's life.

The specific causes of suicidal behaviors among African American children are not known for certain. However, they generally reflect a call for help in addressing emotional and physical pain. This pain is often associated with self-blame for a painful event such as divorce of parents, self-perceptions of having failed at something that is important to oneself or significant others, self-perceptions of not fitting in with peers, not having reached a personal goal, or loss of a loved one.

The need for interventions to deter and modify suicidal behaviors and to prevent suicide among African American children will not be recognized unless parents, teachers, and others who are significant in these children's lives pay attention to these children's emotional and physical pain. This requires that parents and anyone else in these children's lives regularly talk with these youth, ask about their feelings, and observe any negative changes in the behavior of these youth. Once an adult recognizes something of serious concern to the child or something about the child that concerns the adult, action must be taken to assess further what is going on with the child emotionally, physically, and psychosocially. This action needs to include having other family members and family support persons (e.g., minister and physician) as well as a counselor or other mental health professional talk with the child to identify problems that the child is experiencing.

Parents must not let their lack of money to pay for their children to see a physician or a counselor keep them from taking their children to these professionals. Parents can and should seek help from teachers, school administrators, ministers, and community leaders to assist them in getting the professional help that their children should have. With active persistence that might involve calling school administrators or a mental health care facility every day for a week or two, parents and others can get needed assessment and intervention for the suspected and known problems and concerns of their children. When these problems include suicidal behaviors, children ideally should be involved in family counseling by a counselor or psychologist as well as some type of peer group counseling provided by a mental health professional. Furthermore, family members need to mobilize to help these youth feel loved, supported, needed in the family, good about themselves, and have hope for the future. Additionally, involvement of these youth with mentors from church and community organizations who spend quality time with them is recommended.

It is also important for parents, teachers, school administrators, and community and business leaders to work in partnership to arrange for the provision of funding and services to address the problems of youth who are at risk of suicide. Such partnerships can facilitate implementation of strategies recommended by the Centers for Disease Control and Prevention (1995) to prevent suicide among youth. These strategies include doing the following: (1) training school personnel and community leaders to identify youngsters at high risk of suicide; (2) educating youngsters about suicide; (3) implementing screening and referral services; (4) developing peer support programs to address the emotional and other problems that often lead to suicidal behaviors; (5) establishing suicide crisis centers and hotlines;

(6) restricting access to highly lethal methods of suicide (e.g., handguns, drugs); and (7) intervening after a suicide to prevent other youngsters from attempting suicide.

The fact that suicide seems to be significantly increasing among children as well as adolescents, especially among African American males, is alarming. The association of most of these increases with firearms suggests that African American families and communities must take greater responsibility for protecting their youth from the availability of firearms and other destroyers of their lives. Furthermore, African American families and communities simply must be more involved in the lives of their youth and respond immediately to any changes in their behavior or emotions. Simply being concerned and upset about such changes is not enough. Waiting to be sure that an African American child might be suicidal is too risky and often too late.

Conduct Disorders and Delinquent Behaviors

So-called acting-out behaviors that violate social norms are commonly called conduct disorders. These are behaviors such as truancy from school, running away from home, lying, and fighting. In addition to these acting-out behaviors that are antisocial, there are other such behaviors that are also illegal; these are referred to as delinquent behaviors. Delinquent behaviors include behaviors such as theft and burglary. Children younger than a certain age (i.e., younger than from sixteen to twenty depending on the particular state) who engage in delinquent behaviors are labeled delinquents or juvenile delinquents (Erickson, 1992).

The label *conduct disorder* is commonly used to describe the behavior problems of African American children. Yet, according to DSM-IV (American Psychiatric Association, 1994), the term *conduct disorder* may at times be inappropriately applied to individuals in settings where patterns of undesirable behavior are protective (e.g., threatening, impoverished, high-crime neighborhoods). The diagnosis of conduct disorder is appropriate when the acting-out behaviors are reflective of an underlying dysfunction within the individual rather than reactions to the immediate social environment.

Given that many African American youth live in threatening, impoverished, high-crime neighborhoods where some so-called antisocial behaviors are necessary for survival (e.g., fighting, lying), it is reasonable to conclude that the behaviors of these youth that are perceived as antisocial may in fact not be conduct disorders but rather may be survival behaviors. Thus, when addressing behaviors of African American children that are of concern, it is important to consider the cultural and socioeconomic context in which their behaviors of concern occur. It is also important to avoid the use of labels such as conduct disorders to identify behaviors of African American children that seem consistent with this label because the label may not be valid; furthermore, such labels may obstruct the formulation of appropriate culturally sensitive interventions that will likely be effective.

The actual prevalence of conduct disorders and of the subset of these disorders referred to as delinquent behaviors among African American youth is not known. However, there have been reports over two decades suggesting that conduct disorders and delinquent behaviors are disproportionately high among African Americans. It has been reported that African American teens are suspended or expelled from school more often than European Americans for fighting, extortion of money, verbal or physical abuse of teachers, vandalism, and truancy in junior high and high schools (Children's Defense Fund, 1987). It has also been reported that in 1985, 23 percent of all juvenile arrests were African American adolescents. Furthermore, persons of lower socioeconomic status are arrested proportionately more often than their middle-class peers (Erickson, 1992). Given that African Americans are disproportionately represented in the lower socioeconomic classes, they are overrepresented among arrested juveniles.

Among children in general, males show more of the behaviors associated with conduct disorders than do females; the male–female ratio most commonly reported is 4:1 (Earls, 1994). It has been estimated that at least one-half of the teenage population has committed one or more delinquent acts; however, only a very small percentage of teenagers who commit these acts is actually brought to court and convicted (Erickson, 1992). Common delinquent behaviors among adolescents are defiance of authority, truancy, destruction of property, fighting, theft, and sexual aggression (Sykes, 1987). Many studies have found that early onset of conduct problems and delinquent behaviors is related to more serious and persistent antisocial behaviors (Earls, 1994; Tolan & Thomas, 1995). Problems that begin in adolescence as compared to childhood tend to be less severe and tend not to persist beyond adolescence, whereas problems that begin in childhood often persist on into adulthood (Hinshaw, Lahey, & Hart, 1993; Moffitt, 1993).

Nothing is conclusively known about the causes of conduct disorders and delinquent behaviors among African American youth, as research on this topic has been almost nonexistent. We do know from part of a longitudinal study by Farnworth, Schweinhart, and Berrueta-Clement (1985) with 123 African American children that school factors may be major factors in delinquent behaviors of some African American children. In this study, self-reported delinquency was reported when the participants were about age fifteen. Findings included that (1) duration of placement in special education was strongly related to engagement in dishonest activities; (2) school-related attitudes were most important in explaining escape behavior, running away from home, and using drugs, (3) teachers' ratings of the children's conduct in the early years of schooling and the children's self-reports of misconduct in school at age fifteen were both related to law-breaking behavior outside of school; and (4) the strongest relationship was between school attachment and illegal escape from school. It was also found that low IQ and achievement scores were not important predictors of delinquent behaviors by age fifteen. The researchers concluded that schools may affect juvenile misbehavior through various adverse experiences that diminish students' attachment to the school and increase the likelihood of antisocial attitudes and behavior.

It has also been speculated that depression due to feelings of alienation from society and societal racism is a factor in some conduct problems and delinquent behaviors. According to Sykes (1987), delinquent behaviors may be the only way that adolescents see as a means to draw attention to their internal pain. This negative attention appears to give short-term power, status, and self-esteem (Kaplan, Martin, & Johnson, 1986).

Existing theories and research that do not specifically address African American children suggest that the causes of conduct disorders and delinquent behaviors include television violence, negative school experiences associated with the school's insensitivity to cultural differences, parental use of physical punishment, lack of parental supervision, negative peer and adult role models, and failure of parents to teach moral values due to a preoccupation with their own problems (Erickson, 1992). More research is needed to determine whether these are causes of conduct disorders and delinquent behaviors among children and adolescents in the various African American mini-cultures.

It is realistic to conclude that many of the possible contributors to conduct disorders of African American children such as television violence, impoverished home environments with negative role models, and their school environments and experiences will not be easily modified and certainly will not be modified in time to impact the masses of African American children who currently engage in delinquent behaviors and other behaviors consistent with a conduct disorder. Thus, it is reasonable to attempt to modify and prevent conduct disorders and delinquent behaviors with intervention strategies that self-empower African American children for academic and social success in the presence of the external conditions that contribute to these behaviors.

Self-empowerment intervention strategies to address conduct disorders and delinquent behaviors focus on facilitating (1) self-motivation to overcome these problems and to engage in behaviors for social, academic, and life success, (2) self-control of their negative behaviors, (3) self-praise for positive behaviors and using self-control, and (4) adaptive skills for success (i.e., communication, socialization, and daily living skills including skills for expressing negative and positive feelings). This approach based on self-empowerment theory is consistent with the conclusions of others that delinquent behaviors can be viewed as maladaptive coping attempts (to deal with painful emotions) that can be replaced by more adaptive and positive behaviors through skills training (Kantor, Caudill, & Ungerleider, 1992). According to Little and Kendall (1979), an emphasis on skills development with youth who are labeled delinquent is likely to have a considerable long-term benefit in that many of these youth lack the necessary prerequisites for alternative lifestyles.

The present author and her research team tested the effects of a five-week, self-empowerment-based intervention program to facilitate assertiveness (versus aggressiveness), self-esteem, and positive behaviors (i.e., success behaviors) among mostly African American female adolescents who had been labeled delinquent (Tucker, Herman, Brady, & Fraser, 1995). The program was titled Operation Positive Expression. The adolescent participants in the program were from mostly low-income families and were residents of a north central Florida halfway house. Twenty-three of these adolescents participated in the intervention program and eleven served as a treatment control group—a group that did not go through the structured intervention program but participated in routine halfway house activities under the supervision of the halfway house staff that had been trained by the intervention team of counselors.

The intervention program included six components: (1) staff training, (2) nontraditional individual counseling, (3) group discussions and skills training, (4) creation of a poem by each adolescent expressing the personal causes and consequences of her crime(s), (5) creation of an artwork by each adolescent to express something positive about herself, and (6) group planning and execution of an art extravaganza (held at the local city library) to display the creative arts and poems created by the adolescents. A family counseling component was not included given that families were not in contact with most of these adolescents or were in different states from the halfway house where the adolescents were residents. Following are brief descriptions of these intervention components.

Staff Training: Halfway house staff members were trained to teach the adolescents conflict resolution, constructive expression of negative and positive feelings, success behaviors, decision making, strategies for self-esteem enhancement, and self-empowering, step-by-step learning based on Meichenbaum's cognitive modeling and self-instructional method (Meichenbaum, 1977). The self-empowering, step-by-step learning and teaching approach involves writing and modeling the steps to learning any behavior, skill, or task, then instructing the learner to do the behavior, skill, or task independently following the steps, and instructing the learner to self-praise effort and success in following the steps and thus in learning the behavior, skill, or task.

Nontraditional Individual Counseling: Halfway house counselors and the intervention team of counselors involved each adolescent in individual sessions to discuss (1) her emotional pain, (2) the factors in her involvement in crimes, and (3) ways to address these factors so that she could avoid reinvolvement with crimes. Each resident was encouraged to use the following steps in these sessions: (1) think about a time she felt angry or hurt, used drugs, committed a crime, and so on, (2) visualize what happened, (3) express what happened and what she was thinking and feeling at the time, (4) discuss what caused the feelings and thoughts, and (5) discuss how she could have avoided the crime involvement situation that got her into trouble. These steps were first modeled by the counselor who then prompted the resident as needed through each step. The adolescent was praised for sharing through each step and encouraged to feel good about and praise herself for sharing her thoughts and feelings.

Group Discussions and Skills Training: The group sessions with the adolescents focused on identifying future goals and then discussing how the following behaviors and skills contribute to achieving their goals and to being successful in life: (1) success behaviors (e.g., good eye contact, listening while others are talking, making complete sentences), (2) problem solving, (3) assertive behavior rather than aggressive behavior, (4) constructive anger expression, and (5) giving and receiving negative feedback. The adolescents were then taught these skills and behaviors.

Additionally, the adolescents were taught cognitive-behavioral techniques (e.g., progressive muscle relaxation, behavioral rehearsal, positive self-talk, etc.) to manage anxiety and to look and feel self-confident in anxiety-producing situations such as a job interview. Most behaviors and skills were taught using the earlier mentioned self-empowering, step-by-step teaching approach. Public praise from peers and counselors, tangible rewards (pencils, writing paper), and self-praise were used to reinforce learning efforts.

Other training sessions with the adolescents focused on various topics including the following: job interviewing, makeup application, job attire, dining etiquette, dating etiquette, and creative arts for expressing feelings. These sessions were conducted by local business professionals. For example, the job interviewing session was conducted by the personnel manager of a local fast-food restaurant.

Creation of a Poem or Short Story and a Visual Art: With the assistance of a counselor, each adolescent wrote a poem or short story about her needs from parents, friends, and others to help her avoid getting into trouble. Each adolescent also made a collage or other visual art that expressed what she liked about herself. These creations were designed to facilitate self-understanding and acceptance. The poems, stories, and visual arts were displayed at a mini creative arts extravaganza organized by the adolescents and counselors and held at the local city library.

Mini Creative Arts Extravaganza: To organize the extravaganza, the adolescents were divided into committees. Each committee was trained to (1) use a problem-solving method for making committee decisions, and (2) give constructive negative and positive feedback to each other in the process of working together as a group. Feedback to the adolescents during committee work focused on the degree to which they worked cooperatively, expressed disagreement in an assertive but nonhostile manner, self-managed their anger, and compromised when conflicts occurred over how committee tasks should be done.

To prepare for presenting their work to the extravaganza audience of their friends, counselors, and interested local citizens, the adolescents received training in public speaking and then practiced presenting their art; practice sessions were video-taped and used to provide feedback for improving their presentations. Each adolescent received at least a fifth-place award for her poem, story, or visual art, an award certificate, a picture of herself receiving her award, much public praise, and encouragement to self-praise her efforts and accomplishments in association with the extravaganza.

Results revealed that, as hypothesized, both the intervention group and the treatment control group showed increases from preintervention to postintervention in assertiveness, self-control behaviors, and success behaviors. Because the treatment control group was supervised by the staff members who had been trained in the procedures used with the intervention group, it was expected that some improvements in the outcome variables of interest would occur among this group and the treatment intervention group, but that the latter group would evidence greater changes. Only the increases in assertiveness (versus aggressiveness) by the intervention group were statistically significant.

Ratings of the intervention program by the adolescents who participated in it were high. Specifically, on a scale from 1 (strongly agree) to 6 (strongly disagree), these participants gave the following items the indicated mean item ratings: (a) I enjoyed working on this project (1.1); (b) I feel better about myself because I worked on this project (1.3); (c) I felt successful in doing this project (1.1); and (d) I would like to do a project like this again (1.1). Ratings of the project by the halfway house staff were also extremely high and indicated that there were observable clinically significant improvements in the adolescents' self-esteem and success behaviors.

It was concluded by the present author and her research team that the intervention program (Operation Positive Expression) was successful and that with longer than a brief five-week intervention period, greater effects of the program would likely occur. It was also concluded that the program is cost-effective and provides a needed vehicle for counseling professionals and educators, business leaders, and community members to work in partnership to execute their responsibilities for helping youth become responsible and productive community members. Additionally, it was also concluded that future intervention research should include a longer intervention period, assess recidivism rates associated with the implementation of the intervention program, and include behavioral observation data and other objective measures of behavior change in addition to the type of self-report measures used in the study.

Given the many possible factors in conduct problems and delinquent behaviors of African American children, multifaceted intervention programs for social and life success seem needed to modify conduct disorders and delinquent behaviors among these children. Following are several specific intervention strategies and recommendations that should ideally be included in such programs.

1. It is important to change those aspects of the school systems that appear to be fostering rather than deterring delinquent behaviors (Erickson, 1992). Some suggestions for achieving this goal have been offered by Erickson (1992):

a. Train teachers to reward a broad spectrum of behaviors in children and make rewards contingent upon their progress, using prior performance as the progress measure rather than the performance of others.

b. Eliminate criteria that exclude large numbers of children from educational opportunities and advancement, and add ways other than use of grade point averages and standardized test scores as vehicles for these opportunities and advancement.

2. Avoid dependency on token economy based programs, even though these programs have been very effective in teaching children skills important in everyday life. These programs do not facilitate self-control strategies for sustaining behavioral changes over time and in the absence of the token economy system. Furthermore, such programs are not sensitive to the desires of many African American families to not "pay" their children to behave and to not have them controlled by powerful others—a desire that is likely a by-product of the past enslavement of African Americans.

3. Incorporate behavioral contracts when parents acknowledge behaviors that they should change or are willing to change, which their child desires to have changed, and when the child is willing to make some changes in his or her behaviors. Behavioral contracts are especially useful when it is clear that major factors in the child's problematic conduct are power struggles between the child and parents, which have resulted in mostly negative and few or no positive interactions between the child and parents. A behavioral contract is a written agreement that specifies what the parents will do that the child wants and in exchange what the child will do that the parents want. It includes positive consequences for the parents and for the child for following through in doing what was committed to in the contract and negative consequences for failing to follow through with commitments made. The contract is signed by all involved and is reviewed and discussed periodically (e.g., weekly) to determine progress on commitments and any needed changes in the contract. For parents and children who are not willing to entertain the idea of a behavioral contract, it will not be effective.

4. Provide parenting training, especially with parents who have young children with conduct problems. Parents typically have more control and peers have less control with regard to influencing the behavior of younger children versus older children (adolescents). This is perhaps why parenting training is among the most successful intervention approaches with young children labeled as having conduct disorders (Wicks-Nelson & Israel, 1997). The focus of this parenting training with African American parents in particular should include a focus on strategies for facilitating their children's adaptive skills development, using step-by-step learning and teaching methods, teaching children self-control through self-talk, and providing parental praise and encouraging self-praise in response to their children's appropriate behaviors and success behaviors when they occur.

5. Provide parenting training in which parents and other family members are encouraged to focus on looking for and praising what the child does well and right rather than on what the child does wrong. Then when the child does do something wrong, help the child learn to do what is right instead in the future. It is also important to teach parents to focus on one or two specific conduct problems at a time, to observe and record when and how often these problems occur, and to withdraw reinforcers such as attention to the child when these undesirable behaviors occur (Patterson, Reid, & Dishion, 1992). By observing and rewarding the occurrence of target behaviors, parents can better determine what might be contributing to their children's conduct problems and whether or not the decrease in response to an intervention to modify these behaviors is effective. Combining this parenting training approach with teaching children cognitive problem-solving skills has been shown to be effective in reducing antisocial behaviors in children with conduct problems, reducing their parents' stress, and improving their parents' parental functioning (Kazdin, Siegel, & Bass, 1992).

6. When possible, involve the child who engages in conduct problems or delinquent behaviors in family therapy that includes any significant extended family member or family friend who is actively involved in the rearing of the child. Ideally family therapy should be part of a multidimensional intervention approach that includes individual intervention with the child to facilitate the child's skill development as well as modification of the negative influences of the child's peers, school, and neighborhood. This ideal multidimensional approach to conduct problems and delinquent behaviors is called multisystemic therapy (MST; Henggeler & Borduin, 1990). MST has been reported to have significant long-term effects (Borduin, 1994). The problem is that for various reasons many African American families often refuse to participate in family therapy, or participate and soon drop out of this therapy. The dropout is often because the family therapy is not culturally and socioeconomically sensitive and because it does not produce an immediate impact on the conduct problems and delinquent behaviors of concern.

7. It is recommended that communities, businesses, churches, human service agencies, and schools work in partnership with parents, families, and teachers to assist children with conduct problems and delinquent behaviors to discontinue these behaviors and replace these behaviors with success behaviors and adaptive skills. The focus of the partnership needs to be on providing as many learning experiences and educational activities as possible for these children through community-based programs. For example, for an African American child who wants to be a pilot, it can be arranged through a community program for that child to visit an airport and meet some pilots, and by so doing increase the child's self-motivation to become a pilot and to engage in the academic and social behaviors that the pilots communicated were important for becoming a pilot. Given that most African American children who want to be a pilot have never even been close to a plane or pilot, it is clear why such experiences as that in the preceding example are important. Indeed, the reason that many African American children who engage in illegal or inappropriate conduct is because these children are not given alternative experiences and realistic hope for and guidance to successful lives. Long-term partnership-sponsored, community-based, multifaceted training programs (e.g., parenting training, family counseling, skills training for children, plus academic tutoring) to provide such alternatives, hope, and guidance are now being strongly recommended for helping children with so-called conduct disorders and delinquent behaviors overcome these problems and experience social, academic, and life success (Tucker, Chennault, Brady, Fraser, Gaskin, Dunn, & Frisby, 1995; Wicks-Nelson & Israel, 1997).

8. Research to evaluate the short-term and long-term effects of interventions and intervention programs to help African American children modify their conduct problems and delinquent behaviors is needed. It is important that such research include multiple culturally and socioeconomically sensitive outcome measures rather than traditional measures that have excluded African Americans in their development.

Alcohol and Drug Use

Any use of alcohol or other drugs (e.g., marijuana) by children is a concern of parents and many others given the potential of these drugs for becoming addictive, given that use of these drugs is illegal, and given that mild or infrequent drug use in childhood sometimes leads to more serious drug use in adulthood. Children who smoke cigarettes are more likely to later engage in marijuana smoking, and those who use marijuana are more likely to at least try other illicit drugs that may be addictive (Kandel & Logan, 1985). Furthermore, use of any drugs more than occasionally is often associated with other problems including difficulties in school, parent–child conflicts, the occurrence of sexual intercourse and pregnancy, and conduct problems, including delinquent behaviors (Hundleby, Carpenter, Rose, & Mercer, 1982; Huizinga, Loeber, & Thornberry, 1993).

The occurrence and severity of problems in association with use of alcohol or other drugs are often dependent on the age and physiology of the individual and the severity and pattern of alcohol or drug use. Physiological and psychological dependence on alcohol or any drug can occur with very limited use, depending on the individual. When one is physiologically dependent on a drug, typically there is a craving for it; there is a need for increasing amounts of it to experience a satisfactory "high"; and there is an occurrence of physical withdrawal symptoms (e.g., tremors) that are unpleasant following reduction of the drug after heavy use of it. Psychological dependence on a drug is the belief that one cannot function well without the use of it.

Among youth as well as among all age groups, alcohol is the most commonly used drug (National Institute of Drug Abuse, 1992). However, parents of children who use alcohol or other drugs often do not know that their children are doing so because these youth often use these drugs only periodically, and because parents and children now often spend very little structured time together (e.g., eat dinner together) so that parents have limited opportunity to notice the behavioral and psychological changes (e.g., aggressive behavior, impaired judgment) that often come with drug use. Consequently, early intervention to help children discontinue their drug use before it becomes extremely resistant to modification does not occur. Some parents who are aware of their children's use of alcohol or other drugs do not mobilize interventions to help these youth stop this behavior because the parents themselves use drugs and, thus, feel unjustified or incapable of addressing this behavior in their children.

Research on the use of alcohol and other drugs among different ethnic groups generally reports that use of these drugs is more prevalent among European American adolescents than among African American adolescents or Asian American adolescents (National Institute of Drug Abuse, 1992). It is important to note, however, that alcohol and drug use among African American youth is particularly problematic because they often cannot afford treatment. Also, their alcohol and drug use is often associated with lifestyles that include delinquency and selling drugs (Brunswick & Messeri, 1986). Consequently, African American youth who use alcohol or other drugs are often at increased risk of serious social and legal problems.

As with most behavior problems of children, no single factor has been found that explains alcohol and drug use (Morrison & Smith, 1987) among children and adolescents. The research on the factors in alcohol use in children and adolescents has also been limited. Some factors have been suggested as contributors to alcohol use and use of other drugs by children and adolescents. Researchers have found, for example, that teenagers' expectations that drinking would facilitate social interactions predicted initiation of alcohol-drinking behavior. Additionally, those teenagers who held this expectation also drank more over a two-year period; furthermore, their future expectations regarding the effects of drinking were not reduced but rather became more positive (Smith & Goldman, 1994; Smith, Goldman, Greenbaum, & Christiansen, 1995). With regard to use of illegal drugs, research indicates that the earlier that legal drugs are used, the more likely it is that illicit drugs will be used (Kandel & Yamaguchi, 1993).

There are also only a few studies that have focused on the causes of drug use among African American youth. One of these studies was conducted to assess predictors of drug use among African American youth at age sixteen and age seventeen from their behaviors when they were in first grade (Kellam & Brown, 1982). Results revealed that early aggressiveness, especially when coupled with shyness, was positively related to later drug use among males. Wells, Morrison, Gillmore, Catalano, Iritani, and Hawkins (1992) found that self-reported delinquent behavior (e.g., stealing, damaging property) was a significant predictor of drug use initiation by African American males and females by the end of their fifth-grade year. Socioeconomic status and gender did not predict this drug use initiation by the end of the fifth-grade year. Results were the same for the European Americans and Asian Americans who were also included in this study.

The previously discussed research findings concerning the causes of alcohol use and use of other drugs among African American children and adolescents suggest that intervention programs to assist these youth in stopping their use of alcohol and other drugs need to include a major focus on extinguishing aggressive behaviors and antisocial behaviors including delinquent behaviors. In fact, Wells et al. (1992) suggested that early intervention programs are needed that simultaneously seek to prevent drug use and delinquent behavior among African American children because the two problems appear to be linked. Given that alcohol use and drug use occur to some degree in the elementary school years, it is clear that such prevention programs need to be established for children as young as six and seven years old.

It is possible or likely that several of the following occurrences contribute to the use of alcohol and other drugs among children: (1) television beer commercials, (2) being around parents, other family members, and peers who use alcohol and other drugs, (3) living in a community in which use of alcohol and other drugs is common, and (4) trying to cope with the emotional pain of divorce, parent separation, physical abuse, and other family problems. Most of these occurrences are disproportionately high in low-income communities—communities in which African Americans are overly represented. Thus, many African American children are likely at risk for use of alcohol and drugs.

Given the diversity of factors that may influence African American youth to use alcohol or other drugs and given the research suggesting that delinquent and aggressive behaviors may be factors in drug use of these youth, multifaceted intervention programs almost identical to those described in the earlier section on conduct disorders and delinquent behaviors seem needed to extinguish and prevent use of alcohol and other drugs among these youth.

In addition to implementation of the multifaceted intervention programs for academic and social success earlier recommended for modifying conduct disorders and delinquent behaviors by African American children, the following specific intervention strategies are recommended for stopping and preventing use of alcohol and other drugs among these children.

Recommendations for Church and Community Leaders

1. Church leaders and community leaders at community centers can talk with African American children in groups about reasons for or benefits of not drinking alcohol or using other drugs. These adults should avoid lecturing to these youth and instead have the youth come up with the reasons and benefits. This can be done in group formats in which one-half of the group competes with the other in coming up with the most reasons. Following this competition, the children can discuss each of the reasons and benefits generated, with one or two of these youth serving as discussion leaders. Much praise for participation should be given throughout the described activities and self-praise should be encouraged by the children for their good ideas. Focusing on reasons for or the benefits of not using alcohol and other drugs is important because children typically are not given this information; yet, it is needed for wise decision making about their own drug use. Instead, children are typically told all of the reasons why they should not use drugs often in an effort to scare them away from drugs. Because these fear-inducing reasons, which are usually exaggerated, are typically not believed by the children, they are dismissed from the decision-making process about drugs.

2. Church leaders and community leaders at community centers can conduct sessions in which children get opportunities to participate in as well as observe role-plays demonstrating ineffective and effective ways to say no to alcohol and other drugs. It is important that these role-plays are culturally and socioeconomically sensitive; in other words, make sure that they are about situations that African American children and adolescents actually experience in their lives and that all role-plays involve characters that would actually be in their communities. The children should be encouraged to use what is learned in the role-plays in their lives.

3. Church leaders and community leaders at community centers can conduct panel discussions with panelists being African American children who chose to use drugs and wish that they had not. It is advisable for parents or other family members or adult friends of the child to attend these panel discussions so that follow-up discussions of the children's reactions to and learning from the panel discussion can occur. Panel members should ideally include African American children from various socioeconomic levels and mini-cultures.

Recommendations for Psychologists and Counselors

1. Psychologists and counselors can talk with children about their hurt, anger, and other underlying feelings that may be contributing to their use of alcohol or drugs. They can also ask the children what they think would be helpful in stopping and in preventing their use of alcohol and other drugs. What the children share should be respected. Ways of expressing anger and other feelings to their parents and significant others in their lives should be discussed. Perhaps most importantly psychologists and counselors should involve the children in some group counseling in which they can role-play and discuss what they can do and say to resist drugs when in situations in which they feel compelled to use them. The children should also be given opportunities to role-play and discuss ways of respectfully expressing their needs and wants and their negative feelings to powerful adults (e.g., parents and teachers). Family counseling to facilitate each family member's communication of negative feelings and positive feelings about each other as well as their needs and wants to feel supported and loved is also useful in preventing and stopping use of alcohol and other drugs among children and teens. In the process the anger, hurt, self-esteem issues, need for attention, and other factors that contribute to use of alcohol and drugs by the children and other family members will likely surface and can be addressed by the therapist in partnership with the family members.

2. Psychologists and counselors can teach children to use a procedure called covert sensitization to stop the use of alcohol or other drugs. This procedure typically involves having the individual imagine preparing to engage in a problem behavior, engaging in the behavior, experiencing a negative consequence from the behavior, removing oneself from the experience or setting of the behavior, and consequently feeling a sense of relief from having removed oneself from the experience or setting (Cautela, 1967).

Before teaching this procedure to a child, the child should be told that it is a technique that the child can use to better able herself or himself to say no to alcohol and other drugs even in situations in which the child feels pressured to use drugs. To teach the procedure, a child can be told to imagine a scene that is familiar to her or him such as the following scene:

> Imagine being offered a glass of punch mixed with alcohol at a party and feeling "cool" or part of the "in crowd" as you take the glass and bring it up to your lips to drink the alcohol punch. You immediately smell the alcohol and begin to feel sick to your stomach; then you feel sick all over and your stomach begins to hurt. You immediately leave the party and step outside; as soon as you walk outside away from the sight and smell of the alcohol punch you feel much better—your stomach relaxes, your head clears, and you begin to feel good all over and healthy. You return to the party but stay away from the alcohol punch and the friends who gave it to you and you feel great. You feel good about yourself for not drinking the alcohol.

The scene is presented while the child is sitting in a relaxed position with her or his eyes closed. The scene is presented in steps and after each step the child is instructed to raise a finger to indicate that the child has vividly imagined that part of the scene and is ready to go on to the next part of the scene. The psychologist or counselor can go through the scene with the child at least weekly; additionally, the child should be encouraged to practice it herself or himself at least twice a week and to praise herself or himself for doing something to stop or prevent using alcohol or other drugs.

Recommendations for Parents and Teachers

1. Parents and teachers can talk with children about (a) the importance of selecting friends with positive values rather than being selected by whomever wants a friend and (b) how to select friends with positive values, using specific friendship selection criteria. Friendship criteria to discuss might include saying no to drugs, following instructions, paying attention in class, choosing not to be in gangs, being friendly, listening when others are talking, enjoying school, working diligently to make good grades, doing homework, being polite, and talking with respect about one's parents.

2. Parents can provide and teachers can assign family activities that facilitate children and parents spending time together such that children have less time and feel less need to be involved with individuals who provide them with drugs. Parents can involve their children in after-school activities that facilitate their self-esteem and their academic and social skills. It is important for parents to participate with their children in these activities. Teachers can assign activities such as going with parents to the food store and identifying ten low-cholesterol foods there, or interviewing their parents and writing a biography about each. Such activities provide alternatives to drug use and facilitate academic learning and family bonding in the process, all of which discourage drug use.

3. Parents can give up their own use of alcohol or drugs—a step that will likely involve seeking help from a drug rehabilitation or counseling program of some type. Indeed, children do what they see, not what they are told, especially when the two are at odds.

It definitely takes multiple interventions to help African American children avoid using alcohol and other drugs. The popular strategy in the 1980s of telling children to just say no to drugs is much too simplistic. Children additionally need interventions that they can use in their personal war against the many influences in their lives that encourage drinking alcohol and using drugs. Ironically, many of their opposing warriors are family, friends, and neighbors who use alcohol or drugs to temporarily escape their emotional pain, frustration, and anger, or to be "cool." Thus, a major support strategy for helping African American youth win their battles against alcohol and other drugs is to get these drugs out of their homes, out of the hands of their parents, and out of their neighborhoods. Given that making homes and communities drug free will simply not happen, it is crucial to teach children how to resist alcohol and other drugs in the many situations in their lives in which there are powerful influences to use drugs.

Evaluation of Intervention Outcomes

It is important to conduct research to measure the effects on target behavior problems of specific interventions and intervention programs designed to modify these problems. Not only does such research tell us whether the intervention is effective and thus should be used in the future, but it also provides data for getting funding for long-term continuation of the intervention program or intervention that has been evidenced to be effective. Furthermore, information about the intervention or intervention program can be published in journals read by educators, parents, psychologists, and counselors and, consequently, possibly be implemented with other children across the country.

Research to assess the effects of intervention programs and interventions on targeted behavior problems of children should ideally include a control group of children—a group that does not experience the intervention or intervention program but that is similar demographically and in behavior problem occurrence to the group that did experience the intervention or intervention program. Consequently, it can be better determined if reductions in behavior problems targeted by the intervention were actually due to the intervention or intervention program or to some other factor such as maturing or a new school policy.

Research measures used such as questionnaires should be culturally and socioeconomically sensitive; that is, they should be appropriate for use with the African American children that the intervention or intervention program is designed to target. Appropriate standardized measures for African American children are those which have included in the standardization process African American children similar to those with whom the measures are being used to assess intervention or intervention program effects. Standardized measures that have norm scores for representative groups of African American children or for various mini-cultures of African American children (e.g., children from low-income, urban environments) are most ideal.

Multiple measures of the target behavior are strongly advised, especially given that most of the existing paper-and-pencil measures of the behaviors of African American children did not include a representative sample of these youth in their development. Indeed, total reliance on such measures alone is not sensible. Self-reports of the occurrence of behavior problems should be included among the multiple measures used, as these include the children's perspectives, which are very important. For too long African American children have been left out of the process of evaluating their behavior.

Support for the use of self-report measures comes from the findings of a significant association between African American children's self-reports of their drug use and their self-reports of their delinquent behaviors, and from the additional finding that these children's self-reports of their drug use were not significantly associated with their teachers' reports of their delinquent behaviors (Wells et al., 1992). Cultural differences between African American children and most of their teachers likely render teacher reports about children's delinquent behavior to be less reliable than these youth's self-reports about their delinquent behavior. When using self-report measures, teacher report measures, interview measures, and other such measures, the additional use of a social desirability measure is recommended to give some indication of the reliability of the data obtained. The overwhelming majority of existing research on behavior problems of children in general and of African American children in particular has not included a social desirability measure.

Other measures that ideally should be included among the multiple measures to assess change in a behavior problem as a function of an intervention might be behavioral observations of the frequency and prevalence of the behaviors. These observation data can be collected by parents, teachers, therapists, and children whose behaviors are the target of the intervention or intervention program.

Whatever preintervention and postintervention measures are administered to African American children and to their family members, they should be at an educational level that is appropriate for these children and administered in a way that protects their confidentiality. Additionally, these measures should be administered in a culturally and socioeconomically sensitive manner. In other words, administration of the measures should (1) occur in a setting that is comfortable for African American children (e.g., such as a community center in their neighborhood), (2) be preceded by the establishment of a rapport, and (3) be administered by someone who is comfortable with African Americans and familiar with African American cultures. Rapport with African American children and families is established through (1) shows of interest in their efforts to get to the data collection site, (2) expressing appreciation for their willingness to complete the measures, (3) not rushing to begin administering the measures but instead allowing time for participant-generated conversation, (4) inviting questions about the administration of the measures, (5) inviting feedback about anything that is done that makes the participant feel uncomfortable and about what will facilitate the participant's comfort, (6) responding respectfully and patiently to questions, (7) addressing adults with the title Mr., Mrs., Ms., or other appropriate title unless another way of addressing the adult is requested by that adult, and (8) offering refreshments (e.g., low-fat fruit punch and low-fat cookies) to the participants.

Measuring the effects of intervention programs and other interventions to modify behavior problems of African American children typically does not occur. Consequently, many effective intervention programs and interventions that are occurring in towns and cities across the country are not being recognized at the state and national level by educators and therapists who can facilitate their use statewide and nationally. The ultimate result is the current situation of widespread uncertainty about the most effective and efficient ways to reduce and extinguish behavior problems among African American children and facilitate these children's academic, social, and life success. A major solution to this problem is for culturally and socioeconomically sensitive researchers to become partners with community leaders, school administrators, and others who are implementing interventions to address behavior problems of African American children toward the goal of measuring the effects of these interventions using appropriate research methodology.

Culture-Sensitive Interventions

It is generally agreed that most psychologists and counselors regardless of ethnicity can work effectively with African American children with behavior problems and their families toward the goal of modifying the occurrence of these problems. It is also generally agreed that all African American psychologists and counselors are not effective in working with these children and families. Indeed, it is not ethnicity that determines the effectiveness of a therapist or counselor; rather it is the level of general competence as a therapist or counselor, cultural and socioeconomic sensitivity and related knowledge, and use of culturally and socioeconomically sensitive therapy methods when counseling African American children and their families.

In this section, knowledge and counseling methods that are especially important for psychologists and counselors to utilize when addressing behavior problems of African

American children are discussed. Additionally, therapy methods that are uniquely important when addressing behavior problems of African American adolescents are discussed.

Culture-Sensitive Knowledge

Culture-related knowledge is knowledge about certain behaviors, experiences, attitudes, and values that many African American children and their families bring to counseling, which often significantly impacts the counseling process. Additionally, knowledge about certain perspectives and values that psychologists and counselors often bring to the counseling process also typically impacts the counseling process. Both sets of knowledge are important for effective counseling for the purpose of reducing behavior problems among African American children and adolescents. Much of this knowledge is useful when counseling African Americans in general.

To begin with, it is important for psychologists to know how ecological factors such as racism, housing, economic status, and neighborhood impact the social behavior of African American children and families and how these social variables often contribute to behavior problems of African American children (Comer & Hill, 1985). Indeed, a systems approach to understanding an African American child's problem behavior is necessary; thus, getting permission from the child's parents to gain access to all available information about the child such as human service agency records and school records is important.

First, given the economically driven need for short-term therapy and the high counseling dropout rate among African American clients, it is important to access such records to help gather much information quickly. However, this information should not preclude getting the perspective of the child and the child's parents or primary caregivers about the social variables that impact their lives and about how these variables influence the occurrence of the behavior problems of concern.

Second, it is important for psychologists and counselors to become knowledgeable about African American children and their families and the cultural differences among them. All African American families are indeed not alike; thus, generalizations on the basis of seeing just a few African American families, as is common, usually leads to ineffective counseling. Instead of making such generalizations, it is important to read available culturally and socioeconomically sensitive research on African American families and children and to read books about African American cultures. Additionally, to facilitate comfort with as well as knowledge about the lives of African American children and families, it is helpful to interact with them through volunteer counseling and tutoring programs, visit African American churches and neighborhoods, attend events that educate about and celebrate African American cultures, and take courses or enroll in continuing education training sessions that focus on cross-cultural counseling and on counseling African American clients.

Third, having knowledge and understanding of certain common behaviors among African Americans that are often misunderstood by psychologists and counselors is important among these professionals. Following is a brief discussion of some of these commonly misunderstood behaviors.

1. One of these behaviors is the tendency of many African American children and their parents to sit quietly without giving any acknowledgment or verbal reinforcement of what is being said by the therapist such as by nodding, saying "uh-huh," or saying, "I understand." Psychologists and counselors often misinterpret the absence of such feedback as failure of the African American clients to communicate and cooperate; however, to members of their cultural group and themselves they are cooperating by listening in a manner that is the norm for their cultural group. Without this knowledge, psychologists and counselors are often discouraged and, consequently, experience lowered motivation to work with African American clients such as an African American child and her or his family. Such lowered motivation decreases the likelihood of successful therapy outcomes with African American clients.

2. Lack of eye contact by many African American children and parents is another often misunderstood behavior. It is often interpreted as a show of lack of cooperation, low intelligence, resistance, or defiance. This behavior, however, is just the reflection of culture-based experiences. Historically, it was not unusual for African Americans to engage in more than one activity at a time such as sewing, rocking a baby, and carrying on a conversation and, thus, not holding eye contact with persons being engaged in conversation. Historically, it was also the case that African Americans were instructed by European American slave masters not to look in the eyes of European Americans as it was a show of disrespect; the desired subordination from African Americans was communicated through keeping one's eyes focused downward. Consequently, today there are some African American parents who instruct their children not to look at them during verbal exchanges in which the parents are reprimanding the children, as looking downward by the children is a show of respect for the parents and shame by the children for their inappropriate behaviors. Thus, lack of eye contact by African American children and parents in therapy should not be interpreted by psychologists and counselors as meaning that they have social skills deficits or are trying to be antagonistic to the therapy process. Teaching African American children to use eye contact as a success behavior, but not because it represents some underlying "problem," is a reasonable therapy goal.

3. Being late to the counseling session by African American children and their parents is also an often misunderstood behavior as well as a common one among families who have low incomes. This behavior is often perceived by a psychologist or counselor as a show of disinterest in counseling or disrespect for or dislike of the counselor. Instead, this late behavior is often the reflection of the fact that the children and their parents are dependent on transportation by others to get to therapy sessions and, thus, they often do not have control over their arrival time to the sessions. Given the impact that this late behavior can have on the schedules of psychologists and counselors, it is important for these professionals to be aware of this potential late behavior, assess whether this might be a problem, and if so, collaborate with their African American clients to come up with proactive solutions to the potential problem. Taking these actions avoids anger and resentment by counselors and psychologists because their clients are late, and it avoids the anger and resentment of the clients in response to the negative emotions and behaviors by counselors and psychologists because of the clients' late behavior.

4. Another behavior that is common among African American parents with low family incomes that is often misunderstood by psychologists and counselors is that of rescheduling appointments at the last minute. These parents often have to reschedule appointments at the last minute because of the many problems that come with low socioeconomic status that render their schedules unstable. Examples of such problems are having an unreliable babysitter and having one's electricity turned off because of not paying the bill. It is important for psychologists and counselors to plan their schedules to include tasks that can be done should their appointment times with low income African American families get cancelled at the last minute. It is also important for these professionals to be aware of the need to be flexible in their appointment scheduling before agreeing to work with low-income African American clients because these clients often cannot take time off from work for daytime appointments and, thus, require evening or weekend appointments.

Other culture-related knowledge that is important for psychologists and counselors to have when working with African American children with behavior problems concerns the perspectives and values of these professionals themselves that have the potential for impacting the counseling process. One such perspective is that race is not an issue in interactions with African American children with behavior problems and their families. Another such perspective is that all of the behavior problems of African American children and their families can be attributed to cultural and racial conflicts.

Both of these perspectives are extreme and inaccurate. These perspectives can be avoided or modified if psychologists and counselors simply make the effort to get to know their African American clients with behavior problems and their families and make the effort to assess the environmental, economic, cultural, and social influences on the lives of these clients. These actions by psychologists and counselors are important in formulating ideas about the possible causes of and solutions for modifying the behavior problems of African American children. Indeed, racial and cultural conflicts should be explored as factors in the child's manifested behavior problems; however, a fixation on them by the therapist may obstruct the broader view of the multiple factors in the behavior problem and of the approach needed and resources available for assisting the child in modifying the behavior problems.

The other common perspective that race is not an issue in counseling African American children with behavior problems and their families may simply reflect a denial of the significance of race in America and in the lives of African Americans or an insensitivity to the various differences that often exist between the psychologists or counselors and their clients. The reality is that many African Americans do not trust or feel comfortable with European Americans in general; furthermore, many African Americans do not trust or feel comfortable with European American therapists or African American therapists who are perceived as very different from the clients, unable to identify with their problems, and trying to act superior to the clients. Cheek (1976) asserts that there are African American counseling professionals who may be as different from some African American clients as some European American counseling professionals and that there are some European American counseling professionals who communicate well and relate well with African Americans.

Often African American clients feel uncomfortable with African American therapists who have much lighter skin tone than themselves and who talk very "proper." This is because these clients perceive the therapists as not identifying with their race and instead are "trying to be white." African American children and adolescents often do not communicate with European American therapists because in their neighborhoods, European Americans are not to be trusted given the real or perceived harassment of African American relatives by European American police. Psychologists and counselors sometimes have no clue that their race is a factor in such noncommunication; African American clients will likely not come right out and tell them. However, with therapist sensitivity to the possible influence of race in the counseling process, they can assess whether it is a factor, and if so, address this issue with the clients involved. Counselors and psychologists are often surprised by the candid responses that they receive from African Americans clients when they ask these clients how they feel about seeing a European American therapist for counseling and whether they feel that the therapist or counselor can understand and help with their problems of concern given their client–therapist differences.

It is also noteworthy that there are some African American children and families who are very acculturated into the majority culture and have adopted the view that race does not matter in any setting. Some of these individuals report not seeing race. For many African American psychologists and counselors who take pride in their racial identity and understand the major roles that race plays in the education of and opportunities for African American children as well as for African Americans in general, working with "color blind" clients can be problematic and can impact the counseling process (Boyd & Franklin, 1989). The lesson to be learned here is that "one cannot judge the book by the cover"; that is, psychologists and counselors cannot make any assumptions about African American children and families who come into their office. The reverse is also true; African American children and adolescents cannot make assumptions about European American psychologists and counselors or African American psychologists and counselors; indeed, both may or may not be culturally and socioeconomically sensitive.

Finally, it is important to note here that race is an issue in the counseling process when psychologists and counselors feel the need to prove to their African American clients that it is not an issue. When this feeling exists, it is important to process this issue with the client as it might provide some insight into the clients' relationships with others. It is also important for psychologists and counselors to consult with colleagues about their need to prove to African American clients or to themselves that race does not matter (Allen & Majidi-Ahi, 1989). What will usually result is the realization that many therapists experience this need when working with clients who are racially different from themselves, and this experience is frustrating. Such discussions and realizations make it easier to cope with these frustrations and other feelings of psychologists and counselors in counseling and in other interventions (e.g., parenting training workshops) to help African American children modify their behavior problems.

Culture-Related Counseling Methods

Being a competent psychologist or counselor is of central importance in working with African American children and their families just as is the case when working with clients of any other ethnic group. In addition to being competent, it is helpful to use culture-sensitive methods when counseling with African American children and their families. Following are some culture-sensitive methods that are recommended for psychologists and counselors when counseling with these children and families.

1. Consider using family therapy when working with African American children with behavior problems. This is in part because most African American parents are simply uncomfortable with one-to-one therapy with their child and, thus, are often resistant to processing suggestions and therapy discussions that occur in individual therapy of which they were not a part and, consequently, do not understand. Additionally, family therapy provides the opportunity for anxieties and distrust among family members, which impact the child with behavior problems, to be addressed. In fact, in family therapy the patterns of relating among family members can be used to help determine what changes in these patterns are needed to help empower the child client so that the child can better manage her or his own behavior for success in all aspects of her or his own life.

2. It is important to include in therapy extended family members who are significant in the child client's life and who can help provide family support and structure for the child. This support is especially important in families in which there is only one parent or primary caregiver living in the home with the child (Sykes, 1987).

3. When the therapist is of a different race, religion, or socioeconomic level from the child client and her or his family, it is wise to ask the family members how they feel about working with a therapist different from them. It is fair for the therapist to share her or his own feelings about working with African American children and families. Ideally, this discussion should occur in one of the beginning sessions of therapy. The clients will appreciate this honesty, which in turn will facilitate their trust of and comfort with the therapist.

4. Psychologists and counselors should do all that they can to mobilize each African American family to assume part of the responsibility for treatment, thus making therapy a partnership effort. Consequently, the investment in and responsibility for treatment success or failure will be that of the child, the child's family, and the therapist. This partnership therapy approach facilitates empowerment of the child and family to make life changes to facilitate modification of the behavior problems of concern. It is important, however, that parents and the child are not given responsibilities and roles in the therapy process that are inconsistent with their capabilities and level of motivation to execute (Fantuzzo, Davis, & Ginsberg, 1995). For example, a therapist may ask parents to review with their child a problem-solving technique that the therapist reviews in counseling with the child and parents and that the parents indicate does not seem relevant for addressing their child's behavior problems. If the parents have difficulty reading, they will not be capable of executing this therapy responsibility in addition to not being motivated to do so. To avoid such problems, psychologists and counselors should regularly invite feedback from their African American clients about recommended interventions and work in partnership with them to identify alternative interventions when these clients do not approve of or resist the recommended interventions.

5. Psychologists and counselors need to be familiar with and prepared to utilize all community and human service resources that are available to African American children and their families for the purpose of helping them help themselves to address the behavior problems of concern. Such resources include agencies, churches, and organizations that assist with transportation to work and to school meetings, provide free or low-cost health care, provide support groups for African American families, and arrange for mentors for African American children. Indeed, in many cases identification and coordination of support services and assistance in completing paperwork to get needed services are adequate "counseling," especially for African American children and adolescents whose parents cannot pay even for short-term counseling.

Because this coordination of services role to meet the needs of an African American child or adolescent with behavior problems is time consuming, the therapist might, with parents' approval, consider identifying an immediate or extended family member who can execute this role. Over a short time period, the psychologist or counselor can establish a resource directory that can be used in this coordination of services process.

6. Given that behavior problems of African American children are often influenced by multiple factors in different settings, psychologists and counselors should be prepared to use multifaceted assessment and interventions, not only in their offices, but also in these children's schools, homes, and communities. Thus, it is important for these therapists and counselors to figure out how they will charge for this fieldwork, and then advise parents of these costs and the conditions under which such work will be important. This information should be provided to African American families at the time that other regular one-hour therapy fees are discussed.

7. Psychologists and counselors should respect religious and healing beliefs and practices that are important in the lives of African American families that they see in counseling. Additionally, to the degree possible, these beliefs and practices should be integrated in the therapy if the clients view them as potentially therapeutic. For example, if parents feel strongly that prayer and faith can change any behavior problem, the therapist can suggest that in addition to the intervention recommended that family prayer might indeed be helpful. Minimally, it is important for the therapist not to ignore or try to extinguish clients' discussions of prayer or faith and trust in God or some other supreme being(s) or power. Listening to and trying to understand such discussions are consistent with engaging in culturally sensitive counseling.

Counseling Method Recommendations

African American adolescents often bring to counseling (1) the desire for more independence from parents, (2) resentment and resistance toward adults who have tried to control their behavior (e.g., parents and teachers) and who might try to do so (e.g., psychologists and counselors), and (3) frustration and anger due to many reasons including life experiences such as racism, discrimination, and family problems that they are now old enough to recognize, emotionally experience, and attribute blame for. Consequently, psychologists and counselors often find it especially challenging to form a trusting relationship with and facilitate behavior changes among these adolescents. Following are some recommendations for helping psychologists and counselors to meet these challenges in counseling with African American adolescents who evidence behavior problems.

1. Given that African American adolescents often are resistant to anyone who might try to control their behavior, it is important to begin the counseling session with some discussion of the purpose of counseling and the psychologist's or counselor's role. It is especially important to make it clear to the adolescent that it is up to her or him to make any changes in her or his behavior. The roles of the counselor or psychologist that might be shared with the adolescent include the following: to explore why some behaviors of the adolescent are perceived by others as problematic, to determine the adolescent's and others' views of the reasons for the behaviors and how they impact others, to explore the consequences of changing and not changing the behavior, and to assist the adolescent in changing behaviors that the adolescent may decide are in her or his best interest to change.

2. It is recommended that a psychologist or counselor working with an African American adolescent be on the alert for efforts by the adolescent to determine if the psychologist or counselor is prejudiced, has feelings of superiority, is disapproving of the adolescent's dress and ways of being, and will easily reject the adolescent (Gibbs, 1985). It is important for the psychologist or counselor to avoid being placed on the defensive or in the position of trying to prove that he or she is accepting of the adolescent; instead, the therapist should state her or his policies (e.g., such as ending the session on the hour rather than ten minutes after the hour) and adhere to those policies.

3. It is also important for the psychologist or counselor to state her or his preferences but avoid power struggles with the adolescent regarding these preferences. For example, if the psychologist or counselor states the preference for the adolescent client to sit in an office chair and the client insists on sitting on the floor, the counseling professional should avoid any reaction and simply go on with the session.

4. The psychologist or counselor must become aware of and resolve any anger that she or he has toward the African American adolescent because of the adolescent's mistrust and anger, both of which make it difficult for the psychologist or counselor to establish a relationship with the adolescent (Sykes, 1987). This counseling professional might identify and extinguish her or his own anger by directly addressing the adolescent's feelings and acknowledging the legitimate reasons for these feelings. The counseling professional can then help the adolescent be more trusting and comfortable with counseling through words and actions indicating that the counseling process will involve a partnership effort in which the counselor will assist the adolescent, but in which the adolescent will actually make the behavior changes that they both agree are needed.

An analogy for describing this relationship is that the psychologist or counselor will be a very supportive coach in the counseling process, but the adolescent will have to be the quarterback player. As the coach, the psychologist or counselor can help empower the adolescent by teaching her or him self-management skills (e.g., problem-solving skills and anger management skills) and helping the adolescent identify and utilize the adolescent's own strengths and his or her family and community resources and support for making a touchdown (i.e., engaging in behaviors that facilitate social, academic, and life success).

5. It is especially important for the psychologist or counselor to avoid trying to be an instant friend and pretending to have more knowledge about the adolescent client's culture (e.g., language, slang, gang) than is the case. Indeed, the adolescent will recognize this pretense and identify it as disingenuous; this recognition deters trust of the psychologist or counselor by the adolescent. Having the adolescent teach the counseling professional about the adolescent's slang, values, gang, and so on elevates the status of the adolescent toward a counseling partnership that facilitates the self-esteem of the adolescent and the therapeutic process.

6. It is important for psychologists and counselors to show respect for African American adolescents by engaging in the same level of professionalism as that appropriate for their upper-class European American clients. Specifically, it is important for these counseling professionals to dress professionally and to use their attractive offices when seeing African American adolescents as clients. It is also important for these professionals to avoid: being patronizing, using overly simple vocabulary, being late for the therapy session, and answering the telephone during the session (Franklin, 1982). It is also a useful strategy for counseling professionals to seek the opinions and views of their adolescent clients and to show serious consideration of these perspectives rather than give superficial approval of them to earn "brownie points."

7. To overcome an adolescent's resistance to the psychologist or counselor (i.e., an authority figure) and resistance to self-disclosure, it is important for the psychologist or counselor to encourage the adolescent to discuss the adolescent's feelings of anger and other negative feelings. It is also useful for the counseling professional to raise for discussion the adolescent's feelings and fears about being in counseling and to normalize these feelings. Issues regarding confidentiality and its limitations with minors should also be discussed openly and honestly near the beginning of the first therapy session because this too will help build the adolescent's trust of the psychologist or counselor (Gibbs, 1989).

8. In addition to considering the usefulness of family therapy with African American adolescents, it is particularly useful to involve adolescents in group counseling or group adaptive skills training. Massimo and Shore (1963) and Shore, Massimo, Kisielewski, and Moran (1966) showed that therapy with lower-class adolescents labeled as delinquents in which the counselor or therapist taught these adolescents social and practical skills such as how to interview for a job was effective in deterring delinquent behavior and facilitating productive lives among these adolescents.

Among the adaptive skills that are important for African American adolescents to learn include anger management skills, assertiveness versus aggressiveness, how to constructively express negative and positive feelings, problem-solving skills, and interpersonal skills that are particularly important for getting and maintaining a job. A group training approach to adaptive skills training sessions is particularly indicated for use with African American adolescents. This approach gives these adolescents opportunities for active and enjoyable learning through role-plays and demonstrations. This active participation gives African American adolescents important roles in facilitating their own behavior changes and in shaping a positive future for themselves.

Working with African American adolescents with behavior problems is a rewarding challenge for most psychologists and counselors, regardless of their ethnicity. Just because a counseling professional is African American does not assure that the counsellor will be effective in addressing the behavior problems of African American adolescents. All counseling professionals must learn as much as possible about African American mini-cultures and families toward the goal of being culturally and socioeconomically sensitive in the counseling process. This should involve learning about culture-related behaviors that are often misinterpreted and, thus, negatively impact the counseling process, and about culture-sensitive therapy methods that facilitate this process. This learning should also include becoming knowledgeable about the potential impact of race in the therapy process and how to address this issue in constructive ways.

Conclusions

Given the complexity of behavior problems of African American children, especially adolescents, it is most important that the psychologists and counselors who work with them are first and foremost well-trained professionals in basic counseling. It is also important for counseling professionals to accept that the ethnic, social class, and other differences between these professionals and African American youth and their families can potentially impede the counseling process and, thus, should not be ignored. In addition, it is important for African American counseling professionals as well as European American counseling professionals and other counseling professionals who provide counseling to African American youth with behavior problems to become aware of, understand, and prepare to address the various culture-based and socioeconomic-based behaviors, needs, and attitudes that these youth and their families bring to counseling. This requires using methods that encourage African American youth and their families to be partners in the counseling process and that counseling professionals learn as much as they can about African American cultures and life outside of their professional and personal environments.

Effective counseling with African American youth with behavior problems also requires new roles for most counseling professionals including identifying and coordinating human services for African American families and providing adaptive skills training for African American youth. Additionally, it requires that psychologists and counselors avoid making assumptions about the lives, behaviors, and feelings of African American youth. To the contrary, these counseling professionals must learn from these youth and their families about the real and perceived realities that contribute to the behavior problems of these youth.

Given the complexity of the contributors to behavior problems among African American children and adolescents, partnership efforts are needed to address them. The partners in these efforts need to include parents, teachers, school administrators, psychologists or counselors, community leaders, church leaders, and African American children themselves. The work of these partners must include establishing community-based programs that provide these youth with skills and experiences that promote self-motivation, self-control, self-praise, and adaptive skills (communication, socialization, and daily living skills) for deterring behavior problems and facilitating social, academic, and life success. This self-empowerment intervention approach is indicated given that modification of the many negative influences on the behavior of African American children and adolescents (e.g., racism, schools that do not understand and do not have the time, resources, or will to address the behavior problems of African American youth) will take more than the lifetimes of many of these youth to change. Thus, African American youth must learn to self-manage their behavior in violent neighborhoods, to praise themselves for achievements when they do not receive this support from families and teachers, and to establish positive goals and be self-motivated to achieve them.

Modification of behavior problems of African American youth requires the expertise of culturally and socioeconomically sensitive psychologists and counselors. These counseling professionals typically are not born with this sensitivity, but rather they learn it through training and getting out of their offices and neighborhoods and into the communities of African American children and families where they learn about the lives of these individuals, the problems that impact their lives, and the diversity of cultures that these lives reflect. As a result of this learning, these professionals become aware of the multiple factors that influence the behavior problems of African American children and adolescents and gain insight into the importance of culture-related knowledge and methods to address these problems. These methods include family counseling that utilizes the strengths of extended family members and group counseling and training for the development of behavior self-management skills and adaptive skills using a step-by-step teaching and learning method.

The development of multifaceted culturally and socioeconomically sensitive interventions and intervention programs to help African American children modify their behavior problems and self-empower them for social, academic, and life success is in its infancy. A major part of this development must be research to test the effects of these interventions and to provide directions for improving them. It is only with research data evidencing the effectiveness of these interventions can funding from the private and public sectors be obtained for sustaining these interventions. Furthermore, African Americans and others must invest their resources in programs and interventions that truly have a measurable positive influence on the behavior of African American children and adolescents.

Knowing through history the negative impact on African Americans of being controlled and powerless, self-empowering interventions seem clearly indicated. These interventions recognize the importance of moving the focus of counseling from telling African American youth with behavior problems what not to do to teaching African American youth what to do to be successful and giving them the skills and knowledge to do so.

7 Practical Answers to Common Questions and Concerns

This chapter focuses on common questions and concerns about behaviors of African American children that have been presented to the present author through parent and teacher workshops, private practice, consultations with school administrators, and sixteen years of work as guest clinical psychologist on a local call-in television show, which often focused on the African American family, behavior problems of African American youth, and rearing and educating African American children to be successful. One purpose of the chapter is to normalize the questions and concerns of African American parents and teachers regarding behaviors of African American children that are of concern to these adults. This normalization is important given that many African American parents and many teachers feel alone in their need for information to better understand and address the problem behaviors of African American youth.

A second purpose of this chapter is to provide parents and teachers with information and practically useful suggestions that might address their common concerns and questions regarding the behaviors of African American youth. The ultimate objective of this chapter is to provide some guidance and stimulate ideas among parents, teachers, and psychologists and counselors for addressing behaviors of African American youth that are not conducive to their academic, social, and life success.

Indeed, there is no one answer to any question or concern regarding the behavior of African American children or a particular African American child. Furthermore, an effective strategy or response for addressing the behaviors of concern of one child may not be effective with another child. Thus, the responses to the questions and concerns of parents and teachers that are identified in this chapter should only serve as guidelines for ideas in addressing the questions and concerns regarding any particular child. What is appropriate or effective for one African American child or adolescent often will not be appropriate or effective for another child.

Questions and Concerns Raised by Parents

Identity and Self-Esteem

Question.   Are there problems that children are more likely to experience because they are biracial?

Answer.   It is certainly possible that children will experience no particular problems just because they are biracial. However, biracial children are particularly vulnerable to certain problems including differential treatment by their parents and relatives, social rejection by their peers, ambivalent attention in their schools and communities (Gibbs, 1989), and academic and behavior problems as well as identity conflicts (McRoy & Freeman, 1986). Adolescents appear to be particularly vulnerable to conflicts about their dual racial or ethnic identity, social marginality, sexuality, choice of dating and sexual partners, parent–child relationships, and educational or career aspirations. Symptoms of these conflicts may range from mild symptoms of anxiety and depression to severe symptoms of delinquency as well as substance abuse and suicidal behaviors (Gibbs, 1987; Gibbs & Moskowitz-Sweet, 1986).

Racial or ethnic identity appears to be the most widespread area of conflict among biracial adolescents. They sometimes praise and sometimes denigrate each of the two racial groups that form their identity (Sebring, 1985). They also sometimes totally reject their African American identity because of American society's general negative stereotypes of and negative attitudes toward African Americans. Biracial adolescents evidence this rejection by not associating with African American peers in school or in other social situations, avoiding African American dress, music, and so on, and feeling ashamed of their African American features (e.g., dark skin and curly hair). Other biracial adolescents overidentify with their African American parents and reject European American culture and friends. They often adopt the dress, speech, and behaviors reflective of a low-income lifestyle (Gibbs, 1989).

Another major problem of biracial adolescents is their sexual identity and handling dating and sexual relationships. They are often rejected as dating partners and friends by both of the racial groups of which they are a part. This rejection or sexual identity confusion is associated with their general identity confusion and often results in the biracial adolescent being more masculine or more feminine than is typical of their gender, having limited dating options, and being either celibate or sexually promiscuous (Gibbs, 1989).

The behavior problems of biracial adolescents appear to be related to their parents' overprotective behavior in an effort to protect these adolescents from prejudice and discrimination. As a result of this overprotection, some biracial adolescents become overly dependent on their parents and, consequently, are immature, conforming, and depressed or emotionally constricted. In reaction to parental overprotection, other biracial adolescents often rebel against their parents and family members, become confrontational, become risk takers, and engage in delinquent behaviors (Gibbs, 1989).

It is also interesting to note that often biracial adolescents are ambivalent about doing well academically and being upwardly mobile. Some of these adolescents underachieve because of fear of rejection by their African American friends for studying and "acting white." Other biracial adolescents often identify with middle-class European Americans and strive for academic and future success, but often with unclear career aspirations because of knowing that they may be limited in their achievements by prejudice and discrimination (Gibbs, 1989).

Despite the challenges that come with being a biracial adolescent, most of these children grow up to be productive and well-adjusted citizens. These positive outcomes are facilitated by parents and other family members doing the following with their biracial children and adolescents:

1. Encourage them to share their feelings about their identity and the reactions of others to it, and then reassure these youth that their feelings are normal rather than unfounded or irrational (Sebring, 1985).

2. Recognize and praise their healthy coping mechanisms, abilities, and aspirations to facilitate their development of positive self-esteem (Sebring, 1985).

3. Encourage and assist them in exploring both sides of their racial heritage and taking pride in the positive aspects of their ethnic and cultural roots (Lyles et al., 1985). This might be done, for example, through writing reports on achievements of heroes on both sides of their cultural backgrounds, participating in activities that celebrate cultural diversity, participating in activities that celebrate the contributions of each ethnic group that forms their identity, and participating in interracial activities (Gibbs, 1989).

4. Involve adolescents in adolescent peer support groups, which can be established through schools or communities with the help of parenting groups and children's groups in the county and state.

5. Involve them in family counseling to address their identity conflict problems and other problems. This counseling should include adaptive skills training that includes training in expressing feelings, problem solving, establishing friendships, managing stress, and being assertive. The goal of this training should be self-empowering biracial children and adolescents for social, academic, and life success. Self-empowering training has as major objectives self-motivation, self-control, self-praise, and skills and behaviors for academic and social success.

Question.   My young child has low self-esteem because of her dark skin color and short hair. What can I do to make her feel better about herself?

Answer.   This is indeed a common concern among African American parents, especially those whose children attend schools where African American children are clearly in the minority. In such schools and in society in general, positions of leadership, power, and status that typically require intelligence are most often held by European Americans—the Americans who have most often had the opportunities to get these positions. Consequently, there is often an association, especially among youth, between having European American physical features and having status and other desirable attributes that facilitate positive self-esteem.

For some youth, like your child, not having European American physical features, especially in an environment where most peers have them, contributes to low self-esteem. This negative self-evaluation is often reinforced by (1) seeing on television day after day the association of success and beauty with being European American or having European American features, and (2) being jokingly teased or derogated by others, including family, because of dark skin color, "nappy" hair texture, short hair, thick lips, or a broad nose.

It is thus understandable and indeed not uncommon for a child who has a dark skin tone and short hair or any other generally non-European American feature to not feel good about herself or himself for some period of time during her or his life. It is important to realize that this low self-esteem often signals the need for parents and teachers to (1) give positive attention to the child's strengths and beauty, (2) engage the child in experiences to develop her or his strengths, (3) assist the child in setting short-term and long-term goals and working toward those goals, (4) involve the child with African American peers and adults who do not have European American features and who are making important contributions to society, (5) provide the child with experiences that facilitate an appreciation of African American beauty, achievements, and culture, and (6) teach the child skills and strategies for expressing anger and other negative feelings in response to inappropriate and derogatory comments from others.

Some specific actions that you might consider doing to address your daughter's low self-esteem are as follows:

1. Involve her in an after-school program, church group, or other program or organization that provides leadership, communication, assertiveness, and anger management training.

2. Encourage her to express her negative and positive feelings about her physical self and herself in general rather than tell her what she should not be feeling. Listen attentively to her feelings and express understanding of them. Additionally, identify your daughter's specific physical and personality characteristics and behaviors you admire and that will make her successful.

3. Expose her to successful African Americans who come in all shapes and sizes and with varying skin tones and hair textures. Additionally, engage in a project with your daughter to investigate the personal histories of some of these successful individuals—histories that will typically tell how they achieved against all odds and celebrate their African American beauty and culture.

4. Encourage her to enroll in an African American history class, if one is available.

5. Facilitate her motivation and skill development to reach her identified goals. For example, if your daughter thinks that she wants to become a physician, arrange for her to (a) meet and spend time with some African American female (and male) physicians, (b) work or volunteer in a hospital or a physician's office, (c) visit a medical school and talk with African American female (and male) medical students, and (d) receive health care related magazines.

6. Hold a family conference to discuss the reasons for appreciating the differences in skin tone, hair, weight, and other features among family members and why African Americans often reject their own physical features—a major reason being that they allow the majority culture to set their standards of beauty rather than set those standards for themselves.

7. Identify and praise your daughter daily for her positive attributes and success behaviors and encourage her to praise herself for these qualities as well.

8. Role-play with her what to say and do when someone seriously or jokingly teases her about her physical features. The response actions should include stopping and becoming calm before responding, expressing her feelings about the teasing, and stating the appropriate behaviors she expects from the teaser in the future.

Question. I am greatly concerned about the fact that my seven-year-old son has all white friends, likes a little white girl as his "girlfriend," and even has prayed to be white. He attends a predominantly white school, but there are nice black children at the school. What can I do about my son's rejection of his race?

Answer.   When your child expresses the desire to be white, he is likely saying "I want to be like my friends; I want to be accepted." It is likely that the children who choose to play with him and with whom he is around a lot and share common interests are European American children. Thus, his reaction of wanting to be as much as possible like his inner circle peer group is not surprising. Your son's wish to be "white," though understandably a great concern, is likely not a rejection of his race but rather a reaction to his social situation and experiences. At your son's age, a wish to be white is like someone short wishing to be tall given that all of his friends are much taller than he is.

It is extremely important that you do not overreact to your child's behavior by indicating concern or disappointment, and acting upset over his behaviors and prayers, which you perceive as identity confusion or rejection. Instead, it is important for you to involve your son in activities that will allow him the opportunity to meet and interact with many different African American children, including some who are culturally and socioeconomically similar to and different from himself. This can occur through church groups and boys' clubs that are located in mostly African American communities. It is also important for your son to have many opportunities to learn about and gain an appreciation for his African American culture and to have regular contact with many successful African American role models.

Role-playing with your child how to establish friendships when meeting new children like and different from himself is advised. Encourage him to choose his friends rather than be chosen and discuss with him the qualities to look for in friends. After all, what may be more important than the ethnicity of your child's friends are the values and behaviors of those friends. When discussing friend selection, it is a great time to discuss how his current friends came to be friends. This discussion will provide some insight into the role race played in his selection of his friends.

With regard to the prayer to be white, it is a good idea to ask your son in a casual and nonemotional way why he prayed to be white. Discuss with him how his life would be different if he were white. Additionally, discuss with him whatever else he would change about himself if he could. Then tell your son at least three times a week about one or two physical and personality characteristics that you really like about him. It is also important that he identifies what he likes about himself and his behaviors and praises himself for his positive attributes and behaviors. The goal of focusing on your child's positives is to facilitate his self-acceptance. Indeed, rather than focusing on his perceived rejection of his race, focus on facilitating his self-acceptance and showing the love and pride that you feel for him as your son.

Hyperactivity

Question.   We have been thinking about having our child evaluated to determine if he has ADHD (attention deficit hyperactivity disorder). What does such an evaluation involve?

Answer.   You are applauded for your interest in understanding the behaviors of your child that are of concern to you and for wanting to be educated about any evaluations of your child being considered. Should you actually decide to have your child evaluated for ADHD, or for any disorder, it is advisable that you express concern about the confidentiality of the results of the evaluation. Often diagnostic labels such as ADHD that get attached to a child become almost public knowledge in a school system.

A child who becomes aware of a label or diagnosis without a proper explanation can be negatively impacted by the label. Furthermore, for some teachers and parents it becomes difficult to look beyond the label and see the child. It is also the case that the label can be used for placement of the child in special classes—placements that are often undesired by the parent and the child. Because African American children are often at risk of being placed in "special classes" in which often minimal learning occurs, labels that can increase this risk should be obtained and handled with caution.

An evaluation for ADHD involves assessment in many areas using several different procedures. This is because the disorder is complex, meaning that there are biological, psychological, and social factors in its occurrence. It is, in fact, generally conceptualized as a biopsychosocial disorder. Thus, assessment of ADHD includes information on a child's behavior in different settings, and a focus on family functioning and biological functioning. The specific information obtained and how it is obtained depend to some degree on the child's age, because behaviors of children have to be viewed in a changing developmental context (Hinshaw & Erhardt, 1993; Wicks-Nelson & Israel, 1997).

The procedures that are typically included in an evaluation for ADHD are (1) interviews with the parents, the child, and the child's teacher; (2) completion of behavior rating scales and checklists by parents, teachers, and sometimes the child herself or himself, (3) direct observations of the child during structured and unstructured activities while at school and sometimes at home, (4) administration of intelligence and academic achievement tests, (5) execution of a medical examination, if a recent one has not been obtained, and (6) completion of a medical and developmental history questionnaire. Sometimes an EEG and a neuropsychological evaluation are used to evaluate ADHD (Wicks-Nelson & Israel, 1997).

The interviews focus on particular problem situations and seek to determine what the child specifically does that is problematic, the responses of others to these problematic behaviors (e.g., the responses of parents, teachers, and the child herself or himself), and the frequency of each problematic behavior. Behavior rating scales and checklists are also used to identify problem behaviors. Additionally, from such scales and checklists, it can be determined whether the identified problem behaviors are deviant from the norm and whether they indicate ADHD versus some other disorder. The behavior scales and checklists completed by parents and teachers are more appropriate for evaluating children, whereas those completed by adolescents themselves are more appropriate for evaluating adolescents (Wicks-Nelson & Israel, 1997).

The Child Behavior Checklist is now the most widely used behavior rating scale and checklist (Rapport, 1993). There are, however, other popular similar scales. Both interviews and behavior rating scales and checklists are often used to assess family functioning. Family functioning is important given that it plays a role in the development and maintenance of ADHD (Wicks-Nelson & Israel, 1997).

The major purpose of the behavioral observations in the home is to assess compliance of the child and consequences for the child's behaviors; the purpose of these observations at school is to assess social interactions involving the child as well as the child's levels of engagement in off-task behaviors, aggression, and other problem behaviors (Wicks-Nelson & Israel, 1997).

Medical examinations and neuropsychological testing are important to help determine biological factors in ADHD and to better understand the disorder and its treatment.

Standardized tests of intelligence and academic achievement are typically used in planning treatment that facilitates the child's academic as well as social success.

Clearly, an evaluation to determine the existence of ADHD is not simple and requires active involvement of a child's parents and teachers and some degree of involvement of the child herself or himself, with greater involvement of older versus younger children. For an ADHD evaluation to be reliable, parents must prepare to play an active role in the evaluation process, and the evaluators must be culturally and socioeconomically sensitive. Given that how behavior is viewed and interpreted is often culturally influenced, such sensitivity by evaluators of ADHD is very important. It is reasonable for parents to request that someone of the child's race be included in the process to evaluate the existence of ADHD in their child.

Question.   My child's physician is recommending that my husband and I consider giving our son medication to reduce his hyperactivity and inattentiveness. We will discuss this at our next visit. What are the common drugs for hyperactive and inattentive behaviors? Are they effective, and do they have any side effects?

Answer.   Before placing your son on any medication, it is important for him to have a complete physical examination to make sure there are no undiagnosed problems that could be contributing to the problem behaviors and that might be adversely affected by the medications for the hyperactive and inattentive behaviors. It is great that your child's physician will be taking time to discuss the medications with you and your husband. In advance of this meeting, it is a good idea to prepare questions that address your concerns about using medications to modify your child's behaviors. These questions should be discussed to your satisfaction at the scheduled meeting.

Usually stimulant medications are used to treat hyperactivity and inattentiveness in children. The most commonly used stimulants are Ritalin (methylphenidate), Dexedrine (dextroamphetamine), and Cylert (pemoline). It is estimated that over 2 percent of all school-age children are taking these medications (DuPaul & Barkley, 1993).

It is generally agreed that the stimulants mentioned previously work by acting on the central nervous system to influence dopamine, norepinephrine, and epinephrine. The effects of the mentioned stimulants and most stimulants are rapid but short term, typically lasting only a few hours; consequently, they are commonly given two or three times a day.

What is known or has been concluded about the effectiveness of stimulant medications includes the following:

1. About 70 percent of medicated children show increased attention and reduced impulsivity and activity level (Gadow & Pomeroy, 1991; Murphy, Greenstein, & Pelham, 1993). Additionally, research suggests that stimulant medications reduce children's aggressive, noncompliant, and oppositional behaviors (Swanson, McBurnett, Christian, & Wigal, 1995).

2. Among adolescents, stimulants have been shown to reduce inattention, impulsivity, and noncompliance and to improve cognitive functioning; however, further research is needed before making conclusive statements about these effects (Campbell & Cueva, 1995).

3. There are some children with whom stimulants are not effective; children under age four may benefit the least and suffer more adverse side effects from these medications (Barkley, 1990).

4. A review of the literature on the effects of stimulant medications suggests that they are effective (Swanson, McBurnett, Christian, & Wigal, 1995). There is no conclusive evidence that the overall benefits of medications are long lasting (Hinshaw & Erhardt, 1993).

Yes, there are indeed possible adverse side effects of taking stimulant medications. Some of these side effects are biological in nature. Most common among these are insomnia and narexia. Other biological side effects that also sometimes occur are stomach pain, headaches, irritability, rashes, and involuntary muscle movement (Barkley, 1990; Biederman, 1991; Gadow & Pomeroy, 1991). Biological side effects diminish in two or three weeks or after a reduction of the dosage. Given that such effects do occur, it is important for parents to closely monitor their child's physical health for any possible impact on it of the medications.

There have also been reports of growth suppression while taking stimulant medications, but that growth rebounds when the drug is stopped. Furthermore, this side effect can be minimized by not administering the medication to the child during weekends and vacations (Wicks-Nelson & Israel, 1997).

Two other important potential consequences of taking stimulant medications and most other medications are worries about becoming physically and or psychologically addicted to the medication and worry about being stigmatized (e.g., teased by peers) because of its use (Whalen, Henker, & Hinshaw, 1985). When children feel that their behavior is controlled by medications, they may have a lowered sense of competence and self-esteem. However, there is some research that indicates that when medication brings improvement, children may gain feelings of competence and self-control and become better able to realistically appraise their abilities (Milich, 1994). More research is needed before knowing conclusively the psychological impact of taking stimulant medications.

With regard to the physical impact of stimulants, a popular view is that overall they are relatively safe drugs that do cause side effects in some children; thus, their effects should be carefully monitored. Furthermore, because of their side effects, they should not be taken by some children (Wicks-Nelson & Israel, 1997).

It is important to note that two national groups, the Attention Deficit Disorder Association (ADDA) and Children with Attention Deficit Disorder (CHADD), have voiced their criticisms of the use of medications to treat inattention and hyperactivity or the syndrome called attention deficit hyperactivity disorder. Their criticisms and those of others have included that medications are often misused and overused in efforts to provide a quick and easy solution to the problems of inattention and hyperactivity.

Your decision and the decision by any parents to give their child stimulant medications should be done carefully and only after (1) reading about the effectiveness and side effects of these medications for themselves and (2) getting at least two opinions of respected and well-known medical professionals with expertise in treating children and adolescents with inattention and hyperactive behavior problems. Furthermore, it should be realized that the best treatment for most children who evidence hyperactivity or inattention includes individualized educational programs and interventions to facilitate their self-management and social skills. Simply giving these children medications alone will not maximize their likelihood for social and academic success.

Question.   My eight-year old son has been diagnosed as having ADHD. Are children who are diagnosed with ADHD bound for crime or maladjustment as an adult?

Answer.   First of all, not all children who are given the label ADHD are accurately diagnosed. Often African American children and other nonmajority children are given the diagnosis of ADHD without consideration of the cultural and socioeconomic factors in their behavior. For example, being active and beating hands on the desk while in a classroom setting are often considered by the members of the majority culture as signs of ADHD; however, to members of some African American cultures these behaviors are not a reflection of any disorder but rather are learned behaviors resulting from growing up with family and friends who learn by actively participating in a task and who enjoy music and movement. ADHD is sometimes in the eye of the beholder; in other words, the diagnosis ADHD is dependent on the observer and what the observer's culture considers the norm regarding children's behavior in a classroom setting.

It is definitely not true that just because your child or any child is labeled ADHD and really has this disorder, that the child is bound for crime or maladjustment in adulthood. In fact, most children who have been diagnosed as having ADHD grow up to be reasonably well adjusted in adulthood (Campbell, 1995). It is not known how to predict whether a child will or will not be maladjusted as an adult. Many factors such as family functioning, social status, adversity, the severity of the ADHD, and the level of existence of other behavior problems in addition to ADHD influence the future adjustment of a child with ADHD (Campbell, 1995). Whether or not the child received effective interventions to facilitate her or his adaptive skills and academic skills when this problem was first diagnosed is an especially important determinant of the child's future, for it is these skills that are important for the future success of any child.

General Self-Esteem

Question.   My sixteen-year-old daughter has extremely low self-esteem. I just don't understand it. She is smart, makes good grades, is sweet, and has a family that deeply loves her. Her brother teases her about her thick glasses, but she knows that he is just kidding her. What possibly could be causing her not to feel good about herself and what can we do about it?

Answer.   Perhaps the most important thing to realize about self-esteem is that it is influenced directly by how the child sees herself or himself and the degree to which the child has the qualities that the child highly values. The fact that your daughter has the positive qualities that you listed does not mean that she sees she has those qualities; furthermore, even if your daughter does see those qualities that you see, she may not highly value them. For example, she may see herself as smart, caring, and giving. However, she may highly value being beautiful, assertive, and popular. Furthermore, she may not feel the love that your family feels for her. In fact, she may seldom be actually told by family members that she is loved and why she is loved.

Understanding why someone has low self-esteem is difficult given that there are many possible causes of this problem. African American youth may develop low self-esteem because of physical appearance, living in a family structure that does not have two parents in the home, lack of confidence in culturally valued skills (e.g., athletically skilled), and racial victimization (Franklin, 1982; Mayo, 1974). Low self-esteem in African American males and females may also be associated with not having a self-perceived satisfactory level of verbal skills, assertiveness skills, or dressing in style, all of which are important sources of self-esteem to these youth. Males in particular may not feel good about themselves because they are not good athletes and because they are small. In a social context in which most of one's friends play basketball well and are big or tall, it is easy to understand that a male who is not good at basketball and who is physically small may not feel good about himself.

Females in particular may not feel good about themselves because they think they are too fat, have hair that is too curly or nappy, are too tall, or in other ways do not meet the majority culture's established standards of beauty. When these African American girls do not get dates or are overlooked for dates by African American males who choose to date European American girls, the overlooked African American females interpret this as evidence of their unattractiveness, which in turn often lowers their self-esteem. When they are also playfully teased by their siblings about this perceived rejection or about such things as wearing thick glasses, the self-esteem problem is often exacerbated.

Often parents cannot believe that their child's self-esteem could be impacted by experiences so insignificant as not getting a desired date, not having stylish clothes to wear, or being jokingly teased by her or his brother. Yet, among many African American youth, self-esteem is fragile because of not having broad-based support to nurture its development and not knowing how to nurture their own self-esteem. Indeed, African Americans in general and African American youth in particular live in a society where they are often perceived negatively or degraded. Jones (1991) reported, based on research, that African Americans and Hispanics are typically described in less favorable terms than European Americans.

Several strategies that can be used to facilitate the positive self-esteem of your sixteen-year-old daughter include the following:

1. As parents, you can talk with your children, not just your daughter, to find out what would make them feel the happiest possible about themselves and what they would change about their family life and school life if they could bring about these changes simply with a wish. This can be presented and conducted as a family fun activity. This approach will keep your sixteen-year-old daughter from feeling like the problem child and will likely make it easier for her to share what she wants and needs to feel better about herself.

2. You can daily tell your daughter what you like about her physically and what you like about her personality and behavior. This requires thinking ahead and listing these qualities. Most if not all parents love their children; however, many parents do not know what they like about each of them. Furthermore, whatever parents know that they do like about each of their children is seldom actually told to each of them. Children need to hear what their parents like, respect, and admire about them. Simply saying "I love you" to most children is treasured; however, hearing it does not educate them about their strengths—a lesson that children need to learn on a daily basis to help build and sustain their self-esteem. Additionally, you can encourage your children to praise themselves for their achievements, skills, and talents.

3. Your daughter needs to become involved in activities that facilitate her self-esteem— activities that she enjoys and that she does well. She should also be involved in a program or youth group in which experiences to build self-confidence will occur. Involving your daughter with successful female mentors similar to herself is also recommended (e.g., high school girls and first-year African American college students who are honor students, success oriented, and from backgrounds similar to that of your daughter's background).

4. You can save money to get your daughter contact lenses or some different glasses that might make her feel better about her physical self, if she is self-conscious about her glasses.

5. You can make sure that family teasing about physical features is discontinued. This can be facilitated by establishing a family rule that bans teasing and by specifying and implementing consequences for breaking this rule. African American children and adolescents get enough teasing, degradation, and embarrassment from outside of the family to challenge the strongest inner feelings of self-esteem and African American pride; thus, they should not have to deal with these negative experiences at home.

Question.   My twelve-year old son does nothing but spend money on clothes and his hair and hang out with his friends. He feels great about himself even though he has been suspended from school several times for clowning in class and skipping class. What can I do?

Answer.   There are many African American children and adolescents who "act out" and feel good about themselves. Our research suggests that for some African American males, the higher their maladaptive behaviors, the higher their self-esteem (Gaskin-Butler & Tucker, 1995). This finding suggests that there are likely some positive consequences from acting out and these consequences make one feel good about oneself. To change the association between feeling good about oneself and acting out, two things need to occur: (1) Feeling good about oneself needs to become associated with some positive behaviors, consequences, and experiences, and (2) the association between feeling good about oneself and acting out needs to be broken or severed.

In the case of your twelve-year-old son, feeling good about himself is likely associated with looking good, getting positive feedback from his friends about how he looks, and being viewed by his friends as having money with which comes power and status, both of which facilitate self-esteem. One goal needs to be to create an association between feeling good about himself and behaviors such as doing chores, earning an allowance, saving money in his own checking account, attending class every day each week, being on-task in class, studying one and a half hours each evening, learning computer skills, making good grades, following instructions, following rules like being home by his curfew, and engaging in success behaviors (e.g., listening while others are talking, calmly expressing his negative feelings). To reach this goal, you must set clear rules and identify specific behaviors that you require of your son and establish consequences for breaking these rules and not doing the required behaviors. Additionally, it is important to help your son understand how following the rules and engaging in the required behaviors will help him in the future. When the behaviors occur and the rules are followed, strongly praise your son and ask and encourage him to praise himself.

The second goal needs to be to decrease the amount of time that your son spends hanging out with his friends and impressing them with his clothes and good looks. This can be done by keeping your son busy and reducing the money that he has available for clothes that impress his friends. Specifically, you can (1) involve him in an after-school program that provides tutoring and develops leadership skills and other skills for job or career success, (2) encourage him, or require him if necessary, to place at least half of the money that you are giving him in his savings account for college or other postsecondary education training program; (3) help him find a part-time job in an area related to his career interest; and (4) involve him in activities such as karate training in which he will meet new friends who do not waste a lot of time just hanging out.

Finally, it is important to avoid criticizing your son for his inappropriate behaviors like missing class. Instead, specify your rule regarding attending class and the consequence (e.g., withdrawal of a privilege) for not following this rule. Follow through with the consequence in a matter-of-fact way when the rule is broken. Following through should be done without yelling at your son and without upsetting yourself in the process.

Anxiety

Question.   My daughter, who is ten years old, is a very anxious child. She is anxious around new children, when talking with relatives whom she does not see very often, when learning a new game, when she is called on in class by her teachers, and when my husband and I or anyone tells her something she has done wrong. When reprimanded at school, she has actually cried for a long time and vomited. What causes my daughter to be this way and what can be done to help her stop being so anxious?

Answer.   It sounds as though your daughter may be exhibiting general anxiety behavior or overanxiety, which is not uncommon among children, especially girls. It is, however, more common among adolescents (Clark et al., 1994). This overanxiety often lasts for varying numbers of years, but on average, it lasts approximately four and one-half years (Keller et al., 1992).

Children who manifest overanxious behaviors appear to worry about a wide variety of upcoming situations and events (e.g., having to go to a party, being called on by one of her or his teachers) that they perceive to call attention to their competence. These children are not anxious about any particular situation or object. They are, however, very concerned about being evaluated by others in social, academic, and athletic areas, and seem to need a lot of reassurance in these situations and in general. It is not unusual for the symptoms of their anxiety to include headaches, lumps in the throat, digestive problems, and nausea (Erickson, 1992).

What actually causes overanxious behavior is not really known. It is speculated that it is caused by multiple factors including being raised in a family where punishment and criticism are common and praise and provision of other positive feedback are infrequent (Erickson, 1992). Other factors that may be involved in overanxious behavior are being exposed to highly stressful events (e.g., crime and violence in one's neighborhood) and being exposed to overly anxious adults. As a result of such exposure, children may develop problematic ways of thinking regarding the degree to which they have control over what happens to them. Specifically, they may develop cognitions indicating that they have little control over their experiences and that powerful others have much control over their experiences. Such cognitions can lead to great anxiety (King, Mietz, & Ollendick, 1995).

Additionally, cognitions that result in the perception of many situations as hostile or threatening may result in overanxious behavior.

Given that overanxious behavior is likely associated with cognitions, learning, and stressful environments, interventions to address this problem are typically cognitive-behavioral or behavioral. In other words, efforts are made to help children who evidence overanxiety to change their thinking or what they say to themselves and to learn behaviors and techniques to reduce their anxiety. In view of the likely factors in overanxiety or general anxiety, use of medications to modify this problem is not common.

In response to your question regarding what can be done to help your ten-year-old daughter who is seemingly over anxious to overcome her anxiety problem, consider the following recommendations:

1. Facilitate the development of self-confidence and positive self-esteem in your daughter. This involves looking for her strengths and giving her daily positive feedback about them. It is also important to involve her in activities that are consistent with her strengths and through which she will likely get positive feedback from others. For example, if your daughter sings well, you might encourage her to join a community or church choir.

2. Avoid criticism of your daughter's performance of household, academic, and social tasks. Praise her for her willingness to try to learn and for efforts to try to do any task even though she feels anxious, perhaps has a fear of failing, and is not successful in accomplishing the task.

3. Solicit your daughter's feedback regarding how she feels about the way she is punished when she breaks your rules, and ask what she would propose as an alternative punishment. Negotiate a compromise on the punishment. This process will give her a sense of having some control over aversive things that happen in her life.

4. Avoid both yelling at your daughter and getting frustrated with her because she does not do a task as fast as or as well as you would like her to do it. Your expectations may be based on the performance of your other children, and if your daughter senses this, she will experience anxiety and fear about not measuring up to her siblings. When you feel frustrated with your daughter's behavior, say to yourself, "stop, be calm, I can and will respond positively." Then say something positive to your daughter.

5. Try directly to facilitate your daughter's self-efficacy (i.e., the belief that she can do the work or behaviors involved in meeting a challenge, and that if she does this work or engages in the behaviors, she will be successful in meeting the challenge). One way of doing this is to give her tasks that you know she can handle, allow her to do the tasks without your supervision, and praise her performance and successful completion of the tasks.

6. Encourage your daughter's teachers to join with you in following the preceding specified recommendations. Visit your child's class regularly to see if the teachers are praising and encouraging your daughter, and praise and support the teachers for their efforts to support and encourage your daughter. Write a letter of commendation to your daughter's school principal to acknowledge the special efforts that her teachers make to help your child. Teachers are much more likely to give needed individualized attention to your daughter if you show them, not just tell them, that their efforts are greatly appreciated.

7. Involve your daughter in some type of group anxiety management training that focuses on overcoming public speaking anxiety, test anxiety, and interpersonal anxiety. This type of training is often available through after-school education programs, at community counseling centers, and at health centers, especially those that are associated with universities and junior colleges.

Depression

Question.   Do children really experience depression, and if so, how common is it among African American children? How do you know that your child is depressed?

Answer.   Yes, children do get depressed. Attention to depression is important given that suicide in children is often linked to them being depressed. The major symptom of childhood depression includes a sad or apathetic mood that does not seem to go away or improve. The severity of depression in children is typically mild, although it ranges from mild to moderate to severe (Grasha, 1995).

Children who are depressed also tend to evidence social withdrawal, lowered self-esteem, poor academic performance, and changes in their patterns of eating, sleeping, and waste elimination. Some children tend to have a number of somatic complaints.

Depression is one of the few problems of children about which there is quite a bit of research regarding its occurrence, including its occurrence among African American children. However, one must view the results of this research with caution given that culture really influences the manifestation and discussion of depression. Many African Americans never speak of being depressed; rather, they express this emotion by saying "I feel really down." Thus, the occurrence of depression among African American children may be underestimated in existing research studies. In any case, existing studies using school and community participants indicate that the rates of mild to moderate depression in children and adolescents have ranged from 20 percent to 40 percent, whereas rates of severe depression have ranged from 5 percent to 15 percent. Additionally, higher rates of depression seem to be found among African American males and among low-income African American adolescents in these studies (Kaplan, Landa, Weinhold, & Shenker, 1984; Gibbs, 1986; Schoenbach et al., 1983).

If you think that your child is depressed, have your child seen by a culturally sensitive psychologist or counselor without delay. Make sure that this professional talks with your child, you and your partner or spouse, and your child's teacher as part of the professional's evaluation of your child. If the psychologist or counselor administers the Child Depression Inventory (CDI; Kovacs, 1992) to your child, do not consider the results of it as absolutely conclusive because it is just one piece of information that alone is not culturally sensitive. Results of the CDI or any other instrument need to be considered along with the data obtained from the child, the parents, and the child's teacher to determine if the child is depressed, the factors in the depression, and what might be helpful in overcoming it. This comprehensive evaluation approach is indicated given that depression is often associated with suicidal behavior.

Question.   My family physician is convinced that my son is depressed and has recommended that he be seen by a psychologist. What causes depression in children and what can be done to treat this problem?

Answer.   There appear to be several possible causes of depression in children, and these causes are similar to the possible causes of depression in adults. These possible causes are as follows:

1. Feelings of inadequacy due to not being able to satisfactorily meet daily life challenges.

2. The belief that no matter what one does it does not seem to matter with regard to bringing about desired outcomes. This perspective is what has been called learned helplessness (Seligman, 1991).

3. The inability to view negative events in one's life as temporary and as beyond one's personal control and, thus, as not deserving of self-blame (Peterson & Bossio, 1991).

4. A genetic predisposition to depression (Plomin, Defries, & McClearn, 1990).

5. Experiencing a significant loss in one's life (e.g., loss of a parent through divorce or death) that results in decreased reinforcements, especially among children who do not have the adaptive skills to get alternative reinforcement (Ferster, 1974; Lewinsohn, 1974).

6. Demoralization of a parent and the absence of family warmth and positive family activities following the death of a parent (West, Sandler, Pillow, Baca, & Gersten, 1991).

7. Certain chemicals in the brain (e.g., serotonin and norepinephrine) involved in the transmission of nerve impulses; these neurotransmitters keep our nerves firing in ways that make us feel energetic and alert.

8. Focusing on the negatives about one's self, world, and future (Beck, 1967; 1976).

9. Focusing on negatives rather than positives, setting too high expectations and standards for oneself, and giving oneself too little positive reinforcement and too much punishment and criticism (Rehm, 1977).

10. Living around adults who are depressed, especially a depressed mother because mothers typically assume the primary responsibility for providing praise and emotional support for the child. There are likely age and gender differences in the effects of parental depression on the occurrence of depression in children.

All of the foregoing potential causes of depression in children are also potential causes of depression in African American children. Given that many African American children live in environments that help make them feel that they have little control over the events in their lives and over their future, and given that many African American children experience parental separation, racism, discrimination, and financial struggles, many of these children are vulnerable to depression.

Because many African American children have learned from their families not to readily express their thoughts or their feelings, assessing the cause of depression among these youth is not easy. To facilitate an understanding of the cause of depression in an African American child, a parent and psychologist or counselor must enable the child to share her or his thoughts and feelings by providing the child with warmth and support that builds the child's trust in the parent or psychologist to understand what the child thinks and feels. Parents and counseling professionals need to be aware of this fact and act accordingly when trying to understand the child's depression.

In response to your question regarding what can be done to treat depression in your son, it is perhaps most important that you get the help of a culturally and socioeconomically sensitive psychologist or other mental health professional in addressing your son's suspected depression. Ideally, counseling from this person should include family counseling given that family factors often contribute to or help to sustain a child's depression. Furthermore, a child's family can play a major role in helping a child overcome depression. In addition to this counseling, the following intervention strategies are recommended:

1. Talk with your son about his thoughts and feelings regarding loss of a loved one or whatever is a suspected cause of the depression. This discussion might be facilitated by you as parents sharing your own feelings about the event and asking your son if he has similar feelings or different feelings regarding the event.

2. Remind your son daily about how important he is in your family and tell him specifically the ways that he contributes to your happiness and to the family's happiness and well-being. For example, you might tell him that his effort to do things well encourages you to do the same in your job and that his hugs make you feel really loved and needed, both of which make your lives worth living. You can encourage his teacher similarly to remind your son of the contribution he makes to his class and why his teacher enjoys having your son in her life. Such communications help deter thoughts of suicide and low self-worth.

3. Involve your son in a lot of activities such as Boy Scouts, a mentoring program, or some type of after-school training program that focuses on boosting self-confidence and adaptive skills, especially skills for managing anger. Often anger that one has not expressed underlies depression. Expressing this anger with the help of a mental health professional or the help of parents who let a child know that it is normal to be angry can facilitate overcoming depression.

4. Participate with your son in learning and fun activities. Your participation will help make him feel that he is important enough for you to take time to be with him. If his father is not available to participate in learning and fun activities with your son, find a male adult (i.e., a "big brother") who will frequently participate in these activities with him and with you and him.

5. Play family communication games in which each person shares things that they like about themselves, each other, and having a family. Such games do not identify your son as the problem child who needs special attention; yet, these games will help focus your child on his positive attributes and the positives in his environment.

6. If there is a parent or other person who is significant to your son who is depressed, on drugs, rejecting of him, or does not give him positive attention, encourage that person to seek counseling as that person's behavior may be a major factor in your son's depression. Indeed, children are tremendously impacted by emotional and other problems of those whom they love.

7. Focus your son on his future and remind him daily that he can achieve his goals against many odds. The first step is for him to set short-term goals (e.g., to save money to buy a computer) and long-term goals (e.g., to become a computer programmer). The second step is to participate with your son in identifying and participating in activities that will facilitate achievement of each goal (e.g., visiting a computer display, attending a computer-training seminar, meeting with several professionals who work in a computer-related field).

It is very important to praise your son for his efforts related to achieving his goals and to encourage him to praise himself for these efforts and for taking control of his life and his future. You as parents might also set goals and share your plan and progress toward these goals with your son. He thus will learn by your example.

8. Talk with your son about what he can do when he feels really down or sad. Have him come up with suggestions and then offer additional suggestions. You can include in your suggestions that he pay attention to what he is saying to himself and then say something positive to replace any unhappy self-statements or thoughts. For example, if your son reports thinking that his father does not love him and consequently feeling sad, you might suggest that your son replace this thought immediately with the thought that his father, like many fathers, loves him but does not know how to express or show that love. To help your son share his thoughts with you, it might be helpful to invite him to write what he is feeling and then discuss what he wrote with you.

9. Let your son know that everyone feels sad sometimes. However, avoid saying "I understand just how you feel." No one knows just how someone feels. Say something instead like this: "I am not sure exactly how you are feeling; please help me to understand your thoughts and feelings because I care about you, your happiness, and your sadness."

Use of antidepressants for your son's depression should be considered with great caution. It is important for you to be aware that many counseling professionals are opposed to recommending medications for treating depression in children. Furthermore, prescribing antidepressant medications to children is generally controversial because the effectiveness and safety of these drugs are unclear (Johnston & Fruehling, 1994). Additionally, the long-term effects of antidepressants are not known (Johnston & Fruehling, 1994).

School Dropout and School Refusal

Question.   Our sixteen-year-old son wants to drop out of school. His grades are awful. He wants to be a mechanic and feels that what he is learning in school is not going to help him toward that goal. He also wants to have his own money so that he can buy himself a car, which we cannot afford to give him. What can we do to keep our son from dropping out of school?

Answer.   Perhaps the major focus should be on how to help your son achieve his goal of becoming a mechanic. However, before discussing what can be done to achieve that goal, there are two important points that need to be made. One point is that a major positive in this problem situation is that your son has an ambition; he has a goal that he wants to achieve. A second point is that you should not be concerned or feel badly in any way that you cannot afford to buy your son a car. If you gave him a car at this point in his life, he would be even more unlikely to stay in school or get the training that he needs for a job to take care of himself and a family in the future. Indeed, if your son was given a car, he would likely give driving and maintaining it greater priority than studying and preparing for his future.

To keep your son in high school if he is failing may not be possible; however, the likelihood of his staying in school can be increased by having his teachers and his school come up with ways to include mechanics-related training in his education. Incorporation of this training in your son's education can occur by (1) having him spend part of his school day with a mechanics mentor, (2) arranging for him to have independent study courses in the mechanics area (i.e., courses in mechanics in which reading assignments are given and then discussed one-to-one with the student), (3) arranging for him to work as an apprentice under a licensed mechanic once a week, and (4) involving him in a school-based organization or group that is consistent with a hobby or talent (e.g., participation in the drama club). The rationale for the latter suggestion is to increase your son's sense of belonging or connectedness to the school and to build an association between school and having fun, which may help increase your son's interest in staying in school.

It is also important for your son to see the connection between his courses in school and reaching his goal. You, your son's teacher, and two or three mechanics in the real world can all share with your son the knowledge and skills necessary to be a successful mechanic (e.g., computer skills, as many cars now have computerized electrical and other operating systems).

It is also important for you to talk with your son and visit your son's school and teachers to get an understanding of the real problems in his desire not to complete school. These problems may include that your son is not understanding the schoolwork and, thus, does not even pay attention. Such information helps to formulate ideas as to ways to keep him in school. A show of interest in your son by his teachers will certainly be important in keeping him in school.

Another option for keeping your son in school is to allow him to drop out of high school but enroll in some type of vocational training school that includes training in becoming a mechanic and that will assist your son in getting a general equivalency diploma (GED). The vocational rehabilitation program in your state can assist with getting your son into such a training school or program.

Question.   Our five-year-old daughter absolutely refuses to go to kindergarten. She cries and screams when I attempt to get her dressed for kindergarten and then does the same when we get there. Because I hate to see her so upset, the three times that I have carried her to kindergarten I have brought her back home without even going into the kindergarten class. What is causing my daughter to have this fear of kindergarten and how can I get her to overcome this fear and attend kindergarten like other children her age?

Answer.   School refusal is generally considered a symptom of separation anxiety or fear of separating from the mother, the home, or some significant other person in the home; however, this attachment link has not yet been supported by research (Hirschfeld et al., 1992). In fact no causes of school refusal have been evidenced by research. It does seem that, at least in some cases, a child learns the refusal or avoidance response because of some association of school with an existing fear of losing the mother.

Once a child has engaged in this refusal or avoidance response and has been successful in not going to school, the child usually will repeat it. Regardless of what originally caused the refusal response, the repeating of this response is likely reinforced by the attention that it brings from parents and by the positives experienced in being at home versus being at kindergarten (e.g., getting to play with favorite toys and watching television).

With your daughter, as with any child, it is advisable to question her calmly about why she likes to stay at home rather than go to school. This discussion should not occur at a time when you have just tried to get the child to school. The reasons that your daughter gives for liking to stay at home will give some indications about why she does not want to go to school.

Even though we know little about the cause(s) of school refusal, rapid and successful treatment of it has been reported in the research literature (Kennedy, 1965) and in reports of psychologists and counselors who have treated this problem. Generally such successful treatment involves taking the child to school, leaving the child there, and praising school attendance even though it was forced. Following are some specific intervention strategies for your consideration that might be helpful in getting your child to accept attending kindergarten.

1. You should consider whether you are not being more insistent on your daughter staying at kindergarten because you enjoy having her around the house or because of your own anxiety about her being at a place (kindergarten) that is unfamiliar to you and where you cannot keep a protective eye on your daughter. You may be unintentionally showing your anxiety to your daughter and your desire for her to be home; thus, you may be contributing to her refusal to go to school.

2. You should attend kindergarten with your child as a visitor. This will desensitize both of you to this setting and may build your confidence that she will be happy there and have the experience of meeting new friends and doing fun things.

3. It is important to attempt to create excitement in your daughter about going to kindergarten and the fun things that happen there. It should also be made clear that staying at home will not result in her watching all of her favorite television programs all day as may currently be the case. In other words, reduce the positives of being at home.

4. Take your daughter to school with a happy, positive attitude and leave her there no matter how much she cries. Praise her for attending kindergarten when you pick her up to go home. If she complains of a headache or presents other physical complaints when you pick her up, take her to the pediatrician or address these complaints in the way that you have in the past. After school, have the school counselor or another counseling professional teach her through stories about how fears are normal and temporary and about the importance of facing her fears each day. If counseling cannot be arranged, then you can do this teaching. Books and videos to help children deal with fears can be gotten from your local library. Ask your local librarian to help you find these materials.

5. Encourage your daughter to praise herself each day during the day and at the end of the day for attending kindergarten. You should also praise yourself for having the strength and courage to leave your daughter at kindergarten against her wishes.

Behavior Management and Discipline

Question.   Isn't giving children rewards and gifts simply paying them to do what they should be doing? I believe that children should behave appropriately because it is the right thing to do rather than just to get a reward.

Answer.   Indeed, a lot of parents, especially African American parents, do not like giving their children money, candy, or any other tangible rewards or reinforcers to encourage appropriate behaviors. Often reinforcers are needed to encourage appropriate behaviors because other alternatives such as punishment, withdrawal of privileges, and yelling at the child are not effective.

Attention and praise are powerful reinforcers that can be used to encourage children to engage in appropriate behaviors and to do chores or participate in other activities in which their parents want them to participate. For most parents, these nontangible reinforcers are not pay; instead, they are expressions of appreciation that can be given to children for work well done or for engaging in appropriate behaviors. Giving such reinforcers also helps the child realize that you recognize and value that the child succeeded in doing something that was a challenge or simply was worthwhile.

Sometimes tangible rewards such as candy, a trip to Disney World, or other tangible rewards are needed for a few weeks just to establish a behavior that you think is important for the child to learn but which the child is not choosing to learn. Overuse of any given reward can cause it to lose its effect (Grasha, 1995). Tangible rewards should be paired with (i.e., presented at the same time as) social reinforcers such as attention and praise. Gradually the tangible rewards should be withdrawn and only the social reinforcers (nontangible rewards) should be used.

Children should not be given tangible rewards for doing appropriate behaviors that they are already doing without these rewards. Such rewards can cause loss of interest in doing the behavior just because it is right, appropriate, or interesting. If it becomes clear that a child is doing something just to get a reward and the behavior will not be sustained just from praise and attention, then the tangible reward should be discontinued and a new motivational approach should be used. For example, one might point out the positive consequences to the child and to others of doing the behavior.

Regardless of what motivator is used, it is also important for the child's parents or other primary caregivers to model the behavior desired of the child and participate with the child in doing the behavior. For example, if a parent wants her or his child to study after dinner, the parent should help the child study (e.g., help organize the study site and ask questions about the material studied) or read the newspaper or a book rather than watch television or engage in some other activity that will be distracting to the child.

It is also important to encourage children to praise themselves for engaging in appropriate behaviors and accomplishing a task. Self-praise for doing a behavior has a greater probability of sustaining that behavior in the absence of adults being present or in the presence of individuals who do not care about the behavior of African American children as long as they are not disruptive. Given that many African American children do not get much praise and encouragement in their classrooms, these children must learn to praise and encourage themselves for positive behaviors that will empower them for academic and social success.

Obesity

Question.   My eleven-year-old son is fat and, consequently, he just sits at home, watches television, and eats. Obesity runs in our family; both his father and I are overweight. What can I do to help my son lose weight? He says he really wants to lose weight but he does not make the effort to do so.

Response. As you know, your son is facing an increasingly common problem—obesity in childhood. Facilitating weight loss by your son starts with increasing his motivation to lose weight. This can be done by jointly discussing some of the positives of losing weight rather than using scare or humiliation tactics. It is also important that family members do not tease or harass your son about his weight or what he eats; such actions sabotage motivation to lose weight and any progress toward weight loss.

It is also important to address those problems that are associated with obesity. Often these problems include low self-esteem, depression, feeling unloved by significant family members, and not knowing how to make new friends who will not be rejecting. Counseling via a support group for children with weight problems or children with other emotional problems is usually highly recommended. Additionally, you and other family members can look for and praise your son's positives in the area of physical looks and humanistic qualities. Perhaps even more importantly, you can encourage your son to identify his own positives and praise them every day.

You mentioned that obesity runs in your family. Indeed, genetics can play an important role in the size and shape of our bodies. These characteristics and each individual's rate of metabolism all play some role in one's weight gain; however, they do not usually determine whether or not one becomes obese. What one eats, when one eats, the amount one eats, and the amount of exercise that one gets all help influence whether one becomes obese. These are factors over which your son has much control.

Going on a strict diet, which is what most children, adolescents, and adults try to do to lose weight quickly, is usually ineffective over time. First of all, for most individuals losing weight does not happen immediately but is a long-term project. Second, a strict diet slows down the body's metabolism or the amount of energy it expends in a resting state while maintaining basic biological functions such as digestion and breathing. The slower the metabolism, the fewer calories the body needs and the less food you can eat without gaining weight.

Rather than going on a strict diet to lose weight, a much better strategy is to take actions that do not adversely affect your metabolism (Miller, 1983). These actions include the following: (1) Have your son limit his weight gain goal to between one to one and one-half pounds per week, (2) encourage your son to get regular exercise doing something that he enjoys (e.g., playing basketball, riding his bicycle, walking, or some combination of activities), and (3) help your son eat well-balanced meals and encourage him not to skip meals.

Exercise provides a metabolic boost during and after exercising so that more calories are burned than is typical without exercising. Additionally, exercise leads to a loss in weight due to reductions in body fat and this weight loss will likely be much more than would occur from dieting.

Nutritious meals are important for overall general health. These meals should be low in fat and sodium, both of which make losing weight difficult. They should ideally include fresh fruits, vegetables, whole-grain breads and cereals, and meats that are low in fat. High-calorie processed foods and high-fat foods from fast-food restaurants should be avoided or seldomly included in a healthy eating program.

If getting nutritious meals is difficult for your son, it is important that he takes a children's multiple vitamin every day. Not skipping meals keeps metabolic rate high; thus, it is important that your son not skip meals in an effort to lose weight.

Some other suggestions for helping your son to lose weight include the following:

1. Make sure that your son has a physical checkup to rule out a physical factor in his obesity such as a malfunctioning thyroid gland.

2. Let your son know that you can be his coach in the weight loss process, but he will have do the weight loss behaviors. Inform him that you have confidence that he will take control over his eating and activity behaviors for good health whether or not he loses weight.

3. Participate with your son in learning about low-fat and low-sodium foods and about well-balanced meals. Additionally, participate with him in establishing an exercising plan for himself. You can establish a similar weight loss or physical fitness program for yourself. The weight loss program needs to be a family affair in order for it to be nonaversive for your son. If any family member sits around eating potato chips high in fat and sodium that is one of your son's favorite snacks, he will feel frustrated and deprived if he does not share this snack with the family member. Such experiences sabotage a healthy eating plan for weight loss. If the entire family participates in healthy eating, then such sabotaging experiences on a regular basis will be avoided. In addition, this family involvement will make the child feel supported and will help the other members of your family lose weight that they may need to lose or help them prevent obesity in the future.

4. Determine how many calories that your son and other family members are eating each day. Then encourage them to reduce their caloric intake by 200 to 300 calories below the number of calories needed to maintain their current weight. This information can be obtained from a book on nutritious eating, from a consultation with a nutritionist, and possibly from your family physician.

5. Have your son join a weight reduction support group for children or for families that he helps select. Such groups are often run at hospitals or community health or mental health centers. Minimally, these places can help you identify available weight reduction support groups that are in your community for children or families.

6. Talk to your son and other family members about the family being on a healthy eating program rather than a diet. Avoid the word *diet* and avoid weighing your son every day. This often leads to discouragement regarding losing weight when one does not lose as much weight as expected over a two-day or three-day period. Weighing once or twice a month is often sufficient.

7. Talk with your son about the importance of actively seeking new friends using criteria that he identifies for friendship rather than allowing peers to accept or reject him as a friend. It is important for you to discuss this criteria with your son and then role-play with him how to introduce himself to a new potential friend and how to hold a conversation with someone whom you want to get to know.

8. Give your son a lot of praise for his weight reduction activities and efforts; most importantly, encourage him daily to praise and feel good about himself for these efforts.

Negative Parent–Child Interactions

Question.   Often I just lose it and hit my nine-year-old daughter before I know it when she disobeys me. If I feel stressed a lot, her disrespectful behavior is the last straw. What do you recommend that I do?

Answer.   Regarding your daughter's disrespectful behavior, there are several recommendations for your consideration.

1. Make rules for her behavior in relation to you and others (e.g., teachers) and establish consequences for breaking any of the rules—consequences such as loss of telephone use for two days or an added chore.

2. Review and discuss with your daughter the rules for her behavior and the consequences for breaking these rules. Listen to your daughter's feedback about the rules, be open to compromise if you deem compromise is reasonable, and then enforce the rules and consequences.

3. Tell your daughter about alternative behaviors that are acceptable when she does not want to do something that you tell her to do. For example, tell her to do the behavior first, and later make a request to tell you why she did not want to do the behavior.

4. Praise your daughter when she immediately complies with your request.

5. Discuss with your daughter how she would like you to give your requests and instructions differently so as to make her feel better about hearing requests and instructions from you.

6. Discuss with your daughter and other family members how your stress impacts each family member, and what each family member can do to help reduce your stress and the stress that other family members feel.

7. Tell your daughter that you are sorry about hitting her, if you are; additionally, tell her why you are sorry, if you are. Reactive hitting due to stress and anger is not appropriate and is not something that you want to teach your daughter through your example.

Regarding your stress that leads to hitting your daughter, it is clear that you must reduce the stressors in your life and learn to manage stress more effectively when it occurs. Additionally, the stress in the family associated with your stress and any other stress must also be reduced or managed effectively. Ideally, family counseling should occur to address not only stress management but also the anger, resentment, and hurt feelings that have contributed to or are the result of the stress of one, two, or all family members.

In addition to the negative impact of stress on parent–child relationships, there are other negative consequences of stress that should influence you to get family counseling or to at least learn stress management strategies. Physiological consequences of stress include increases in blood pressure and heart and respiration rate; the release of adrenalin; increases in muscle tension; lowering of digestive functioning needed to enable blood to be diverted to the heart, lungs, and muscles; and reduced mobilization of the immune system to destroy bacteria and viruses (Selye, 1976). Stress also can cause one to overreact to behaviors of others and events, to be easily irritated, and to be defensive in response to any questions or comments about one's performance.

There are several stress management strategies that you and your family members can use, which are as follows:

1. You can change the negative statements that you say to yourself or negative thoughts in response to a negative or stressful incident. To illustrate this, imagine your daughter saying the following to you when you ask her to wash the dishes stacked in the kitchen sink: "Hell will freeze over before I wash the dishes; let your angel son wash them since he messed them up." Now imagine saying to yourself in response the following: "I can't believe she said that to me. For being so nasty to me, I could kill her." Having said this, now say to yourself the following more positive and constructive statement about your daughter's statement to you: "She must be feeling really unloved and feeling that I love her less than my son. We need to talk about this a little later tonight when she and I are more calm." This strategy is often called cognitive restructuring.

2. Use effective time management, which involves setting priorities, scheduling time to do these priorities, and including in priorities some activities for happiness.

3. You can use the following quick relaxers (Grasha, 1995): (a) Lie down or sit in a chair, tense all muscles and relax them while engaging in slow-rhythmic breathing, (b) while relaxing, imagine a pleasant scene in your mind and then place yourself in the scene and experience the pleasure of being there (i.e., guided imagery), and (c) whenever you feel yourself becoming tense in the future, immediately stop what you are doing and thinking, take a deep breath, tell yourself to relax, and then concentrate on something in the room (e.g., a chair) for two to three minutes.

4. Talk with friends or family members who are very close to you about your stress and ways of reducing your stress. Such family and social support is often psychologically helpful and may result in other needed help such as financial support or just a place to be away from your present stressful environment.

5. Integrate more physical exercise into your life. Indeed, when physical endurance increases, we become fatigued less easily and have more mental and physical energy to deal with the demands of life (Smith, 1993).

6. Stop at a safe and quiet place on your way from work for at least fifteen minutes just to relax. You can just experience the peacefulness or think about something positive.

7. Establish an agreement with your family that no one is to talk with you for the first thirty minutes after you arrive home so that you can have a work-to-home transition period for your health. You might choose to meditate during this time.

Question. When I was a child and an adolescent, my mother and father whipped me with a belt when I misbehaved, and today I am grateful that they did, because it kept me from getting into trouble. I now whip my children when they misbehave. However, the last time I whipped my ten-year-old daughter, she threatened to call the department of children and families to report me for physical abuse. Is physical punishment wrong?

Answer. If you are asking whether you have the right to physically punish or whip your child, the answer is yes. However, it is indeed illegal to physically abuse your child; in other words, it is illegal to mishandle and inflict bodily damage such as by seriously bruising or breaking the skin. Indeed, whippings that involve heavy impact licks to the skin can cause bodily damage and could be found by legal authorities to be physical abuse.

Whippings that involve light impact licks to the skin with the intent to teach a child that the child has done something wrong are generally not considered physical abuse. The fact is that whippings can range from light to heavy and painful and the intensity as well as the motive behind the whipping determines whether or not it can be legally called physical punishment. Physical abuse is often an appropriate label if the motive of the whipping is to express rage and anger and to hurt your child as opposed to trying to call attention of the child to a problematic or wrong behavior. Because the line between a whipping and physical abuse can often be thin and unclear and thus puts you or anyone who whips a child at risk for a child abuse charge, you might want to reconsider using whippings as a means of punishing your daughter and other children.

Many parents do use physical punishment with their children. They use this discipline method for the same reason that you do. It is a discipline tradition or a part of your culture and it has often been effective in the past in deterring the reoccurrence of a problem behavior. Whether or not physical punishment is effective, for some children there are associated immediate or long-term side effects of physical punishment that you and other parents may or may not realize. In addition to the buildup of resentment toward their parents, many children learn in the process to hit and inflict pain in response to negative emotions. Yet, most parents whose children end up hitting and fighting do not realize that their children may have learned this behavior as a result of their parents' use of physical punishment in association with feelings of anger, frustration, and disrespect. Children act the way they see significant others act in their lives.

You might want to consider using alternatives to physical punishment such as withdrawing a privilege, adding chores, and using negative consequences that involve making your child think about her behavior (e.g., having to write an essay on why the behavior was wrong). With all types of punishment, it is important to teach your child alternative behaviors to the inappropriate behaviors for which she was punished. It is also important to calmly discuss with your child why her behavior was inappropriate. Additionally, it is important to express before and after the punishment your love for her.

Peer Pressure

Question.   Every time my fifteen-year-old child has gotten into trouble at school or in the community it is because of peer pressure. He can't seem to say no when someone is leading him astray. What can I do to help my child say no to peer pressure?

Answer.   One of the most important things you can do to help your son resist peer pressure that gets him into trouble is to encourage him and show him how to select friends who will not negatively impact his life. Too often parents do not even know their children's friends until their children get in trouble with these friends. It is important for you to get to know your son's friends and to let him know whom you would like for him to make the decision to discontinue having as friends and why you think that they are not desirable friends. Equally as important is for you to support friendships with children whom you feel will have a neutral or positive impact on your child. You can support such friendships by including your son's desirable friends in family activities and by allowing activities (e.g., cookouts) at your home with these friends. It is also important for you to help your child select criteria for his friends to meet and then encourage him to choose friends on the basis of these criteria.

You can also help your son avoid negative peer pressure by involving him in training to strengthen his adaptive skills for social and academic success, especially skills in effectively saying no to a request in the face of peer pressure. Help your son learn that success in life does not just happen, you have to make it happen. You can facilitate your son's success by assisting him in setting short-term and long-term goals and by helping him learn adaptive skills to achieve these goals. Adaptive skills include communication skills, socialization skills, and daily living skills. These skills can be learned through after-school skills training programs, leadership training workshops, involvement in a local boys' club, and youth organizations that focus on development of leadership skills. Indeed, resistance to peer pressure requires being a leader, not a follower.

Saying no to peer pressure can be practiced through role-plays with your son in your home. This simply involves describing a situation involving peer pressure in which your child might be confronted, discussing some appropriate ways of handling the situation, and then acting out the situation and one of the ways discussed for appropriately handling the situation. For example, a situation that you might describe to your son is as follows: You are at a party where everyone seems to be drinking punch that has liquor in it, and your friend, Gerald, insists that you and your girlfriend drink the cups of punch that he has brought to your table. Your girlfriend immediately drinks her punch and joins Gerald in encouraging you to drink your cup of alcohol-based punch.

Some of the ways of handling this situation that you, your son, and other children you have might generate are: (1) Simply say "Thanks, but no thanks," (2) say "I am not drinking tonight, I am driving," and (3) say "I appreciate you getting the drink for me, however, I would prefer having a Coke." If Gerald or the girlfriend insists on your son having the drink in the role-play, then your son should simply continue to repeat his earlier response calmly each time the drink is offered. Your son should give a reason for not drinking as in the second and third examples only if he feels that it will be beneficial to another person present such as his girlfriend, who might feel badly because she did not have the courage to say no to the drink offer.

The first response of simply saying no politely is the best response and the type that should usually be given and repeated if necessary. In this response no reason is given. Giving a reason may weaken the stand that one has taken and allow the opportunity for counterarguments to encourage one to agree to something one does not want to do or should not do (Grasha, 1995). After the role-play, participants can share their feelings in the role that they each played.

Role-plays and discussions about how to respond to specific types of peer pressure situations are very important because they provide your child with ammunition to resist peer pressure. Too often children and adolescents are told to say no to peer pressure without being taught how to say no. Yet, children need this knowledge ammunition because resisting peer pressure is an ongoing battle. Children and parents must treat it as such by working together to prepare for this battle.

Questions and Concerns Raised by Teachers

Parent–Teacher Relations

Question.   Why is it that when I call to talk with an African American parent about her or his child's behavior or grades in my class, the parent is usually not very pleasant, distant, and seemingly resentful that I called? It makes me feel that most African American parents are not concerned about their children's education.

Answer.   Most African American parents want their children to get a good education and be successful in school. The majority of these parents have many stressors in their lives associated with low incomes, the high costs of living, blue-collar jobs, racism, and discrimination. The last thing that they want is to receive a telephone call about a problem with their child's grades or behavior from a teacher who (1) has never called before to say anything positive about their child, (2) does not begin the telephone call with something positive about the child or about having the child as a student, (3) lectures to the parent about what the parent needs to do and has not done, and (4) did not take time to ask whether the time of the call is inconvenient and whether it would be better to schedule another time to talk. Yet, according to many African American parents who have attended parent workshops conducted by the present author, the preceding descriptions of telephone calls from teachers are typical of the telephone calls that they receive from teachers of their children.

The preceding descriptions of telephone calls from teachers offer some insight into the verbal behaviors and attitudes of some African American parents when talking with some teachers who call to give these parents "bad news" about their children. Teachers' responses to these descriptions when they are discussed in teacher training workshops by the author have typically been that the teachers had not thought of calling children's parents to give "good news," and even if they had thought about it, they do not have time to make such calls. Furthermore, teachers have expressed that given the difficulty involved in catching parents at home before leaving school for the day, they are forced to talk with parents at times that may not be convenient for parents. The teachers also reported being glad to reschedule a call, if a parent requested doing so. Additionally, they commented that including positive feedback in telephone calls to parents is a good idea that they will put into practice.

Based on the foregoing information from parent workshops and teacher workshops and from other discussions in workshops by the author on improving parent–teacher relations, there are several implications for how teachers may avoid unsatisfactory and disappointing responses from African American parents in telephone calls to discuss the school performance of these parents' children. These implications follow.

1. A teacher ideally should find something positive to say about each child in her or his classroom and then share this with that child's parents at the beginning of or in advance of a telephone call to them for any reason.

2. A teacher can send a note, a card, or make a call to parents at least twice a year to say something positive about their child. As an alternative the teacher can send a note or a card asking the parents to call the teacher for some positive feedback about their child. The teacher can specify times and days that she or he can be reached and the telephone number to use.

3. Schools need to arrange for classroom assistants or office secretaries to arrange parent–teacher telephone contacts at mutually satisfactory times for parents and teachers.

4. Strategies can be implemented to increase the participation of parents in parent–teacher conferences where face-to-face discussions between parents and teachers can occur and friendly relationships can be established, possibly making future telephone calls by teachers to parents and vice versa more pleasant.

5. Teachers should be compensated and recognized for their extra efforts and for taking time to talk with parents about their children's school performance and for their efforts to make these conversations positive and constructive.

Question.   What can be done to increase the attendance of African American parents to parent–teacher conferences? I just do not understand why they do not attend these conferences.

Answer.   The reasons that African American parents often give for not attending parent–teacher conferences include the following: (1) not having transportation to get to the meetings, (2) having difficulty finding their children's teachers' rooms in situations in which they have to meet with several different teachers, (3) not having a babysitter for their small children, and (4) having some anxiety about talking with teachers who are so different from the parents and who are only going to give them "bad news" about their children. Following are some recommendations for increasing the attendance of African American parents to parent–teacher conferences.

1. Hold parent–teacher conferences at community centers and church education centers that are easily accessible to African American parents and that are familiar types of settings for these parents.

2. If the parent–teacher conferences must occur at a school, then have teachers centrally located on the first floor and arrange for high school students to escort parents to the teachers with whom they are to meet. This escort service would make attending the meetings less anxiety producing and more pleasant for parents who have difficulty reading room numbers and teachers' names. To facilitate a culturally sensitive atmosphere, it is recommended that more than a few of these escorts be African American.

3. Arrange for there to be a supervised room for parents to leave their children while in the parent–teacher conference, as most African American parents cannot afford babysitters. Additionally, provide snacks for these children and their parents. Doing this would help to create a more social and friendly atmosphere for the parent–teacher conference, thus making it more appealing to attend.

4. In conjunction with parent–teacher conferences, hold other brief programs that will be of great interest to African American parents such as a one-hour workshop on "everything you've always wanted to know about how to lose weight." Such a workshop could be fun and could facilitate friendly relations among attending parents and teachers.

5. Each teacher should ideally begin the interaction with a child's parents with getting-to-know-you conversation such as talk about each other's families, original home location, jobs, or hobbies. Then the teacher can give the parents a chance to share their views of how their child is doing in school and to ask questions or share concerns about their child's school behavior and academic performance. Next, the teacher can provide the parent with positive feedback and then any negative feedback about the child. The conversation ideally should end with a plan of action to address any identified concerns regarding the child's behavior. The conversation should also end on an optimistic or positive note. It is important for the parent to walk away from the parent–teacher conference feeling positive about having attended the conference.

6. The teacher should talk about what the parent and the teacher can do together to address social or academic problems of the child. This avoids blaming the parent. Responsibility for the child's problems and efforts to overcome these problems should be shared by the teacher and parent. In other words, a partnership approach should be used when discussing with parents ways to address the social and academic problems of their children.

Peer Relations among Children/Adolescents

Question.   Given all of the negative associations with the word *nigger* and the anger that it elicits in African Americans when they are called niggers, why is it that many of the African American guys at our school call each other nigger? I think that this is bad because it is not a good word to use and because it gives students from other ethnic groups permission to use the word only to be ostracized or physically and verbally abused for doing so.

Answer.   It is indeed true that many African Americans in general, not just African American youth, use the word *nigger* (i.e., the *n* word), but they use it in a culturally defined way that only members of their ethnic group understand and thus have permission to also use. In many African American cultures the *n* word is used affectionately to indicate a common bond and friendship. It is often used when expressing a feeling in a joking way, so that the feeling will not be responded to negatively. It is also sometimes used to threaten someone in an argument; in other words, it is used to indicate one's anger or rage.

Historically, the majority culture has used the term to degrade, humiliate, and label African Americans as subhuman. Thus, when European American youth or others who are not African American use the *n* word, it is assumed that it is used in the way that it was historically used; consequently, it generates anger, hurt, and other negative emotions in most if not all African Americans.

Many African American youth use the *n* word casually, thinking that it will not be misconstrued by their peers who are "cool" and who are far removed from the "ancient" use of the *n* word. These youth have not been victims of the pain and humiliation that in the past came with the label *nigger;* thus, it is easy for them to use the word and give it all kinds of meanings that are consistent with hip conversations.

Most adult African Americans use the *n* word more discretely than African American youth. The adults usually only use it with close friends or family. Most African American adults and most African American youth realize that the word is easily misconstrued by others who do not know them very well and would not understand their nonracist usage of the word. Thus, most African Americans wisely do not use the *n* word.

Efforts are needed by parents and teachers to teach African American students and other students about the historical use of the *n* word and how the label *nigger* has negatively impacted the lives of African Americans. African American students also need to be taught how their use of the word, no matter how they have defined it, will forever have associations that reflect negatively on the intellect and status of African Americans.

Community forums on the use of the *n* word are encouraged. Such forums would call the attention of parents, teachers, students, and community leaders to the history of the word, its contemporary uses, and the problems that its use causes given that all Americans do not speak the same language. Ultimately, parents, teachers, and communities must work in partnership to discourage the use of the *n* word by all Americans.

Classroom Behavior

Question.   What can be done to get African American children and adolescents to follow classroom rules regarding appropriate behavior in the classroom?

Answer.   Many African American children are from family situations that require much less structure than what is required in the classroom setting and encourage children to be active. The result of this cultural influence is that many African American children have some difficulty adjusting to the structure and rules regarding appropriate classroom behavior. Consequently, they often need more individualized instruction and support to successfully make the home-to-school transition than is the case with their peers who have come from families who value structure and have rules similar to those of the school environment.

African American children are capable of learning and following classroom rules. Teachers must approach these children with this knowledge and with the expectation that they will learn and follow classroom rules. Teachers must also assume the responsibility of teaching African American children classroom rules in a culturally sensitive manner, as the following guidelines suggest.

1. Teachers can provide a copy of their classroom rules to the parents of each African American child with the request that the parents or someone designated by the parents do the following: Review the rules with the child regularly, quiz the child regarding his or her knowledge of the rules, and discuss with the child why each rule is important. The reasons generated regarding why the rules are important will likely be culturally sensitive and, thus, have true meaning and significance to the child. The copy of the classroom rules gives the child's parents the opportunity to see what is expected of their child in the classroom and to determine if there are any rules with which they disagree and thus should discuss with the teacher.

2. Teachers can use games in which teams compete to come up with the best reason for each rule; African American children will likely enjoy this more active and fun way of learning about the importance of classroom rules and, thus, be more motivated to follow them.

3. Teachers can praise African American children whenever they see these children following classroom rules, and the teachers can share with these children the positive feelings experienced in response to this compliant behavior.

4. Teachers can ask the parents of the African American children in their classrooms to visit their classrooms to observe and rate how well they feel that their children are following classroom rules. This will motivate parents to discuss these rules with their children at home because these parents will see for themselves where they need to concentrate their energies in encouraging their children to follow all classroom rules. These observation times will also give parents a chance to input to teachers some suggestions for helping their child follow any rules that the child is not following. It might be difficult, for example, for a child who has a bladder control problem to wait to be recognized in order to ask permission before going to the bathroom.

5. Teachers can encourage African American children to self-monitor and self-praise their rule-following behavior. For example, a teacher can give African American children a sheet with the rules clearly stated and can ask the children twice a day (i.e., in the morning and in the afternoon) to rate how well they followed the rules on a scale of 1 to 5. Additionally, the children can be told to praise themselves for high ratings and for improvements in ratings. The teacher can praise the children in accordance with their actual observations of rule-following behaviors. They can also make comments on the children's rating sheets and send them home to their parents.

The advantage of having children self-monitor target behaviors is that it focuses the children on their behaviors and what they should be doing. The self-praise gives them some control in calling attention to what they do well. Both self-monitoring and self-praise promote self-empowerment of African American children, which helps to reduce the powerlessness that they often feel as minorities in majority-controlled schools.

Question.   How can I get African American children to participate in class? They seldom volunteer to answer a question and almost never ask a question.

Answer.   Very often African American children do not participate in class for several reasons including the following: (1) They feel that they will be viewed negatively or laughed at because of their language style, which is often not consistent with the rules of standard English; (2) they do not feel that it is important to participate, and that being quiet and following rules is all that is important to their teachers; (3) they do not want to appear as though they are "acting white," which means trying to show that you have knowledge to impress the teacher and thus get a good grade; (4) they have not had experiences that relate to the topics being discussed and thus feel that they do not have anything to share; and (5) they want to avoid the embarrassment of not knowing the answer to a question and thus avoid being perceived as not smart. Regarding the latter reason, many African American children believe that their teachers and their European American peers assume that they are not smart and thus have low expectations of them. Indeed, children live down to or up to the expectations of significant others in their lives among whom are teachers and their peers.

When you add to the preceding reasons the fact that African American children often are in the minority in their classrooms and, consequently, are very aware of how different they are from their peers and teachers, it is not surprising that they would feel hesitant to participate in class. Furthermore, elementary school classrooms and high school classrooms are often settings in which very little occurs to inform students about African American culture and about the many extremely smart African Americans who have made extraordinary and valuable contributions to our nation in the fields of science, medicine, and so on. Such information helps to extinguish the many negative stereotypes about African Americans and their cultures, provide discussion topics to which African American students can relate, and helps to elevate the expectations and self-confidence of African American students. High self-confidence is usually needed by most people in order to ask questions and share views in settings that are anxiety producing for them.

With an understanding of the nonparticipation of African American children in their classrooms usually comes the patience and motivation to provide these children with the skills, opportunities, and the type of supportive environments necessary for them to participate in classes and thus facilitate their learning. The skills that these children especially need for verbally participating in class are public speaking skills and study skills. The latter skills facilitate the knowledge acquisition that is needed to have something to say in class when class discussions focus on academic information taught by the teacher. Parents should be advised to get tutoring or training to help their children develop public speaking and study skills. Parents should also be advised of places to solicit this skills training (e.g., after-school tutoring programs, their church, family members who are educators, and community organizations such as boys' clubs). Ideally, schools begin as early as first grade teaching students public speaking skills, study skills, and other adaptive skills for academic and social success.

The following example of teaching a child public speaking skills will serve to show how simple and fun teaching such skills can be. This example shows how to use a step-by-step approach to teach public speaking skills to a child whose name is Gerald.

Step 1: Tell Gerald that most children feel a little nervous when they are thinking about or getting ready to talk before a group, especially when they have not done this a lot.

Step 2: Ask Gerald about what he was thinking or saying to himself the last time he remembers his teacher calling on him to talk in front of his class.

Step 3: Teach Gerald to interpret his thoughts or self-talk so that they cause less or no anxiety. (In other words, ask Gerald to reframe his thoughts, which means to give a different meaning to thoughts and feelings such that they are viewed more positively.) For example, Gerald reported feeling his jaws shake and his heartbeat increase, and saying to himself, "Oh man, it ain't no way I am going to go up there; I don't know what to say." Gerald can be taught to instead say the following to himself in response to his shaking jaws and fast-beating heart: "The fact that my jaws are shaking and my heart is beating fast does not mean that I am going to freeze up or do poorly when I go up to the front to talk before the class. Instead, my shaking jaws and fast-beating heart are my body's way of making me alert so that I can do a good job when I speak before the class."

Step 4: Teach Gerald to relax when feeling anxious or nervous by taking three deep breaths, slowly inhaling and exhaling.

Step 5: Teach Gerald about standing straight, projecting his voice, taking his time to think, and focusing on a person or spot in the audience when talking to a group (e.g., his class).

Step 6: Teach Gerald to praise himself for speaking in front of his classmates and for using good posture and good eye contact and projecting his voice while talking.

Children can also be taught mental practice to help them with public speaking. This involves rehearsing to themselves what they want to say, imagining themselves saying it, and imagining themselves feeling good about saying what they wanted to say. Of course, it is also great to have children actually practice speaking at home before a mirror, in front of two or more family members, and at church. Practice facilitates skill development (e.g., use of good eye contact) and public speaking self-confidence.

Teachers must provide culturally sensitive opportunities for African American children in their classrooms to participate in class discussions and activities. One way to do this is to include in their class discussion topics about which African American children are familiar, thus rendering them the "experts" in the classroom. These topics might include discussions of family traditions, the pros and cons of gang membership, their experiences with racism and discrimination and how these experiences have impacted their lives, the places they would like to visit and why, and the causes of school dropout and how to prevent it. When class discussions instead focus on topics such as children's travels to other states and countries, the experience of flying on a plane, their favorite restaurants, and what they can access with the CD-ROM on their computer, most African American children have little to contribute. This is because many if not most African American children have not even been near a plane or a pilot, have not experienced fine dining at a restaurant, do not have home computers, and have not traveled much beyond their home state or even their home county.

Another way of providing opportunities for African American children to participate in class is through having them demonstrate their talents and skills and discussing the history of the development of the talent or skill and the role that it has played in their lives to date. African American children are eager to share with others something that they do well, thus facilitating their self-esteem. Most African American children love to perform before an audience because this is something that is often done in African American families. Given that many African American families do not have money to travel, go bowling, send their children to summer camp, and so on, family members often entertain themselves through performing for each other. Having such experiences in the classroom will help desensitize them to the audience there—their peers and teachers.

Giving African American students opportunities to invite successful African Americans of their choice to class to be interviewed by them in front of the class is also a creative way of both involving these students in class and exploding the stereotypes of African Americans that many European American children have. The children could practice their interviews and, thus, be confident of having a successful experience in front of their classmates. Such experiences encourage future class participation. With some creative thinking and brainstorming with other teachers including African American teachers, many such learning experiences that encourage class participation among African American children in their classrooms can be identified.

Teachers can create supportive environments for African American children to participate in their classes in several ways. One way is by having African American cultures represented in the physical structure of the classroom. For example, pictures of African American leaders in science, medicine, politics, and so on as well as African American art can be included in the classroom in some meaningful way.

Another way of creating a supportive environment is to reduce speech anxiety among the African American students in the classroom. Many African American students have speech anxiety because they pronounce some words and sometimes use sentence structures in ways that are inconsistent with the standard English that is spoken by their European American peers and by other African American students, especially those from middle-class families. The African American students who do not consistently use standard English often fear that they will be laughed at or viewed as not very smart by their peers. Reduction of their speech anxiety can occur by facilitating an understanding of the reasons for different ways of speaking that exist among different cultural groups and by making it clear to students that these differences have nothing to do with intelligence.

It is recommended that an expert on "black English" be invited to classrooms that include African American children to talk about the evolution of speech differences among African Americans and between African Americans and European Americans. It is also recommended that students from the various racial groups have the opportunity to read poems and stories written in "black English" by African American writers. African American storytellers can also be invited to schools to read stories that include some written in nonstandard English. Such experiences help reduce speech anxiety among African American students and criticisms of language differences among all students.

It is indeed important to also teach African American youth standard English so that they can effectively communicate in the language of the majority culture in the United States and with individuals in other countries. While standard English is being taught and encouraged among African American students, any nonstandard English that they use should be not be criticized, rejected, or viewed as problematic in general. Furthermore, it is important to teach African American children that speaking both standard English and nonstandard English are legitimate, but that they need to practice standard English most often because it is associated with making better grades, is required in job interviews, facilitates getting into and being successful in college, and increases the likelihood of life success. Regarding the latter, it is important for African American students to understand that most people who control the great opportunities inside and outside of the United States expect and require those with whom they associate to speak standard English.

When teaching African American students to use standard English, it is important not to interrupt them to correct them while they are speaking; doing so will only generate speech anxiety and discourage them from participating in class discussions. Instead of such interruptions, teachers can give the students individual feedback and individualized exercises to facilitate learning standard English. Teachers can also help African American students experience success in using standard English by having them write about topics of interest to them and then providing them with assistance in modifying the writing to be consistent with standard English. Then students can be given the opportunity to read their modified papers to the class. Doing this will give these students opportunities to participate verbally in class with confidence that their public speaking will not be negatively viewed.

It is especially important to encourage African American children to ask questions in class about what they do not know or understand. Otherwise, they end up graduating from high school with substandard educations that are not conducive to future academic, social, and life success. African American children can be encouraged to ask questions about what they do not know or understand by making this a success behavior that is encouraged and praised in the classroom. Asking such questions should be associated with intelligence by saying that it is smart to ask about what you do not know. African American children should also be encouraged to praise themselves and to feel good all over about speaking up to get the knowledge that they need and want.

Conclusions

It is clear from the questions in this chapter from African American parents and from many European American teachers that these individuals want and need guidance in their efforts to teach, support, and promote success behaviors among African American children and adolescents. It is also clear that these efforts require partnerships in which parents, teachers, community leaders, health providers, and mental health professionals work together and support each other rather than blame each other for the problems of African American youth.

Because the problems of African American children and adolescents do not occur in a vacuum, it is important that significant others in the lives of these youth recognize and accept their contributions to the problems and their roles in addressing the problems. In other words, the behaviors of parents and teachers are not always appropriate and sensitive in their interactions with African American children and adolescents. Thus, parents and teachers often must not only be the facilitators of behavior change in these youth but also often need to change their own behaviors and address their own problems that impact the youth about whom they are concerned. Indeed, parents and teachers are human beings with feelings, stressors, and responsibilities that impact their behavior with African American children.

Parent training workshops, teacher training workshops, and parent–teacher communication workshops are clearly needed to provide teachers and parents with answers to the questions that they have regarding the behaviors of African American youth. Such workshops provide opportunities for relationship building and for the development and exchange of ideas for helping parents and teachers work more effectively together and for finding creative and cost-effective ways of addressing behaviors, attitudes, skill deficits, and cultural differences of African American youth that impede their academic, social, and life success.

Because parenting is not a skill with which one is born, it makes sense that parents often need consultation, training, counseling, support, and normalization of their feelings, mistakes, and questions in the parenting process. Similarly, because teaching is not a skill with which one is born and because all children cannot be taught in the same manner, it makes sense that teachers need help and support in educating the many different children in their classrooms.

The questions and concerns often raised by parents and teachers that are covered in this chapter make it clear that African American children face many challenges in their lives, not the least of which are peer pressure, self-acceptance, and development of adaptive skills (communication, socialization, and daily living skills) for social, academic, and life success. To meet these challenges African American parents must be actively involved in their children's lives. These parents must provide their children with as much learning as possible outside of the classroom as well as participate in their learning in the classroom. Parents must also participate with their children in fun activities to get to know their children's friends. Additionally, parents must engage in the positive behaviors in which they want their children to engage. Indeed, it is not reasonable and is certainly ineffective to tell a child not to smoke while puffing on a cigarette or while smelling like the cigarette that was secretly smoked. Children and adolescents do what they see.

Yet, because African American parents often have the desire but not the means, resources, or strength to do all that is needed to facilitate their children's academic and social success, it is crucial that churches, boys' and girls' clubs, community leaders, and potential mentors reach out to offer assistance in providing needed training, counseling, friendship, and adaptive skills training to African American youth and their families. It is important that these supportive actions include recognition and praise of what these youth and their families are doing well often under the most adverse life circumstances.

8 Prevention of Behavior Problems

Real-World Solutions

A national focus on prevention of behavior problems is essential in order to ensure that most African American children will have a reasonably good chance to achieve social, academic, and life success. Indeed, Americans in general and African Americans in particular realize that the economic, social, and emotional costs of behavior problems to African American children, their families, and their communities are too high. They also realize that the counseling resources and the family, school, and community resources needed to address these problems often are not available even though they are desperately needed. Furthermore, there is the realization that when African American children disrupt classrooms, engage in delinquent behaviors, or drop out of school, all Americans are negatively impacted. Clearly, programs and other methods to prevent behavior problems among African American children and other children as well are in the best interest of all Americans.

There are many in the United States who believe that more programs for African Americans and, thus, programs to prevent behavior problems among African American children are not needed. These people argue that there are more than enough school counselors, psychologists, and social workers available to address any behavior problems among these children. The fact, however, is that traditional counseling is typically not available to African American children and families, especially those with low family incomes. When traditional counseling is available, it is often culturally and socioeconomically insensitive and, thus, ends up being ineffective, abandoned, and avoided in the future (Sue, 1977).

The scarcity of licensed African American psychologists and counselors, the preference for them by many African American families, and the high cost of individual and family counseling further suggest that counseling alone will not successfully prevent behavior problems among African American children. Consequently, it is absolutely necessary to develop and implement multidimensional strategies and programs to prevent the occurrence of behavior problems and facilitate adaptive skills and success behaviors among African American youth. It is also sensible that these strategies and programs be cost-effective, culturally and socioeconomically sensitive, long term, and conducive to self-empowerment of African American children.

Programs and strategies to prevent behavior problems among African American youth can be made cost-effective through the active involvement of volunteers, utilization of churches and community centers as prevention sites, and partnerships such as school-community-education department partnerships in which resources are shared. African American families, community leaders, educators, and psychologists and counselors must play leading roles in these partnerships. Furthermore, these leaders must give of their time and talents and consider them humanistic and economic investments in their own future and the future of our nation. Indeed, from among African American youth must come responsible employees and employers on whom many Americans will depend.

Programs and strategies to prevent behavior problems among African American children can be made to be culturally and socioeconomically sensitive by involving these children and their parents as well as professionals who are culturally and socioeconomically sensitive in the planning and implementation of these programs. These programs and strategies can also be made more sensitive by utilizing community services that are consistent with the realities of the lives of the families that each program is meant to serve. For example, a parenting training workshop series that is culturally and socioeconomically sensitive and that occurs in a low-income, urban African American neighborhood would likely (1) occur on days and times that a survey revealed were convenient for most parents in the neighborhood, (2) be conducted at the neighborhood community center, (3) provide babysitting services at the parenting workshop site, (4) provide a hearty snack, (5) coordinate car pooling for those parents who do not have transportation, (6) encourage very casual attire, (7) involve African Americans and members of the neighborhood in the planning and implementing of the workshop, (8) address topics that were generated by parents in the neighborhood that the workshop serves, (9) include role-plays and other activities that incorporate the real-life parenting issues of the low-income parents in the neighborhood where the workshop is conducted, (10) recruit members from the nearby local church to assist with babysitting services and preparing the snack, (11) be free, and (12) include some fun activities like singing a song or two, and giving away inexpensive prizes to three parents with lucky numbers.

Because the social (e.g., racism), family (e.g., parental separation), environmental (e.g., neighborhood violence), economic (e.g., poverty), and school (e.g., low teacher expectations) variables that place African American children at risk for behavior problems are usually multidimensional, institutionalized, and resistant to change, programs and strategies to prevent behavior problems among African American youth need to be long term and need to focus on self-empowering African American youth and their family for life success despite conditions counterconducive to this success. The programs and strategies need to be long term because the modifiable factors in behavior problems, such as teachers' expectations and culturally insensitive school systems, typically take a long time to modify. Indeed, there is no quick-fix program or strategy for preventing behavior problems. The programs and strategies need to be self-empowering so that African American youth and their parents will gain the motivation, self-control, skills, and behaviors needed to resist negative influences in their lives and to engage in success behaviors and learning experiences that are designed to eradicate behavior problems.

The nature of the factors in behavior problems of African American children suggests that successful implementation of prevention programs and strategies to deter these problems will require the efforts of children themselves, their parents or primary caregivers, teachers, school administrators, and community leaders, as well as psychologists and counselors. This chapter will focus on the roles that of each of these groups can execute to help prevent behavior problems among African American children.

Roles of Children

African American children are seldom if ever asked their views regarding behavior problems among African American children. Yet, these children are perhaps the real experts regarding problems that occur among themselves. Thus, in a recent study the present researcher and her associates (Tucker, Herman, Pedersen, & Vogel, 1997) interviewed mostly low-income, urban African American elementary school children ($n = 24$) and high school children ($n = 19$) to determine their perspectives regarding behavior problems of African American children. Two of the interview questions concerned prevention of behavior problems. These two questions, the responses of the children to them, and the percentage of time each response was given among all responses given follows.

Question
What can African American children do to prevent themselves from acting inappropriately in the classroom or at school in general?

Responses
Elementary School Children
Engage in learning activities and success behaviors (46.7%)
Use self-control and self-respect (17.8%)
Avoid children who get into trouble (6.7%)
Miscellaneous responses (28.8%)

High School Children
Engage in learning activities and success behaviors (40.7%)
Use self-control and self-respect (22.2%)
Avoid children who get into trouble (22.2%)
Miscellaneous responses (14.9%)

Question
What can African American children do to resist the temptation to do the wrong thing wherever they are?

Responses
Elementary School Children
Use self-control (35.7%)
Engage in positive activities and think about your goals (21.4%)
Think about the consequences and whether the behavior is right or wrong (10.7%)
Miscellaneous responses (32.2%)

High School Children
Think about the consequences and whether the behavior is right or wrong (41.7%)
Be in the right places and be with friends who do not get you into trouble (29.1%)
Engage in positive activities and think about your goals (16.7%)
Miscellaneous responses (12.5%)

The preceding interview data from children support the view that self-empowering African American children and adolescents through teaching them self-control, self-motivation, and adaptive skills and behaviors (i.e., success behaviors) is an important strategy for preventing behavior problems among such children. It is interesting to note that the majority of the elementary school children and African American children gave cognitive-oriented recommendations for resisting the temptation to do the wrong thing. It is also interesting to note that these children realize the important influence of peer pressure in their lives and that they must avoid peers who get into trouble. Clearly, children need to be given help in establishing criteria for choosing good friends in order to avoid peer pressure that often gets African American children and adolescents into trouble.

Several of these children interviewed also recognize the importance of self-control for resisting temptations to engage in wrong or inappropriate behavior. This skill is especially important given that African American children, especially those in low-income neighborhoods, are constantly exposed to environmental stressors, social problems, and other conditions that elicit problematic behaviors. These children must be able to use self-talk, problem-solving skills, anger management skills, stress management skills, and other self-management strategies to control their own behavior in the presence of conditions or stimuli that elicit inappropriate behavior.

It is also important to note that many of the children interviewed recognize the need to have goals and to be involved in alternative behaviors to problem behaviors. In other words, these children indicate a need for positive activities in their lives and goals that dictate and encourage positive behaviors and learning activities. Indeed, if African American children were kept busy engaging in appropriate behaviors, they would be less vulnerable to problem behaviors.

Yet, many African American children spend many hours of their day being quiet or controlled in classes so that other children can learn, watching violence on television, or hanging out in the street with nothing to do. Their idle minds often place them at risk for disruptive behaviors, delinquent behaviors, and other problem behaviors that get them some attention and offer challenge in their lives. Indeed, children need attention; often when they cannot get positive attention, they will gladly take negative attention. A national challenge must be to engage African American children in positive, constructive learning activities in school and after school.

After-school activities for African American children can occur at schools in the evening, at the girls' and boys' clubs, and at neighborhood churches and community centers. These activities should ideally focus on (1) development of communication skills (e.g., how to make complete sentences, how to use body language effectively, and negotiation skills); (2) public speaking skills (e.g., how to manage speaking-related anxiety, how to organize a speech, how to project confidence when speaking, and use of standard English); (3) socialization skills (e.g., anger management skills, how to chair a meeting, how to make introductions, proper etiquette, how to order from a menu and calculate gratuity, how to select and keep good friends, how to say no to negative peer pressure, and how to effectively manage interpersonal anxiety); and (4) age-appropriate daily living skills (e.g., how to interview for a job, prepare a résumé, balance a checkbook, set a table, and use a computer).

Involvement of African American children in field trips such as a trip to a bank to open a checking account, dinner at an elegant restaurant, and a visit to a business to experience going through a job interview can facilitate learning adaptive skills (communication skills, socialization skills, and daily living skills), boost self-esteem and self-confidence, and increase verbal participation in class. Field trips also give African American children interesting and positive experiences to share in class. The objectives of these field trips should be to further prepare African American children for jobs in the real world or owning and operating their own businesses, and for academic, social, and life success.

Roles of Parents

One of the major roles of African American parents and other primary caregivers is to teach children values, strategies, and skills that will enable them to resist engaging in problem behaviors and that will facilitate their engagement in behaviors for academic, social, and life success. In other words, the role of these parents in the prevention of behavior problems among their children is to empower them for success. African American children ultimately must prevent themselves from engaging in behavior problems; however, these children must be empowered to do so by parents, teachers, school administrators and other educators, community leaders, and psychologists and counselors.

Parents can empower their children to avoid engaging in behavior problems in several ways including the following:

1. Parents must teach their children beginning by age two to value learning, reading, studying, delay of gratification, and the golden rule—"Do unto others as you would have them do unto you." This teaching must be by example, as children do what they see. Thus, parents must practice the golden rule and engage in learning activities such as participating in community-sponsored workshops and seminars, taking a computer class, reading the newspaper, and reading books. Such parent activities as well as engagement in learning activities by their children require that parents impose a daily study or reading time in the home, include learning activities and materials in their budget, and conduct weekly or biweekly family discussions about the human values that the parents view as important in living positive lives (Gary & Booker, 1992).

2. Parents must assist their children in identifying the behaviors, attitudes, and values that children should look for in peers whom they choose as friends. Parents must also teach their children to choose their friends and not wait to be chosen by peers. Just as importantly, parents must teach or see to it that their children are taught how to initiate and keep a positive friendship. This teaching can ideally be done through role-plays. Such teaching is important given that children are often attracted to gangs and other groups that encourage inappropriate behaviors.

3. It is important for parents and others (teachers, church school teachers, club leaders, and coaches) to use and teach children to use strategies for controlling their behaviors rather than have their behaviors controlled by others. Parents and children must refuse to allow others to control their behavior or "push their buttons" to make them yell, hit, and use vulgar language. Parents and children can use cognitive and behavioral strategies to control their own behaviors.

A useful cognitive strategy is to covertly talk to oneself for the purpose of controlling one's own behavior. For example, one might say the following: "I know that she is just trying to upset me so that I will do something that will get me in trouble or that I will regret doing; however, I am too smart for that. I am going to remain calm and tell her what I feel about what she just said and did. I will not yell and scream. Yes, I feel upset and angry and I will tell her my feelings as soon as I am calm; however, I am going to remain in control of my behavior."

It is important for children and parents to express their angry and upset feelings as soon as they can do so in a calm way. Expression of feelings is important because if these feelings do not get expressed, they often get displaced or expressed toward some innocent object or person. For example, a child may get angry with his teacher, not tell her calmly how he feels, and then later slap a classmate or kick the trash can for seemingly no just reason. In this example, the anger toward the teacher is channeled away from the source that elicited the anger (i.e., the teacher) and toward the innocent classmate or trash can. Yet slapping the classmate and kicking the trash can result in the child being punished and labeled "a behavior problem."

Another cognitive strategy that parents and teachers can use to control their own behavior is to think about the likely negative and positive consequences of an anticipated behavior before doing the behavior. Following this thinking, it is important to decide on actions that have positive consequences and no or minimal negative consequences or risk of negative consequences. For example, if a boy is thinking about pushing a girl down the stairs for calling him dumb, two likely positive consequences of this action are that the boy who is thinking of pushing the girl would feel vindicated and the girl will likely not call him dumb again in his presence. Two likely negative consequences are that the girl would be seriously injured and the boy who did the pushing would be expelled from school and punished by his parents. After comparing the negative consequences with the positive consequences, the boy would likely think of an alternative behavior to pushing the girl down the stairs.

Children should be taught by their parents how to respond to provocations. Children should also be taught to engage in behaviors that will not result in consequences like feeling guilty, getting punished, or getting put out of school, but instead will result in positive feelings about managing their own behavior to stay out of trouble and to stay on track for success.

Parents can also teach their children to think about their goals whenever they feel angry or frustrated and, consequently, want to hit, fight, or otherwise retaliate against the person who elicited the anger or frustration. This requires that children have short-term and long-term goals. A short-term goal, for example, might be to pull up their grades in math and science from C's to A's; a long-term goal might be to be accepted into college at the University of Florida. In addition to helping children set their goals, it is important to teach them that hitting, fighting, and any other such behaviors that might get them in trouble will not help them and may obstruct them for reaching their goals. It is also important to teach children that success behaviors such as walking away from a fight, studying, treating others with respect, and asking questions about what is not understood will facilitate achievement of their goals.

Reframing is another cognitive strategy that parents can use and teach their children for controlling their own behavior. Reframing is simply reinterpreting the meaning of behaviors and statements such that they do not elicit negative emotions and behaviors. For example, in response to being yelled at by the teacher to sit down and listen, a child can be taught to reframe the teacher's behavior by telling himself that the teacher is telling the child how much she cares about his education. Typically, in response to such yelling, a child automatically interprets the teacher's yelling to mean that the teacher does not like the child. The latter interpretation often motivates the child to engage in negative classroom behaviors. Reframing the teacher's behavior will likely elicit positive feelings and behaviors from the child.

Some useful behavioral strategies that parents can use and teach their children to use to control their own behavior include (1) walking away from someone who is engaging in inappropriate behaviors or is trying to entice others to engage in inappropriate behaviors, (2) walking away from a situation that generates feelings of anger or frustration, (3) taking a few deep, slow breaths to calm oneself when feeling angry or frustrated, and (4) associating with individuals who stay on task, are success oriented, and have the positive qualities desired in a friend.

It has been recommended that parents start teaching their children by age three the importance and methods of controlling their behavior, delaying gratification, and constructively expressing their emotions. This early education is indicated given that by age three, the cultural values and beliefs of many African American children are in place, and so is their awareness of race (Spencer, 1982). Given this race awareness, it is especially important for these children to express their feelings about their race, including the negative feelings elicited by subtle and not so subtle negative messages about their race-associated differences.

Parents should strongly praise children for expressing their feelings and using cognitive and behavioral methods that they are taught to control their own behavior. Of course, there will be many times that children will engage in self-control behaviors and in other positive behaviors and will not receive praise or support for doing so; thus, it is important that these children learn to praise and support themselves for resisting negative behaviors and instead doing the right thing. Self-praise is saying things such as, "I am so proud of myself for not cursing her because she cursed me. I feel good all over for doing the right thing. Let me wrap my arms around myself and give myself a big hug. I deserve it."

Parents can also help prevent behavior problems among African American children by specifying rules for their children's behavior at home, at school, and at places outside of home and school. In addition, parents must clearly specify consequences for breaking these rules and follow through in implementing these consequences. Often children engage in problem behaviors such as yelling at their parents when angry because there was no rule saying that parents always will be spoken to calmly, using eye contact with the parent, even when angry.

Rules should be clear, written, and reviewed regularly with the children in the family. The rules should be posted to serve as a reminder to the child that rules exist that are to be followed. Rules for expected appropriate behaviors help to prevent children from engaging in inappropriate behaviors. If a rule states what a child should not do, it should also include what the child should do instead. For example, a rule that states that there will be no smoking of cigarettes anywhere should go on to say that if you get a desire to smoke, discuss that desire with your parents before you actually do it.

Parents can also engage in the prevention of behavior problems by African American children by modeling the appropriate behaviors that they expect of their children. If they expect their children to speak calmly when angry, then the parents must speak calmly when angry. Parents who yell, scream, and hit each other will likely have children who yell, scream, and hit each other and other people.

Parents must immediately get help with marital or family problems that cause family stress and discord because both contribute to the occurrence of behavior problems. This help can come from a psychologist, counselor, minister, or someone else that parents trust and who has the skills and interest in helping. Providing children with a calm, loving, supportive family environment is the foundation for efforts to prevent behavior problems among African American children.

Prevention of behavior problems among African American children can also be facilitated through involving them in activities, organizations, and learning experiences to facilitate development of their adaptive skills (i.e., communication, socialization, and daily living skills). Just as importantly, parents must participate in these activities with their children in order to see their children's strengths and weaknesses and, thus, know firsthand what the children need to be successful in college, in a job, and in life in general. Adaptive skills development in children can be facilitated in many ways including through participation in available after-school tutoring and skills training programs, boys' and girls' clubs, community- and school-sponsored field trips, participation in church youth groups, and participation in karate classes.

Parents can also prevent behavior problems among their children by meeting and entertaining their children's friends, given that negative peer influences are major forces in the promotion of problem behaviors in children. Many children will do almost anything including stealing for peer acceptance and approval. Thus, it is important that parents encourage their children to discontinue friendships with children who engage in problem behaviors. Parents, however, will not know about the behaviors of their children's friends without hosting and otherwise participating in parties and other activities with their children and their children's friends. In other words, parents must know what their children are doing in order to prevent the development of behavior problems among their children.

Another way that parents can help prevent their children from developing behavior problems is to weekly visit their children's schools and interact with their children's teachers. This will allow parents to know firsthand what is going on at school with their children, and it will enable parents to better formulate rules for their children's behavior at school and better facilitate their children's adherence to classroom rules specified by the teacher. Children must see their parents and teachers working in partnership toward the same goals—to facilitate success behaviors and academic learning among the children and to empower these children to be active participants in self-managing their behaviors and their success.

A major role that African American parents can play in the prevention of behavior problems among their children is to lobby their community and state leaders and politicians to provide after-school programs for teaching African American children adaptive skills, leadership skills, and self-management skills for social, academic, and life success. An example of such programs is described in Chapter 12 of this book. The program described in Chapter 12 is a research-based model partnership education program to facilitate academic achievement and adaptive skills and to reduce maladaptive behavior among African American children.

The program is community based and involves parents, teachers, children, community leaders, businesses, university student volunteers, community volunteers, a state department of education, philanthropic foundations, and an African American church, which is the site of the program. Such programs are needed in African American communities because schools either cannot or will not provide African American children with adaptive skills training and self-management skills needed to achieve against the many odds that most of these children face on a daily basis. It is such training that will not only play a major role in preventing behavior problems among African American youth but also will equip or empower them for achieving social, academic, and life success.

Roles of Teachers

Teachers, like parents, play major roles in preventing behavior problems among African American children. These roles include (1) providing a supportive, orderly, disciplined learning environment, (2) engaging the children in diverse learning experiences to deter idle minds, (3) teaching the children success behaviors and adaptive skills, and (4) facilitating appreciation of racial and cultural diversity among all students in their classrooms. Ironically, many teachers feel that their only job is to teach children academics and that they should not have to and are not trained to deal with behavior problems in the teaching process. Given this not uncommon perspective, it is particularly important for teachers to be active in preventing behavior problems among African American children and all other children in their classrooms. The resulting absence or low number of behavior problems will not only promote academic achievement among all students but may also reduce job stress among teachers and facilitate their work-related quality of life.

Providing Supportive Learning Environments

In order for teachers to provide supportive, orderly, and disciplined learning environments toward the goal of preventing behavior problems among African American students, teachers can use several strategies.

1. They can actively try to develop positive teacher–student relationships with the African American students in their classrooms. According to Wentzel (1994), such relationships during the middle school years especially may prevent some of the problematic social behavior and low levels of motivation that are typically displayed by young adolescent students. Teachers can develop positive relationships with African American students by:

   a. Talking with these students during free-time activities about their hopes and aspirations and encouraging them to pursue their hopes and aspirations.
   b. Expressing whatever positive feelings they have about having these students in their classes.
   c. Catching the students doing something well and praising that behavior.
   d. Giving the students important responsibilities in the class that make them feel trusted by the teacher.

e. Asking for and then respecting the students' opinions on topics discussed in class.

f. Punishing the students in ways that do not involve public humiliation.

g. Showing the students affection with a public hug, handshake, touch on the shoulder, warm and sincere voice tones, and smiles of approval and admiration.

h. Giving the students many positive experiences in the classroom, such as the opportunity to show their talents.

2. Teachers can set classroom rules, individually review those rules with African American students, and engage the students in sharing reasons as to the importance of each rule. Teachers must also specify the consequences for breaking the rules. These consequences and the fairness of them should also be discussed with the students. It is crucially important to follow through consistently on the consequences rather than merely threaten to follow through. Following disciplinary actions, it is important for teachers to note and praise appropriate behaviors by the disciplined students and to continue positive relationship-building efforts with the students. In other words, it is important to pair consistent, firm discipline of African American students with consistent shows of support and caring.

3. It is important for teachers to have well-planned teaching days. Such structure deters students from feeling that the class is disorganized and that they can engage in acting-out behaviors. Even though some African American students are culturally influenced to enjoy learning through vervistic experiences, which connote a low tolerance for monotony and a preference for movement, these students must learn to tolerate longer and longer periods of concentrated reading, studying, and listening without off-task or acting-out behaviors (Chimezie, 1988). It is indeed important to be culturally sensitive to the preference for and responsiveness of some African American students to verve, but it is also important to empower them for success, which requires being self-disciplined to doing sometimes boring tasks such as writing an essay or listening to a lecture on subject–verb agreement.

Teachers can make structured activities culturally sensitive by, for example, assigning or allowing students to choose to write essays on culturally relevant topics and by using sentences that relate to African American culture in their demonstration of subject–verb agreement. The bottom line is that teachers must praise and must encourage African American students to self-praise tolerance of passive and active learning without off-task, disruptive behaviors.

Providing Diverse Learning Experiences

Prevention of behavior problems among African American students through providing them with diverse learning experiences can be fun for teachers and students. Diverse learning experiences ideally should include in-class learning and out-of-class learning activities, active learning and passive learning, individualized and group learning, as well as many opportunities for African American students to experience independent teaching and learning. Such diversity facilitates students' excitement about learning and deters attention to off-task behaviors. Furthermore, when a learning activity is boring, it can more likely be tolerated knowing that there will be different types of learning activities to which one can look forward.

Out-of-class learning experiences such as a visit to a hospital to learn about the various activities, jobs, and roles of professionals who work there are particularly important in preventing behavior problems. This is because such experiences are engaging and they help to formulate realistic and exciting goals for African American students, especially those who have not had much exposure to the world beyond their apartment building. Goals in turn facilitate self-motivation to succeed in the classroom, especially when teachers explain the relationship between academic work in the classroom and achievement of one's goals.

Active learning and teaching through role-plays and skits and through presentations by students about their own work and learning experiences are also helpful in preventing behavior problems among African American children. This is because these experiences give these youth positive attention and alleviate the need for negative attention through acting-out or inappropriate behaviors. These experiences also are self-empowering; in other words, they place the children in teaching roles that facilitate self-control over the learning process. Given that many African American youth often feel powerless in typical classes and schools because of their minority status, experiences that empower them and give them positive attention are valued, motivating, and engaging and, thus, help deter problem behaviors.

Teaching Success Behaviors and Adaptive Skills

Teaching students success behaviors and adaptive skills is indeed a major contribution of teachers to the prevention of behavior problems among African American students. Yet, because of the many responsibilities that teachers have (e.g., teaching basic course work, correcting homework, keeping records, and attending teacher meetings), they often simply do not have the amount of time needed to teach and encourage most effectively the development of students' success behaviors and adaptive skills. However, teachers can significantly impact the occurrence of these behaviors and skills even with the very little available time to do so.

Success behaviors include behaviors that contribute to a positive self-presentation and that are typically needed to get and keep a job and to receive and take advantage of opportunities in life. Success behaviors include using good eye contact, studying to be prepared for class, listening when others are talking, using good manners, asking questions about what is not understood, using complete sentences, and following appropriate instructions. Teachers can make and post a list of success behaviors, review and discuss the list with all of their students, review and discuss the list individually with African American students, and then praise the occurrence of these behaviors.

Behaviors such as making complete sentences and listening while others are talking will likely need to be taught by teachers and require patience in the teaching process. Because these behaviors are culturally influenced, they are sometimes difficult to establish. For example, because in many African American cultures spontaneity is valued, it is difficult for some African American children to listen while others are talking or to wait their turn (Chimezie, 1988). Thus, teachers must be patient and supportive in teaching these behaviors. It is important in this teaching process that teachers take the position that there is a time and place for each kind of behavior and that some behaviors that are fine at home are not acceptable at school or in a job setting.

Teaching African American children adaptive skills, which include communication skills (e.g., how to express feelings, make a complete sentence, and write a business letter), socialization skills (e.g., how to resolve conflict, problem solve, initiate a conversation, and interview for a job), and daily living skills (e.g., how to calculate gratuity, write a check, and make an emergency telephone call), is something that most teachers agree is important. Yet, many teachers feel that most of these skills should be taught at home. The problem is that many African American parents feel inadequate in this teaching role and so do many teachers. Furthermore, many teachers feel that it is difficult enough to teach math, reading, science, and other courses without adding adaptive skills. Yet, if teachers do not teach adaptive skills, many African American students and other students likely will not learn them. Learning adaptive skills is important for social, academic, and life success, all three of which are front-line deterrents to behavior problems.

One thing that teachers can do to teach adaptive skills is integrate them into teaching academics. For example, when teaching math, the math assignment could be to calculate the cost of the listed items and then write a check to pay for them. This assignment adds interest to the task and prepares students for something that they will do in real life. Fortunately, there is finally a growing recognition that what is taught in the classroom needs to be directly linked to what students must do in real-world jobs to be successful in life.

Teachers can also help children learn adaptive skills through real-world field trips in which students learn by doing. They can learn about banking, check writing, saving money, and so on through a trip to a bank. The bank professionals then can actually teach the students the adaptive skills related to their profession. In this process, some students may decide to become a bank teller or bank president rather than a school dropout. The bank could then provide mentors for those children who become interested in the banking field.

Another creative way that teachers can help children learn adaptive skills is by inviting guest professionals to periodically teach these skills. For example, a psychologist or counselor who is experienced in working with children can come to a classroom and teach anger management via role-plays and videotapes that are fun and interesting. The children and teacher can actively participate in these learning activities, and the teacher will learn how to teach anger management.

Facilitating Appreciation of Racial and Cultural Diversity

Prevention of behavior problems among African American students is facilitated through having all students in a classroom learn to appreciate racial and cultural differences among them. This is because many of the behavior problems of African American children are associated with feeling angry about being perceived as and treated as though they are inferior by peers, teachers, and society in general. This anger is often expressed in destructive ways that result in these children being labeled as behavior problem children. This label often becomes a self-fulfilling prophecy. By facilitating an appreciation of racial and cultural differences, teachers can help stop racial and cultural discrimination in their classrooms and schools and, thus, deter or minimize the anger and associated behavior problems that such discrimination often brings. An appreciation of racial and cultural differences in the classroom also facilitates a sense of belonging at school and in the classroom among

African American students. Such feelings of belonging in school facilitate academic achievement and self-regulation (Eccles, 1983).

There are several actions that teachers can take to promote an appreciation of racial and cultural differences.

1. Teachers can assess their own feelings about African Americans and challenge any stereotypes and prejudices that they have through reading about African American cultures and the many contributions of African Americans to this country. Indeed, teachers must gain an appreciation of racial and cultural differences before they can adequately promote this appreciation among the students in their classrooms.

2. Teachers can gain an appreciation for and a commitment to multiculturalism, which can facilitate positive interactions with all students in their classroom. Multiculturalism refers to valuing and respecting diversity, understanding that equality means neither sameness nor inferiority, and believing in the intrinsic worth and dignity of individuals (Asante, 1991). Attending training workshops on teaching culturally different students and on multicultural education facilitates gaining a multicultural perspective in the classroom.

3. Teachers can use cooperative learning in which small groups of children of different races, cultures, and competency levels work together on academic tasks. Such groups have been shown to promote interpersonal attraction and positive attitudes toward each other among group members across race (Johnson, Johnson, Tiffany, & Zaidman, 1983).

4. African American and other nonmajority professionals can be invited to classrooms by teachers to help extinguish race-based stereotypes and to facilitate racial pride among African American students.

5. Teachers can make their classroom decor reflect an appreciation of cultural and racial diversity by having pictures on the walls that include African Americans and other nonmajority individuals and art that represents different cultures.

Roles of School Administrators

Schools can play central roles in preventing behavior problems because the majority of children spend many of their waking hours there. Furthermore, African American families are more likely to go to schools to participate in activities and services designed to prevent behavior problems than to go to mental health facilities for these services and activities (Allen & Majidi-Ahi, 1989).

It is up to school administrators to establish services and activities to prevent behavior problems and to take leadership in finding funding for them. It is also the responsibility of these administrators to take leadership in creating school environments that encourage African American children and their parents to utilize these services and activities. Finally, school administrators must arrange and find funding to support culturally and socioeconomically sensitive research to evaluate the effects of services and activities to prevent behavior problems. Such research will avoid wasting money on programs that do not work.

There are several services and activities that school administrators can spearhead to prevent behavior problems among African American children.

1. School administrators can establish after-school and summer tutoring, adaptive skills training, and computer skills training programs for African American children and other youth as well. They can actively recruit participation in these programs by African American youth. Furthermore, they can make participation possible and attractive by doing the following: (a) making program participation free, (b) providing assistance with transportation to and from these programs for those who need this assistance, (c) providing a healthy snack for the participating youth midway through each program session, and (d) including several African American teachers and other professionals to provide tutoring and skills training.

2. School administrators can work in collaboration with mental health facilities to arrange for at-school family counseling and parent training activities that will deter behavior problems and that will help parents self-empower their children for social, academic, and life success. Counseling and training can occur after school at a cost that families can afford to pay. African American psychologists and counselors should be invited to donate their time to help with these interventions. School administrators can network with businesspersons to help financially support these prevention programs, pointing out that when African American children experience behavior problems and academic failure at school, all children are negatively impacted as the teachers' time and energy are diverted from teaching to addressing these problems.

3. School administrators can establish school–work training partnerships designed to (a) engage African American children and other children in learning by helping them see the relationship between what is being taught in school and what they will be doing in real-world jobs or professions, and (b) prepare African American children for summer and weekend jobs. Jobs provide alternatives to delinquent behaviors and they facilitate self-empowerment of children by giving them skills and knowledge for future learning and for social, academic, and life success. School–work partnerships actively involve businesspersons in preparing the well-trained future work force that they desperately need.

4. Through the leadership of school administrators, partnerships can be formed with local politicians, churches, and parents to provide recreational activities (e.g., computer classes, sports, karate classes, drama classes, music classes) for African American students on the weekends and at night. Such activities provide great alternatives to hanging out in the neighborhood and getting into trouble.

School administrators can also take a leadership role in creating school environments that embrace multiculturalism and that empower African American children. Following are some actions that school administrators can take to help create such school environments.

1. School administrators can publicly acknowledge and reward teachers (e.g., give them vacation time with pay) for initiatives in their classrooms that promote multiculturalism.

2. School administrators can make sure that African American and other nonmajority professionals are well represented among the faculty and staff at their schools.

3. School administrators can make sure that African American art, music, plays, and portraits are well represented among all art, music, plays, and portraits at the school.

4. Administrators can actively recruit and train African American students to participate in and assume leadership roles in student organizations such as the student government and student newspaper. Often African American students do not participate in such organizations because they have not had the opportunity to learn parliamentary procedure and other leadership skills necessary to have leadership roles in such organizations.

5. School administrators can establish school advisory councils to which African American students and parents can be appointed for the purposes of advising school administrators on (a) ways to help African American students and their parents become more actively involved in their children's schools, and (b) ways to help African American students receive the knowledge, skills, and experiences necessary for their academic, social, and life success.

6. School administrators can advocate teaching and learning methods that actively involve African American children and their parents in the learning process. These administrators can also advocate self-instruction-based learning, which self-empowers African American children by enabling them to teach themselves.

Roles of Churches and the Community

Churches have traditionally played leadership roles in the lives of African Americans, providing spiritual and social support to families and opportunities for learning and skill development among African American youth. Given the negative plight of many African American youth due to behavior problems and academic problems, churches and community leaders must assume more formal and active roles in educating and training African American youth and in providing positive social activities for them. Churches have the accessible, physical structures for such training and social activities, and the human resources needed to educate and train the youth can generally be recruited from the surrounding community.

Schools cannot or will not meet all of the training needs of African American youth. Churches and community leaders must work in partnership with schools to prevent behavior problems and self-empower African American youth for school and life success. There are several specific actions that African American churches and community leaders can take to achieve these goals:

1. Churches and community leaders can establish community-based partnership education programs that emphasize teaching African American children adaptive skills and provide tutoring in a very supportive environment. Such programs can emphasize individualized step-by-step, self-instruction-based learning that self-empowers children for academic and social success. Parents, community volunteers, business leaders, teachers from the community, and participating children's teachers can be involved in teaching children academics and skills in the community-based partnership education programs.

Funding and instructional materials for these programs can come from multiple sources including community members, church members, education departments, foundations, church and community fund-raising activities, and fund-raising by the participating children themselves. The latter activity provides yet another way for actively involving African American children in their own education. A detailed description of a successful community-based partnership education program is presented in Chapter 12.

2. Churches can provide opportunities for African American youth to practice their public speaking skills and their leadership skills through giving speeches at church-sponsored programs and holding offices in church youth organizations.

3. Churches and community leaders can raise funds for academic scholarships to help students with college or trade school expenses. Churches and community leaders can also assist students in enrolling in postsecondary education training and in getting financial assistance to pay for this education.

4. Churches can arrange for appropriate mentors for African American children—mentors who can help these children form goals that facilitate self-motivation to learn.

5. Churches can solicit volunteer support from medical professionals and monetary donations from community members to host health evaluations and arrange for needed health care (e.g., eyeglasses, school breakfast and lunch tickets) for children whose families cannot pay for this health care. Indeed, children cannot learn well when they are hungry, cannot see well, are malnourished, and so on.

6. Churches can host teacher–parent meetings and community-funded and school-funded parent workshops to help African American children succeed in school and in life.

7. Churches, community leaders, and school administrators can work in partnership to raise funds for culturally and socioeconomically sensitive research to evaluate the effects of programs to prevent behavior problems of African American children. Such research can ensure long-term financial and volunteer support of these programs.

Conclusions

Prevention of behavior problems and the often associated school failure, school dropout, and crime need to be national priorities, because the future of all Americans is negatively impacted by these problems. Because African American children are at high risk of behavior problems because of poverty, racism, discrimination, and other negative conditions external to themselves, special attention needs to be given to the development of programs and strategies to prevent behavior problems among these youth. It is true that the last thing that many Americans want is to pay for more programs for any disadvantaged group. Yet, the alternative of letting behavior problems occur among African American children is potentially much more costly to all Americans, for when African American children disrupt classrooms, all other children in those classes are negatively impacted.

Because of the multiple factors in the occurrence of behavior problems among African American children, including family, social, economic, neighborhood, school environments, and self-factors, multidimensional prevention efforts are indicated to prevent these problems. These efforts must actively involve parents, teachers, school administrators, churches, businesses, community leaders, communities, and the target African American children themselves. These groups must work in partnership to provide programs that are cost-effective and result in measurable positive outcomes.

The major objectives of programs and strategies to prevent behavior problems among African American youth should include teaching children adaptive skills, providing them with academic tutoring, and providing them with alternative recreational activities to hanging out in the neighborhood where they are at risk for negative activities such as drug use and other crimes. The ultimate goals of these programs and strategies should be not only to prevent behavior problems among African American youth but to also self-empower these youth for social, academic, and life success. These goals can be facilitated by using self-instruction based teaching and learning methods and by providing the participating children and adolescents with real-world and in-class learning experiences that encourage self-control, self-motivation, self-praise, success behaviors, and adaptive skills development. These goals can also be facilitated by creating learning environments that embrace multiculturalism and that respect culture-based learning styles (e.g., a preference for oral communication based learning) while teaching alternative learning styles (e.g., written communication based learning) that are necessary to be successful academically, economically, and socially in this country and in other countries.

History continues to teach us that schools alone cannot prevent behavior problems or meet all of the educational needs of African American children and adolescents. As well stated by an old and now very popular African proverb, "it takes a village to raise a child." All Americans must assist in empowering African American children to resist engaging in problem behaviors and to be successful in school and in life. Indeed, when African American youth are successful, all other youth around them and all Americans are positively impacted.

CHAPTER

9

Factors Underlying Academic Failure of African American Children

It is difficult to identify conclusively the factors in academic performance (i.e., level of academic failure or success) of African American children that are now known, especially given the cultural, gender, and linguistic biases that exist in the commonly used measures to assess the academic performance of these children. Outcomes of the existing research on factors in academic performance of African American children suggest that there are likely multiple external and internal factors that influence the academic performance of African American children. Additionally, the existing research outcomes suggest that the particular combination of factors that influences academic performance of African American children likely differs across the various groups of African American children (e.g., low-income urban children versus middle-class urban children).

The existing research is inconclusive regarding the major factors in academic performance among African American children in part because of the tendency of researchers and clinicians to lump groups of African American children together, failing to respect socioeconomic, developmental, gender, and cultural differences among the youth. Indeed, the major predictors of academic performance among low-income urban African American children, for example, may be different from the predictors of academic performance among middle-class urban African American children. Thus, to lump these groups together in studies of factors in academic performance of African American children renders findings from such studies inconclusive.

There are several theories about the determinants of academic failure versus academic success of African American children. Some of these theories emphasize the role of external factors in academic performance such as social, cultural, family, school, and teacher factors. Other theories emphasize the role of internal factors in the academic performance of African American children, that is, factors such as academic self-concept, academic self-efficacy, perceived social support, and perceived control over academic outcomes.

Given that some African American children experience academic success under external conditions conducive to academic failure, more and more attention is being given to the role of internal factors in academic performance, especially psychological and psychosocial factors. Yet, the fact that some African American children who evidence psychological strengths that have been associated with academic success actually underachieve or fail suggests that factors in academic performance are diverse and complex.

Research to test the theories regarding academic performance of African American children is needed. Much of the existing research is not theory driven, although some of it can be construed to support one or more of the existing theories to explain level of academic performance of African American children. Theory-driven research that adheres to a Difference Model research approach (Oyemade & Rosser, 1980) is particularly needed to determine the factors underlying academic performance. This type of research recognizes and respects cultural differences among African Americans as well as differences between African Americans as a group and other ethnic groups. Thus, in this type of research children who are similar (e.g., a group of middle-class urban fourth graders) are studied as a group and generalizations are not made to all African American children and adolescents based on the findings from a particular group of African American youth.

This chapter will review major theories and theoretical models that explain academic performance of African American children. Included are those theories that recognize the influence of direct and indirect cultural and socioeconomic influences on the academic performance of these youth. Research on the factors in the academic performance of African American children is also briefly reviewed. The implications of this research for future research and theory development are discussed.

Family Culture and Communication Theory

Clark (1983) suggested that high versus low academic achievement of African American children is determined by mental structures that are produced or shaped by family members' beliefs, activities, and overall cultural style. Specifically, Clark asserted that high academic achievement and appropriate social behavior by children are facilitated by a "sponsored independence" style of parent communication. This is parental communication that involves teaching children to master educational, social, recreational, and daily living tasks and activities. This teaching involves explaining, creating, demonstrating, monitoring, role-playing, and practicing what is being taught. In these activities, parents are warm and supportive, and they model success behaviors (e.g., following rules) in which they would like to see their children engage. As a consequence of family activities and parental modeling, it is believed that children learn certain cognitive operations such as creative problem solving, self-regulation, initiating oral and written communication, and memorizing and following rules for social encounters and rules in general. It is also believed that learned knowledge and skills facilitate children's academic and social success at school.

According to Clark (1983), low academic achievement and inappropriate social behaviors are facilitated by an "unsponsored independence" style of parent communication, which is just the opposite of a "sponsored independence" style of parent communication. An "unsponsored independence" style of parent communication is characterized by low frequency of parents being involved with their children, low frequency of parents being engaged in teaching their children activities, and much criticism and little praise of children by their parents.

Clark (1983) hypothesized that both parents' and other family members' communication patterns (with their children, kin, friends, and other community members and groups) are influenced by the way that they themselves experienced life when they were young. This researcher also hypothesized that (1) parents' sense of well-being, their academic aspirations for their children, and their perceived ability to academically empower their children are directly influenced by their contacts within community structures, including schools; and (2) that children's aspirations and expectations are also influenced by these community contacts. Clark further postulated that these same communication dynamics and processes account for the success or failure of children across families regardless of ethnic, occupational, income, and structural differences between families.

Conflict Model

Bond (1972) identified two major and very different conceptualizations of the academic achievement of African American students based on the existing relevant literature. One conceptualization links the academic achievement of these students to their environmental circumstances. Bond labeled this conceptualization the "deficit model" of academic achievement. Specifically, this model suggests that African American students who evidence low academic achievement have deficiencies in critical academic skills because of an "impoverished" intellectual environment, little encouragement toward intellectual pursuits, lack of parental discipline, and poor academic instruction.

Bond's other conceptualization links the academic achievement of African American students to their learning history, which is not deficient, but rather is simply in conflict with effective instruction in American classrooms dominated by the majority culture. Bond labeled this conceptualization the "conflict model" of academic achievement and stated that this model is more contemporary than the deficit model. The conflict model suggests that African American children like all other children experience a substantial amount of intellectual growth and learning in their environments, but that the skills and competencies that African American children acquire in their learning histories are often in conflict with those needed in U.S. classrooms to be academically successful. For example, the development of oral nonstandard English communication skills among some African American students is in conflict with the expectation and often demand in most U.S. classrooms for the use of standard English in oral and written form (Labov, 1972).

Identity and Cultural-Ecological (ICE) Model

The ICE model as proposed by Ogbu (1986) suggests that academic failure among African American students is likely due to the external limits placed on the ability of minorities to succeed in taking advantage of educational, economic, social, professional, and political opportunities. According to the ICE model, minority persons such as parents and students reject their low status and develop strategies in response to this oppression that may not facilitate academic success. For example, African American and other minority parents might undervalue education because they do not believe education can rid individuals and our nation as a whole of political and social biases (Okagaki, Frensch, & Gordon, 1995). Furthermore, poor school performance by African American students may be a kind of adaptation to the limited social and economic opportunities they perceive ahead for them in adult life (Ogbu, 1978).

Modified Cultural-Ecological Model

The modified cultural-ecological model was offered by Fordham and Ogbu (1986). It suggests that some African American students experience academic failure or do poorly in school to avoid "acting white." Specifically, these authors suggest that African American students experience ambivalence and affective dissonance in regard to academic effort and success because of the view of African American students that to strive for academic success means that you are "acting white," which implies rejection of one's African American identity and culture. The authors further explain that this negative association of academic success with "acting white" arose from the traditional refusal of European Americans to acknowledge that African Americans are capable of intellectual achievement, and from subsequent doubting by African Americans of their own intellectual ability. Additionally, the authors explained that African Americans began to define academic success as the prerogative of European Americans and began to discourage their peers, perhaps unconsciously, from emulating the behaviors and attitudes of European Americans to be academically successful.

According to Fordham and Ogbu (1986) some African American students form an oppositional collective identity, which means that they unite as a people in opposition to the perceived enduring and collective oppression of the European American majority with whom they will never be allowed to assimilate and by whom they will never be treated equally no matter what their individual physical appearance or economic status happens to be. Additionally, according to these authors, these students develop an oppositional cultural frame of reference; that is, they identify a set of behaviors, events, symbols, and meanings that is appropriate for European Americans and they identify a different set of behaviors, events, symbols, and meanings that is appropriate for African Americans. To behave in a way that is consistent with what is appropriate for European Americans is considered "acting white" and is negatively viewed. Interestingly, speaking standard English is among the attitudes and behaviors that Fordham and Ogbu (1986) found that some African American students consider "acting white." Fear of "acting white" might explain why many African American students consistently speak black English or use a lot of slang in their verbal communication. Adoption of the oppositional cultural frame of reference by some African American students may explain why they often harass and tease their African American peers who speak standard English for doing so.

Fordham and Ogbu (1986) went on to state that because of oppositional collective identity, some students (1) become underachievers who avoid studying and thus avoid being called a brainiac, (2) become athletes or cheerleaders who thus avoid being labeled brainiac; or (3) simply act less smart than they are. In contrast, other students pursue academic success and use some of the following specific strategies to cope with or avoid the anxiety and negative consequences associated with "acting white": (1) act like a clown or comedian, (2) give the appearance of not putting forth much effort to get good grades, (3) deny being a brainiac, and (4) make good but not excellent grades. In addition, females use low profiling, meaning that they avoid participating in academic societies and activities (Fordham & Ogbu, 1986).

Indeed, all African American students do not identify with the oppositional identity and oppositional cultural frame of reference of their group. Some students only marginally identify and some repudiate these identifications (Fordham, 1985). Consequently, there are differences in levels of academic success and in levels of engagement in academic success behaviors (i.e., "acting white" behaviors) among African American students.

Identification-Participation Model

Finn (1989) proposed an identification-participation model that can be used to explain academic failure and school dropout. According to this model, children and adolescents fail academically and sometimes drop out of school because of their own social withdrawal in response to not identifying with the school, not feeling a sense of belonging to the school, and not feeling valued or respected by teachers, staff, peers, and others at the school.

Consistent with the identification-participation model is the assertion by others that the school culture (e.g., values, beliefs, norms, and unspoken rules) at predominantly European American operated schools is very different from the home cultures among the African American children who find themselves in these schools (Hale-Benson, 1986; Hilliard, 1979). Consequently, African American children may experience some difficulty adjusting to the school culture, especially given that they must move back and forth from their home culture to their school culture (Ford, 1992). This adjustment difficulty likely negatively impacts on the academic performance of children whose school culture and home culture are very different. Furthermore, these culture differences may impede a sense of identification with the school and, thus, contribute to social withdrawal that is antagonistic to the development of adaptive skills for academic and social success.

Context-Specific Model

The context-specific model of minority development as advocated by Delgado-Gaitan (1992) suggests that cultural context affects social and cognitive development and that individuals from different cultures will likely have different cognitive and social behaviors. Therefore, it is likely that children from minority cultures as compared with children from the majority culture will likely have different cognitive and social behaviors that they bring to the classroom. In schools where majority culture is dominant and where the cognitive and social behaviors of majority children are valued, the cognitive and social behaviors of children from minority cultures are likely devalued and may not be functional for the academic challenges, learning, and social situations presented in these schools. Consequently, many African American students and other minority students in such schools may not reach their potential for academic and social success.

Connell's Process Model of Motivation

Connell and his colleagues (Connell, 1991; Connell & Wellborn, 1991; Skinner, Wellborn, & Connell, 1990) have proposed a process model of motivation to explain academic performance outcomes such as grade point averages and aptitude test scores. According to this model, student action patterns such as school attendance, study behaviors, shows of interest in learning, and satisfaction with school are what directly influence academic performance or achievement (Connell, 1991; Skinner, Wellborn, & Connell, 1990); however, important variables influence or shape student action patterns. Specifically, Connell and his associates proposed that the following process occurs: A student's perceived social context (e.g., parent support, teacher support) directly influences the self-system variables (i.e., perceived competence, perceived autonomy, and perceived relatedness), which in turn influence student action patterns. The student action patterns reflect engagement in learning, which involves initiation of action, effort, persistence, and emotional investment.

Perceived competence refers to "the sense that doing well in school is possible and that there are known and workable strategies for achieving success and avoiding failure in school" (Connell & Wellborn, 1991; p. 59). Perceived autonomy refers to "the experience of choice in the initiation, maintenance, and regulation of behavior, and the experience of connectedness between one's actions and personal goals and values" (Connell, 1991; p. 63). Perceived relatedness refers to "the experience of connection and emotional security with other individuals in the school setting" (Connell, Halpern-Felsher, Clifford, Crichlow, & Usinder, 1995; p. 58). Perceived competence is closely associated with the familiar construct of self-efficacy, and autonomy is similar to the construct of self-regulation (Herman, 1997).

Connell's process model of motivation helps us to understand why social context variables such as socioeconomic status, parenting behaviors, ethnic composition of schools, and others are only sometimes found in research to be associated with academic performance. According to this model, the influence of social context variables is not direct; their impact is really determined by the self variables (e.g., academic self-efficacy), which have been influenced by the social context variables but also add their own influence as they directly impact student action patterns or engagement in learning. Therefore, the strength of the self-variables will determine to some degree the impact of the social context variables and vice versa. This is perhaps why some African American youth achieve academic success in spite of impoverished backgrounds and limited educational support from parents and teachers.

Self-Empowerment Theory

Self-empowerment theory (SET) recognizes that social, economic, cultural, and home environmental factors (i.e., social context variables) significantly influence the academic achievement of African American children and asserts that the nature and degree of these influence variables likely differ across individual and/or groups of African American children. SET also recognizes the reality that most social context variables that negatively influence academic achievement of African American children are intractable, especially given the negative attitudes toward and limited resources for social programs to modify these variables. SET is based on the assumption that ultimately the most direct and modifiable influences on African American children's academic achievement are the following self-empowerment variables: (1) self-motivation to achieve, (2) self-control necessary to engage in academic behaviors and to avoid behaviors that are antagonistic to academic success, (3) self-praise to sustain achievement efforts and behaviors, (4) adaptive skills (i.e., communication skills, socialization skills, and daily living skills) and (5) success behaviors (e.g., asking questions about what is not understood). SET advocates the modification of realistically modifiable social context variables, such as teacher and parent behaviors, toward the goal of facilitating self-motivation, self-control, self-praise, adaptive skills, and success behaviors of African American children.

In sum, SET asserts that the academic achievement of African American children is dependent on the self-empowerment of these youth for academic, social, and future economic success, which will occur through helping them develop the previously described achievement-related self-motivation, self-control, self-praise, adaptive skills, and success behaviors. Through this self-empowerment approach to educating African American children, these youth will be able to experience academic and social success both under ideal conditions for such success and under realistic conditions in which parent and teacher support may be limited and in which racism and discrimination challenges to their academic and social success are significant. In other words, this self-empowerment approach necessarily prepares African American children to achieve against the odds that they will inevitably face in school and in future efforts to realize their goals of lives worth living.

Interventions that address the self variables to facilitate the self-empowerment of African American youth are numerous and include teaching students how to study and learn using a step-by step approach, helping them establish motivational goals, teaching them how to constructively express anger as well as other negative feelings and positive feelings, teaching them social skills such as how to introduce themselves to their teachers, and teaching them behaviors that constitute good manners. Interventions to modify social context variables (e.g., lack of parent involvement in their children's education, family conflict, few educational resources due to family poverty, racism in schools, and low teacher expectations regarding the academic achievement of African American children) are also important for facilitating the self-empowerment of African American children; however, for most African American children, many of these social context variables will not be changed within the duration of their childhoods.

It thus makes sense to concentrate more on interventions that address self variables in efforts to self-empower African American children. This view is consistent with the conclusion of Connell et al. (1994) from a study with over a thousand African American students to examine predictors of these students' academic achievement. These researchers concluded that it is self-variables that regulate the actions in school of African American children and that the influences of self-variables on these actions are far greater than the influences of these children's gender and economic conditions.

Relevant Research

There has been a great deal of research conducted to identify factors in the academic performance (i.e., level of academic failure or success) of African American students. Perhaps this is because of the very high school dropout rates among urban, low-income, and minority students, among whom African Americans are highly represented (Ford, 1993). Several studies have focused on factors in academic achievement that are external to African American children themselves. These are factors such as socioeconomic status, parents' behaviors and attitudes, teacher behaviors and attitudes, and learning methods used in the classroom.

Several other studies have focused on internal factors or self-factors in academic achievement. Internal factors are those that have to do with the child's own psychosocial functioning, values, attitudes, behaviors, and skills. These internal factors include such variables as self-control, academic self-efficacy, and achievement motivation. Research has also been conducted to simultaneously examine both internal and external factors in the academic achievement and performance of African American children and adolescents.

Research on External Factors

Parent Behaviors.   The present author and her colleagues examined the association of selected parent behaviors with the academic achievement among a group of African American children and a group of European American children (Tucker, Harris, Brady, & Hermann, 1995). The participants in this study were 266 African American children and their primary caregivers and 414 European American children and their primary caregivers. Both of the participating ethnic groups consisted of a disproportionately high number of low-income families; however, the European American group consisted of slightly more middle-income families than the African American group. The student participants were either in second, fourth, or eighth grade in one of several schools in a mostly rural southern county. Most of the primary caregivers who participated were mothers. The measures of academic achievement used were grade point averages (GPAs) and the Metropolitan Achievement Test scores, which is a standardized measure of academic achievement routinely given in the schools of the participating students.

Results of the study revealed numerous associations between parents' self-reports of their use of selected behaviors and the measures of children's academic achievement; however, these associations differed by grade level. Specifically, the following associations were found:

1. For second graders across ethnicity, mothers' grade expectations of C were associated with lower GPAs than mothers' grade expectations of A or B or no particular grade expectation.
2. For fourth graders across ethnicity, mothers' grade expectations of C were associated with lower GPAs.
3. For fourth graders across ethnicity, parental use of restrictions for unsatisfactory grades was associated with lower GPAs.
4. For fourth graders across ethnicity, church attendance by mother never or occasionally versus frequently was associated with lower GPAs.
5. For fourth-grade African Americans, fathers' grade expectations of A versus fathers' grade expectations of B or C or no particular grade expectation were associated with higher GPAs; for European American fourth graders, fathers' grade expectations of C were associated with lower GPAs than fathers' grade expectations of A or B or no particular grade expectations.
6. For eighth graders across ethnicity, parental use versus no use of verbal reprimands for unsatisfactory grades was associated with lower MAT scores.
7. For eighth graders across ethnicity, mothers' grade expectations of A versus B or C or no particular grade expectations were associated with higher MAT scores.

8. For eighth graders across ethnicity, frequent mother praise versus occasional mother praise for satisfactory grades was associated with higher MAT scores.

9. For eighth graders across ethnicity, frequent father praise versus occasional father praise for satisfactory grades was associated with higher MAT scores.

Tucker and her colleagues concluded from these findings that certain parent behaviors may be important influence factors in the academic achievement of African American children; however, the type of parent behaviors and the level of their influence likely depend on various child variables such as the age or grade level of the child and the psychosocial development needs of the child. It was also concluded that providing some African American youth and European American youth with encouragement and praise for satisfactory grades likely facilitates high academic achievement and that negative responses to unsatisfactory grades by these youth likely facilitates low academic achievement.

Additionally, it was concluded that communication by parents to some African American youth and European American youth that making a C grade or at least doing average work is satisfactory may not challenge some students and in fact may result in them making lower grades than would occur with higher parent grade expectations or than expressing no particular grade expectation at all. Surprisingly, A grade expectations by African American fathers were associated with higher GPAs among fourth-grade African American children, thus suggesting that African American fathers have the potential for facilitating academic success of some African American children.

Finally, it was concluded that parental support of academic achievement may be more important to the academic success of African American adolescents and European American adolescents than to the academic success of younger children of both of these ethnic groups. This is ironic given that parents tend to be more encouraging of and more involved with the academic achievement of younger children. Perhaps this is because of the general desire of adolescents for more independence from parents or because parents feel less adequate at evaluating and being involved in the academic work of children in secondary school. In any case, it appears that parental support of academic achievement is important for some adolescents.

The researchers also indicated the need for the execution of future research on the association of actual parent behaviors (versus self-reported parent behaviors) with academic achievement of African American children and adolescents. Yet, it was concluded that the present research provides support for encouraging African American parents and European American parents to praise and support the academic efforts and success of their children.

Peer Values and Ethnicity.   Values of friends and ethnicity of friends have also been found to be associated with achievement efforts and grades of African American students. In a study with African American adolescent students, Patchen (1982) found that the adolescents with friends who had high academic values engaged in more efforts to achieve than did adolescents with friends who had low academic values. The following variables were used to determine achievement effort: time spent doing homework, whether or not homework was completed, number of days absent from school, frequency of being late to class, and number of missed classes.

Another major finding in this study was that the African American adolescents who did versus those who did not develop friendships with European American students put forth more achievement effort and made higher grades. Given the strong impact of peer influence, it may be that through modeling success behaviors such as studying, European American students influenced their African American friends to engage in the same behaviors. The friendship may also result in African American students buying into the notion that working hard to do well academically will result in getting a good job, a home, an accumulation of money, and the other aspects of the American dream.

Cauce (1986) found friends' values or attitudes regarding the importance of education and school to be important factors in academic failure of African American students from lower-class families. Specifically, this researcher found that students who experienced academic failure tended to have friends who did not value education and school. Additionally, Cauce (1986) found that students who valued education, had the best academic records, and perceived themselves as academically competent had friends who highly valued education.

Socioeconomic Status (SES). SES has continued to be investigated as a factor in the academic performance of African American children. In a study involving families of African American children and Hispanic children in urban schools, Carter (1984) found a significant positive relationship between SES level and academic performance. Specifically, this researcher reported that those children from higher SES-level families performed better academically.

Teacher Attitudes. Bond (1982) concluded from a review of several studies that both European American teachers and African American teachers generally have negative attitudes regarding the education potential of minority children. Specifically, according to Bond, minority children are often viewed by their teachers as less able academically, less academically motivated, and less educable than majority children.

Teachers' Self-Efficacy. Teachers' beliefs concerning their instructional efficacy (e.g., their beliefs that they have the skills and competencies to teach and that their students will learn as a function of their teaching) have been found to be significant predictors of students' levels of mathematical and language achievement, controlling for students' ability (Ashton & Webb, 1986). According to Woolfolk and Hoy (1990), teachers' personal efficacy affects their instructional practices. Specifically, teachers with a low sense of instructional efficacy are typically controlling and rely on extrinsic incentives, threats, and negative sanctions to get students to study, whereas teachers with high instructional efficacy facilitate the development of their students' intrinsic interests and motivate their students to learn and to engage in self-directed learning that is intrinsically reinforcing. Gibson and Dembo (1984) reported finding that teachers who have high instructional efficacy spend much time on academic tasks, give extra help to students who need it, and praise even small amounts of progress and success, whereas teachers with low instructional efficacy spend more time on nonacademic activities, easily give up on students who have difficulty learning, and criticize failures.

A school staff's collective sense of efficacy that staff members can successfully facilitate academic learning among the students at their school has also been found to be a significant factor in their school's actual level of academic achievement (Bandura, 1993). It was also found by Bandura (1993) through the use of a path analysis that student body characteristics such as socioeconomic levels and racial composition influence students' academic achievement more strongly by the beliefs of the teaching staffs about their collective efficacy to motivate and teach their students than through any direct effects on school achievement. Bandura concluded that with teaching staffs who believe that by their determined efforts they can motivate and teach students no matter what the students' backgrounds, schools with many minority students with low socioeconomic backgrounds can achieve the highest rankings for math and language competency scores based on national score norms.

Learning Method.   The association of minority children's and European American children's academic achievement with learning method was investigated by Johnson, Johnson, Tiffany, and Zaidman (1983). Participants in their study were twenty minority fourth graders from a large inner-city elementary school (eighteen African Americans, one Native American, and one Spanish-speaking student) and twenty-eight Caucasian, middle-class fourth graders. The learning methods investigated were individual learning and cooperative learning. Findings were that cooperative learning as compared with individualistic learning promoted (1) higher academic achievement for the mostly African American group of minority children, (2) more interactions that involved students from different ethnic backgrounds for the purpose of supporting and regulating efforts to learn and that involved all of the students in the learning process, and (3) greater cross-ethnic interpersonal attraction.

It has also been asserted that (1) cooperative learning in small mixed-race groups results in a greater likelihood of participating students helping each other and feeling less threatened socially by students who are racially different from themselves, and (2) both European American students and nonmajority students who participate in cooperative learning do better on subsequent measures of achievement (Rosenholtz & Wilson, 1980; Slavin, 1978).

Research on Internal Factors

Learning Styles.   Various writings and research examined collectively suggest that there is an association between academic failure among African American children and the learning styles that these children bring to their classrooms. According to Cohen (1969) and Hilliard (1976), African American students tend to use learning styles that are inconsistent with those of the majority culture of which most schoolteachers are a part and thus promote; consequently, African American students are at risk of academic failure. These researchers describe the learning styles of African American students to be more relational than analytical.

Cohen (1969) and Hilliard (1976) concluded that students with more relational versus analytical learning styles often are more global in their focus, tend to exhibit more emotive behavior, find more meaning in text, have shorter attention spans, may tend to devalue linear relationships, and try to find personal relevance in the content. Additionally, these authors suggested that more analytical versus relational learners often are more global in focus, find linear relationships easily, have longer attention and concentration spans, can often extract information embedded in text, and may have more perceptual vigilance.

According to Cushner, McClelland, and Safford (1992), because analytical learners (who tend to be European Americans) as compared to relational learners (who tend to be African Americans) tend to do better on school-related tasks, and because analytical learning is likely emphasized and reinforced by the mostly European American teachers in our classrooms, one might expect that a majority of African American students will be at an achievement disadvantage (i.e., unfamiliar with the preferred analytical learning and teaching styles) when they enter the school environment.

Cushner, McClelland, and Safford (1992) also have reported that there are within-group differences in learning styles. The fact that some African American students have analytical learning styles suggests that African American children are capable of both analytical and relational learning styles. According to Cushner et al. (1992), all children should be exposed to different learning styles in the classroom, and this should be done in a manner that is sensitive to the preferred learning styles of each child. In other words, it is important for teachers to adapt the teaching and learning in their classrooms to the learning styles that African American children and other children bring to these classrooms. Teachers should gradually expose these children to new learning styles without condemning their existing learning styles.

Motivation, Ability, and Self-Concept.   Jordan (1981) examined the association of academic achievement in African American children with three self-variables—academic motivation, verbal ability, and academic self-concept. The term *academic self-concept* was operationalized as one's self-evaluation of one's general academic ability. Participants in the study were 328 inner-city African American adolescents. Results were that academic achievement of these youth was significantly associated with all three of the investigated self-variables.

Success/Failure Attributions.   What African American children tell themselves about academic failure may be a factor in some of these children's academic performance. In a study with African American fourth through eighth graders, Willig, Harnish, Hill, & Maehr (1983) reported finding that those children who attributed failure to lack of luck tended to have lower math scores than did those who attributed failure to lack of ability, lack of effort, or task difficulty. Luck-oriented attributions reflect a lack of perceived control over academic outcomes, which could result in a lack of academic effort and, thus, academic failure.

Perceived Teacher Support.   In a study by Wentzel (1994), perceived academic support from teachers was indicated as a factor in the academic performance of African American students. Participants in this study were 475 adolescents (i.e., sixth graders and seventh graders), 23 percent of whom were African Americans. The two major findings in this study were that (1) the more teacher support the students reported receiving, the more academic effort they put forth, and (2) the African American students reported receiving significantly less support from their teachers than did the European American students.

The author concluded that if these findings are in fact accurate, then academic failure by some African American children is likely due at least in part to their perception of receiving inadequate support from their teachers. Based on this research, it appears that future research is needed to determine the specific types of teacher behaviors that various groups of African American students perceive as supportive. Such information would be helpful in designing teacher training programs focused on effectively teaching African American students.

Perceptions of Parents' Achievement-Related Beliefs and Values. In a study with 148 low SES African American fifth and sixth graders who attend urban schools, Ford (1994) examined the association of students' perceptions of their parents' beliefs regarding education with the students' own attitudes, beliefs, and values about schooling, particularly their level of support of the American achievement ideology. In essence, the American achievement ideology includes the beliefs that school is important, that doing well in school will lead to a good job, and that with hard work and effort anyone can become whatever he or she wants to become, including becoming president of the United States.

The participating students were in either a gifted program, a high-achieving program, or a regular program. Among the results reported by Ford were that (1) the students who strongly agreed that their parents consider school and gifted programs important were more optimistic and indicated stronger support of the American achievement ideology, and (2) primary caregiver variables (including father's presence or absence in the student's home) and parents' educational level, occupation, and employment status had little association with the level of the students' support of the American achievement ideology. Ford concluded that the messages that African American parents in some way communicate to their children and the children's perceptions of these messages influence the children's achievement orientation.

Research Regarding Internal and External Factors

Fisher (1988) examined a combination of several internal variables and external variables as potential factors in the academic achievement of African American high school students in inner-city schools. The investigated variables were socioeconomic status, gender, educational aspirations, occupational aspirations and expectations, perceived opportunity for success in school, academic self-concept (one's self-evaluation of general academic ability), awareness of limited opportunity for the future, and perceived support from parents, teachers, and friends. The measures of academic achievement used were the California Achievement Test (CAT) scores and grade point averages (GPAs).

The author reported finding that academic self-concept, perceived academic support, and perceived opportunities for success in one's academic environment were significant factors in the academic success or failure of the students in this study. Specifically, academic self-concept was found to be the best predictor of both CAT scores and GPAs and the relationship was positive. High levels of perceived academic support and perceived opportunities for success in the academic environment were also found to be significantly associated with high CAT scores and GPAs.

It is noteworthy that the self-variable of academic self-concept rather than socioeconomic status and the other external support related variables was found to be the most salient factor in the academic achievement of the students in this study. Support is provided for intervening with African American students themselves to facilitate their academic achievement, especially given that external factors such as socioeconomic status may not be modifiable.

In a study with 1,470 African American children and 69 Hispanic children from among 26 urban kindergarten schools, Reynolds (1991) investigated the association of several external and internal factors with these children's achievement following kindergarten (i.e., in year 1 and year 2 of school). The external factors that were investigated were the experience of attending prekindergarten, level of parental involvement with their child's education in kindergarten, and whether or not the child changed schools following kindergarten. The internal factors that were investigated were prekindergarten cognitive readiness (e.g., skills for listening and vocabulary) and prekindergarten motivation to learn (e.g., enthusiasm and eagerness to work). Results showed that only prekindergarten cognitive readiness and remaining at the same school where one attended kindergarten were significantly associated with participating children's achievement in year 1 and year 2 of school, which were the two years that these children were followed in this study. Specifically, cognitive readiness was positively associated with achievement, and the children who remained in their kindergarten school during first grade as compared to those who transferred to a new school learned more in first- and second-grade math and more in second-grade reading. The author concluded that there are likely multiple factors that impact the academic achievement of children such as the African American children and Hispanic children in this study.

Using a group of 301 urban adolescents, among whom were 96 African Americans, Goodenow and Grady (1994) investigated the association of general school motivation (beliefs and feeling that attending school is important, satisfying, and worthwhile), the expectation for academic success, and the value attributed to academic schoolwork with multiple adolescent variables including an external variable (i.e., friends' level of value of doing well in school) and the following internal variables: a sense of belonging to one's school (perceptions of being accepted, respected, and encouraged) and level of expectation that one will do well in school. When examining the specified associations looking only at the 96 African American students, the researchers found that the higher their sense of school belonging, the higher their expectation to do well in school, the higher their general school motivation, and the higher their friends' level of valuing doing well in school. These findings further support that there are likely multiple factors in the academic failure or success of African American children. This research also suggests that many of these factors are likely internal psychosocial variables.

Connell, Spencer, and Aber (1994) conducted a study of factors in academic achievement of African American students using data sets from a total of 1,065 African American seventh, eighth, and ninth graders from schools in Atlanta, New York, Boston, and Washington, D.C. The study was designed to test these researchers' process model of motivation—a broad theoretical framework set forth for understanding academic performance. In sum this model asserts that students' perceived social context (e.g., teacher support) directly influences the self-system (i.e., perceived competence, perceived autonomy, and perceived relatedness), which in turn leads to student action patterns that reflect engagement in learning (e.g., study behaviors).

The specific variables investigated in the study being described were parental involvement (social context variable), perceived competence and relatedness with others (self-system variables) and emotional and behavioral involvement (student action patterns/ engagement in learning). Support was provided for the model; that is, parental involvement significantly influenced African American children's perceived competence and relatedness to others, which in turn significantly influenced their emotional and behavioral involvement in their schoolwork and school. Given that perceived competence is similar to the construct of self-efficacy and autonomy is similar to the construct of self-regulation (Herman, 1997), these findings provide support for self-empowering African American youth for academic success. In other words, these findings support teaching African American children self-control, self-motivation, self-praise, success behaviors, and adaptive skills for academic and social success.

Based on the findings of Connell, Spencer, and Aber (1994), it appears that the influence of the external variable of parental support is significant, but its influence on academic engagement behaviors is indirect; it is African American children's internal or self-variables such as perceived competence that directly impact their academic engagement for academic success. It is also noteworthy that Connell, Spencer, and Aber (1994) view the engagement behaviors as just as important or perhaps more important than simply looking at culturally defined grade point averages and standard achievement test scores, which are influenced by the engagement or action behaviors. These researchers have suggested that for some students such as African American males, the ultimate goal may be establishment of the engagement or action behaviors, as they have long-term benefits (Connell, Halpern-Felsher, Clifford, Crichlow, & Usinder, 1995). Indeed, given that grade point averages and standardized test scores are often not reliable measures of achievement for African American students and other nonmajority students, factors of student action or engagement behaviors should be the major criteria when evaluating the achievement of these students.

Clark (1983) examined multiple external and internal factors that differentiated five low-income, high-achieving high school seniors from five low-income, low-achieving high school seniors. This researcher used in-depth interviews, participant observation, and attitudinal questionnaires for data collection. Achievement level was assessed based on student-reported grades and class rank, student-reported reading and math achievement scores, teacher perception of the child's "promise," and student perception of ability. Some of the findings from this research were that high achievers were distinguished by the facts that they had parents who initiated frequent school contact, expected their child to get postsecondary training, had achievement-centered rules, enforced rules, deferred to their child's knowledge in intellectual matters, were nurturant and supportive, and engaged in achievement training activities. Additionally, the high achievers were distinguished by their long-term acceptance of rules and norms, active involvement in their schooling, exposure to little family conflict, and reports of having some stimulating and supportive teachers.

Clark (1983) concluded from the findings of his research that across gender, high external support plus high internalized control and a high personal sense of intellectual power are needed for the high achievement of some African American students. He clarified that intellectual power facilitates academic achievement only when it pertains directly to academic achievement. The findings from this research provided empirical support for his earlier discussed family and culture communication theory (Clark, 1983).

In a study by Lee (1984) multiple psychosocial factors were evidenced in the academic success of African American adolescents from rural, low socioeconomic families. These factors included family-related factors, school-related factors, and social relationship factors. Family-related factors included clear rules that were enforced, guidance from grandparents, academic encouragement, frequent and positive family communication, and strong family values. Among the school-related factors were positive feelings toward school and teachers, regular studying, few race-related and personal-social problems, a desire to do well in school, and active involvement in school activities. Social relationship factors included spending time with friends of different gender and ethnicity, spending time with role models outside of home and school (e.g., pastors and godparents), and spending time learning about the accomplishments of celebrated individuals.

Future Research and Theory Development

The reviewed research suggests the need for future research that simultaneously examines multiple factors in the academic achievement of African American children and adolescents. These factors need to include external factors such as culture, family, and peers and internal factors such as academic self-efficacy, perceived control of academic outcomes, perceived social support, and sense of belonging in one's school. Additionally, modifiable skills, behaviors, and environmental conditions that directly influence academic achievement also need to be examined.

It is especially important that research with African American children is culturally and socioeconomically sensitive; that is, it is important for the research to include large samples of students who are similar in culture and socioeconomic status. With such large samples the need to separately examine factors in the academic performance of males and females by age group can be addressed. It is also important to realize that the results of research with a group of African American children cannot be generalized to groups that are culturally and socioeconomically different.

The reviewed research also suggests the need for research examining factors in the academic achievement of middle-class African American students and gifted African American students, many of whom are underachievers. Such research recognizes the diversity among African Americans and the need for different intervention strategies to facilitate the academic achievement of different groups of African Americans. Indeed, one intervention package does not fit all, as many who have a monolithic view of African Americans tend to believe.

Another implication of the reviewed research is that there is a need to use multiple measures of academic achievement as outcome variables, among which are culturally and socioeconomically sensitive measures. Given that grade point averages and standardized test scores are often not reliable measures of academic achievement of African American children, it is not sensible to use only these types of scores as indicators of academic achievement in African American youth. Students' self-evaluations of their academic achievement and engagement in learning actions (Connell & Wellborn, 1991), such as study frequency, satisfaction with school, level of interest in schoolwork, frequency of completing homework, and frequency of class attendance, should perhaps be included as measures of academic achievement.

Finally, more theory-driven research is also needed. Furthermore, research is needed to test the existing theories of academic performance of African American youth. Future modifications of these theories or development of new theories should include a focus on the most direct and salient influences on academic achievement. Such theories will provide the needed directions for cost-effective practical interventions for addressing the serious problem of academic failure among African American students, which has the potential of negatively impacting the lives of all Americans.

Conclusions

Clearly, there are multiple factors that impact the academic achievement of African American children and adolescents. These factors include external factors such as family factors (e.g., parents' academic involvement and achievement-related family rules) and teacher factors (teacher instructional self-efficacy and teacher attitudes) as well as internal factors such as psychosocial factors (e.g., perception of belonging at one's school), perceived competence, academic self-efficacy, learning style, and achievement motivation. In sum, the existing research seems to suggest that the relationship between these multiple factors and academic achievement is complex and that the effects of some of these factors are likely indirect and minimized by the existence of other influence factors.

Much of the research that exists is not theory driven and the existing theories are not adequately supported with empirical research. Clearly, more research with diverse groups of African American students is needed. This research must be culturally and socioeconomically sensitive. Specifically, this research must include measures that give a broader and more reliable indication of the academic achievement of African American students than is given by the commonly used measures (i.e., grade point averages and standardized achievement test scores). Furthermore, this research must be conducted with large samples of African American students with each sample including students who are similar culturally and socioeconomically and large enough to examine factors in academic achievement by grade level and gender. These samples also need to include middle-class African American students and gifted students—two groups often overlooked in research on factors in academic achievement of African American youth. Indeed, academic underachievement and academic failure commonly occur in these two student groups.

More attention needs to be given to the role of internal factors in academic achievement of African American youth given that internal factors such as self-control of academic outcomes, achievement motivation, and academic self-efficacy tend to be implicated in several studies as important factors in academic achievement of these youth. The fact that some African American students experience academic success under external conditions conducive to academic failure further suggests giving more attention to examining the role of internal factors in the academic performance of these students. The fact that some African American youth who evidence psychological and psychosocial strengths that have been associated with academic success actually underachieve academically or experience academic failure suggests that external factors certainly play a role in the academic achievement of these students and, thus, also must be included in research models that seek to understand the academic achievement of these youth.

10 Assessment of Academic Performance among African American Children

Children's academic performance is typically assessed to determine: (1) the degree to which the children are achieving instructional objectives, (2) what they need to reach these objectives, (3) the appropriate curriculum for them, (4) whether they should advance from one grade to the next, (5) any improvement or worsening in their academic performance, especially as a result of an intervention effort, and (6) causes of or contributing factors to low academic performance when it is evidenced. Usually grades, standardized achievement tests, and intelligence tests are used as measures of academic performance.

When it is suspected that a child has impaired academic performance due to some type of disorder (e.g., a learning disorder), neurological and neuropsychological assessments are often conducted. Additionally, the child is usually observed in her or his classroom and interviewed by a school psychologist or counselor. The parents and teachers of the child are also usually interviewed by the psychologist or counselor to obtain their views of the child's academic ability and performance.

Assessment of academic performance of African American children often meets with much controversy and concern given that the assessment methods and procedures typically used are biased, and the consequences of these assessments are often negative for African American children and their families. These consequences for some African American children include being mislabeled as learning disabled, being inappropriately placed in special classes, being viewed as having low academic and intellectual potential, experiencing low academic self-confidence and efficacy, feeling like an academic failure, and experiencing little motivation to do well academically. The consequences for many African American parents include frustration, worry about their child's academic future, and feeling powerless regarding actions to move their child from academic failure to academic success.

This chapter discusses the methods used to assess academic performance of African American children, the limitations of and biases in these assessments methods, and some culturally and socioeconomically sensitive recommendations for assessing academic performance of African American children. Additionally, suggestions are made regarding what African American parents can do in response to their concerns about both the academic performance of their child and test results and recommendations from evaluations of their child's academic performance.

Assessment of Academic Performance Level

Often assessment of academic performance level includes assessment of both intellectual functioning and academic achievement. Assessment of intellectual functioning is usually included because it is considered a central defining feature for disorders such as mental retardation and learning disabilities that impair academic performance.

Intellectual Functioning Assessment

There continues to be disagreement among theorists and educators as to just what intelligence is and is not; thus, it is not clear what intellectual functioning actually reflects. There is some agreement that intellectual functioning refers to level of manifested knowledge, level of ability to learn or think, and level of capacity to adapt to new situations (Wicks-Nelson & Israel, 1997).

Intellectual functioning is measured in African American children and other children using intelligence tests such as the Stanford-Binet—Fourth Edition (Thorndike, Hagen, & Sattler, 1986), the Kaufman Assessment Battery for Children (Kaufman & Kaufman, 1983), or one of the Wechsler tests. The Wechsler tests that tend to be used are the Wechsler Preschool and Primary Scale of Intelligence—Revised for four- to six-year-olds (Wechsler, 1989), or the Wechsler Intelligence Scale for Children—Third Edition, which is for six- to sixteen-year-olds (Wechsler, 1991). All of these intelligence tests are individually administered and yield an intelligence quotient (IQ) score. The average IQ score is 100. Any evaluated child's IQ score indicates how far the child's score is above or below the IQ score of an average child of the same age (Wicks-Nelson & Israel, 1997).

Most intelligence tests are designed to emphasize the assessment of verbal abilities, which are important in academic achievement. They, however, also are designed to measure other abilities that are important for academic success. For example, the Stanford-Binet is designed to measure abstract/visual reasoning, quantitative reasoning, and short-term memory as well as verbal reasoning. The correlation of IQ scores with school grades and reading, spelling, and mathematics achievement scores have been reported (Berger & Yule, 1985) to range from low (.40) to moderately high (.75).

Academic Achievement Assessment

Both standardized achievement tests and grades in school are commonly used to assess academic achievement of African American children and other children. Standardized achievement tests are used to assess functioning in particular areas such as math, reading, spelling, and arithmetic skills. Some of these tests are individually administered and others are group administered.

Two often used group administered tests are the Iowa Test of Basic Skills (Hieronymous & Hoover, 1985) and the Stanford Achievement Test (Gardner, Rudman, Kurlsen, & Merwin, 1982). Two often used individually administered measures of academic achievement are the Wide Range Achievement Test (Jastak & Wilkinson, 1984) and the Woodcock Master Tests (Woodcock, Mather, & Barnes, 1987). In general, achievement tests include only a sample of the possible specific behaviors or competencies that comprise a particular skill area. These tests are designed to provide an estimate of a child's performance relative to that of her or his peers (Erickson, 1992).

Grades awarded by children's teachers in math and reading as well as overall grade point averages in all academic subjects taken are also commonly used as measures of academic achievement. These grades are typically based on multiple criteria that vary across teachers. These criteria include teacher-constructed tests on subject matter discussed in class, student oral participation in class, and the quality and grammatical accuracy of written assignments. Grades typically are at least to some degree subjectively determined by teachers.

Assessment of Academic Performance Impairments

It is not unusual for undiagnosed physical problems and mental disorders to significantly impair children's academic performance. Assessment of these problems is important to understand a child's academic performance and to determine needed interventions to help the child perform up to her or his academic potential. The methods of assessing possible impairments of children's academic performance often include obtaining family and child histories, conducting a physical examination of the child, and conducting an evaluation of nervous system functioning through the combined use of a neurological assessment and a neuropsychological assessment.

Family and Child Histories and Physical Examinations

Family and child histories and physical examinations may reveal genetic problems that are treatable such as phenylketonuria (PKU)—a recessive gene condition that affects cognitive functioning. Most of the cognitive problems associated with PKU can be prevented by avoiding phenylalanine in the child's diet (Wicks-Nelson & Israel, 1997). Family and child histories and physical examinations can also reveal something as simple as poor vision and hearing, both of which can significantly impact academic performance.

Neurological Assessment

A neurological assessment directly assesses nervous system functioning. An evaluation of nervous system functioning is important in understanding mental retardation, autism, learning disabilities or disorders, and attention deficit disorders, all of which can impair academic performance. Modern neurological assessments often include some combination of the following: an electroencephalograph (EEG), a computerized tomography or a CT scan (commonly referred to as a computerized axial tomography or CAT scan), positron emission tomography (PET) scans, and magnetic resonance imaging (MRI). An EEG records activity of the brain cortex. The CT scan and CAT scan are used to get images of the brain that can reveal abnormalities of the brain, such as blood clots or tumors. PET scans allow determination of the rate of activity of different parts of the brain. MRI gives images of the brain. Brain and other neurological dysfunctions that might be revealed from a neurological assessment are thought to be associated with abnormal physical reflexes, motor coordination problems, and sensory and perceptual deficits that impact scores on intelligence tests and on school performance.

Neuropsychological Assessment

A neuropsychological assessment indirectly assesses nervous system functioning. It consists of tests that include learning, sensorimotor, perceptual, verbal, and memory tasks. These tests are primarily used to distinguish groups of learning and behavioral disorders that are presumed to have a neurodevelopmental etiology (Wicks-Nelson & Israel, 1997). Test results are also used to discriminate learning disabled learners from normal learners (Taylor, 1988) and to evaluate level of recovery from a head injury.

Among the most widely used batteries for neuropsychological assessments are the Halstead-Reitan and the Luria-Nebraska test batteries (Hynd, Snow, & Becker, 1986; Slomka & Tarter, 1993). The Halstead Neuropsychological Test Battery is used for children between the ages of nine and fourteen. The Reitan-Indiana Neuropsychological Test Battery is used for children five to eight years of age. The Luria-Nebraska Neuropsychological Battery—Children's Revision is used for children eight to twelve years of age. Each of these batteries consists of several subtests or scales, and each of the subtests or scales is designed to assess one or more abilities. In addition to one of the age-appropriate batteries or parts of these batteries, it is typical to include some or all of the following tests: (1) the Wechsler Intelligence Scales, (2) achievement tests, and (3) the Bender Visual-Motor Gestalt Test.

Assessment of Influences on Academic Performance

Classroom behavioral observations are commonly used by behaviorally oriented psychologists and counselors to assess negative and positive environmental influences and other influences on children's academic performance. Psychologists and counselors in general often use informal, unstructured interviews with teachers and parents to determine factors that might have a negative or positive impact on the academic performance of children. Sometimes children themselves are also interviewed.

Classroom Behavioral Observations

Observation of a child in a classroom setting often provides the following types of information that might be helpful in understanding the child's academic performance: (1) the frequency within a specified time period (e.g., a five-minute time period) that the child is engaging in off-task behaviors that preclude academic learning such as daydreaming or talking with others, (2) whether the child sits in a social group of peers who engage the child in off-task behaviors, (3) the frequency and duration of positive attention and negative attention that the child receives from the teacher, (4) whether the child appears sluggish and uninvolved in class, and (5) whether the child appears anxious when called on by the teacher to participate in class. Classroom observations ideally should be conducted at different times during the day and for periods long enough for the reactivity to the observer to disappear or to be minimized before actual observation data or notes are taken.

Informal Interviews with Teachers and Parents

Psychologists and counselors often conduct academic assessment interviews with a child's teachers and parents or primary caregivers to get their perspectives as to the child's level of academic performance and what might be significant influences on the child's academic performance. The interviews with teachers often focus on their perceptions of the child's level of attentiveness to class activities, level of off-task behaviors, ability to learn, reactions to failure and success, level of motivation to learn, level of assistance with homework at home, level of support from parents for academic success, academic deficits, and needs in order to perform up to the child's academic ability.

The interviews with parents by psychologists or counselors often focus on parents' perceptions of their child's academic performance level, academic weaknesses and strengths, needs for academic success, level of motivation to learn, level of interest in school, learning style, classroom behavior, level of support at home, level of encouragement and assistance from the child's teachers, and feelings about the child's teachers, classmates, and school. The interviews with parents also focus on whether the child has a study place and structured study time, receives help with homework, and engages in problem behaviors at home. Parents' grade expectations, reactions to unsatisfactory grades and to satisfactory grades, level of involvement and satisfaction with the child's teachers, and level of involvement in the child's school activities are also often assessed in parent interviews.

Informal Interviews with Children

Academic assessment interviews by psychologists and counselors with children usually focus on the child's perceptions of her or his level of academic performance as well as the child's perceptions of the levels of academic help and support that she or he receives from teachers and parents. The views of these youth as to how important it is to study and make good grades and as to what would help them make better grades are also sometimes assessed. Additionally, questions are often asked to assess the child's study habits and skills and test-taking attitudes and skills.

Whether the focus of an academic performance assessment is on assessing the level of academic performance or on identifying any impairments of academic performance, multimethod assessments and multidimensional assessments are ideal. This is because it is important for a child or adolescent to be understood in the context of her or his family, peer, and school systems, which requires gathering information from various sources such as parents, teachers, and so on. Furthermore, the assessment methods should be socioeconomically and culturally appropriate for the child being assessed. For example, assessment of a European American child's level of academic performance might include grades, standardized achievement test scores, an intelligence test for children, and interview data regarding the child's, parent's, and teacher's perception of the academic performance level being assessed. Because of the agreement among some professionals that intelligence tests are culturally biased and have led to social injustice (Kamin, 1974; Kaplan, 1985), an intelligence test may not be appropriate for inclusion in the assessments to evaluate the academic performance of an African American child. If an intelligence test is included, results from it should be viewed cautiously and should not be used alone as the basis for conclusions about a child's academic problems and needed interventions to address the child's academic problems.

Because most schools have limited financial and human resources for academic performance assessments, multimethod and multidimensional assessments often do not occur; and when these assessments do occur, they are often done by professionals who are not skilled in working with children and families who are culturally and socioeconomically different from majority children and families. Consequently, sometimes inappropriate decisions are made about programs and interventions to meet the academic performance needs of children. To avoid such occurrences, more resources are needed in schools for the execution of multimethod and multidimensional assessments of the academic performance of adolescents by professionals who are skilled in the administration of these assessments and familiar with and sensitive to cultural and socioeconomic differences among children who are evaluated.

Given that academic assessment resources are not and will not be available in many schools, especially public schools, parents must take it upon themselves to be actively involved in the decision making about educational programs and interventions for their children with problematic academic performance. Parents must insist on the reevaluation of decisions about educational programs and interventions for their children that were not based on multimethod and multidimensional assessments, especially when these programs or interventions do not appear to be facilitating their children's academic success.

Limitations and Biases in Assessments

Standardized achievement tests, intelligence tests, and neuropsychological assessments have known limitations and biases, which suggest that reliance on these tests alone is inappropriate. Such limitations and biases can result in misdiagnoses of students' strengths and weaknesses and placement of children in educational programs that are not consistent with their academic needs.

Limitations of Standardized Tests

Standardized measures of academic performance have the following important limitations: (1) They are not sensitive to small changes in achievement, (2) they are not reflective of local school curriculum, and (3) they may not measure the content that students actually experience (Bergin, Hudson, Chryst, & Reseter, 1992). Additionally, standardized academic performance tests cannot measure other important outcomes such as continued interest in learning (Maehr, 1976), increased learning efforts, improved social competence, or a preference for challenging versus easy tasks (Bergin, Hudson, Chryst, & Reseter, 1992), all of which may be important indices of academic progress.

It is also noteworthy that test reliability studies suggest that cultural, gender, linguistic, and other types of biases may exist in standardized tests such that a given achievement test score or other standardized test score is influenced by factors other than actual achievement or ability (Bergin, Hudson, Chryst, & Reseter, 1992). Such biased results then often provide the basis for decisions regarding the educational opportunities that a child is capable of experiencing. For example, low scores on reading tests by students for whom English is a second language or students with undiagnosed visual problems could result in these students being placed in special decelerated reading classes that do not challenge these students and cause them to miss participation in reading competitions and related activities that foster self-pride and opportunities for awards and scholarships.

Limitations of Intelligence Tests

A major limitation of intelligence tests is that although they indicate deficiencies in abilities, they do not indicate the reasons for these deficiencies. Other limitations of intelligence tests are associated with how intelligence scores have come to be interpreted and used over the years. For example, for many professionals, stability of low intelligence test scores has been misinterpreted to mean that educational intervention programs will be useless for a child with such consistent scores. Yet, such consistent scores could really reflect that the child's deprived home and school environments have remained fairly constant over time.

Among the many criticisms of intelligence tests is that they are culturally biased (Kamin, 1974; Kaplan, 1985). Yet, they continue to be used in educational placement and in labeling of African American children and other culturally diverse youth groups. Because the tests are likely culturally biased, placements and labels based on them may be inaccurate and result in inappropriate expectations of and educational interventions for nonmajority youth.

Other criticisms of intelligence tests are that these tests often view intelligence as a real entity rather than as a concept and that these tests view intelligence as a rigid and fixed attribute rather than as something complex and subtle (Wicks-Nelson & Israel, 1997). A common view today is that improvement is needed in the construction of and in the degree of caution used in the administration of intelligence tests and in the interpretation of results from these tests (Kamphaus, 1993; Kaufman, 1990). When it comes to use of intelligence tests with African American youth and other nonmajority youth, there is little evidence that such caution is being taken.

Biases in Neuropsychological Assessments

It is mistakenly assumed that the behaviors and skills that are assessed with neuropsychological assessments and the assessments themselves are free from social and environmental influences. Making this assumption is a mistake because there is little empirical justification for it (Taylor & Fletcher, 1990) and because of found relationships between the occurrence of brain damage and social class. For example, brain damage has been found to be correlated with social class and family variables that are disadvantageous to social adjustment and physical health (Sameroff & Chandkler, 1975). These social and family variables may also underlie the brain damage and the observed behavior problems or learning problems often revealed in neuropsychological assessments (Wicks-Nelson & Israel, 1997). The typical lack of sensitivity to these variables can result in implications for treatment that are inadequate and perhaps culturally and socioeconomically insensitive.

Biases and Limitations of Interviews
and Behavioral Observations

Informal, unstructured interviews with parents, children, and teachers that are commonly used in academic performance assessments are likely biased to some degree by social desirability or the desire to present oneself in a positive light. Consequently, parents, teachers, and children may be guarded against giving responses that reveal them to be less than adequately involved in the educational process; thus, their responses have questionable reliability. Lack of trust of European American assessment professionals by African American parents and some African American children may further contribute to the providing of responses by these parents and children that may not be reliable.

Behavioral observational data in the classroom can also be biased. This is especially likely when the observer and the child being observed are from different cultures and socioeconomic backgrounds. This is because behaviors that are considered off-task, inappropriate, or hyperactive behaviors in one culture may not be viewed as such in another culture. For example, a low-income African American child who interrupts her middle class teacher and peers to add her views to the class discussion and who actively moves around in her seat may be viewed by a European American observer who is not culturally sensitive as hyperactive or as having a behavior control problem, whereas the child's parents and a culturally sensitive observer may more likely view the behavior of the child as energetic behavior but not "problematic." Indeed, many African American children have a culture-based preference for spontaneity and verve and, thus, it is inappropriate to label these behaviors as deviant or problematic, even though they may need to be substituted for other behaviors in the classroom setting to facilitate these children's academic success.

It is also the case that many European Americans who assess academic performance bring to their jobs certain stereotypes of African Americans and other groups. One such stereotype is that African Americans are lazy. An academic performance assessor who holds this stereotype may consequently see more unmotivated, off-task behavior in an African American child than one who does not hold this stereotype. Thus, it is important that behavioral observations and interviews to assess academic performance be conducted by more than one person and include individuals who are culturally and socioeconomically sensitive. The resulting data taken together will likely give a more accurate assessment of the child and will allow determination of the interrater reliability of data obtained. The latter provides some indication of the level of confidence one can have that the data obtained are accurate.

Culture- and SES-Sensitive Assessments

The many limitations and biases that plague the methods commonly used to assess children's academic performance have implications for assessing the academic performance of African American children, who typically are socioeconomically and culturally different from the psychologists, counselors, and teachers who spearhead or execute leadership roles in these assessments. These implications are discussed next in the form of culturally and socioeconomically sensitive recommendations for assessing the academic performance of African American children.

1. Avoid using intelligence tests or only use these tests as hypotheses generators when assessing the academic performance of African American children. This is because intelligence tests and most other psychological tests tend to be standardized on European American, middle-class children and are insensitive to cultural differences (Flaugher, 1978; Sattler, 1988). Even when there are African American norms, intelligence tests do not provide information about the absolute abilities of any child. How a child is feeling physically and emotionally on a particular day, the testing and interpersonal skills of the tester, the child's test-taking skills, and what the child is told regarding the purpose of the test can all affect the child's performance on the test.

2. Make every effort to have African American professionals or other professionals who are culturally and socioeconomically sensitive administer psychological tests and intelligence tests to African American children. Multiple assurances of confidentiality from a European American assessor may have little effect on the feelings of African American youth who are suspicious of and mistrust European Americans because of experienced racism or because of having been taught to feel this way by African American families who have been victimized by European Americans. This mistrust of European Americans is acceptable normative behavior for many African American youth (Allen & Majidi-Ahi, 1989).

3. Multiple assessment methods and assessment dimensions should be used in assessing the academic performance of African American children. It is important that an assessment team be involved in the assessment and that this team is not only skilled but also aware of the limitations of and the biases in the assessment methods and in the sources of assessment data. Minimally, it is important that members of the assessment team be culturally and socioeconomically sensitive.

4. Given that African American youth often do not perform well on standardized tests, it is especially important that assessment of their academic performance includes grades, level of their active engagement in academic learning (e.g., average number of hours of study and percentage of school days at school), their teachers' ratings of their academic performance, their self-ratings of their academic performance, and achievement test data that are directly related to what they are taught in the classroom. Shultz (1993) reported using such achievement tests with minority children in urban schools because the content is more instructionally valid; that is, it is more representative of what is actually being taught in schools. Specifically, Shultz (1993) used the Basic Achievement Skills Individual Screener (BASIS) to measure academic performance rather than a standardized achievement test. Fantuzzo, Davis, and Ginsberg (1995) also have advocated for using curriculum-based assessments as academic performance measures. These researchers concluded that such assessments are closer to students' daily work and are more sensitive to change rather than tests based on a more global set of expectations.

5. Efforts should be made by the assessor of academic performance to reduce the potentially negative impact of lack of test-taking skills on an African American child's test performance. These efforts ideally should include rehearsal of the test-taking instructions and procedures, explanation of the different types of tasks on the tests, building rapport with the child before testing begins, and allowing time for the child to ask questions before the testing begins. Regarding the latter, Zigler and his colleagues found that rapport with the examiner was strongly related to academic performance for African American students but not for European American students (Zigler & Butterfield, 1968; Zigler, Abelson, & Seitz, 1973). This finding suggests that it is particularly important for an assessor of academic performance to make the effort to establish rapport with an African American child prior to the assessment process in order to increase the likelihood of obtaining valid and reliable academic performance assessment data from that child.

6. Level of school engagement (e.g., effort to learn and school attendance) should be included in academic performance measures rather than just grades, test scores, and subjective ratings of academic performance because eliciting student engagement may be the most important ultimate goal. Connell, Halpern-Felsher, Clifford, Crichlow, and Usinder (1995) concluded that "African American males' engagement in their school work in junior high school has long-term benefits over and above its relations with contemporaneous education performance and adjustment indicators" (p. 58).

7. Include some standardized assessments in multimethod assessments of academic performance, primarily because such data are typically needed to get funding to conduct research for development and evaluation of alternative academic assessment methods and procedures. Furthermore, standardized inventories can be used to obtain baseline information on language and cognitive achievement; over the years, changes in these areas of achievement can be evaluated. Alternative assessment measures to standardized tests that can be used and tested for their usefulness as academic assessment methods include behavioral observations, examples of academic work collected over time, anecdotal notes, and structured subjective evaluation rating scales and checklists (Hale-Benson, 1986).

8. Use individualized approaches to assessing academic performance. In such approaches a child is compared to herself or himself to determine improvements over time. Assessment strategies that measure individual achievement relative to a particular starting point often provide a clearer picture of an individual's growth in a given area. Changes in perceived self-control over academic performance, self-motivation to learn, self-praise frequency, and skills for academic success (e.g., study skill level) are especially important assessment areas because it is these areas that will help children succeed academically whether or not they get desired academic support and encouragement from teachers and parents.

9. When interviewing African American parents as a part of the assessment of their child's academic performance, it is recommended that the following questions be included in the interview.

   a. What are your feelings about answering some questions about your child's grades and school-related behaviors, attitudes, and experiences? Are there any questions that you would like to ask before I ask you some questions? Is there anything that you would like explained or done to make answering my questions more comfortable for you?

b. What is the typical routine of your child from the time he or she leaves school each day?

c. How comfortable are you in helping your child with homework, if he or she needed help? Are there others in the home who feel comfortable helping your child with homework?

d. Do you know all of your child's teachers? To what degree do you think each of them is genuinely interested in teaching and supporting your child?

e. How comfortable are you talking with your child's teacher(s)? How frequently do you talk with each of them?

f. What is your understanding of how your child's grades are determined?

g. How satisfied are you with your child's grades? What happens when your child brings home a grade that is not satisfactory? What happens when your child brings home a grade that is satisfactory?

h. Do you feel that your child is making grades and earning test scores that reflect her or his true ability? What kinds of grades should your child be making? What do you think would help your child make better grades?

i. Do you feel that your child's race or ethnicity affects the education that she or he receives or her or his grades? If so, how?

j. Do you encourage your child to study every day?

k. What are your child's goals and what are you and your child doing to prepare her or him to meet those goals?

l. How often do you or someone else take your child for a regular physical health checkup, including examination of his or her sight and hearing?

m. How satisfied are you with the amount of sleep your child gets and the kinds of food she or he eats? What is your child's sleeping and eating schedule?

n. How do you feel about our interview? Are there any comments you would like to add about your child? Are there any questions you would like to ask about my questions or the reasons for them?

10. When interviewing African American children as part of the assessment of their academic performance, it is recommended that the following questions be included as part of the interview.

a. How do you feel about talking with me about your grades and school-related behaviors, attitudes, and experiences? Are there any questions that you would like to ask me before I begin asking you some questions? Is there anything that you would like for me to explain or do to make answering my questions more comfortable for you?

b. Do you feel that you belong at your school?

c. How comfortable are you with your teachers and classmates? Is there anything that your teachers or classmates could do to make being with them more comfortable?

d. Do you ask questions in class about what you do not understand? If not, why not?

e. How do you feel about taking tests in class? What would make taking tests better for you?

f. How satisfied are you with the grades that you are making? What would help you make better grades?

g. Do you get the help and encouragement that you need from your teachers? What would you like for your teachers to do that they are not doing? What would you like for them to stop doing?

h. Does your race have anything to do with your grades? If so, what?

i. Do you think that you know how to study successfully? How often do you study? When you study and come across something that you do not understand, what do you do? What would make it easier for you to study at home?

j. How often and when do you eat each day? Describe what you ate throughout the day yesterday.

k. When you make a grade that is unsatisfactory to you, how do you feel and what do you do? How do your parents react to a grade that is unsatisfactory to them?

l. How important is it for you to make good grades? Why? Who controls what grades you make?

m. When you make grades that are satisfactory to you, how do you feel and what do you do?

n. When you make grades that you think are good, what do your parents say and do?

o. How much effort do you make to earn good grades?

p. What are your future short-term goals and long-term goals? What are you doing to help yourself meet these goals?

q. How do you feel about our interview? Is there anything that you would like to tell me about yourself or your experiences with school? Are there any questions you would like to ask about my questions or the reasons for them?

11. When interviewing teachers of African American children as part of the assessment of these children's academic performance, it is recommended that the following questions be included as part of the interview.

a. How do you feel about talking with me about John's grades and school-related behaviors, attitudes and experiences? Are there any questions that you would like to ask me before I begin asking you some questions? Is there anything that you would like for me to explain or do to make answering my questions more comfortable for you?

b. How do you feel about having John in your class? What do you see as his strengths and weaknesses?

c. What do you think are the causes of John's academic weaknesses? What is needed to help John overcome these weaknesses?

d. What do you think needs to happen for John to make better grades in your class?

e. What have you done in an effort to help John learn better and make better grades?

f. Do you feel that the grades John makes are reflective of his true ability?

g. How involved are John's parents in his education? How often do you speak with John's parents about his academic performance and behavior in your class? Who initiates these conversations?

h. Does John participate in class discussions? If not, why do you think this is the case?

i. Do you think that John's race or ethnicity has anything to do with his academic performance in your class? If so, in what way?

j. How do you recognize and facilitate acceptance of cultural differences in your class?

k. How much experience have you had teaching African American children? Is there anything that you do differently in teaching these children? If so, what?

l. Is there anything else that you can tell me about John that might be helpful in understanding him as a student?

m. How do you feel about our interview? Is there anything that you would like to tell me about John or your experiences in teaching him? Are there any questions you would like to ask about my questions or the reasons for them?

Recommendations for Concerned Parents

It is not unusual for African American parents not to be involved in assessments of their children's academic performance and then be told of a special class or program that academic assessment results suggest is appropriate for their children. These parents often worry that such placements are not in the best interest of their children; yet, they feel unprepared to argue with test data and experts in evaluating the academic performance of their children. Furthermore, many parents are not aware of the biases and limitations of the assessment methods used to assess academic performance. Without this information, they are especially unlikely to appeal the decisions of school administrators and teachers about their children's educational needs. Because school administrators and teachers are perceived by many African American parents as having much power over the academic futures of their children, challenging the perspectives of these education professionals is particularly difficult or impossible for many of these parents.

Parents who are concerned about test results and the recommendations of school administrators and teachers based on these results have several constructive actions available to them. Following are some of these constructive actions.

1. Parents can calmly express their concerns to the school administrators of their child's school and to their child's teachers. Additionally, parents can ask to have their child reevaluated by a nonmajority professional with expertise in working with African American children. It is advisable for parents to get help from a church member, family member, or friend in education in formulating these concerns so that they can be most effectively presented. It is important to have concerns and requests in letter form so that the letter can guide the discussion and document the parents' concerns and requests. Parents should copy the letter to all involved (e.g., the school principal and the child's teachers) and request that a copy of the letter be placed in the child's academic record.

2. Parents can request that any labels used in the academic assessment report of results be removed so as to not have your child stigmatized by the label. Teacher expectations of students are often tied to such labels. Children often live up to or down to teachers' expectations.

3. Parents can become actively involved in their child's education, insisting on participating in decisions about their child before they are made. Parents should come up with alternatives to placing their children in special classes for slow learners and volunteer to help implement these alternatives. For example, parents can get their child into an after-school academic tutoring and academic skills training program and make sure that at least one parent attends with the child. Another example is that parents can arrange for individual tutoring of their child in collaboration with the child's teachers to make sure that the child's academic weaknesses are addressed in this tutoring.

4. Parents can visit their child's class and talk with their child's teachers at least twice weekly. In other words, parents must translate their concern about assessment results into actions to make sure that their child gets the academic assistance that she or he needs. To do this parents must be prepared to commit time and energy to letting school administrators and teachers know by their actions that they are willing to work diligently to ensure that their child gets the best available education. Teachers and school administrators tend to join the efforts of parents when parents show by actions their intent to get the best possible education for their child.

Conclusions

It is clear that assessment of the academic performance of African American children is challenging given the limitations and cultural biases and other biases that plague the commonly used academic assessment methods. Multimethod and multidimensional assessments of academic performance of African American youth are important. It is also important that the assessments be conducted by African Americans or others who are culturally and socioeconomically sensitive.

Multimethod assessments with African American children might include standard achievement tests, curriculum-based assessments, grades, subjective ratings of academic performance by parents, teachers, and children themselves, and level of academic engagement (level of school attendance, academic effort, etc.). This latter measure is important because it will determine whether the student will stay in school and have learning experiences. Given the cultural and other biases in commonly used intelligence tests, such tests should only be used with African American children to generate hypotheses about academic strengths and weaknesses.

It is especially important that assessments to identify impairments of and factors in academic performance be multidimensional; that is, the assessments should include data on family influences, physical influences, and school influences. Such assessments require obtaining data from parents, teachers, the children being assessed, and professionals who conduct physical examinations and neurological and neuropsychological evaluations of the child. It is important that the results of these assessments be considered in light of the child's family, social, and environmental contexts.

It should also be considered that parents, teachers, and children who are interviewed may give responses that are socially desirable rather than totally accurate and that what one sees when conducting behavioral observations is often subjective.

It is very useful to individualize assessments such that performance of the child is measured over time in particular areas. These areas ideally should include perceived self-control over academic performance, self-motivation to learn, self-praise of academic success, and level of academic success behaviors and skills (e.g., level of study skills); after all, it is these characteristics, behaviors, and skills that will ultimately ensure academic success whether or not children receive the support of parents and teachers.

African American parents have the right and responsibility to be actively involved in assessments of their children's academic performance and in decisions about placement of their children in special programs. When this right is abused, parents can take positive, constructive actions to make sure that their opinions, concerns, and wishes regarding their children's education are heard and respected. These actions can include having their child's academic performance reevaluated by culturally sensitive academic performance assessors and proposing alternative educational interventions for their children. When parents express concerns about academic evaluations of their children and take constructive actions to address these concerns, school administrators and teachers tend to join with these parents to come up with the best possible education for their children.

CHAPTER

11

Fostering Academic Success

General Intervention Approaches and Strategies

Even when some African American youth say that they do not care that they are failing, it is important to remind ourselves that these youth like all Americans find it much more desirable to succeed than to fail in school and life. When these children experience academic failure, they often use defense or coping mechanisms such as rationalization to deal with the emotional pain of failure. Rationalization involves telling themselves and others that it was not important to succeed and, thus, they did not try to succeed. Such defense mechanisms often mislead teachers and parents into thinking that these African American children do not want to be academically successful. Consequently, teachers and parents may lower their expectations of these youth and experience low instructional and motivational self-efficacy in their educational roles with these children. In other words, teachers and parents may give up or reduce their efforts to help these children experience academic and social success because they feel that their efforts will be in vain. Children and adolescents live down to these lowered expectations and efforts.

There is some research support for the view that African American children do want to be academically challenged and want to finish school. For example, in a survey conducted by Garibaldi (1992) with 2,250 African American male students in schools in New Orleans, it was found that 95 percent of these male students expected to graduate from high school and 60 percent felt that their teachers needed to push them harder to succeed. Additionally, it was found that 40 of the male students surveyed believed that their teachers did not set high enough goals for them. Ironically, in a survey of 500 teachers in New Orleans, Garibaldi (1992) found that almost 60 percent of the teachers surveyed did not expect that their African American students would go to college. The author reported that 70 percent of these teachers were elementary school teachers and 65 percent were African American.

In order to move African American children from academic failure or academic underachievement to academic success, parents, other family members, teachers, and other educators involved in these youth's education must minimally (1) believe that these youth want to be academically successful, no matter what they say and do to the contrary, (2) have high expectations of these youth for academic success, (3) believe that the parents, other family members, teachers, and other educators have or can get the knowledge and skills to help these youth be academically successful, and (4) use culturally and socioeconomically sensitive approaches and strategies, including self-empowerment strategies, to facilitate academic and social success of these youth.

Additionally, parents, other family members, teachers, and other educators must be diligent in using approaches and strategies for effectively moving African American youth from academic failure or underachievement to academic success. Indeed, these academic interventions will not be effective unless they are used over a period of time. According to Watson and Tharp (1993), when desired behavior changes do not occur, it is usually because the behavior interventions are not used or are used inconsistently; it is not because they do not work.

This chapter presents some general intervention approaches and strategies for helping African American children and adolescents who are academically failing or underachieving to experience academic success. The importance of these interventions and some suggestions for evaluating their effectiveness are also discussed. Additionally, some recommendations are made for psychologists and counselors in their efforts to help move African American children from academic failure or underachievement to academic success.

The Importance of a Self-Empowerment Approach

A self-empowerment approach to achieving academic success focuses on facilitating self-motivation for academic achievement, self-control of academic progress (e.g., self-instruction-based learning), self-praise of academic progress and success, skills for academic success, and academic success behaviors. The goal of this approach is to enable children to help themselves learn, to teach themselves, and to motivate and support themselves in the educational process. Given that African American students often will find themselves in families that are not actively involved in their education and in classrooms with teachers who get frustrated with their academic weaknesses, overlook their academic strengths, and do not recognize their need for support and encouragement, it is especially important for these students to be empowered to facilitate their own academic success. In other words, it is important for them to be able to experience academic success even when they do not receive the academic assistance, encouragement, and support from others (e.g., parents, teachers, schools, educational systems) that they deserve. A self-empowerment approach to achieving academic success helps prepare African American children for achieving success in whatever learning environment they find themselves.

A sense of powerlessness or lack of control over one's academic learning or one's success or failure has been reported to be associated with diminished academic effort and performance (Boggiano & Katz, 1991). Many African American children in majority-controlled classrooms and schools have this sense of powerlessness, which is in part because of the existence of few or no African Americans in positions of power in their schools, the predominance of the majority culture throughout their schools, and their total dependence on teachers for their academic learning, evaluation, and advancement. In response to finding that African American urban elementary school students rely on teachers for their evaluations of success and failure, Merchant (1991) asserted that schools must find ways to promote self-responsibility among students in general and African American students of low socioeconomic status in particular.

Views of Children, Parents, and Teachers

It is seldom that African American children, parents, and teachers are asked their views as to what is needed to facilitate academic success among African American students. Yet, many of these individuals have culturally and socioeconomically sensitive perspectives on the academic challenges that these students face and what is needed to meet these challenges. African American students and some of their parents have particularly good insights into the psychosocial needs of African American students.

Thus, the present author and her colleagues, using structured interviews, assessed the recommendations of African American students and their parents (or primary caregivers) and of African American teachers regarding what African American children, parents, and teachers should do to help African American students make better grades—the quintessential measure of academic achievement. This was done as part of a larger study of the views of African American students, parents, and teachers regarding the academic behaviors and performance of African American students (Tucker, Herman, Pederson, & Vogle, 1997). Elementary school students ($n = 24$) and teachers ($n = 5$) as well as high school students ($n = 19$) and teachers ($n = 8$) were among the interviewees. All participants lived in a small city in the South. The student participants were from low-income families. All of the parent participants were mothers or mother figures. Ninety-one percent of the teacher participants were female.

The recommendations of all participants in response to each of the three questions asked in the interviews regarding strategies for helping African American students improve their grades were summarized by participant group (i.e., elementary school children, high school children, elementary school parents, high school parents, elementary school teachers, and high school teachers). The responses by question and the percentage of times each response was given among all responses given to the question within each participant group follow.

Question
What should African American students do to help themselves make good grades?

Responses
Elementary School Children
Participate in class (ask questions, listen, and follow instructions) (52.2%)
Study and do homework regularly (23.9%)
Be self-determined and self-motivated (8.7%)
Various other recommendations (15.2%)

High School Children
Study regularly (43.6%)
Participate in class (ask questions, listen, and follow instructions) (30.8%)
Be self-determined and self-motivated (12.8%)
Various other recommendations (12.8%)

Question
What should African American parents do to help African American children make good grades?

Responses
Elementary School Children
Help students with homework and help them study (51.1%)
Visit students' school and teacher (14.0%)
Encourage and praise students (9.3%)
Various other recommendations (25.6%)

High School Children
Help with homework (25.9%)
Discuss school and schoolwork with students (25.9%)
Encourage and praise students (25.9%)
Various other recommendations (22.3%)

Elementary School Parents
Discuss school and schoolwork with students and structure study time (29.0%)
Help with homework (19.4%)
Visit students' school and teacher and volunteer to help the teacher (16.1%)
Various other recommendations (6.5%)

High School Parents
Help with homework (25.0%)
Discuss school and schoolwork with students and structure study time (25.0%)
Talk with students' teachers and attend school conferences (25.0%)
Various other recommendations (25.0%)

Elementary School Teachers
Help students with reading and studying (33.3%)
Encourage students (33.3%)
Give students extra academic work (33.3%)
Various other recommendations (0.0%)

High School Teachers
Help students with homework (28.6%)
Encourage and praise students (28.6%)
Talk with and visit students' teachers and school administrators (14.3%)
Various other recommendations (28.5%)

Question
What can teachers do to help African American students make good grades?

Responses
Elementary School Children
Ask if students understand; if not, give more explanation or help (54.5%)
Spend more time teaching and explaining (15.2%)
Be patient and encourage questions (12.1%)
Various other recommendations (18.2%)

High School Children
Ask if students understand; if not, give more explanation or help (40.0%)

Encourage and praise students (24.0%)
Be patient and encourage questions (12.0%)
Various other reasons (24.0%)

Elementary School Parents
Talk regularly with other parents and students (45.5%)
Give extra homework and help or explanation (22.7%)
Encourage, praise, and be sensitive (13.6%)
Various other recommendations (18.2%)

High School Parents
Give extra help or explanation (25.0%)
Encourage students and be sensitive (25.0%)
Talk regularly with parents (20.0%)
Various other recommendations (30.0%)

Elementary School Teachers
Specify and elevate students' expectations (33.3%)
Encourage students (33.3%)
Give extra work and effort to help (33.3%)
Various other recommendations (0.0%)

High School Teachers
Encourage and praise students (42.9%)
Seek extra help for students (14.3%)
Help develop students' study skills (14.3%)
Various other reasons (28.5%)

The foregoing data suggest that there is a great deal of agreement among the elementary and high school students and their parents and the high school teachers who participated in the interviews regarding what should be done to help African American students make better grades. There are also several noteworthy observations from these data. Particularly noteworthy is that the majority of elementary school children and high school children agree that they can help themselves make better grades by studying and participating in class through asking questions, listening, and following instructions from teachers.

These findings are interesting because they suggest that some African American students do not engage in important academic behaviors that lead to good grades not because they do not view these behaviors as important but perhaps because of other reasons. Perhaps some of these students do not engage in behaviors needed to make good grades because they do not know how to do the behaviors. Indeed, many African American students do not know how to study and have anxiety about participating in class and asking questions, especially when they have very little understanding of the subject matter and do not want to let on that this is case. It could also be the case that some African American students do not realize the importance of making good grades and, thus, are not motivated to engage in the behaviors that they know lead to good grades.

A common view among both the elementary school students and the high school students that teachers can help them make good grades by asking the students if they understand what has been taught and by giving more time to explain and teach what students do not understand further suggests that some African American students may be anxious about and reluctant to acknowledge what they do not know by asking for more in-depth teaching. The ultimate outcome of such anxiety and reluctance is not learning what is covered in class and then making poor grades.

Interestingly, it was also a common view among the elementary school parents and high school parents interviewed that teachers could help African American students make good grades by giving more in-depth explanations of what is taught in their classrooms. Similarly, it was a common view among teachers interviewed that teachers could help African American students make better grades by giving or arranging for them to receive extra help with their academic work or studying.

Another noteworthy observation from the preceding interview data is that both the elementary school students and high school students reported viewing encouragement from parents and teachers and having these two groups communicating as important in helping African American children make good grades. Some teachers interviewed also viewed parent encouragement and teacher encouragement as ways to help African American children make good grades; this view was more common among high school teachers. Teacher encouragement was also frequently reported among parents as a way to help students make good grades; this view was more often expressed among the high school parents. Surprisingly, the parents interviewed did not view encouragement by parents as a way that parents could help African American children make good grades.

Perhaps African American parents see teachers as playing a more significant role in encouraging their children when they are being taught; yet, a very popular view among the high school students interviewed was that encouragement by both parents and teachers is important in helping African American students make good grades. The association of self-reported parental encouragement with making good grades by African American high school students has been documented (Tucker, Harris, Brady, & Herman, 1995). Yet, parents often think that younger children as compared to older children need more encouragement and praise and, thus, tend to give them more.

Finally, it is noteworthy that a very common view of both the elementary school students and parents and the high school students and parents interviewed was that provision of help with homework by parents is a way to help African American students make good grades. Yet, in workshops with African American parents conducted by the present author, it is frequently expressed by these parents that they feel unprepared to help their children with homework, especially the children in fourth grade and higher. They reported feeling unprepared because of the new math being taught in schools and because of the new ways of teaching various academic subjects. Furthermore, it is common for African American parents to not be knowledgeable about computers and, thus, many feel inadequate in helping their children with computer-based learning exercises.

The findings from the foregoing interview data suggest the following:

1. Routine communication is needed among African American students and their parents and teachers about ways to help the students be academically successful. Each of these individuals must take responsibility for arranging and facilitating the occurrence of meetings for this communication to occur on a regular basis. These meetings should occur at an agreed upon time and place that does not have to be the school. For example, it might

be more comfortable for parents to have such meetings at a community center or at a fast-food restaurant in their community.

2. Parents need to find academic tutoring for their children during school hours and after school. In reality teachers are limited in the extra help that they can provide to any student. School administrators can and usually will assist parents in finding tutoring for their children.

3. Teachers must help enable parents to help their children be academically successful. For example, parents can be shown ways to help their children with homework. Teachers can also encourage parents to identify another family member to provide homework help to their child in cases where the parents question their capability to provide this help.

4. Teachers must not assume that African American students understand the subject matter just because these students do not ask questions. These students often need to be encouraged to ask questions; furthermore, this encouragement may initially need to occur one-on-one because African American students may feel uncomfortable asking questions in classrooms where there are low expectations of them or where they feel uncomfortable for various reasons. Teachers should also work to create a classroom atmosphere in which asking questions about what is not understood is viewed as intelligent and as engagement in learning that is respected and praised.

5. Teachers and parents need to help African American students with learning how to study effectively. Indeed, parents, psychologists, counselors, teachers, and other educators frequently tell African American students that they must study, but very seldom if ever has someone helped these students learn how to study.

6. Teachers and parents must self-empower African American children for academic and social success. In other words, teachers and parents must (a) teach these children to motivate themselves to study and learn, to teach themselves, and to reinforce themselves for their academic effort and progress; and (b) teach these children adaptive skills (communication skills, daily living skills, and socialization skills) and behaviors for academic and social success. It is just the reality that teachers will not always have the time and parents will often not have the resources, talent, time, or confidence to teach African American children what they need to learn. Additionally, parents and teachers will not always be available to support and encourage African American children.

Other General Intervention Strategies

Given that there are teacher, parent, school, neighborhood, social, psychosocial, psychological, cognitive, and physical factors that may influence the academic performance of any African American child, interventions to successfully facilitate children's academic success will need to be multidimensional. Because of the cultural and socioeconomic diversity among African American youth, the needed interventions will often differ across groups of African American students and across individual African American students within groups. However, there are some general intervention strategies that existing academic achievement theories and research suggest are particularly important in helping most African American children experience academic success, regardless of their specific academic problem (e.g., a reading disability). General interventions are ideal adjuncts to most intervention programs to help move African American youth from academic underachievement or failure to academic success.

Because academic failure or underachievement could be due to undiagnosed or unsuspected physical problems, it is important to make sure that any child who is failing or underachieving have a physical examination. This physical examination should be a part of the assessment process to identify factors in the achievement problems. Indeed, interventions designed to deal with physical problems, such as provision of eyeglasses, a modified teaching approach to address a learning disability, establishment of a bedtime schedule to address sleep deprivation, and removal of a tumor that is causing blurred vision and memory problems, may be needed to overcome academic failure or underachievement. Yet, even in such cases, general intervention strategies to facilitate the academic success of African American children will also be helpful.

Self-Empowerment Strategies

These general intervention strategies include self-motivation for academic achievement, self-control of academic progress, self-praise of academic effort and progress, and teaching of adaptive skills and behaviors for academic success. The goal of these strategies is to provide children with tools for succeeding under whatever learning conditions exist, including conditions where they will receive very little academic support and encouragement.

Strategy 1. Self-Motivation.   African American youth like other youth must be motivated to achieve, not because it will lead to higher grades or standardized achievement test scores but because it may lead to a greater sense of competence, value for learning, and utilization of their potential for success (Shultz, 1993). However, unlike the majority of children in America, African American children are victimized by racism and discrimination, which directly or indirectly negate the American achievement ideology for them. Thus, many of these youth do not see the links between their academic success and achieving their goals. Thus, they are often not motivated to achieve. Because many African American children will not have significant others (e.g., teachers, parents, siblings, and ministers) who can make time to motivate them to achieve, it is important that they become and remain self-motivated to achieve. Following are some ways to help African American children become self-motivated to achieve academic success.

1. Parents and teachers can help African American children establish short-term and long-term goals and frequently talk with these children about these goals. It is particularly important to discuss what the children need to do to reach these goals. For a fourth grader, a short-term goal might be to make a grade of A on the next math test, which will occur in three weeks. Reaching this goal might include having a specified number of hours to study each night, getting tutored three times a week in math, and asking the math teacher for extra math practice assignments.

A long-term goal for a fourth grader might be to get a summer job in two years as a library computer assistant. The plan for reaching this goal might include meeting some students who already have this job and finding out what they actually do and have to know to do this job; spending some time with library computer assistants on the job; and taking some computer courses in school or in the community.

2. Teachers can include learning activities that are consistent with children's goals. For example, teachers can have guests in class who are members in the professions in which the students are interested. Teachers can also make the extra effort to explain why school-work, such as learning standard English, is important for applying to college, for writing an essay to get a college scholarship, and for being an accountant or other professional.

3. Teachers and parents can encourage even young children to save their money for college. This is something that children can continue independently. It can help focus children on their future goals and also the academic achievement required to reach these goals.

4. Children can be challenged by their parents and teachers to do something each week on their own that will help them reach their short-term and long-term goals. They should be encouraged to share this information in class and with their families.

5. Parents and teachers can encourage children to read books and articles about successful African Americans whom they know and who came from backgrounds similar to their own.

6. Children can be constantly reminded that they are in charge of their success and that they must work toward some academic goal every day in order to reach their future goal. In other words, we can inject African American children with the American achievement ideology.

Strategy 2. Self-Control of Academic Progress.   Facilitation of self-control of academic progress is needed among African American children, especially those who feel quite powerless in their majority-controlled and majority-dominated classrooms. Self-control of academic progress increases the likelihood of academic success because it allows progress to occur in a step-by-step fashion. Furthermore, it allows small reinforcing successes to occur along the way to a successful outcome.

This type of learning is often called self-regulation learning and has been found to be significantly associated with high scores on standardized achievement math tests by African American high school students (Payne, 1991). There are several ways of facilitating self-regulation learning.

1. A step-by-step teaching and learning method based on Meichenbaum's cognitive modeling and self-instruction approach (Meichenbaum, 1977) can be used in the teaching and learning process. This method enables the learner to experience self-control that counteracts feelings of powerlessness—feelings that often accompany minority status and that often result in active or passive disengagement from the teaching and learning process.

The step-by-step teaching and learning process involves (a) breaking the skill or behavior to be learned into steps; (b) having the teacher model the skill or behavior using the steps and saying each step aloud (i.e., cognitive modeling); (c) having the student perform the same skill or behavior (as modeled by the teacher) while the teacher instructs the student using the steps; (d) instructing the student to perform the skill or behavior while using the steps to instruct himself or herself aloud and then silently (i.e., covert self-guidance); (e) having the student memorize the steps and practice the skill or behavior using the steps covertly; and (f) having the student self-praise progress toward and attainment of the behavior or skill throughout the learning and practice processes. An outline of the general steps in the step-by-step teaching and learning method is presented in Table 11.1.

An example of use of the step-by-step teaching and learning method when teaching long division to a child is provided in Table 11.2.

2. A step-by-step learning file can be established in the classroom for storing index cards with the steps written on them for learning various academic tasks such as taking a test, multiplying fractions, looking up a word, diagramming a sentence, and so on. Students can be given the freedom and encouraged to use these step-by-step cards to independently learn or practice academic tasks.

3. Students can be given individualized learning tasks that have step-by-step instructions. A teacher's aide or other class helper can be made available to help the children if they get stuck on one of the steps.

TABLE 11.1   The Step-by-Step Method for Teaching New Behaviors and Academic Tasks

---

1. The teacher figures out what steps are involved in doing the behavior or task by doing it prior to meeting with the learner.
2. The teacher writes the steps on a large index card or sheet of paper using clear print and simple wording (For example, "Step 1. Read instructions carefully.").
3. The teacher explains to the learner what will be taught using the steps on the sheet or index card.
4. The teacher shows the learner how to do the behavior or task by reading aloud and then doing each step (i.e., the teacher models for the learner). The learner is told to listen and observe the demonstration and to feel free to ask questions as the teacher demonstrates each step.
5. The teacher instructs the learner to read aloud and then do each step. The teacher assists the learner in getting a step correct when an error is made or when the learner has forgotten how to do a step. It is important to make sure that the learner does not skip any steps.
6. The teacher instructs the learner to read silently and then do each step.
7. The teacher instructs the learner to study the steps in an effort to memorize them.
8. The teacher instructs the learner to think and then do each step without looking at the card or paper on which the steps are written.

Notes

a. The teacher praises effort as well as successful accomplishment of each step.
b. When the learner has great difficulty with any step, the teacher directs the learner to an earlier step that can be done successfully and then instructs the learner to move to the next step.
c. Give the learner a copy of the steps for use in practicing the behavior or task at a later time.
d. On a day soon after the training in doing the behavior or task, the teacher asks the learner to do it without the paper with the steps. If the learner is not able to successfully do this, then the teacher repeats the step-by-step method for doing the behavior or task.

TABLE 11.2   A Step-by-Step Method for Long Division

Get ready to divide by doing A, B, and C.

    A. Read the problem.

    B. Say to yourself, "I can do this math division problem. I will relax and do it
       step by step."

Example

    C. Take three slow, deep breaths to relax. Now begin to do the problem.

$$4\overline{)268}$$

Step 1. *Divide*

    Divide the divisor into the first number or numbers in the dividend into which it is
    small enough to fit. 4 into 2 will not fit. 4 into 26 will fit 6 times. Write this num-
    ber of times as the first quotient number.

$$\overset{6}{4\overline{)268}}$$

Step 2. *Multiply*

    Multiply the quotient times the divisor and write your answer under the dividend.
    $6 \times 4 = 24$

$$\overset{6}{4\overline{)268}} \\ 24$$

Step 3. *Subtract*

    Subtract your answer. $26 - 24 = 2$

$$\overset{6}{4\overline{)268}} \\ -24 \\ \overline{2}$$

Step 4. *Bring Down*

    Bring down the next number in the dividend, which is 8.

$$\overset{6}{4\overline{)268}} \leftarrow \\ -24 \quad\downarrow \\ \overline{28} \leftarrow$$

Step 5. *Start over with Step 1.*

    1. *Divide*   Divide 4 into 28. It will fit 7 times. Write this number in
                the quotient.

    2. *Multiply*   Multiply the new quotient number times the divisor
                and write your answer under the dividend. $7 \times 4 = 28$

$$\overset{67}{4\overline{)268}} \\ -24 \\ \overline{28} \\ -28 \leftarrow$$

    3. *Subtract*   Subtract your answer.

                    The number left at the bottom is called the remainder.
                    The remainder is zero.

$$\overset{67}{4\overline{)268}} \\ -24 \\ \overline{28} \\ -28 \\ \overline{0}$$

    4. *Bring Down*   There is no number left in the dividend to bring down. This means
                    that you have finished the division problem.

Step 6 *Self-Praise*

    Praise yourself for having finished the long division problem. Feel good about
    yourself.

4. Tutors who work with African American children can be trained in using the step-by-step teaching method in tutoring. The tutor can make step-by-step cards for academic tasks taught and file these cards so that the tutored children can later independently do similar academic tasks.

Strategy 3. Self-Reinforcement of Academic Effort, Progress, and Success.   Reinforcement of academic effort, progress, and successful outcomes increases the likelihood of these occurrences; yet, effort and incremental progress are often not recognized by teachers and parents of African American students. Sometimes this is because academic effort and progress are overshadowed by the children's academic failures and behavior problems associated with these failures. Furthermore, there are teachers and parents who feel that they should not have to or do not have time to praise every little academic accomplishment that a child experiences or achieves. Therefore, it is important to encourage African American youth to praise themselves and to feel good for academic effort, progress, and success outcomes.

Edgar and Clement (1980) reported that self-controlled reinforcement is significantly more effective than teacher-controlled reinforcement in changing targeted academic behaviors of underachieving African American fourth-grade boys. The reinforcers were points for being focused on the assigned academic task at the time that a buzzer on a variable interval schedule was sounded. The points could be exchanged for a fun activity.

Given that some teachers and African American parents are opposed to tangible rewards for what they feel that their children should do without rewards, overt and covert self-praise plus self-imposed positive affect (feeling good about oneself) plus external praise from parents, teachers, and others can be used in combination as alternatives to tangible reinforcers. Frequent external praise is important initially in conjunction with self-praise and self-imposed positive affect in order to establish the self-praise and self-imposed positive affect. After a few weeks of this praise combination, the external praise can be reduced to a periodic level that is realistic for parents, family members, and teachers over time.

Ideally, self-praise or self-reinforcement is not to serve as a substitute for external praise or reinforcement; instead, self-praise is an important support for African American youth whether or not external praise or reinforcement is given. It facilitates students' self-confidence and perseverance for goal attainment. Self-praise or self-reinforcement is indeed an alternative support for children in environments in which they receive little or no praise or encouragement for their academic effort, progress, or success. Following are some specific self-praise and other self-reinforcement strategies that students can use.

1. Students can say aloud and silently to themselves statements such as "I am proud of myself for trying really hard to do this math, even though I have only completed one problem."

2. Students can wrap their arms around themselves and give themselves a hug and say aloud or silently, "I feel so really good all over about finishing my math; I deserve this big hug for staying focused until I finished it."

3. Students can set academic goals and decide on a self-reward (e.g., play time, calling a friend, or going to a movie with allowance money that they routinely receive) following the accomplishment of each goal. The idea is to make fun activities in which one already engages contingent upon academic effort, progress, or an academic success outcome. By doing so these fun activities become self-rewards.

4. Students can set up an academic success wall or academic success board in their home to display academic work of which they are proud.

5. Students can draw smiling faces on work in which they invested much effort. They can also be encouraged by teachers to write a self-evaluation of their work in class and of their homework. In fact, they can give themselves the grade that they think that they deserve for effort and progress.

Strategy 4. Teaching Adaptive Skills. Adaptive skills are communication skills, socialization skills, and daily living skills. Communication skills include speaking and writing skills for effectively expressing ideas and thoughts and for relating to others. In society, to a great extent, individuals are judged and given opportunities on the basis of their verbal and written communication skills. In school communication skills are important for the learning process to occur. Demonstrations of verbal communication skills are using complete sentences when speaking, enunciating words, and projecting one's voice. Demonstrations of nonverbal communication skills are standing erect and using good eye contact when speaking, and writing complete sentences that express ideas in a clear and organized manner.

Socialization skills include skills for interacting responsibly and sensitively with others. These skills are especially important for developing meaningful relationships at school and, thus, for developing a sense of belonging in one's school environment. Demonstrations of socialization skills include initiating and engaging in a conversation with a teacher or peer, introducing oneself and others appropriately, working cooperatively with a group to accomplish a task, and using good manners.

Daily living skills are basic self-care skills that are necessary for successful independent functioning. These skills are important for overall life management for effective academic, physical, mental, and social functioning. Demonstrations of daily living skills are managing time wisely to get studying and other important tasks done, setting up and following a budget, managing a checking account, and using proper etiquette.

Detailed exercises for teaching adaptive skills to students in different grade levels can be found in *Handbook for Increasing Academic and Adaptive Skills and Reducing Maladaptive Behaviors of African American Children* (unpublished) that can be requested from the author (Tucker, Brady, Herman, & Lowenberg, 1996). Suggestions for teaching adaptive skills follow.

1. Teachers can spend thirty minutes daily or every other day teaching an age-appropriate adaptive skill such as how to write a check and how to introduce oneself to a teacher. Teachers can model the skill and then have the students role-play the skill. It is also possible to include some of these skills as part of regular academic exercises such as reading a poem in English class. The students can be challenged to use their best public speaking skills including good eye contact, projecting their voices, standing erect, and so on. Teachers can provide these students with step-by-step public speaking guides so that the students can independently practice public speaking at home and at school.

2. Parents can practice adaptive skills with their children and adolescents at home. Teachers can facilitate this home practice by assigning it as homework. For example, a homework assignment could be for students to plan a study schedule and practice reading a poem to their parents while following the step-by-step public speaking guide.

3. Parents and teachers can praise and encourage students to self-praise efforts to use adaptive skills. These adults can also provide many opportunities for students to use adaptive skills through participating in church activities, writing for the school newspaper, assuming leadership roles in organizations, and participating in the family's financial management activities (e.g., paying bills and balancing their parents' and their own checkbooks).

Strategy 5. Self-Management or Self-Control for Reducing or Extinguishing Maladaptive Behaviors. Maladaptive behaviors are behavior problems such as aggressive behaviors (e.g., hitting and fighting), defiance, inattentiveness, threatening violence, and off-task, disruptive behavior in class. Because these problem behaviors deter students from learning and may result in school suspension or school expulsion, they are often major factors in the occurrence of the academic failure of students. Maladaptive behaviors are also often the result of academic failure. Whether these behaviors are causes or effects of academic failure, it is important to extinguish the occurrence of these behaviors by African American youth.

Because maladaptive behaviors are often associated with anger, frustration, and other negative emotions, it is important to address these underlying causes through teaching students self-management methods such as a step-by-step approach for anger management that can be used to constructively express negative emotions. It is also important to teach students cognitive (e.g., self-talk) and cognitive-behavioral interventions (e.g., problem solving) to avoid engaging in maladaptive behaviors. Self-management strategies that students can use to deter or modify engagement in maladaptive behaviors have been earlier discussed in Chapter 5. Self-management strategies for deterring or modifying specific maladaptive behaviors such as inattentiveness, aggressive/disruptive behaviors, and oppositional defiant behaviors are included in Chapter 6.

Strategy 6. Teaching Academic Success Behaviors. Academic success behaviors will help African American students be successful in the classroom. These success behaviors are numerous and include the following:

1. Introducing oneself to teachers.
2. Helping teachers get to know one's goals, family background, strengths, and weaknesses that one expresses motivation to change.
3. Sitting near the front of the class and paying attention in class.
4. Volunteering to respond to questions from teachers.
5. Asking questions about what one does not understand that is covered in class.
6. Asking for extra work to better learn concepts taught and doing assigned homework neatly and on time.
7. Staying after school to study.
8. Letting the teacher know one's desire and willingness to work diligently to make A's in all classes.

9. Reviewing notes with the teacher after class.
10. Asking for and regularly using the help of a tutor before starting to make poor grades.
11. Being polite to the teacher and classmates.
12. Sitting upright in class.
13. Taking notes in class.
14. Expressing positive feelings to the teacher about the teacher's efforts to help one learn.

Some African American children often consider success behaviors such as the preceding behaviors to be "acting white." Such behaviors were discussed by Fordham and Ogbu (1986) and addressed earlier in this chapter. One of the many academic and social challenges facing teachers, parents, family members, and community leaders is to relabel so-called "acting white" behaviors as academic success behaviors. Additionally it is important for adults to explain to children the connections among success behaviors, learning, and receiving good grades. Teachers, parents, family members, and community leaders can also call attention daily to African American children's success behaviors, and encourage and praise their occurrence. Children can also be asked to post a list of success behaviors, self-monitor their occurrence (i.e., place a check mark by those that occurred each day), and then praise themselves for their occurrence.

Other General Strategies for Parents to Use

African American parents and primary caregivers can play major roles in helping their children who are underachieving or failing experience academic success. Yet, many of these parents feel intimidated by schools and teachers and by the new and different learning that children are experiencing in today's modern classrooms; consequently, these parents often become disengaged from the learning process. They often lovingly empathize with their children's failure and low grades, realizing that these children's academic challenges are great and that their teachers are not always emotionally invested in children's learning as "in the good old days." Indeed, African American parents often reflect on the days when African American teachers would come to their homes and to their churches to discuss their children's academic performance and when parents and teachers worked as teams to make sure that the children obeyed school rules and did their schoolwork or faced some very negative consequences at school and at home for not doing so.

Yet, parents must realize that today teachers have very limited punishment options in the classroom and that most teachers are culturally different from their African American students and, thus, do not feel comfortable visiting parents' homes and churches to discuss their children. Furthermore, because of a lack of trust between many teachers and African American parents, many parents would not welcome teachers to their homes as "in the good old days." Thus, parents cannot judge teachers' commitment to their children's academic success on the basis of outdated teacher behavior norms.

The changes in schools, school rules, teachers, and parents over the years make it extremely important for parents to be actively involved with rather than intimidated by and disengaged from their children's teachers, schools, and schoolwork. No matter what their educational level, parents have the rights, responsibilities, skills, and access to resources necessary to facilitate their children's academic success.

Following are some specific strategies that parents can use to facilitate their child's academic success.

1. Parents can first of all become knowledgeable about what their children's grades are, when report cards come out, what help is available for students who are underachieving or failing, and what their rights are regarding the education of their children. This information can be gotten from their local school board office.

2. Parents can regularly meet with their child's teacher to find out what they can specifically do to facilitate higher achievement by their child. Indeed, just as parents have rights, they also have responsibilities to assist the teacher with the educational process. Parents can get help from school board members, church leaders, community leaders, family members, and friends. For example, if the teacher says that a child needs help with homework, then parents must find that help and make sure that the child is physically at home to get that help.

3. It is important for parents to regularly and directly monitor their children's academic progress, academic failures, and academic successes. Parents cannot rely on their children to show them all grades and schoolwork, for these youth are often embarrassed by their performance and do not want to disappoint their parents. Consequently, parents must ask about and insist on looking at all report cards, test scores, and graded assignments. Additionally, parents must both observe their children in their classrooms and talk with their teachers regularly.

Garibaldi (1992) found in a survey of 3,523 African American parents that one-fourth of these parents reported having never gone to their children's school for regular or specially scheduled parent–teacher conferences; yet, at these conferences children's report cards and academic performance in their classes are usually discussed. It is important for parents to recognize that not attending regular and teacher-requested parent–teacher conferences is often interpreted by teachers and principals to mean that the parents are not interested in their child successfully finishing school or simply do not have positive educational aspirations for their child (Garibaldi, 1992).

4. Parents can challenge African American youth to perform better than average. Parents' expectations that their children simply will pass with a C grade and do so regardless of what is learned is not associated with making high grades (Tucker, Brady, Harris, Tribble, & Fraser, 1993). Yet, these expectations are not uncommon.

5. Parents can expect their child to show much academic effort and academic progress (i.e., improvement) and clearly express these expectations to the child. It is important to be specific about the effort behaviors that are expected such as studying two hours an evening at home, doing all homework on time, and so on. Additionally, it is important for parents to state the specific demonstrations of progress that they expect from their child. For example, parents might state that they expect a grade improvement in math from an F to a D. However, parents cannot simply express expectations; they must also work in partnership with their child to help their child meet the stated academic effort and progress expectations.

6. It is important that parents show interest in the homework even if they do not have a clue about how to do it. Parents can show interest in their children's homework by (a) asking their children to describe their homework and inquiring whether they understand it,

(b) getting needed assistance for helping the children understand their homework, (c) asking their children questions about what they learned from doing their homework and the relationship between the homework and what they learned in school that day, (d) looking over the completed homework and asking questions about it whether or not the parents understand it, and (e) asking the children study questions that are often given to students to prepare for a test. If a tutor is working with the children, parents can make sure that the tutor provides detailed, specific, constructive feedback to the children after reviewing their homework or other academic work. Indeed, parents must supervise whomever tutors their children.

7. Parents can establish quiet, low-stimulation zones and times in their home for their children to study or get quiet tutoring. A low-stimulation zone is simply a room or section of a room to be used only for studying, reading, and tutoring. A low-stimulation time is at least a two-hour period each day or evening, when all children are to read, study, do homework, or get quiet tutoring. During these times, parents are to assist with or quietly discuss homework, engage in quiet tasks such as paying bills, or model reading for the children by reading a magazine, newspaper, the Bible, or other books of interest.

Most importantly, there should be no television, radio, or social conversation in the house that will disturb or compete with the children's focus on studying or homework. Boykin (1982) found that African American children from low-stimulation homes were able to learn under both very varied and interesting learning conditions and under very dull learning conditions; that is, they were found to be cognitively versatile and flexible rather than dependent on a lot of stimulating activity in order to learn.

8. Parents can set bedtimes that provide adequate sleep for their child and arrange for their child to get breakfast and lunch. These actions increase the likelihood that the child will have the levels of mental and physical energy needed to learn successfully.

9. Parents can praise and celebrate their child's academic initiative and persistence. These parent involvement behaviors have been linked to increases in self-rated academic and behavioral self-concepts by urban elementary school African American students considered to be at risk (Fantuzzo, Davis, & Ginsburg, 1995). Additionally, parents can encourage their child to praise herself or himself and feel good all over for this initiative and persistence. For example, a parent could say the following:

> I am so impressed that you kept working on your math problems until you got them all right. Such persistence shows that you have the determination needed to reach your goal of becoming a nurse. I am so proud of you and respect you so much for your effort and determination to succeed. You have earned the pleasure of feeling really proud of yourself and of feeling extra good all over. You should give yourself a hug and let me give you a hug for your hard work.

10. Rather than feeling a sense of failure and being immobilized because of their child's unsatisfactory academic performance, parents can attend available parenting classes, workshops, and groups that include a focus on effective parenting and helping children be successful in school. If such training is not available, parents can challenge their ministers and community leaders to organize such training. Additionally, parents can ask their local churches to establish tutoring and adaptive skills training programs to help self-empower

African American children for academic and social success. A model training program is described in Chapter 14 of this book.

Hill (1972) appropriately reminded us that the African American church has traditionally played a major role in educating African American children. The African American church has been and continues to be a place for African American youth to develop their leadership, listening, speaking, and problem-solving skills. Because of its location and stature in the African American community and its human and financial resources, the African American church is an ideal place to implement educational programs to empower African American children for academic and social success. It is also an ideal site for conducting church-sponsored or community-sponsored parenting workshops to empower parents to facilitate the academic and social success of their children. Church-sponsored, academically oriented activities are growing in popularity across the country.

11. African American parents must insist that their child is not simply given a passing grade just to have the child moved out of a teacher's class. Giving passing grades to students who cannot adequately read, write, and do math calculations is a travesty. Having them eventually graduate without the basic academic knowledge and skills for life success is close to criminal.

Rather than simply passing African American students who are not learning, parents, teachers, and schools must assess the causes of the learning difficulty, try to address these causes, and ultimately decide on the very best possible educational option for the student. The last option to consider should be special class placement because often students in such placements are labeled "slow," are expected to learn very little over time, and, consequently, work at a level that is consistent with these low expectations rather than at a higher level consistent with their academic potential.

Other General Intervention Strategies for Teachers and School Administrators to Use

Teachers play major roles in the academic achievement of all the children in their classrooms. Teachers can and must play especially important roles in helping African American children who are underachieving or experiencing academic failure perform up to their academic potential. Because teachers are faced with these challenges along with making sure that all children in their classrooms are academically challenged, meeting the needs of African American children who need extra academic help and emotional support is not easy.

Many teachers have the additional challenge of understanding and accepting the cultural and socioeconomic differences between the majority children and the African American children in their classrooms. These differences include differences in communication skills, learning styles, and social interaction styles. Some teachers are confused and frustrated by the social withdrawal, lack of participation in class, and hostile attitudes of some African American children. Having never walked in these childrens' shoes, these teachers do not understand such behaviors and attitudes.

Many excellent teachers will be less effective than they could be in teaching African American children unless they are provided with the needed emotional and behavioral support from schools and from these children's parents and communities. Teachers cannot do it all when it comes to educating African American children. Yet, they can do a lot with (1) knowledge about and understanding of their African American children, which involves taking time to know them as individuals, (2) a repertoire of culturally and socio-economically sensitive teaching strategies, and (3) the belief that they can help any African American child reach the child's academic potential and the determination to do so (i.e., high instructional self-efficacy with African American children).

There are no culturally and socioeconomically sensitive strategies that teachers and school administrators can use that will facilitate the academic success of all African American children because groups of African American children vary in their cultural and socio-economic backgrounds. However, there are some strategies that will be helpful in facilitating the academic success of many African American children. Varying combinations of these strategies as determined by the cultural and socioeconomic backgrounds and the resulting skills and competencies of each child will likely facilitate the academic success of most African American children.

Following are some culturally and socioeconomically sensitive strategies that teachers and school administrators can use in facilitating the academic success of African American students in their schools.

1. It is important for teachers and school administrators to have high expectations of African American students with regard to their academic abilities and performance. In a study by Hall, Howe, Mërkel, & Lederman (1986) with European American teachers, it was found that these teachers rated the abilities of the European American junior high school students in their classes higher than the abilities of these students' African American peers with similar academic achievement scores.

Indeed, some European American teachers may have lower expectations regarding the abilities of African American students; students often live down to or up to the expectations of them. Lower expectations regarding the abilities of African American students by teachers may contribute to academic failure by these children and to academic performance below the capabilities of these students. Cooper (1979) asserted that teacher expectations can sustain an achievement gap between student groups that might otherwise be narrowed.

A tremendous amount of research has been done over the past twenty-five years on the effect of teacher expectations on student achievement (Good & Brophy, 1986). This research suggested that some teachers expect students of color as well as students from lower socioeconomic groups to perform more poorly on school-related tasks than their middle-class peers. Furthermore, according to Good and Brophy (1987), when these expectations are upheld, the teachers' expectations of and associated beliefs about students of color and students from low socioeconomic backgrounds are reinforced; thus, this expectation-performance cycle continues.

2. Teachers can assess the learning styles of their students, avoid labeling any found nonanalytical learning styles as inferior, and gradually teach new learning styles such as an analytical learning style that will help students be academically competitive and successful in school, college, in most careers, and in life in general. In this teaching process, teachers can incorporate the use of various learning styles to facilitate some successes among all children while teaching new learning styles that the children will need to learn. Teachers should also make sure that all students recognize and respect that due to cultural and individual differences—not deficits—children vary in their learning styles. Teachers should also remind themselves that not all African American students use relational learning styles as is commonly believed; rather, some African American students are great analytical learners and thinkers just as are many European American students. Indeed, teachers must not assume all African American students are the same.

3. Given that encouragement by teachers is very important to African American students and seems to be linked to their academic success, it is indeed important for teachers to actively look for, find, and praise any academic effort toward learning among African American students who are failing or underachieving. Teachers can praise looking at a math problem to be done, trying to work it, asking questions about it, not playing around when unsuccessful at doing the math problem, asking for help with the problem, and so on. It is also important for teachers to encourage the students to praise themselves for their academic efforts.

4. Teachers and school administrators can help African American students feel that they belong in and are a part of their school and class. Teachers can do this, for example, by encouraging African American students to participate in classroom and school activities and by asking for and showing interest in their opinions during class discussions. Teachers can also informally ask each of their African American students what could be done to help her or him feel a greater sense of belonging in the classroom. According to Goodenow and Grady (1993), increasing a sense of school belonging (i.e., perceptions of being liked, accepted, included, respected, and encouraged to participate in school and classroom activities) may reduce school dropout among African American students and other students as well.

School administrators can conduct student surveys and interviews to identify what African American students think would increase their sense of belonging at their school and their sense of being encouraged and supported. African American students can be involved in administering the surveys and conducting the interviews. Even more importantly, these students can be involved in reviewing the obtained data and developing and implementing strategies to facilitate their sense of belonging and their feelings of being supported by teachers, school administrators, and other members of their school environment. Involving African American students in determining such school actions may not only improve their sense of belonging at school but also facilitate their self-empowerment for academic and social success.

5. School administrators can provide teachers with training and other assistance that promote teachers' coping efficacy, instructional efficacy, instructional strategies, and motivation needed to optimally address the academic needs of their African American students. Chwalisz, Altmaier, and Russell (1992) provided evidence that teachers with high perceived coping efficacy manage academic stressors by directing their efforts toward resolving academic problems, whereas teachers with low coping efficacy try to avoid such problems and instead focus on relieving their own emotional distress. The latter avoidance behavior ultimately results in occupational burnout that can be unpleasant for teachers and that can have an indirect negative impact on their students. Gibson and Dembo (1984) found that teachers who have a high sense of instructional efficacy as compared to those with a low sense of instructional efficacy are more patient, positive, and focused on teaching.

Training to facilitate teachers' coping efficacy, instructional efficacy, instructional strategies, and motivation for teaching African American students should include the following:

a. stress management and problem-solving training specifically tailored to teachers;

b. motivational discussions of the fact that when African American students fail, all other students and all Americans are negatively impacted;

c. presentations by European American teachers, African American teachers, Latino American teachers, and teachers from other ethnic groups who have successfully improved the academic achievement of African American students who were underachieving, failing, or being disruptive in their classrooms;

d. presentations by African American students who are no longer underachieving or academically failing because of the efforts of European American teachers as well as other teachers and who want to thank these teachers and share what these teachers did to facilitate their movement from academic underachievement or failure to academic success;

e. presentations by African American parents which address the support, patience, and encouragement that their children need from their teachers and that their children have actually received from European American teachers and other teachers;

f. sharing among teachers about strategies that they have found to be effective for teaching African American students who may have inadequate academic backgrounds, skills, or motivation for certain subjects; and

g. sharing among teachers about strategies for coping with their own stress, frustration, and feelings of incompetence that often occur when teaching underachieving students and students who are academically failing.

6. Teachers can create learning environments such as those advocated by Bandura (1993) in which teachers reinforce the view that ability is a skill that can be acquired and in which each individual student competes with herself or himself to meet higher and higher goals that the individual sets for herself or himself. The result of such learning environments, according to Bandura, is an increased sense of self-efficacy that promotes academic achievement. Such a learning environment is culturally and socioeconomically sensitive.

7. Teachers can constructively utilize the cultural preference of some African American children for oral teaching and learning modalities toward the goal of helping these children learn to comprehend and communicate in written form at the highest possible levels of excellence for each child. For example, a child might be invited to compose a song and sing it to the class. The child can then write the song using her or his preferred grammatical style, be assisted in preparing a second version in standard English format with no grammatical errors, told the value of both versions, and reinforced for having prepared both versions. The child's song as written in standard English format might additionally be placed on display in the classroom for some period of time.

8. Teachers can teach the value of waiting one's turn to speak and of thinking about what to say before speaking. The benefits of doing these behaviors in various jobs and careers should be included in these discussions. Additionally, it is important for African American students to generate individually their own perceived benefits of these behaviors in order to maximize the likelihood that those students who have not adopted these behaviors will become self-motivated to do so. In order to not extinguish or destroy their enthusiasm for class participation due to having to wait and think, it is important to give African American students as many opportunities as possible to speak after thinking and raising their hands.

9. Teachers can find something constructive to say in response to an African American student's or any student's incorrect response to a question. Saying that the response is wrong or incorrect is often especially devastating to an African American child who may already feel that she or he is not smart because of her or his cultural or socioeconomic based differences that are interpreted as deficits. Teachers could instead give responses such as the following to an incorrect answer from students: "That is an interesting answer even though it is not the answer that I am looking for. It shows that you are really thinking and that is great! Keep up the great effort!"

10. Teachers can be informed that there are likely cultural factors (Boykin, 1983) and possibly environmental factors (Boykin, 1982) and genetic factors (Guttentag, 1972; Morgan, 1976) in the seeming need for stimulation, lively activity, and varied learning activities among many African American children. Teachers can then be encouraged to incorporate hands-on learning activities in their teaching and can show excitement about what is being taught. Exciting, interesting, and captivating teachers who energetically move around among their students and use their hands, voice intonations, and facial expressions to teach and explain the subject matter facilitate the academic achievement of many African American students. Teachers with such verve have been found to be the most effective teachers for African American first graders (Prestrup, 1973).

Teachers can also vary their teaching format and modality (e.g., use of television, a videotape, a game, a writing exercise, a guest lecturer, an experiment, a field trip) to captivate the interest and energy of many African American students and other students who enjoy motor activity and have a low boredom threshold. Using a combination of teaching format presentations has been found to be effective in teaching African American fourth graders (Prestrup, 1973). Just as importantly, teachers can regularly discuss with these students the short-term and long-term benefits of learning that requires reading, studying, and concentrating for long periods of times. Teachers should assist these students in setting study duration goals and study schedules and in arranging self-reinforcements for meeting their study duration goals and for adhering to their study schedules.

11. Teachers can utilize reciprocal peer tutoring in their classes where dyads tutor each other and the dyad members participate in designing, evaluating, and managing their own reward procedure (i.e., a cooperative reward system). Given the reported success of this method (Fantuzzo, Davis, & Ginsberg, 1995), parents can also encourage siblings to do this at home.

12. Teachers can teach African American children how to take notes and study. Research suggests that when taking notes, students capture important points by summarizing or paraphrasing ideas in their own words and later organizing the information into an outline of the key points (Carrier & Titus, 1979; Kiewra, Dubois, Christian, & McShane, 1988).

Bonwell and Eison (1991) report that teaching and learning strategies that encourage active practice enhance the acquisition and retention of information. Study techniques such as the SQ3R method (i.e., survey, question, read, recite, and review) encourage active practice. Using this method, a student glances over the chapter and notices what is covered and how it is organized. The student then asks and writes questions about the first section before beginning to read it. Next, the student reads the section and then recites answers to the written questions. If the student finds that she or he cannot answer the questions written, the student reviews the section to find the answers (Robinson, 1970).

13. It is important for teachers to actively encourage African American students to ask questions about what they do not understand, which is a success behavior. Minority students are often uncomfortable asking such questions because they are concerned that their questions are silly or dumb and they will appear to be inadequate or stupid (Eaglin, 1992). According to Eaglin (1992), minority students are often especially uncomfortable asking questions if the teacher is ethnically different from themselves because doing so will reflect badly on the students' ethnic group.

14. Teachers can help promote high academic self-concepts among African American students in their classrooms. This can be done by simply encouraging and valuing their class participation, creating a sense of community in the classroom where it is expected that everyone will succeed, and reframing failure as only one step on the road to achieving academic success (Cushner, McGelland, & Safford, 1992).

15. Teachers can survey their African American students and other students to find out their views as to what they might do and what the teacher might do to make each subject area of greater interest to them. This will self-empower the students; that is, it will give them some control over and responsibility for their own learning. It will also make teaching easier by reducing the stress of trying to find ways to teach students who are bored and by reassuring themselves that they have gone the extra mile to try to meet the learning needs of their African American students and all students.

16. Teachers can use teacher attention (including verbal praise, smiles, frowns, handshakes, and pats on the back) to help decrease disruptive behavior by African American children and to increase appropriate on-task behavior. Ward and Baker (1968) used teacher attention to increase the task-relevant productive behavior of twelve African American first graders who attended an urban public school. For seven weeks the participating teachers systematically ignored maladaptive behaviors and systematically reinforced task-relevant, productive academic behavior with attention and praise. During the last five weeks of this intervention, deviant behavior dropped from 74 percent to 57 percent. The effects of such interventions will likely be enhanced by having children practice saying to themselves that they can focus on their work and follow the teacher's instructions and by encouraging them to praise themselves for engaging in such task-relevant behaviors.

17. Teachers can use a low-group contingency learning approach that has been found to be quite effective in enhancing the academic performance of some African American students. In this approach, the performance of low-performing students determines the reinforcement for the entire group. Group members are told that they can work together to prepare for a test on material covered in class on a particular topic. In a study involving thirty-eight African American inner-city children, Hamblin and colleagues (1974) showed this approach to be effective in improving math, reading, and spelling performances of participating low-performing students. The low-group contingency learning approach increased the level of performance of both slower students and gifted students.

18. Teachers can try different strategies to build the confidence and test-taking skills of African American students. For example, teachers might routinely give students practice tests as homework after giving them a step-by-step guide for taking tests successfully. Teachers can also encourage students to say to themselves statements to minimize their test anxiety such as the following statement: "I will be calm, do one question at a time, skip questions I do not know and come back to them, and remember that I will simply do my best."

19. Teachers can ideally use methods other than written tests to assess the achievement of African American students. Use of oral examinations where students can be coached a bit in giving their answers to questions is such an alternative to written tests. Eisenman (1991a, 1991b) reported finding that African American students would sometimes fail to answer test items when they seemed to know the answers. In giving makeup exams to students who had missed the regular exam, Eisenman found that if coached slightly, African American students could often give correct answers to test questions when prodded to do so.

Partnership Intervention Strategies

Parents, teachers, and school administrators cannot do all that is important for facilitating the academic success of African American students, especially those students who are underachieving or experiencing academic failure. Parents, teachers, schools, community and local business leaders, African American churches, school board leaders, and state education leaders must work in partnership to provide African American students with activities and experiences to facilitate their academic success. These partnerships will likely need to be facilitated by parents and the African American leaders and other community leaders in the partnership because they have the most direct interest in the education of the African American youth in a particular community. However, the active participation of individuals who are concerned about the plight of African American youth regardless of their ethnicity, position, or location should be invited to join the partnership to make education work for African American students.

Following are several intervention strategies that members of such partnerships can use to move African American youth from underachievement and academic failure to academic success.

1. The partners can conduct self-empowerment for academic success seminars in the community to teach African American children the importance of self-motivation to achieve; self-control of their academic progress and success; self-reinforcement of their academic effort, progress, and success; and adaptive skills and success behaviors for academic and social success. These seminars should include a focus on the role of children's health and nutrition in their academic performance. A program such as a health-conscious ethnic food festival or a student recognition program ideally should be paired with the seminars to increase the likelihood of attendance to the seminars.

2. The partners can arrange motivational career and job festivals for African American children where African Americans and others in various skilled jobs and professions come to meet these children and talk with them about their work and about how math, reading, English, and so on are used in their work. Following the festivals, arrangements can be made for the adult participants in the festivals to take interested children to visit their work site and see what their work actually entails. Such experiences can be used to assist participating students in setting long-term goals that facilitate achievement motivation.

3. Community-based talent contests with reading and writing contests as the major features should be regularly (e.g., monthly) held to desensitize African American children to competition and to facilitate development of their reading, writing, and public speaking skills. Competition prizes might include mini academic scholarships or savings bonds for future attendance to college or trade school.

4. Community-based, after-school partnership educational programs can be established to teach African American children adaptive skills, computer skills, and success behaviors, and to provide them with academic tutoring. Such a program can be conducted after school for two hours each day and can involve volunteer active and retired teachers, parents, university and high school student tutors, church and community leaders, and business leaders. The author and her colleagues have conducted such a program since 1989 (Tucker, Chennault, Brady, Raser, Gaskin, Dunn, & Frisby, 1995). This program is discussed in Chapter 14 of this book.

5. The partners can conduct parent workshops and teacher workshops on culturally and socioeconomically sensitive strategies for teaching and self-empowering African American youth for academic and social success.

6. The partners can set up mentoring programs that recruit and train mentors and pair them with African American children. The mentor training should ideally focus teaching mentors on how to facilitate self-empowerment of African American youth for academic, social, and economic success and should emphasize developing their academic self-concepts. This mentor training should also include encouraging African American children to see the relationship between their course work and their career ambitions to facilitate their motivation to do well in their academic courses.

7. The partners can conduct workshops for youth and their families on economic empowerment through education as a way of motivating African American youth to achieve academically and to resist involvement with drugs to make money. Participants in these workshops can include successful African American business owners, investors, and other entrepreneurs. The idea is to talk with African American youth about making money, which is a tremendous reinforcer for them, and linking this to what they are learning in school. After all, economic empowerment is a major key to empowering African Americans; that is, acquisition of money and money management are critical vehicles for moving African Americans from dependency and powerlessness to independence and self-sufficiency, thus breaking the cycle of poverty that underlies much of the academic failure and crime among African American youth.

Conclusions

African American children and adolescents, like other youth, want to be successful in school and in life; however, they often do not have the skills, behavioral repertoires (e.g., knowledge of success behaviors), and the parent, teacher, school, and community support needed to achieve this goal. Enabling African American youth to experience academic and social success requires not only the active effort of their families, schools, teachers, and communities but also academic and social training that is intense and that is culturally and socioeconomically sensitive.

A self-empowerment approach is needed to facilitate the academic and social success of African American children. This approach focuses on promoting in these youth self-motivation for academic achievement, self-control for academic progress and success, self-praise of progress and success, and adaptive skills and success behaviors for achieving academic and social success. Such an approach is indicated given that many African American children and adolescents often feel powerless and without control in majority-controlled classrooms and schools, and that such feelings are often associated with decreased effort and performance. Furthermore, this approach recognizes the fact that African American children can and must play a major role in helping themselves to learn, as they will not always have parents, teachers, or others around who can, will, or desire to teach them.

Interestingly, interview research data obtained from African American elementary school students and high school students and their parents and from African American teachers support the view that African American children need to be actively engaged in their learning, need to be self-empowered for academic and social success, and need help and structure from teachers and parents to do so. The African American students interviewed reported that for African American students to make good grades they need to actively participate in class (e.g., listen and follow instructions, ask questions about what they do not understand), study and do their homework, and be self-motivated. Additionally, the students, parents, and teachers interviewed agreed that active parent involvement in their children's education, teacher–parent communication, help with studying and homework, and more explanations from teachers about the subject matter taught in class were important for the academic success of African American students.

African American children must be taught how to study, and other behaviors and skills for academic success. Even though most African American children have well-developed, culture-influenced learning skills and strategies, these skills and strategies often are inconsistent with those needed both in classrooms dominated by the majority culture and also to compete for jobs or have successful businesses in the United States or other countries. To acquire needed skills for school and life success, many African American children must be taught by culturally and socioeconomically sensitive teachers who respect and utilize the learning strategies, skills, and competencies that these children bring with them to their classrooms and who gradually teach them new learning strategies, skills, and competencies for success in the twenty-first century. These teachers must view African American students' academic and social differences from their majority peers as merely differences—not deficits.

Teachers cannot teach African American students all of the skills and behaviors that they need for academic success. Parents, school administrators, African American churches, community and business leaders, school boards, and teachers must work as partners to facilitate the academic success of African American children. These partnership efforts must have as a major focus the self-empowerment of African American children for academic, social, and economic success. Such empowerment is necessary to help break the cycles of poverty and powerlessness that nurture academic failure among many African American children and impede the movement of these children from academic failure to academic success.

12 Overcoming Specific Academic Problems

Practical Intervention Approaches and Strategies

Given the importance of academic achievement to the life success of African American children, it is important to do all that is possible to help these children overcome academic problems that impede their learning. Overcoming these problems is not easy because there are usually multiple factors that cause the problems, thus creating the need for multidimensional intervention strategies. Furthermore, because of individual, cultural, and socioeconomic differences among African American children, intervention strategies must be sensitive to these differences. Thus, interventions for the same academic problem may differ across African American children. The following section presents some specific, common academic problems among African American students and offers some intervention strategies for consideration in addressing these problems.

Test Anxiety

Test anxiety, which is common among African American children, is a feeling of concern, apprehension, and worry about an upcoming test or exam. It often involves a worry about not finishing the test and about making a low grade on or failing the test. The feelings themselves are usually associated with negative or self-defeating thoughts such as the following:

> I can't handle this exam. It is going to blow me away and I am going to surely get an F on it. Oh, my mind is blank. I know that I am going to fail this test.

Students may engage in such negative thoughts or self-talk because they have not adequately studied for the test. It is also often the case that the students have studied for the test, but they still have a fear of failing it. In both of these situations, the students may not perceive that they have behavioral control over academic outcomes (e.g., test performance) because of any number of reasons including having failed a test in the recent past that they expected to pass and the expectations of others that they will not do well on the test.

The first step in helping students learn to overcome test anxiety is to convince them that they can significantly increase the likelihood of doing well on a test by studying long and hard for the test, beginning several days before the test. The second step is to inform the students of the importance of (1) getting a full night of sleep before the day of the test, (2) having breakfast the day of the test, and (3) getting to the test site early to have time to become calm before the test starts.

There are several intervention strategies that students can use to help calm themselves before and during a test.

1. Students can take three deep breaths, slowly inhaling and exhaling.

2. Students can substitute success-oriented thoughts for their negative or self-defeating thoughts about failing the test. In other words, students can take control of their thoughts and their emotions; by changing their thoughts, they can change or reduce the anxiety. By controlling their thoughts and emotions, students can usually improve test performance (Grasha, 1995). Students can be taught to replace their negative thoughts with the following coping thoughts or self-statements:

> I studied hard for this test, I know the material, and I will do well on the test. I know enough information to think up good answers to questions that I do not immediately know the answers to. I will write whatever I know that is related to the question if I do not know the exact answer. I will just concentrate and focus on one question at a time. I will do well on this test.

3. If children have been taught at home to pray, children can also say a brief prayer, which might include the request for help to think clearly and be calm in order to do well on the test.

4. Students can take a couple of minutes to tense and then relax their muscles, holding the tension for about five seconds and then relaxing them. They can tense the muscles in their faces, arms, stomachs, legs, and feet in sequential order.

5. Students can spend one or two minutes thinking about a very pleasant and quiet place and activity that they like (e.g., sitting comfortably by an old oak tree in the backyard with eyes closed as a breeze pleasantly cools their warm skin).

Before the test is received, the student should ask how much time is given for completing the test. When the test is received, the student can use the following successful test-taking steps.

Step 1. Place your name on the test and provide any other requested information such as the test date.

Step 2. Carefully read the test instructions.

Step 3. Look through the test to see how much there is to do. Figure out what is the halfway point of the test and note it. Then figure out what time it will be when half of the testing time is over. You should strive to be more than halfway through the test when half the time is over so that you can be sure to finish the test and have time remaining to do any questions that you skipped, or to review answers about which you were not sure.

Step 4. Start with the first test question, focusing on one question at a time, and read each question carefully. Skip the questions that you do not know and come back to them. Place a check mark by the answers about which you are not certain and may want to review if you have time. If you skip questions, remember that you must leave time to come back to them.

Step 5. When you have answered the questions that you know, go back to the questions that you skipped. Think of anything you know about the question and write what you remember as it relates to the question, or choose the best answer based on what you know.

Step 6. After finishing the test, read over the answers by which you placed a check mark and erase your check marks. Then proofread the remainder of the test.

Step 7. Tell your teacher that you studied hard and did your best after turning in your test.

Step 8. Praise yourself. Tell yourself that you made a very good effort to do well on this test and that you are proud of your effort, regardless of the grade that you make. Then give yourself a hug and feel good all over for your effort.

Step 9. When the graded test is received, read over the answers that were incorrect and then ask your teacher to tell you the correct answers. Thank your teacher for giving you this information. Then repeat Step 8. Later make sure you learn the correct answers.

Difficulty with Studying

Children are frequently told by parents and teachers that they need to study to keep from failing. However, little attention is given to assessing whether the child knows how to study or to instructing students in how to study effectively. The present author and her associates (Tucker, Herman, Pedersen, & Vogel, 1997) found that 45.2 percent of the responses of African American elementary school students and 50 percent of the responses of African American high school students to an interview question about what parents can do to help prevent academic failure among African American students were that parents could help by assisting these students with studying and structuring their study behavior. Even though there is no set way to study and each individual must experiment to find out what helps her or him to study effectively, there are study behaviors, strategies for memorizing what is studied, and study do's and don't's that facilitate achievement of the goal of studying, which of course is learning. Following are some important study behaviors.

1. *Get motivated to study.* This can be done by thinking about the positive consequences of studying. For example, you can think about the following positive consequences: (a) Studying will help you achieve your goal of making the honor roll each semester this year; (b) you will feel good about yourself for doing something to help yourself reach your goal; (c) studying will make your parents feel happy and proud that you are serious about learning; (d) you will feel proud when you can answer questions about what you studied in class the next day; (e) studying will help you make a good grade on your upcoming test; and (f) you will feel good about having engaged in a success behavior.

2. *Get physically ready to study.* This involves doing the following: (a) getting into comfortable attire, (b) getting the books, pencils, and other study materials needed, and (c) going to the designated quiet zone in your house for studying at the regular study time that you, with the support of your parents, have set for daily studying. This place should be quiet and comfortable, and ideally should be at a desk or table, as opposed to lying on a bed or sofa. The latter often facilitates sleeping and, thus, is not conducive to studying or learning. The radio and television should be off throughout the house because they are distractors. You should plan to study for at least two hours with one to two five-minute breaks.

3. *Get mentally ready to study.* Tell yourself the following through self-talk: "I am going to study for two hours and I will focus and concentrate without interruptions. I will not allow anyone to keep me from enjoying the positive consequences of studying. If I do not understand what I am studying, I will try harder to understand, and then I will get help from my parents or other available family member. If no one at home can help me, I will study another subject and get needed help with what I do not understand the next day from my teacher. If I become frustrated or stressed, I will take three deep breaths, inhaling and exhaling slowly."

4. *Survey the material to be studied and then begin studying.* Look over what needs to be studied and begin with what needs to be done by the next day and with what is most difficult about this work. Read over the study materials that you have identified as the first study task. Highlight with a marker what you feel was emphasized by the teacher in class or what you think is most important. Place a question mark by what you do not understand after reading it twice. After you finish reading through the first task, ask someone in the home to explain what you have not understood. Next, read over everything that you highlighted again, trying to think of examples and related life experiences to the subject matter that will help make what you studied meaningful to you.

5. *Test yourself on what you have read twice.* First look through what you have read twice and write questions from it. Read each question and try to answer it, first without looking at the material that you read and then while looking at the material that you read. See how similar your answer is to what was stated in the material that you read. Adjust your answer to be consistent with what was in the material you read.

6. *When possible, ask a family member to test you on what you read.* This should be done using the questions that you wrote and any other related questions that the family member wants to ask. Together discuss any answers about which you and the family member disagree based on the reading material.

7. *Praise yourself for studying.* Indeed, studying takes effort, energy, and concentration. It is work for which you should praise yourself. Feel good about having the self-discipline to delay recreational activities to give schoolwork priority.

Following are some strategies for memorizing what is studied.

1. *Repeatedly review.* Children should read over and over what they want to memorize. It is usually necessary to repeat this reading several times a day for more than one day.

2. *Use rhythm to help you memorize.* Most African American children have rhythm as part of their cultural heritage. They can use this to help them memorize by creating a rhythm of their own for the information to be memorized. They can also use "rapping," which tends to be rhythmic, to memorize science facts as well as a poem.

3. *Use chunking.* Chunking simply means grouping information so that it can be more easily remembered. To memorize the names of ten states, for example, children can group together those states that begin with the same letter, or the ones that have been visited versus the ones that have not been visited. Additionally, chunking can be used to remember several numbers by dividing the numbers into small sets of numbers. For example, the number 378007387 can be chunked as 378 007 387, which is likely to be easier to remember.

4. *Use creative visual memory.* Children can make a drawing that orders information in a way that they can remember it. For example, they can draw a language house that has three steps on which there is one of each type of verb and three windows on the door with one of each of the three parts to a sentence written on each window.

5. *Memorize through storytelling.* Part of the cultural heritage for many African Americans is storytelling. Children can use storytelling to memorize almost anything. For example, if children had to remember the seven continents, they could make up a story about sitting at home in North America and getting phone calls from Aunt Agnus in Asia, and Uncle Edward in Europe that an ancestor from Africa had left them a lot of money, but that they would have to get the money from a bank in cold Antarctica. However, they could leave the cold and vacation for months in the warmth of South America or Australia.

6. *Memorize through use of association.* Children can learn something new by associating it with something they already know. For example, children can learn the meaning of a new word by first thinking of what the word reminds them of and then incorporating the association within the actual definition of the word given when the word is looked up in a dictionary. For instance, one can learn the meaning of the word *aesthetic* by associating it with the word *athlete,* which comes to mind when seeing the word *aesthetic.* The definition of *aesthetic* is having to do with being beautiful. A child then can remember the meaning of the word *aesthetic* by associating it with a very beautiful athlete.

7. *Outlining.* Children for whom outlining is easy can rewrite their notes into an outline of major points to make the information simpler and easier for them to remember.

Following are several study guidelines for children who want to study effectively.

Do study...
1. before it gets late into the evening when you are tired.
2. at your regular study time.
3. before rather than after doing something fun.
4. every day to avoid having to cram for a test.
5. based on a prioritized list of reading and study assignments such that what is done first is what must be done for the very next day, starting with the most difficult task.
6. from borrowed notes if you miss class. Borrow notes from someone who studies regularly and makes good grades when you must borrow notes because of missing class.
7. after reviewing your study notes with your teacher in situations where you have written unclear or incomplete notes.

8. after you have first mentally and physically prepared for studying.

9. with the plan to praise yourself for studying at your planned study time and for studying with much concentration and effort.

Don't study...

1. with a group of friends in a social atmosphere.

2. while eating a meal.

3. after consuming alcohol or other drugs.

4. while reclining in a comfortable position.

5. when you are emotionally upset, as you will likely not be able to concentrate.

Developmental Language and Learning Disorders

Academic failure among African American children and other children as well is often an associated outcome of developmental language disorders and learning disorders and disabilities. Children with one or both types of these disorders typically evidence near average intelligence but also show some specific impairments that are inconsistent with their general intellectual ability. These impairments can negatively impact not only academic outcomes but also overall life success (Wicks-Nelson & Israel, 1997).

Developmental Language Disorders

Developmental language disorders are communication disorders that are often categorized as expressive and receptive disorders. These disorders involve problems with producing and understanding oral language. Specifically, there are problems in making sounds (phonology), understanding meanings of words and sentences (semantics), knowing the rules of word formation (morphology), and knowing the rules of sentence formation (grammar) (Rice, 1989). These problems are due to or associated with the misuse or disuse of sounds, meanings of words and sentences, and rules of word formation and sentence formation. The underlying cause of developmental language disorders is not known, as the associated research is very confusing (Bishop, 1992).

Evaluation of expressive and receptive language disorders usually involves auditory, psychological, and language testing along with interviews and medical evaluations. The tests typically used to conduct this evaluation are the Peabody Picture Vocabulary Test—Revised (Dunn & Dunn, 1981) and the Arthur Adaptation of the Leiter International Performance Scale (Arthur, 1952).

Assessment to determine the presence of expressive and receptive language disorders usually occurs when a child's vocal language is significantly delayed and the delay is not associated with a hearing impairment, mental retardation, or infantile autism. Other problems that sometimes occur along with these disorders are impairment in auditory, auditory discrimination, and reading and spelling skills (Erickson, 1990).

There are three specific types of expressive and receptive language disorders: phonological disorders, expressive language disorders, and receptive language disorders. These disorders are often referred to as specific learning disorders (SLDs) (Wicks-Nelson &

Israel, 1997). It is estimated that these disorders occur in 2 percent to 5 percent of the general population, varying in occurrence with type of disorder and age (American Psychiatric Association, 1994).

Interesting to note, however, is that SLDs are estimated to occur in 25 percent to 97 percent of children who attend clinics and do so primarily because of referrals for other problems (Cohen et al., 1993). This is particularly interesting because clinics are more often used by families of low socioeconomic status whereas private psychologists and psychological services groups are more often used by middle- and upper-class families (Wicks-Nelson & Israel, 1997). It is indeed likely that diagnoses of SLDs are influenced by who is making the diagnoses, where the diagnoses are being made, and who are being diagnosed.

To make the diagnosis of SLD the language impairments cannot be accounted for by general intellectual or sensorimotor deficits or by insufficient environmental stimulation; furthermore, the impairments must be severe enough to interfere with daily functioning (Wicks-Nelson & Israel, 1997). Following is a brief discussion of each of the three types of SLDs.

1. Phonological disorders involve problems in the production of speech sounds such as saying "wed" for "red." These disorders are usually diagnosed between ages three and six (Wicks-Nelson & Israel, 1997). Given cultural differences in the pronunciation of words, pronunciation norms for a cultural group as well as developmental norms must be considered in making the diagnosis of a phonological disorder. If cultural norms are not considered, which has often been the case, then many African American children would be inappropriately diagnosed with this disorder. This is because in many African American mini-cultures, it is historically common to say words differently from the way that they are used in the majority culture. For example, among many African Americans, some words beginning with *t* are pronounced as though they begin with *d* (e.g., "the" is pronounced as "dee" and "this" is pronounced as "dis").

2. Expressive language disorders involve problems with the production of speech with regard to language. For example, a child with an expressive language disorder may have a limited vocabulary of simple words and thus use very short, simple sentences; however, the child understands age-appropriate communication (Wicks-Nelson & Israel, 1997). Caution, however, is indicated in making this diagnosis as well, given that such language production could simply reflect environmental and cultural influences. Some African American children, for example, are raised in families where for various reasons the adults do not spend very much time talking with these children and, thus, the children have few opportunities for learning language. Such family communication patterns often occur in families of low socioeconomic status, thus placing children in these families at risk for a false diagnosis of an expressive language disorder.

Children are also placed at risk for a false diagnosis of an expressive language disorder when standardized measures of language development and measures of nonverbal intellectual capacity used to assess expressive language disorders are not culturally and linguistically sensitive. It is important for these measures to be culturally and linguistically sensitive when used to diagnose expressive language disorders (American Psychiatric Association, 1994).

3. Receptive language disorder involves difficulties with understanding the communication of another person. This disorder is usually diagnosed between the ages of four and seven or older. A child with this disorder may appear deaf or respond inappropriately. The child may show disinterest in television and may also have problems with words, phrases, word order, past tense of words, multiple meanings of words, expression, articulation, and other similar problems. When a child shows both significant receptive and expressive impairments, the child is typically diagnosed as having a mixed receptive-expressive language disorder.

Learning Disorders and Learning Disabilities

Learning disorders (once commonly referred to as learning disabilities) are specific developmental disorders characterized by deficits in or impairments of specific skills including reading, arithmetic, spelling, and writing. The deficits are significant such that a child's achievement scores in these areas are much lower than expected given the child's intelligence, age, or education. To be considered a learning disability, the skill deficit must be severe enough to significantly interfere with the child's academic achievement or daily living and must not be due to a sensory deficit (Wicks-Nelson & Israel, 1997).

Children with learning disabilities usually have average or above average IQ test scores but have more variable subtest scores. In other words, their subtest scores suggest that some of their abilities are adequate to excellent and some are extremely poor (Erickson, 1992). These children often evidence behavior problems such as inattentiveness, impulsivity, task incompletion, perceptual-motor deficits, memory deficits, and overactivity. They also tend to have low self-esteem and to think of themselves as not very smart (Erickson, 1992).

The prevalence of learning disorders is estimated to range from 2 percent to 10 percent depending on the definition or criteria used to make the diagnosis. It is also estimated that approximately 5 percent of students in public schools have a learning disorder. Boys are approximately three to five times more often diagnosed as having a learning disorder than girls; however, this may reflect a referral bias (American Psychiatric Association, 1994).

There are no reported estimations of learning disorders among African American children. This is likely because African American children were underrepresented in the limited research on learning disorders. This underrepresentation is likely in part because for many years prior to 1980, African American students with learning disorders often went undiagnosed for these disorders. African American students with learning difficulties were simply placed in "special classes" for "slow" students without adequate assessment of the factors in their academic performance and, thus, without identification of appropriate assessment-based interventions to address their academic problems.

Since the early 1980s, significantly more African American students have been diagnosed with learning disorders and not just stuck in "special classes" for "slow" students (i.e., classes for the educable mentally retarded). This change is likely due to social and political pressures for schools to recognize the cultural bias in standardized tests that has led to inappropriate labeling of African American children as mentally retarded, the stigma against mental retardation, and the social and political pressures for appropriate educational placement of students to optimize the learning of all students (Chinn & Hughes, 1987). Yet, in many places in the United States a disproportionate number of African American students are still inappropriately placed in "special classes" for "slow" students; many of these students likely have undiagnosed learning disorders or other problems that do not warrant such placements.

Today, there are three commonly recognized learning disorders: reading disorders, mathematics disorders, and written expression disorders. Following is a discussion of each of these disorders.

1. *Reading disorders.* A reading disorder is characterized by the inability to read with normal proficiency even with the following conditions: having received normal academic instruction in reading, living in a culturally adequate home, having received proper motivation to read, and having intact senses, normal intelligence, and freedom from gross neurological defect (Eisenberg, 1966). Reading disorders are estimated to occur in approximately 4 percent of school-age children and are by far the most common of the learning disorders (American Psychiatric Association, 1994).

A reading disorder is evidenced by a significant discrepancy between a child's expected reading achievement level (based on the child's chronological age, grade placement, and mental age) and the child's actual reading achievement level. The discrepancy is such that the child's actual reading level is substantially lower than expected. In addition to this discrepancy, children with reading disorders often make errors on tests such as failing to discriminate both letters within words and similar words, omitting letters or words within sentences, and mispronouncing words. These errors are significant in that they interfere with daily life activities that require reading.

2. *Mathematics disorders.* The major distinguishing characteristic of a mathematics disorder is that there is a substantial discrepancy between a child's mathematics ability, as measured by individually administered standardized achievement tests of mathematical calculation or reasoning, and the child's expected mathematics ability given the child's chronological age, measured intelligence, and age-appropriate education. The discrepancy is such that the child's actual mathematics ability is substantially lower than expected. The resulting disturbance in math skills significantly interferes with academic achievement or with daily life functioning requiring mathematical skill. A child who has a mathematics disorder may have deficiencies in some or all of the needed computational, visual-spatial, memory, and mathematical reasoning skills.

It is estimated that a mathematics disorder occurs in approximately one in every five cases of learning disorders (American Psychiatric Association, 1994). Often a child with a mathematics disorder who has high IQ scores will not be diagnosed with this disorder until in fifth grade or later because this disorder usually does not become apparent until then.

3. *Disorders of written expression.* The major feature of a disorder of written expression is that there is a substantial discrepancy between a child's writing skills, as measured by an individually administered standardized test or functional assessment of writing skills, and a child's expected writing skills given a child's chronological age, measured intelligence, and age-appropriate education. The discrepancy is such that a child's actual writing skills are substantially lower than would be expected. The resulting disturbance in written expression significantly interferes with academic achievement or with daily life functioning activities that require writing skills (American Psychiatric Association, 1994).

Evaluation of a written expression disorder is often based on a comparison between extensive samples of a child's written schoolwork and other assigned writing tasks (e.g., the task of writing spontaneously) and expected performance for her or his age and IQ.

Such comparisons are often used because, except for spelling, the standardized tests for assessing a written expression disorder are not well developed.

The prevalence of written expression disorders is not known; however, it is known that it usually occurs in conjunction with one of the other learning disorders (American Psychiatric Association, 1994).

There is no reported research on the causes of learning disorders among African American children. Furthermore, the existing research suggests the actual causes of learning disorders in the general population are not completely clear. However, brain dysfunction has been reported to be the primary causal factor in learning disorders (Wicks-Nelson & Israel, 1997).

It is also suspected that genetic factors, pregnancy complications, premature delivery, and neurological dysfunction are factors in the occurrence of reading disorders—the most prevalent disorder and the one on which most research has been done. There is a developing view that deficits in phonological awareness and coding may be central factors in specific reading disorders. There is much evidence that most specific reading disorders are associated with phonological processing (Stanovich, 1994).

It has been reported that factors in specific learning disorders (SLDs) include genetic causes, damage to the central nervous system, and minimal brain dysfunction (Erickson, 1992). Bishop (1992) concluded from her review of the literature that at least in some SLDs, the causes of them may be the combination of auditory deficits and limited processing of information capacity. She also concluded that the research on the causes of SLDs is confusing.

It is important to note that most researchers and clinicians acknowledge that environmental factors such as social class and parental attitudes play some causal roles in learning disorders (Wicks-Nelson & Israel, 1997). It has also been suggested that motivation may be a factor in learning disorders. According to Licht and Kistner (1986), children with learning disorders begin to doubt their intellectual abilities when they fail and, thus, give up easily, resulting in more failure and low achievement motivation. Additionally, success comes to be viewed by these children as the result of external factors such as luck or the teacher's help rather than their own effort and ability. Furthermore, the results of many studies suggest that some peers, teachers, and parents of children with learning disabilities view these children negatively and often reject them (Gresham & Elliott, 1989; Margalit, 1989). Clearly, such attitudes also negatively impact the motivation of these children to learn.

Assessment of Developmental Language and Learning Disorders and Disabilities

There are some researchers and clinicians who believe that environmental, social, cultural, political, and economic influences are major factors in the diagnosis of language and learning disorders and that many children diagnosed with one of the language or learning disorders do not have neurological dysfunctions that are severe enough to impair learning and academic achievement. These researchers and clinicians believe that it is the specified influence factors that are the culprits in the impairments in learning and academic achievement that these children evidence (Coles, 1987). This is a culturally and socioeconomically sensitive view of language and learning disorders.

A culturally and socioeconomically sensitive view of language and learning disorders recognizes the importance of multidimensional and multimodal assessments of African American children with learning and achievement problems who often are suspected of having language or learning disorders. In addition to the traditional administration of standardized achievement, language, and intellectual assessments and other paper-and-pencil tests, assessments of African American children suspected of having one of the language or learning disorders should include the following: (1) interviews with parents, teachers, and the children suspected of having a learning disorder; (2) classroom and home behavioral observations, (3) evaluation of the children's study habits and behaviors, and (4) examination of the children's schoolwork.

Furthermore, the standardized tests for diagnosing language and learning disorders should be administered in a very supportive environment with highly trained test administrators who are culturally and socioeconomically sensitive. Ideally, one of these test administrators should be an African American who is culturally and socioeconomically sensitive. Coaching of the children on these test is also recommended. Additionally, test norms for African American children, when available, should be used; otherwise, the test scores of other African American children of a similar socioeconomic background to the child being assessed for a learning disorder should be considered when interpreting the standardized test scores and schoolwork of the child being assessed.

A culturally and socioeconomically sensitive view of language and learning disorders also recognizes the importance of using caution in assigning the label of language disorder or learning disorder or disability and of identifying environmental, social, cultural, and economic factors that may be operant in the learning and achievement problems of children whether or not they have a learning disorder diagnosis. Indeed, there are likely children with a language or learning disorder diagnosis who do meet the criteria for the label(s) and children with a learning or language disorder diagnosis who do not meet the criteria for the label(s).

Intervention Strategies for Developmental Language and Learning Disorders and Disabilities

Intervention strategies to help African American children with language or learning disorder diagnoses and children with learning problems characteristic of these disorders must be designed to facilitate the children's academic progress and success. High achievement expectations and high levels of individual effort are needed by those who use these intervention strategies. The specific intervention program used with a particular child must be tailored to the child's needs as indicated by a multidimensional and multimodal assessment of the child's academic and behavior problems. Special attention must be paid to the factors in the child's academic strengths and weaknesses, as academic intervention strategies must capitalize on the child's strengths and remediate the child's weaknesses.

Given that majority youth who experience language or learning disorders often experience a lack of a sense of personal control over academic success and low achievement motivation from the experience of ineffective effort, it is likely that African American youth with language or learning disorders or characteristics of these disorders may have these experiences even more intensely. This is because many African American youth may be at higher risk of feeling powerless over their academic learning given their minority status and their high risk of having teachers with low expectations of them. Furthermore, many of these youth have families who are not sufficiently educated about language and learning disorders and, thus, do not provide them with needed support and encouragement.

It is clearly important to facilitate the self-empowerment of African American youth with language or learning disorders or the characteristics of these disorders; that is, it is important to promote in these youth the self-motivation for achievement, self-control of their academic progress and success, self-praise of their academic progress and success, adaptive skills (i.e., communication skills, socialization skills, and daily living skills), and success behaviors for academic and social success. Given the behavior problems and the social rejection that African American children often experience with or without the label of a language or learning disorder, teaching African American children with language or learning disorders adaptive skills and success behaviors is particularly important.

It is also important to explain to African American children and adolescents diagnosed as having a language or learning disorder just what such a disorder is and why they may be having difficulty in learning. The explanation should be age appropriate and should include that the disorder does not mean that they are mentally retarded—a hurtful label often given them by some of their peers.

General Education Strategies. It is also important for teachers, parents, and tutors who participate in the education of African American youth with learning disorders or characteristics of these disorders to use the following general education strategies suggested by Taylor (1989).

1. Provide the children with as much academic work as possible, devoting a great deal of this time to individual instruction in which the teacher directs learning and provides feedback to the children.

2. Give the children much opportunity to practice a technique that has been learned by giving learning problems very similar to the one used to teach the technique. In other words, facilitate overlearning through practice as this overlearning is important to establish firmly what has been learned.

3. Establish realistic goals and provide incentives for reaching these goals.

4. Provide training to address all of the academic deficiencies rather than focus on one or two deficiencies in hopes of learning generalization, given that this generalization seldom occurs. Start with mastery of lower-order skills and knowledge, because this is important for learning higher-order skills and knowledge.

Specific Intervention Strategies to Facilitate Academic Success. Following are some specific educational intervention strategies that parents, teachers, and tutors can use to facilitate academic progress and success of an African American child (including adolescents) with a developmental language or learning disorder or characteristics similar to those of such a disorder.

1. Teachers and tutors can provide the child with instruction that is directed to addressing the child's specific deficiencies. For example, if the child has a limited vocabulary, then the child should be involved in activities that include learning new words and their meanings. It is also important that a teacher trained in working with children with language and learning disorders spend some individual time with the child each day. Such a teacher will have a wide range of activities for teaching specific academic knowledge and skills and can efficiently and effectively respond to the child's motivational and other self-empowerment needs.

2. Programmed instruction can often be effectively used. This type of instruction involves presenting the academic work in small, sequential steps, after which the child receives feedback before going on to the next step. The child moves along each step at her or his own pace, getting assistance from the teacher or tutor as needed. The child also receives individualized reinforcers for successes or progress. To facilitate self-empowerment of the child, it is recommended that the child give herself or himself reinforcements from a group of possible predetermined reinforcers.

3. A step-by-step teaching method is highly recommended because this teaching method allows the child to successfully practice what is taught on her or his own. Thus, it facilitates in the child a sense of power and self-control over her or his academic achievement and progress. This method is based on Meichenbaum's cognitive modeling and self-instruction (Meichenbaum, 1977). It provides the structured, directed learning that children with learning impairments typically need.

The step-by-step teaching method involves (a) breaking the skill or behavior to be learned into steps and writing these steps; (b) having the teacher model the skill or behavior using the steps and saying each step aloud (i.e., cognitive modeling); (c) having the child perform the same skill or behavior (as modeled by the teacher) while the teacher instructs the student using the steps; (d) instructing the student to perform the skill or behavior while using the written steps to instruct herself or himself aloud and then silently (i.e., covert self-guidance); (e) having the child memorize the steps and practice the skill or behavior saying the steps covertly; and (f) having the child self-praise progress toward and attainment of the behavior or skill throughout the learning and practice processes. If the child cannot read, the steps can be tape recorded for the child to listen to and follow.

It is recommended that realistic, task-specific goals be set for the child and that the child play a major role in setting these goals. Accomplishment for achieving these goals should primarily be reinforced with self-praise along with teacher praise and parent praise. Because of the history of African Americans being controlled and subjugated, many African American parents do not support controlling children's academic or social behavior with tangible rewards. Thus, self-controlled reinforcers, especially self-praise, are most appropriate. If stronger reinforcers are needed, especially initially in working with a child with learning impairments, then have the child self-select these reinforcers with assistance from the teacher, parent, or tutor and with parental approval of the reinforcers from which the child may select. The reinforcers can be educational such as free time on the computer and putting together an educational puzzle.

A common reward system for reaching goals is to have children give themselves a predetermined number of points for reaching each goal and then have these points exchangeable for identified reinforcers that have predetermined point values. Alternatives to this reward system are limitless and include (a) having the child or teacher place an excellent grade and smiling face or star on the child's work and then post the work on an outstanding work board at school or home, (b) publicly praising the student in class for excellent academic progress, and (c) giving the child an academic progress certificate. Ideally, self-praise should be encouraged in conjunction with all reinforcers from others. Indeed, the ultimate goals are to facilitate academic achievement and self-rewarding of academic progress and success to help sustain this achievement.

4. Teachers, parents, and trainers can provide the child with training in adaptive skills (e.g., socialization skills such as how to initiate a new friendship), self-management of maladaptive behaviors (e.g., self-management of frustration), and success behaviors (e.g., staying focused on assigned work and asking questions about what is not understood). These skills and behaviors were discussed in Chapter 11 in the section on other general intervention strategies.

Because of the need for intense focus on academic deficiencies while the child is at school, parents must play an active role in providing or arranging for the provision of adaptive skills training and training to teach their child school success behaviors. Additionally, teachers can encourage and praise these skills and behaviors to facilitate and sustain their occurrence.

5. Children can be taught to use problem solving, which involves understanding their own cognitive processes and regulating cognitive activity (Palincsar & Brown, 1986). This can be done using the step-by-step teaching approach. Following are steps that can be used to teach problem solving.

Step 1. Teach the child to identify what a task requires.

Step 2. Have the child attempt to do the task, and when the child cannot do so, discuss the child's approach, why it did not work, and the importance of using specific strategies to master the task.

Step 3. The teacher suggests some specific strategies for doing the task and models using these strategies, saying them aloud while doing the task. (The strategies ideally should be simply written and followed by the teacher.)

Step 4. The child practices doing the task following the strategies modeled by the teacher. Initially the child reads the strategies aloud to do the task and then practices the task while reading the strategies silently. Next, the child studies and practices the strategies so that the child can do the task using her or his memory of the strategies.

Step 5. The child praises herself or himself for following the strategies and for successfully doing the task. The child may also give herself or himself some other self-reward such as task completion points that can be later exchanged for some fun activity approved by the child's parents. The teacher also praises the child.

A similar problem-solving approach has been successfully used to teach mathematics, reading, study skills, and other academic skills to children with learning disorders (Lyon & Moats, 1988). This approach has also been used to teach junior and high school students with learning disorders (Palincsar & Brown, 1987; Schumaker, Deshler, Alley, Warner, & Denton, 1984).

6. It is recommended that a child with a language disorder receive training from a speech therapist or a speech pathologist (Erickson, 1992; Wicks-Nelson & Israel, 1997). It is generally agreed that parents should be educated about both the treatment plan used by the speech therapist or speech pathologist and its rationale; however, there is much disagreement as to whether parents should be trained to provide some speech therapy for the child. Yet, it is agreed that parents must be encouraged to be patient and very supportive of the child in the treatment process.

7. Parents should get as much consultation as possible about the best treatment program for their child. They ideally should consult with the child's teacher, school administrators, and specialists at the school who are trained in working with children who have language and learning disorders (e.g., a speech therapist). It is also advisable for parents to consult with individuals outside of the child's school who are trained in working with children who have language and learning disorders about (a) available treatments, (b) what might be the best treatment program for their child, (c) parents' rights in decision making about their child's treatment, and (d) the state's responsibilities in meeting the child's education needs. This outside consultation is important because the school may not have the ideal treatment resources or staff for a child with a language or learning disorder and may not be up with current treatment information. With information from professionals outside of the child's school, parents can often work with school administrators, the local school board, and their state's department of education to get the help for their child that may not be initially available at their child's school.

8. Schools should provide at least semiannual workshops for parents and children who have language or learning disorders. These workshops can provide accurate as well as positive and motivating information about how to be successful despite these disorders. Such information should include the fact that more and more students with language or learning disorders are going to college and to other postsecondary education training settings (Hughes & Smith, 1990) and that most colleges have or will make accommodations (e.g., provision of tutoring, counseling, and special test-taking schedules and formats) in an effort to meet the needs of their students with these disorders. The workshops can also provide opportunities for children with language or learning disorders and their parents to ask the questions that they want to ask about these disorders.

9. Parents and schools can work together to find successful adults with language or learning disorders who can serve as mentors for children with similar problems. These mentors can attend the previously mentioned workshops. Such mentors can greatly facilitate the motivation to learn of children with language or learning disorders and can encourage these children to form long-term career goals that help facilitate their self-motivation to achieve.

10. Teachers who have children with language or learning disorders in their classrooms can explain these disorders in talks to their students about respecting differences among peers and how differences help make each child unique and special. This action will decrease the likelihood of children with language or learning disorders being teased and mislabeled as mentally retarded by their peers.

11. Teachers must be trained to teach students with language or learning disorders if such children spend any time in their classrooms. Given the current movement to include students with language or learning disorders and other disorders in regular classrooms (Hammill, 1993), this training is especially important and should be sought by teachers in preparation for future teaching of children with disorders.

12. Parents must provide and assist classroom teachers and resource teachers in getting whatever help (e.g., teacher assistants) and resources (e.g., computers and computer software) needed to teach their child and other children with language or learning disorders. Through consultation with and monetary support of African American churches, businesses, and community organizations, parents can get the resources that their child and other children with learning disorders need in their school. Parents must also facilitate recognition and rewarding of teachers who work with children who have learning disorders because this work is difficult and challenging.

Educational Placement Intervention Options.   Currently, most children with language or learning disorders receive their education through one of the following arrangements: (1) They are placed in regular classrooms, (2) they spend time in both regular classrooms and resource rooms for children with language or learning disorders and children who may have other special needs, or (3) they are placed in self-contained special classrooms. Intervention plans to teach children with language or learning disorders include one of the following:

1. placement in a regular classroom with a teacher trained in working with children who have a language or learning disorder;

2. placement in a regular classroom with a teacher who is not trained in working with children who have a language or learning disorder but who gets consultation and teaching materials for teaching such children from a resource teacher (a teacher trained in teaching children with language or learning disorders and other special needs);

3. placement in a regular classroom that includes a resource teacher who separately teaches the children with language or learning disorders and does so in the regular classroom;

4. placement in a regular classroom part of the day and placement the rest of the day in a resource room where the child gets small group or individual instruction by the resource teacher and teaching assistants;

5. full-time placement in a self-contained special classroom with other children with language or learning disorders and children with other special needs.

Because of inadequate research, it is not known which of the preceding placements or which of the preceding general and specific intervention strategies are most effective for children with learning disorders. Yet, clinical experiences, existing case studies, and research as well as known and tested principles of learning suggest that the recommended intervention strategies are worthwhile efforts that have much potential for facilitating the academic achievement of African American and other children with learning disorders or learning difficulties similar to those of children with learning disorders.

Mental Retardation

Mental retardation is also a developmental learning disorder. Technically, a child who is diagnosed with mental retardation has received a general intelligence test score of 70 to 75 or below on tests such as the Wechsler Scales, and evidences limitations in adaptive functioning associated with intellectual limitations.

According to the American Association on Mental Retardation's 1992 publication entitled *Mental Retardation: Definition, Classification, and Systems of Support,* mental retardation is defined as follows:

> Mental retardation refers to substantial limitations in present functioning. It is characterized by significantly subaverage intellectual functioning, existing concurrently with related limitations in two or more of the following applicable adaptive skill areas: communication, self-care, home living, social skills, community use, self-direction, health and safety, functional academics, leisure and work. Mental retardation manifests before age 18 (p. 5).

Limitations due to cultural differences are not supposed to be used in establishing a diagnosis of mental retardation. In many cases in the past and to some degree presently, limitations in adaptive functioning due to any reasons are used to establish a mental retardation diagnosis. Because of this practice and given the cultural bias in commonly used IQ tests, some African American children (and other children as well) have been unjustly labeled as mentally retarded. Many of these youth have become highly successful adults in careers that require high intellectual functioning and extraordinary adaptive skills. This should not be surprising given the reported low correlation ($r = .40$) between IQ test scores and out-of-school achievements (Baumeister, 1987). Furthermore, the reported correlations between IQ test scores and school grades have ranged from low ($r = .40$) to moderately high ($r = .75$) (Berger & Yule, 1985; Matarazzo, 1992).

Prevalence of Mental Retardation

The prevalence of mental retardation depends on the criteria used to make the diagnosis of mental retardation. The prevalence is estimated to be at about 2 percent to 3 percent of the general population when IQ alone is the criterion; however, when both IQ and adaptive behavior are used to establish the diagnosis of mental retardation, its prevalence drops to less than 1 percent.

The prevalence of mental retardation among African Americans is presumed to be disproportionately high. This presumption is based on the fact that most African Americans fall in the low socioeconomic groups and these groups have been reported to have disproportionately high numbers of individuals diagnosed as having mental retardation; furthermore, mental retardation is reported to be more prevalent among some nonmajority groups (Crnic, 1988; Scott, 1994). There is, however, a problem with the basis of this presumption, which is the failure to consider that the standard measures of IQ are culturally biased, and research on nonmajority groups (minorities) typically does not independently investigate the effects of race and social class (Helms, 1992).

Clearly, research to develop culturally and socioeconomically sensitive measures of intellectual functioning are needed before empirically sound research on the prevalence of and the factors in mental retardation among African Americans can be conducted. In such research the socioeconomic and cultural differences among African Americans must be considered. African Americans are not a homogenous group.

A New View of Mental Retardation and Its Assessment

Because of the bias in IQ test scores and lack of cultural and socioeconomic sensitivity in assessments of mental retardation, a disproportionately high number of African American youth have been labeled as mentally retarded. This is likely in part why since 1982, the American Association on Mental Retardation (AAMR) has advocated consideration of cultural, linguistic, and behavioral diversity when making a diagnosis of mental retardation. The AAMR has also advocated judging adaptive skills on the basis of typical community environments, recognizing an individual's personal capabilities and strengths in the adaptive skills areas, and making treatment recommendations on the basis of this environmentally sensitive evaluation. Additionally, the AAMR also revised its old position of viewing mental retardation as an absolute trait to viewing it as the product of limited intellectual functioning and environmental influences (Wicks-Nelson & Israel, 1997).

This new view of mental retardation does not allow someone with an IQ of 60 to be labeled mentally retarded if the person is functioning adequately in her or his environment. The new emphasis is on how the individual is functioning; if functioning changes, then the diagnosis might change (Wicks-Nelson & Israel, 1997). Indeed, this is a more culturally and socioeconomically sensitive view of mental retardation; yet, there is no guarantee that this view has been or will be adopted in educational settings, clinical practice, or research.

With this new emphasis on adaptive functioning has come new ways of classifying people considered to be mentally retarded. Classifications in the past have been used for treatment and residential placements and for research purposes. For example, educators have used the placements *educable* (mild retardation), *trainable* (moderate to severe retardation), and *custodial* (profound retardation). The new classification model recommended by the AAMR does not classify individuals by IQ; instead, each individual is classified on four dimensions. These dimensions were summarized by Wicks-Nelson and Israel (1997):

1. The individual's strengths and weaknesses in intellectual functioning and adaptive skills
2. The individual's strengths and weaknesses with regard to psychological/emotional functioning
3. The individual's strengths and weaknesses with regard to physical functioning and health
4. The current environment and the optimal environment that would facilitate continued growth (p. 246)

Wicks-Nelson and Israel (1997) further state that the foregoing information is used to develop a profile, which stipulates for each dimension the level of support required. The possible support levels required are intermittent, limited, extensive, or pervasive. Thus, the resulting diagnosis should not only state that the person has mental retardation but also state the level of support needed and in which specific areas from among the four previously specified dimensions (e.g., daily living skills).

The emphasis on adaptive skills by the AAMR has also resulted in new views of these skills. Specifically, it is now clearly recognized that these skills change and that they depend to a large degree on the situation in which the person must function (Scott, 1994). For example, if an African American child is in a classroom in which all of her or his classmates are European Americans and the teacher gives the child little attention, and the child is too anxious and embarrassed to ask questions about the class work that is not understood, the child's adaptive skills will likely not develop. With one-on-one instruction by a tutor, support and encouragement by the tutor and teacher, and involvement of the child in an adaptive skills training program, the child will likely show significant improvement in adaptive skills.

Adaptive skills are usually measured using the Vineland Adaptive Behavior Scales (Sparrow, Balla, & Cicchetti, 1984), which has versions for parents or other primary caregivers and a version for teachers. These scales use semistructured formats and assess communication skills, daily living skills, socialization skills, and motor skills. The parent version includes a measure of maladaptive behavior.

Two of the more recently developed assessments of adaptive functioning are: (1) the Adaptive Behavior Scales-Residential and Community (ABS-RC) for use with individuals in communities or institutions who are from age three through adulthood (Nihira, Leland, & Lambert, 1993), and (2) the Adaptive Behavior Scales-School Edition for children (primarily those with mild to moderate levels of retardation) ages three through sixteen (ABS-SE) (DeStefano & Thompson, 1990).

Causes of Mental Retardation

The causes of mental retardation can be organic, genetic, and psychosocial (Scott, 1994). Organic factors include brain impairment due to abnormal genetic mechanisms and prenatal, birth, and postnatal variables. The genetic mechanisms include chromosome abnormalities, which are associated with syndromes of mental retardation, particularly Down syndrome—the most common genetic mental retardation (Thapar, Gottesman, Owen, O'Donovan, & McGuffin, 1994). One can also inherit single-gene patterns such as the X-linked pattern associated with the X syndrome—an inherited disorder associated with mental retardation and ranked second to Down syndrome as a genetic cause of mental retardation (Bregman & Hodapp, 1991).

Types of prenatal factors in mental retardation include exposure to disease, chemicals, drugs, radiation, poor nutrition, and Rh incompatibility. Among the birth-related causes of mental retardation are low birth weight and prematurity (Bregman & Hodapp, 1991) and birth complications and anoxia (Scott, 1994). The postnatal causes commonly cited include seizures, malnutrition, head injuries, lead poisoning, and a host of other variables (Scott, 1994). Organic causes are believed to be the primary cause of approximately 25 percent of all cases of mental retardation (Scott & Carran, 1987).

The polygenic factors in mental retardation involve the combining of effects of multiple genes such that mental retardation is produced (Scott, 1994). It is estimated that 50 percent of the variation in tested intelligence in populations is due to genetic transmission of multiple genes (Plomin, DeFries, & McClearn, 1990).

The reported psychosocial factors in mental retardation include social isolation and inadequate social stimulation. The latter may be due to parents not having the knowledge or skills or not taking the time to stimulate children's language and cognitive development. Lack of such stimulation is believed to be more common among low socioeconomic families. Limited empirical support has been provided for this view. However, some researchers have reported that psychosocial variables (e.g., parental practices and attitudes), social class, and measured intellectual functioning of children are significantly associated (Hart & Risley, 1992; Sameroff, 1990).

Problems Associated with Mental Retardation

There are several problems that often come with mental retardation in children that must be addressed when planning interventions to facilitate these children's academic and social success. These problems typically include behavior problems, academic failure, finding appropriate education placements, physical disabilities, social stigma, psychological problems, and family problems such as stress.

According to Scott (1994), children and other persons with mental retardation may evidence various clinically significant behavior problems and as a population evidence three to four times more of these problems than in populations without mental retardation. These problems may include conduct problems, depression, self-injury, aggressive behavior, attention problems, and other such problems. Scott suggested that neurological, genetic, biological, and psychosocial factors (e.g., social isolation that limits exposure to appropriate role models) influence these behavior problems. Furthermore, certain kinds of institutional care, use of certain medications, social stigma, and the home environment may contribute to behavior problems (Scott, 1994).

Parents are usually psychologically, emotionally, socially, and financially impacted by their child's mental retardation diagnosis. Indeed, parents of children with mental retardation often experience a range of emotions in response to their child's diagnosis and functional limitations including depression, embarrassment, guilt, and anger. African American parents of low socioeconomic status especially experience great stress and hardship because of the knowledge acquisition and money often needed to meet these children's educational and social needs. Siblings of African American children with mental retardation often initially experience embarrassment as well as resentment over their increased responsibilities due to having to help care for the child with mental retardation.

How well the child with the mental retardation and her or his parents and siblings cope with the related problems depends on many factors. These factors include severity of the mental retardation, parental beliefs and coping skills, the parents' marital adjustment, the parents' level of intellectual functioning, social class variables, available professional services, and level of social support that the family and child receive (Atkinson et al., 1995; Flynt, Wood, & Scott, 1994).

Intervention Strategies for Mental Retardation

The intervention strategies to facilitate the academic and social success of children with mental retardation need to be multidimensional in that they must address the educational, behavioral, social, psychological, emotional, and physical needs of the child and the family. The needed interventions must also be multimodal in that they ideally must involve the child's parents, family, school, physician, community, and state service agency. All children, including those with intellectual and adaptive skills limitations, are among this nation's most precious resources. Therefore, these children must be helped to help themselves reach their highest attainment.

Because most youth with mental retardation typically want to be seen as "normal" and to function independently like their peers without mental retardation and because youth with mental retardation often experience social rejection and low expectations from others, a self-empowerment intervention approach with these youth seems indicated. It other words, it is especially important to teach and encourage children with mental retardation to teach themselves, to be self-motivated, to use self-reinforcement in pursuit of academic and social success, and to develop adaptive skills and success behaviors.

Preliminary to any interventions with African American children or any children with mental retardation must be an appropriate attitudinal set by all involved. Efforts need to be made to help these children understand that they can learn and will learn but that it is going to take a lot of determination and hard work. The idea needs to be conveyed that they will learn step-by-step and that those working with them believe that they can and will learn step-by-step. In other words, positive and high expectations need to be communicated to these children toward the goals of helping these youth experience self-motivation and self-empowerment for successfully meeting a series of academic and social goals.

The attitudinal sets of teachers, parents, and psychologists who provide the intervention for these children and adolescents must be humanistic, positive, supportive, realistic, and patient. These adults must see these youth as human beings with strengths and much undiscovered potential. Furthermore, these adults must provide structured instruction that allows the children to experience as much independence as possible so that they can make self-attributions regarding their success. Such independence and self-attributions will facilitate positive academic self-concepts and positive self-esteem—both of which are often lacking in children with intellectual and functional limitations.

Educational Placement Intervention Options.   Selecting the appropriate educational setting for a child with mental retardation is perhaps the first major intervention decision to facilitate the child's academic and psychosocial development. The educational setting will need to be one that is based on the child's strengths and limitations and associated objectives and goals for the child. However, every effort should be made to place the child in an educational program that allows the child to have her or his limitations addressed and to spend as much time as possible in regular classroom settings with peers who are not retarded.

Children with mild retardation clearly should be placed in regular classrooms for a great deal of their school time. There is some evidence that placing children with mild retardation primarily in special classrooms for children with mental retardation or other disorders can result in the children with mild retardation receiving a lesser-quality education (Ysseldyke, Thurlow, Christenson, & Muyskens, 1991). There is also some evidence that children with severe retardation evidence greater social and communication skills development in regular schools than in separate schools (McDonnell, Hardman, Hightower, & Kiefer-O'Donnell,1991).

Even though there is not enough well-designed empirical research evidence to conclude that students with mental retardation are better off with more integration into regular class settings than in full-time special class placement (Wicks-Nelson & Israel, 1997), common sense and logic suggest that youth with mild and moderate retardation would benefit from having positive nondisabled role models. Howlin (1994) has made this argument well and has pointed out that integration of children and adolescents with mild retardation or moderate retardation may help avoid them being stigmatized and may orient them toward integration in society as adults.

When making the decision about placing a child with mental retardation into an educational setting and program, there are typically four options (Patton, Beirne-Smith, & Payne, 1993): (1) education in a regular classroom that includes use of special materials and equipment, participation in a resource room with a resource teacher specially trained in working with children with disabilities, and provision of other special education activities to address the child's limitations and needs; (2) education in a special classroom that involves students with extensive special education needs spending all their time there and for students who do not have extensive special education needs spending part of their time in a regular classroom; (3) education in a special school that involves being taught at a special day school or special residential school, and (4) non-school-based education that involves receiving hospital instruction or homebound instruction.

Specific Intervention Strategies Parents Can Use. Parents of African American children with mental retardation must play a central role in their children's education and psychosocial development. There are several specific intervention strategies that these African American parents can use to facilitate their child's academic achievement, psychosocial adjustment, and social success.

1. Parents can and must utilize all educational evaluations and interventions available to their child. This will require learning all that they can about mental retardation in children and learning what services their children have the right to receive because of their disabilities. These rights are specified in the Education for All Handicapped Children Act (Public Law 94-142), which was expanded in the early 1990s under the title the Individuals with Disabilities Education Act. Parents can get a copy of this act from their local school board office, state department of education, or their local children and family services department.

In sum, this act ensures that students with handicaps (e.g., mental retardation) get free public education that is tailored to the student's special needs. The act requires that each child with a disability have an individualized education plan (IEP) that considers the child's functioning and that specifies educational objectives and goals, needed services to meet these objectives, and evaluation procedures for measuring progress toward achieving these objectives. This plan must be reviewed annually by a committee and parents of the child.

The act also requires that students with disabilities be educated with children who do not have disabilities to the degree that is appropriate with the goal being the least restrictive educational environment possible. If the child requires placement in a program that requires living outside of the child's home, then an appropriate program nearest to the child's home must be chosen.

Parents of a child with mental retardation can and should also get a copy of the Americans with Disabilities Act of 1990, which ensures access to education and jobs and other opportunities such as assistance with independent living for individuals with disabilities. Of great importance is that parents actively involve themselves in the formulation of the individualized educational plan (IEP) for their child.

2. Parents can initiate getting training from resource teachers to use teaching strategies and behavior management strategies for facilitating their child's academic achievement and for teaching their child adaptive skills. Parents can also seek this training by sitting in on classes at the local junior college and attending workshops on facilitating the achievement and adjustment of children with mental retardation.

3. Parents can get a member of their church or community to assist them in working with their child's school to ensure that culturally and socioeconomically sensitive evaluations of their child's functioning are conducted and that all aspects of the individualized education plan for their child are culturally and socioeconomically sensitive. Because many African Americans feel intimidated by medical, educational, and psychological professionals, parents often do not ask all of the questions that they would like of these professionals and they often do not challenge recommendations from these professionals that legitimately should be challenged. Thus, it is important for many African American parents to have partner advocates for their child and for themselves.

4. Parents can talk with their child about the meaning of mental retardation, making the point that it involves having to learn in different ways from the way that most children learn and having to take much time and effort to learn. Additionally, it can be communicated that with a positive attitude and hard work, learning for them will be interesting, sometimes frustrating, and very rewarding just as it is for many children who do not have mental retardation. It is especially important for parents to also communicate that mental retardation does not mean that one cannot learn.

5. Parents can get their child involved in group counseling to help deal with her or his feelings, psychological symptoms (e.g., withdrawal, hostility), and behavior problems associated with mental retardation. Such counseling can indeed be beneficial for children and adolescents with mental retardation (Szymanski & Kaplan, 1991). Additionally, parents can get family counseling to address the feelings of the child's siblings and their own feelings associated with the child's mental retardation and to learn ways that the family can be supportive of each other and of the child toward the goal of facilitating the child's achievement and adjustment.

Parents can also attend support groups for parents. Such groups as well as family counseling often help to reduce parents' feelings of anger, frustration, guilt, and depression and to teach parents information and interventions that other parents with children who are mentally retarded have found to be helpful to their children and themselves.

6. Parents can involve their child in as many activities as possible with children their own age and adults who are not mentally retarded so as to provide much exposure to role models who engage in appropriate social behaviors.

7. Parents can spend as much time as possible teaching their child what is being taught in their academic classes and teaching them adaptive skills and success behaviors using the step-by-step teaching approach discussed earlier in this chapter in the section on learning disorders under specific intervention strategies to facilitate academic success. This approach helps the child to learn independently by breaking the task into steps, modeling the steps, having the child independently follow the steps, and then using self-praise as well as receiving praise for task progress and success.

Teaching children with mental retardation adaptive skills (i.e., communication, socialization, daily living, and motor skills) and success behaviors (e.g., asking questions about what is not understood) is critical in facilitating the achievement and psychosocial adjustment of these children (Danforth & Drabman, 1990; Matson & Coe, 1991). The adaptive skills and success behaviors that the parent should focus on teaching the child should depend on the child's level of competency and psychosocial development, the parents' judgment, and recommendations of the child's teacher and psychologist or counselor. Family members can all praise the adaptive skills, success behaviors, and academic progress of the child with mental retardation, as such praise encourages and helps sustain the occurrence of these skills and behaviors.

8. Parents can set rules of behavior for the child with mental retardation and set consequences for breaking these rules. Parents cannot out of guilt or sympathy ignore maladaptive behavior by the child. Rules must be reviewed with the child daily if necessary and consequences such as withdrawal of privileges should occur when it is certain that the rule is understood but disobeyed. Similar consequences should also occur for maladaptive behaviors such as hitting or fighting.

9. Parents and siblings of the child with mental retardation cannot let their entire lives revolve around this child, as over time such attention can lead to feelings of resentment or anger toward the child and to stress and unhappiness or depression among all family members. Parents can get supportive in-home or out-of-home part-time respite day care for their child with mental retardation. It is important that they do so without guilt because this will enable them to have the energy and patience to provide quality care and support when they are with their child.

Strategies That Teachers and School Administrators Can Use. Teachers and school administrators who work with African American children with mental retardation can use many strategies to help these children reach their academic potential. Following are some of these strategies.

1. School administrators can play major roles in arranging for and getting funding for the training that teachers need to work effectively with children who are African American and have mental retardation. This training should include how to be culturally and socioeconomically sensitive when working with these children and their families. Even teachers who are not resource teachers designated to work with these children need some level of such training given that most of these children are going to spend some time in regular classrooms with regular classroom teachers. Anytime that a child is with any teacher is a time when that teacher can encourage and praise adaptive skills and success behaviors by the child and can facilitate reduction in maladaptive behaviors. Regular classroom teachers can also facilitate the child's sense of belonging in their classrooms.

2. School administrators and teachers can identity new program learning materials, computer software, and other materials that will help educate children with mental retardation. They can also establish adaptive skills training programs for these children.

3. In teaching an African American child with mental retardation, teachers can use the step-by-step, self-empowering teaching approach and programmed learning that were earlier discussed in this chapter. Teachers can also use frequent praise and privileges to reinforce the child's academic effort, progress, and success. Self-reinforcement should be emphasized and the child should be involved in the selection of the possible reinforcers that the child will have the option to choose for self-reinforcements.

4. Teachers can work in partnership with counselors or psychologists who work with these children to modify their behavior problems and other psychological problems. Typically behavior management techniques such as timeout, setting specific behavioral goals, reinforcing goal attainment, shaping, ignoring inappropriate behaviors, and immediately praising appropriate behaviors are used to facilitate the children's positive behaviors and reduce their negative behaviors. For many African American children and some other children with mental retardation, timeout may be particularly humiliating and isolating. Both of these emotional experiences too often impact these children's lives and thus should be avoided. Thus, every effort should be made to interrupt inappropriate behavior of children with mental retardation without much attention to it (e.g., use whispers to say "please stop talking and focus on your work"). It is also important to teach these children alternative appropriate behaviors to inappropriate behaviors.

5. Teachers can instruct parents on a regular basis as to how they may help their child academically. For example, they can do this by giving the parents homework assignments to do with their child.

6. Teachers can invite to their class African American young adults who are mentally retarded and who have completed high school or other advanced training programs and youth who are retarded but gainfully employed. Teachers can also include success stories about individuals with mental retardation in their reading classes and other classes. Such activities will facilitate the self-motivation of students who are mentally retarded. These activities will also change negative stereotypes about children and adolescents with mental retardation and, thus, facilitate the acceptance of youth with retardation by their classmates.

7. Teachers can be creative in conducting class activities and activities with the African American child who is retarded to make the child feel desired and supported in the class. These activities might include talking with the class about individual differences, mental and physical challenges, and how each child is different and special. Teachers can also engage their classes in fun group discussions and exercises that involve coming up with ways to make students who are different feel supported.

8. Teachers and school administrators can be advocates for African American children with mental retardation to be placed in regular classrooms to the extent that such placements do not obstruct meeting these students' academic and social needs. Such placements involve additional responsibilities for regular classroom teachers who typically are already overworked and underpaid. Yet, such placements are believed to be conducive to the academic and social development of many mentally retarded youth. Furthermore, such placements may result in nondisabled classmates of children with mental retardation having improved attitudes and perceptions of these children and others with disabilities (Patton, 1990).

9. School administrators can advocate for increased salaries and bonuses (e.g., paid vacation time) for teachers who teach or assist in teaching children with mental retardation and other disabilities and who demonstrate efforts to actively teach these students and make them feel a sense of belonging in their classrooms.

Strategies that Psychologists Can Use.   Psychologists are often involved in evaluating and in recommending and providing group counseling and family counseling to help African American children with mental retardation overcome emotional and behavior problems and learn adaptive skills and success behaviors. These professionals also identify the need for and make the proper referral for a child with mental retardation to be evaluated for psychotropic medications for psychotic behavior or severe behavior problems such as extreme overactivity. However, given the lack of knowledge about the long-term effects of medications on children, medications are often the last treatment alternatives. Behavioral and cognitive behavioral interventions for behavior management and self-management of behavior are usually the much more desirable treatment options.

Following are some important intervention strategies that psychologists can use in evaluating and providing treatment to African American children with mental retardation.

1. Psychologists can consult with colleagues who are experienced in working with African American children who are retarded and their families both in the evaluation and intervention processes.

2. In the assessment or evaluation of a child with mental retardation, a psychologist can use interviews with the child and the child's family, interviews with the child's teachers, and behavioral observations of the child in academic and social settings. It is also useful for the psychologist to conduct at least one home visit to get a sense of family interaction patterns and the family's intervention resources (e.g., space for one-to-one tutoring, availability of extended family members to assist in teaching the child, neighborhood resources such as a library and church). Home visits also often facilitate comfort of the clients with the therapist through a more informal interaction in their home environment.

Family interaction patterns and cultural norms identified through home visits help in the development of realistic goals for the child and in developing interventions to modify interaction patterns that are not conducive to the child's independent functioning and self-empowerment. Identification of intervention resources is helpful in suggesting interventions that are realistic and culturally sensitive.

3. Psychologists can read about African American cultures and families to facilitate culturally sensitive counseling delivery. They can also get training in cross-cultural counseling to facilitate their skill development in working with African American children and families.

4. Psychologists can assess the religious beliefs of the child and family members because these beliefs and their religious affiliations can be very useful resources for coping with the challenges that mental retardation brings.

5. In family counseling, psychologists can use practical problem-solving approaches and can actively involve family members in coming up with problem solutions toward the goals of problem resolution and of enabling these families to solve their own problems. Psychologists can also encourage family members to identify their emotional and other needs and to share what they need from each other to meet those needs. Emphasis also needs to be on having all involved share their feelings constructively using "I" statements and specifying the behaviors that lead to their negative feelings or positive feelings.

6. Psychologists can teach children with mental retardation and their families behavioral and cognitive-behavioral interventions to modify behavior problems. Such interventions might include contingency management, self-monitoring of behaviors, goal setting, shaping, self-talk for controlling frustration and stress, muscular relaxation, self-imposed timeout (e.g., relaxation of head on the desk for ten minutes to calm down when frustrated or stressed), and cognitive progressive relaxation. Priority should ideally be given to self-regulation interventions to the degree possible so as to facilitate the self-empowerment of these youth. A step-by-step approach is discussed earlier in this chapter in the section on learning disorders under specific interventions to facilitate academic success.

7. Psychologists can use brief family therapy and group therapy approaches because families of children with mental retardation often have many problems (e.g., transportation difficulties) that deter long-term regular participation in counseling. Furthermore, action-oriented therapy is recommended to address specific problems and to set specific therapy goals that family members play a major role in addressing. Self-attribution of therapy success by the clients should be a major therapy objective especially for those African Americans who do not trust having European American psychologists due to race relations in the United States.

8. When group counseling for the child with mental retardation is a part of treatment, it is important for the psychologist to make an effort to involve African American children among the group members. It is also helpful to have someone who is mentally retarded and who has graduated from high school or is in college to serve as a group facilitator. It would be ideal if that person were culturally and racially similar to the African American child client, given that such a group facilitator would be a great role model for the child client.

9. Psychologists can identify and help arrange local services (e.g., involvement with Big Brothers and Big Sisters, Parents without Partners, Alcoholics Anonymous, a rape survivors group), which may be needed but that were not in the child's individual educational plan. Psychologists have a great deal of influence as advocates for children and families to get needed services.

10. Psychologists can be cognizant of and sensitive to the negative psychological and emotional impact on African American children and their families in dealing with the double dose of social stigma, negative stereotypes, and social rejection often associated with being African American and being labeled as mentally retarded.

11. If an African American child or the child's family feels uncomfortable with the psychologist, this professional can discuss this situation without bad feelings with the family and assist them in finding another more suitable therapist if this is the preference of the family or child.

Partnership Intervention Strategies. Parents, schools, community leaders, political leaders, local businesspersons, and African American churches can work in partnership to meet the academic, social, and recreational needs of African American children with mental retardation and their families. Schools can take leadership in identifying the needs of these children. For example, schools can identify and publicize their needs for computers in their homes as well at school, their need for activities to facilitate their adaptive skills and success behaviors, and their needs for social activities that facilitate their integration into their community.

Parents can do much to further publicize these needs and to assist in the implementation of funded activities for their children. Community leaders, political leaders, businesspersons, and churches can play major roles in finding the financial and human resources to meet the identified needs and can rally public support of and involvement in activities and programs to meet the needs of children with mental retardation and their families. Community leaders, political leaders, and ministers of African American churches are often ideal coordinators of intervention programs and activities that can benefit these children and their families.

Specific intervention programs and activities that such partnerships can provide for children with mental retardation and their families include the following:

1. Seminars and workshops in the community on the truth about mental retardation that have as major objectives the extinction of negative stereotypes associated with individuals who have this label and facilitation of acceptance and involvement of these children and their families in the community.
2. Part-time job programs for adolescents with mental retardation—jobs such as bagging groceries, stocking shelves, observing for store theft, collecting tickets at football games, serving food, and doing office jobs such as running the copy machine.
3. Training to participate in various sports activities for fun and safety (e.g., swimming, karate).
4. Community Special Olympics activities.
5. Scholarship programs that provide money for college and for vocational training
6. Achievement Against All Odds Festivals to provide opportunities to celebrate children with mental retardation and other disabilities.
7. Ongoing after-school programs in African American communities that are specially equipped to tutor and to teach adaptive skills and success behaviors to children with mental retardation and that involve nondisabled high school and college students and adults as tutors and adaptive skills trainers.
8. Family resource centers that include spiritual and psychological counseling and support groups for children with mental retardation and their families, which are led by culturally and socioeconomically sensitive professionals.

African American youth with mental retardation and their families should be involved to the degree possible in planning and implementing all educational and counseling activities to meet their needs. Furthermore, it is important for such activities to be ongoing, as the challenges that African American youth with mental retardation and other disabilities face are ongoing and long-term. Indeed, unless supportive instructional environments are maintained their effects will diminish with time (Natriello, McDill, & Pallas, 1990).

Conclusions

There are several problems that can impede or deter the academic success of African American children and thus threaten their future life success. Whether the academic problem is as seemingly benign as test anxiety or difficulty studying or as significant and complex as having a learning disorder or mental retardation, it can have serious negative consequences for an African American child. These consequences include academic failure, school dropout, social stigma, social rejection, behavior problems, and a host of other problems often leading to a future of poverty, crime, and despair. Thus, it is the responsibility of and to the advantage of all Americans to participate in efforts to facilitate the academic success of African American children with academic problems, for when these children fail, all in their communities and all Americans are negatively impacted.

Given that the academic performance of African American children with significant academic problems may be and usually is influenced by school, social, family, physical, psychological, and community factors, interventions to facilitate the academic and social success of these youth usually must be multidimensional and multimodal. The intervention strategies to address these problems need to be multidimensional in that they usually must address educational, behavioral, social, psychological, emotional, and physical needs of these children and their families. The interventions need to be multimodal in that they usually must involve the child's parents, teachers, family, school, physician, community, church, and state child and family service agency. Furthermore, these individuals and organizations must work in partnership to the degree possible to most effectively meet the academic and social needs of children with significant academic problems that impede or deter their academic success.

The objectives of interventions for African American children with learning disorders and mental retardation ideally should include facilitation of their academic achievement, modification of any manifested behavior problems, meeting their physical, emotional, social, and health needs, and facilitation of the following self-empowerment variables: self-motivation to achieve, self-control of academic progress and success, self-praise of academic progress and success, adaptive skills, and success behaviors. Additionally, interventions must focus on facilitating these children's sense of belonging in their classrooms, schools, and communities.

African American students with learning disorders and those with mental retardation need self-empowerment for academic and social success, culturally and socioeconomically sensitive teachers, and much family and community support and involvement in their education. In addition, they need educational placements, special education resources, and teachers that are appropriate given their functional limitations. It is agreed by many professionals that regular classroom placement integrated with needed special education is in the best interest of most youth with disabilities.

African American youth with learning disabilities and mental retardation especially need as many learning experiences and activities and as much community awareness as possible to avoid, negate, and overcome the social stigma, social stereotypes, low expectations, and social isolation traditionally associated with the labels of learning disorder and disability and mental retardation. African American youth also especially need careful evaluations of their strengths and weaknesses and to have this information rather than their IQ scores determine their academic placements and needed academic, social, and physical interventions. Given the general agreement that IQ scores are not culturally sensitive and thus not reliable, these scores should not solely determine intervention programs for African American youth with mental retardation or disabilities.

The good news is the growing recognition of the need for (1) more culturally and socioeconomically sensitive evaluations of the academic, psychological, and behavioral functioning of African American youth with academic problems, (2) research on the most effective assessment and intervention approaches and methods addressing academic problems of African American youth, and (3) partnership efforts to facilitate the academic and social success of African American youth, especially those with significant academic problems and learning disorders or mental retardation. With such recognitions will surely come strategies that make education work for African American children with major academic and social challenges, thus assuring them of quality lives worth living

13 Prevention of Academic Failure

Real-World Solutions

Academic failure typically refers to making poor grades and not doing well on standardized achievement tests. Yet, these measures often are not reliable reflections of the competencies or the learning that has been acquired by African American youth. Perhaps a more appropriate definition of academic failure is disengagement from the learning process that results in poor grades and poor standardized achievement test scores. Because colleges, universities, and other academic institutions typically use grades and test scores as major factors in decisions about college entrance and college scholarships, these assessments are given much more attention and importance than level of academic engagement. Yet, in fact, level of academic engagement is a major determinant of academic failure or success. Thus, interventions to prevent or modify academic failure should ideally focus on facilitating academic engagement.

According to Skinner (1990), engagement "encompasses children's initiation of action, effort, and persistence on schoolwork, as well as their ambient emotional states during learning activities" (p. 24). Thus, lack of academic engagement can be and is being viewed by the present author as not engaging in academic success behaviors such as studying, doing homework, making a genuine effort to learn, asking questions about what is not understood, showing concern about lack of academic progress, and showing interest in and having a positive attitude toward learning and school.

Prevention of academic failure among African American children must begin early in the preschool years, as once academic failure begins, the associated attitudes (e.g., lack of achievement motivation) and behaviors (e.g., behavior problems and avoidance of school) become established and in turn contribute to or sustain academic failure. These attitudes and behaviors often require much time, energy, expertise, and money to modify and extinguish. Prevention of academic failure is indeed not easy; however, it is easier, less costly, and more positive in nature than is trying to modify academic failure.

African American parents must execute major roles in preventing the academic failure of their children and they must execute these roles throughout their children's school years. The degree to which African American parents are successful in executing these roles significantly influences the degree to which others (e.g., teachers) are successful in executing their roles to prevent academic failure of children. The most important prevention role of African American parents is that of early intervention to prepare their children for academic success in school. This process of preparation for success involves (1) creating a home environment for learning to occur, (2) promoting the expectation among all in the family that academic success will occur, (3) promoting the attitude in their children that they can and will achieve through hard work and perseverance, (4) helping their children establish motivational short-term and long-term goals, and (5) making sure that these children have the behaviors, skills, and knowledge to succeed in any classroom and school, including especially those classrooms and schools in which education is primarily a reflection of majority culture.

This chapter discusses specific strategies that children, parents, teachers, school administrators, and community leaders can use to prevent academic failure among African American children. Most of these strategies focus on facilitating these children's academic success. Throughout this chapter, the importance of self-empowering African American children and of facilitating their engagement in "acting African American" is emphasized. "Acting African American" is a new label for engaging in success behaviors—behaviors mistakenly considered in the past by African American youth as "acting white" behaviors.

Views of African American Students

Consistent with the perspective of empowering African American children for academic success and, thus, for preventing academic failure is the view that these children and their parents should be involved in the identification of strategies for promoting academic success and preventing academic failure among African American youth. Thus, the present author and her colleagues, using structured interviews, assessed the views of African American students and their parents (or primary caregivers) and of African American teachers regarding what African American children, parents, and teachers should do to prevent African American students from making poor grades—a quintessential measure of academic achievement. This assessment was done as part of a larger study of the views of African American students, parents, and teachers regarding the academic behaviors and performance of African American students (Tucker, Herman, Pederson, & Vogle, 1997). Elementary school students and teachers as well as high school students and teachers were among the interviewees. All participants lived in a small city in the South. The students were from low-income families and ranged in grade level from first grade to twelfth grade. All of the parent participants were mothers or mother figures. Ninety-one percent of the teacher participants were female.

The views of all participants in response to each question asked in the interviews were summarized by participant group (i.e., elementary school children, high school children, elementary school parents, high school parents, elementary school teachers, and high school teachers). The three questions that were asked regarding views on preventing African American students from making poor grades, the responses to each question, and the percentage of times each response was given among all responses given within each participant group follow:

Question
What should African American students do to prevent themselves from making poor grades?

Responses
Elementary School Children
Pay attention, follow instructions, and do schoolwork (33.3%)
Study and do homework regularly (28.9%)
Don't talk or misbehave in class; be nice (17.8%)
Various other recommendations (20.0%)

High School Children
Pay attention (27.3%)
Study and do homework regularly (24.2%)
Ask questions about what is not understood and get tutoring (21.2%)
Various other recommendations (27.3%)

Question
What should African American parents do to help prevent African American students from making poor grades?

Responses
Elementary School Children
Help with homework, studying, and study structure (45.2%)
Encourage and praise students (16.1%)
Talk with students' teachers regularly (12.8%)
Various other recommendations (25.9%)

High School Children
Help with homework, studying, and study structure (50.0%)
Talk with students' teachers regularly (17.9%)
Encourage and praise students (14.3%)
Various other recommendations (17.8%)

Elementary School Parents
Talk to and spend time with students (23.1%)
Talk with students' teachers regularly (19.2%)
Help with homework (15.4%)
Various other recommendations (42.3%)

High School Parents
Encourage studying; reading together (38.5%)
Get academic help (e.g., from tutors and role models) (19.2%)
Help with homework, studying, and study structure (15.4%)
Various other recommendations (26.9%)

Elementary School Teachers
Help with homework, studying, and study structure (45.5%)
Emphasize education and reading at home (18.2%)
Talk with teachers regularly (13.6%)
Various other recommendations (22.7%)

High School Teachers
Encourage students (30.9%)
Help with homework, studying, and study structure (23.0%)
Talk with students' teachers and visit school regularly (23.0%)
Various other recommendations (23.1%)

Question
What can teachers do to help prevent African American students from making poor grades?

Responses
Elementary School Children
Give students extra and individual help and provide tutoring (45.2%)
Encourage students and do not give up on them (19.4%)
Talk with students' parents regularly (9.7%)
Various other recommendations (25.7%)

High School Children
Ask if students understand; if not, give more explanation (28.0%)
Encourage students and do not give up on them (24.0%)
Be patient and encourage questions (24.0%)
Various other reasons (24.0%)

Elementary School Parents
Encourage students and show interest in them (29.0%)
Give extra help to students and ask them if they understand (25.8%)
Talk with students' parents regularly (12.9%)
Various other recommendations (32.3%)

High School Parents
Give extra help, explain in more detail (26.3%)
Encourage students and be sensitive (26.3%)
Talk regularly with parents (15.9%)
Various other recommendations (31.5%)

Elementary School Teachers
Give extra help, explain in more detail (41.3%)
Have higher expectations (17.6%)
Make learning fun and varied (17.6%)
Various other recommendations (23.5%)

High School Teachers
Encourage and praise students and do not give up on them (33.3%)
Give them extra help; explain in more detail (41.7%)
Have high expectations (8.4%)
Various other reasons (16.6%)

The preceding data suggest that there is a great deal of agreement across the elementary and high school students and their parents and the high school teachers who participated in the interviews regarding what should be done to prevent African American students from making poor grades. There are also several noteworthy observations from these data, particularly that the majority of elementary school children and high school children agreed that African American students could keep themselves from making poor grades by studying and paying attention in class. Additionally, the older students reported that asking questions in class and getting academic tutoring would help prevent African American students from making poor grades.

There was also much agreement across the participating students, parents, and teachers regarding what African American parents can do to prevent African American students from making poor grades. Specifically, across all groups there was much agreement that parents can help students with homework and studying. Across all groups except the high school parents there was much agreement that parents can help prevent African American students from making poor grades by talking with their children's teachers. The teachers of elementary school students added that parents can emphasize education and reading at home, whereas the teachers of high school students added that parents can encourage their children.

With regard to what teachers can do to prevent African American students from making poor grades, it appears that there was much agreement across all of the students, parents, and teachers that teachers can give more help and explanation to African American students. Across all participant groups except the elementary school teachers and the high school parents, there was also much agreement that teachers can help prevent poor grades among African American students by encouraging students and not giving up on them. Additionally, some elementary school teachers said that teachers can help prevent African American students from making poor grades by making learning fun and varied. Some of the high school parents added that teachers can get outside help and talk with parents regularly to help prevent African American students from making poor grades.

Clearly, these interview data provide support for preventing academic failure through actively engaging African American children in the learning process through teaching them "acting African American" behaviors (i.e., success behaviors such as studying). Additionally, support is provided for encouraging parents to be actively involved in their children's education through encouraging their children's academic efforts, assisting their children with their homework, creating an environment and plan for their children to study, and regularly talking with their teachers. Support is also provided for encouraging teachers to be very actively engaged in the teaching process through asking their African American students if they understand what is being taught and through engaging in behaviors to make these students feel supported and encouraged in the teaching and learning process. Finally, support is provided for preventing academic failure among African American youth by providing them with tutoring when needed and by teaching skills and behaviors for helping themselves achieve academic success.

Strategies Children Can Use

The existing culturally and socioeconomically sensitive theories, the research on academic achievement that has included African American children, and the clinical experience of the present author together suggest some specific strategies that African American youth and children can use to avoid experiencing academic failure and to facilitate their academic success. In other words, strategies are suggested for self-empowering African American children for academic achievement. Following are brief discussions of these strategies.

Strategy 1. Children Can Engage in "Acting African American" Behaviors (i.e., Success Behaviors)

It is important for African American children to engage in success behaviors for academic and social success. Indeed, there is empirical support for the self-empowerment perspective that African American children must be taught engagement in learning behaviors and skills that directly and positively impact their academic performance in the classroom. For example, Connell, Spencer, and Abner (1994) showed that behavioral engagement (i.e., prosocial school behaviors such as on-task behaviors in the classroom and study behaviors) and emotional engagement (e.g., level of school satisfaction, boredom, and nervousness) were both significant predictors of academic performance (e.g., grades) of African American students.

Traditionally, some African American students have considered such behaviors "acting white" behaviors. Consequently, these students have avoided or minimized their own engagement in these behaviors and have discouraged and ridiculed the occurrence of these behaviors among their African American peers (Fordham & Ogbu, 1986). Clearly, prevention of academic failure by African American youth must involve engagement in behaviors that are associated with academic success. These youth must take ownership of academic success behaviors and consider them "acting African American" behaviors. See Table 13.1 for a list of "acting African American" behaviors for preventing academic failure and facilitating academic and social success.

Strategy 2. Children Can Practice Expected Classroom Learning Behaviors that Are Inconsistent with Their Learning Preferences

It is reported in the literature that African American children have a preference for oral-aural learning modalities, spontaneity of expression, and vervistic experiences (Boykin, 1983). According to Boykin (1983), a preference for oral-aural learning modalities refers to a special sensitivity to or appreciation for knowledge gained through oral modes of communication and the tendency to use oral communication to express one's thoughts, meanings, and feelings. Spontaneity is expressing one's feelings, thoughts, and environmental reactions as they are experienced without delay and without filtering this information based on environmental circumstances (Chimezie, 1988). A preference for vervistic experiences refers to being able to relate to and become involved in what is stimulating, lively, and animated, and a dislike for and often rejection of what is dull, passive, routine, or boring (Boykin, 1983). Yet, these preferred behaviors among some African American youth are inconsistent with behaviors that are required to be academically successful in

TABLE 13.1   Success Behaviors

The following behaviors are encouraged, supported, and reinforced at the Model Program. Please encourage and support your child in developing these behaviors that we feel are important in achieving academic and personal success.

1. Always arrive on time and be prepared.
2. Complete all assigned tasks.
3. Follow directions.
4. Maintain a positive attitude.
5. Use complete sentences.
6. Project your voice and speak clearly.
7. Maintain eye contact during conversations.
8. Listen attentively when others are speaking.
9. Be enthusiastic about doing a good job.
10. Participate actively in group discussions.
11. Cooperate when working with others.
12. Be helpful to others and considerate of their feelings.
13. Avoid the use of insulting and criticizing remarks.
14. Maintain self-control, especially when angry.
15. Identify your strengths and compliment yourself for your achievements.
16. Compliment others for their successes.
17. Understand that you are an important person, today and every day.
18. Set goals and work hard to reach them.
19. Don't say "I can't." Say "I'll try."
20. When you start something, finish it.
21. Never give up.

U.S. classrooms and to compete for jobs and business opportunities nationally and internationally.

Indeed, throughout the world, written communication is emphasized, and there is much structure and insistence on taking one's turn to express thoughts, reactions, and feelings. Additionally, much time is spent sitting, concentrating, reading, and listening to lectures that lack verve (Chimezie, 1988). Furthermore, in most careers and in our increasingly technologically oriented society, success as well as adequate functioning will require adaptation to written communications, nonanimated interactions, and ordered and organized presentation of ideas in a deliberate manner. Thus, African American children must adapt to such behaviors because they are critical to successful school learning and performance (Chimezie, 1988).

It is recommended that parents teach African American children to engage in concentrated learning activities when they are very young (i.e., two to three years of age). Furthermore, it is important that before kindergarten, these children spend much time in activities that require concentration, reading, and writing. Ideally, these activities should be required to occur in a structured setting (e.g., sitting at a desk) for increasing lengths of time. The idea is to have African American children practice behaviors expected in classrooms even though the behaviors may not be those that these children prefer.

Strategy 3. Children Can Use Self-Management
Strategies to Facilitate Engagement
in Nonanimated Learning

It is not unusual to find some learning boring because of the subject of the material being taught or the way that it is taught. Often what is considered boring are lectures and readings related to math and science. Yet, knowledge in these areas is critical for getting into and doing well in college and for functioning well in the twenty-first century. Given the importance of learning that is boring, children must use techniques for overcoming the boredom. Following are some techniques that children can use.

1. Children can reframe their thoughts that material to be read and learned is boring to thinking of it as a challenge to find ways to make it interesting. Thus, children can focus on doing things such as reading the material in an interesting way, thinking of how it relates to their own lives and making up a funny story about it to help remember it.

2. Children can use self-talk or thoughts to remind themselves of the advantages of learning material that is boring to them, such as having the opportunity to go to college, trade school, or into the armed services and getting jobs or establishing careers that will make them a lot of money to buy things that they want. Such self-talk can help motivate children to learn what is boring.

3. Children can use self-talk to enable themselves to learn. For example, a child can say, "I can and will sit still and pay close attention to what the teacher is saying. I will write notes about the important points and what I do not understand, and I will ask questions about what I do not understand. I can do this because I am smart and I want to learn all that I can for my future. I will make every effort that I can to learn this material. It may not be easy, but I will keep trying to learn this material. I will not give up!"

4. Children can arrange positive consequences for their efforts to learn. These positive consequences should ideally include self-praise of their efforts. For example, a child might say, "I am really proud of myself for spending two hours trying to learn how to multiply fractions."

Strategies Parents Can Use

Parents must be informally or formally trained in implementing their roles to prevent failure. They are not born knowing how to raise academically successful children. The many young African American parents with very limited parenting experience especially need such training. This training should include learning what it takes for their children to go to college or a trade school—a desire of most African American parents. Indeed, most African American children also want postsecondary educational training and have ambitious goals such as becoming a lawyer, physical therapist, nurse, or teacher.

The problem is that often neither African American parents nor their children realize that getting into college usually takes a certain grade point average and SAT scores, and that remaining in college with the plan to reach their ambitious goal requires having taken advanced math and science courses in high school. Parent training can provide this type of knowledge and other knowledge necessary for parents to steer and coach their children toward academic engagement that will take these children to the careers to which they aspire. Parents then can assist teachers in establishing the often missing link between what is learned in their kindergarten, elementary, and high school classrooms and achieving their career goals—the link that often facilitates self-motivation for sustained learning.

Parents can play many different roles in the prevention of academic failure by their children. Ideally, these roles should start months before their children start walking and continue throughout their high school education. Some of the roles are even appropriate throughout the college years. The work of parents to help prevent academic failure of their children is not easy, but anything worth doing is not easy. Surely, investing in the future success of one's children is worth doing well.

The good news is that most African American parents want to promote the academic development of their children to prevent academic failure and they want education on strategies for doing so (Frisby, 1992). Following are several strategies that parents can use to help their children avoid academic failure and experience academic success.

Strategy 1. Parents Can Make Their Home "Learner Friendly" for Their Children

Making one's home learner friendly for children means making the home a place that facilitates and invites learning by children, makes children's learning a top priority, integrates learning by their children into all aspects of family life, and keeps to a minimum distractors to learning. Following are several ways that parents can help make their home learning friendly.

1. Parents can make every effort to eliminate family discord in the form of behaviors such as verbal and physical fighting, social withdrawal, and unfriendly or hostile nonverbal interactions. Dunn and Tucker (1993) found that perceived family conflict by African American children from mostly low-income families was a significant predictor of maladaptive behavior among the children in these families; maladaptive behavior has in turn been found to be significantly associated with low standardized achievement test scores of a large low-income skewed sample of African American second graders, fourth graders, and eighth graders (Tucker, Chennault, Brady, Fraser, Gaskin, Dunn, & Frisby, 1995).

Family discord usually requires some form of counseling from a professional such as a psychologist, counselor, or minister trained in pastoral counseling. Awareness of the fact that even subtle tension in the family can negatively impact children's motivation and cognitive set for studying may provide the needed impetus for African American parents to seek counseling. Given that cost of counseling is often a deterrent to getting needed counseling, parents need to be aware of the fact that counseling fees are often based on one's ability to pay and that such counseling can be located through calls to a local child and family services program, psychology clinics at local colleges, and local community health clinics.

2. Parents can actively engage their children in conversation throughout the day. Furthermore, parents can encourage their children to think about what they want to say before saying it, to formulate what they want to say into clear, complete sentences, and to wait until the person speaking has stopped speaking before beginning to talk. When each child has finished her or his comments, a parent can give the child feedback on the child's sentence structure, articulation, and social etiquette, with an emphasis on what the child did well.

The importance of standard English and of thinking before speaking are great dinner conversation topics. Such group conversations give children practice listening to others and waiting one's turn to speak just as in class, meetings, and church school. Consequently, children will be prepared for handling group conversations in these settings in the future. Furthermore, children learn important information from listening to their parents and siblings during family meals and at other family activity times.

3. Because writing and reading are emphasized at school and are important ways of communicating in classrooms, it is important for parents to create an area in their home for reading and writing to occur routinely. The area should be a quiet zone; that is, it should be the one place that anyone can go to read, write, study, or just to think that is off limits to social conversation or any noisy activity. The quiet zone may be a corner in the dining room that includes only a desk and chair.

Because of space limitations, the quiet zone may only be usable during an established quiet time each day. This quiet time should be at least two hours after school. During this time, there should be no television or other social activity. It should be the time for children to study, read the paper, write a poem or letter, do homework, or get tutoring. The quiet time should also be a time when parents can read the paper, pay bills, read a novel, read a magazine, or help their children with their homework.

To encourage children to read and write, parents must keep plenty of books, magazines, and writing tablets in the home. Children and their parents should also make frequent trips to the library for the joint selection of appropriate reading materials. It is important for parents to save their money to buy a home computer and software to promote the development of reading and writing skills.

It is likely that most low-income African American families and, thus, most African American families do not have computers in their homes, as parents in these families depend on schools to provide computer access. African American children need computers in their home for the level of practice needed to become computer literate, which is essential to be successful in the twenty-first century. Parents must see computers as necessities for making their homes learner friendly.

Children and adolescents should be required to study and do homework in the quiet zone just as in school. These youth should also be encouraged by their parents to write stories, articles, and poems especially about the following topics: (a) African Americans who achieved against many odds, (b) African American culture, (c) the career they aspire to have, (d) what it takes to go to college, (e) their role model, and (f) their personal strengths. Written work can be presented to the family as a group, praised, and posted in the quiet zone for family recognition. Children should be encouraged to praise themselves for spending time reading and writing.

4. Parents can restrict their viewing and their children's viewing of television. Children will more likely read, write, and study at home when these activities are not competing with television. When children are allowed to watch television, parents can encourage them to watch educational and news programs because such programs are wonderful educational vehicles. Those children who tell parents that they cannot study without the television or radio should be encouraged to learn to study with the radio and television off. Indeed, through practice at home, learning in the classroom without the benefit of radio or television will likely occur.

Strategy 2. Parents Can Engage Prekindergarten Children in Preschool Readiness Activities

Long before their children begin kindergarten, it is important for parents to ready their children for academic learning and school success. There are several ways that parents can ready their children for the academic and social challenges that come with entry into school.

1. Parents can engage their prekindergarten children as young as two years old, or even younger, in many different activities to develop their cognitive skills, which include problem solving, memory, reasoning, creativity, and language skills. Parents can consult with any prekindergarten or kindergarten teacher as to specific activities and exercises for learning each of these skills. Recommended activities will likely include assembling age-appropriate puzzles, learning simple math from flash cards, learning short lists of words, learning crayon colors, and reading and telling a story.

2. Prekindergarten children can be encouraged to have short-term and long-term goals so that specific learning activities can be related to their goals and, consequently, facilitate self-motivation to do the activities. For example, if a four-year-old child says she or he wants to be a police officer, the child can be told that the child must learn about numbers in order to read street numbers when going on an emergency call to help someone in trouble.

A young child whose short-term goal is to save money for a bike can be encouraged to learn to count, add, and subtract by linking learning activities for teaching these skills to being able to keep a record of money being saved for the bike and being able to actually transact the business involved in purchasing the bike. The children in both of the foregoing examples will likely have more math achievement motivation when learning math is associated with their goals. The importance of motivation to learn among African American children is reflected in the following Nigerian proverb: "Not to know is bad, not to wish to know is worse" (cited in Gary & Booker, 1992).

3. It is important for parents to psychologically prepare prekindergarten children to respond constructively to academic failure experiences (e.g., getting a poor grade on a test) and disappointments in their academic-related performance (e.g., forgetting lines in a class play and being very upset about it). Parents can socialize children when they are very young to believe that (a) what is important in school and in life is doing the best that they can in areas under their control such as putting forth their best effort to study, to understand what is taught, and to learn, and (b) even with their best effort, they will sometimes not get positive outcomes because outcomes are often under the control of others. Parents can also teach children to praise themselves for their efforts to learn regardless of the outcomes of their efforts. When negative outcomes occur despite children's efforts to learn, parents can encourage them to keep trying to learn using more and perhaps different studying strategies. Perhaps most importantly, parents must normalize failure experiences and perseverance as parts of the learning process for most children and adults.

4. Parents must address children's maladaptive behaviors such as hitting and defiance. Such behaviors have been found to be significant predictors of standardized achievement test scores of low-income elementary and junior high school students (Brady et al., 1992). One way to modify or extinguish these behaviors is to provide children with alternative appropriate behaviors to these maladaptive behaviors.

For example, seven-year-old Clarence can be taught that rather than hitting his brother Jacob when angry, he can do the following: walk away from Jacob, take a few deep breaths to calm down, later tell Jacob why he was so angry with him, and discuss with Jacob a solution for avoiding a reoccurrence of the kind of interaction that led to Clarence's anger. It is very useful for parents to teach children and adolescents how to manage anger using a step-by-step teaching approach such as that described in Chapter 6.

A most important strategy for avoiding the occurrence of maladaptive behaviors is for parents to specify rules for their children's behavior with specific rules for each of the following settings: home, school, church, and social settings such as parties. Often parents get upset with the behavior of their children, even though the parents had not told the children before the problem behavior occurred the kind of behavior that was expected or would be viewed as appropriate in a particular setting. It is important for children to know the rules to be followed and the behaviors expected of them in a particular setting; such knowledge deters inappropriate or maladaptive behaviors by the children.

It is extremely important that both parents or primary caregivers in the home be involved in setting rules for their children. It is important for parents to review these rules with their children and give their children a chance to express their feelings about the rules and consequences for breaking them. Parents, however, should have the final word with regard to the rules and the consequences for breaking them.

Parents should also use a "united front" as a way of helping to prevent maladaptive behaviors and academic failure by their children. A united front by parents means supporting each others' decisions regarding the children's behavior and rule enforcement while in the children's presence. In other words, if one parent says no to a child's request, the other parent should support that position. When parents disagree, regarding their children's behavior and rule enforcement, it is important that the parents later discuss this disagreement in privacy and decide how the request should be handled in the future.

Finally, prevention of behavior problems and perhaps prevention of academic failure may be facilitated by frequent praise by the mother for various appropriate behaviors and by actively involving children's fathers in their lives. Tucker, Brady, Harris, and Fraser (1993) found that mother reports of frequent praise of their second-grade African American children for appropriate behaviors were associated with lower maladaptive behaviors in these children as reported by their mothers. These researchers also found that most discipline of these children by their fathers as reported by their mothers was significantly associated with fewer maladaptive behaviors in the children as reported by their mothers.

Strategy 3. Parents Can Meet Their Children's Physical and Mental Needs for School Readiness

Because children typically cannot perform up to their academic potential when their physical needs are not met, it is important for parents to address these needs. Specifically, parents must make sure that their children each have a physical checkup yearly that includes an eye examination to assess the need for eyeglasses. Health problems found and problems that occur during the year must be addressed without delay.

It is also important for parents to give priority to their children getting a nutritious breakfast and lunch in order to be able to think well and focus on their schoolwork. Just as importantly, parents must make sure that their children have a set bedtime that allows them to get at least eight hours of sleep each night. Parents should also insist on their children having some regular physical exercise. The children's physician can be helpful in providing a nutrition guide and some exercise recommendations that are individualized for each child. Making sure that children get proper nutrition, sleep, and exercise requires that parents take charge of their families, providing schedules and rules regarding these health issues and enforcing these rules. Parents can perhaps best do this by modeling the health behaviors that they require of their children.

Parents must also immediately address any psychological or emotional problems such as depression, stress, social withdrawal, and prolonged sadness that their children may experience in association with a divorce, obesity, death of a parent, a physical disability, a developmental learning disorder or disability, or other problem. It is advisable that parents seek consultation with a psychologist or counselor for these problems. Such a professional can usually recommend a treatment plan for each child that should include having the child seen by a physician to determine whether there are any undiagnosed physical problems that might be factors in or consequences of the psychological or emotional problems. This plan might involve a few sessions of family counseling, involvement of the child in group therapy with children who have similar problems, or some other treatment intervention. Parents often begin their help-seeking process by consulting with their children's physician, school counselor, or a counselor at the local child and family services program. Starting with the latter may be most appropriate when parents know that they do not have money to pay for counseling or medical treatment for their children.

Strategy 4. Parents Can Be Actively Involved in Their Children's Formal Education

Throughout the literature on educating African American children, it is generally concluded that African American parents must be actively involved in their children's education and that this involvement must continue throughout the school life of their children. The latter is suggested by the finding that more parent behaviors are associated with the academic performance of African American adolescents than with the academic performance of younger children (Tucker, Harris, Brady, & Herman, 1996).

Indeed, most African American parents want to be involved in the education of their children, but many of these parents are not sure what they can specifically do to prevent the academic failure and promote the academic success of their children. There are many actions, however, that parents can take toward these goals. Some suggestions follow.

1. African American parents can engage in specific behaviors that some African American children, parents, and teachers believe to be important in preventing poor grades among African American students. In a study earlier mentioned by Tucker, Herman, Pedersen, and Vogel (1997), a group of low-income African American elementary school students and high school students and their parents and a group of African American elementary school teachers and high school teachers evidenced much agreement that African American parents can help prevent their children from making poor grades by helping these students with their homework and their studying.

Additionally, across all participant groups except the high school parents, there was much agreement that parents can also help prevent African American children from making poor grades by regularly talking with their children's teachers. The teachers of elementary school students added that African American parents can emphasize education and reading at home as a way to prevent their children from making poor grades, whereas the teachers of high school students added that parents can encourage their children to accomplish this prevention goal.

2. Because African American students tend to do less well academically as they progress in grade level (Garibaldi, 1992; Tucker, Chennault, Brady, Fraser, Gaskin, Dunn, & Frisby, 1995), parents must become more involved in their older children's education. Ideally, this involvement should include providing or arranging for someone to provide their children with homework assistance and talking with their children's teachers about specific academic interventions that will facilitate each child's academic success. Volunteer tutors can usually be recruited through a local college or a volunteer center in one's community.

Yet, there is evidence that some African American parents are less involved in the education of their older children or adolescents than they are in the education of their younger children (Hart, 1988; Ziegler, 1987). Furthermore, it has been reported that school visits by preschool and elementary school parents are qualitatively different from the school visits made by secondary school parents. Specifically, the school visits of parents of the younger children tend to be more regular and frequent and tend to grow out of an interest in the children's skill acquisition, emotional adjustment, and social integration at school, whereas the school visits of the parents of the secondary school children tend to be more distant and tend to grow out of the necessity of having to address a problem, such as fighting by their children at school (Gotts & Purnell, 1987).

3. African American parents must especially provide needed academic tutoring, support for doing homework, and academic encouragement to their male children. This is because of the many indications that these youth are at particular risk for academic failure and underachievement. Garibaldi (1992) reported finding that up to third grade African American males and females did equally well on mathematics and reading criterion-referenced tests, but that by fourth grade the African American males experienced a sharp decline on both of these tests; furthermore, the percentage of African American males in the top reading group from among eighteen counties dropped from grade four to grade six. The present author and her associates found that among first through twelfth graders from low-income families, the male students as compared to the female students had significantly lower overall grade point averages and reading grade point averages (Tucker, Chennault, Brady, Fraser, Gaskin, Dunn, & Frisby, 1995).

4. Parents can engage in parenting behaviors that have been found to be associated with high academic achievement of some children. In an interview study with inner-city parents of fourth and fifth graders, Rankin (1967) found the following parenting behaviors to be associated with high achievement:

a. providing activities such as playing games, talking with children, and attending church;

b. requiring high grades;

c. giving help with homework;

d. talking about school activities;

e. promoting an interest in reading; and

f. initiating discussion with school personnel.

Tucker, Harris, Brady, and Herman (1996) found in an interview study with parents of second, fourth and eighth graders that certain parent behaviors were significantly associated with grade point averages of these students and that these behaviors differed by grade level. The following parent behaviors were significantly associated with high grade point averages and standardized achievement test scores by grade level:

For Second Graders

1. Mother's grade expectation of A or B or mother having no particular grade expectation versus mother's grade expectation of C (A C grade expectation by mother was associated with low grade point averages.)

For Fourth Graders

1. Same as for second graders

2. Avoidance of use of restrictions for unsatisfactory grades

3. Frequent church attendance by mother

4. Father's grade expectation of A versus B, C, or no particular grade expectation

For Eighth Graders

1. Avoidance of use of verbal reprimands for unsatisfactory grades

2. Frequent mother praise

3. Frequent father praise

4. Mother's grade expectation of A versus B, C, or no particular grade expectation

Clark (1983) found in a case study of families of African American adolescent students that in families of the high achieving students the following parent behaviors occurred:

1. Frequent talks between the parents and the children in the family

2. Strong parental encouragement of academic pursuits

3. Clear and consistent limits for the children

4. Warm and nurturing interactions

5. Consistent scheduling of how time is used among family members

Clark (1983) also reported that parents of high achievers in his study felt responsible for part of their children's education such as providing basic literacy skills, giving priority to their children's education above their own growth and development, viewing their children as responsible for pursuing knowledge, expecting their children to get postsecondary education, and viewing parent involvement in their children's school as important.

Strategy 5. Parents Can Involve Their Children in After-School Learning Activities

Because teachers and schools cannot or will not provide African American children with all of the skills that they need for academic and social success, parents of African American children must assume responsibility for providing their children with the needed knowledge and skills that schools do not provide adequately. These skills include adaptive skills (i.e., communication, socialization, daily living skills) and success behaviors (e.g., asking questions about what one does not understand). Additionally, parents must make sure that their children learn self-management of their frustration, anger, and desires that often lead to maladaptive behaviors (e.g., hitting, fighting), which in turn are associated with academic failure.

Yet, most African Americans do not have the knowledge or time to teach their children adaptive skills and success behaviors, to teach or promote in their children self-empowerment for academic and social success through self-motivation for academic achievement, self-control of academic effort, progress, and success, and self-reinforcement of their academic progress and success. Thus, these parents must involve their children in after-school activities in which they can acquire self-empowerment knowledge, skills, and behaviors for academic and social success. It is important for parents to be actively involved with their children in these activities so that they can learn along with the children and thus help transfer this learning to their home environment. Some recommended after-school activities for promoting self-empowerment of African American children for academic and social success follow:

1. Trips to the library for the librarian to teach the children how to use the library as well as guide them in selecting age-appropriate books on topics related to their career interests, learning adaptive skills (e.g., books on social skills), and overcoming academic problems (e.g., books on how to study, books on tips for writing effectively)

2. Viewing of educational videotapes obtained from the local community or school library

3. Participation in after-school tutoring and adaptive skills training programs, such as those which are being established in churches, schools, and community centers in many communities throughout the country

4. Home tutoring or school tutoring requested or arranged by the parents

5. Involvement in after-school church programs, Girl Scouts, Boy Scouts, and other activities that provide opportunities for children to learn and practice social skills and success behaviors

6. Participation in church school classes in which children learn the importance of self-control and values that promote academic and social success and in which children have success experiences such as reading the scriptures or giving a church service welcome address

Strategy 6. Parents Can Facilitate Self-Acceptance and Racial Pride in Their Children

It is important for parents to facilitate self-acceptance and racial pride in their children to counteract negative stereotypes of African Americans and common denigration of African American culture. By so doing parents will facilitate their children's feelings of belonging with their peers and their self-confidence to participate in class and enjoy learning. Furthermore, arming children against emotional and psychological self-image problems due to racism can allow them to focus on their academic studies rather than on these problems. Such a focus likely helps to prevent academic failure.

Parents can promote self-acceptance and racial pride in their children by teaching them about African American culture and history (Hale-Benson, 1986; Kunjufu, 1984). Specifically, parents can talk with their children about (1) the beauty of their skin color and their hair, (2) accepting and respecting individual differences, (3) their physical and character strengths, (4) the many contributions of African Americans to the United States in the areas of science, medicine, architecture, art, and many other areas, and (5) the history of African American language patterns.

Strategies Teachers Can Use

Teachers, most of whom are culturally and socioeconomically different from most African American students, must also play major roles in preventing academic failure of African American students. For teachers to be successful in these prevention roles, they must minimally expect that African American students will be successful and realize that, because of their cultural and socioeconomic differences, students often will need extra time, energy, and effort from teachers to adjust to the success requirements in classes and schools that are dominated by the majority culture. There are many specific strategies that teachers can use and often must be trained to use to prevent academic failure and to facilitate the academic and social success of African American children.

Strategy 1. Teachers Can Get To Know Each African American Child and Her or His Preferred Ways of Learning before Teaching New Ways of Learning

Because African American children differ individually and often as a group from the majority children in their classrooms and from their teachers, it is important for teachers to assess these differences, including differences in learning styles, preferred ways of participating in class, and academic strengths and weaknesses (Bergin, 1992). It is also important that teachers respect African American children's differences and not see the differences as deficits.

Teachers, however, must not set different academic standards for African American children; instead, teachers must teach these children learning strategies that will enable them to meet the academic performance standards for all students. This process must involve teaching that (1) utilizes the strengths and learning strategies that each African

American child brings to the classroom, and (2) gradually incorporates new learning strategies and skills that facilitate academic success in the classroom and future life success (Chimezie, 1988).

For example, a teacher can use African American children's possible preferences for oral, rather than written, expression and enthusiasm for singing to facilitate the improvement of their writing skills by having each child first write down a song that they would like to sing. The teacher can use the written songs to teach the class a writing lesson. An edited copy of the song can be distributed so that the class can sing along as whichever child wrote the song leads. For the entire class, singing each song will likely reinforce the writing skills just learned. This collective singing may also facilitate each African American child's sense of belonging to the group, and teach their European American classmates something about African American culture.

Teachers can learn about the personal and learning characteristics of an African American child through closely observing that child in class, individually teaching the child for short periods in class, talking with the child during recess and immediately after school, and talking with the child's parents. It is recommended that teachers avoid making assumptions about an African American child on the basis of another teacher's experience with the child or on the basis of records that may have various negative comments and labels to describe the child. It is respectful and positive to respond to the child on the basis of what the child does rather than what the child did in the distant past.

Strategy 2. Teachers Can Create a Family-Like Class Atmosphere

Teachers can do much to prevent academic failure and associated low class attendance, school absenteeism, and school dropout by creating teaching and learning environments that are family-like and that accept and respect cultural, socioeconomic, and individual differences. Following are ways that teachers can create such environments.

1. Include pictures and artwork by African Americans on the walls and in other places in the classroom.
2. Use successful African Americans in examples and stories used in the teaching process.
3. Invite African American professionals to the classroom as well as professionals from other ethnic groups.
4. Invite students to make culture-related presentations in class.
5. Invite an expert on cultural differences to conduct cultural sensitivity exercises in the classroom.
6. Give children opportunities to showcase their talents.
7. Conduct activities that involve having classmates interview each other about their families, interests, hobbies, ambitions, and so on.
8. Ask for and be responsive to each student's recommendations for making the class comfortable for her or him.
9. Look for and praise the children's success behaviors.
10. Avoid embarrassing children through humiliating public punishments such as standing in a corner on one leg.

Strategy 3. Teachers Can Use Culturally and Socioeconomically Sensitive Teaching Strategies

It is very important that teachers use culturally and socioeconomically sensitive strategies that keep African American children engaged in the learning process and that facilitate self-empowerment of these children for academic and social success. Self-empowerment involves learning self-motivation for academic achievement, self-control for academic effort, progress, and success, self-reinforcement of academic progress and success, and success behaviors and adaptive skills for academic, social, and economic success. Given that most African American children tend to perceive little internal control (Edgar & Clement, 1980) and have little power in their classes and schools, strategies that self-empower them and actively engage them in their own learning seem indicated. Following are some self-empowerment teaching strategies that teachers can use in their classrooms:

1. Teachers can use step-by-step teaching strategies which involve having children teach themselves by following the steps for doing a task after these steps have been written, modeled by the teacher, and practiced by the children with feedback and praise from the teacher. (See a detailed description of the step-by-step teaching method in Chapter 6.)

2. Teachers can teach children to use self-monitoring and self-reinforcement of their academic behaviors. Bergin and Clement (1980) showed that student-controlled reinforcement as compared to teacher-controlled reinforcement was significantly more effective in teaching on-task math and reading behaviors to underachieving African American children. Furthermore, the children did not give themselves more reinforcers (e.g., points that could be later exchanged for a fun activity) than did the teachers.

3. Teachers can spend one-to-one time asking African American students if they understand the subject matter, asking them questions to be sure they understand, and patiently and willingly giving any additional needed explanations of what is being taught in class. Research evidence suggests that these actions by teachers will help prevent academic failure by African American children (Tucker, Herman, Pedersen, & Vogel, 1997).

4. Teachers can engage in culturally sensitive instruction, which according to the Educational Research Service (1991) includes the following: teacher flexibility to accommodate cultural traits (e.g., a preference for oral learning modalities) and needs of students (e.g., encouragement and praise) as individually assessed, high teacher expectations, and confidence in students' abilities.

5. Given the literature, which suggests that many African American students are from cultures that embrace vervistic experiences (Chimezie, 1988), teachers can include some type of activity relevant to a learning task and can use varied teaching formats in the teaching process. Support for including some activity-based learning with African American students comes from the research of Prestrup (1973), which showed that vervistic teachers were most effective in teaching reading to first-grade African American children.

Support for using varied teaching formats comes from research showing that a combination of using oral, written, and pictorial formats facilitates the learning of prose material among fourth-grade African American children (Rohwen & Harris, 1975). Boykin (1979) also found that format variability was associated with better performance of a variety of tasks by African American children.

6. Teachers can model and help create excitement about learning activities, as such affect is highly valued in many African American cultures. The importance of this integration of affect into the classroom is suggested by Boykin (1983), who stated that "affect implies integration of feelings with thoughts and action, such that it would be difficult to engage in an activity if one's feelings toward the activity ran counter to such engagement" (p. 345).

Strategies School Administrators Can Use

School administrators can do much to help prevent academic failure and facilitate academic success by African American students. However, first, school administrators must be committed to multiculturalism and to retaining all African American students through providing them with quality education and through supporting community-based efforts to meet the academic needs that schools simply cannot or will not meet. This commitment can be facilitated by reminding these school administrators and boards of education that when African American children fail, all other children and all of our communities are negatively impacted. Once committed to the goals of preventing academic failure and facilitating academic success of African American children, school administrators can use the following potentially effective strategies for meeting these goals.

Strategy 1. School Administrators Can Promote Multiculturalism and Empowerment of African American Students

Multiculturalism has been explained as valuing and respecting diversity, seeing equality as neither sameness nor inferiority, respecting the dignity of all individuals, and being objective when faced with differing views among others (Asante, 1991). School administrators must embrace and promote multiculturalism toward the goal of operating schools committed to creating a sense of belonging for all students. Given that African American students are often in no positions of power in schools and are in the minority in terms of numbers, their concerns and needs for academic and social success are overlooked. These students often need empowerment that facilitates making schools aware of and responsive to their needs and concerns. There are several actions that school administrators can take to promote multiculturalism and empowerment of African American students.

1. School administrators can invite ideas for activities that promote an understanding of and an appreciation for different cultures, and then they can find money for executing these activities.

2. School administrators can give speeches about and encourage teachers to teach about the importance of accepting and respecting others who are individually, culturally, or socioeconomically different from oneself.

3. School administrators can provide training for teachers that facilitates their instructional self-efficacy with African American students in general and with African American students with special needs (e.g., learning disorders). Such training is important given that teachers' sense of instructional efficacy has been positively linked to parents' participation in children's scholastic activities (Hoover-Dempsey, 1987) and to both teacher perseverance in efforts to help students who are not quick to learn and teacher support of such students (Bandura, 1993).

4. School administrators can provide cultural sensitivity training for all school staff and for interested students, and offer some incentive for attendance to this training.

5. School administrators can recognize and reward teachers who implement creative ideas to promote multiculturalism and to empower African American students and other nonmajority students in their classes or in the school in general.

6. School administrators can involve African American parents and students in the development and implementation of low-cost programs to prevent academic failure of African American students and find funding to support these programs.

7. School administrators can provide teachers with training in how to respond effectively to behavior problems of African American children and students. (Chapters 5 and 6 discuss strategies for modifying behavior problems of African American children.)

8. School administrators can promote leadership training among African American students to increase their election to student government and other student academic organizations at the school.

9. School administrators can actively recruit African American students for involvement in school-sponsored academic and social activities such as scientific competitions (e.g., the state science fair and public speaking contests), the school band, and school exchange programs in other countries.

10. School administrators can hire more African American teachers and school administrators, especially African American males, who can serve as mentors and role models for African American students and who can call attention to cultural and socioeconomic concerns and problems that need to be considered in efforts to prevent academic failure and facilitate the academic and social success of African American students. Indeed, there is evidence that models (e.g., African American teachers and school administrators) are more influential on the behavior of observers (e.g., African American students) when the models are more similar to the observers (Schunk, 1987). There is also evidence that African American male teachers are positively experienced by African American male children (Edgar & Clement, 1980). Yet, African American male teachers are underrepresented in the public schools in the United States (Ascher, 1992).

Strategy 2. School Administrators Can Help Involve African American Parents in the School's Education of Their Children

Many African American parents, especially those from low SES groups, do not know what they can do to prevent academic failure and facilitate academic success of their children. Following are two important specific actions that school administrators can take to provide African American parents with this knowledge.

1. School administrators can provide school-based training for parents on ways that they can prevent the academic failure and facilitate the academic success of their children. They can also actively encourage parents' participation in this training given research indicating that many nonmajority parents feel intimidated by and awkward about approaching school personnel (Williams & Chavkin, 1985).

School administrators might encourage African American parents to participate in parent training at their schools by doing the following: (a) mailing and verbally giving them personal invitations to the training, (b) requiring comfortable dress such as jeans by all trainers (i.e., teachers and school administrators) and trainees (i.e., parents), (c) assisting parents with transportation, (d) inviting parents to bring a friend, (e) arranging for school-based supervision of children for whom parents cannot get babysitters, and (f) arranging for escorts to personally accompany parents to the classrooms from the school entrance.

2. School administrators can actively invite African American parents to regularly meet with their children's teachers, especially parents of older children. Research suggests that African American parents of students in secondary schools tend to only visit these schools when it is necessary to address a problem involving their child (Gotts & Purnell, 1987); yet, high-achieving African American students tend to have parents who are actively involved in their children's schools (Clark, 1983; Rankin, 1967).

Strategies Churches Can Use

Because African American churches play a major and powerful role in the lives of many African Americans, these churches can be a major force in the prevention of academic failure and facilitation of academic success among African American youth. Many of the most successful African American national leaders were closely aligned with African American churches and grew up actively attending church (e.g., Dr. Martin Luther King, Jr. and Dr. Jesse Jackson). There are several major strategies that African American church leaders can play in preventing academic failure among African American youth.

Strategy 1. Churches Can Establish Long-Term Mentoring Programs for African American Youth

One of the most likely places to find African American role models and mentors, especially males, is in an African American church. Thus, church leaders, especially African American ministers, can establish mentoring programs that train mentors to tutor African American children and to emphasize academic engagement among these youth. Because African American ministers tend to be very influential and highly respected by their congregations, they can influence African American males and females to commit to long-term, voluntary mentoring relationships with African American children.

Strategy 2. Churches Can Provide Opportunities To Learn and Practice Adaptive Skills and Success Behaviors

Churches historically provide opportunities for African American youth to participate in church service programs and other programs that facilitate their development of academic skills and behaviors, adaptive skills (i.e., communication and socialization skills), and success behaviors in very supportive environments. For example, children read scriptures in church school and participate in discussions of what they read, which facilitate reading and comprehension skills. Additionally, many African American churches sponsor statewide African American history and public speaking contests.

Thus, to actively prevent academic failure, African American churches can sponsor academic brain bowls on particular topics or books and public speaking contests for African American youth whether or not they attend church. Such experiences facilitate academic engagement and skill development for academic and social success. These experiences can also teach African American youth how to study and compete, how to relate effectively with others, and how to appropriately use standard English. Indeed, such outcomes can do much to prevent the academic failure of African American children.

Strategy 3. Churches Can Promote Valuing Education and Being African American

African American ministers can include in their sermons and work with youth messages about the value of education, what is great about being African American, and the connections between education and the money and careers that African American youth desire. These ministers and their associate church leaders can also sponsor seminars and workshops on ways to prevent the academic failure of African American children. These workshops can be for African American families whether or not they attend church. Parents of academically successful African American youth and the successful youth themselves can be seminar leaders. Such experiences facilitate self-empowerment of African American families for the prevention of academic failure and the facilitation of academic success among African American children.

Strategy 4. Churches Can Provide Long-Term Parent Consultation and Training for Preventing Academic Failure

African American churches are ideal for hosting parent consultation and training to prevent the academic failure and facilitate the academic success of African American youth. This is because African American churches have the physical structures for this training and they tend to be centrally located in African American communities, thus making them easily accessible to African American families. Furthermore, churches can usually mobilize teachers, psychologists and counselors, parents, and church members to volunteer their time to either provide training or consultation on a regular basis or organize and host the training.

Frisby (1992) reviewed much of the literature on parent training for African American parents and its association with the academic achievement of African American youth. This researcher concluded that there is support for parent training to facilitate the academic achievement of African American children given the large amount of literature that documents that optimal cognitive development and achievement of African American children and adolescents are generic correlates of related parent training.

A Partnership Education Approach

Teachers and parents cannot alone prevent academic failure among African American youth. A partnership approach is needed to achieve this goal. This partnership must involve parents, teachers, school administrators, psychologists and counselors, and community leaders, especially leaders of the African American church and local business and political leaders. The roles of the partnership must include (1) providing teachers and African American parents with the training and support that they need to enable African American youth to avoid academic failure, and (2) facilitating the self-empowerment of African American children for academic, social, and economic success. Self-empowerment of African American youth involves teaching them self-motivation for academic achievement, self-control for academic progress and success, self-praise for academic effort, progress, and success, and adaptive skills and success behaviors (i.e., acting African American behaviors). There are several partnership strategies that can be implemented as part of a partnership approach to prevent academic failure and facilitate self-empowerment of African American children.

Strategy 1. Establish Long-Term, Community-Based, After-School Partnership Education Programs (PEPs)

Given the high academic failure and underachievement among African American students, it is clear that schools alone cannot or will not prevent academic failure by African American students. Communities must work in partnership with schools to meet the academic needs of African American students and to self-empower these students for long-term academic, social, and economic success. Specifically, schools and communities can work in partnership to operate community-based, after-school partnership education programs (PEPs) for African American students, which provide self-empowerment training, academic tutoring, assistance with homework, computer training, and a mentoring program.

The PEPs ideally should include parent training to facilitate students' academic success and activities for children that facilitate positive academic self-concepts, positive self-identity, and an appreciation of African American history and cultures. These programs can be conducted at churches under the leadership of psychologists, teachers, and other educators. Other teachers as well as parents, community leaders, and volunteer college or high school students can serve as tutors, student activity planners, coordinators, parent trainers, and trainers who teach adaptive skills and behaviors for academic and social success. The focus of the academic tutoring and the adaptive skills should ideally be based on consultations with or reports from the regular schoolteachers of participating children regarding these children's individual academic and social strengths and weaknesses.

Psychologists at universities and colleges can play major roles in establishing, conducting, and empirically evaluating these PEPs. These professionals can write research-training grants to help financially support the programs. They can utilize their professional training to help develop the self-empowerment training components, to identify interventions to deter and modify behavior problems of the participating students, and to help develop the parent training. Psychologists can also assist with the implementation of all components of the PEPs. Particularly, the psychologists can use their research skills and experience to develop and implement evaluations of the effects of PEPs and to write articles about the PEPs and their impact. This latter role can facilitate dissemination and institutionalization of PEPs toward the goal of preventing academic failure among African American students across the nation.

Community leaders including business leaders, political leaders, and church leaders can help acquire the funds, equipment (e.g., computers), and human resources needed to operate the PEPs on a long-term basis. These leaders can also participate in all aspects of the PEPs, especially the adaptive skills training (e.g., provide training in job interviewing) and the student activities component.

A detailed description of a successful PEP is found in Chapter 14. The roles of the partners in the PEP as well as its program components are described in some detail, thus providing a model for individuals interested in setting up a PEP in their community.

Strategy 2. Conduct Communitywide Workshops on Preventing Academic Failure by African American Youth

Given that all members of a community are negatively impacted when African American children fail, all community members have a vested interest in preventing academic failure by African American students. Communitywide workshops are needed to help community members see this reality and to actively involve them in formulating strategies for preventing academic failure among African American youth as well as all youth. Identification of ways that community members can support schools in meeting the needs of African American students and low-income students can be among the major focuses of these workshops. The outcomes of these workshops will likely be improved community relations and, thus, a more supportive environment for the academic and social success of African American students and all other students.

Perspectives of Two African American Teachers

What Parents and Teachers Can Do to Help African American Children
Be Academically Successful: Perspectives of an African American Teacher
Parents and teachers can be energized to promote the success of African American children by reflecting on the Philosophy of our Research-Based Model Partnership Education Program, which is as follows:

All children can learn and all adults can teach. They simply need to be challenged.

All children can achieve some measure of success and all adults can help them succeed. They only need to be motivated.

All children have strengths and all adults can help discover them. They simply must make time to do so.

All children are different and all adults can play a role in making these differences positive and special.

African American children are like all children. They too are different and special.

What parents say and do at home is important in preparing children for success in life. Parents who are positive role models tend to encourage their children to become positive and productive adults. Parents should provide their children with the things that they need for academic, social, and personal success. It is not wise for parents to give their children all of the things that they want, such as stylish tennis shoes or clothing.

Children need to receive the love and attention that they need and want from their family. This love and attention helps them develop a sense of security. Children need to have people in their "corner" who believe in them.

When children enter school, they need to have been exposed to an environment where parents and others have a high regard of reading. Parents should let children start reading at an early age and they should read to them as often as possible. Books, magazines, and newspapers should be highly visible in each child's home.

Parents should talk about their family history, what grandma and grandpa did to reach their goals, and the importance of goals for the future. Parents should also talk with their children about the mistakes that they made in the past that prevented them from realizing their full potential. Such talks motivate children to achieve and to use their time constructively. These talks boost children's self-confidence about their success potential and help direct their lives toward success.

To help African American children succeed academically, it is important for teachers and parents to teach these children to be independent, self-sufficient, and patient. It is also important for teachers and parents to communicate regularly with each other. Parents should not wait until there is a crisis to start communicating with their child's teacher. Teachers should keep parents informed about their children via letters, newsletters, and/or direct contact.

Parents should attend open house programs at their child's school as often as possible to learn policies and regulations of the teachers. When parents meet with their child's teacher, they should let the teacher know of their child's special needs. Teachers should inform parents of their child's academic skills early in the school year so the student and parents can take early steps to work on academic problems.

Parents should plan to help out at the school occasionally. Parents can be classroom volunteers, chaperones on field trips, booster club members, PTA members, etc. Parents are viewed by their children in a positive light when they actively participate in school events. Teachers and parents can teach African American children about the world of work and teach them skills for getting part-time or full-time jobs. Before the child starts looking for a job, it is suggested that teaching approaches can be used. For example, children can be asked to interview relatives or neighbors to find out about their jobs and how they got these jobs. Parents can talk with their children after each interview to see what they learned.

Last but not least, parents and teachers should talk to their children about the values and benefits of getting a good education. They should tell the children that with hard work and a determination to succeed, THE SKY IS THE LIMIT.

Mrs. Cynthia E. Mingo
4th Grade Teacher
Prairie View Elementary School
Gainesville, Florida

What Parents and Teachers Can Do to Help African American First Graders Be Academically Successful: Perspectives of an African American Teacher

African American children, like all children, enter first grade eager to learn to read, write, and solve problems. This is great, given that what a child learns in first grade lays the foundation for higher order learning in more advanced grades.

The level of successful learning that first-graders actually experience in school is strongly linked to the level of involvement of their parents in the education that these children receive. Indeed, parental involvement plays a major role in a first-grader's school behaviors, attitudes toward learning, and overall academic success. Thus, it is important that parents and their child's teacher work as partners for the child's success.

Teachers can contribute to this partnership by inviting parents to visit their child's classroom, to eat lunch with their child, and to participate in learning activities with their child at school and at home. It is especially helpful for teachers to provide parents with a monthly calendar of school activities to assist parents in planning their schedules to accommodate school activities. Teachers can also encourage parents to check their child's bookbag for homework or any other correspondence sent from the teacher. Furthermore, it is extremely important for parents to help their children do assigned homework. When parents help their children with homework, grades and self-esteem go up.

Parents can also play a major role in helping their first-grader learn social skills for developing positive relations with peers in their classroom. Specifically, parents can involve their child or children in group activities such as little league sports and scouting. Participation in such activities helps children build character, as well as leadership and problem solving skills, all of which foster success in the classroom and in everyday life.

African American first-graders especially enjoy and benefit from hands-on learning experiences that are varied in nature. Parents can expose these children to different learning environments by taking them on trips to the local library, museum, park and/or historical sites.

Teachers can, in addition, incorporate diverse learning experiences in their classrooms. For example, teachers can invite professionals to their classrooms to discuss and show pictures of what their careers involve. Teachers can also take their first-graders on educational field trips as well as involve them in roleplays that involve real world experiences beyond the classroom. In addition, teachers can provide students with access to and instructions for using computers and the internet, both of which enable children to teach themselves and help motivate themselves to do so.

Most important of all, African American first-graders, like all children, need love from their parents and teachers to be successful in school and in life in general. Specifically, these children need to hear what they do well and right much more often than what they do wrong and need to change. In sum, African American children need parents and teachers who love and teach rather than yell and preach.

Mrs. Priscilla Strickland
First Grade Teacher
Jeter Primary School
Opelika, Alabama

Conclusions

Given that grades and standard achievement test scores are not always accurate measures of the academic knowledge and competencies of African American students, academic failure of these students should be more broadly defined to include lack of academic engagement. Academic engagement is the involvement in academic success behaviors such as studying, doing homework, making a genuine effort to learn, asking questions about what is not understood, showing concern about lack of academic progress, and showing interest in and having a positive attitude toward learning and school. For African American youth, failure to be academically engaged typically results in failing grades—the widely accepted traditional measure of academic failure. Thus, interventions to prevent academic failure among African American children need to include a major focus on facilitating these children's academic engagement.

African American students themselves as well as their parents and teachers play major roles in preventing academic failure among these students. Their efforts must be coordinated such that academic material that teachers cover in their classrooms is reviewed in the homes of their students by the students with the needed support from parents to facilitate further understanding and learning of the material. Parents who feel that they do not have the knowledge and skills to help their children with their schoolwork at home must take the responsibility for getting their children the academic help that they need. Parents also need to be in regular contact with their children's teachers and school administrators to discuss ways of best meeting their children's needs for academic success.

Teachers and schools administrators must actively empower African American parents for involvement in the education of their children. These teachers and school administrators can do this by conducting parent training on how parents can help prevent academic failure and facilitate academic success of their children and by doing all that they can to make attendance to this training by African American parents possible and comfortable. Additionally, teachers and school administrators can invite African American parents to meetings to discuss ways that schools can best meet their children's academic needs and concerns and ways to make their children feel a part of their school.

It is important for school administrators, teachers, other school staff, and all students at schools to be culturally and socioeconomically sensitive. This can occur through a commitment by school administrators and teachers to accept and respect individual and group differences and to view differences in learning styles and backgrounds as just that—differences, not deficits. Such commitments should be reflected in school activities, teaching methods, and classrooms that are culturally and socioeconomically sensitive and to a family-like school atmosphere in which each student is a valued and respected member of the student body.

Because of the historical negative stereotypes of African Americans, the racism that still exists in this country, and the dominance of the majority culture in most schools, many African American students often feel their minority status; that is, they often feel little control over their academic destinies. Additionally, African American students often are not understood and are not expected to succeed and, thus, they often do not get the support and motivational experiences that they need for academic success. To help prevent academic failure of African American students, teachers must individually assess the strengths and weaknesses of each African American child and facilitate the assessed strengths and extinguish the assessed weaknesses in a culturally and socioeconomically sensitive manner.

Additionally, culturally influenced learning strategies and classroom behaviors of African American students that are not optimum for academic success must be accommodated and utilized in the process of teaching these students new learning strategies and behaviors that are necessary for them to be academically successful in U.S. classrooms and in getting jobs and establishing careers in the future. The academic standards should not be lowered for African American students; rather, academic support must be provided to ensure that African American students meet these standards.

In addition to the efforts of parents, teachers, and school administrators, preventing academic failure of African American students requires the efforts of church leaders and community members including political and business leaders and academic psychologists. Even with needed parental support, teachers and schools alone cannot or will not meet the educational needs of African American students for academic, social, and economic success. Communities must actively involve themselves in providing after-school activities such as community-based partnership education programs (PEPs) that supplement the academic efforts of teachers and schools. Academic psychologists involved in education can play major roles in organizing and implementing PEPs and in conducting research to evaluate the effects of these programs and, thus, ensure their institutionalization.

The underlying objective of interventions and other strategies to prevent academic failure of African American students ideally needs to be to facilitate self-empowerment of these youth for academic, social, and economic success. In other words, efforts must be made by parents, teachers, school administrators, and community leaders to facilitate among African American students self-motivation to achieve, self-control of their academic progress and success, self-praise of their academic effort, progress, and success, and adaptive skills and success behaviors to prevent academic failure and facilitate academic and life success.

14 Self-Empowering African American Children for Academic and Social Success

A Successful Model Program

The Research-Based Model Partnership Education Program (Model Program) is based on self-empowerment theory to facilitate academic achievement and adaptive skills and to reduce maladaptive behaviors in socially and economically disadvantaged African American children. The Model Program was developed by the present author and her research colleagues and is conducted at the Mt. Olive Education Center (an annex to the Mt. Olive AME Church) in Gainesville, Florida. The Mt. Olive Education Center is located in the heart of a low-income community.

The partners who work together to operate the Model Program include psychologists and psychology graduate students at the University of Florida, surrounding elementary and high schools, parents of participating students, volunteer community members, business leaders, and two major foundations—the Jessie Ball duPont Fund and the Hitachi Foundation. The ultimate goal of the Model Program is to self-empower African American children with academic or behavior problems for academic, social, and life success.

This chapter will discuss the educational statistics indicating the need for the Model Program, the theory and supporting research that provided the basis for the content of the Model Program, the components of the Model Program, the operation of the Model Program, the effectiveness of the Model Program, and the plans to replicate the Model Program across the nation.

Need for the Model Program

There is general agreement that public schools are having less success in meeting the educational needs of African American students as compared to European American students. These schools seem to be having particular difficulty with meeting the academic needs of economically and socially disadvantaged African American students. Following are some educational statistics, which suggest that public schools are not effectively meeting the academic needs of many African American children, especially those from low-income families.

1. Proportionately, more African American students in general and more African American students from low-income families in particular drop out of school as compared to their European American counterparts. In 1995, about 12.1 percent of all African Americans between the ages of sixteen and twenty-four were school dropouts; comparatively, only 8.6 percent of European Americans were school dropouts. In 1995, for this same age group, the status school dropout rate was much higher for African American students in low-income families (20.1%) than for African American students in middle-income families (8.7%) and those in high-income families (3.2%). Comparatively, the status school dropout rate for European American students in low-income families (18.6%) was much higher than that for European American students in middle-income families (8.8%) and those in high-income families (2.6%).

[Low-income families as used here are those families with incomes in the bottom 20 percent of all family incomes for 1995; middle-income families are those families with incomes between 20 percent and 80 percent of all family incomes in 1995; and high-income families are those families with incomes in the highest 20 percent of all family incomes in 1995 (unpublished data from the U.S. Department of Commerce, Bureau of the Census, Current Population Survey, October 1995 reported in *Dropout Rates in the United States: 1995* published by the National Center for Education Statistics, 1995)].

2. There are some data that suggest that more African American students repeat one or more grades than European American students. For example, in 1989, 49 percent of African American thirteen-year-olds were in seventh grade or below, whereas only 32 percent of their European American counterparts were in seventh grade or below. Furthermore, some studies have shown that students who repeat at least one grade are more likely to drop out of school (*The Condition of Education: 1997,* National Center for Education Statistics, 1997).

3. The academic proficiency in reading, mathematics, and science, as measured at age nine by the National Assessment of Educational Progress, is lower for African American children than for European American children, and this racial/ethnic difference persists through age seventeen, though it does not widen (*The Condition of Education: 1997,* National Center for Education Statistics, 1997).

4. African American sophomores (51%) as compared to their European American counterparts (37%) are more likely to report that disruptions by other students interfere with their learning. Additionally, in 1990 it was found that African American sophomores (13%) as compared to the European American counterparts (7%) were more likely to report that they did not feel safe at their school (*The Condition of Education: 1997,* National Center for Education Statistics, 1997).

The preceding data suggest that public schools need help in meeting the educational needs of African American children, especially those from low-income families. The Model Program is designed to provide such help in a constructive manner that involves schools, teachers, parents, communities, businesses, local colleges and universities, foundations interested in education, and psychologists working in partnership to facilitate academic and social success and to reduce and prevent academic failure and behavior problems of African American children and, thus, all children.

Indeed, when African American children fail, all other children and all Americans are negatively impacted. Other children in the classrooms of African American children who fail often learn less because of the increased attention of teachers to the children who are failing and their failure-related behavior problems. The children's parents often feel they too have failed and thus they experience frustration and hopelessness. Teachers of African American children who fail often must deal with their parents' emotional response to this failure and with their own resentment and anger.

Communities often feel the impact of the failure of African American children when this failure leads to school dropout, which in turn leads to crimes such as theft, vandalism, and drug use. Additionally, businesses in communities are impacted by academic failure of African American children because this failure reduces the quality and quantity of the work force from which they must recruit competent workers. Indeed, businesses lose money when their workers cannot adequately follow instructions and communicate in oral and written forms, resulting in poor job performance and reduced profits for the business owners. Of course, the ultimate result when businesses lose money is economic pain and an associated reduced quality of life for all Americans.

Clearly, it is in the best interest of all Americans to help facilitate the academic and social success of African American students, especially those who are economically and socially disadvantaged and, thus, at high risk of academic underachievement and academic failure. The Model Program makes this point in its recruitment efforts to recruit partners to help make education work for economically and socially disadvantaged African American children, many of whom have academic weaknesses, adaptive skill weaknesses, and behavior problems.

Underlying Theory and Research

The Model Program is based on the present author's self-empowerment theory of academic achievement, which asserts that academic achievement by African American children is determined by levels of self-motivation to achieve, self-control of academic progress and social behavior, self-reinforcement of progress toward academic and social success, and by levels of adaptive skills (i.e., communication, socialization, and daily living skills) and engagement in success behaviors. In other words, for African American children to achieve, they must:

1. be self-motivated to do so;
2. learn to teach themselves;
3. learn to self-manage their social behavior;
4. praise themselves for academic and behavior management efforts, progress, and success; and
5. be taught success behaviors and adaptive skills, including communication skills, socialization skills, and daily living skills.

Self-empowerment theory recognizes that multiple external factors often negatively impact the academic achievement and social behaviors of African American children.

These factors include social, cultural, physical, economic, political, school, neighborhood, family, and parental factors. Yet, most of these factors are difficult or impossible to change in the school life time of a child. Thus, African American children must be taught to achieve under whatever conditions exist.

Self-empowerment theory asserts that to facilitate the academic achievement of African American children, we must give priority to modifying internal influences on children's academic and social behaviors such as self-control while making efforts to modify the most direct and modifiable external influences such as parents' and teachers' behaviors.

Connell's process model of motivation (Connell, 1991; Connell & Wellborn, 1991) offers support for this view. According to this model, social context variables (e.g., neighborhood and parental and teacher support) impact self-variables (e.g., perceived competence, which is often called self-efficacy and self-control; and perceived relatedness to school), which in turn impact children's actions or engagement in school (e.g., interest in school, attention in class, and study behaviors) that directly impact academic outcomes (e.g., grades and aptitude test scores). This model can explain why some poor children with little or no parental support and who live in disadvantaged communities are academically successful. Indeed, it may be because of the strength of the self-variables and their engagement in school behaviors.

Connell, Spencer, and Aber (1994) provided empirical support for self-empowering African American children when they showed with a sample of African American fifth graders to ninth graders that self-variables such as perceived competence and perceived control directly influenced the children's engagement in learning behaviors (e.g., studying), which in turn most directly influenced the children's grades and standardized achievement test scores. Parental support (a social context variable) also had a significant but indirect influence on the children's grades and standardized achievement test scores.

Findings from five studies by the present author and her research colleagues with samples of low-income African American families led to the self-empowerment theory of academic achievement. These research studies utilized a Difference Model research approach (Oyemade & Rosser, 1980), which advocates identifying determinants of differences among African American students rather than focusing on their deficits compared to European American students.

The Difference Model research approach respects cultural differences between groups and, thus, separately examines factors in target behaviors for each group. This research approach suggests that because of different socialization experiences, customs, and traditions between African Americans and both European Americans and other ethnic groups, these groups likely differ sometimes in their responses to the same behavior influence variables. Thus, for example, behaviors found to be effective in modifying certain behaviors among European American children may or may not be effective in modifying the same behaviors among African American children. The Difference Model research approach also asserts that conclusions based on research with European Americans may not be valid for African Americans.

In contrast, the more commonly used Deficit Model research approach compares the performance of African American and other nonmajority groups to the performance of European Americans, uses the performance of the European Americans as the comparison standard, and invalidly views lower performance by African Americans as inferior or deficit performance. The Deficit Model approach incorrectly assumes that there are equal opportunities available to both African Americans and European Americans and fails to consider the cultural, economic, and socialization factors in differences in their performances that might have implications for understanding and positively impacting the performances of African Americans and European Americans.

The children in the samples for the five studies by the present author that led to the self-empowerment theory of academic achievement were first graders through twelfth graders who had one or more low grades, a weakness in math or reading, and mild behavior problems. Over 90 percent of the children had below a 2.5 grade point average (GPA), a weakness in math or reading, and mild behavior problems. Following is a summary of each of the studies conducted and the major findings that are relevant to self-empowerment theory.

1. We examined adaptive skills (i.e., communication, socialization, and daily living skills), maladaptive behavior (e.g., hitting and off-task behavior), frequency of school defiance, and school fighting as predictors of African American children's grade point averages (Tucker, Chennault, Brady, Fraser, Gaskin-Butler, Dunn, & Frisby, 1995). Results revealed that all of the examined variables were significant predictors of grade point averages.

2. We examined expressiveness, cohesion, and conflict in the family as predictors of children's maladaptive behavior and adaptive skills (Dunn & Tucker, 1993). Only conflict in the family was found to be a significant predictor of maladaptive behavior.

3. We investigated self-esteem as a predictor of African American children's grades, adaptive skills, and maladaptive behavior (Gaskin-Butler & Tucker, 1995). Results revealed that self-esteem was not a significant predictor of the children's grades. However, for females, high self-esteem did predict high adaptive skills and low maladaptive behavior. Surprisingly, for males, the results were just the opposite; that is, high self-esteem predicted high maladaptive behavior and low adaptive skills. In other words, the African American males who were feeling great about themselves were those who were engaging in problem behaviors and had low skills.

4. We investigated African American children's math achievement motivation, self-control, and perceived social support from their primary caregiver as predictors of maladaptive behavior (Tucker, Vogel, Keefer, & Reid, 1997). Results revealed that self-control was a significant predictor of maladaptive behavior, accounting for 55 percent of the variance in maladaptive behavior. The math achievement motivation scores were uniformly low and, thus, may be why this variable was not a significant predictor. Other studies have shown academic motivation to be significantly associated with academic achievement of low-income African American children (Jordan, 1981).

5. We conducted a structured interview study with African American elementary school students and high school students and their parents and a group of African American teachers to determine their views on the academic performance and school behaviors of African American students (Tucker, Herman, Pedersen, & Vogel, 1997). Among the questions asked of the two student groups was what African American students, African American parents, and teachers can do to help prevent poor grades by African American children. The responses to this question were highly consistent across the elementary school students and the high school students who were interviewed. These student groups highly agreed that to prevent poor grades, African American students can pay attention in class, follow instructions given by the teacher, and ask questions about what they do not understand. The student groups also highly agreed that African American parents can help their children with their homework and studying, encourage them, and talk regularly with their teachers. Additionally, the students interviewed highly agreed that teachers can help prevent poor grades among African American children by giving them extra individual help, explaining what is taught in class in more detail, encouraging them, and not giving up on them.

In addition to providing support for self-empowerment theory and the need to self-empower African American children from low-income families for academic and social success, the preceding research suggested that the Model Program must meet the following criteria.

1. It must teach African American children adaptive skills (i.e., communication skills, socialization skills, and daily living skills) given that these skills appear to be associated with making high grades.

2. It must teach African American children to self-manage their anger, frustration, and other negative feelings that often lead to maladaptive behaviors.

3. It must teach African American children success behaviors and sever the relationship between positive self-esteem and engaging in maladaptive behaviors that was found in African American males. The Model Program must instead associate positive self-esteem with engaging in success behaviors (i.e., acting African American), learning adaptive skills, and all efforts toward academic and social success.

4. It must provide children with supplemental instruction to that provided in their classes; furthermore, this instruction must be individualized and provided using a step-by-step teaching method that involves more detailed teaching or tutoring.

5. It must teach African American children to self-praise their academic efforts, progress, and success, because many of these children will not have parents and teachers around to praise them for these occurrences.

6. It should perhaps facilitate academic self-motivation to achieve as some African American children have low achievement motivation and many of these children will not have teachers and parents who will motivate them to achieve.

7. It must teach parents to self-manage their anger and other negative feelings that contribute to or reinforce family conflict, which in turn contributes to the occurrence of maladaptive behavior in their children. Additionally, the Model Program must encourage parents to encourage their children and to be actively engaged in their learning and with their school. Furthermore, the Model Program must teach parents how to encourage and be supportive of their children for academic and social success.

8. It must train teachers to be firm and supportive with African American students, to praise them frequently for positive behaviors, and to use step-by step teaching methods in their classrooms.

9. Given the indication that teachers already may find it difficult to provide children with needed extra help and given the multiple factors that appear to be associated with the academic achievement of low-income African American children, the Model Program most ideally should be community based.

Components of the Model Program

Given the foregoing research-based criteria for the Model Program, it was decided that the Model Program should consist of the following components: (1) individualized academic tutoring, (2) group training to teach adaptive skills and to reduce maladaptive behavior, (3) computer skills training, (4) sharing, (5) group field trips, (6) individual field trips, (7) parent training, and (8) teacher training. Following is a discussion of each of these components.

Individualized Academic Tutoring

In this component children are provided with one-on-one academic tutoring in areas in which they have academic weaknesses. These areas are identified monthly by their teachers and by the children themselves. Additionally, children are provided with individual tutoring as needed to understand and correctly do their homework and some strategies for effective studying. It is recognized that African American children, especially those who are disadvantaged, need individual attention for academic success (Gary & Booker, 1992). The tutoring in the Model Program is provided by University of Florida undergraduate students, community volunteers, and parents, all of whom are trained to use a teaching/tutoring method called the Step-by-Step Teaching/Learning Method. Teachers from the regular school system who participate in the Model Program supervise the academic tutoring to make sure that the participating children are provided with academic materials that best address their academic weaknesses.

The Step-by Step Teaching/Learning Method is based on Meichenbaum's cognitive modeling and self-instruction approach (Meichenbaum, 1977). This method involves (1) breaking the skill or behavior to be learned into steps; (2) having the teacher model the skill or behavior using the steps and saying each step aloud (i.e., cognitive modeling); (3) having the student perform the same skill or behavior (as modeled by the teacher) while the teacher instructs the student using the steps; (4) instructing the student to perform the skill or behavior while using the steps to instruct himself or herself aloud and then silently (i.e., covert self-guidance); (5) having the student memorize the steps and practice the skill or behavior using the steps covertly; and (6) having the student self-praise progress toward and attainment of the behavior or skill throughout the learning and practice processes. Edgar and Clement (1980) showed that self-reinforcement (e.g., self-praise) was more effective than teacher-controlled reinforcement in facilitating the math academic achievement of African American males.

Once children have learned how to do a behavioral or academic skill to do an assigned problem or behavior using the step-by-step method, they are assigned very similar problems or skills so that they can practice the learned skill(s) toward the goals of overlearning and repeated successes. Such successes likely facilitate African American children's academic self-concept, which has been found to have a significant positive association with academic achievement in inner-city African American children (Fischer, 1988).

The step-by-step method is particularly useful in teaching African American children because it allows them to make self-attributions for academic progress and success, which are self-empowering. In the Model Program, the steps that are written for a child (e.g., the steps for doing long division) are kept and filed in a step-by-step library (i.e., a file cabinet); consequently, when another child needs to learn the same behavioral or academic skill, the tutor can simply retrieve the steps for learning that skill from the step-by-step library. Additionally, in the process of tutoring, students are taught memorization and problem-solving skills. These cognitive skills have been found to be associated with high academic achievement in African American children (Clark, 1983; Reynolds, 1991).

Group Skills Training

In this component children are taught the following adaptive skills:

1. communication skills such as how to effectively express positive and negative feelings, public speaking skills, how to write and speak using complete sentences, and how to form paragraphs and organize them in a letter or manuscript. The goal of these skills is to enhance each student's ability to understand, speak, read, and write standard English. According to Hale-Benson (1990), interventions with African American children must include a focus on expressive language such as responding to questions in complete sentences and engaging in conversations with adults.

2. socialization skills such as how to resist peer pressure, chair a meeting, introduce oneself to a teacher or other person, interview for a job, and effectively handle conflict. The goal of these skills is to improve each student's ability to interact with others in a responsible and sensitive manner and to enjoy constructive leisure time.

3. daily living skills such as how to use the telephone, proper etiquette, time management, and how to write a check. The goal of these skills is to increase each student's ability to attend to her or his daily living needs such as eating, dressing, and hygiene, and to attend to the need to manage her or his time, money, and life effectively.

In addition to teaching adaptive skills, students in the Model Program are taught behavior self-management strategies to avoid engaging in problematic or maladaptive behaviors such as hitting, fighting, and cursing. These strategies include use of self-talk, selection of friends who are academically and socially successful, use of a feedback formula for expressing upset feelings, and an anger management strategy. These strategies are discussed in Chapter 5.

We use the earlier described step-by-step method to teach the children adaptive skills and behavior self-management strategies. Peer modeling, role-plays, and real-world experiences are also used to teach these skills and strategies. According to Shunk (1987), observation of models similar to oneself provides valuable information about a student's own self-efficacy regarding doing the observed behavior. Regarding the real-world experiences, children are involved in experiences in which they can actually use what they are taught.

For example, when children were taught about proper etiquette, they first role-played using proper etiquette during a meal, and then were taken out to dinner at a fine local restaurant where they could actually use the skills that they learned. The local restaurant donated the costs of the children's meals.

We also use cooperative learning to facilitate learning what was taught during adaptive skills training. Usually this learning occurs via a *Jeopardy* game format where groups compete to answer questions about adaptive skills, behavior self-management strategies, and academic skills that they have been taught. The student on each team who must attempt to answer the question must be a different student each time; however, the student's group must discuss with her or him the answer before it is given. Teachers and tutors applaud correct answers and recognize the group that accumulates more points. The other group that did not get as many points is also applauded. The groups are told to self-praise their academic efforts and successes. Cooperative learning has been found by Johnson, Johnson, Tiffany, and Zaidman (1983) to be associated with high academic achievement in African American students. We have found it to be highly effective in facilitating learning of adaptive skills, academic skills, and behavior self-management strategies.

Computers Skills Training

In this component students are taught basic computer programming and word processing skills using the step-by-step method. During this component, students are also helped with their academic weaknesses through the use of appropriate educational software. Indeed, computer skills training will empower any child and any adult for life in the twenty-first century.

Sharing

In the sharing component, tutors and all other Model Program staff give students public, positive feedback about their academic and adaptive skills development effort, progress, and success, and about their self-management and success behaviors. The students are also given the opportunity to give public, positive feedback about the help they received or about the success behaviors that they observed in any staff member(s). Additionally, students are given the chance to share about their self-perceived academic and skills development progress and any accomplishment or success behaviors used about which they feel proud.

Success behaviors are behaviors such as (1) talking with the teacher about what is not understood, (2) listening when others are talking, (3) using complete sentences, (4) projecting one's voice, and (5) study behaviors. The Model Program staff members constantly look for success behaviors and then enthusiastically praise the children immediately following their occurrence and then again during sharing. Staff members also encourage the participating children to praise themselves for their successes and success efforts and progress.

Fordham and Ogbu (1986) reported that some African American children label engaging in success behaviors "acting white." In the Model Program, we label engaging in success behaviors "acting African American," and we tell students that doing so is "cool." Furthermore, we try to sever the relationship between feeling good about oneself and engaging in problematic or maladaptive behaviors that has been found among low-income African American males (Gaskin-Butler & Tucker, 1995); simultaneously, we try to develop and strengthen the association between engaging in success behaviors and feeling good about oneself.

During the sharing component and during other program components, public and private positive feedback is given using what we called the feedback formula. The feedback formula is a technique for expressing both positive and negative emotions or observations in specific and assertive terms. It facilitates the expression of feelings and communicates desired behaviors from others in a constructive manner.

The feedback formula consists of three parts: (1) a statement or description of the specific observed negative behavior or positive behavior that is the subject of the feedback, (2) a description of the various feelings that the behavior generated, and (3) a statement of what is desired in the future instead of the negative behavior or a statement indicating that you would like the positive behavior to occur again in the future. Two examples using the feedback formula to give positive feedback follow.

> When you took out your homework and questions to ask me about it immediately at the beginning of tutoring, I felt proud of you and happy to be your tutor. Your readiness to work also made me feel that you are serious about learning, and that you value my time as your tutor. I hope that you will continue being prepared for tutoring and showing such interest in learning.

> Man, when you broke line in front of me, you made me feel angry and disappointed. In the future if you want to get in front of me, just politely ask me, and I will likely let you get in front of me.

Two examples of using the feedback formula to give negative feedback follow.

> I noticed that when I left the classroom to get some water, you stopped doing your math problems and started playing around in your seat and talking aloud, thus disturbing your other classmates. Your off-task behavior makes me feel upset and that you do not respect me. I would appreciate it if you will stay on task with your work and remain quiet when I leave the classroom. This would make me feel very proud of you."

> Mrs. Jones, you publicly criticized me three times today for pronouncing words incorrectly. I felt so embarrassed. I would appreciate it if you would privately tell me how to correctly pronounce words that I say incorrectly. Thank you for considering this request.

It is important to teach African American children to express positive feelings as well as negative feelings in order to help explode the stereotype that these children are negative and hostile, and because expressing positive feelings to their teachers, parents, and peers will increase the likelihood of children getting the academic help and support that they need. Indeed, people move toward others who often express positive feelings and away from those who express no feelings or frequently express negative feelings.

It is important to teach African American children to constructively express negative feelings because doing so avoids having others make incorrect assumptions about their feelings and because suppressing rather than expressing negative feelings often results in displaced aggression and hostility. For too long African American children have been told to shut up and be quiet. Furthermore, for too long these children, especially African American males, have been taught that holding their feelings on the inside is a show of strength. African American children and their parents must be taught to constructively express their feelings to avoid the potential negative consequences of not doing so. The feedback formula facilitates this constructive expression.

Group Field Trip

This component involves taking children on group field trips to increase their knowledge, give them an opportunity to practice learned skills, facilitate their self-esteem, and facilitate their pride about being African American. Field trips have included taking a train from Florida to Atlanta, Georgia, to visit the Martin Luther King Center, visiting an African arts museum, visiting a local center for the performing arts, and touring university campuses. Such field trips provide the children with opportunities to practice their success behaviors and adaptive skills and to practice self-praise for doing so beyond the Model Program setting. Participation in such field trips also enables African American children to contribute to class discussions about travel and interesting experiences.

Additionally, the field trips help make the participating children feel advantaged rather than disadvantaged, which in turn contributes to positive self-esteem. Learning about African American culture and the contributions of African Americans to the United States and the world facilitates self-acceptance and racial pride, both of which often need to be enhanced in African American youth who must live with racism and discrimination that threaten their self-esteem. Phinney (1992) found that for nonmajority groups, ethnic identity is positively linked to self-esteem.

Individual Field Trip

In this component a mentor or tutor helps each child establish both short-term and long-term goals and assists the child in formulating a plan for reaching these goals. Indeed, successful individuals have goals early in life (Gary & Booker, 1992). The mentor or tutor also plans an individual field trip for the child that is consistent with one or both of the child's goals. For example, a student whose long-term goal is to become a nurse might participate in a field trip to a hospital where the student will spend a few hours with a nurse who has been instructed to explain to the child about the nursing profession and about how the math, English, and science that the child is taking in school are needed in nursing. The goal is to facilitate the child's academic achievement motivation. Such motivation has been found to be significantly associated with the academic achievement of inner-city African American adolescents (Jordan, 1981).

Anecdotal evidence suggests that the individual field trips do impact positively the academic achievement of low-income African American children. For example, one of the children in the Model Program showed academic improvement following his individual field trip. This student wanted to be a pilot; however, he reported never having met a pilot and never having been in an airplane. It was arranged by a tutor for the student to meet a pilot who told the student how his courses in school would help him become a pilot. With parental approval, the pilot also took the student for his first airplane ride. The student could not wait to share his experience with the other students in the Model Program during the sharing component. He also had an increased enthusiasm about becoming a pilot and making good grades, both of which seem to be major factors in his improved academic engagement and grades.

Parent Training

The purposes of the parent training are to teach parents to use the methods and strategies used with their children in the Model Program and to consult with parents on how to address particular problem behaviors of their children and their own problem behaviors that negatively impact their children's academic and social behavior. Parent training occurs through monthly parenting workshops and through practicum experiences in which the parents observe the use of the Model Program's methods and strategies with their children and their children's positive responses to these interventions.

Dinner is served at these workshops and babysitting services are provided at the training site to encourage parents' participation. The training also usually includes a period of time for parents to anonymously write questions about any topic (e.g., sex problems, marriage problems, and obesity problems) and have those questions answered. The questions are dropped in a hat from which they are randomly drawn and then answered by the workshop leaders and other parents present. This activity and planned brief talks about popular topics such as weight loss strategies increase attendance to the parent training workshops. The effectiveness of using incentives to motivate attendance to self-help types of meetings has been documented (Miller & Miller, 1970).

In the parent training component, the major focus is on training parents to facilitate the self-empowerment of their children for academic and social success. Thus, parents are trained in the Model Program's methods and strategies (e.g., use of the feedback formula) so that the methods used with the children in the Model Program also are used at home. We particularly emphasize having the parents look for and praise the children's self-management behaviors, success behaviors, and use of adaptive skills.

We also teach parents ways to talk with their children about their schoolwork and we encourage them to do so daily. Given that many African American parents do not feel that they have the skills and knowledge to give their children much needed help with their homework, we encourage parents to find tutors, family members, church members, or others to regularly tutor their children during the evenings when the children are not in the Model Program.

During parent training, emphasis is also given to encouraging parents to use the feedback formula in self-managing their own anger, given that family conflict has been found to be associated with maladaptive behavior of children in the family (Dunn & Tucker, 1993). Additionally, we encourage these parents to engage in positive parenting behaviors that have been found to be significantly associated with higher academic achievement, adaptive skills, and lower maladaptive behaviors among low-income African Americans. These behaviors include frequent praise, use of encouragement rather than verbal reprimands and restrictions in response to low grades, high grade expectations, frequent church attendance, and provision of most discipline by the father (Tucker, Harris, Brady, & Herman, 1996; Tucker, Brady, Harris, Tribble, & Fraser, 1993). Parents are asked to read the Positive Parenting Pledge (see Table 14.1).

To facilitate children's positive self-esteem in association with positive aspects of themselves, parents are encouraged to give their children positive feedback about their physical characteristics, attitudes, and personality. To facilitate the occurrence of this parent feedback, parents are asked to generate a list of the qualities, behaviors, and characteristics of each of their children that they like, respect, or admire. These lists provide a repertoire of information for frequently giving their children praise and expressions of positive feelings.

Such lists seem necessary given that when parents have been asked to share what they like about one of their children, they typically can only think of one or two things. These parents acknowledge that they tend to focus on what their children do wrong and on their weaknesses rather than on their strengths or positive qualities. Consequently, many African American children receive more negative feedback than positive feedback from their parents; this feedback pattern is conducive to resentment, noncompliance, and defiance in children.

TABLE 14.1 Positive Parenting Pledge

Please read, sign, and post this pledge where you and your child will see it every day.
Please also continue to read it at least once a week:

I will do my very best
to contribute to my child's success

by responding constructively
when my child acts negatively, and

by responding affectionately
when my child acts positively.

I will also find a positive way
to express my love to my child each day,

and to tell my child what I view positively
and what I value especially.

Then I will do my very best
to contribute to my own success

by praising myself quietly
and treating myself lovingly.

Signed _____   Signed _____
　　　　　Father or Father Figure　　　　　　　　　　Mother or Mother Figure

Date _____   Date _____

　　　　Child's Name _____

Teacher Training

In this component the regular schoolteachers of the children in the Model Program and other interested teachers are trained in the Model Program's methods and strategies (e.g., the Step-by-Step Teaching/Learning Method). At present this training occurs bimonthly through large workshops followed by individual practicum training at the Model Program. In the individual practicum training each teacher is paired with a member of the Model Program staff who makes sure that the teacher gets to see all of the Model Program's methods and strategies used with a child in the Model Program. Teachers receive continuing education units for their participation in the training.

The teacher training is provided so that the children in the Model Program can experience in their classrooms the same methods and strategies used in the Model Program to self-empower them for academic and social success. Other interested teachers are invited to participate in the teacher training workshops and follow-up individual practicum so that the impact of the Model Program's methods and strategies can be experienced by a larger number of African American children than those in the Model Program.

In addition to training teachers to use the Model Program's methods and strategies, we encourage teachers who participate in the teacher training component to be assertive and supportive of African American children. Being supportive requires asking them what they do not understand, patiently giving them needed extra academic help, and giving extra academic help with a positive attitude. Being assertive requires stating and reviewing classroom rules and consequences for breaking these rules and then following through with these consequences when the rules are broken. Eaves (1997) found that African American teachers had fewer classroom discipline problems than did their European American peer teachers because the African American teachers as compared with the European American teachers were more likely to follow through on the consequences for breaking rules and failing to follow directions.

Teachers who are trained by Model Program staff are also encouraged to positively view the relational learning style and the preferences for spontaneity, verve, and oral learning modalities that many African American children bring to the classroom (Boykin, 1983; Chimezie, 1988). In addition, we encourage these teachers to incorporate these learning styles and preferences as well as the children's talents in the teaching and learning process, thus resulting in more varied teaching methods. However, in agreement with Chimezie (1988), we strongly encourage teachers to also gradually and respectfully teach African American children to think analytically, to learn what is boring but important, to problem solve, to wait their turn to be recognized, and to write and speak standard English. Abstractly, one might say we challenge teachers to teach African American children to write well the songs that they want to sing, to wait their turn to sing them well, and to feel good all over about the writing and the singing.

Operation of the Model Program

Program Location and Participants

The Model Program operates on Tuesdays and Thursdays for two hours each day after school. It operates out of the Mt. Olive Education Center, which is an annex to the Mt.

Olive AME Church, located in a low-income neighborhood in Gainesville, Florida. The Model Program serves approximately fifty-five students from first grade to twelfth grade with academic problems, behavior problems, or some adaptive skill weaknesses. The older children (seventh graders to twelfth graders) attend the Model Program on Tuesdays and the younger children (first graders to sixth graders) attend on Thursdays.

Program Partners in Its Operation

The partners in the partnership and their roles and responsibilities follow.

1. *The Hitachi Foundation and the Jessie Ball duPont Fund.* Both of these granting agencies have provided large grant funding to help develop, test, and institutionalize the Model Program and to disseminate its methods and strategies beyond the Model Program.

2. *The local Burger King (Mr. Chuck Gatton, owner),* The New York Times *and our local* Gainesville Sun *newspaper (Mr. John Fitzwater, editor), and other local businesses.* These businesses have participated in the adaptive skills training and associated field trips and have donated funds and in-kind services needed to help operate the Model Program.

3. *The University of Florida (president, Dr. John Lombardi).* The University of Florida has funded some of the graduate students who help conduct the Model Program. Graduate and undergraduate students help tutor the participating children, assist with the adaptive skills training, help arrange all field trips, and assist with the collection of research data to identify determinants of African American children's academic performance and school behavior and to evaluate the effectiveness of the Model Program. The undergraduate students each receive course credit for their work in the Model Program. Graduate students get the opportunity to co-author publications reporting research related to the Model Program.

4. *Eleven teachers from the regular school system who teach in the Model Program.* These teachers provide individualized teaching in the Model Program to address the participating children's academic weaknesses, supervise the tutors who work in the Model Program, and help train the regular schoolteachers who participate in the teacher training component of the Model Program. These teachers receive small monetary rewards for their work.

5. *The regular schoolteachers of the children in the Model Program.* These teachers monthly inform the teachers in the Model Program about the academic weaknesses and strengths and about the behavior problems and behavioral strengths of the children whom they teach who participate in the Model Program. This information is used by the teachers in the Model Program to direct the tutoring that each child receives and to identify teaching materials and methods to address each child's academic weaknesses. It is also used to help structure the adaptive skills and behavior self-management training. The teachers of the children in the Model Program also participate in the teacher training workshops so that they can work in partnership with the Model Program to self-empower the children in it for academic and social success.

6. *Parents of the children in the Model Program and volunteer parents.* Parents execute many different roles in the Model Program including tutoring, preparing a snack for the children, operating the Model Program's library, and assisting teachers with copying and disseminating teaching materials. The parents of the children in the Model Program also participate in the parent training workshops so that they can work in partnership with the Model Program to self-empower their children for academic and social success. Some of the parents who work in the Model Program such as those who regularly prepare a snack for the children and those who regularly work as tutors receive a small monetary honorarium for their work.

7. *The present author and her research team of four graduate students in psychology and fifteen undergraduate psychology majors.* This team assists with and supervises all aspects and components of the Model Program and plans and conducts the research to assess the effects of the Model Program. The undergraduate researchers receive a research course grade for their work and the associated learning.

8. *The executive board.* This board consists of twelve members of the community among whom are educators and business leaders and owners. The board assists with finding resources for and disseminating information about the Model Program. Board members also participate in the adaptive skills training and the individualized and group field trip components of the Model Program.

A Typical Two-Hour Session in the Model Program

Tutoring occurs during the first hour of the Model Program. Following tutoring, students participate in snack time, which is a fifteen-minute period when a nutritious meal is served to the students and Model Program staff. During snack time, students practice using good table manners and engaging in appropriate dinner conversation. They discuss their short-term and long-term goals and their regular school day with their tutors and other Model Program staff.

Snack time is particularly important because it helps energize the students for the next part of the Model Program session—the thirty-minute group skills training to teach adaptive skills and behavior self-management strategies to deter or reduce maladaptive behaviors. Following this skills training is the last activity of the day, which is sharing. This activity lasts fifteen minutes.

Research on Program Effects

Research Participants

The effects of the Model Program on participating children's overall grade point average (GPA), math GPA, and reading GPA were investigated using 148 mostly low-achieving and low-income African American students living in Gainesville, Florida (Tucker, Chennault, Brady, Fraser, Gaskin, Dunn, & Frisby, 1995). These students were used to form four groups: (1) an experimental group of 20 third graders (71%), and 8 ninth graders (29%); (2) a planned control group (*n* = 48) of 27 third graders (56%), and 21 ninth graders (44%); (3) a default control group (*n* = 29) of 8 third graders (28%) and 21 ninth graders (72%); and an enrichment group ($n = 43$) ranging in age from first graders to twelfth graders.

The enrichment group included 28 students (65%) in the lower grade level (sixth grade and below) and 15 children (35%) in the upper grade level (seventh grade and above). The experimental group, the planned control group, and the default control group consisted of students who were randomly selected from a computer printout of third-grade and ninth-grade students who lived in the low-income area of the local school district and met the following program eligibility criteria: (1) overall GPAs of 2.5 or below for the first semester of the preintervention academic year, and (2) performance levels below grade level for reading and/or math.

All selected students were invited and required to participate in both the research and intervention components of the Model Program. Those who agreed to participate were randomly assigned to the experimental group or planned control group. The default control group consisted of students initially assigned to the experimental group or the planned control group but who did not follow through in participating as they had agreed. The default control group, the planned control group, the experimental group, and the enrichment group did not significantly differ in mean overall GPA or in their mean reading GPA and math GPA at preintervention.

The enrichment group students were extended an invitation to participate in the Model Program because they and their families were members of the Mount Olive AME Church, which housed the Mount Olive Education Center where the Model Program was conducted. These enrichment students were not required to meet the program participation criteria; however, 80 percent of these children were from low-income families and, as mentioned earlier, had GPAs similar to those of the other participating groups of students.

The four groups in this study had similar family income distributions. The income profile for the families of the entire sample is as follows: 33 percent of the families had incomes below $15,000; 40 percent had incomes between $15,000 and $25,000; 10 percent had incomes between $25,000 and $35,000; and 17 percent had incomes slightly above $35,000.

Data Collection

The primary caregiving parent of each student (who for 97 percent of the students was the mother or mother figure) was verbally administered the Vineland Adaptive Behavior Scale (Sparrow, Balla, & Cichetti, 1984) to obtain adaptive functioning data and maladaptive behavior data. The primary caregivers were also verbally administered a demographic data questionnaire.

Academic performance data were obtained from the local school board office for the schools attended by the children in this study. Specifically, mean overall GPA, mean math GPA, and mean reading GPA for the preintervention academic year and for year 1 and year 2 of the Model Program were obtained.

Parent behavior self-monitoring sheets were used to assess parents' follow-through in praising their children's success behaviors and in using the Step-by-Step Teaching/ Learning Method to (1) manage their own stress, (2) constructively express their own negative emotions (e.g., anger) and positive feelings, and (3) assist their children with constructively expressing emotions and learning academic and adaptive skills. Parents rated their follow-through on engaging in these behaviors on a five-point Likert scale ranging from 1 = never did the behavior to 5 = frequently did the behavior.

Procedure

Students in the enrichment group and the experimental group began participating in the Model Program in year 1 following the end of the preintervention baseline year. The planned control group began the program one year later, at the beginning of year 2 of the program. The default control group never participated in the Model Program; therefore, it was the only control group for the entire two-year intervention period.

With one exception, the intervention program was the same for the enrichment group, the experimental group, and later for the planned control group when it joined the intervention program in year 2. The exception is that the enrichment group received individualized one-on-one academic tutoring in whatever academic areas that the students reported needing help, whereas the other intervention groups (i.e., experimental group in year 1 and year 2; the planned control group in year 2) received small group academic teaching in math and reading rather than individualized tutoring. Data collection to assess the effectiveness of the Model Program discontinued at the end of year 2 when this research phase was complete.

Results

None of the four groups in the Model Program differed significantly in either mean math GPA or mean reading GPA at baseline. Extremely low scores at baseline in reading and math by two students in the default control group made the mean scores in math and reading for that group lower than the mean scores in these courses for the other three groups; however, this difference was not statistically significant.

Two repeated measures analyses of covariance (ANCOVAs)—one with reading GPA data that used baseline reading GPA as a covariate and the other with math GPA data that used baseline math GPA as the covariate—were used to assess effects of the Model Program on the participating children's academic performance. Results indicated that participation versus nonparticipation in the Model Program had some gradual but significant beneficial effects on targeted GPAs (Tucker et al., 1995). At the end of year 2 of the Model Program, children in the program for this entire period evidenced significantly higher mean math GPA and mean reading GPA than did a control group of children not in the Model Program over the entire two-year investigation period.

Specifically, from the baseline year to the end of year 2 of the Model Program, the children not in the Model Program during year 1 or year 2 (i.e., the default control group) showed a decrease in mean math GPA, whereas the children in the Model Program (i.e., experimental group, the enrichment group, and the planned control group—the group that was not in the program in year 1 but was in the program in year 2) showed no change in math GPA. It was also found that from the baseline year to the end of year 2, the enrichment group—the only group to receive individualized one-on-one tutoring—showed an increase in reading GPA, whereas the other groups showed a decrease in mean reading GPA.

Behavioral observations by program staff members, written comments on students' report cards by their regular public school teachers, and verbal feedback from the students' public school teachers during monthly telephone calls to them from program teachers indicated yearly increases in all students' adaptive skills and decreases in their maladaptive behaviors and reported school misconduct.

Data from the parent behavior self-monitoring sheets (PBSMS), which were used to assess parent workshop participants' follow-through in use of what they were taught in the parent workshops, were collected only for three months, beginning midway in year 1 of the Model Program. After this period of time, parents discontinued the self-monitoring as indicated by a continuing increase in the number of parents who did not return their PBSMS to the Model Program staff. Because this unwillingness of parents to provide the requested self-monitoring data seemed to result in them feeling embarrassed and in decreased attendance to the parent workshops, this self-monitoring procedure was discontinued.

The data from the PBSMS that were obtained from thirty parents (42%) over the three-month period in which the PBSMS were used were summarized. Parent follow-through self-ratings on the PBSMS could range from 1 = never did the behavior to 5 = frequently did the behavior. Results revealed the following mean parent follow-through self-ratings for the specified behaviors: used stress management (4.4); constructively expressed anger and other negative emotions (4.1); expressed praise and positive feelings (4.7); and taught child adaptive skills (3.5), academic skills (2.8), and stress management behaviors (4.6) using the Model Program methods and strategies. Anonymous workshop evaluations from parents concerning how beneficial the parent workshops were to them received ratings ranging from 4.6 to 4.9 on a five-point scale on which 5 = very beneficial and 1 = not beneficial.

A MANOVA was used to determine if there were differences in baseline adaptive functioning skills or in maladaptive behavior in association with gender, grade level [first grade to sixth grade (lower grade level) versus seventh grade to twelfth grade (upper grade level)], or group. Results revealed nonsignificant overall effects for gender, grade level, and group.

An ANOVA was used to determine if there were differences in baseline overall GPA in association with gender, grade level, and group. Results revealed the following: (1) females had a higher baseline mean overall GPA than did the males; and (2) students in the lower grade level had a higher baseline mean overall GPA than the students in the upper grade level.

A MANOVA was used to determine if there were differences in baseline math GPA and reading GPA in association with gender, grade level, and group. Results revealed the following: (1) students in the lower grade level had significantly higher baseline mean math GPA than did children in the upper grade level; (2) females had significantly higher baseline mean reading GPA than did males, and (3) children in the lower grade level evidenced significantly higher baseline mean reading GPA than did the children in the upper grade level.

Nationwide Replication of the Model Program

Given the findings indicating that the Model Program has gradual but significant effects on the academic achievement and adaptive skills of low-income African American children and given the realization that teachers and schools alone cannot meet all of the academic and social needs of these children, it seems clear that partnership programs similar to the Model Program should be in communities across the nation to help facilitate academic and social success of low-income African American children. These programs seem especially needed for high school students and males because these groups evidenced lower academic achievement in math and/or reading than elementary school students and females, respectively.

Early intervention to self-empower African American children for academic and social success when they are young may deter the seemingly downward trend in academic achievement as children advance in grade level. As of now, it appears that self-empowerment of African American children in all grade levels is needed in order to facilitate their present and future academic and social success and to increase the likelihood of them having successful future careers.

At present, plans are underway for training teachers across Florida and the nation in the use of the Model Program's methods and strategies and for setting up satellite programs similar to the Model Program across Florida and the nation. These statewide and nationwide dissemination initiatives are being funded by grants from Florida's department of education and from the Hitachi Foundation, respectively. Two satellite programs have already been successfully launched, showing that the Model Program is replicable and can be operated without large grant funding.

Even in communities without access to university students who can provide tutoring, the Model Program can still be operated. High school students, retired teachers, and other community volunteers can serve as alternative tutors to university students. An adaptive skills handbook and a videotape of a day in the Model Program have been produced to aid others interested in setting up satellite partnership education programs. These materials and information about the teacher training and satellite training workshops can be obtained from the author.

Conclusions

The Research-Based Model Partnership Education Program is an example of how communities, schools, African American parents, and African American children themselves can work together to facilitate the academic and social success of low-income African American children. Research to assess the effectiveness of the Model Program suggests that it (1) prevents or minimizes decreases in academic achievement, which seem to come with increase in grade level, (2) contributes to some gradual improvements in academic achievement, (3) increases subjectively assessed adaptive skills, and (4) decreases subjectively assessed maladaptive behavior.

The research leading to the Model Program suggests that maladaptive behaviors or defiant behavior, adaptive skills, and self-control are significant predictors of academic achievement in low-income African American children. Given that defiance is somewhat culture specific and subjectively assessed, it is important that teachers and other school personnel clearly identify for African American students and their parents what specific behaviors are defiant. This information may help African American parents, communities, and African American students work in partnership with teachers and schools to modify those defiant behaviors that negatively impact African American students' grades.

Other research suggests that academic-specific achievement motivation, self-control, self-reinforcement of academic progress and success, perceived self-competence, and other self-variables facilitate academic achievement of African American children. In sum, the research on the academic achievement of African American children suggests that we must self-empower low-income African American children to facilitate their academic and social success under whatever external environmental conditions exist (e.g., school conditions, family conditions, neighborhood conditions, and social conditions).

The Model Program offers a cost-effective and practical way of self-empowering African American children for academic, social, and future life success. It addresses the need for all members of a community to help make education work for all children. Furthermore, it advocates total community involvement in the education of African American children in general and low-income African American children in particular. It motivates this involvement by calling attention to the great reality that is often ignored—the reality that when African American children experience academic and social success, all other children in their classrooms, all communities, and all Americans are positively impacted. Conversely, when African American children experience academic failure and behavior problems, which in turn lead to school dropout and associated crime, all Americans are negatively impacted.

CHAPTER

15

When All Else Fails

What to Do and Not to Do

When an African American child fails academically or repeatedly engages in behavior problems, parents, teachers, and psychologists and counselors who have tried to intervene to stop the failure or behavior problems often are negatively impacted in direct and powerful ways. These adults often feel a sense of failure and, consequently, they sometimes question their competencies in their roles as they relate to the child.

Usually parents, teachers, and psychologists and counselors realize that no matter what they do, they cannot force a child to learn or behave in ways that are appropriate based on society's norms; yet, these adults still often feel inadequate when they cannot influence and motivate a child to engage in academic and social success behaviors.

Some parents, teachers, and psychologists and counselors respond to a child's academic or behavior problems with total rejection of any responsibility for the child's persistent problems. This reaction may make the adults feel better, but it does nothing to address the emotions or lack of emotions of the child who continues to have academic or behavior problems. Furthermore, the classmates of the child continue to be negatively impacted by the child's problems.

This chapter identifies and seeks to normalize common specific reactions of parents, teachers, and psychologists and counselors when each perceives having done everything possible to modify the academic or behavior problems of a child and has been unsuccessful in all efforts. It also presents some recommendations for parents, teachers, and psychologists as to what they might do and avoid doing when they have been unsuccessful in modifying a child's academic or behavior problems. Included in this discussion are the views of African American parents and teachers regarding what parents and teachers can do when academic and behavior problems persist despite seemingly every possible effort to modify these problems.

Common Reactions of Parents

In response to their child's academic failure or behavior problems, parents often engage in one or more of the following common behaviors.

1. Parents often blame themselves and past family problems for their child's continuing academic failure or behavior problems. Consequently, parents may become very tolerant of the child's academic performance and behavior problems. Their child often perceives this self-blame and family blame and, consequently, uses this information to justify not making efforts to be academically and socially successful.

2. Parents often blame the child for doing things (i.e., academically failing and acting out) to hurt them. This blame is often accompanied by anger by the parents toward the child and anger and resentment by the child in response to the parents' blaming reaction. The child becomes even more resistant toward actions to help her or him be academically and socially successful.

3. Parents often blame the teacher for not caring about the child and for not getting help to stop the child's academic failure or behavior problems. The parents also begin to view their child's teachers as being racist and, thus, not making efforts to help their child. Teachers resent this perceived blame and avoid contact with the parents, thus eliminating any hopes of a parent–teacher partnership effort to facilitate the child's academic and social success.

4. Parents may take their child to a psychologist or counselor with the hopes that this professional can "fix the child" or prescribe actions that will quickly get the child to become academically engaged and socially successful. Parents often become disenchanted with the psychologist or counselor who spends time assessing the problems rather than modifying them.

5. Parents often punish the child more and more harshly for the academic failure and behavior problems. The child becomes determined to teach the parents that the perceived unfair punishment will not influence the child's academic or social behavior. The child may deliberately act out to punish her or his parents.

6. Parents often give up and wait for the child to come to her or his senses. The parent typically feels disappointed and upset with the child's academic and behavior problems and regularly tells the child this. The result is an even greater focus on all that the child does wrong, resulting in even more criticisms and negative feedback to the child. This negative attention becomes reinforcing to the child, viewing it as better than no attention at all.

Common Reactions of Teachers

Teachers' responses to a child's academic failure or behavior problems is often limited by the fact that the child is only one of many children in the classroom. Their responses often depend on whether the problem is academic or behavioral and on the attitude of the child's parents. Regarding the latter, teachers will engage in more effort to be positive, supportive, and helpful with a child whose parents are highly involved in actions to help the child—actions that include joining with the teacher in partnership efforts to address the child's academic or behavior problems. Regarding the type of problem, teachers are often much more reactive to a child with a behavior problem than to a child who is academically failing.

Teachers Reactions to Academic Failure

The teachers of an African American child who is academically failing often respond in one or more of the following ways.

1. Teachers often read the child's records to find out information such as family factors that might explain or justify the child's academic failure or behavior problems. This information is often distorted or negatively biased because it was not obtained in a culturally and socioeconomically sensitive manner.

2. Teachers often talk with other teachers who have taught the child; if these consultants feel that the child is simply not motivated to learn and the parents are not invested in helping the child or are hostile toward teachers, then the child's failure may simply be accepted. This acceptance is especially likely if the child's present teacher concludes that there is nothing more any teacher can do and if the child is not causing any disruption in the classroom. If the teacher finds out that the child has been doing much better academically in other teachers' classes and concludes that child is simply not relating to her or him as a teacher, the teacher may experience some self-blame, frustration, and resentment toward the child for causing these unpleasant feelings.

3. Teachers often blame the parents for the academic failure, especially if the parents do not attend parent–teacher conferences. In such cases, the teacher often will try to give the child extra help but may be impatient in doing so because of feeling that help will be wasted time without additional academic help for the child outside of school.

4. Teachers often refer the child for assessment to determine if the child has a learning disorder or disability or other problem that is causing the academic failure. Indeed, sometimes evaluators for learning disorders find what they are looking for, especially when it comes to African American children for whom the evaluation may not be culturally and socioeconomically sensitive.

5. Teachers often feel frustrated with the child when additional time and effort to provide extra academic help for the child does not result in improved academic performance.

6. Teachers often give up on trying to help the child academically, after having tried on several occasions and in several ways to help the child do better academically.

Teachers' Reactions to Behavior Problems

The teachers of an African American child who is engaging in behavior problems often respond in one or more of the following ways to these problems.

1. Teachers often punish the child for the inappropriate behaviors by withdrawing a privilege such as participating in recess period or by using timeout, which involves separating the child from other class members and from interesting or stimulating activity (e.g., having the child stand in a corner of the classroom facing the wall). For many African American children, such separation reinforces perceptions of discrimination and associated resentment, even when the punishment has nothing to do with discrimination.

2. Teachers often send the child to the principal's office where the principal tells the child the potential consequences of her or his behavior and appeals to the child to stop engaging in problem behaviors. These principal–student discussions often involve threats regarding the consequences of the child's inappropriate behaviors. Whether or not the latter is the case, the child misses valuable class time and, thus, gets behind or further behind academically.

3. Teachers sometimes request that the child be removed from their classes and/or suspended, often resulting in continued academic failure or mounting academic weaknesses.

Common Reactions of Psychologists and Counselors

A psychologist or counselor will often refer an African American child and the child's family to another psychologist or counselor when provided counseling is ineffective in modifying the child's academic and behavior problems. It is not uncommon for the psychologist or counselor who makes such a referral to feel as though she or he has failed in her or his professional efforts. This feeling sometimes occurs even though the psychologist or counselor knows that no matter what counseling skills and commitment to positive therapy outcomes she or he brings to the counseling process, therapy is sometimes not effective.

It is also common for a psychologist or counselor to talk with peer professionals to validate that the counseling provided was most appropriate, especially given the many variables influencing children's academic performance and behavior at school and at home. Furthermore, this professional may look for and find reasons external to herself or himself to explain unsuccessful counseling for academic and behavior problems of an African American child. These reasons are usually legitimate; yet, they do not address the fact that the children continue academic and social paths that do not lead to successful lives.

The reactions of parents, teachers, and psychologists and counselors to an African American child who is academically failing or engaging in problem behaviors typically are the product of their desire for the child to be academically and socially successful at school. Unfortunately, no matter how well intentioned, these reactions often have no significant, positive outcomes for the child. Furthermore, these reactions often exacerbate rather than reduce the frustrations, guilt, feelings of adequacy, and stress that parents, teachers, and psychologists often feel when their efforts to modify the academic failure or behavior problems of an African American child are not successful.

The reactions of parents and teachers often reinforce a child's undesirable behaviors because the reactions provide negative reinforcement. When a child does not receive much positive attention or reinforcement because of the focus on her or his unsuccessful behaviors, the child often will become satisfied with negative attention such as reprimands from parents and teachers. This satisfaction often results in the child continuing to do what is not desired in order to get parents' and teachers' attention—a needed validation by the child that she or he is important.

The reactions of psychologists often make the psychologist or counselor feel better but can result in the parents feeling hopelessness and despair. Even though referral of the child and the child's parents is clearly justified, parents often feel that their child is beyond help and do not follow through with seeking what might be more effective counseling for their child from the psychologist or counselor to whom they were referred. The child who does not want to participate in counseling anyway may view discontinuation of counseling as a positive outcome and, thus, continue the counseling-related behaviors (e.g., resistance behaviors) and the academic and behavior problems that made the psychologist or counselor simply discontinue counseling efforts.

Recommendations When Efforts Have Failed

There are no easy answers as to what should be done when parents, teachers, and psychologists or counselors feel that they have done all that they can do to modify the behavior problems or academic failure of an African American child. Yet, answers must be sought and implemented, because the cost of simply giving up on modifying academic and behavior problems of any African American child is extremely costly to the child, the peers in the child's classroom, the child's family, and eventually to all Americans. Indeed, when African Americans fail academically and engage in behavior problems they become at risk for many negative consequences including school dropout, long-term poverty, teenage pregnancy, drug use, and involvement in crime; these consequences in turn have a negative economical and social impact on all Americans.

Recommendations from African American Parents and from Teachers

As part of an interview study with African American students and their parents and with African American teachers regarding their views of African American students' academic performance and classroom behaviors, the present author assessed the views of the participants as to what parents and teachers should do when their efforts to address the behavior problems or academic failure of an African American child have failed (Tucker, Herman, Pederson, & Vogel, 1997). Elementary school students and teachers as well as high school students and teachers were among the interviewees. All participants lived in a small city in the South. The students were from low-income families and ranged in grade level from first grade to twelfth grade. All of the parent participants were mothers or mother figures. Ninety-one percent of the teacher participants were female.

Following are the responses of the study's participants to four specific questions regarding what parents and teachers can do when they perceive that all efforts to address academic or behavior problems of an African American child have failed. The responses to each question and the percentage of times each response was given among all responses given within each participant group follow.

Question
What should African American parents do and not do when everything that they have done to help their child stop making poor grades has failed?

Responses
Elementary School Parents
Get outside help (i.e., counseling and tutoring) (36.1%)
Do not give up on the child (25.0%)
Engage in learning activities that might help the child (19.4%)
Various other recommendations (19.5%)

High School Parents
Get outside help (i.e., counseling and tutoring) (34.6%)
Do not give up on the child (34.6%)
Do not criticize or ridicule the child (11.5%)
Various other recommendations (19.3%)

Elementary School Teachers
Get outside help (i.e., counseling and tutoring) (40.0%)
Do not give up on the child (40.0%)
Talk with the child regularly to motivate her or him (20.2%)
Various other recommendations (0.0%)

High School Teachers
Get outside help (i.e., counseling and tutoring) (46.2%)
Do not give up on the child (43.8%)
Various other recommendations (10.0%)

Question
What should teachers do and not do when everything they have done to help an African American child stop making poor grades has failed?

Responses
Elementary School Parents
Do not give up on the child; keep trying new strategies (41.8%)
Do not criticize, ridicule, or label the child (8.3%)
Use timeout (8.3%)
Various other recommendations (41.6%)

High School Parents
Do not give up on the child (28.0%)
Talk with parents to find a solution (24.0%)
Get outside help (i.e., counseling and tutoring) (20.0%)
Various other recommendations (28.0%)

Elementary School Teachers
Do not give up on the child (25.0%)
Regularly talk with the child to assess the cause(s) of the problem (16.7%)
Consult with other teachers and a psychologist; rule out a learning disability (16.7%)
Various other recommendations (41.6%)

High School Teachers
Encourage and praise the child and do not give up on the child (33.3%)
Give the child extra help and explain lessons in more detail (33.3%)
Have higher expectations (22.2%)
Various other recommendations (11.2%)

Question
What should African American parents do and not do when everything that they have done to modify their child's problem behaviors has failed?

Responses
Elementary School Parents
Get outside help (i.e., counseling) (30.0%)
Talk with the child and encourage the child to behave better (20.0%)
Do not give up on the child (16.0%)
Various other recommendations (34.0%)

High School Parents
Do not give up on the child (34.6%)
Get outside help (i.e., counseling and role models) (34.6%)
Consult with other parents (7.7%)
Various other recommendations (23.1%)

Elementary School Teachers
Get outside help (i.e., counseling) (40.0%)
Do not give up on the child (40.0%)
Talk with the child regularly to motivate the child (20.2%)
Various other recommendations (0.0%)

High School Teachers
Get outside help (50.0%)
Do not give up on the child (33.3%)
Tough love; punish immediately after the problem behavior (8.3%)
Various other recommendations (8.4%)

Question
What should teachers do and not do when everything they have done to modify an African American child's problem behaviors have failed?

Responses
Elementary School Parents
Do not give up on the child; keep trying new strategies (41.8%)
Get outside help (12.5%)
Do not criticize, ridicule, or label the child (8.3%)
Various other recommendations (37.4%)

High School Parents
Do not give up on the child (28.0%)
Talk with parents to find a solution (24.0%)
Get outside help (i.e., counseling and consultation) (20.0%)
Various other recommendations (28.0%)

Elementary School Teachers
Get outside help (i.e., counseling and consultation) (41.7%)
Do not give up on the child (25.0%)
Remove the child from the classroom (8.3%)
Various other recommendations (25.0%)

High School Teachers
Do not give up on the child (53.9%)
Get outside help (i.e., role model and consultation) (23.0%)
Talk with parents to find a solution (7.7%)
Various other recommendations (15.4%)

In sum, the preceding data suggest that there is much agreement across the elementary school and high school parents and across elementary school and high school teachers that when all efforts of parents and teachers to modify academic failure and behavior problems of an African American child have failed, it is important for the child's parents and teachers not to give up on the child and to get outside help for the child. This help can come from psychologists or counselors and from others such as other teachers, role models, and mentors who are appropriate for the student.

Many of the teachers and parents in this study also agree that the modification of academic and behavior problems requires talking with parents in an effort to find solutions to these problems. Also important is talking with the child who is having problems to find out possible causes of the problems so that solutions can be found. This is particularly noteworthy given that getting the perspective of an African American child regarding how to modify her or his problem behaviors and academic failure is indeed uncommon though a potentially effective intervention strategy.

Other Recommendations for Parents, Teachers, and Psychologists or Counselors

Recommendations for Parents.   Because parents have more opportunities to talk with their child, they and their child are most suited to assess the underlying causes of the child's academic failure or behavior problems. Indeed modification of these problems will not likely be successful without an understanding of the factors involved. Often the underlying causes of the problems must be addressed before the child will even participate in or allow efforts to modify academic or behavior problems. For example, a child who blames her mother for her parents' divorce may be failing just to punish her mother for the perceived "wrong" by her mother. Thus, when all efforts to modify academic or behavior problems have failed, it is important for parents or primary caregivers to spend time with the child to find out what might be the underlying cause(s) of these problems.

Indeed, assessment of the underlying causes of a child's academic failure or behavior problems might require the additional help of a culturally and socioeconomically sensitive psychologist or counselor. Such a person should be sought through others who might know such professionals. It is important that parents be patient with the assessment process as implemented by themselves, other family members, or counseling professionals. This is because an African American child with underlying problems that are impacting the child's grades or behaviors will not readily disclose those problems unless the child can trust and be comfortable with whomever is conducting the assessment.

In addition to taking time to understand the underlying causes of a child's academic failure or behavior problems, there are several other recommendations that will likely be helpful to parents who feel that all their efforts to modify these problems have failed. Following are these recommendations.

1. It is important for parents to focus on what the child does right or well in the classroom and at home. This will require that parents regularly observe their child at school and at home. Focusing on the child's positives and praising these positives will renew or create hope and patience in the parents that are needed for them to not give up on helping their child become academically and socially successful.

Parents ideally should also encourage the child to praise herself or himself along with the parental praise. Both the external encouragement and self-praise can facilitate the child's perceived self-competence and perceived parental support—two variables positively associated with African American children's academic and social success.

2. It is important for parents to work in partnership with schools and communities to get their child needed help for academic and social success. Mentors and role models who can give the child much one-on-one guidance, tutoring, and encouragement can be found in the community. Furthermore, it is important to involve the child in any available after-school program that provides tutoring and training in self-management of one's behavior. It is also recommended that the child be involved in groups such as a church or community choir, church school, and a boys' and girls' club where the child receives much exposure to peers who will likely be positive role models.

3. It is important for parents to take time out daily for themselves to relax and spend time doing something that makes them happy rather than worrying about their child's academic failure or behavior problems. Such relaxation will deter or lessen resentment of parents toward their child for having to spend so much time, energy, and money to address the child's problems.

4. It is important for parents to discuss their frustration, resentment, guilt, or anger related to their child's problems with someone that they trust and with whom they feel comfortable. This someone could be a family member, friend, psychologist or counselor, minister, or other person. Parents should also take needed actions to address any marital or family problems that are likely impacting their child emotionally.

5. It is important to involve the child in some type of learning activities in which the child can be successful and receive much praise for her or his accomplishments. For example, the child can be taught to use a computer, to play chess, play piano, and so on.

6. Parents can consider and investigate alternative educational programs for their child—programs such as home schooling, vocational training that includes getting a general equivalency diploma (GED), private schooling, and regular private tutoring.

7. Parents can consult with their child about what the child needs to stop failing and engaging in problem behaviors.

8. It is recommended that the parent have their child undergo a neuropsychological evaluation to determine if there are any brain or nervous system problems as well as psychological problems that might be contributing to the child's academic or behavior problems. Most psychologists and schools can arrange for such evaluations. The evaluation itself ideally should be conducted by a psychologist who is culturally and socioeconomically sensitive.

9. It is important for parents to publicly recognize and praise the efforts of their child's teacher and school administrators to address the child's academic and behavior problems. Such actions by parents motivate these professionals to do more to assist their child in getting the help needed to experience academic and social success.

10. Parents should avoid blaming themselves for their child's academic or behavior problems, as is commonly done. If the parents feel that their actions have contributed to their child's problems, it is important for the parents to acknowledge this to their child and apologize to the child for their actions. Consequently, the parents can feel better about themselves and focus their energies on getting their child the required help rather than on self-blame.

11. Parents can avoid ridiculing and criticizing the child and the child's teacher for the academic failure or behavior problems that the child is experiencing. Usually multiple factors impact the child's academic and social behaviors. Ridiculing teachers only angers them and decreases their motivation to help the child; furthermore, it gives the child justification for not trying to modify her or his own academic or behavior problems.

12. It is strongly recommended that parents avoid comparing their child who has academic or behavior problems with any other child. Such comparisons contribute to the child feeling unloved and feeling resentment toward their parents and siblings which in turn decrease the child's motivation to make positive changes in her/his academic and social behavior.

Recommendations for Teachers.   Indeed, most teachers want all of their children to engage in appropriate behaviors and to be academically successful. These teachers typically make extra efforts to help their students; yet, because these efforts are often not recognized and appreciated by parents or school administrators, it is challenging for even the most dedicated teachers to continue these efforts over an extended period of time without successful outcomes.

Following are some recommendations for teachers who have experienced repeated failure in their efforts to modify an African American child's academic and behavior problems.

1. It is recommended that teachers document their efforts to modify a child's academic and behavior problems so that they can verify for themselves and others such as parents and school board members the extensiveness and nature of their intervention strategies. This documentation can help alleviate guilt and feelings of inadequacy that a teacher might experience from lack of success in addressing a student's academic failure and behavior problems. Furthermore, it deters blame from parents and others for the child's academic failure and behavior problems. This documentation might also provide some guidance as to what is ineffective with the child; this information can help in generating new intervention strategies that might be helpful in facilitating the child's academic and social success.

2. Teachers should be proactive in contacting parents and the school principal to present the idea of a group meeting that includes the child's parents to brainstorm on ways of addressing the academic and behavior problems of an African American child. With parental permission, a psychologist or counselor and a couple of veteran culturally sensitive teachers should participate in this meeting. At least for part of the meeting, the child should also be involved to share her or his views as to what will be helpful for her or him to do better academically and to avoid specific problem behaviors of concern to the child's parents and teachers.

The ultimate goal of the meeting should be to come up with a multidimensional plan for addressing the child's academic and behavior problems. Indeed, group thinking is often more effective than the thinking of one person when trying to address the problems of a child that seem very resistant to change.

3. It is recommended that teachers make a list of the strengths and positive characteristics of the child who has academic and behavior problems that are resistant to change. The goal of this exercise is to get the teachers to focus on the child's positives and to feel affection toward and hope for the child in the process. It is difficult to experience and communicate these feelings to the child when frustrated and aggravated by the child's academic failure and behavior problems. Yet, what an African American child often needs most from teachers and other adults is unconditional love and support and the expectation that the child can and will learn and behave.

When an African American child continues to fail and act out, the child particularly needs expressions of caring and support and an unwillingness to give up on her or him. Such relentless support and encouragement from a teacher will build the child's trust in the teacher and, thus, the child's willingness to talk about what might be factors in her or his academic failure and behavior problems. Furthermore, such relentless support and encouragement will help motivate the child to achieve and behave appropriately.

4. Teachers can talk with trusted colleagues about the frustration, anger, inadequacy, and other feelings that they have as a result of an African American child's academic failure and behavior problems. Because most teachers have experienced failure in their efforts to modify a child's academic and behavior problems, teachers can typically help normalize feelings of their colleagues regarding such failure. Such normalization often reduces teachers' stress associated with a lack of success in modifying academic failure and behavior problems of a child in their classroom. This normalization also helps validate teachers' instructional efficacy, which is associated with more creative and positive teaching.

5. When the teacher has done all that she or he knows to do to modify the academic failure and behavior problems of an African American child and finds herself or himself truly angry with and resentful toward the child, then the teacher should consider and discuss with the child's parents the need for and the advantages and disadvantages of transferring the child to a different teacher.

Indeed, children sense when they are not liked by their teachers and respond to these feelings with retaliation, which in turn exacerbates the negative feelings of the teacher toward the child. This negative cycle makes it nearly impossible for successful teaching and learning to occur.

6. Teachers should not delay in getting help for a child's academic and behavior problems. Immediate help might be to get a teacher's assistant (e.g., a teacher's aide or family member) to work with the child one-on-one in the classroom to help teach the child and respond constructively to the child's behavior problems. In response to the latter the assistant and the teacher can tell the child how the behavior makes them feel, identify the alternative behavior(s) in which the child should engage, state the school rule regarding the problem behavior, and follow through on administering the consequences for breaking school rules.

7. Teachers should avoid yelling at and criticizing a child who is failing or engaging in behavior problems. Such behaviors by teachers only teach a child that yelling and being derogatory are appropriate behaviors that the child can also use when feeling frustrated or dissatisfied with something or someone.

8. It is recommended that teachers not let their perceived failure in modifying the behavior problems or academic failure of a child negatively impact their teaching and interactions with the other children in the child's classroom. It is easy to get frustrated with one child, become preoccupied with that frustration and the child, and, consequently, give less time and positive attention to other students in the classroom.

9. Teachers should avoid letting the child with behavior problems control them by making them upset. When a child learns how to push teachers' buttons to get reactions (e.g., anger, frustration, etc.) that keep teachers from focusing on the child's academic and behavior problems, then the child continues to push those buttons. Thus, the child takes control of the teachers and also takes control of what happens in the classroom.

Recommendations for Psychologists or Counselors.   Because African Americans are very underrepresented among licensed psychologists, it is typical that the psychologist who will be asked to help address the academic failure and behavior problems of an African American child will be a European American. Because African Americans do not readily seek the help of psychologists for their children's academic and behavior problems (Hall & Tucker, 1985), most psychologists typically do not have much experience addressing these problems in African American children.

Consequently, it is not unusual for psychologists, regardless of ethnicity, to sometimes find themselves baffled as to what to do to modify academic and behavior problems of an African American child. Furthermore, because of the multiple external factors beyond the control of the psychologist or the child that impact the behavior and academic performance of an African American child (Bronfenbrenner, 1979), it is usually not easy to modify such a child's academic failure and behavior problems.

Following are some recommendations for psychologists when every intervention that they have tried has failed to result in modification of an African American child's academic failure and behavior problems.

1. It is recommended that a psychologist who is having difficulty facilitating modification of academic and behavior problems of an African American child consult with other psychologists about these problems, including one or more psychologists who are African American and culturally and socioeconomically sensitive.

2. The psychologist should also further assess the factors causing the academic and behavior problems of the child. When interventions to modify these problems are not working, it often means that what is being targeted by the intervention is not central in the occurrence of the problems. Further assessment such as home observations, school observations, neuropsychological evaluations, and more in-depth interviews of the child and family members may be helpful. The assessment process cannot be done quickly because it often takes time to build the trust of an African American child and family to the degree that they will give the personal information needed to come up with more effective intervention strategies to modify a child's academic failure and behavior problems.

3. It is recommended that the psychologist working with an African American child identify services and resources in the child's community (e.g., after-school tutoring and adaptive skills training programs, a big sisters and big brothers program, and a church-based mentoring program for African American youth) that might facilitate modification of the problems that the child is manifesting. Furthermore, the psychologist will likely need to assist with paperwork and arranging transportation and social services assistance necessary for the child and the child's parents to utilize these services and resources. Indeed, these are new roles for psychologists, but they are now being recognized as needed roles in order for many low-income African American children and their families to get needed help for academic and behavior problems and other problems.

4. Psychologists like teachers often experience feelings of failure when they are not successful in modifying academic and behavior problems of their clients. The problems become challenges rather than evidence of failure when psychologists have their feelings normalized by talking with colleagues about their perceived failure in modifying the academic and behavior problems of an African American child. Such talks are thus highly recommended.

Because psychologists typically spend most of their work time seeing clients for which they are paid, it is difficult for them to simply take time to consult with colleagues about their feelings. Yet, such time can extinguish feelings of inadequacy by the psychologist and possibly generate new perspectives and intervention strategies for modifying the academic failure and behavior problems of an African American child client.

5. It is important for the psychologist to recognize and praise the intervention efforts of parents and teachers even when these efforts are not successful and may not be of the quality or consistency desired by the psychologist. In many instances the efforts of teachers and parents represent the best that they can do when considering the many demands on their time and all of the other children whose needs must be met. Any hopes of getting more help from parents and teachers will only come through acknowledging their many responsibilities and the intervention efforts that they have made. Criticizing them for not doing all that an intervention program with a child client requires of them will likely cause them to disengage from the intervention process.

6. It is important for the psychologist to avoid using the disadvantages in a child's life (e.g., poverty and absence of a father figure) as excuses for the failure of interventions used to modify the child's academic failure and behavior problems. Furthermore, when parents and teachers of the child are disappointed with the continuation of these problems even with psychological intervention, it is not the time to give excuses but rather it is time to work even more closely with parents and teachers to come up with a plan to address the academic and behavior problems that the child continues to manifest.

7. It is important for a psychologist to avoid using psychological labels or diagnoses to conveniently describe the behaviors of an African American child given that these labels are often inappropriate when consideration is given to the cultural and socioeconomic factors in the behaviors. Because psychological reports on a referred child that are paid for by the school tend to remain in the referred child's school file and tend to be read by various individuals (e.g., future teachers of the child), these reports can set up negative expectations of the child that become self-fulfilling prophecies. It is especially important that psychological reports include the child's strengths and those of the child's family and emphasize the type of teaching and behavior management strategies that might be effective in facilitating the child's academic and social success.

Conclusions

When African American children and adolescents experience academic failure and behavior problems, all children in their classrooms and all other Americans are negatively impacted. It is not unusual for the parents, teachers, and psychologists who are often directly involved in trying to help modify the academic and behavior problems of African American children to fail in their efforts. This is often because of the multiple external factors in these problems that are beyond the control of parents, teachers, psychologists, and the children themselves.

It is common for parents, teachers, and psychologists to have a range of negative emotional reactions to their failure to bring about positive behavior changes in the academic achievement and behavior problems of African American children. These reactions include feelings of inadequacy, frustration, anger, and hopelessness. Blaming themselves or others also often occurs when academic and behavior problems persist despite efforts to address these problems. These reactions, though normal and understandable, do nothing to facilitate the academic and social success of the children who are manifesting academic and behavior problems.

There is no easy solution to the problem of what to do when seemingly all efforts to modify the academic failure and behavior problems of an African American child have failed. A group of African American parents and teachers interviewed to assess their views regarding such a situation evidenced much agreement that those involved must not give up on the child or ridicule the child. There was also much agreement among the interviewees that parents and teachers of the child should communicate among themselves and get outside help in continued efforts to address academic and behavior problems that seem to be resistant to change.

Parents, teachers, and the psychologist or counselor involved in trying to address persistent academic failure and behavior problems of an African American child must realize that there is no "quick fix" for these problems. They also must recognize and support the efforts of each other toward successfully modifying these problems. When the interventions continue to fail, then further assessment is indicated to identify the underlying factors in the child's academic and social behavior. Active involvement of the child and the child's parents in this assessment process and in planning interventions to address the child's problems is important.

Obtaining helpful information from the child and the child's parents for modifying the child's academic and behavior problems will require taking time to build trusting relationships with them and utilizing culturally sensitive assessors and assessment methods. Conclusions about the child's academic and behavior problems nee]d to emphasize the strengths of the child and the child's family and implications of the assessments conducted for additional interventions to address the child's academic and behavior problems. Psychological labels and diagnoses should be avoided in these reports as these labels are often inappropriate when cultural and socioeconomic factors are considered. Furthermore, such labels and diagnoses often become known by the child's future teachers and serve only to lower their expectations of the child—expectations that often become self-fulfilling prophecies.

Parents, teachers, and psychologists must also take care of themselves in the intervention process; that is, they should seek help from friends and colleagues to deal with their own negative emotional reactions to having their efforts fail to modify the academic failure and behavior problems of a child. Such reactions impede the thinking and energy needed to come up with new intervention strategies to address these problems. Furthermore, these reactions make their lives more stressful and, thus, unpleasant and impede their effectiveness with the other children in their lives.

Parents, teachers, and psychologists must support each other in the intervention planning and implementation process, recognizing and praising each other's efforts whether or not these efforts meet one another's expectations. Such mutual support serves to motivate and energize new intervention efforts by parents, teachers, and the psychologists involved.

Given that parents, teachers, school administrators, and psychologists often cannot meet the academic and social needs of many African American children so that they can become academically and socially successful, it is important that these adults identify and utilize resources and services in the community (e.g., after-school educational programs and mentoring programs) that can assist with meeting these needs. There is a growing realization that interventions to facilitate the academic and social success of many African American children will require the involvement of individuals and groups throughout their communities. There is also the growing recognition that when African American children experience academic and social success, all Americans are positively impacted.

It is indeed true that the modification of academic failure and behavior problems of some African American children will involve much time, effort, energy, and heart. No, modification of these problems is not easy. However, "anything worth doing ain't easy!"

REFERENCES

Achenbach, T. M. (1978). The child behavior profile: I. Boys aged 6–11. *Journal of Consulting and Clinical Psychology, 46,* 478–488.

Achenbach, T. M. (1993). *Empirically based taxonomy: How to use syndromes and profile types derived from the CBCL/4–18, TRF, and YSR.* Burlington, VT: University of Vermont Department of Pyschiatry.

Achenbach, T. M., & Edelbrock, C. S. (1981). Behavioral problems and competencies reported by parents of normal and disturbed children aged four through sixteen. *Monographs of the Society for Research in Child Development, 46,* 82.

Achenbach, T. M., & Edelbrock, C. S. (1983). *Manual for the child behavior checklist and revised child behavior profile.* Burlington: University of Vermont.

Allen, L., & Majidi-Ahi, S. (1989). Black American children. In J. T. Gibbs, L. N. Huang, & Associates, (Eds.) *Children of color: Psychological interventions with minority youth* (pp. 148–178). San Francisco, CA: Jossey-Bass.

American Psychiatric Association. (1994). *Diagnostic and statistical manual of mental disorders,* (4th ed.). Washington, DC: American Psychiatric Association.

Arthur, G. (1952). *The Arthur adaption of the Leiter International Performance Scale.* Los Angeles: Western Psychological Services.

Asante, M. (1991). *Afrocentricity.* Trenton, NJ: African World Press.

Asante, M. K. (1991, September 3). Putting Africa at the center. *Newsweek,* 446.

Ascher, C. (1988). Improving the school-home connection for poor and minority urban students. *Urban Review, 20,* 109–123.

Ascher, C. (1992). School programs for African American males...and females. *Phi Delta Kappan,* 777–782.

Ashton, P. T., & Webb, R. B. (1986). *Making a difference: Teachers' sense of efficacy and student achievement.* White Plains, NY: Longman.

Atkinson, L., Scott, B., Chrisholm, V., Blackwell, J., Dickens, S., Tam, F., & Goldberg, S. (1995). Cognitive coping, affective distress, and maternal sensitivity: Mothers of children with Down Syndrome. *Developmental Psychology, 31,* 668–676.

Avery, R. D., & Ivancenvic, J. M. (1980). Punishment in organizations: A review, propositions, and research suggestions. *Academy of Management Review, 5,* 123–132.

Bandura, A. (1977). *Social learning theory.* Englewood Cliffs, NJ: Prentice-Hall.

Bandura, A. (1986). Fearful expectations and avoidant actions as coeffects of perceived self-inefficacy. *American Psychologist, 41*(12), 1389–1391.

Bandura, A. (1993). Perceived self-efficacy in cognitive development and functioning. *Educational Psychologist, 28*(2), 117–148.

Barbarin, O. (1993). Emotional and social development of African American chidren. *Journal of Black Psychology, 19*(4), 381–390.

Barkley, R. A. (1990). *Attention-deficit hyperactivity disorder.* New York: Guilford.

Barkley, R. A., Anastopoulos, A. D., Guevremont, D. C., & Fletcher, K. E. (1992). Adolescents with attention deficit hyperactivity disorder: Mother-adolescent interactions, family beliefs and conflicts, and maternal psychopathology. *Journal of Abnormal Child Psychology, 20*(3), 263–288.

Baumiester, A. A., (1987). Mental retardation: Some conceptions and dilemmas. *American Psychologist, 42,* 796–800.

Beck, A. T. (1967). *Depression: Clinical, experimental, and theoretical aspects.* New York: Harper & Row.

Beck, A. T. (1976). *Cognitive theory and emotional disorders.* New York: International Universities Press.

Berger, M., & Yule, W. (1985). IQ tests and assessment. In A. M. Clarke, A. D. B. Clarke, & J. M. Berg (Eds.), *Mental deficiency. The changing outlook.* New York: The Free Press.

Bergin, D. A., Hudson, L. M., Chryst, C. F., & Reseter, M. (1992). An afterschool intervention program for educationally disadvantaged young children. *The Urban Review, 24*(3), 203–217.

Biederman, J. (1991). Psychopharmacology. In J. Wiener (Ed.), *Textbook of child and adolescent psychiatry.* Washington, DC: American Psychiatric Association.

Bishop, D. V. M. (1992). The underlying nature of specific language impairment. *Journal of Child Psychology and Psychiatry, 33,* 3–66.

Boggiano, A. K., & Katz, P. (1991). Maladaptive achievement patterns in students: The role of teachers' controlling strategies. *Journal of Social Issues, 47*(4), 35–51.

Bond, H. M. (1972). *Black American scholars: A study of their beginnings.* Detroit, MI: Balamp.

Bonwell, C., & Eison, J. A. (1991). *Active learning: Creating excitement in the classroom: ASHE-ERIC Higher Education Report No. 1.* Washington, DC: The George Washington University School of Education and Human Development.

Borduin, C. M. (1994). Innovative models of treatment and service delivery in the juvenile justice system. *Journal of Clinical Child Psychology, 23,* 19–25.

Boyd-Franklin, N. (1989). *Black families in therapy: A multisystems approach.* New York: Guilford.

Boykin, A. W. (1982). Task variability and the performance of Black and White school children: Vervistic explorations. *Journal of Black Studies, 12,* 469–485.

Boykin, A. W. (1983). The academic performance of Afro-American children. In J. Spence (Ed.), *Achievement and achievement motives.* San Francisco: Freeman.

Brady, B. A., Tucker, C. M., Harris, Y. R., & Tribble, I. (1992). Association of academic achievement with behavior among Black students and White students. *Journal of Educational Research, 86*(1), 43–51.

Bregman, J. D., & Hodapp, R. M. (1991). Current developments in the understanding of mental retardation: Part I. Biological and phenomenological perspectives. *Journal of the American Academy of Child and Adolescent Psychiatry, 30,* 707–719.

Bronfenbrenner, U. (1979). *The ecology of human development: Experiments by nature and design.* Cambridge, MA: Harvard University Press.

Brunswick, A., & Messeri, P. (1986). Drugs, life style and health. *American Journal of Public Health, 76,* 52–57.

Bynum, A. S. (1991). *Black student/white counselor: Developing effective relationships,* (Expanded second edition). Indianapolis, IN: Alexandria Books.

Byrnes, D. A., Shuster, T., & Jones, M. (1994). Parent and student views of multiage classrooms. *Journal of Research in Childhood Education, 9*(1), 15–23.

Camp, B. W. (1977). Verbal mediation in young aggressive boys. *Journal of Abnormal Psychology, 86*(2), 145–153.

Campbell, M., & Cueva, J. E. (1995). Psychopharmacology in child and adolescent psychiatry: A review of the past seven years. Part I. *Journal of the American Academy of Child and Adolescent Psychiatry, 34,* 1124–1132.

Campbell, S. B. (1995). Behavior problems in preschool children: A review of recent research. *Journal of Child Psychology and Psychiatry, 36,* 113–149.

Carrier, C. A., & Titus, A. (1979). The effects of notetaking: A review of studies. *Contemporary Educational Psychology, 4,* 299–314.

Carter, L. (1984). The sustaining effects study of compensatory and elementary education. *Educational Researcher, 13*(7), 4–13.

Cauce, A. (1986). Social networks and social competence: Exploring the effects of early adolescent friendships. *American Journal of Community Psychology, 14,* 607–628.

Cautela, J. R. (1967). Covert sensitization. *Psychological Reports, 20*(2), 459–468.

Centers for Disease Control (1995). Suicide among children, adolescents, and young adults—United States, 1980–1992. *Morbidity and Mortality Weekly Report, 44,* 289–291.

Cheek, D. (1976). *Assertive black, puzzled white.* San Luis Obispo, CA: Impact Publishers.

Children's Defense Fund (1987). *A children's defense budget.* Washington, DC: Children's Defense Fund.

Chimezie, A. (1988). Black children's characteristics and the school: A selective adaptation approach. *The Western Journal of Black Studies, 12,* 77–85.

Chinn, P. C., & Hughes, S. (1987). Representation of minority students in special education classes. *Remedial and Special Education, 8,* 41–46.

Chwalisz, K. D., Altmaier, E. M., & Russell, D. W. (1992). Causal attributions, self-efficacy cognitions, and coping with stress. *Journal of Social and Clinical Psychology, 11,* 377–400.

Clark, D. B., Smith, M. G., Neighbors, B. D., Skerlec, L. M., & Randall, J. (1994). Anxiety disorders in adolescence: Characteristics, prevalence, and comorbidities. *Clinical Psychology Review, 14,* 113–137.

Clark, R. (1983). Family life and school achievement: Why poor Black children succeed or fail. Chicago: University of Chicago Press.

Cohen, R. (1969). Conceptual styles, culture conflict and nonverbal tests of intelligence. *American Anthropologist, 71,* 828–856.

Cohen, P., Cohen, J., Kasen, S., Velez, C. N., Hartmark, C., Johnson, J., Rojas, M., Brook, J., & Streuning, E. L. (1993). An epidemiological study of disorders in late childhood and adolescence: Age and gender-specific prevalence. *Journal of Child Psychology and Psychiatry, 34,* 851–867.

Coie, J. D., Dodge, K. A., & Coppotelli, H. (1982). Dimensions and types of social status: A cross-age perspective. *Developmental Psychology, 18*(4), 557–570.

Coles, G. S. (1987). *The learning mystique.* New York: Pantheon.

Comer, J., & Hill, H. (1985). Social policy and the mental health of Black children. *Journal of the American Academy of Child Psychiatry, 24*(2), 175–181.

Connell, J. (1991). Context, self, and action: A motivational analysis of self-system processes across the life span. In D. Cicchetti & M. Beeghly (Eds.), *The self in transition: Infancy to childhood* (pp. 61–97). Chicago: University of Chicago Press.

Connell, J., Halpern-Felsher, B. L., Clifford, E., Crichlow, W., & Usinder, P. (1995). Hanging in there: Behavioral, psychological, and contextual factors affecting whether African-American adolescents stay in school. *Journal of Adolescent Research, 10,* 41–63.

Connell, J. P., Spencer, M. B., & Aber, J. L. (1994). Educational risk and resilience in African American youth: Context, self, action, and outcomes in school. [Special issue: Children and Poverty]. *Child Development, 65*(2), 493–506.

Connell, J., & Wellborn, J. (1991). Competence, autonomy, and relatedness: A motivational analysis of self-system processes. In M. Gunnar & A. Sroufe (Eds.), *Minnesota symposium on child psychology, 23.* Hillsdale, NJ: Erlbaum.

Cooper, H. M. (1979). Pygmalion grows up: A model for teacher expectation communication and performance influence. *Review of Educational Research, 49,* 389–410.

Corder, L. J., & Quisenberry, N. L. (1987). Early education and Afro-Americans: History, assumptions and implications for the future. *Childhood Education, 63,* 154–158.

Craig, M. A., Cauce, A. M., Gonzales, N., & Hiraga, Y. (1994). An ecological model of externalizing behaviors in African American adolescents: No family is an island. *Journal of Research on Adolescence, 4*(4), 639–655.

Crnic, K. A. (1988). Mental retardation. In E. J. Mash & L. G. Terdal (Eds.), *Behavioral assessment of childhood disorders: Selected core problems.* New York: Guilford.

Cushner, K., McClelland, A., & Safford, P. (1992). *Human diversity in education: An integrative approach.* New York: McGraw-Hill, Inc.

Dancy, B., & Handal, P. (1984). Perceived family climate, psychological adjustment and peer relationships of Black adolescents: A function of parental marital status or perceived family conflict? *Journal of Community Psychology, 12,* 222–229.

Danforth, J. S., & Drabman, R. S. (1990). Community living skills. In A. M. LaGreca, L. J. Siegel, J. L. Wallander, & C. E. Walker (Eds.), *Stress and coping with child health.* New York: Guilford.

Delgado-Gaitan, C. (1992). School matters in the Mexican-American home. *American Educational Research Journal, 29,* 495–513.

DeRosier, M. E., Cillessen, A., Coie, J. D., & Dodge, K. A. (1994). Group social context and children's aggressive behavior. *Child Development, 65*(4), 1068–1079.

DeStefano, L., & Thompson, D. S. (1990). Adaptive behavior: The construct and its measurement. In C. R. Reynolds & R. W. Kamphaus (Eds.), *Handbook of psychological and educational assessment of children: Personality, behavior, and context.* New York: Guilford.

Dillon, D. (1994). Understanding and assessment of intragroup dynamics in family foster care: African American families. *Child Welfare, 73,* 129–139.

Dornbusch, S. M., Ritter, P. L., & Steinberg, L. (1991). Community influences on the relation of family statuses to adolescent school performance: Differences between African Americans and Non-Hispanic whites. *American Journal of Educational Research, 99,* 543–567.

Drabman, R., & Spitalnik, R. (1973). Social isolation as a punishment procedure: A controlled study. *Journal of Experimental Child Psychology, 16,* 236–249.

Dunn, C. W., & Tucker, C. M. (1993). Black children's adaptive functioning and maladaptive behavior associated with quality of family support. *Journal of Multicultural Counseling and Development, 21,* 79–87.

Dunn, L. M., & Dunn, L. M. (1981). *Peabody Picture Vocabulary Test: Revised.* Circle Pines, MN: American Guidance Service.

DuPaul, G. J., & Barkley, R. A. (1993). Behavioral contributions to pharmacotherapy: The utility of behavioral methodology in medical treatment of children with attention deficit hyperactivity disorder. *Behavior Therapy, 24,* 47–65.

DuPaul, G. J., Guevrement, D.C., & Barkley, R. A. (1991). Attention-deficit hyperactivity disorder. In T. R. Kratochwill & R. J. Morris (Eds.), *The practice of child therapy.* Boston: Allyn & Bacon.

Earls, F. (1994). Oppositional-defiant and conduct disorders. In M. Rutter, E. Taylor, & L. Hersov (Eds.), *Child and adolescent psychiatry: Modern approaches* (3rd ed.). London: Blackwell Scientific Publishers.

Eaves, R. C. (1975). Teacher race, student race, and the behavior problem checklist. *Journal of Abnormal Psychology, 46,* 23–24.

Eccles, J. (1983). Expectancies, values, and academic behaviors. In J. T. Spence (Ed.), *Perspective on achievement and achievement motivation* (pp. 75–146). San Francisco: Freeman.

Edelbrock, C., Costello, A. J., Dulcan, M. K., Kalas, R., & Conover, N. C. (1985). Age differences in the reliability of the psychiatric interview of the child. *Child Development, 56,* 265–275.

Edgar, R., & Clement, P. (1980). Teacher-controlled and self-controlled reinforcement with underachieving Black children. *Child Behavior Therapy, 2*(4), 33–56.

Educational Research Services (1991). Educating a culturally diverse population: Teaching methods and the learning process. Arlington, VA: Author.

Eisenberg, L. (1966). The epidemiology of reading retardation and a program for preventive intervention. In J. Money (Ed.), *The disabled reader* (pp. 1–19). Baltimore: Johns Hopkins University Press.

Eisenman, R. (1991a). *From crime to creativity: Psychological and social factors in deviance.* Dubuque, IA: Kendall/Hunt.

Eisenman, R. (1991b). Successful coaching of black students on college exam questions. *Education, 112,* 155–156.

Erickson, M. T. (1992). *Behavior disorders of children and adolescents* (2nd ed.). Englewood Cliffs, NJ: Prentice Hall.

Fantuzzo, J. W., Davis, G. Y., & Ginsberg, M. D. (1995). Effects of parent involvement in isolation or in combination with peer tutoring on student self-concept and mathematics achievement. *Journal of Educational Psychology, 87,* 272–281.

Farnworth, M., Schweinhart, L. J., & Berrueta-Clement, J. R. (1985). Preschool intervention, school success and delinquency in a high-risk sample of youth. *American Educational Research Journal, 22*(3), 445–464.

Faulstitch, M. E., Moore, J. R., Roberts, R. W., & Collier, J. B. (1988). A behavioral perspective on conduct disorders. *Psychiatry, 51,* 398–413.

Felner, R. D., Abner, M. S., Primavera, J., & Cauce, A. M. (1985). Adaptation and vulnerability in high-risk adolescents: An examination of environmental mediators. *American Journal of Community Psychology, 13,* 365–379.

Ferster, C. B. (1974). Behavioral approaches to depression. In R. J. Friedman & M. M. Katz (Eds.), *The psychology of depression: Contemporary theory and research.* Washington, DC: Winston.

Finn, J. (1989). Withdrawing from school. *Review of Educational Research, 59,* 117–142.

Fisher, T. A. (1988). *Academic achievement motivation of Black adolescents.* Dissertation Abstracts International, 50,02A. University of Illinois.

Flaugher, R. L. (1978). The many definitions of test bias. *American Psychologist, 33,* 671–679.

Flynt, S. W.,Wood, T. A., & Scott, R. L. (1994). Social support of mothers of children with mental retardation. *Mental Retardation, 30,* 233–236.

Ford, D. Y. (1992). Determinants of underachievement as perceived by gifted, above-average, and average black students. *Roeper Review, 14*(3), 130–136.

Ford, D. (1993). Black students' achievement orientation as a function of perceived family achievement orientation and demographic variables. *Journal of Negro Education, 62* (1), 47–66.

Ford, D. Y. (1994). Nursing resilience in gifted Black youth. *Roeper Review, 17* (2), 80–85.

Fordham, S. (1985). *Black student school success as related to fictive kinship. Final Report.* Washington, DC: The National Institute of Education.

Fordham, S., & Ogbu, J. (1986). Black students' school success: Coping with the "burden of 'acting white.'" *The Urban Review, 18,* 176–206.

Forehand, R., & McMahon, R. J. (1981). *Helping the non-compliant child: A clinician's guide to parent training.* New York: Guilford.

Forgatch, M. S., & Stoolmiller, M. (1994). Emotions as contexts for adolescent delinquency [Special issue: Affective processes in adolescence]. *Journal of Research on Adolescence, 4,* 601–614.

Foxx, R. M., & Azrin, N. H. (1972). Restitution: A method of eliminating aggressive-disruptive behavior of retarded and brain damaged patients. *Behaviour Research and Therapy, 10,* 15–27.

Franklin, A. J. (1982). Therapeutic interventions with urban black adolescents. In E. E. Jones & S. J. Korchin (Eds.), *Minority mental health.* New York: Praeger.

Freedman, B. J. (1974). An analysis of social-behavioral skills deficits in delinquent and nondelinquent adolescent boys. Unpublished doctoral dissertation, University of Wisconsin, Madison.

French, A. P. (1977). *Disturbed children and their families: Innovations in evaluation and treatment.* New York: Human Sciences Press.

Frisby, C. L. (1992). Parent education as a means for improving the school achievement of low-income African-American children. In S. L. Christenson & J. C. Conoley (Eds.), *Home school collaboration: Enhancing children's academic and social confidence* (pp. 127–153). Silver Spring, MD: National Association of School Psychologists.

Frisby, C. L., & Tucker, C. M. (1993). Black children's perception of self: Implications for educators. *The Educational Forum, 57,* 146–156.

Gadow, K. D., & Pomeroy, J. C. (1991). An overview of psychopharmacotherapy for children and adolescents. In T. R. Kratochwill & R. J. Morris (Eds.), *The practice of child therapy.* Boston: Allyn & Bacon.

Garbarino, J. (1982). Who owns the children? An ecological perspective on public policy affecting children. *Child and Youth Services, 5,* 43–63.

Gardner, E. F., Rudman, H. C., Kurlsen, B., & Merwin, J. C. (1982). *Stanford Achievement Test.* San Antonio, TX: The Psychological Corporation.

Garibaldi, A. M. (1992). Educating and motivating African American males to succeed. *Journal of Negro Education, 61*(1), 4–11.

Gary, L., Beatty, L., & West, J. (1982). *The delivery of mental health services to Black children.* Washington, DC: Mental Health Research and Development Center, Institute for Urban Affairs and Research, Howard University.

Gary, L. E., & Booker, C. B. (1992). Empowering African Americans to achieve academic success. *NASSP Bulletin* [October—Urban Education].

Gaskin-Butler, V. T., & Tucker, C. M. (1995). Self-esteem, academic achievement, and adaptive behavior in African American children. *The Educational Forum, 59,* 234–243.

Gibbs, J. T. (1981). Depression and suicidal behavior among delinquent females: Ethnic and socio-cultural variations. *Journal of Youth and Adolescence, 2,* 159–167.

Gibbs, J. T. (1982). Personality patterns of delinquent females: Ethnic and sociocultural variations. *Journal of Clinical Psychology, 38,* 198–206.

Gibbs, J. T. (1985). Treatment relationships with Black clients: Interpersonal versus instrumental strategies. In C. Germain (Ed.), *Advances in clinical social work practice.* Silver Spring, MD: National Association of Social Workers.

Gibbs, J. T. (1988). Conceptual, methodological, and sociocultural issues in Black youth suicide: Implications for assessment and early intervention. *Suicide & Life-Threatening Behavior, 18*(1), 73–89.

Gibbs, J. T., & Moskowitz-Sweet, C. (1986). *Clinical and cultural issues in the treatment of biracial and bicultural adolescents.* Paper presented at the National Association of Social Workers Conference, San Francisco.

Gibson, S., & Dembo, M. H. (1984). Teacher efficacy: A construct validation. *Journal of Educational Psychology, 76,* 569–582.

Gillis, J. J., Gilger, J. W., Pennington, B. T., & Defries, J. C. (1992). Attention deficit disorder in reading disabled twins: Evidence for genetic etiology. *Journal of Abnormal Child Psychology, 20,* 305–315.

Gillum, R., Gomez-Marin, O., & Prineas, R. (1984). Racial differences in personality, behavior, and family environment in Minneapolis school children. *Journal of the National Medical Association, 76*(11), 1097–1105.

Glassford, D., Ivanoff, J., Sinsky, A., & Pierce, W. (1991). Student generated solutions to the alcohol/drug problem: A Wisconsin profile. *Journal of Alcohol and Drug Education, 37*(1), 65–71.

Golombok, S., Spencer, A., & Rutter, M. (1983). Children in lesbian and single-parent households: Psychosexual and psychiatric appraisal. *Journal of Child Psychology and Psychiatry and Allied Disciplines, 24,* 551–572.

Good, T. L., & Brophy, J. E. (1986). School effects. In M. C. Wittrock (Ed.), *Handbook of research on teaching,* (3rd ed.). (pp. 570–602). New York: Macmillan.

Goodenow, C., & Grady, K. E. (1994). The relationship of school belonging and friends' values to academic motivation among urban adolescent students. *Journal of Experimental Education, 62*(1), 60–71.

Gotts, E., & Purnell, R. (1987). Practicing school-family relations in urban settings. *Education and Urban Society, 19*(2), 212–218.

Gould, M., Wunsch-Hitzig, R., & Dohrwend, B. S. (1981). Estimating the prevalence of childhood psychopathology. *Journal of the American Academy of Child Psychiatry, 20,* 462–476.

Graham, S., Hudley, C., & Williams, E. (1992). Attributional and emotional determinants of aggression among African American and Latino young adolescents. *Developmental Psychology, 28*(4), 731–740.

Grasha, A. F. (1995). *Practical applications of psychology,* (4th ed.). New York: Harper-Collins College Publishers.

Gresham, F. M., & Elliott, S. N. (1989). Social skills deficits as a primary learning disability. *Journal of Learning Disabilities, 22,* 120–124.

Guttentag, M. (1972). Negro-white differences in children's movement. *Perceptual and Motor Skills, 35,* 435–436.

Hale-Benson, J. E. (1986). *Black children: Their roots, culture, and learning styles.* Baltimore, MD: Johns Hopkins University Press.

Hall, L. E., & Tucker, C. M. (1985). Relationships between ethnicity, conceptions of mental illness, and attitudes associated with seeking psychological help. *Psychological Reports, 57,* 907–916.

Hall, V. C., Howe, A., Merkel, A., & Lederman, N. (1986). Behavior, motivation, and achievement in desegregated junior high school classes. *Journal of Educational Psychology, 78*(2), 108–115.

Hamblin, R. L., Hathaway, C., & Wodarski, J. (1974). Group contingencies, peer tutoring, and accelerating academic achievement. In R. Ulrich, T. Stachnik, & J. Mabry (Eds.), *Control of human behavior, 3.* Glenview, IL: Scott, Foresman.

Hammill, D. D. (1993). A brief look at the learning disabilities movement in the United States. *Journal of Learning Disabilities, 26,* 295–310.

Hammond, J. M. (1979). Children of divorce: A study of self-concept, academic achievement, and attitudes. *Elementary School Journal, 80,* 55–62.

Hare, B. R. (1988). Black youth at risk. In J. D. Williams (Ed.), *The state of Black America 1988.* New York: National Urban League.

Harrison, A. O., Wilson, M. N., Pine, C. J., & Chan, S. Q. (1990). Family ecologies of ethnic minority children. *Child Development, 61,* 347–362.

Hart, B., & Risley, T. R. (1992). American parenting of language-learning children: Persisting differences in family-child interactions observed in natural home environment. *Developmental Psychology, 28,* 1096–1105.

Hart, T. (1988). *Involving parents in the education of their children.* Eugene, OR: Oregon School Study Council (ERIC Document Reproduction Service No. 300 930).

Harvey, M. R. (1980). Public school treatment of low income children: Education for passivity. *Urban Education, 15,* 279–323.

Hechtman, L. (1991). Resilience and vulnerability in long-term outcome of attention deficit hyperactivity disorder. *Canadian Journal of Psychiatry, 36*(6), 415–421.

Helms, J. E. (1992). Why is there no study of cultural equivalence in standardized cognitive ability testing? *American Psychologist, 47,* 1083–1101.

Henggeler, S. W., & Borduin, C. M. (1990). A multisystemic approach to the treatment of serious delinquent behavior. In R. J. McMahon & R. D. Peters (Eds.), *Behavior disorders of adolescence: Research, intervention, and policy in clinical and school settings* (pp. 63–80). New York: Plenum Press.

Herman, K. (1997). *Engaging Latino-American students in school: Evaluating a causal model for understanding and predicting academic achievement.* Unpublished doctoral dissertation, University of Florida, Gainesville.

Hieronymus, A. N., & Hoover, H. D. (1985). *Iowa tests of basic skills,* forms G and H. Chicago: Riverside.

Hill, R. (1972). *The strengths of Black families.* New York: Emerson Hall.

Hilliard, A. (1976). *Alternatives to IQ testing: An approach to the identification of gifted minority children.* Final report to the California State Department of Education.

Hilliard, A. G. (1979). Standardization and cultural bias as impediments to the scientific study and validation of "intelligence." *Journal of Research and Development in Education, 12*(2), 47–58.

Hinshaw, S. P., & Erhardt, D. (1993). Behavioral treatment. In V. B. VanHasselt & M. Hersen (Eds.), *Handbook of behavior therapy and pharmacology for children: A comparative analysis.* Boston: Allyn & Bacon.

Hinshaw, S. P., Lahey, B. B., & Hart, E. L. (1993). Issues of taxonomy and comorbidity in the development of conduct disorder. *Development and Psychopathology, 5,* 31–49.

Hirschfeld, D. R., Rosenbaum, J. F., Biederman, J., Bloduc, E. A., Farone, S. V., Snidman, N., Reznick, J. S., & Kagan, J. (1992). Stable behavioral inhibition and its association with anxiety disorder. *Journal of the American Academy of Child and Adolescent Psychiatry, 31,* 103–111.

Hoover-Dempsey, K. V., Bassler, O. C., & Brissie, J. S. (1987). Parent involvement: Contributions of teacher efficacy, school socioeconomic status, and other school characteristics. *American Educational Research Journal, 24,* 417–435.

Howlin, P. (1994). Special education treatment. In M. Rutter, E. Taylor, & L. Hersov (Eds.), *Child and adolescent psychiatry: Modern approaches.* Cambridge, MA: Blackwell Scientific.

Hughes, C. A., & Smith, J. O. (1990). Cognitive academic performance of college students with learning disabilities: A synthesis of the literature. *Learning Disabilities Quarterly, 13,* 66–79.

Huizinga, D., Loeber, R., & Thornberry, T. P. (1993). *Public Health Reports, 108* (Supp 1), 90–96.

Hundleby, J. D., Carpenter, R. A., Ross, R., & Mercer, G. W. (1982). Adolescent drug use and other behaviors. *Journal of Child Psychology and Psychiatry, 23,* 61–68.

Hynd, G. W., Snow, J., & Becker, M. G. (1986). Neuropsychological assessment in clinical child psychology. In B. B. Lahey & A. E. Kazdin (Eds.), *Advances in clinical child psychology,* vol 9. New York: Plenum.

Jastak, S., & Wilkinson, G. S. (1984). *Wide range achievement test—revised.* Wilmington, DE: Jastak Associates.

Jencks, C., Smith, M., Acland, H., Bane, M. I., Cohen, D., Gintis, H., Heyns, B., & Michels, S. (1972). *Inequality: A reassessment of the effect of family and schooling in America.* New York: Basic Books.

Johnson, D. N., Johnson, R., Tiffany, M., & Zaidman, B. (1983). Are low achievers disliked in a cooperative situation? A test of rival theories in a mixed ethnic situation. *Contemporary Educational Psychology, 8,* 182–200.

Johnston, H. F., & Fruehling, J. J. (1994). Pharmacotherapy for depression in children and adolescents. In W. M. Reynolds & H. F. Johnston (Eds.), *Handbook of depression in children and adolescents.* New York: Plenum Press.

Jones, R. L. (1980). *Black psychology* (2nd ed.). New York: Harper & Row.

Jordan, T. J. (1981). Self-concepts, motivation, and academic achievement of black adolescents. *Journal of Educational Psychology, 73,* 509–517.

Kagan, J., Reznick, J. S., & Snidman, N. (1990). The temperamental qualities of inhibition and lack of inhibition. In M. Lewis & S. M. Miller (Eds.), *Handbook of developmental psychopathology* (pp. 219–226). New York: Plenum Press.

Kalyanpur, M., & Rao, S. S. (1991). Empowering low income Black families of handicapped children. *American Journal of Orthopsychiatry, 61,* 523–532.

Kamin, L. J. (1974). *The science and politics of IQ.* Potomac, MD: Erlbaum.

Kamphaus, R. W. (1993). *Clinical assessment of children's intelligence.* Boston: Allyn & Bacon.

Kandel, D. B., & Logan, J. A. (1984). Patterns of drug use from adolescence to young adulthood: I. Periods of risk for initiation, continued use, and discontinuation. *American Journal of Public Health, 74,* 660–666.

Kandel, D., & Yamaguchi, K. (1993). From beer to crack: Developmental patterns of drug involvement. *American Journal of Public Health, 83,* 851–855.

Kanfer, R. (1990). Motivation and individual differences in learning: An integration of developmental, differential and cognitive perspectives. *Learning and Individual Differences, 2,* 221–239.

Kantor, G. K., Caudill, B. D., & Ungerleider, S. (1992). Project Impact: Teaching the teachers to intervene in student substance abuse problems. *Journal of Alcohol and Drug Education, 38,* 11–29.

Kaplan, H. B., Martin, S. S., & Johnson, R. J. (1986). Self-rejection and the explanation of deviance: Specification of the structure among latent constructs. *American Journal of Sociology, 92,* 384–411.

Kaplan, R. M. (1985). The controversy related to the use of psychological tests. In B. Wolman (Ed.), *Handbook of intelligence.* New York: Wiley.

Kaplan, S. L., Landa, B., Weinhold, C., & Shenker, I. R. (1984). Adverse health behaviors and depressive symptomatology in adolescents. *Journal of the American Academy of Child Psychiatry, 23*(5), 595–601.

Kaufman, A. S., & Kaufman, N. L. (1983). *Administration and scoring manual for the Kaufman Assessment battery for Children.* Circle Pines, MN: American Guidance Service.

Kaufman, A. S., Swan, W. W., & Wood, M. M. (1980). Do parents, teachers, and psychoeducational evaluators agree in their perceptions of the problems of black and white emotionally disturbed children? *Psychology in the Schools, 17,* 185–191.

Kaufman, J. M., Lloyd, J. W., & McGee, K. A. (1989). Adaptive and maladaptive behavior: Teachers' attitudes and their technical assistance needs. *Journal of Special Education, 23,* 185–200.

Kazdin, A. E. (1972). Response cost: The removal of conditioned reinforcers for therapeutic change. *Behaviour Therapy, 3,* 533–546.

Kazdin, A. E., Siegel, T. C., & Bass, D. (1992). Cognitive problem-solving skills training and parent management training in the treatment of antisocial behavior in children. *Journal of Consulting and Clinical Psychology, 60,* 733–747.

Kellam, S. G., & Brown, H. (1982). *Social adaptational and psychological antecedents of adolescent psychopathology ten years later.* Baltimore, MD: Johns Hopkins University.

Keller, M. B., Lavori, P. W., Wunder, J., Beardslee, W. R., Schwartz, C. E., & Roth, J. (1992). Chronic course of anxiety disorders in children and adolescents. *Journal of the American Academy of Child and Adolescent Psychiatry, 31,* 595–599.

Kennedy, W. A. (1965). School phobia: Rapid treatment of 50 cases. *Journal of Abnormal Psychology, 70,* 285–289.

Kerckhoff, A. C., & Campbell, R. T. (1977). Black-White differences in the educational attainment process. *Sociology of Education, 50,* 15–27.

Kessler, J. W. (1980). History of minimal brain dysfunctions. In H. E. Rie & E. D. Rie (Eds.), *Handbook of minimal brain dysfunctions.* New York: John Wiley.

Kiewra, K. A., Dubois, N. E., Christian, D., & McShane, A. (1988). Providing study notes: Comparison of three types of notes for review. *Journal of Educational Psychology, 80,* 595–597.

King, N.J., Mietz, L. T., & Ollendick, T. H. (1995). Psychopathology and cognition in adolescents experiencing severe test anxiety. *Journal of Clinical Child Psychology, 24,* 49–54.

Kovacs, M. (1992). *Children's Depression Inventory.* North Tonawanda, NY: Multi-Health Systems.

Kovacs, M., Krol, R. S. M., & Voti, L. (1994). Early onset psychopathology and the risk for teenage pregnancy among clinically referred girls. *Journal of the American Academy of Child Adolescent Psychiatry, 33,* 106–113.

Kunjufu, J. (1984). *Developing positive self-images and discipline in black children.* Chicago: African-American Images.

Kurdek, L., & Sinclair, R. (1988). Relation of eighth grader's family structure, gender, and family environment with academic performance and school behavior. *Journal of Educational Psychology, 80,* 90–94.

Labov, W. (1972). *Language in the inner city.* Philadelphia: University of Pennsylvania Press.

Larue, A., & Majidi-Ahi, S. (1989). Black American children. In J. T. Gibbs, L. N. Huang, and Associates (Eds.), *Children of color: Psychological interventions with minority youth.* San Francisco, CA: Jossey-Bass.

Lee, C. C. (1982). The school counselor and the black child: Critical roles and functions. *Journal of Non-White Concerns in Personnel and Guidance, 10,* 94–101.

Lee, C. C. (1984). An investigation of psychosocial variables related to academic success for rural Black adolescents. *Journal of Negro Education, 53*(4), 424–434.

Lee, C. C., & Lindsey, C. R. (1985). Black consciousness development: A group counseling model for Black elementary school students. *Elementary School Guidance and Counseling, 19,* 228–236.

Leler, H. (1983). Parent education and involvement in relation to the schools and to parents of school-aged children. In I. R. Haskins & D. Adamson (Eds.), *Parent education and public policy.* Norwood, NJ: Ablex.

Lewinson, P. (1974). A behavioral approach to depression. In R. J. Friedman & M. M. Katz (Eds.), *The psychology of depression: Contemporary theory and research.* Washington, DC: Winston.

Licht, B. G., & Kistner, J. A. (1986). Motivational problems of learning-disabled children: Individual differences and their implication for treatment. In J. K. Torgensen & B. Y. L. Wong (Eds.), *Psychological and educational perspectives on learning disabilities.* New York: Academic Press.

Lochman, J. E., Nelson, W. M., III, & Sims, J. P. (1981). A cognitive behavioral program for use with aggressive children. *Journal of Clinical Child Psychology, 146–148.*

Lyles, M., Yancey, A., Grace, C., & Carter, J. H. (1985). Racial identity and self-esteem: Problems peculiar to bi-racial children. *Journal of the American Academy of Child Psychiatry, 24,* 150–154.

Lyon, G. R., & Moats, L. C. (1988). Critical issues in the instruction of the learning disabled. *Journal of Consulting and Clinical Psychology, 556,* 830–835.

Madsen, C. H., Becker, W. C., Thomas, D. R., Koser, L., & Plager, E. (1970). An analysis of the reinforcing function of "sit down" commands. In R. K. Parker (Ed.), *Readings in Educational Psychology.* Boston: Allyn & Bacon.

Maehr, M. L. (1976). Continuing motivation: An analysis of a seldom considered educational outcome. *Review of Educational Research, 46,* 443–462.

Mancini, J. K. (1980). *Strategic cycles: Coping in the inner city.* Hanover, NH: University Press of New England.

Margalit, M. (1989). Academic competence and social adjustment of boys with learning disabilities and boys with behavior disorders. *Journal of Learning Disabilities, 22,* 41–45.

Mason, C. A., Cauce, A. M., Gonzales, N., & Hiraga, Y. (1994). An ecological model of externalizing behaviors in African-American adolescents: No family is an island [Special Issue: Affective processes in adolescence]. *Journal of Research on Adolescence, 4*(4), 639–655.

Massey, G. C., Scott, M. V., & Dornbusch, S. M. (1975). Racism without racists. *Black Scholar,* 10–19.

Massimo, J. L., & Shore, M. F. (1963). The effectiveness of a comprehensive, vocationally oriented psychotherapeutic program for adolescent delinquent boys. *American Journal of Orthopsychiatry, 33,* 634–642.

Matarazzo, J. D. (1992). Psychological testing and assessment in the 21st century. *American Psychologist, 47,* 1007–1018.

Matson, J. L., & Coe, D. A. (1991). Mentally retarded children. In T. R. Kratochwill & R. J. Morris (Eds.), *The practice of child therapy.* Boston: Allyn & Bacon.

Mayo, J. (1974). The significance of sociocultural variables in the psychiatric treatment of black outpatients. *Comprehensive Psychiatry, 15,* 471–482.

McAdoo, H. P., & McAdoo, J. L. (Eds.) (1985). *Black children: Social, educational, and parental environments.* Beverly Hills, CA: Sage.

McCartin, R., & Meyer, K. A. (1988). The adolescent, academic achievement and college plans: The role of family variables. *Youth and Society, 19,* 378–394.

McDonnell, J., Hardman, M., Hightower, J., & Kiefer-O'Donnell, R. (1991). Variables associated with in-school and after-school integration of secondary students with severe disabilities. *Education and Training in Mental Retardation, 26,* 243–257.

McGee, R., Feehan, M., Williams, S., & Anderson, J. (1992). DSM-III disorders from age 11 to age 15 years. *Journal of the American Academy of Child and Adolescent Psychiatry, 31,* 50–59.

McGee, R., Partridge, F., Williams, S., & Silva, P. A. (1991). A twelve-year follow-up of preschool hyperactive children. *Journal of the American Academy of Child and Adolescent Psychiatry, 30,* 224–232.

McMahon, R. J., & Wells, K. C. (1989). Conduct disorders. In E. J. Mash & R. A. Barkley (Eds.), *Treatment of childhood disorders* (pp. 73–132). New York: Guilford.

McRoy, R. G., & Freeman, E. (1986). Racial identity issues among mixed-race children. *Social Work in Education, 8,* 164–174.

Meichenbaum, D. H. (1977). *Cognitive behavior modification: An integrative approach.* New York: Plenum Press.

Merchant, G. J. (1991). A profile of motivation, self-perception, and achievement in Black urban elementary students. *The Urban Review, 23,* 83–99.

Milich, R. (1994). The response of children with ADHD to failure: If at first you don't succeed, do you try, try again? *School Psychology Review, 23,* 11–28.

Miller, L. K., & Miller, O. L. (1970). Reinforcing self-help group activities of welfare recipients. *Journal of Applied Behavior Analysis, 3,* 57–64.

Miller, P. M. (1983). *The Hilton Head metabolism diet.* New York: Warner.

Moffitt, T. E. (1993). Adolescence-limited and life-course-persistent antisocial behavior: A developmental taxonomy. *Psychological Review, 100,* 674–701.

Monihan, D. P. (1965). *The Negro family: The case for national action.* Washington, DC: Office of Policy Planning and Research, U.S. Department of Labor.

Morgan, H. (1976). Neonatal precocity and the black experience. *Negro Educational Review, 27,* 129–134.

Morrison, M. M., & Smith, Q. T. (1987). Psychiatric issues of adolescent chemical dependence. *Pediatric Clinics of North America, 34,* 461–480.

Murphy, D. A., Greenstein, J. J., & Pelham, W. E. (1993). Pharmacological treatment. In V. B. Van Hasselt & M. Hersen (Eds.), *Handbook of behavior therapy and pharmacotherapy for children: A comparative analysis.* Boston: Allyn & Bacon.

National Center for Education Statistics. (1992). *Dropout rates in the United States.* Washington, DC: U.S. Department of Education.

National Center for Education Statistics. (1992b). *A profile of American eighth-grade mathematics and science instruction* [Tech. Rep. No. NCES 92–486]. Washington, DC: U.S. Government Printing Office.

National Commisssion on Excellence in Education. (1983). *A nation at risk: The imperative for educational reform.* Washington, DC: U.S. Department of Education.

National Institute of Drug Abuse (1992). National Household Survey on Drug Abuse. *Statistical Abstract of the United States 1992* (112th ed.). Washington, DC: U.S. Department of Commerce, Bureau of the Census.

Natriello, G., McDill, E. L., & Pallas, A. M. (1990). *Schooling disadvantaged children: Racing against catastrophe.* New York: Teachers College Press.

Neighbors, H. W. (1985). Seeking professional help for personal problems: Black Americans' use of health and mental health services. *Community Mental Health Journal, 21,* 156–166.

Nihra, K., Leland, H., & Lambert, N. (1993). *AAMR Adaptive Behavior Scales—Residential and Community.* Austin, TX: Pro-Ed.

Nobles, W. W. (1988). African American family life: An instrument of culture. In H. P. McAdoo (Ed.), *Black Families* (pp. 44–53). Newbury Park, CA: Sage.

Odom, S. L., & Strain, P. S. (1984). Peer-mediated approaches to promoting children's social interaction: A review. *American Journal of Orthopsychiatry, 54,* 544–557.

Ogbu, J. U. (1978). *Minority education and caste: The American system in cross-cultural perspective.* New York: Academic Press.

Ogbu, J. U. (1986). The consequences of the American caste system. In U. Neisser (Ed.), *The school achievement of minority children: New perspectives* (pp. 19–56). Hillsdale, NJ: Erlbaum.

Okagaki, L., Frensch, P. A., & Gordon, E. W. (1995). Encouraging school achievement in Mexican-American children. *Hispanic Journal of Behavioral Sciences, 17,* 160–179.

O'Leary, K. D., Kaufman, K. F., Kass, R. E., & Drabman, R. S. (1970). The effects of loud and soft reprimands on behavior of disruptive students. *Exceptional Children, 37,* 145–155.

O'Leary, K. D., O'Leary, S., & Becker, W. C. (1967). Modification of a deviant sibling interaction in the home. *Behavior Research and Therapy, 5,* 113–120.

Oyemade, U. J., & Rosser, P. L. (1980). Development in Black children. *Advances in Behavioral Pediatrics, 1,* 153–179.

Palincsar, A. S., & Brown, A. L. (1986). Interactive teaching to promote independent learning from text. *The Reading Teacher, 39,* 771–777.

Palincsar, A. S., & Brown, D. A. (1987). Enhancing instructional time through attention to metacognition. *Journal of Learning Disabilities, 20,* 66–75.

Patchen, M. (1982). *Black–White contact in schools: Its social and academic effects.* West Lafayette, IN: Purdue University Press.

Patterson, C. J., Kupersmidt, J. B., & Vaden, N. A. (1990). Income level, gender, ethnicity, and household composition as predictors of children's school-based competence. *Child Development, 61,* 485–494.

Patterson, G. R. (1976). The aggressive child: Victim and architect of a coercive system. In E. J. Mash, L. A. Hamerlynck, & L. C. Handy (Eds.), *Behavior modification and families.* New York: Brunner/Mazel.

Patterson, G. R., & Reid, J. B. (1973). Intervention for families of aggressive boys: A replication study. *Behaviour Research and Therapy, 11*(4), 383–394.

Patterson, G. R., Reid, J. B., & Dishion, T. J. (1992). *Antisocial boys.* Eugene, OR: Castalia Publishing Company.

Patton, J. R., Beirne-Smith, M., & Payne, J. S. (1990). *Mental retardation.* New York: Macmillan.

Payne, O. L. (1991). *An examination of factors influencing the verbal and mathematics SAT scores among Black secondary students.* (Doctoral Dissertation, University of Houston, 1991) Dissertation Abstracts International, 52;05A.

Peters, M. (1981). Parenting in black families with young children. In H. McAdoo (Ed.), *Black families.* Newbury Park, CA: Sage.

Peterson, C., & Bossio, L. M. (1991). *Health and optimism.* New York: Free Press.

Phinney, J. S. (1992). Ethnic identity in adolescents and adults: Review of research. *Psychological Bulletin, 180,* 499–514.

Pintrich, P. R., & DeGroot, E. J. (1990). Motivational and self-regulated learning components of classroom academic performance. *Journal of Educational Psychology, 82,* 33–40.

Plomin, R., DeFries, J. C., & McClearn, G. E. (1990). *Behavioral genetics: A primer* (2nd ed.). New York: W. H. Freeman and Co.

Preator, K. K. (1990). *Teacher tolerance, responsibility and efficacy: Responding to adaptive and maladaptive student behaviors.* (Doctoral Dissertation, University of Utah, 1990) Dissertation Abstracts International, 51;03A.

Prestrup, A. (1973). *Black dialect inference and accommodation of reading instruction in first grade.* Monograph No. 4, Language behavior research laboratory. University of California, Berkeley.

Quay, H. C., & Peterson, D. R. (1983). *Interim manual for the revised Behavior Problem Checklist.* Coral Gables, FL: University of Miami.

Rankin, P. (1967). *The relationship between parent behavior and achievement of inner-city elementary school children.* Paper presented at American Educational Research Association Convention, New York.

Rapport, M. D. (1993). Attention deficit hyperactivity disorder. In T. H. Ollendick & M. Hersen (Eds.), *Handbook of child and adolescent assessment.* Boston: Allyn & Bacon.

Rehm, L. P. (1977). A self-control model of depression. *Behavior Therapy, 8,* 787–804.

Reynolds, A. J. (1991). Early schooling of children at risk. *American Educational Research Journal, 28*(2), 392–422.

Rice, M. L. (1989). Children's language acquisition. *American Psychologist, 44,* 149–156.

Robinson, F. P. (1970). *How to study.* New York: Harper Colllins.

Rohwer, W. D., & Harris, W. J. (1975). Media effects on prose learning in two populations of children. *Journal of Educational Psychology, 67,* 651–657.

Rosenbaum, M. (1980). A schedule for assessing self-control behaviors: Preliminary findings. *Behavior Therapy, 11,* 109–121.

Rosenholtz, S. J., & Wilson, B. (1980). The effect of classroom structure on shared perceptions of ability. *American Educational Research Journal, 17,* 75–82.

Rutter, M., Tizard, J., & Whitmore, K. (1970). *Education, health, and behaviour.* London: Longmans.

Sameroff, A. J. (1990). Neo-environmental perspectives on developmental theory. In R. M. Hodapp, J. A. Burak, & E. Zigler (Eds.), *Issues in the developmental approach to mental retardation.* New York: Cambridge University Press.

Sameroff, A. J., & Chandkler, M. J. (1975). Reproductive risk and the continuum of caretaking casualty. In F. D. Horowitz (Ed.), *Review of child development research,* Vol. 4. Chicago: University of Chicago Press.

Sandoval, J., Lambert, N. M., & Sasson, D. (1980). The identification and labeling of hyperactivity in children: An interactive model. In C. K. Whalen & B. Henker (Eds.), *Hyperactive children: The social ecology of identification and treatment.* New York: Academic Press.

Sarason, I. G., Sarason, B. R., Pierce, G. R., Shearin, E. N., & Sayers, M. H. (1991). A social learning approach to increasing blood donations. *Journal of Applied Social Psychology, 21,* 896–918.

Sattler, J. M. (1988). *Assessment of children* (3rd ed.). San Diego, CA: Jerome M. Sattler.

Schaughency, E., McGee, R., Raja, S. N., Feehan, M., & Silva, P. A. (1994). Self-reported inattention, impulsivity, and hyperactivity at ages 15 and 18 years in the general population. *Journal of the American Academy of Child and Adolescent Psychiatry, 33,* 173–184.

Schultz, G. F. (1993). Socioeconomic advantage and achievement motivation: Important mediators of academic performance in minority children in urban schools. *The Urban Review, 25*(3), 221–232.

Schumaker, J., Deshler, D., Alley, G., Warner, M., & Denton, P. (1984). Multipass: A learning strategy for improving reading comprehension. *Learning Disability Quarterly, 5,* 295–304.

Scott, K. C., & Carran, D. T. (1987). The epidemiology and prevention of mental retardation. *American Psychologist, 42,* 801–804.

Scott, S. (1994). Mental retardation. In M. Rutter, E. Taylor, & L. Hersov (Eds.), *Child and adolescent psychiatry: Modern approaches.* Cambridge, MA: Blackwell.

Sebring, D. (1985). Considerations in counseling interracial children. *Journal of Non-White Concerns in Personnel and Guidance, 13,* 3–9.

Seligman, M. E. (1991). *Learned optimism.* New York: Knopf.

Selye, H. (1976). *The stress of life.* New York: McGraw-Hill.

Semrud-Clikeman, M., Filipek, P. A., Biederman, J., Steingard, R., Kennedy, D., Renshaw, P., & Bekken, K. (1994). Attention-deficit hyperactivity disorder: Magnetic resonance imaging morphometric analysis of the corpus callosum. *Journal of the American Academy of Child and Adolescent Psychiatry, 33,* 875–881.

Shoenbach, V., and others. (1983). Prevalence of self-reported depressive symptoms in young adolescents. *American Journal of Public Health, 73,* 1281–1287.

Shore, M. F., Massimo, J. L., Kisielewski, B. A., & Moran, J. K. (1966). Object relations changes resulting from successful psychotherapy with adolescent delinquents and their relationship to academic performance. *Journal of the American Academy of Child Psychiatry, 5,* 93–104.

Shultz, G. F. (1993). Socioeconomic advantage and achievement motivation: Important mediators of academic performance in minority children in urban schools. *The Urban Review, 25*(3), 221–232.

Shunk, D. H. (1987). Deer models and children's behavioral change. *Review of Educational Research, 57,* 149–174.

Silverman, W. K. (1994). Structured diagnostic interviews. In T. H. Ollendick, N. J. King, & W. Yule (Eds.), *International handbook of phobic and anxiety disorders in children and adolescents* (pp. 293–315). New York: Plenum Press.

Simmons, W., & Grady, M. (1990). *Black male achievement: From peril to promise.* Prince Georges County, MD: Prince Georges County Schools.

Skinner, E. A., Wellborn, J. S., & Connell, J. P. (1990). What it takes to do well in school and whether I've got it. A process model of perceived control and children's engagement and achievement in school. *Journal of Educational Psychology, 82,* 22–32.

Slavin, R. E. (1978). Separating incentives, feedback, and evaluation: Toward a more effective classroom system. *Educational Psychologist, 13,* 97–100.

Slomka, G. T., & Tarter, R. E. (1993). Neuropsychological assessment. In T. H. Ollendick & M. Hersen (Eds.), *Handbook of child and adolescent assessment.* Boston: Allyn & Bacon.

Smith, G. T., & Goldman, M. S. (1994). Alcohol expectancy theory and the identification of high risk adolescents. *Journal of Research on Adolescence, 4,* 229–248.

Smith, G. T., Goldman, M. S., Greenbaum, P. E., & Christiansen, B. A. (1995). Expectancy for social facilitation from drinking: The divergent paths of high-expectancy and low-expectancy adolescents. *Journal of Abnormal Psychology, 104,* 32–40.

Smith, J. C. (1993). *Creative stress management.* Englewood Cliffs, NJ: Prentice Hall.

Sonuga-Barke, E. J. S. (1994). On dysfunction and function in psychological theories of childhood disorder. *Journal of Child Psychology and Psychiatry, 35,* 801–815.

Sparrow, S. S., Balla, D., & Cicchetti, D. V. (1984). *Vineland Adaptive Behavior Scales.* Circle Pines, MN: American Guidance Service.

Spencer, M. B. (1982). Personal and group identity of Black children: An alternative synthesis. *Genetic Psychology Monographs, 106,* 59–84.

Spencer, M. B. (1990). Development of minority children: An introduction. *Child Development, 61,* 267–269.

Sprich-Buckminister, S., Biederman, J., Milberger, S., Faraone, S. V., & Lehman, B. K. (1993). Are perinatal complications relevant to the manifestation of ADD? Issues of cormorbidity and familiarity. *Journal of the American Academy of Child and Adolescent Psychiatry, 32,* 1032–1037.

Stanovich, K. E. (1994). Does dyslexia exist? *Journal of Child Psychology and Psychiatry, 35,* 579–595.

Steinberg, L. (1987). Single parent, stepparents, and the susceptibility of adolescents to antisocial peer pressure. *Child Development, 58,* 269–275.

Stormont-Spurgin, M., & Zentall, S. S. (1995). Contributing factors in the manifestation of aggression in preschoolers with hyperactivity. *Journal of Child Psychology and Psychiatry, 36,* 491–509.

Street, S., Kromrey, J. D., Reed, J., & Anton, W. (1993). A phenomenological perspective of problems experienced by high school seniors. *High School Journal, 76*(2), 129–138.

Streissguth, A. P., Barr, H. M., Sampson, P. D., Darby, B. L., & Martin, D. C. (1989). IQ at age 4 in relation to maternal alcohol use and smoking during pregnancy. *Developmental Psychology, 25,* 3–11.

Sue, D. W., & Sue, D. (1977). Barriers to effective cross-cultural counseling. *Journal of Counseling Psychology, 24,* 420–429.

Swanson, J. M., McBurnett, K., Christian, D. L., & Wigal, T. (1995). Stimulant medications and the treatment of children with ADHD. *Advances in Clinical Child Psychology, 17,* 265–322.

Sykes, D. K. (1987). An approach to working with black youth in cross-cultural therapy. *Clinical Social Work Journal, 15,* 260–270.

Szymanski, L. S., & Kaplan, L. C. (1991). Mental retardation. In J. M. Wiener (Ed.), *Textbook of child & adolescent psychiatry.* Washington, DC: American Psychiatric Association.

Tao, K. T. (1992). Hyperactivity and attention deficit disorder syndrome in China. *Journal of the American Academy of Child and Adolescent Psychiatry, 31,* 1165–1166.

Tatara, T. (1992). *Characteristics of children in substitute and adoptive care,* (Based on FY82 through FY88 data.) Washington, DC: American Public Welfare Association.

Taylor, E. (1994). Syndromes of attention deficit and hyperactivity. In M. Rutter, E. Taylor, & L. Hersov (Eds.), *Child and adolescent psychiatry: Modern approaches.* New York: Blackwell Scientific.

Taylor, H. G. (1988). Neuropsychological testing: Relevance for assessing children's learning disabilities. *Journal of Consulting and Clinical Psychology, 56,* 795–800.

Taylor, H. G. (1989). Learning disabilities. In E. J. Mash & R. A. Barkley (Eds.), *Treatment of childhood disorders.* New York: Guilford.

Taylor, H. G., & Fletcher, J. M. (1990). Neuropsychological assessment of children. In G. Goldstein & M. Hersen (Eds.), *Handbook of psychological assessment,* (2nd ed.). New York: Pergamon.

Tesman, J. R., & Hills, A. (1994). Developmental effects of lead exposure in children. Social Policy Report. *Society for Research in Child Development, VIII*(3), 1–16.

Thapar, A., Gottesman, I. I., Owen, M. J., O'Donovan, M., & McGuffin, P. (1994). The genetics of mental retardation. *British Journal of Psychiatry, 164,* 747–758.

Thorkildsen, T. A., Nolen, S. B., & Fournier, J. (1994). What is fair? Children's critiques of practices that influence motivation. *Journal of Educational Psychology, 86*(4), 475–486.

Thorndike, R. L., Hagen, E. P., & Sattler, J. M. (1986). *Stanford-Binet Intelligence Scale* (4th ed.). Chicago: Riverside.

Tolan, P. H., & Thomas, P. (1995). The implications of age of onset for delinquency risk II: Longitudinal data. *Journal of Abnormal Child Psychology, 23,* 157–181.

Tucker, C. M., Brady, B. A., Harris, Y. R., & Fraser, K. (1992). The association of selected parent behaviors with the adaptive and maladaptive functioning of black children and white children. *Child Study Journal, 23,* 39–55.

Tucker, C. M., Brady, B. A., Harris, Y. R., Tribble, I., & Fraser, K. (1993). The association of selected parent behaviors with the adaptive and maladaptive functioning of black children and white children. *Child Study Journal, 23*(1), 39–55.

Tucker, C. M., Brady, B. A., Herman, K. C., & Lowenberg, D. L. (1996). *Handbook for increasing academic and adaptive skills and reducing maladaptive behaviors of African American children.* Unpublished manuscript.

Tucker, C. M., Chennault, S. A., Brady, B. A., Fraser, K. P., Gaskin, V. T., Dunn, C., & Frisby, C. (1995). A parent, community, public schools, and university involved partnership education program to examine and boost academic achievement and adaptive functioning skills of African-American students. *Journal of Research and Development in Education, 28,* 174–185.

Tucker, C. M., Harris, Y. R., Brady, B. A., & Herman, K. C. (1996). The association of selected parent behaviors with the academic achievement of African American children and European American children. *Child Study Journal, 26*(4), 253–277.

Tucker, C. M., Herman, K., Brady, B. A., & Fraser, K. (1995). Operation positive expression: A behavior change program for adolescent halfway house residents. *Residential Treatment for Children and Youth, 13*(2), 67–80.

Tucker, C. M., Herman, K., Pedersen, T., & Vogel, D. Parent, student, teacher, and counselor perceptions of African-American students' performance and behaviors. Manuscript in progress.

Tucker, C. M., Herman, K., Reid, A., Keefer, N., & Vogel, D. The research-based model partnership education program: A four-year outcome study. Manuscript in progress.

Tucker, C. M., & O'Leary, S. G. (1982). Reasons and reminder instructions: Their effects on problematic behavior of kindergarten children. *Cognitive Therapy and Research, 6*(2), 231–234.

Tucker, C. M., Vogel, D., Keefer, N., & Reid, A. Self-control, achievement motivation, and parental support: Predictors of maladaptive behavior in African American children. Manuscript in progress.

Tuma, J. M. (1989). Mental health services for children: The state of the art. *American Psychologist, 44,* 188–189.

United States Bureau of the Census (1986). *Statistical abstract of the United States: 1986* (106th ed.). Washington, DC: U.S. Department of Commerce.

Viadero, D. (1988). Big-city gang culture spreading to new turf. *Education Week, 7* (1), 18–19.

Wahler, R. G. (1976). Deviant child behavior within the family: Developmental speculations and behavior change strategies. In H. Leitenberg (Ed.), *Handbook of behavior modification and behavior therapy.* Englewood Cliffs, NJ: Prentice-Hall.

Wall, S. M., & Paradise, L. V. (1981). A comparison of parent and teacher reports of selected adaptive behaviors of children. *Journal of School Psychology, 19,* 73–77.

Ward, M. H., & Baker, B. L. (1968). Reinforcement therapy in the classroom. *Journal of Applied Behavior Analysis, 1,* 323–328.

Watson, D. L., & Tharp, R. G. (1993). *Self-directed behavior: Self modification for personal adjustment.* Pacific Grove, CA: Brooks/Cole.

Wells, E. A., Morrison, D. M, Gillmore, M. R., Catalano, R. F., Iritani, B., & Hawkins, J. D. (1992). Race differences in antisocial behaviors and attitudes and early initiation of substance use. *Journal of Drug Education, 22*(2), 115–130.

Wentzel, K. R. (1994). Relations of social goal pursuit to social acceptance, classroom behavior, and perceived social support. *Journal of Educational Psychology, 86*(2), 173–182.

Weschler, D. (1989). *Weschler Preschool and Primary Scale of Intelligence-Revised (WPPSI-R).* San Antonio, TX: The Psychological Corporation.

Weschler, D. (1991). *Manual for the Weschler Intelligence Scale for Children-Third Edition (WISC-III).* San Antonio, TX: The Psychological Corporation.

West, S. G., Sandler, I., Pillow, D. R., Baca, L., & Gersten, J. C. (1991). The use of structural equation modeling in generative research: Toward the design of a preventative intervention for bereaved children. *American Journal of Community Psychology, 19,* 459–480.

Whalen, C. K., Henker, B., & Hinshaw, S. P. (1985). Cognitive-behavioral therapies for hyperactive children: Premises, problems, and prospects. *Journal of Abnormal Child Psychology, 13,* 391–409.

Wicks-Nelson, R., & Israel, A. C. (1997). *Behavior disorders of childhood* (3rd ed.). Upper Saddle River, NJ: Simon & Schuster.

Wilkin, H. A. (1967). A cognitive-style approach to cross-cultural research. *International Journal of Psychology,* 2:237–238.

Williams, C. D. (1959). The elimination of tantrum behavior by extinction procedures: Case report. *Journal of Abnormal and Social Psychology, 59,* 269.

Williams, D., & Chavkin, N. (1985). *Final report of the parent involvement in education project.* Contract No. 400–83–007, Project P-2. Washington, DC: National Institute of Education.

Willig, A. C., Harnisch, D. L., Hill, K. T., & Maehr, M. L. (1983). Sociocultural and educational correlates of success-failure attributions and evaluation anxiety in the school setting for Black, Hispanic, and Anglo children. *American Educational Research Journal, 20*(3), 385–410.

Winfield, L. F. (1988). *An investigation of the characteristics of high versus low literacy proficient Black young adults.* Philadelphia: Temple University, Center for Research in Human Development and Education.

Winfield, L. F. (1991). Resilience, schooling, and development in African-American youth: A conceptual framework. *Education and Urban Society, 24,* 5–14.

Winfield, L. F., & Lee, V. E. (1990). *Gender differences in reading proficiencey: Are they constant across racial groups?* Baltimore, MD: Prince Georges County Schools.

Woodcock, R. W., Mather, N., & Barnes, E. K. (1987). *Woodcock Mastery Tests-Revised: Examiner's Manual, Forms G and H.* Circle Pines, MN: American Guidance Service.

Woolfolk, A. E., & Hoy, W. K. (1990). Prospective teachers' sense of efficacy and belief about control. *Journal of Educational Psychology, 82,* 81–91.

Ysseldyke, J. E., Thurlow, M. L., Christenson, S. L., & Muyskens, P. (1991). Classroom and home learning differences between students labeled as educable mentally retarded and their peers. *Education and Training in Mental Retardation, 26,* 3–17.

Ziegler, S. (1987). *The effects of parent involvement on children's achievement: The significance of home/school links.* Toronto: Toronto Board of Education (ERIC Document Reproduction Service No. 304 234).

Zigler, E., Abelson, W., & Seitz, V. (1972). Motivational factors in the performance of economically disadvantaged children on the Peabody Picture Vocabulary Test. *Child Development, 44,* 294–303.

Zigler, E., & Butterfield, E. (1968). Motivational aspects of changes in IQ test performance of culturally deprived nursery school children. *Child Development, 39,* 1–14.

Zimmerman, B., & Martinez-Pons, M. (1988). Construct validation of a strategy model of student self-regulated learning. *Journal of Educational Psychology, 80,* 284–290.

INDEX

THE IMPRINT OF MAN

edited by

Emmanuel Anati

Also in this series:

André Leroi-Gourhan
The dawn of European art: an introduction to palaeolithic cave painting

THE IMPRINT OF MAN

Rock art of the Spanish Levant

Rock art
of the Spanish Levant

ANTONIO BELTRÁN

Dean of the Arts Faculty, University of Saragossa

Translated by Margaret Brown

CAMBRIDGE UNIVERSITY PRESS

CAMBRIDGE
LONDON NEW YORK NEW ROCHELLE
MELBOURNE SYDNEY

Published by the Press Syndicate of the University of Cambridge
The Pitt Building, Trumpington Street, Cambridge CB2 1RP
32 East 57th Street, New York, NY 10022, USA
296 Beaconsfield Parade, Middle Park, Melbourne 3206, Australia

Originally published in Italian as *Da cacciatori ad allevatori l'arte rupestre del Levante Spagnolo* by Editoriale Jaca Book, Milan, 1980, and © Editoriale Jaca Book 1979

First published in English by Cambridge University Press (1982) as *Rock Art of the Spanish Levant*
English translation © Cambridge University Press 1982

Printed in Italy

Library of Congress catalogue card number: 81-21694

British Library Cataloguing in Publication Data
Beltrán, Antonio
Rock art of the Spanish Levant—(The Imprint of Man)
1. Rock paintings—Spain
2. Art, Prehistoric—Spain
I. Title II. Da cacciatori ad allevatori. *English*
III. Series
759.01'13'0946   N5310.5.S/

ISBN 0 521 24568 0

Contents

Illustrations

The distribution of rock art sites

1 Colungo (Huesca)
2 Os de Balaguer (Lérida)
3 Cogul (Lérida)
4 Mas de Llort, Rojals (Tarragona)
5 Mas de Ramón de Bessó, Rojals (Tarragona)
6 Cabra Feixet, Perelló (Tarragona)
7 Cova de l'Escoda, Vandellós (Tarragona)
8 Racó d'en Perdigó, Vandellós (Tarragona)
9 Cova del Ramat, Tivissa (Tarragona)
10 Cova del Cingle, Tivissa (Tarragona)
11 Cueva de la Moleta de Cartagena, San Carlos de la Rápita (Tarragona)
12 Abrigos de la Esperanza, Ulldecona (Tarragona)
13 Roca dels Moros, Calapatá, Cretas (Teruel)
14 Barranco dels Gascons, Calapatá, Cretas (Teruel)
15 Els Secans, Mazaleón (Teruel)
16 Caidas del Salbime, Mazaleón (Teruel)
17 Val del Charco del Agua Amarga, Alcañiz (Teruel)
18 Abrigo del Arquero, Ladruñan (Teruel)
19 El Pudial, Ladruñan (Teruel) (¹)
20 El Torico, Ladruñan (Teruel)
21 Abrigo de la Vacada, Castellote (Teruel)
22 Covacho Ahumado, El Mortero, Alacón (Teruel)
23 Los Trepadores, El Mortero, Alacón (Teruel)
24 Abrigo de los Borriquitos, El Mortero, Alacón (Teruel)
25 Abrigo de los Recolectores, El Mortero, Alacón (Teruel)
26 Covacho Ahumado, Cerro Felío, Alacón (Teruel)
27 Pared de la Tia Mona, Cerro Felío, Alacón (Teruel) (¹)
28 Cueva de Eudoviges, Cerro Felío, Alacón (Teruel)
29 Fronton de los cápridos, Cerro Felío, Alacón (Teruel) (¹)
30 Cueva del Garroso, Cerro Felío, Alacón (Teruel)
31 Abrigo de la Cañada de Marco, Alcaine (Teruel)
32 Barranco de la Fuente del Cabrerizo, Albarracín (Teruel)
33 Toricos del Prado del Navazo, Albarracín (Teruel)
34 Cocinilla del Obispo, Albarracín (Teruel)
35 Arquero de los Callejones cerrados, Albarracín (Teruel)
36 Cueva de Doña Clotilde, La Losilla, Albarracín (Teruel)
37 Abrigo de las figuras diversas, La Losilla, Albarracín (Teruel)
38 Covacho del Ciervo, La Losilla, Albarracín (Teruel)
39 Abrigo del medio caballo, La Losilla, Albarracín (Teruel)
40 Abrigo de los dos caballos, La Losilla, Albarracín (Teruel)
41 Abrigo del Huerto, Las Tajadas, Bezas (Teruel)
42 Paridera, Tajadas, Bezas (Teruel)
43 Barranco del Pajarejo, Albarracín (Teruel)
44 Cerrada del Tio José, Albarracín (Teruel)
45 Ceja de Piezarrodilla, Albarracín (Teruel)
46 Prado del Barranco de las Olivanas, Tormón (Teruel)
47 Peña del Escrito, Villar del Humo (Cuenca)
48 Abrigo de la Selva Pascuala, Villar del Humo (Cuenca)
49 Fuente de la Selva Pascuala, Villar del Humo (Cuenca)
50 Cueva de Bullón, Villar del Humo (Cuenca)
51 Marmalo, Villar del Humo (Cuenca)
52 Cueva de El Polvorin, Puebla de Benifaza (Castellón de la Plana)
53 Cueva alta de la Masía, Morella la Vella, Morella (Castellón)
54 Cueva del Roure, Morella la Vella, Morella (Castellón)
55 Cueva Remigia, barranco de Gasulla, Ares del Maestre (Castellón)
56 Cingle de la Mola Remigia, Gasulla, Ares del Maestre (Castellón)
57 Racó de Molero, Gasulla, Ares del Maestre (Castellón)
58 Racó de Gasparo, Las Solanas, Ares del Maestre (Castellón)
59 Les Dogues, Ares del Maestre (Castellón)
60 Mas Blanc, Ares del Maestre (Castellón)
61 El Single, Ares del Maestre (Castellón)
62 Racó de Nando o Corvarjos, Benasal (Castellón)
63 Roca del Senallo, Villafranca del Cid (Castellón)
64 Cuevas de El Civil, Barranco de la Valltorta, Tirig (Castellón)
65 Cueva dels Tolls, Alts Valltorta, Tirig (Castellón)
66 Cueva Rull, Valltorta, Tirig (Castellón)
67 Cueva dels Cavalls, Tirig (Castellón)
68 Cueva del Arco, Valltorta, Tirig (Castellón)
69 Abrigo de Mas d'en Josep, Valltorta, Tirig (Castellón)
70 Cueva alta del Llidoné, Valltorta, Cuevas de Vinromá (Castellón)
71 Cueva Saltadora, Valltorta, Cuevas de Vinromá (Castellón)
72 La Joquera, Borriol (Castellón)
73 Gilet, Albalat (Valencia)

74 Cinto de las Letras, Dos Aguas (Valencia)
75 Abrigo de la Pareja, Dos Aguas (Valencia)
76 Cinto de la Ventana, Dos Aguas (Valencia)
77 Barranco de las Cañas, Millares (Valencia)
78 Cuevas de la Araña, Bicorp (Valencia)
79 Barranco Garrofero, Bicorp (Valencia)
80 Barranco Gineses, Bicorp (Valencia)
81 Balsa Calicanto, Bicorp (Valencia)
82 Abrigo Gavidia, Bicorp (Valencia)
83 Abrigo del Sordo, Ayora (Valencia)
84 Abrigo de Tortosilla, Ayora (Valencia)
85 Abrigo Boro, Quesa (Valencia)
86 Cuevas de la Sarga, Alcoy (Alicante)
87 Cantos de la Visera, Monte Arabí, Yecla (Murcia)
88 Cueva del Queso, Alpera (Albacete)
89 Cueva de la Vieja, Alpera (Albacete)
90 Abrigos de la Fuente de la Arena, Alpera (Albacete)
91 El Mugrón, Almansa (Albacete)
92 Minateda (Albacete)
93 Rinconada del Canalizo del Rayo, Minateda (Albacete)
94 Barranco de la Mortaja, Minateda (Albacete)
95 Abrigo I de la Casa de los Ingenieros, Nerpio (Albacete)

96 Abrigos del Prado del Tornero, Nerpio (Albacete)
97 Hornacina de la Pareja, Nerpio (Albacete)
98 Abrigo de las Cabritas, Nerpio (Albacete)
99 Abrigo de la Llagosa, Nerpio (Albacete)
100 Abrigo Sautuola, Nerpio (Albacete)
101 Abrigo de la Mujer, Nerpio (Albacete)
102 Abrigo de Solana de las Covachas, Nerpio (Albacete)
103 Cueva del Peliciego, Jumilla (Murcia)
104 Barranco de los Grajos, Cieza (Murcia)
105 Cañaíca del Calar, El Sabinar (Murcia). La Risca, Moratalla (Murcia)
106 Fuente del Sabuco, El Sabinar (Murcia)
107 Lavaderos de Tello, Vélez Blanco (Almería)
108 Estrecho de Santonge, Vélez Blanco (Almería)
109 Cortijo de los Treinta, Vélez Rubio (Almería)
110 Peñón de la Tabla de Pochico, Aldeaquemada (Jaén)
111 Prado del Azogue, Aldeaquemada (Jaén)
112 Cueva de la Pretina, Benalup de Sidonia, Casas Viejas (Cádiz)

(¹) On unprotected cliff-faces.

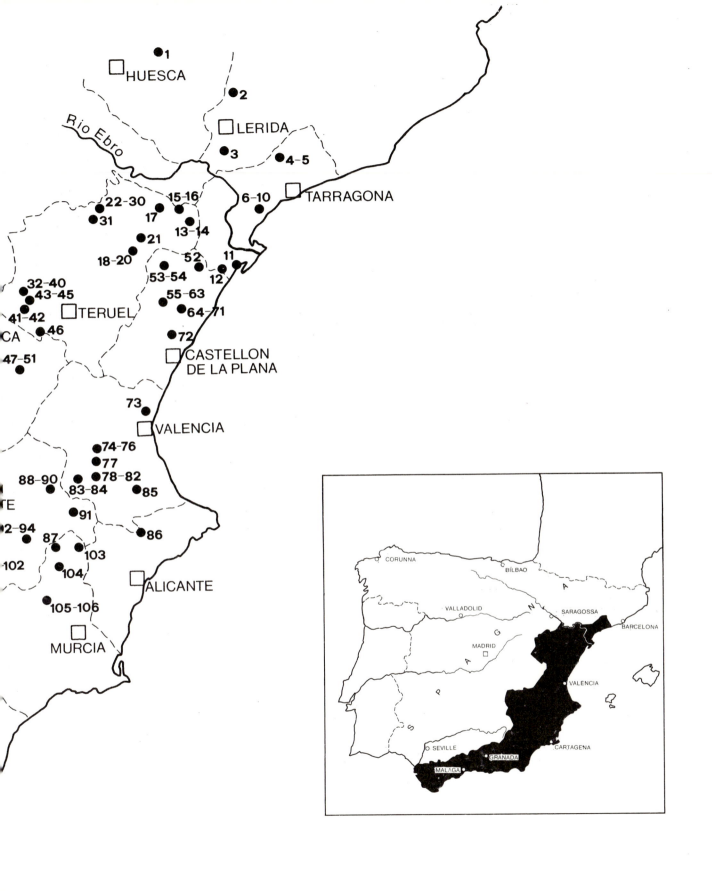

CHAPTER ONE

Introduction

The rock art of eastern Spain is the most vivid of the artistic legacies surviving from European prehistory. It is not easy to find anything of its period which is analogous and this, together with its originality, enhances the mystery of its appearance and the pleasure it affords. It stands quite distinct both from palaeolithic art and from the schematic art of the Spanish Bronze Age.

The distribution map shows the art to be geographically centred in eastern Spain – whence the term 'Levantine art' – along the mountainous borders of the Mediterranean watershed. The paintings, and the few engravings which exist, are found in shallow hollows or 'rock-shelters' which are loosely referred to as 'caves'. Bathed in sunlight, the sites lie amidst rugged territory cut by deep ravines and often difficult of access. There would probably have been a dense forest cover of Mediterranean type, though today this has practically disappeared. Most of the painted rock-shelters are between the 600 m and 1000 m contours. The climate is continental and extreme, but moderated by the proximity of the sea among the more easterly groups. These latter are close to the coastal plain, and some in Castellón within sight of the sea, but there are no sites in flat country.

This is the territory of hunters and gatherers, or latterly of pastoralists: inhabitants of isolated mountainous country where cultural elements could easily survive whilst fundamental changes were taking place in the more accessible areas near by. The mountains and the chase will be seen to be decisive factors in the art of these people.

The zone defined by the distribution of Levantine rock art extends south from the sub-Pyrenean region in the province of Huesca (to judge from an unpublished find at Alquézar) and south of present day Catalonia (Os de Balaguer and Cogul in Lérida, and rock-shelters in Tarragona). Its maximum penetration westward, through Cuenca and Teruel, is 130 km and it reaches its southern limit in Albacete, Murcia and, apart from occasional examples among the schematic art of Andalusia, essentially in Almeria. Castellón and Valencia are central to its distribution, with the maximum density of rock-shelters. The map on page 11 shows this distribution more precisely.

Geologically, the territory is diverse. The Catalan rock-shelters lie at a fairly low altitude (about

400 m on average), in tableland of somewhat irregular structure. Immediately to the south the sierras round the lower Ebro and the harsh ranges in the interior of Tarragona already exhibit landscape more characteristic of the mountain-dwellers' art. In Teruel the rock-shelters in the region of Cretas and Alcañiz open from the sides of gorges or deep valleys cut through oligocene or miocene formations of continental type; but in the Albarracín range, and in Cuenca, we return to high mountainous country, of fine, reddish, triassic sandstone, deeply cut by erosion. Still in Teruel, the valleys of the rivers Martín and Guadalope, and the Maestrazgo massif which separates the province from Castellón and the sea, provide caves along deep faulted ravines, steeply bordered by limestone cliffs. In the inland mountains of Valencia there is once more a mesa-like relief, with vertical scarps and deep crevices. Finally, the geotectonic slope descending from the tableland of La Mancha de Albacete to the eastern coastlands of Alicante or Murcia contains the caves of Alpera and Minateda, along the steep sides of ancient inland-draining valleys. The Nerpio range in northern Murcia, often isolated by winter snows, encompasses a series of shelters containing both Levantine and schematic paintings. Sites in the inaccessible mountains of Murcia relate to finds in the sierras and woodlands of eastern Almeria, although there the art is essentially schematic, with some slight Levantine influence which might also be seen in the region of Cadiz.

In sum, landscape, geography and geology do not account for the uniformity of Levantine art. Rather, this derives from a common mountain environment, in isolated or hardly accessible country with a harsh continental climate, particularly suited to hunting. The reason why Levantine rock painting developed in these remote regions, without external contacts, must be sought in historical causes.

Rock-shelter Arpán L, Colungo (Huesca). Deer, fully coloured in red (after Beltrán and Baldellou).

13

CHAPTER TWO

Discovery of the art and the problem of conservation

Val del Charco del Agua
Amarga, Alcañiz (Teruel).
The complete frieze,
containing many scenes
(after an old drawing by
Cabré).

Although local scholars had described some rock paintings in the late nineteenth century, their accounts, like the much earlier confused reports of Lope de Vega, did not gain the attention of scientific observers; nonetheless, there are references to the *toricos* or bulls at the Cocínilla del Obispo site and at Cogul as early as 1892.

Juan Cabré's discovery of deer paintings at the Roca dels Moros, Calapatá, near Cretas (Teruel) in 1913, published four years later, met with some response, probably because interest had already been generated by the finds at Altamira. The Cogul group, found in 1908, with its astonishing phallic dance scene, contributed to the increasing awareness of Levantine art. Its foremost exponent was the Abbé Breuil, writing in *L'Anthropologie*. A considerable group of scholars, such as Hugo Obermaier and his students (among them P. Wernert) and the Spanish investigators Cabré, Serrano and Motos, became active in the search for new finds, and within three-quarters of a century the number of known sites has risen to over a hundred, comprising thousands of figures. Early finds included Albarracín, Alpera, Cantos de la Visera at Monte Arabí,

14

Yecla, and, above all, Minateda. Matching his work at Altamira on palaeolithic art, the Abbé Breuil worked out a chronological and evolutionary scheme on the basis of these sites, especially the last, which he subsequently applied, unmodified, to new discoveries. To their discredit, all contemporary writers accepted his hypothesis without question.

In 1915 Juan Cabré published the first complete survey of Levantine art, adding unpublished finds from Val del Charco, Els Gascons and Tortosilla. His book, *El arte rupestre en España*, disagreed with Breuil's doctrines and was severely and unjustly criticized by that author, who extended his objections to the work of the Comisión de Investigaciones Prehistóricas y Paleontológicas, under Eduardo Hernández. The latter published studies of the Morella la Vella

rock-shelters (Castellón) in 1917, and the Araña caves at Bicorp (Valencia) in a fundamental work in 1924.

For his part, Professor Obermaier, who was establishing a school in Madrid, wrote about the Valltorta rock-shelters in 1919, in a scarcely scientific attack on members of the Institut d'Estudis Catalans of Barcelona and on Cabré. With Wernert, he also published studies of El Civil, Els Cavalls and Mas d'en Josep, while his opponents produced brief notes on Saltadora and other minor rock-shelters. Breuil and Obermaier combined to study and publish details of El Prado de las Olivanas, Tormón and the Remigia cave, as well as other paintings from the Gasulla gorge.

In recent years Spanish investigators – including Almagro, Ripoll and many others – have been legion in this field, and their numerous publications are listed in the bibliography.

Increasing accessibility, and a diversity of circumstances, are conspiring against the conservation of these unique sites. Despite the fact that the rock-shelters are so shallow that the paintings have been subjected to the direct action of rain, sun and temperature change through the millennia, at

Cueva Remigia in the
Gasulla gorge, Ares del
Maestre (Castellón). The
central group in the frieze
(after Obermaier).

the time of their discovery they have almost invariably been in an amazingly good state of preservation. This can be attributed to the relative dryness of the atmosphere, and also to the loss of binding agents used with the mineral pigments, which then remain on the rock-face as though fossilized. Sometimes the paintings are further protected by a film of calcite or a superficial patina.

Factors which affect the paintings and underlying rock today may be natural or induced by man. Sun, rain, wind and abrupt temperature change may wash them away, or cause erosion or flaking. Humidity, by capillary action or seepage, encourages the disintegration or deformation of the rock-face, and micro-organisms, mosses and vegetation are also active. Wind-blown sand causes erosion, and there is dust deposition as well as the effects of chemical action, from salts etc. Stalagmite deposits are often encountered (Saltadora, Cavalls, Nerpio, Araña), as well as vegetable staining (Racó Molero, Paridera at Bezas).

But the principal threat to conservation is human. Through ignorance, shepherds have frequently utilized the sites for shelter, the fleece of their flocks rubbing paintings from the walls, or smoke from their fires obliterating them. Other destruction stems from intentional actions: for example, paintings are dampened and rubbed to increase their effect, obliterating their surface and increasing risk from damp. Even worse is the barbarous conduct of tourists, who scratch or remove the paintings: there are examples of this at Els Secans and Cañada de Marco,

16

Alcaine, and other sites where the art has partly or totally disappeared. Barcelona Museum harbours paintings removed from Calapatá by Cabré, and the museum at Cervara has an archer stolen from the Cuevas del Civil by some irresponsible person. At Valltorta, a supposed expert is removing figures in order to study the mystery of their excellent state of conservation. At some rock-shelters – like Minateda or Els Cavalls – all the figures are nowadays virtually invisible. The schematic art of one shelter at Velez Blanco is well-preserved only high up on the walls, out of reach of man. As a result, progressive study of the art has become difficult, when not impossible.

Recently, in October 1978, a symposium organized by the governor took place at Argel, with support from UNESCO and the International Centre for the Study of Preservation and Restoration of Cultural Property, to study the problem. Man himself was recognized as the worst enemy of rock art; though given the isolation of the sites it was not thought possible to guard all of them by wardens, or by fencing. But a campaign against deterioration from natural causes, and the suppression of damage by man, could allow the conservation on site of what remains of this prehistoric art.

Barranco del Cabrerizo, Albarracín (Teruel). Rough engravings of a horse and a deer.

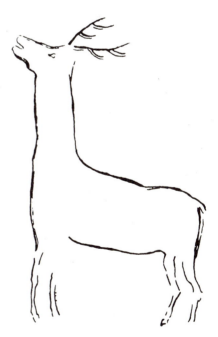

CHAPTER THREE

The characteristics of Levantine art

In any complex feature such as Levantine art, which is geographically extensive and lasted (as we shall see) for several thousand years, it is inevitable that we encounter diversity, or even contradictory features, combined with the common and unifying characteristics to form nonetheless an acceptable whole. Thus, as a general rule, figures in rock art exhibit great vivacity, to the point of wild movement. Scenes involving men and animals are full of life and complexity. It is only exceptional paintings which depict animals standing at rest, or on their own (though even these invariably lie near other animal figures, or near men who are fully active, even launched in swift or headlong career).

Similar variety is present in the style, as well as in the size of the figures. We may contrast the great bull from the Cuevas de la Araña, some 1.10 m long, with the small figures in the same rock-shelter, or with diminutive examples, only 3 cm in length, from El Polvorín. Apart from some rare engravings, the figures are usually painted and, except for a few examples rendered in white from the Albarracín range, the standard colours are red and black only. The reds however can be found in such distinct and various shades that geographical or chronological differences may be involved, especially in the contrast between light or orange reds and the purple or chestnut reds.

There is no perspective in the modern sense, nor any arrangement dictated by pre-ordained rules. Nonetheless, certain established notions seem evident in the composition, such as the circular scheme adopted for the conflict of archers at Morella (Cueva del Roure, p. 45), or the diagonal disposition of the running archers at Val del Charco del Agua Amarga (pp. 14–15). Elsewhere a purely incidental order is followed, as in the wild boar hunt at the Cueva Remigia in the gorge of Gasulla (p. 16), even to the point of conveying anarchy.

Variety in subject-matter and the manner of its presentation is a feature common to all the sites, as well as being a characteristic source of the pleasure they afford. In Levantine art we are spared the monotony of formal rules.

Our account has concentrated on the paintings, since the engravings known at present are few in number and of uncertain date and stylistic affinity. They represent single animals, for example at Barranco de la Fuente del Cabrerizo, Albarracín (two examples: p. 17), and Racó de Molero,

Ares del Maestre. Otherwise they are simple incised profiles, intended as outlines for the painting. There is no engraving except on the rock-shelter walls.

Perhaps the most outstanding feature of Levantine art is its depiction of men and animals together, in a range of activities. Man, undoubtedly, is the protagonist. Normally he appears as a hunter, wounding, pursuing or closing in on his prey. At times he is represented as a warrior, armed with a bow, and fighting or dancing; or, exceptionally, as a sorcerer, or as a masked figure. Women appear frequently, although never as huntresses. At Cogul and Barranco de los Grajos (pp. 48–9) they are dancers. Often they stand alone, and frequently without apparent relationship to other figures. At times they are handling digging-sticks, as at Alacón. At Alpera a woman leads a child by the hand and there are scenes of animated conversation.

Other economic activities depicted will be described below. They include the collection of honey, training (or hunting) the horse with a lasso, and possibly riding. Evidence for agriculture and domesticated animals is also present.

There are no rules governing the position of the paintings, though normally they will occur over the whole length of the cave walls and at heights easily accessible from the floor. The shallowness of the caves and rock-hollows, open to the daylight and barely affording protection from the elements, stands in marked contrast to the sites of palaeolithic art, where darkness and, almost invariably, distance from the cave entrance are essential features. Furthermore, in a number of instances Levantine friezes were painted in the open, on almost vertical cliffs (for example, at Cerro Felío at Alacón, or the Barranco Gomez de Santolea), though that these sites do provide some protection is obvious from damage caused by the fires of shepherds nearby.

Orientation of the rock-shelters is variable also. A good many do point west, which might perhaps imply rites connected with the setting sun.

None of these accounts has furnished a reasonable explanation of how the rock-shelters were utilized. As occupation sites, they would not offer the least protection against the severe climate, with its seasonal and even daily extremes of temperature. These conditions of contrasting summer heat and winter hail and snows, in a region where there are no sheltering caves, must always be borne in mind.

CHAPTER FOUR

Techniques, materials and subject-matter

Techniques employed in the paintings and rare engravings are well known. There is no sculpture or relief in Levantine art, nor is it related to trial sketches found on small stone plaques, or on bone or other materials, as in mesolithic or neolithic contexts.

TECHNIQUES AND MATERIALS

Engraving

Those rare examples of engraving used to outline paintings are executed in light, and at times almost imperceptible, incision purely secondary in purpose. Since it has been possible to identify these at Cogul, Cretas and elsewhere, it is probable that the practice is in fact more widespread. The technique serves only to define the area to be painted. In a similar way we often find a harder and deeper outline of the same colour round painted figures.

Turning to fully engraved figures, we first need to eliminate those natural markings and supposed examples which have been reported in the region around Cretas and the Val del Charco del Agua Amarga. We are left with two very crude examples at the Barranco del Cabrerizo, Albarracín (p. 17), the supposed wild ass and a deer. Both are unevenly drawn, with deep and wide incisions, resulting in inaccurate representation which is difficult to relate stylistically to the nearby painted rock art. Nor can we dismiss the doubts sometimes expressed about the dating of the figures. There is little comparison with the fine engraving of a bull, drawn with a fairly firm and sharp line, which has been discovered at the Racó de Molera in the Gasulla gorge. More of these finds will be needed before any general theory can be proposed about their affinities.

Painting

For the painting, by contrast, we are able to classify the techniques employed, without reference to the significance of the art. First, we find simple outlines, almost invariably of animals in profile,

20

leaving the central parts unpainted. We next encounter profiles with a partial rendering of modelling, especially of the head, neck, thorax and upper portion of the forelegs: the rest of the animal remains in outline only, or with a few simple lines of hatching. There are examples at Cogul (cf. p. 47). There is a curious parallel with palaeolithic art, where both the red and the black figures show the same process from linear outline to full colour, with an intermediate phase representing modelling in part.

A further stage in Levantine art extends the painted area by the use of long strokes of colour, mainly parallel though occasionally contingent. Beyond these striped and partially coloured figures we reach flat washes which cover the whole surface fairly uniformly, and are outlined in a more intense shade of the same colour. However, there is never any indication of different parts of the body by the use of deeper or lighter tones. Two-colour painting did not develop. Most of the large figures, especially those of animals, are painted in monochrome wash.

Later we shall consider whether the various techniques fall into any chronological order, whether they can be assigned to distinct or regional schools, or if they show any appropriate relationship between style and the size of figures.

Human beings are represented on a smaller scale, leaving more restricted areas for painting. Moreover, the figures are now governed by different pictorial conventions: drawn with continuous strokes which are linear, though with inflection and flourishes, to achieve an impressionistic rendering of parts of the body and of the movement which pervades the scenes – a calligraphic style, according to the painter Porcar. However, wherever possible, the bodies are coloured in, although there are some examples of unfilled outlines or partial, striped colouring, as at Minateda (pp. 68–9) or Alpera.

Brushwork is often still discernible, showing the progressive loss of colour in the course of long sweeps, down to the heavily painted, uneven, strokes used in the irregular colouring between profiles. This last practice presupposes an earlier outline, and the deeper colour shown by these

Cuevas del Civil in the Valltorta gorge, Albocácer (Castellón). Technique in a linear profile, seen in an unfinished human figure.

could derive from deliberation in the painting, or from the need for the defining line to be thick enough. As we saw, a lightly engraved outline was occasionally substituted. Afterwards, the colouring was enhanced by the application of thin, uneven layers, using a coarser brush. We cannot exclude the occasional use of feathers, or the spreading of a very liquid paint with the aid of a stick. However, in many paintings the use of brushes is demonstrable, and includes some very fine ones.

Pigments. The minerals which provided colouring matter were not applied directly or in a pastel form, but were used in solution or suspension. The required bases have not been definitely identified, but water or other liquids, as well as fatty substances, will have served the purpose.

As already noticed, there is a complete absence of polychromy or two-tone painting in Levantine art. Any apparent appearance of it in fact derives from repainting, in different colours which are never contemporary. A similar process accounts for the white outlines sometimes found round red figures, as in the Cuevas del Civil, Valltorta, and at other sites in the Albarracín mountains. The original paintings there were in white, and a faint white line remains visible round figures subsequently repainted in red, or in black.

Red, in its variety of tones, is the colour most frequently encountered, followed by black. Only a few examples of white paintings are known. Each colour (especially the red) can occur in numerous shades, though these do not always represent true chromatic differences, but rather variation in the strength of the solution or the quality of the pigment, or possibly the result of chemically or mechanically effected changes to the paintings through time, as well as that resulting from the amount of paint used. Condition, coloration, surface hydration or the absorptive capacity of the rock-face are other possible factors. A painting may also become patinated, with consequent dessication or the hardening of its surface layers; or a film of calcite may cover it. This depends on many factors such as air, water, micro-organisms, dust, damp and organic agents.

Results of chemical analysis to date are confined to the confirmation of the advanced state of fossilization observable among the paintings, and to establishing the presence of iron, aluminium, manganese and traces of copper. These tests were made at Barcelona Museum, from samples obtained from rock-shelters at Santolea. The basic minerals used were ochre, oxides of iron and manganese, cinnabar, haematite, limonite, blood, vegetable carbons and kaolin. They will have been ground down and mixed with various bases – either water, vegetable juices, blood, liquid honey, egg-white or possibly resins or animal fat, although we are not able to confirm these hypotheses. Equally, we are uninformed about any preliminary work which may have been undertaken to prepare the rock surface, by cleaning or smoothing, prior to painting. The brushes used could have been made from animal hair or vegetable fibres.

Painting in white. This is confined to a few rock-shelters in the mountains of Albarracín. Characteristically it is in a yellowish-cream shade, which at times can be made to look pink from the underlying red sandstone (*rodeno*). We cannot say why the colour was chosen. It was absent in the palaeolithic, and is very rare in Spanish schematic art. Desire to achieve a contrast with the red sandstone background is not a sufficient explanation, since red or black figures in the same rock-shelters stand out quite distinctly.

It is interesting to consider one example of repainting. At Ceja de Piezarrodilla, in the Albarracín range, so exactly does the later painting in black follow the original white figure of a bull that a residual white outline is barely perceptible. It might in fact be missed, were it not for the one change: white, lyre-shaped, horns remain visible between the crescentic contour of new horns in black. It remains to wonder how many of the red or black figures in this region might have originated as works in white. Something analogous could also have taken place in other areas. Some figures outlined in white do occur in the Cuevas del Civil sites, Valltorta, and there are, too, some schematic figures painted in white at the unpublished El Single rock-shelter, near the Montalbana, also in Castellón.

Painting in black. Generally, black painting is less well preserved than other colours, and it lies between the red and the white in frequency of its occurrence. The colour variation encountered (apart from subsequent changes in the paints) include brownish tones, the violet-black derivative from manganese, and the bluish or grey shades which result from varying thickness in application. For comment on the quality of the paint, we may recall Breuil's observation on the poorly preserved figures at Vélez Blanco (Almería): that whereas red paintings are brightened by the application of water, the black figures are washed away. Manganese oxide was utilized, but so was soot or charcoal. Regional differences in material also account for the variable state of conservation.

Painting in red. Red is the commonest colour in Levantine painting, but among the diversity of shades found are some probably better considered as different colours in their own right. The light or orange reds are a case in point.

Once again, colour differences due to accidental change, or the thickness of the paint, must be discounted. There are, then, the darker, purple or chestnut, tones – sepia, wine and the like; the clearer vermilions, crimsons and bright reds; and finally light reds of varying shades, and orange. Each of these shades can be found described by a variety of terms in the literature, though in practice they are easily distinguishable and this confusion could be avoided by reference to a colour-chart. It must be remembered, too, that the effects of changing seasons, humidity, light intensity and so on have influenced past reports. In summary, we propose to reduce distinctions in the reds to purple, chestnut, bright red and light and orange-red tones.

Working methods

Techniques of painting differ according to the condition of the rock surface, the size of the figures and the area to be covered. Regional differences, or 'schools', derive essentially from the personal style of the artists, and their modes of working furnish some indication of the way Levantine art developed and of the chronological differences within it.

Levantine rock art contains no strict parallels to the practice of utilizing natural surface irregularities to suggest, enhance or complete the representation, so common in palaeolithic art. Instead we find that the positioning of men, animals and objects has been adapted to the projections, hollows or contours of the rock to express surroundings, or a virtual landscape. Landscape as such is never depicted, but in a cave at Alpera, or at Cingle de la Mola Remigia,

Gasulla, for example, we see arrows or receptacles shown in hiding-places formed by little cracks in the surface. At other times it is men who are protected or hidden by jutting rock: like the two archers, one old and one young, in the latter cave, who have concealed themselves to escape the notice of a wounded ox some distance away. One of them is indicating the animal by pointing. The tiny archers at the Abrigo Sautuola, Nerpio, see their battlefield delineated by a red line which follows a feature on the cave wall, while a similar line is painted round a natural hollow in the Cueva de la Vieja, Alpera. In the Barranco de los Grajos shelter, Cieza, a small figure is enclosed in a break in the rock shaped like a man's body; another archer makes use of a crevice for concealment, in order to attack the bulls at the Prado del Navazo at Albarracín with impunity. At the Cuevas de Araña, Bicorp, certain natural holes have assumed the rôle of hives, with bees shown flying round them. A painting of wooden supports crosses the mouth of one, to secure a ladder being climbed by a honey-collector, carrying a bag (p. 51).

Numerous other examples show how Levantine artists took into account the rocky surfaces they were about to decorate, making their choice for technical reasons in addition to artistic considerations. Each irregularity could be endowed with significance beyond its utility for enhancing depiction or indicating an otherwise absent perspective.

A problem which has so far remained unanswered is that of incomplete or unfinished figures. I believe they are the result not of technical difficulties or abandonment of work but of deliberate decision. Examples include a man in the Cuevas del Civil, Valltorta, represented only by a lower limb and a line for the body (p. 21); a goat in the Prado del Tornero shelters, Nerpio, with a completely painted head but just a simple oval for the body; or the not infrequent 'half-men',

24

Cueva de la Vieja, Alpera (Albacete). The complete frieze, showing a man with feathered head-dress, and bulls with added deer antlers, in the central group.

lacking the lower part of their bodies. Corrected or repainted figures on the other hand are more easily explained, whether the latter are exact copies of the original or include alteration. We shall return to this topic when discussing the significance of Levantine art.

Quality and conventions

In its artistic, aesthetic or stylistic qualities Levantine art may vary from the exquisite to the crude or feeble. These extremes may be encountered within a single frieze, without any apparent difference in date which would explain the contrast. Generally, standards are inferior to those of palaeolithic art, though Levantine art surpasses this in its expression of movement and vitality.

At the same time, it is important to note the distinct treatment given to the presentation of animals, as opposed to that of human beings. In general terms, one feels conscious of an evolutionary process, departing from a tranquil realism and love of detail (cf. the Albarracin bulls, or deer at Calapatá, pp. 34–5), indicative of keen observation on the part of the artist, to arrive at analytical images which observe intellectual rules, becoming stylized or even schematic. With the human figure, emphasis is on movement and gesture, impressionistically conveyed, while in the paintings of animals detailed naturalism is the norm. Consequently, realistic animals are found in the same scene as archers whose bodies and limbs are reduced to a simple line. Idealization of the human form, seen in those portrayals with attenuated waists, no abdomens, triangular thorax and a strongly marked musculature of the calves, however, is sometimes combined with the representation of detail: eyes, nose, chin, fingers, sex or numerous forms of adornment. Later we

25

Abrigo de las Figuras
Diversas, La Losilla, Albarracin
(Teruel). Naturalistic animals
and human figures
approaching the schematic
(after Almagro).
Right. Los Cantos de la Visera,
Yecla (Murcia). The central
frieze (after Cabré).

26

shall see that conventional figures arrive at a thread-like form, in which a single stroke suffices to convey the body, arms or limbs.

Comparison of Levantine art with that of the palaeolithic, or an emphasis on their common naturalism in the portrayal of animals, serves little purpose. In essence, both reflect the activity of hunting; and this is proper to both the palaeolithic and mesolithic, as well as remaining basic to the economies of the neolithic. But the presence of men in Levantine art, and its inclusion of agricultural and pastoral scenes, invalidates all the similarities.

We can assert that Levantine art underwent progressive development towards stylization, showing a clear tendency to a conceptual approach in principle and to impressionism in execution. Its forms became ever more flat and angular and the figures more elongated, including those of animals. We find a disproportion between the scale of component elements which is characteristic of stylization and of schematic art.

However, we cannot establish any rigid sequence, for at the Cuevas de la Sarga, Alcoy, at Cantos de la Visera, Yecla (below), and in the Cuevas de la Araña, Bicorp, there is clear evidence of naturalistic figures either superimposed on, or cutting into, abstract features. Thus the theory of evolution from naturalism/realism to stylized or schematic art is not absolutely demonstrable, although the general tendency may prevail. In either case, it is wiser not to propound unduly clear-cut chronological theories when these are based on artistic sequence.

The artistic conventions of Levantine art exclude any attempt to render the pliancy or physiology of either human or animal forms. Nor is polychromy or modelling included. Instead, the aim is to portray movement and vivacity, both in the separate figures and the complete scenes.

A feeling for composition may be considered one of the dominant characteristics of Levantine art. Admittedly, single figures are found: for example, the Los Callejones Cerrados archer in Albarracín, resting on the ground as though about to shoot from his bow, or the realistic bull painted high on the rock-face at El Pudial, Ladruñán. But these exceptions serve only to confirm the rule that generally we find scenes composed of numerous figures, frequently dominated by man. They are set out in striking arrangements, which are rarely found repeated.

In some friezes one large figure is dominant, although it does not apparently stand in any direct relationship to the others – like the deer at Val del Charco del Agua Amarga (pp. 14–15), a bull in the Cuevas de la Araña, and the man at the Cueva Remigia. We cannot propose any rational explanation for the differences in scale between adjacent figures or scenes, especially if we remember that no attempt is made to convey perspective. But variation in size, from 1.10 m down to 3 cm, must be intended to indicate the relative importance of the figures found mingled together within any composition, and this seems to be independent of the rôle they play in the depicted scene. Changes in scale are deliberate and not fortuitous. In extreme instances, large figures are in proportion ten times bigger, and we have to assume they predominate in their

groups: such examples are the tall woman on the extreme right at Val del Charco (p. 15), or the men with plumes in the Cueva de la Vieja, Alpera (pp. 24–5). What is difficult is to determine the significance of this distinction.

In the portrayal of the human figure we should notice how various parts of the body are shown in different proportions, with exaggeration of the trunk and limbs. This could be taken as evidence of an impressionistic approach, or perhaps it is merely artistic convention. There are conventions, too, for conveying certain activities: for running or pursuit, both human and animal figures are shown descending diagonally across the field. The best known example is at Val del

Cueva Remigia in the Gasulla gorge (Castellón). Bull, possibly pursuing an archer.

Charco del Agua Amarga, where a band of archers, whose legs form a line parallel to the notional ground, are running from top right to lower left of the scene (pp. 14–15). There is a similar arrangement in the wild boar hunt at Cueva Remigia (p. 16). But we also find examples of upward diagonal movement, as well as many horizontal lines of figures, like the file of archers at El Cingle de la Mola Remigia, Gasulla (p. 45), or the Abrigo de Boro, Quesa. Additionally, there are natural poses, depicting a particular activity or movement: for example, the swift horse with lowered head among the Araña caves, the slaying of an ox at El Cingle de la Mola Remigia, the slain hind with pendent neck at the Prado de las Olivanas; and, finally, standing, walking and running animals, and men similarly engaged.

Animals are normally shown in profile, with simple, flat colouring. Each leg is visible. Antlers, horns, hooves and crania are viewed from the front, although the body is in profile – termed *perspective tordue* by the Abbé Breuil when he applied it to Aurignacian/Périgordian art. Although we leave aside any discussion of the chronological significance of this perspective, we cannot fail to wonder at its identical appearance in both palaeolithic and Levantine art. We can adduce very few exceptions to its use, apart from a semi-twisted or normal perspective of the beasts in the Racó de Nando, Benasal (p. 29), Covarjos or Riu de Montllor.

Alongside these general features, there are marked regional differences in Levantine art. These could be attributed to distinct 'schools', such as those of the Maestrazgo massif, Albarracín, Alacón, La Araña, Dos Aguas, Alpera, Minateda or Nerpio, which seem to define the particular, original zone, round which there are extensions in all directions. Although opinions differ, in general artistic quality decreases towards the south as one leaves northern Castellón.

SUBJECT-MATTER

Animals

Although the subjects treated in Levantine art can be very varied, scenes of hunting are the most numerous. Other topics are warfare, dance, daily life and, as an exception, agricultural or pastoral activities. Landscape is not depicted, apart from a few trees or bushes, such as we see in the Cueva de Doña Clotilde, Albarracín, in the La Sarga caves, Alcoy, or in the Los Trepadores rock-shelter, Alacón. In the Abrigo de la Vacada, Santolea, there are some painted lines near the muzzle of an ox which may represent pasture-land. Animals may appear on their own, without the hunters, in herds grazing, or on the alert and expectant. Others are shown singly, running or at rest. Normally however, animals form part of a hunting scene, where there are archers shooting arrows at them, as in the Cueva dels Cavalls, Valltorta, or pursuing, surrounding or closing in on their prey. Frequently the animals are shown wounded, or even dead, with feet retracted (the ruminant in the Abrigo de Tortosilla), head hanging (the hind in the Prado de las Olivanas), or rushing away vertically down the rock-face (like the La Araña horse). Sometimes the animals are running towards the archers who are shooting at them, as is the case at the Cueva dels Cavalls, or they may be escaping from them, either wounded or unharmed. The Cueva Remigia, in the Gasulla gorge (p. 16), provides a good example: one group of the hunted boar is in flight, pursued by some of the archers while others surround the herd. A few animals have been felled and lie dead with their feet in the air. At El Cingle de la Mola Remigia an animal is being cut up and skinned. In short, animals

Racó de Nando (Els Covarjos), Benasal (Castellón). Horses being hunted (after Gonzalez Prats).

29

La Araña, Bicorp (Valencia). The middle rock-shelter, including the honey-gatherer and a horse in headlong flight: there are schematic symbols under some of the naturalistic animals (after Hernández Pacheco).

are shown in many different situations, but with the basic contrast between those on their own and those being hunted.

A good number of the large or medium sized animals painted naturalistically are shown stationary, with the head held high as though scenting a hunter. However, many can be regarded as significant in their own right, without reference to people or other beasts. We shall return to this theme when considering possible cults of the bull or deer.

Occasionally an animal is represented with the head turned, but it is most rare to find a front view. Male and female are almost always distinguished, especially among cervids and young animals. The commonest detail is of horns, tails and ears.

The species represented are not very sensitive to climate; the fact that there is not a single type from beyond the Pyrenees is of crucial importance for any supposed palaeolithic dating of Levantine art. The red deer (*Cervus elaphus*) is the commonest animal in the paintings, followed by mountain goat (*Capra ibex* or Pyrenean goat). Cattle are also frequently found (*Bos taurus*), as are wild boar (*Sus scropha*). There are far fewer horses, while fallow deer, chamois, canines, birds – like

the stork and crane – and arthropods are extremely rare. A fox, a canine which could be a dog, and a bear in the Cañaica del Calar seem to be exceptional, and the identification of felines in the Covacho Ahumado, Alacón, and the Abrigo de la Vacada, Santolea, is not so clear. The palaeolithic animals (onagers, bison, elk, saiga antelope, rhinoceros) which Breuil and Obermaier claimed to recognize in various rock-shelters may be rejected.

It must be admitted that frequently the animals are very difficult to identify, when insufficient detail, or smallness of scale, prevents determination of class, or when figures become indistinct or poorly preserved. Horns, antlers and ears allow greater precision. The progressive stylization of Levantine art, however, creates further confusion, so that often a figure may be identified only as a quadruped.

Cattle. These seem to correspond to the oldest phases of Levantine art. In many of the red examples the paint is very faded or fissured, and in cases of superimposition it is this type of painting which is covered. The figures are generally large, naturalistic in style and stationary. The

31

presentation develops, however, and in later phases they appear repainted and restored, smaller in scale but more animated. They have almost disappeared by the final phases of the art.

The group of white bull paintings in the Albarracín mountains is of especial interest. The animals, with prominent heads and heavy bodies, are shown in repose, paying no attention to the archers who may at times surround them. In rock-shelters discovered at La Losilla, however, it is remarkable to find that deer and horses are numerous, and the bull rare. This is the first appearance of the horse, for none was previously known in the Albarracín district. For the evolution of bull paintings, evidence already cited from Ceja de Piezarrodilla is important: there, a black bull is superimposed over a white one. At Los Cantos de la Visera (Murcia) a deer, in dark red, covers a reddish bull, demonstrating a sequence of colours, or the primacy of the bull over the deer. Another bull at this site has been changed into a deer, while in the Abrigo de Mas d'en Josep, Valltorta, it is a boar which replaces the bull. Again, in the Cueva de la Vieja, Alpera, antlers have been painted over bull horns (p. 25), but at the Prado de las Olivanas (Teruel) it is complete figures of bulls which are found covering earlier deer, of which details alone remain. Notwithstanding this contradiction, it is certain that in the majority of cases the bull should be designated the oldest animal.

We may also draw attention to the fact that these large figures of bulls are often shown to be wounded by tiny darts or arrows, which could be later than the original painting, and added to

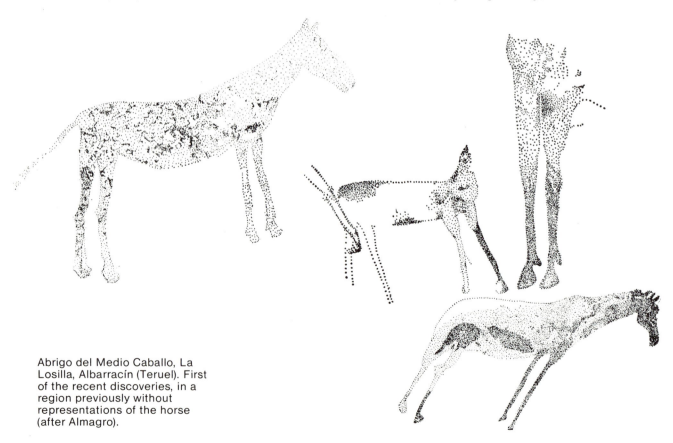

Abrigo del Medio Caballo, La Losilla, Albarracín (Teruel). First of the recent discoveries, in a region previously without representations of the horse (after Almagro).

32

complete its significance. We find examples of this in the Cuevas de la Araña (pp. 30–1), El Cingle de la Mola Remigia, Gasulla, or in the Riparo di Santolea, and it is not surprising that the original sense of any painting should later become modified, requiring revision in the representation (addition of wounds, change in the horns, hooves, etc.).

We should notice one exceptional case, which may be interpreted as a man being pursued by a bull, in the Cueva Remigia, Gasulla (p. 28). This seems to be the sole instance in which man is not depicted as the dominant figure in any encounter with either the bull or any other type of animal.

It is only at an advanced stage of the art that bulls are shown as objects of the chase, and then they are numerically fewer than the gregarious deer, goats or wild boar. The most interesting examples would be, in chronological order, the Albarracín sites, Cuevas de la Araña, Cogul, Minateda, those at Alpera, El Cingle de la Mola Remigia, at Villar del Humo, Cantos de la Visera, at Ladruñán and Abrigo de la Vacada.

At the point when Levantine art reached the height of its animation and began to become stylized, the figures of bulls disappeared, although they are present again smong the schematic art of the Bronze Age.

Horses. Examples of the horse family are uncommon, and the majority of them represent horses proper. Notable instances include the figure in the Cuevas de la Araña, rushing vertically down the rock-face and crossing a zigzag line; three from the new shelters at La Losilla, Albarracin, one with only the fore part of its body; and the lassoed horse in the Abrigo de la Selva Pascuala. At the Racó de Nando, Benasal, two archers are pursuing four extraordinary creatures (p. 29), with strange bodies and very short necks, though from their heads they appear to be horses. In general, the manes of horses are barely distinguishable. Asses, on the other hand, are clearly characterized by their long ears and short bodies. Sometimes they are ridden, as in the Los Borriquitos shelter, El Mortero de Alacón. Others are led off on a halter, as in the Cueva de Doña Clotilde, Albarracin, although this site already belongs to the phase of schematic art. In the Abrigo de la Vacada there is a very dubious example of an onager. However, it is quite possible that this animal would be found in Levantine art, since the wild ass (*encebro*) survived in the sierras of Teruel late into historical times.

Deer and goats. These animals are found in abundance and are present in almost every rock-shelter throughout each of the regions. Although they appear in a wide variety of poses, the conventions of representation are repeated. There are large, striking paintings of deer in repose, like those which dominate the rock-shelters of Val del Charco del Agua Amarga (pp. 14–15) or Cañaica del Calar. But most often they are shown in herds, and running, the males with large antlers and the females with their young. There is a curious composition at the Roca dels Moros, Calapatá, where one of the three naturalistic deer lies with one foreleg folded. The observation proposed in the case of the bull paintings may be repeated: namely, that there was evolution from large figures seen walking peacefully, or stationary, to those shown in active motion or agitation.

In the more realistic paintings, the antlers are clearly outlined, in the 'twisted' perspective, and there is careful depiction of ears and tail. Fawns are shown with mottling on the body, to correspond to actual dappling of the skin: for example, at the Racó Gasparo (p. 37) or the Cueva dels Cavalls.

Turning to the goat, we find none of the large-scale figures dominating scenes, and in general there are few paintings which belong to the oldest phase of the art. The horns may be shown large and strong, or alternatively small and fine, though they are always well delineated and clearly distinguished from the ears. We may notice the goat balanced on its hind legs to browse on a notional, but unpainted, tree in the Cueva Remigia (p. 16), or again the herd in the Cañada de Marco rock-shelter, which some have supposed to be controlled by the tall figure, as a shepherd, but which, given the superimposition of animals over the man, is preferably interpreted as a sequence of scenes. The goat in the Cueva del Queso at Alpera, which was changed into a deer by repainting, is of especial importance, since flaking of the rock-face along the lower margin of the head has given this animal the appearance of an elk. It was published as such by Breuil and his followers, who used it as evidence that Levantine art was palaeolithic in date.

Goats may be shown in herds, being preyed on by hunters. At Peña del Escrito, Villar del Humo, we find stylized representations, with very long horns. It therefore seems probable that one phase in the art, which was dominated by bulls and deer, was followed by another, characterized by the deer and the goat.

Chamois. There is an unquestionable example at the Prado del Tornero shelter at Nerpio, with long, fine horns, curving backward at the tip. The one at La Tortosilla, Avora, is an undefinable ruminant, seen with the head face-on, having small, straight horns, with a little ear to either side. It would not be impossible for the chamois to have survived in the cold Albacete mountains until neolithic times.

Wild boar. The figures are always crude, representing coarse and powerful animals. One example is the painting at the Val del Charco del Agua Amarga, where the boar is very large in proportion to the small archer in pursuit. The ones at El Polvorin, La Cenia, or at La Peña del Escrito, Villar del Humo, are more realistic. The most vivid scene is that of the herd in the Cueva Remigia (p. 16), with many beasts in different positions, most of them running, though some are dead. Evolution of the paintings follows the pattern noticed for other animals.

34

Dog family. Identification is more doubtful than in the case of cattle or deer. Wolves are certainly present at El Polvorín, one with its jaws open, and a thin, stylized body. Dogs or wolves may be represented at Fuente Sabuco, El Sabinar, or in the Los Trepadores and Los Borriquitos shelters at Alacón. The supposed dogs assisting a hunter at Alpera pose the question of their domestication, and whether this scene should be assigned to the mesolithic or the neolithic. But in either case there is more than reasonable cause for doubt.

A fox has been identified in the Cuevas de la Araña, and there may be others, poorly characterized, among animals shown with thick tails.

Birds. Identification again presents difficulties. There is one comparatively realistic instance, at El Polvorín, which could be a crane with wings open in flight. By contrast, the supposed stork – or at least wading-bird – at Los Cantos de la Visera is entirely schematic; it is partly covered by a naturalistic animal. All other alleged examples are dubious: for example, stylized symbols at Morella la Vella and Dos Aguas, where bisected angular signs have been interpreted as birds.

Insects. An interesting topic is the alleged portrayal of spiders catching flies, represented by fairly large red blobs, with several radial lines for the legs, and with small crosses nearby, double or single, which would be the flies. There are two clear examples, and a possible third, among rock-shelters in the Gasulla gorge. Hugo Obermaier was the first to identify these marks as spiders. He justified their disproportionate size, compared with surrounding paintings, as an indication of the hunters' admiring response to the spider's sinister technique for securing its prey. Some later writers have proposed instead that what we see are bee-hives, suspended by cords; for them, the little crosses are the homing bees.

Although as spiders the markings are admittedly not commensurate with adjacent paintings of men and beasts, this argument does not seem conclusive. Levantine painters in general pay little attention to the actual relative dimensions of their subjects, and, furthermore, it is quite possible that they might express their admiration for the spider's skill by deliberate exaggeration. Moreover, we do know of three pictures of honey-combs and bee-hives, in the Araña caves at

Roca dels Moros, Calapatá, Cretas (Teruel). Deer figures (after Cabré), discovered in 1903 and subsequently removed. Now in Barcelona Museum.

35

Mas d'en Josep, Valltorta, Tirig
(Castellón). Beating of deer
(after Obermaier). One animal
remains unfinished.

Bicorp (p. 51) and at the Solana de las Covachas, Nerpio; here natural holes in the rock have been chosen to represent the hives, twice without any painted modification. At La Araña, a bar of wood is shown supporting an access ladder for the honey-collector. Interpretation of the lines issuing from the painted features as cords would then be quite as much a conventional usage as their identification as spider legs. And it should be recalled that near one of the Gasulla examples, at Cueva Remigia, there is a closed spiral which could be a spider web. The hypothesis that these enigmatic painted blobs represent spiders, surrounded by flying insects, seems therefore plausible.

Bear. A case can be made for the depiction of a brown bear at Cañaica del Calar, although much of the figure is covered by a very dark vegetable stain. There are blackish, broad claws, in threes or fours; the head is only partially preserved.

36

Animal spoor. Closely related to the theme of the animal figures are the tracks, footprints or trails of blood on which the hunters depended for following their prey, or retrieving the wounded. We interpret as tracks those lines which follow a sinuous course, either continuous, or delineated by dots or parallel dashes. Shown one way or another, we find these in many of the shelters, and they are at times of considerable length. Their significance is most obvious either when they lead to an animal, wounded or no, or they run back from one towards a following hunter. In the Cueva Remigia (p. 16) a diminutive archer is bending over some tracks to examine them. Rejecting the hypothesis that they are human footprints, which would be contrary to the general significance of these hunting scenes, it is certain that when we encounter discontinuous paired dashes we are dealing with the tracks of cloven hooves. Lines of dots will represent the trail of blood from wounded animals. In the Riparo di Santolea an archer is shown with a wounded and bleeding animal. There is less certainty about the interpretation of continuous lines, which could indicate either of the situations above; they are not necessarily marks in the snow, or traps, as has been suggested at Cinto de las Letras. There are numerous examples, and they confirm our general proposition. In the Cueva Remigia, for instance, a kid which has been wounded by two arrows leaves a trail of parallel lines. Almost at the end of them is an archer. There are seven additional examples at this site, some without the animal which left the trail, and one showing a goat encountering his attacker at the end of a line which the latter had not followed.

In sum, these lines do in the main represent animal tracks, whether they should be understood as footprints or trails of blood. This is not to say that every group of dots has this significance. For example, the crude ones in the Abrigo del Huerto, Bezas, widely separated by a rough painting of a deer, and, furthermore, forming a triple line joined at the ends, should be excluded.

The question of the palaeolithic animals claimed by Breuil and accepted, with some reserve, by Obermaier, who also saw a supposed onager engraved at La Fuente del Cabrerizo, Albarracín, will be examined later. The possible domestication of animals, especially of the ass and the dog, will also be discussed below.

Human figures

Human beings are depicted less realistically than the animals; their representation shows greater stylization or idealization. The paintings are of conventional types, without any attempt at portraiture and only very occasionally with individualistic features. Certain details, like the nose

Racó Gasparo, Gasulla, Ares del Maestre (Castellón). Two phases are present: the woman with the fawn is painted over a quadruped.

37

Cuevas del Civil, Valltorta,
Albocácer (Castellón). A group
of ribbon-like ('cestosomatic')
men, in various poses (after
Obermaier).

or mouth, and, more rarely, the eyes or sex, are however frequently indicated. By contrast, head-gear, belts, limbs and joints, and different modes of dress, both masculine and feminine, are scrupulously portrayed. As we have said, the paintings are not of individuals but of types, though among these occurs a wide range of variation. There are formulas which apply not only to the shape and proportions of the body, but also to positioning and attitudes, but, though applied with monotonous repetition, they never deprive the figures of their vivacity and spontaneity in movement.

A classification of human forms was worked out by Obermaier and Wernert. Although not fully inclusive, it makes a valid distinction between realistic figures and those conventional representations which ignore natural proportions, to follow preconceived, notional rules. The authors called their classes (a) the realistic or Alpera type, (b) ribbon-figured ('cestosomatic'), (c) heavy-

Archers. 1, 2, 6, 7: Cueva Saltadora, Valltorta. 3: Cuevas del Civil, Valltorta. 4, 5, 9: Cueva de la Vieja, Alpera. 8: Covacho Ahumado, Alacón. 10: Mas d'en Josep, Valltorta. 11: Els Cavalls, Valltorta. (Figure 6 does not represent archers but men in conversation.)

limbed ('pachypod') and (d) thread-like ('nemetemorphic') forms. Since their evidence derived almost exclusively from figures in the Barranco de Valltorta, the scheme is somewhat limited in its application, although it is acceptable in general terms.

The ribbon figures stand on average about 25 cm high and have exaggeratedly stretched and elongated bodies, with a flattened, discoid head and broad, triangular chest, narrowing to an exiguous waist which turns into a very long and thin lower torso, supported by lengthened and robust legs. The calf muscles are clearly indicated. The heavy-limbed type, by contrast, is relatively short, with a large head and angular profile. The torso is short and thin, and the legs are shown gross and strong. Finally, in the thread-like figures we meet a linear technique combined with extreme stylization, with marked disproportion between different parts of the body. None of this, however, detracts from the vivacity and movement of these figures.

We are not in fact dealing with anthropological differences, but with distinct conventions of portrayal. It is difficult to understand them, since there is no valid chronological explanation and the various types co-exist in rock-shelters within the same geographical region. It must moreover be repeated that the classification is too simplistic and should be used only in a general way. The number of variants makes it virtually inapplicable.

In many rock-shelters, furthermore, we do find arrays of distinct physical types, showing marked physical differences, but who nonetheless belong within a single scene. We may cite Les Dogues, Ares del Maestre (p. 44), El Molino de las Fuentes, Nerpio, or El Polvorin at La Cenia. Here, two armed bands confront each other in battle, and the scenes appear to indicate that it is racially distinct groups which have come together in conflict. Evidence at Racó Gasparo (p. 63) is of greater importance, for two men with differently shaped heads are painted one above the other, suggesting a sequence of types. The older figure, in light red, has a rounded head and a pear-shaped coiffure, held in place by a diadem. He is overlain by the second figure, bright red in colour, whose head is greatly elongated, leaving us to suppose that an earlier, brachycephalic group was displaced by a dolichocephalic one. It would appear that we are observing pictures of historical, or commemorative, import. This assumption requires the problematic hypothesis of successive painters, each recording his own people: first the earlier inhabitants, and then those who drove them out.

In a scene of warfare at Minateda there is a group of very large warriors, with painted lines covering their bodies, who are armed with enormous triple-curved bows, which have often been identified as Asiatic. We shall return to this claim, but in the meantime note that some writers have seen negroid figures among the paintings at Cinto de las Letras, Dos Aguas. These few examples of possible racial features apart, however, it must be emphasized that paintings of men are almost always impressionistic, rendering and adapting the various parts of the human body in accordance with the dictates of chronological, geographical or artistic schools.

Men and their activities. Most of the male figures are nude (we leave aside for the present the implications for the contemporary climate). However, some clothing is shown, though not in full detail. It is certain that there were skirts or loin cloths, which do not stand out from the line of the body except when displaced by movement: on the climbing figures at El Cingle de la Mola Remigia, or in the La Araña caves, for example. Many of the nude male figures have a simple indication of the sex organs. Occasionally, however, the penis is painted realistically, and this is

Archers. 1: Cueva Saltadora (bearded). 2: Cueva Remigia. 3: Els Secans (with breeches). 4: La Araña (just after releasing the arrow). 5, 6: Cueva de la Vieja, Alpera. 7: Las Olivanas, Tormón

usual on the tiniest figures, or it is exaggerated, as on the Prado de las Olivanas warrior, or deliberately ithyphallic, as at Cogul (p. 47) or the Barranco de los Grajos (pp. 48–9). Sometimes it is difficult to decide whether the painted feature is a penis or a phallic shield.

Men are seen engaging in the most diverse activities. Hunting is the most frequent, and there they may be beaters, following a trail, pursuing or shooting animals, tracking the wounded or retrieving the slain. There are times when they seem to close up on the prey to put it to flight. When he goes armed to the chase, the hunter carried his bow hanging low, with a bundle of arrows in the same hand. The archer may be standing when he discharges his bow, both while it is drawn and when it retracts after the arrow is shot, or he may kneel, or even lie on the ground, as in the Callejón del Arquero, Albarracin. There is a splendid collection of shooting archers in rock-shelters in the Valltorta gorge, especially in the Cueva dels Cavalls. And there are many scenes of men, either armed or not, walking slowly, like the beautiful example at El Prado de las Olivanas,

Left. Men in bull-masks from Racó Molero and El Cingle de la Mola Remigia. *Above.* Horseman with helmet at El Cingle de la Mola Remigia (Bronze Age).

Tormón (p. 41); or climbing ladders, as in the Cuevas de la Araña (p. 51) and the Los Trepadores rock-shelter at Alacón, or the figure at El Cingle de la Mola Remigia; in the Abrigo de Solana de las Covachas, Nerpio, a file of men is seen climbing up a rock.

A convention frequently repeated is that used for running men; their speed is indicated by their legs being forced apart to form a continuous straight line. The best known example is at Val del Charco del Agua Amarga (p. 14), in a poorly preserved scene, but there are many more, showing the whole sequence from legs placed simply at an angle, to such widening as to show them as a single stroke, parallel to the ground. Archers in the Cueva del Tio Garroso, or the thread-like figures in the Valltorta rock-shelters, illustrate such series.

Among the range of other activities, we may mention men participating in dance scenes (Barranco de los Grajos, p. 48, or Cogul), or the archers' own dance at Santolea; numerous everyday tasks, such as flaying animals (El Cingle de la Mola Remigia), though many others are indecipherable; events inspired by military affairs, like marching, or executions; and other assemblages of people, for diverse ends.

Amidst this variety, nonetheless, we find repetition, if not identity, in the scenes and conventions used, sufficient not only to discern different schools within Levantine art, but also to establish its basic unity. However, some writers would prefer to exclude certain, more distinctive, paintings, such as the grave figure at Los Trepadores, holding his knees with both hands, or the stylized figures in the frieze in the Pared de la Tia Mona (both these sites are in Alacón).

It should be emphasized that the different human types, and varying degrees of stylization, described above occur together in single scenes. The various problems this poses for the dating of the paintings and for interpreting the conceptual approach of the artist will be considered below. While attempts to resolve complex friezes into their related artistic styles may not have reached definitive conclusions, it is always easy to determine the rôle which each figure is playing in them.

Alongside the general simplification, or idealization, of the human form, rare cases of detail should be considered: of nose, mouth, chin, pointed beard, sex organs, and hands and feet, sometimes with the fingers and toes shown in groups of three or five. It is exceptional to find the foot carefully delineated; usually a rough line suffices, at an angle to the leg. The figure with painted toes in the Abrigo de Solana de las Covachas is quite unusual. It is possible that the general elimination of detail derives both from the smallness of many figures and from their idealized representation.

By contrast, great care is taken to portray ornaments. This emphasis reflects not only a primitive instinct for self-adornment and the attraction of the opposite sex, but also, and more essentially, a need to express status, authority or position, including any ranking based on magical powers. Pending further discussion below, we may say that the head-ornaments may be feathers, worn two or more together, and at times with ostentation. There are hats or caps of very special forms: flat-topped and wide (Cinto de las Letras and Cueva de Doña Clotilde), with a high crown and brim (Prado de las Olivanas, p. 41, and El Cingle de la Mola Remigia), caps with little ears or horns (Cueva de la Vieja, p. 39, and Cueva Saltadora, p. 39), and others with features difficult to identify. We find paintings of pendants, which would have been of shell, or perforated teeth. Some figures wear tassles, or tufts, notably the complicated ones seen on the wounded man, falling onto his face, in the Cueva Saltadora (p. 45), or the large feathered head-dresses on the men in the Cueva de la Vieja (p. 41). Another detail to be carefully recorded is the way in which the hair is arranged. The different styles are found repeated many times. In one, a fillet or diadem is used to secure the hair over the temples, drawing it flat across the head, with a bunch falling onto the shoulder on either side. There are also pear-shaped *coiffures*, or the hair may be left to fall

Cogul and Cinto de las Letras, Dos Aguas. Women, one with a digging-stick.

Les Dogues in the Gasulla gorge, Ares del Maestre (Castellón). Combat between two bands of archers (after Porcar).

abundantly about the neck and shoulders. Often it appears to have been cut, and on occasion it looks curly or frizzy. But in most cases the form of the head prevents us from seeing how the hair was worn.

Men in the Cueva Saltadora, Cuevas del Civil, at Los Recolectores, Alacón, and other sites are bearded. At El Cingle de la Mola Remigia, a bearded man is contrasted with a young man by his side, whom he is instructing by pointing at a bull.

On the arms were worn bracelets, or ornaments suspended from the elbow or fore-arm, in the form of strands of vegetable fibres, feathers or even tassles. These could have symbolized authority or status. No necklaces, or other neck ornament, are known. Any asserted examples seem in fact to be pouches, bags, quivers, or simply bundles of arrows carried on the shoulder.

Trappings worn round the waist were at once decorative and practical, serving to suspend squared pieces of cloth or skin, as well as feathers or ribbons. They become visible when men walk quickly, or run, streaming behind in fast motion, or displaced from the body in climbing (the sites of La Araña and El Cingle de la Mola Remigia have already been mentioned in this context). These short skirts, or aprons, were in general use, though only occasionally are they distinguished from the outline of the body. This is why most men appear to be nude, and the protecting loin cloths would also explain why there is only occasionally an indication of sex.

Leg ornaments are attached at the knee by bindings, and sometimes shown flaring out over the calf, very much as among modern primitives. Conventionally they have been called 'garters', and it is possible they were indeed simple bindings of cord or bands, rather than, as some have supposed, fringes or laced fastenings at the bottom of breeches or trousers. It has also been suggested that they were the upper part of leggings, or protective leg coverings. They would seem however to have nothing to do with either wide or narrow breeches which reach to the knee, since these are on occasion clearly depicted, as at Els Secans, Mazaleón (p. 41), or El Garroso at Cerro Felío. Moreover, they appear on otherwise naked figures, or those wearing the simple loincloth.

The discovery of masked men, who could be sorcerers, has excited particular interest. Whatever their significance, there are clear examples at Racó Gasparo and Racó de Molero (p. 42), both sites being near the Montalbana and the Gasulla gorge. The painting in the Abrigo de la Vacada is more doubtful. The first two are standing figures, with human body and limbs, though

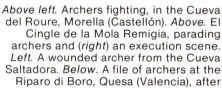

Above left. Archers fighting, in the Cueva del Roure, Morella (Castellón). *Above.* El Cingle de la Mola Remigia, parading archers and (*right*) an execution scene. *Left.* A wounded archer from the Cueva Saltadora. *Below.* A file of archers at the Riparo di Boro, Quesa (Valencia), after Gonzales Prats.

in an unusual front-facing position, and with a long tail and a bull's head having clearly marked horns. They are carrying a bow, or a javelin. These are certainly men, with the head or mask of a bull on their heads. Possibly they are representing the spirit of the chase, in a masked dance, or we may imagine a totemic rite, or alternatively a bull cult. The painting at La Vacada is of a bull's head on its own, and there has never been an animal body attached. It may be interpreted as a mask. We can point to numerous parallels elsewhere, again specifically relating to bulls: at Val Camonica, Fezzan, Tassili and so on. The meaning of other figures wearing decorative feathers remains quite problematical: at Val del Charco and Cañada de Marco, Alcaine, for example. They could be hunters, disguised to allow an unobserved approach to their prey.

The appearance of horsemen in Levantine contexts is of critical importance for dating. Domesticated on the Pontic steppes towards 3000 BC, the riding horse spread widely in the Near East during the second millennium, reaching the eastern Mediterranean during the Middle Helladic, about 1500 BC. Necessarily therefore, it will have arrived in the western Mediterranean rather later than this, that is to say, during the Late Bronze Age. A careful analysis of evidence for domesticated and riding animals is thus of importance – signs of the appearance of bits, or saddles, for example. Two horses being led on a rein or a halter appear at Los Canforos, Peñarrubia, and the Cueva de Doña Clotilde, Albarracin, but both these rock-shelters undoubtedly belong to an

already stylized phase of the art. Nor are these horses being ridden. We find a quite different scene in the Abrigo de la Selva Pascuala at Villar del Humo, where a horse is being hunted with the lasso by a highly stylized figure of a man. It is possible to distinguish the rope round the animal's neck; with his back towards us, the man is casting, rather than pulling on, it.

Although not absolutely established, in the rock-shelters of Los Borriquitos and Los Trepadores in the Mortero gorge (Alacón) there appear to be men mounted on asses. There is no doubt, on the other hand, about the figure of a horseman at El Cingle de la Mola Remigia in the Gasulla gorge (p. 42), mounted on a horse he controls by reins, and himself wearing a splendid crested helmet, which dates him securely to the Bronze Age. In drawing, colour and general style, however, he is quite distinct from the other work in the cave, apart from the crude, schematic figures of goats painted nearby. It should be emphasized that naturalistic and schematic paintings are frequently found together in the rock-shelters and that they derive from different periods. The same dating cannot be applied to them all.

Women. There are far fewer paintings of women than of men, although, apart from a few difficult cases, they are clearly distinguishable. Diagnostic features may be breasts and prominent buttocks, the skirts worn, the type of activity engaged in and the absence of weapons. Absence of the penis is not indicative, since often it is not shown even when men are naked. Nor is there much evidence from the hair or its arrangement, which is similar in men and women. Of the breasts, which are shown pendent and in profile, only one may be included, or, if two, painted either together, or one to each side of the body.

The shape of the women at the Alpera sites, who have straight skirts, prominent hips and bound hair, differs sharply from the forms at Cogul (pp. 43 and 47), where the breasts are elongated and hanging, the hair dressed into a triangular or pear-shaped outline, and the skirts bell-shaped. We find something similar at Val del Charco del Agua Amarga, with a narrow waist and prominent buttocks. A different pattern appears at Dos Aguas (p. 43), and a very distinctive form emerges in the two figures at the Abrigo de Solana de las Covachas, who seem to have heavy breasts, shown one to each side, repeating the convention found in the Barranco de los Grajos, Cieza (pp. 48–9). Surprisingly, this last site contains fourteen female figures, out of a total of forty-nine. Women are generally shown with prominent buttocks. Furthermore, in the Cueva de el Polvorin and at Racó Gasparo, this feature is combined with angularity in the line of the skirt. Compared with the heaviness of the lower part of the body the upper half looks slender, and even linear, apart from the breasts.

Skirts worn are generally bell-shaped and brought in to the waist, as though held by a tie or belt; at Dos Aguas (p. 43) we see this knotted at the back. They are very full at the bottom, falling either into points on each side, or ending in a straight hem, as on the women seen gossiping in the Cueva de la Vieja. The usual width of the skirt is reduced at the Cueva de el Polvorin, while at the Barranco de los Grajos (pp. 48–9) we find a very short skirt among long ones. One woman at Dos Aguas is wearing a loose ceremonial gown. A very small woman at Fuente de la Arena is exhibiting a wide band, attached to her waist, which she is waving in the air. At Minateda (pp. 68–9), a woman leading a child by the hand wears a tight, straight hemmed skirt; another there is arrayed in a type of divided skirt, of which no other example is known in Levantine art.

Breasts and hips, together with the skirts worn, are thus the important features used to differentiate women. In addition we may notice that they never take part in the hunting scenes, or carry any type of weapon. However they do participate in dance scenes, and in later paintings they may have a digging-stick. Frequently the figures are on their own, and they are never shown in direct relationship with the men. The two women talking together in the Cueva de la Vieja, Alpera, are gesticulating, while at Minateda a woman holds the hand of a little girl. Those at Val del Charco and in the Cuevas de la Araña are large in scale, and may be thought to preside over their section of the frieze, although they appear to have no relationship to the figures which surround them.

I do not consider that the unsexed figures with a triangular chest, even though this is shown to be full, represent women; this is a convention used for men. Compare the three black paintings, the men wearing eared caps, their arms linked, and possibly jumping or dancing, at the Cueva Saltadora (p. 39), or the figure painted over the goat-herd in the Abrigo de la Cañada de Marco, Alcaine.

Ornaments for women hardly differ from those for men and the same is true of hair styles. Generally the hair is bound in a fillet, which gives a pear-shaped outline to the head. Common ornaments are feathers in the hair, ribbons hanging from the arms, and bracelets, together with the skirts, which leave the upper parts of the body free. Only exceptionally is a woman completely dressed: for example, the one in the Abrigo de la Pareja, Dos Aguas, who is wearing a full and heavy garment, with a profusion of trimmings. Other objects which are possibly proper to women are castanets, or clappers, used to accompany dancing, and found in the Barranco de Pajarejo or Cinto de las Letras, Dos Aguas (p. 43).

We may conclude by noting that in Levantine art any grouping of female figures into types must

derive from distinctions in dress or ornaments, since physical or anatomical detail is generally similar throughout. Subject to this reservation, the following division might be accepted: first, the Alpera and Minateda type; next, Cogul and Los Grajos; thirdly, Val del Charco, the Araña caves, El Polvorin, Santolea and Racó Gasparo; and, finally, the exceptional instances at Solana de las Covachas, Cinto de las Letras at Dos Aguas and the shelter of La Pareja nearby, and El Pajarejo, Albarracin. There remains some doubt about the figures at Las Olivanas, at Gasulla, Racó de Molero and Saltadora (the latter are probably men).

Social and economic activities

The majority of the scenes in Levantine art, as we have seen, are concerned with hunting, and no aspect of the chase is overlooked. Man is always triumphant and the animals – pursued, trapped, wounded or slain – are his victims. The rôle of every individual depicted in the task of the chase can be distinguished, despite the complexity of some of the friezes. It is possible that the Cueva Remigia (p. 28) may record a wounded bull (with its mouth comically open) pursuing an archer, who is running swiftly in front of him. If this is so, it is the sole instance of a man put to the worse by an animal.

Warriors and conflict. These highly significant scenes can represent actual or simulated fighting as well as war dances. It is not always easy to isolate separate incidents, since the figures tend to become mixed with neighbouring themes, nor can we be sure which dances are bellicose. However, the meaning seems clear in the Cueva del Roure at Morella la Vella (p. 45), at Les Dogues (p. 44) and in the Molino de las Fuentes shelter, Nerpio. At El Roure four thread-like figures confront three archers, whose attentions seem centred on the plumed leader of the first

Barranco de Los Grajos, Cieza (Murcia). Dance scene (after Beltrán)

group. Physically, all the men are of the same type, and all adopt similar poses, with the forward leg bent and the other braced and straight. It may just be possible to discern slight, ear-like projections on the second group. Les Dogues shows the meeting of two bands of archers. The eleven men in the one group have elongated bodies, and hold their legs moderately far apart. Their leader has high plumes on his head, others projecting from the small of his back, and wears a loincloth. Two of his followers also have feathered caps. The group is sustaining an attack by some twenty warriors, all of slighter build, who are rushing at them, their legs stretched apart into a horizontal line. The forces are separated by a blank zone. It could be said that the group defending itself occupies the upper left, and the anthropologically distinct attackers the lower right of the scene. It is evident that we are looking at an actual battle which took place between the inhabitants of a country and invaders who attacked them.

At El Molino de las Fuentes (or the Abrigo Sautuola) at Nerpio there is an encounter between some fifteen archers, occupying the top left-hand corner of the scene, and some twenty attackers on the upper right. The defenders appear to be protected by a stalagmite deposit projecting from

Cave II at Barranco de Los Grajos, Cieza (Murcia). Women in a dance scene, with a quadruped.

the cave wall, which is emphasized by a red line. The attackers are shown in one pose, leaning far forward and discharging their bows, and drawn up in a line, with four men on the upper flank and one on the lower. One group, standing upright with their feet slightly apart, appear to be directing their attention to an area below that occupied by their enemies. Although less marked than at Les Dogues, at this site too there are some differences between the two groups of archers, especially with respect to size, since none in the band of attackers exceeds 3 cm in height.

It may be that other scenes of confrontation among archers are represented by the dances of armed men. At the Cueva de el Polvorin, two archers of differing type, who are separated by a rocky protuberance, appear to be making towards each other with their arms outstretched. One assemblage of more than sixty men in the Cuevas del Civil, Valltorta, all ribbon-like figures of the same scale, could involve a war-like dance; there are four scenes but they fall into two bands.

El Cingle de la Mola Remigia contains an especially interesting scene where some fifty archers, each armed with a simple bow, are divided into two bands, running towards each other. The group on the left is headed by a file of five men (p. 45) marching in step and at speed, to judge from their widespread legs, each of which lies parallel to the corresponding one of his fellows. Their leader is wearing a high crowned hat, and each has a handful of arrows, held upright, the men on their left and the chief on his right, with the bow carried aloft in the free hand. This file of men was unique in Levantine art until a recent discovery in the Riparo di Boro at Quesa (Valencia: p. 45). Here, four nude warriors, with their penises depicted, are seen wearing knee ornaments and sometimes ample head-gear or head-dresses, marching in step carrying a bow and a bunch of four arrows. The latter are in the left hand, and two of the men hold their right arm raised.

Whatever the exact interpretation of these, and many other scenes of archers in confrontation, there is no doubt about their familiarity with the disposition and deployment of armed men. We must suppose, first, that the painters were deeply versed in fighting with the bow and arrow; and also that war-like encounters between native groups and invaders were being commemorated. The efforts taken to convey which people belonged to each side is clearly illustrated at La Fuente de Sabuco at El Sabinar. A small group of three, thread-like archers is seen in the lower left of the picture, opposing twelve archers with round heads and sometimes triangular body, almost all of them grouped in the upper right. Without entering into further detail, we may remark that these marked distinctions in human 'type' do not correspond in this instance to any chronological difference. They derive from the desire to differentiate, by physical representation, between two separate groups.

Related to scenes of conflict are those which show archers raising their bows over the dead, or those of archers who have been wounded, undoubtedly intentionally. Such is the famous figure in the Cueva Saltadora (p. 45), with his head-plumes falling forward as he is about to collapse over bended knee, arrows fixed in his body. A similar case might be that of a man on the ground, headless, with arrows in his body in the Cueva Remigia, who, it could be surmised, was a chieftain sacrificed at the end of his term of office. From the same cave in the Gasulla gorge, and from that of El Cingle nearby, there are five examples of scenes where a regular line of men stand with bows raised above their heads, before a wounded or dead figure, or sometimes one on all fours or halted, with arrows in his body (p. 45). This could represent an execution squad, with their arms raised in jubilation. They occupy the upper part of the scene, with the victim at the bottom (or, in one case, on the left).

There is something analogous in the shelter of Los Trepadores, Alacón, where a symmetrically

arranged group of seven stylized archers are raising their bows over an indistinct human figure, lying at their feet. The exact significance of these scenes remains questionable, but it is beyond dispute that we see real or symbolic executions, dealing with enemies, prisoners, malefactors or possibly evil spirits. They could even be the conclusion of a ritual dance, or some other rite. Manifestly, the scenes demonstrate military organization, devoted to duties regulated by pre-ordained rules.

Dance. Associated with warfare, fertility rites, or simply pleasure, there are many differing forms of dance in the art. We have already suggested that opposed pairs, or groups, of warriors may denote dancing, especially when they are of the same physical type, or are unarmed, as in the Abrigo del Arquero, at Ladruñán. Two men in bird-disguise in the Cueva Remigia also seem to be so engaged. Elsewhere, women participate in the dancing. A single figure, with arms crooked above her head, at El Polvorín is clearly dancing, and in this attitude she can be compared with another at La Fuente de la Arena at Alpera. We should first explain that the women's dances were executed with the upper part of the body, especially with movement of the arms, while the feet stayed still. The best groups of dancers are at Cogul (p. 47), Barranco de los Grajos (pp. 48–9), Barranco del Pajarejo and Cinto de las Letras. At Cogul, the so-called 'phallic' dance is made up of ten women around a tiny nude and ithyphallic figure, perhaps repainted over an analogous man, also in black. The women are either black in colour, or light red, at times reinforced with black strokes. Their heads are pear-shaped and, on some, one or two large pendent breasts are clearly shown. All have bell-shaped skirts, which fall in a point on either side; sometimes there is a bracelet at the elbow, or ribbon ornaments. It appears that the painter attempted to place the dancers in their correct relationships. Thus the first two are holding hands, while others must be viewed from behind, since the breasts are invisible. The figure which completes the scene has an

51

arched body, whereas the others are upright. Together, this indicates an intention to show the figures in a circle, with the small man in the centre. Nonetheless, it is clear that the scene was made up in successive stages: two of the women are the oldest figures, the rest being added on at least two later occasions. We must however concede that the significance of repaintings might require some modification to this interpretation, in which the man in his 'phallic' state would be the final addition to the scene.

Most writers agree that Cogul records a phallic dance, though it has also been suggested that the painting deals with a tribal investiture. Others, seeking an Aegean precedent, have proposed a 'bull-fight' on the Cretan model, in which animals and women take part, the man then belonging to a nearby hunting scene, with phallic archers. But the obvious intention of the scene at Los Grajos confirms the first interpretation of Cogul. At both sites, the phallic dance constitutes an initiative ceremony, like that practised by modern primitive hunters during the breeding season (of bison, for example), to ensure increase in the herds.

The dance at the Barranco de los Grajos (pp. 48–9) is extraordinary to a degree, in respect both of the principal scene at the rock-shelter, and of the two women with an animal painted in a little cave to the side. There are some twenty women in the main frieze, with a few men among them. Their bell-shaped skirts are of medium length, falling to lateral points at the hem. The women adopt a range of poses. One holds her arms akimbo, another, above her head in a circle. The right arm of a third is curved towards the body, while the left is thrown upwards so violently as to swing the breasts. The first line, of seven women, is headed by a fairly schematic male figure, and there are three or four more men behind them. A small figure painted above the dance scene has a monstrous penis, shown as a continuation of the line of the body, a common Bronze Age convention. To the right of the frieze, three women mingle with four men, one markedly ithyphallic.

The dance at Los Grajos is unique in Levantine art. The various gestures and movements of the dancers are remarkable, especially those of the arms, and the swaying from the waist, which is sometimes so vigorous as to double the body backwards. The women's legs remain stationary, drawn as parallel lines crooked at the end for the feet, which are usually shown facing in the same direction. Doubts begin to arise when the relationship between the women and the men is examined. As possibly at Cogul, the small schematic and phallic man is of a period later than the women, and it is difficult to encompass the further file of men seen at the top of the picture in the women's dance. There is also the male group, shown in agitation, whose movement extends to their feet as well as to the arms: an interesting contrast between the dances of men and women. It is however indisputable that their dance centres on a quadruped, which is itself moving.

The painting in the little adjacent cave is of two women dancing behind another animal, while all the figures move towards the right. The women are strongly inclined in that direction. They wear the bell-shaped skirt, reaching to the knee. The breasts are clearly shown, one to either side of the body. The left arms are thrown forward, while the right of one is bent back toward the waist. As in the main frieze, the animal cannot be identified.

A scene in the Barranco del Pajarejo, Albarracin (p. 51), was also published as a phallic dance on the supposed evidence of a little figure showing a large, erect penis, with three women holding objects which were identified as castanets. A careful study allows us to say that the man is not 'phallic', but shows no sexual organs, whereas the instrument in the hand of one of the women is an angled digging-stick, analogous to others found in Levantine art (cf. the section on gathering).

The same may be said of Cinto de las Letras, Dos Aguas, where we find two women, very different in stature, one wearing a long, heavy skirt, the other a simpler one, tied at the back. They are holding in their hands sticks, one of which is also angled, like a pick. The smaller figure is bending well forward, as though to fix these objects in the ground. One of the women at El Pajarejo was curved into a similar position, although here the angled tool is much bigger. Furthermore, at El Cingle de la Mola Remigia, alongside the figure in the bull's head mask, is a man with two sticks in either hand.

The question to decide is whether these are simply harvesting scenes, or whether they represent fertility dances performed by the women, designed to invoke yield from the soil by beating it with sticks and breaking it with picks, as if fertilizing a human body.

Gathering. The evidence above can be related to known scenes of gathering; the cultural and chronological import of these depends on whether they depict the simple collection of wild plants or tasks in an agricultural cycle. If the latter, then the scenes are neolithic in date, as indeed would be the case if the dance scenes are in fact fertility rites. Relevant tools would be a simple stick (the digging-stick of the Bushmen, or other tribes), since a weighted stick is never shown, although perforated spherical stones have been found in the Cueva de la Sarga, Valencia. Additionally, there are the angled picks, in varying sizes. Occasionally, the sticks are so short that we must think that what is painted is symbolic, rather than of actual size. Apart from those quoted above, there are further, very clear, examples of the digging-stick at Cinto de las Letras, as well as at the Los Recolectores rock-shelter (Alacón). At both these sites, men are shown bending over, as though breaking the soil. In the Covacho de las Trepadores, also in Alacón, it is possible to distinguish people gathering from bushy trees.

Another important product collected was honey. Supposed examples in many caves are dubious, but the evidence in the Cuevas de la Araña (p. 51) is quite clear. The convention of representing hives by natural hollows or crannies in the rock-face has already been discussed. At La Araña, two crossing strokes are painted which could depict bars of wood, from which are hanging three ropes, tied horizontally at intervals, to form a ladder. A man has climbed up alongside a hive, gripping the ladder with his legs, and with one hand in the crevice and a basket or container in the other. Another man is also climbing the ropes, carrying a bag like that of his companion on his shoulder; only a third of the way up, he is not supported by a rung, but grips the ropes with hands and legs – without, however, clutching them to himself, or between his knees. The existence of the ropes tells us something about textile working; they would certainly be made from esparto, and its fibres would need to be twisted. On the technique of collecting the honey, we know that in this region it is possible to take the honey-comb without protective clothing at times when the bees are immobilized by cold. In this painting, however, there are fourteen insects, indicated by crosses, buzzing round the collector.

Domestication of animals. Possible examples of dogs among the paintings are highly questionable, especially the one already mentioned with a hunter at the Cueva de la Vieja, Alpera (pp. 24–5). Examples of mounted men in several sites in the El Mortero gorge are however far clearer; in particular the cavalryman controlling his mount with reins at El Cingle de la Mola Remigia (p. 42). The Abrigo de la Selva Pascuala, as we have seen, shows the lassoeing of a horse by a schematic figure of a man. Another is being led on a halter in the Cueva de Doña Clotilde, Albarracín. The problem is to distinguish hunting scenes from representations of domesticated animals and, where the latter are shown, to determine the date of the rock-shelter and whether the paintings are neolithic. With the Selva Pascuala animal, the line of what some have supposed to be a tether reaches the neck, and somewhat below, and does not issue from the mouth. In the case of the rider at El Cingle, what we know about the helmet and the bridle, as well as independent dating for the spread of horse riding, requires a very late date, well after 1500 BC.

Arms and equipment

Weapons. Bows and arrows are the commonest weapons. There are exceptional cases of other projectiles, such as a light spear or javelin, and of lassos. A high proportion of the male figures are archers. They adopt various postures when drawing their bows. When they are running, or walking, they carry a bunch of arrows in their hand, generally with one at the ready and the rest in reserve. At times, the bow is raised above the head, in excitement or jubilation.

The bows can be very large, sometimes even longer than the body. Some examples are triple-curved, or possibly reflexed or semi-reflexed, as at Els Gascons, in the Cueva de la Vieja, Alpera (p. 41), or El Pudial, Ladruñán. More frequently, the bows are small and simple. If we imagine the El Pudial archer to be about 1.70 m tall, then the large bow would measure more than 1.55 m in length. However, we need to consider what margin of exaggeration may be involved in conventional representation of the bows, both large and small. Possibly, actual measurements should be looked for between the two extremes. The Abbé Breuil compared the recurved and triple bows at Minateda (pp. 68–9) with neolithic, but non-Oriental, examples from North Africa, and supposed that in Spain they were 'foreign', or imported. It is not, however, certain that Levantine art does depict a true composite bow, nor is it essential that these should derive from the Near East. There is also the theory that they originated in the west, and passed from there to North Africa during a meso-neolithic phase when cultural currents were running from the Peninsula to the Maghreb. With certain reservations, we may judge that the strings of the Levantine bows were between 0.50 m and 1.50 m long, but bearing in mind the simplification of detail which was usual in the art, the more or less conventional outline painted will not always show the full nature of the weapon.

The arrows used were usually long, at least in proportion to the bow. When an archer is shooting, he may bring at least one other arrow up parallel with the bow, held in his left hand. Generally an archer is painted with a handful of three or four arrows, which are grasped in the middle of the shaft, so that the ends spread out, to show one angular, as the point, and the other lanceolate or spearhead-like, for the feathering. The kneeling archer in the Cueva de la Vieja, Alpera, has three arrows upright behind him, as though supported on the rock-face (p. 24); these have barbed heads, though without any visible feature at their ends. A hunter at El Tortosilla, Ayora, and one in El Cingle de la Mola Remigia, Gasulla, are carrying weapons of this type upright in their hand, as though they may be lances. Whatever their use, these heads would seem to be conventional representations of flint points, which would be attached by means of resin or other vegetable substances to the shaft. There is nothing to prevent other arrows from being simple wooden darts with a pointed end, or with bone or horn points; mostly the points are not differentiated, apart from those with angled heads. The lanceolate shaft end represents feathering to steady the flight; it could be a simple leaf, fixed into a slot. Some arrows at Alpera are shown as angular at one end and oval at the other. At the Cueva Saltadora it is the oval end which is turned towards the archer's body, whereas in most cases, when the arrows are carried, it is with points forward. But to dispel doubts about the interpretation, it can be recalled that when arrows are shown sticking in an animal's body it is the lanceolate end which is seen to be protruding.

In seeking to prove that Levantine art could not be palaeolithic, F. Jordá Cerda claimed that it included arrow forms – leaf or laurel-shaped, rhomboidal, with terminal points, or barbed and tanged – which were quite outside the range of trapezes, triangles, crescents etc. used in epi-palaeolithic or mesolithic times, and that furthermore the existence of the bow at those times remains unproven. However, the arrows represented in Levantine art have only a simple tip, like the pointing of a wooden shaft – except for those with a barbed head. If these last are accurately portrayed, they do admittedly raise some difficulties, which, as will be seen, Jordá would resolve by supposing them to be of metal.

Receptacles. Quivers for carrying arrows are very rarely depicted. They are seen hanging from an archer's shoulder, or by themselves, as though left on the ground. Arrows, too, are painted on their own: at the foot of archers, or in hiding-places, though also simply lying about, as if lost. There are five places in the Gasulla gorge where arrows are painted along with pouches or baskets, with bindings or handles for attaching all these objects to a transverse carrying-stick. Occasionally a bow is shown too. In the Cueva Saltadora the container has a lateral handle, and there are arrows in the quiver (p. 51). Bags and baskets, which would be of leather, or woven from vegetable fibres, reeds or osiers, are not uncommon. They vary in size and shape, though almost always the profile is ovoid or globular and there is a substantial handle, or bindings for lifting. Sometimes they are being carried, hanging on a man's shoulder like a haversack or game-bag. One of the honey-gatherers in the Cuevas de la Araña has a pouch suspended in this way, while his companion holds a container by the handle. It would appear that, in addition to simple baskets for provisions and receptacles for water and honey, there were sets of such bags, with arrows, quiver and carrying stick, which were specific to the hunter. Not every suitable bag in these contexts need be a quiver; they could serve for food or other necessities – perhaps even for venom for poisoning arrows, in which case the accompanying stick or rod might be not for transport, but for stirring the liquid.

Slings and lassos. Very simple examples of these have been recognized. Identifying possible snares presents more difficulty, because of the subjective element in the interpretation. They are basically trip ropes, as at Cinto de las Letras. The Abrigo de la Selva Pascuala at Villar del Humo shows a lasso being cast over the head of a horse, to fall round its neck. A cord-like symbol painted in the Araña caves might indicate another lasso; in the El Polvorín rock-shelter an archer has caught a quadruped with one.

Their uses of rope occasion no surprise. We have seen very long ropes utilized for honey collection, as well as for other purposes. Cords can occur in connection with men and women's clothing, to form a belt, for example. There are also a few examples of halters. Short lengths could be thongs, but manufacture from twisted strands must have been usual.

CHAPTER FIVE

The significance and cultural contribution of Levantine art

Spanish Levantine art, like any other, made a contribution to the society to which its painters and their viewers belonged. It is important to exploit it as an historical source, whether its primary intention was magical, religious, narrative, or simply descriptive of everyday life and customs. Consequently, it is useful to consider the reasons for which the paintings were undertaken, before approaching the question of its dating. The most appropriate method is through a simple, general assessment of the themes and subjects which we have already described.

In the first place, almost all writers agree about the obsessive concern with hunting displayed in Levantine art, in all its manifestations, and conclude that the paintings must have had a religious aim. Although aware of reservations nowadays felt about the hypothesis of magical intent, this too is recognized as a component in the art – in the same way as it is allowed to be an explanation of the art of palaeolithic hunters, despite obvious differences. The presence of men in Levantine art, and the way they are shown to dominate animals, weakens the notion of invoking help from supernatural powers in finding, hunting and catching animals on the one hand, and for ensuring their supply on the other. Religion, and the idea of hunting magic, convert the rock-shelters into sanctuaries, strategically sited outside habitation zones and normally without evidence of being occupied on a permanent basis. Certain rock-shelters, however, do have signs of settlement nearby, or at their mouth. The religious and reverential nature of the art caves and their surroundings will perhaps explain the accumulation of paintings at certain sites, and in certain areas, while suitable and accessible caves remain unpainted and whole areas inside the Levantine zone are quite devoid of art. The density of painted shelters in the mountains of Albarracín or the 'Barrancos' of Gasulla and Valltorta cannot be fortuitous. Like the richly painted friezes of Cerro Felío, Alacón, and those at Alpera and Nerpio, they must reflect the aura of certain localities, either magical or religious. Persistent usage of the same sites through time, furthermore, including repainting to preserve figures, or making additions in different styles, is also an expression of their special status. Whether this quality counts as 'manna' will depend on the weight accorded to theories of magic. The many layers of paint observed at Minateda, for example, denotes a considered conviction, whether – as Ripoll claims – only four or five are

56

visible, or thirteen, as Breuil asserted. There are similar findings in many other shelters: the most significant may be Abrigo V at Solana de las Covachas, Nerpio, and especially Cogul. At this last site, Iberian and Latin inscriptions have been added to the repainted figures. The one reading *Secundio votum fecit* could relate to the phallic dance scene (p. 47) and fertility rites, should we in fact have discovered a true sanctuary with a potency which survived into historical times.

If we allow that rock-shelters with paintings are sanctuaries, and accept the significance of their constant repetition of hunting scenes, then the interpretation of detail becomes of secondary importance, beside the general conclusion that Levantine art represents the fulfilment of a religious (or magical) rite. The art does relate to the activities of the chase, activities basic to the economic life of the community. It is necessary to relate the paintings of slain, wounded or imperilled animals, of sorcerers or men with bovine masks, and of propitiatory dances, to the depicted rites of death, execution or the wounded, to activities concerned with attracting and destroying, as well as conserving, game and to the ceremonies of secret societies. Together they may constitute a sort of animal mythology, and possibly imply the cult of certain species, especially the bull.

The phallic dances, and those performed around an animal, would relate to fertility ceremonies. Ethnographic comparisons are hazardous, but there is remarkable similarity with the rites of many modern hunting peoples, which take place during the breeding season of the animals whose increase they seek to ensure. There could be a similar intention in the activity of the women shown with sticks pointing towards the ground, to beat and break the soil in a rite of penetration and insemination. Comparable agricultural dances have persisted until very recent times.

Possibly the most telling argument in support of ritual, religious or magical purposes in the art would derive from the repainting of figures, and their repetition, in identical form, nearby. I have been able to confirm that this occurs very frequently. It is obvious that repainting was not undertaken simply to revive fading colours, since these were sometimes changed, or an analogous form painted, not over the original figure, but beside it and sometimes overlying the model. There are superimpositions of black paintings over red ones, of dark red over light, and of both these colours over white. These afford a relative chronology of colour, but with the perpetuation of animal forms, despite the change in fashion indicated by the chromatic succession. Superimposition is not always obvious, even when it exists, since there can be absolute coincidence, both in the linear outline of the figures and in their overall flat colouring. But it is evident in many rock-shelters and in a few, like that in the Barranco de los Grajos, Cieza, it would be possible to say that all the figures had undergone a colour change. One of the most informative examples has already been described: the white bull at Ceja de Piezarrodilla, Albarracín, repainted in black, but retaining his original white horns between added crescentic ones. It is possible, too, that an early short and massive body has been elongated, and somewhat deformed; this would indicate that the heavy archaic bulls, after being displaced from their privileged position by deer and goats, were modified when they survived through repainting to suit the new tastes of the later artists, according to current fashion. At Prado de las Olivanas, Tormón, there are early bulls in light red repainted in varying shades of black and with obvious retouching of the hooves in bright red.

The implications are clear. As colouring which was lost, or was not wanted in its original shade, was renewed or changed, the general lines of an animal's earlier form were retained, in order to preserve and prolong the value – whatever its nature – attributed to the primitive figure. Thus we shall have to allow that pictorial practice in Levantine art was governed by considerations other than purely aesthetic. One consequence of the exact reproduction of the silhouette when repainting is to remove any chronological significance from particular combinations of form and colour. Any artistic evolution which might have differentiated between paintings was constrained by this determination to respect the ancient forms, at least in part. This respect will have been derived from spiritual or religious conviction.

The same conclusions hold in the case of the repeated figures, partly overlapping, in the Prado del Azogue at Aldeaquemada. Among schematic figures here are two naturalistic and rather clumsy paintings of deer in light red, partly repainted in a somewhat deeper shade of the same colour, but with modification of the antlers into unduly long horns to change the animals into goats, leaving them markedly disproportionate in their measurements.

Figures found repeated alongside, and partly cutting into, each other could have analogous significance, although each could retain its own autonomy and meaning. In the case of the two goats at Cogul, for example, where the black one cuts across the other, almost identical, in red, there is no doubt but that the first was modelled on the second. A similar sequence is found in the two beautiful deer, one black and the other red, at Els Gascons; here, the head of the first covers the body of the second. The copy is less exact in the Cuevas de la Araña, Bicorp: the light red deer and the deep red one which interrupts it are similar in attitude and general appearance, but there are many differences in detail. At El Prado de las Oliveras, Tormón, two successive deer figures, with barely indicated antlers, are painted almost identically in the same shade of bright red.

To all this evidence for attempts to perpetuate the ideal qualities of the animal figures may be added the fact that some were converted into different animals, rather than painting the new types *ex novo*. We saw this at the Prado del Azogue, where deer were changed into goats, at the Cueva de la Vieja, Alpera (bulls into deer: pp. 24–5), at Cantos de la Visera, Yecla (bull into deer: p. 27) or the Riparo di Santolea (deer into goat). We have therefore to suppose that the power of original figures could be prolonged by modifying them into different types of animal, as well as by making exact copies. We have mentioned the unusual case among the black bulls at the Prado de las Olivanas, where short crescentic horns are at variance with delicate hooves which had belonged to grazing deer, and where the original forelegs were not erased during repainting, thus leaving an animal with three pairs of legs.

In sum, while it was normal in successive phases to introduce new figures into Levantine friezes, which frequently blend into previous scenes, it is not unusual to prolong the power of existing figures by repainting, to conserve their value. It might also be asked whether the very act of painting might not itself be essential to the rite, or whether the mutable image was the object of religious observance.

There is one instance in the Abrigo de Solana de las Covachas which could be interpreted as evidence of destructive magic. Here a deer is crossed by vertical lines, which extend beyond the outline of the body, similar to those in palaeolithic paintings at Altxerri in Guipúzcoa. This is, however, an exceptional case. Usually, the slaughter of animals is invoked by pictures of those wounded or dead, or occasionally we find small arrows over large animals – the La Araña bull, for example – which leads us to postulate a 'wounding' ceremony, subsequent to the time when an animal was first painted in full vigour.

At all events, though hunting magic or religious ceremony concerned with the chase is

important this does not exhaust the character of Levantine art. There remain the mythical, or the totemic, episodes with which the 'sorcerers' are connected, or the numerous incomprehensible abstract symbols. A commemorative, or narrative, component must also be acknowledged, including that expressed through banal and everyday activities which were recorded for contemporary eyes, and for preservation in the future. These scenes include conflict between armed bands of men of differing physical type; hunting episodes which seemed especially significant; and scenes of a domestic character, difficult to reconcile with notions of religion or magic. The woman leading a child by the hand at Minateda falls into this class, as do the women in conversation in the Cueva de la Vieja, Alpera. And if the scene at El Cingle de la Mola Remigia (p. 28) does in fact show a man being chased by a wounded bull, this would be quite extraordinary, and contrary to the practice of sympathetic magic.

Such considerations have led certain authors to believe that the paintings in Levantine art are simply *ex votos*, recording events in everyday life rather than success at the hunt. The supposed battles would then be no more than dances (the views of Ripoll and Jordá). However, even if we concede that these are *ex votos* which seek to conserve the life and customs of the people, we are still involved with 'religious' or social concepts, since record of battle and triumph (perhaps against invaders), replacement and execution of chieftains, of human sacrifice, and of obsessive concern with hunting cannot be deprived of its significance simply by the presence of other scenes which to us seem banal or futile, perhaps because we do not know how to explain them.

Supposed quarternary
animals in Levantine art.

CHAPTER SIX

Identity of the artists and the date of their work

The question of chronology is a constant preoccupation of the prehistorian. For help in dating such cultural remains as the rock-shelter art, several types of evidence may emerge. The superimposition of paintings, for instance, may indicate a relative chronology, or fallen pieces of painted rock could become embedded in a layer of habitation débris, or such remains might be left to cover part of a frieze. In the context of Levantine painting only the first type of evidence is available. But since examples of superimposition are limited, we also have to rely for our chronology on the comparative analysis of style, along with rather dubious accounts of occupation material from the rock-shelters, and the internal evidence of the paintings themselves, as they provide clues to economic and social structure. The dating of Levantine art has however given rise to embittered polemic. Years ago, this centred on the possible palaeolithic character of the paintings; today, it is the question of their survival into the Bronze Age which is contentious.

From a simple glance at Levantine painting the differences between it and both palaeolithic and schematic art in Spain become obvious, even though there are some signs of schematization (at times even older than the naturalism) in a few Levantine rock-shelters. In the main, however, the painted Levantine friezes retain their own characteristics, which differentiate the art from the palaeolithic and the Bronze Age alike. The Abbé Breuil who, with certain eminent colleagues, maintained until his death that part of Levantine art was palaeolithic in date, nonetheless did not include a single example from it in his work of synthesis, *Quatre cents siècles d'art pariétal.* Other questions which have to be considered are the appearance of schematic symbols in all stages of Levantine art (they exist in palaeolithic contexts as well); evolution towards stylization, with the simplification of human and animal figures; and, as a separate topic, the introduction of a whole range of schematic painting, which reflects quite new and different concepts.

From the evidence of either total or partial over-painting, together with the study of stylistic development, we should be able to establish a more or less reliable relative chronology. But when considering absolute dates it is necessary to distinguish between temporal and cultural considerations. Put in another way: the hunting and gathering economy which is apparent in the majority of Levantine paintings is appropriate to a mesolithic way of life, but in mountain regions this could have persisted while neighbouring areas had already changed to neolithic ways, or even experienced the introduction of metal-working. There may have been little or no contact between the mountain zones and the cultivators and pastoralists on the coastal plain, so that sporadic introduction of the new ways among normal hunting activities would be limited and delayed. It is therefore hazardous, not only to transfer dates between two such different areas, but also to claim cultural change. A wiser aim is to concentrate on establishing the incontrovertible social features of the distinctive upland regions.

It is worth recounting earlier discussion about the chronology of Levantine art, before examining the present arguments. From 1903, when finds at Calapatá and Albarracín began to be discovered and published, the Abbé Breuil, who was active in publicizing them, treated them as being unequivocally contemporary with palaeolithic art. The important book, *El hombre fosil*, of Hugo Obermaier gave wide currency to this view, and the Spanish archaeologist P. Bosch Gimpera always maintained that Breuil's early dating could not be refuted. His conclusions were moreover in accordance with the accepted interpretation of the Spanish palaeolithic in general. The art of Cantabria – 'Franco-Cantabrian' as it was called – was thought to be the work of a Nordic people, settled in geographically defined areas of the Peninsula, while Levantine art, as its contemporary, was held to be due to penetration from North Africa, by a Capsian folk. In 1960, after his views had been strongly criticized for a great many years, Breuil gave the following, seemingly simple, summary of his position. Enjoying a Mediterranean climate more clement than that of Cantabria or Aquitaine lived other, but equally upper palaeolithic, tribes – Gravettian, Solutrean and Magdalenian. Being separated by the expanse of the Pyrenean range from their place of origin, they developed an original and conceptually distinctive art, though not without relation to the north, as seen in the adoption of the Perigordian *perspective tordue*. There was probably a mixture of local schematic art, with subsequent additions of a Mediterranean nature.

Today the first part of this argument cannot be maintained; and it is entirely arbitrary and impossible to suppose that there could have been any derivation of schematic or Mediterranean elements during palaeolithic times. Breuil himself acknowledged difficulties. He proposed that work in the Cueva de Doña Clotilde, at Villar del Humo, and in the three final phases at Minateda should not be counted as Levantine painting, while Cantos de la Visera and Meca would represent its final phase. In his view, furthermore, there would be no examples of Levantine art, either in central Spain or the southern part of eastern Spain. An analysis of this partial revision of Breuil's theories would be lengthy. He later conceded that one group of rock-shelters is neolithic in date, and allowed a progressive evolution towards stylization and schematic work. However, in certain of the rock-shelters cited by him, various styles – Levantine, neolithic and Bronze Age – are in fact mixed, and his sweeping generalisations do not hold. Next, concerning the chronology of the art, Breuil asserted that finds in the more northern part of the region would be older, since their artistic quality is higher; further south, a tendency to degenerate becomes, in his view, apparent, with the gradual emergence of characteristics which become dominant in that region during later phases. But these conclusions seem equally unacceptable, since Breuil is presuming that the art derives from the palaeolithic, and attributes stages in its stylistic evolution to the geographical distance of particular Levantine rock-shelters from centres of palaeolithic cave art. Recent finds, of both palaeolithic and Levantine art, however, show how complex the problem really is. Firstly, there is not the slightest similarity between any set of Levantine paintings and the palaeolithic work which is nearest to them. Comparison of paintings at Alquézar with the Basque caves, for example, or of rock-shelters in Albarracín with the Los Casares and La Hoz finds in Guadalajara, support this observation. Nor do the Nerpio group of finds resemble the Cueva del Niño at Aine, in the same province of Albacete. Other recent discoveries have added little to the evidence, apart from extending the distribution of the art somewhat to the north in Catalonia (Cueva de Os, Balaguer) and increasing the density of finds in some areas, for example round Benasal or Bicorp. It is difficult to assess a find (which has now disappeared) at La Moleta de Cartagena, near San Carlos de la Rápida (Tarragona), which combined a naturalistic bull in palaeolithic style with stylized, Levantine figures of people.

It is hardly possible, either, to agree with a further contention of Breuil's: that Levantine art is not the pictorial expression of a people relegated to the mountains, but rather that it was not necessary for the artists to seek out deep caves for sanctuaries or occupation sites, because the climate of eastern Spain was relatively clement. In fact, the climate of the region is harsh and extreme. The art is found exclusively in upland country: the sites are always at a high altitude, wild and rugged, and in isolated places difficult of access. Such circumstances would account for the survival of archaic life styles; and many of the paintings themselves indicate the alternation of extremes of heat and cold, both seasonal and daily.

The depiction of pleistocene animals in Levantine art is also central to Breuil's argument. In 1960 he still maintained that there were two bison at Cogul and possibly others at Tormón and Minateda, an elk at Alpera, and a feline, a rhinoceros and an *Equus hydruntinus* with a fallow deer at Minateda. It has not been possible to identify any of these. Chamois at Minateda and Tortosilla, however, seem plausible, and we shall return to an assessment of the evidence from La Moleta.

In his pronouncement of 1960 Breuil was also concerned to revise his earlier interpretation of the evidence at Minateda. He now treated his original division of this frieze into thirteen successive layers of painting as provisional, and applicable elsewhere only to the Cueva de la Vieja at Alpera and Cantos de la Visera, Monte Arabí (and thus certainly not to regions further north). This revision is crucial, since Breuil's scheme for Levantine art had been dependent on his reading of the Minateda evidence.

Not surprisingly, Breuil's earlier hypothesis had immediately attracted criticism. Based, however, not on proof, but on the personal impressions which would arise in any observer comparing the cave art of northern Spain with work in Levantine rock-shelters, this was inconclusive. Personal quarrels sometimes intruded. Different hypotheses were put forward by Spanish archaeologists: at first rather timidly, by members of the Institut d'Estudis Catalans (Colominas, Durán and Sanpere) then, in 1925, in a firm and well documented case, by Eduardo Hernández Pacheco, who opted for a post-palaeolithic date.

Racó Gasparo, Gasulla (Castellón). A dolichocephalic man superimposed over a brachycephalic one (after Beltrán).

The simple scheme for the Spanish palaeolithic which had prevailed, moreover, was overturned by the new site of Parpalló (Valencia). Finds there of painted and engraved plaques in dated upper palaeolithic layers undermined Breuil's theories on the ordering of palaeolithic cave art. Furthermore, the French prehistorian R. Vaufrey was able to show that the Capsian industry, which Breuil had sought to link to the authors of Levantine art, had in fact a far more limited distribution in North Africa than previously imagined, and anyway it is probably largely later than the European palaeolithic. Hernández Pacheco's views were espoused by a younger generation of Spanish specialists, including J. Martinez Santa-Olalla and Martín Almagro. The latter's publications in particular led to general acceptance of a post-palaeolithic date for Levantine art, though this was not without bitter debate in the scientific world, since Breuil, and Bosch Gimpera, held to their views. It must be admitted, too, that the more recent interpretation still does not provide a clear and coherent synthesis to match the comprehensive simplicity of the old scheme. In general, it can be said that no-one today maintains that the art is palaeolithic in date, nor is it thought to derive directly from that period. However, the mesolithic-neolithic date generally accepted has begun to be questioned from another viewpoint: by Martinez Santa Olalla, who thinks that the paintings belong to the Bronze Age, and also by Francisco Jordá Cerdá, who also prefers a later dating, since he thinks that their position in the mesolithic has not been sufficiently demonstrated.

In Jorda"s view, the subject-matter of the paintings denotes an agricultural and herding community, who also practised hunting, rather than epi-palaeolithic hunters and gatherers. He postulates instead an art which originated in parallel with the schematic, to develop during the eneolithic and Bronze Age. He feels unable to allow the survival of Gravettian peoples, through thousands of years, to emerge as the authors of Levantine art at just the moment when their life style was about to encounter the alien neolithic. Jordá maintains he knows no evidence of an

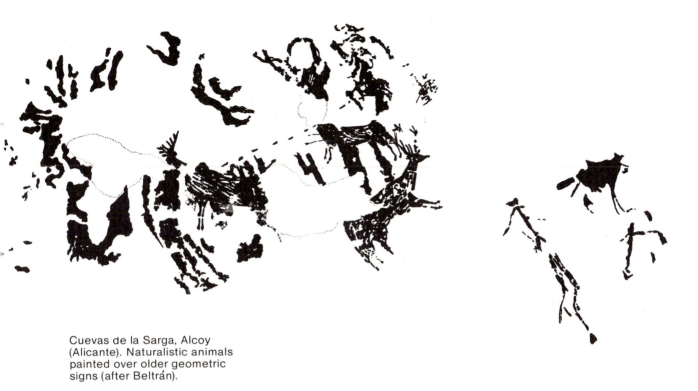

Cuevas de la Sarga, Alcoy
(Alicante). Naturalistic animals
painted over older geometric
signs (after Beltrán).

upper palaeolithic complex, cultural or artistic, in the mountains of eastern Spain which could support this hypothesis – the 'mammoth' in the confused scene at La Moleta de Cartagena hardly clarifies the issue. He thus finds the case for an epi-palaeolithic origin unproven, or even questionable, since the little art known to be of this period is strictly abstract. The arrowheads shown in the art, moreover – leaf-shaped, lanceolate, barbed and tanged or hooked – bear no relation to the geometric microliths of the known industries, nor is the existence of the bow in Spain certain during this early period. In the face of these uncertainties, Jordá prefers the evidence of the art's neolithic scenes, and believes that local specialization will explain the absence of animal art in other regions where related cardial pottery is found.

Accordingly, Jordá ascribes the beginning of Levantine art to a late phase of the neolithic, the time of the first neolithic villages and initial metallurgy – alongside the linear and geometric emphasis of schematic art. This hypothesis, however, is not followed by the majority of his colleagues.

In order to establish a chronology for Levantine art it is helpful to begin by distinguishing those characteristics which separate it from both the palaeolithic and the schematic. Firstly, there is the different topographical context of the Franco-Cantabrian sites: in contrast to the shallow and sparsely protected Levantine rock-shelters, palaeolithic art in the north is found in deep caves, where darkness adds to its significance. Next, the standard inclusion of complex scenes is an exclusively Levantine feature. It is rare in the palaeolithic, and the descriptive element is lost during the schematic. Turning to dimensions, even the smallest palaeolithic figure in the region – the small horse at Le Portel – at 18 cm in length matches the average size of Levantine paintings. These rarely exceed one metre and include many tiny figures, down to 2.5 cm high. The majority range between 15 and 18 cm. Stylistically, both palaeolithic animals and the schematic figures are shown at rest, while Levantine art emphasizes movement, sometimes to the point of impetuosity, with the figures 'flying' about (though there are occasional exceptions to this generalization). A further distinction lies in the palaeolithic use of polychromy – sometimes achieved by incorporating base colouring – in place of the Levantine or schematic flat painting restricted to reds, black and occasionally white. Nor are the later styles found except as rock paintings – never on portable objects.

Features common to palaeolithic and Levantine work are thus reduced to the naturalistic treatment of the older animal figures (in flat colours) in Levantine art, the *perspective tordue* of the horns and antlers and the occasional appearance of abstract elements along with the animals.

One important piece of evidence may be the co-existence of these different styles of art within the same region, or even at the same site. There is the exceptional case, still unpublished, of Alquézar in the province of Huesca: there, palaeolithic, Levantine and schematic art has been found, each in its own cave or rock-shelter, but close together. The first surprising discovery was at Parpalló, in Valencia, where there were rich finds of art on stone plaques. The site refuted Obermaier's scheme of dividing the palaeolithic in the Peninsula into a Franco-Cantabrian and a Capsian zone, and added evidence to that of the cave paintings known as La Pileta, Ardales, La Cala and later Nerja in Andalucia. Finds of Aurignacian engravings at Los Casares and La Hoz, not far from the Albarracin rock-shelters, attracted even more interest. With further discoveries since then, the old hypothesis of a Pyrenean art dependent on more northerly European influence, alongside a Levantine art related to the Capsian of North Africa has been disproved. Sites such as Oña, Atapuerca, El Requerillo, Maltravieso, Escoural, La Griega and El Niño now demonstrate that palaeolithic art spread over the entire Peninsula. The same is true of schematic art, while Levantine art remains restricted to a well-defined geographical zone. The argument of Breuil and Obermaier that all naturalistic animal painting was the contemporary work of similar peoples, with environment alone accounting for local differences between the Franco-Cantabrian and Levantine, was bound to collapse.

On the evidence of supposed pleistocene fauna among Levantine animals, Obermaier himself questioned or refuted some of Breuil's examples. Among those so dismissed are the 'bison' at Cogul, which is a crude and poorly preserved drawing of a bull; the 'wild ass' in the Abrigos de la Fuente del Cabrerizo (p. 17), a crude engraving of a horse; the 'elk' in the Cueva del Queso at Alpera, which is no more than a goat repainted as a deer – the rock-face has in fact flaked below the jaw to change the profile. Furthermore, no bones have been found from this last animal, which requires a marshy habitat not found in the Spanish Levant. The 'chamois' claimed at La Tortosilla is an indefinable ruminant, although there is a clear example of this animal among the Prado del Tornero rock-shelters. Its presence however is inconclusive, since it is not known how long the type may have survived in the east Spanish mountains, where a mountain goat is still found. The so-called 'rhinoceroses' at Minateda can still be seen well enough to proclaim themselves as poorly differentiated quadrupeds: badly preserved and confusing, but with no definitive features of these animals, which became extinct in Spain from the beginning of the upper palaeolithic. Much the same can be said of Minateda's two 'elks', 'saiga antelope' and 'feline' or lion; any claim that a reindeer is depicted there must be met by the fact that this animal never crossed the Pyrenees, even during periods of maximum cold. The 'elk' from the Cueva Remigia is also questionable, since the copy published has been heavily reconstructed and the surviving original has become ill defined.

Turning to internal evidence, we find that the analysis of development patterns may override similarities between the different forms of art suggested by a comparison of their techniques or stylistic features in isolation. All used pigments derived from oxides of iron and manganese and lamp-black; and there are common points of technique, such as flat washes or simple stroke or line work. Quaternary art, however, began with linear, and then developed pictorial, representation. In Levantine art, on the other hand, if we exclude the few samples of early stroke-symbols, the tendency is reversed, beginning with the colour-work and proceeding later to the linear, with stylization and schematic art, like that of the Bronze Age. Breuil himself abandoned the sequence of styles he worked out at Minateda. There is little of substance in the isolated comparisons proposed with figures at Lascaux, Le Portel, Pasiega and the shelter of Labatut at Sergeac in the Dordogne. The famous small red horse at Le Portel has little in common with Levantine art apart from size and the flat red wash: the stylistic treatment is quite different. By contrast, the use of *perspective tordue* for depicting the horns and antlers of animals seen in profile is a convention common to both cave art and Levantine paintings. According to Breuil, it was first used in the Perigordian, while a *semi-tordue* version was adopted in the Magdalenian. Thus, he argued, Levantine art would have to overlap with the earlier of these periods. Pericot thought this came about through an epi-Gravettian, which was linked to the Gravettian or Perigordian after a number of episodes and (at Parpalló) superimposed layers of cultural material. In fact this gap is very difficult to explain, and any exact chronology for the *perspective tordue* must remain in suspense – as Breuil had to acknowledge. The same convention is found in neolithic painting in North Africa, and even later, in situations which can have nothing to do with the palaeolithic. The occasional appearance of a normal perspective in Levantine art moreover precludes unqualified generalization. It should however be emphasized that some similarities are striking: the much quoted deer painting which fell from the cave wall to become embedded in the Perigordian III layer at Labatut in the Dordogne, for instance, is extraordinarily like examples found in eastern Spain. The same may be said of the hooves and heads of many of the animals shown full frontal while their bodies are seen in profile.

Attempts to compare representations of the human figure in palaeolithic and Levantine art scarcely merit attention. If there is any subject in which differences are marked it is this. The simplified sketches on the *bâton de commandement* from the Cueva de Valle have no distinguishing features, and the same can be said of the suggested evidence on stone plaques from Pechialet or Parpalló, on bone from Teyjat, Limeuil or Chaffaud, and in wall engravings at Los Casares and Addaura.

If we are to establish a chronology for Levantine art it is essential to utilize the evidence contained within the rock-shelters themselves, especially through the assessment of super-impositions in the paintings. It is obvious that the use of black paint came later than the red (or, in Albarracín, than white); also that there is an orange-red which followed the black, and a shade of light red which is older than the dark or purplish-red. Then, with good reason, it has been usual to assign the naturalistic and the schematic figures in the rock-shelters to different periods. The first, I maintain, were mesolithic, developing during the course of the neolithic tendencies to stylization and simplification which eventually engulfed the style. Schematic figures and symbols were substituted during the eneolithic and Bronze Age, degenerating finally into mere strokes, geometric shapes and crude emblematic forms. It would be a grave mistake to confuse Bronze

Minateda (Albacete). The left
(above) and right (below)
halves of the frieze.

Age schematic features with the figurative signs – albeit at times indecipherable – contemporary with naturalistic Levantine art. These are comparable with the so-called *tectiforme* symbols of the palaeolithic, which likewise were indistinguishable, chronologically, from the naturalistic animal paintings with which they occur. There are frequently examples of schematic paintings on the Levantine friezes and generally they cut across the naturalistic work. However, there are a few exceptional instances – no less significant because they are scarce – in which schematic paintings underlie naturalistic ones, demonstrating that here they are older. There are examples in the Cueva de la Sarga (pp. 64–5) at Alcoy: one dark red deer, its body coloured by close set parallel lines, interrupts a roughly painted bright red symbol; and a similar but incomplete animal, more densely painted, lies over another wide stroke painted in deep red. At Cantos de la Visera, Monte Arabí, a deer which has been repainted over a bull just covers the wing and foot of an apparently schematic figure, taken to be a wading-bird, and lies squarely across groups of parallel and wavy lines and a hatched symbol (p. 27). Finally, in the Cuevas de la Araña an obvious zigzag is crossed by the antler of a deer.

Thus it can be confidently asserted that the oldest phase recognizable in Levantine art comprised linear and geometric work, earlier than the naturalistic red figures. Afterwards, their evolution must have proceeded through successive changes in colour, movement and style. It must however be admitted that attempts by the author to distinguish these stages, at the Cueva de los Grajos, Cieza, had no success. Separating out elements from the whole of its paintings on the

Ulldecona (Tarragona), rock-shelter I. Hunting scene (after Viñas).

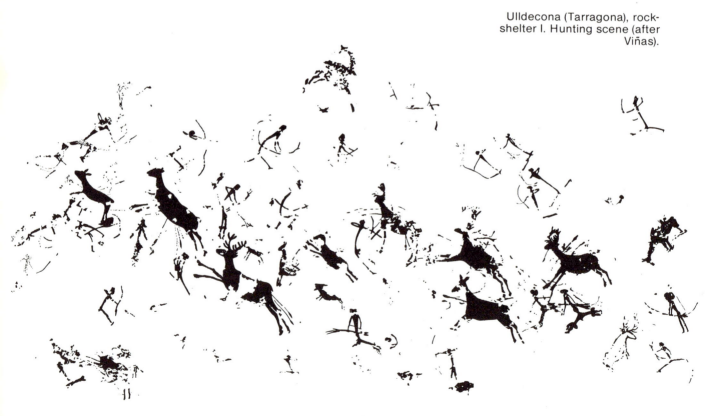

70

grounds of common colour or style led simply to fragmentation and dissolution of the scenes.

Another line of investigation has examined art found on small portable objects from archaeological contexts. Obermaier, for example, proposed to relate painted Azilian pebbles with similar schematic symbols in the art of the rock-shelters. He argued that since Levantine art is admittedly earlier than the schematic, it must also precede the Azilian, and hence be palaeolithic in date. There are also geometric designs on stone plaques found with a microlithic flint industry at La Cocina, Valencia. Finally, there is the question of flint industries found at sites near the painted rock-shelters. Almagro considers that they represent epi-palaeolithic hunters who survived until eneolithic times, and were responsible for Levantine art. But it is not proved that the two are contemporary, and doubts could remain even if the flints lay at the very foot of a painted rock-face, for it would still be necessary to determine which of the possibly various art styles in a frieze they belonged to. There have been studies concerning the Cueva de la Rabosa (Valltorta), Cogul, La Cocina, Ladruñán, Alacón, Albarracin and Val del Charco del Agua Amarga, as well as those of Vallespi in lower Aragon, with revisions by F.J. Fortea. The general conclusion is that the flints represent an epi-palaeolithic tradition in the process of acculturation, and surviving alongside a neolithic or eneolithic in other regions: that is to say, they are not epi-palaeolithic in a chronological or cultural sense. Thus, while it is not certain that the workers in these industries were responsible for any or all of the paintings, the meso-neolithic dating proposed for them by Almagro and by Ripoll is consistent with the general evolutionary processes we postulate.

We may conclude that evidence from the paintings themselves allows us to distinguish at least four phases. The first comprises linear and geometric work, and this might be linked with the engraved plaques found at La Cocina. Its cultural context is poorly defined. Next come the single, large animals, scarcely ever shown with human figures. The following phase is dominated by hunting, in its various aspects, with occasional pictures of gathering, and also dancing and other activities. Finally, there are culturally neolithic scenes: gathering, agricultural work using digging-sticks, spades and picks, and the domestication of animals. This last phase coincided with highly developed forms and colour-work, for example in the horses at the Cueva de Doña Clotilde and Los Canforos at Peñarrubia. Our account has shown that there was no break in continuity from the beginning of Levantine art to its end and it is clear that this occurred well after the introduction of metals, after the loss of some characteristic features. It should however be emphasized again that hunting and gathering could very well have persisted in the coastal sierras while agriculture and herding were being practised on adjacent plains, though it is not possible to say how far this can be explained by lack of contact between peoples.

In the cirumstances, it is difficult to reach a decision about the possible metal objects mentioned by Jordá. Only the cavalry helmet at El Cingle de la Mola Remigia, Gasulla, is obvious. Nor does comparison of weapons and clothing, or objects and activities which will have survived long periods, help towards closer dating, and the same is true of palaeo-ethnological features, like masking, or sorcerers. For this reason, the evidence of basketry, ropes and, for example, of breeches or skirts can be set aside.

CHAPTER SEVEN

A scheme and chronology for Levantine art

Here it is taken as self evident that Levantine art was post-palaeolithic in date and that it declined and was replaced by another style during the eneolithic. By contrast, it is very difficult to fix any absolute chronology, even if it is accepted as a meso-neolithic phenomenon. Recent neolithic discoveries close to an area of Levantine paintings at Verdelpino in the province of Cuenca serve to illustrate how thorny this problem of chronology can be. The site produced radio-carbon dates of about 6000 bc for neolithic plain pottery and 3200 to 2680 for decorated ware. The first figure corresponds to the dates for epi-palaeolithic flint industries in Cantabria; for plain ware it is surprising and without parallel in the western Mediterranean, apart from Corsica. It would indicate a very early stage of the neolithic in eastern Spain, prior to that represented by cardial ware. Nor should a date obtained from the Barranco de los Grajos, Cieza, be forgotten, where the paintings appear to be of an advanced phase: at 5220, this is earlier than dates associated with Valencian cardial pottery of the type of the Coveta de l'Or (and this is without allowance for corrections which raise the Cieza date to 5470).

This means that to arrive at a chronology the few dates available – and even these are not consistent – will have to be combined with out proposals for the relative ordering of Levantine art. These in turn are based on the evidence of overlying colours and styles, stylistic development and on the hazards of comparative method. Even if it is conceded that the ultimate roots of Levantine work lie in palaeolithic art, Perigordian or Gravettian, we still do not know when and where the transition took place, or how the Magdalenian stage, which left no art in the Spanish Levant, was surmounted. Nor do we know why caves were abandoned in favour of rock-shelters, or what brought about the radical change apparent in the concept of the art.

In estimates for an absolute chronology, even accepting the postulate of some, albeit indeterminate, unbroken heritage from palaeolithic art, it is difficult to allow Levantine art a beginning before 6000. Gradually it gave way to novel ideas and the new schematic art which arrived in the eneolithic. According to Almagro's Los Millares date, this period could begin about 2300, and last until 1500 or a little later.

We cannot agree that the art's older phases lie in the north, spreading thence southwards, as

72

Breuil has said, for the discovery of Cañaica del Calar and Nerpio has disproved this hypothesis. Moreover, a common territory, or coincidence in the same rock-shelter, does not prove that Levantine and schematic art were contemporary. An entirely fresh spirit inspires the new style, although for reasons we do not understand, the former rock-shelters were maintained as 'sanctuaries', where it was felt appropriate that painting should continue.

It would seem that, as a hypothesis, the following chronological and stylistic phases may be proposed for Levantine art:

(1) A phase with simple linear and geometric paintings, contemporary with the decorated stone plaques in layer II at La Cocina; this could last until the year 5000. The phase is recorded only in

Os de Balaguer (Lérida). Group including naturalistic and schematic figures (after Diaz Coronel).

the Cuevas de la Sarga (pp. 64–5), at Cantos de la Visera (p. 27) and in the Cuevas de la Araña, but it no doubt exists unpublished in other rock-shelters.

(2) An early or naturalistic phase, epi-palaeolithic or mesolithic, datable between 6000 and 3500. Its subjects are flat-painted, large animals, showing little movement and there are no human figures. It includes the white and red bulls of Albarracín, the large bull at La Araña, the red bulls with patination at the Cueva Remigia in the Gasulla gorge, the deer at the Roca dels Moros, Calapatá (pp. 34–5) and Val del Charco del Agua Amarga (pp. 14–15), and bulls from Ladruñán, at the Riparo de Santolea, Mas de Llort and analogous sites. This corresponds to the first of Ripoll's phases (with its two periods). The deer with linear colouring on their bodies, from the Cuevas de la Sarga, Alpera, possibly belong to the very end of this phase.

(3) The culmination of the art. In this phase bulls become progressively fewer, replaced by numerous deer (into which they may be transformed, by repainting). The human figures which now appear are barely naturalistic but animals continue in the tradition of phase 2, though

showing an increased sense of movement. The principal change lies in the complexity of the scenes. The starting point could be a little after 4000, and this coincides with Ripoll's *b* phase, of 'static stylization'. The clearest example is the great central scene in the Cueva Remigia (p. 16). The tall female figure at Val de Charco (0.60 m high: p. 15), and the leaning man in the Remigia cave, could signal the start of this phase, if not the transition between phases 2 and 3. According to Breuil's sketches, at Minateda (where up to five chronological stages may still be distinguished) a few animals belong in our phase 2, but the majority are of this phase. Other examples can be found at Els Gascons, and in most of the material at Cogul, Cañaica del Calar or in the Abrigo de Solana de las Covachas.

(4) A phase of development, contemporary with the neolithic of the coastal plains, but still lacking agricultural or pastoral scenes. It could run from something after 3500 to 2000. These are the paintings which combine so beautifully the figures of running men and animals. Characteristic features include alignment of the outstretched legs of sprinting men; a diagonal tendency in composition; naturalism in animals modified by movement; stylization of the human figure towards the calligraphic, with conventions like a triangular thorax. The archers at Val del Charco del Agua Amarga (pp. 14–15) will serve as example: the style is found widely among sites in Castellón, at Gasulla and Valltorta, and in lower Aragon. The phase is more or less Ripoll's 'stylized movement' group, his phase *c*.

(5) The final phase, from 2000 until the art died out. It represents a return to the static, while the unskilful rigidity of the stylization tends to the schematic. Reference to agriculture – for example the digging-stick – is included, with domestication of certain animals, like the supposed dogs at Alpera. There is also riding; the horseman at El Cingle de la Mola Remigia, who cannot date earlier than 1200, must obviously belong at the end of the phase.

It is possible that certain animal figures, representing the final products of Levantine art, are datable to an eneolithic or full Bronze Age phase, after the schematic style was fully established. This may apply to many animals at Aldeaquemada (Jaén), the large deer at Los Letraros, Lavaderos de Tello (Almeria), and the single deer at Tejo de la Figuras (Cadiz). What is not acceptable is the idea that the spirit of Levantine art inspired the schematic, which by contrast is symbolic and ideographic in character. The latter evolved in response to novel religious, funerary and artistic ideas, dependent on an entirely distinctive concept of life, which arrived as metal-working was introduced.

It must be stressed that the above divisions, and especially the absolute chronology, proposed for the art are put forward only as hypotheses, since we lack exact dating evidence. Nor do the criteria established above for the relative order of the paintings apply invariably. It is, for example, confusing that each of the colours and shades distinguished can occur, more or less certainly coincidently, in every one of the phases. In principle, there is generally a known order between the different colours, but particular instances may be more complicated. The bull in the Ceja de Piezarrodilla in Albarracin, for example, belongs to phase 2, both in its original white form and in the blackish repainting, yet the white deer at Las Tajadas, Bezas, are from the third phase, while a stylized human figure in white at El Single, near the Montalbana, is Middle Bronze Age in date. Again, the figures at the Barranco de los Grajos, at Cieza, which belong for the most part to the fifth and final phase, were painted in light red or red, with repainting in deep red or black respectively. We could quote further instances, all of which lead to the conclusion that, though there is a recurrent pattern in the superimposition of colours, there are no absolute rules from which to establish a chronology. The same is true of degrees of stylization, especially in the human figures, or of differences in their size. The tall woman at Val del Charco, from the transition between phases 2 and 3, is in the same style as smaller figures in the frieze belonging to phase 3, and analogous to others we suppose to be of phase 4. Thus, the proposed divisions in the art, like the very similar phases distinguished by E. Ripoll, should be considered merely as indicative: only the upper and lower limits appear to be fixed.

This discussion of absolute dating ends with a consideration of proposals by F. Jordá, since they differ greatly from views which are generally accepted (by Almagro, Bandi, etc.). This author maintains that Levantine art began in parallel with the start of schematic art, after 2500. From this it derived the convention of the wide-angled, outstretched legs of runners, the elongation of figures, as well as certain static qualities, as exemplified in the southern sites of Cantos de la Visera, at Alpera (the static figures), some rock-shelters at Nerpio, and perhaps certain elements in the Cuevas de la Sarga. Jordá's second phase would correspond to the introduction of bull-paintings (Cantos de la Visera, Alpera, La Sarga), possibly relating to a bull cult which, like other features in the neolithic of eastern Spain (cf. wheat and barley), could be of Anatolian origin. From a first phase, which also included sites in Almeria, the bulls and their attendant female figures reached lower Aragon and the Maestrazgo in phase 2, perhaps through migration. Jordá's third phase is dominated by the deer, and here movement is adopted, with the elongated, calligraphic human figures which lead to impressionistic scenes like those in the rock-shelters at Ares del Maestre and the battle at Les Dogues. The fourth phase is one of decline and return to the schematic (though not the static), seen in the 'bull-fight' at Cogul and the dance of the women round a phallic god at the Barranco de los Grajos. The horseman from the Gasulla gorge, which Jordá would date about 800 BC, is the final representative of the art.

Present evidence does not seem to sustain Jordá's arguments, especially his contention that Levantine and schematic art are contemporary. Levantine work was obviously practised for a very long time, without any break in continuity. The original friezes were continued, either by adding new figures, for example the stylized men in the rock-shelter of Los Toricos, Albarracín, by repainting existing figures in an identical or similar form, like the Ceja de Piezarrodilla bull, by altering bulls into deer, as at Alpera or Monte Arabí, or simply by introducing new figures into existing scenes, using new styles, as we saw at Cogul. Painting of the same rock-shelters, or in others nearby, continued right into the Bronze Age, as is seen at Nerpio or in the Cañaica del Calar, perpetuating the tradition even up till Iberian or Roman times, as shown at Cogul.

CHAPTER EIGHT

Levantine art and schematic art

This chapter discusses the definition and mutual relationships of these two styles of art. Certainly, instances of lines and symbols within Levantine art which can be classified as schematic are almost as numerous as animal figures which may be characterized as naturalistic. The figuration of human beings needs separate consideration: most diverge sufficiently from the naturalistic to qualify as schematic, though without ever losing the evident preoccupation of the artists with movement. Furthermore, cases where naturalistic animal figures are superimposed on very varied examples of schematic work have been noticed above. Most commentators suppose that there was no break in an evolution which began with Levantine art and ended with the schematic. Beyond this, interpretations vary. Breuil would make his 'levantino' begin in the Gravettian, to reach its apogee during the epi-Gravettian and Magdalenian (his phases 8–9 at Minateda); thence naturalism died out during the mesolithic, with schematization continuing into the neolithic and Bronze Age. For Pericot, the art derives from a very obscure period, connected with the epi-Gravettian and the Magdalenian, and lasted until the neolithic,, when it died out as schematic art appeared. This then survived throughout the Bronze Age, to reach Iron Age times. Almagro and Bandi propose a mesolithic origin for Levantine art, with development throughout the neolithic; for them, schematic art belongs to the Bronze and Iron Ages, with differing characteristics appropriate to each.

From the evidence of the fifth phase as presented above, during the eneolithic there was migration from the eastern Mediterranean, bringing artistic 'factories', first to Andalucia where they encountered no established tradition, and later to the Spanish Levant, where the deeply rooted native art came under their influence – though not without itself leaving its stamp on what was new. The much quoted horseman in El Cingle de la Mola Remigia, for example, who from his helmet and horse-trapping cannot pre-date 1200 BC, is nonetheless decidedly naturalistic in style.

There has been a tendency to treat schematization as the outcome of unilinear evolution, beginning with Levantine art and passing through semi-naturalistic and semi-schematic stages. Bosch Gimpera and Ripoll have propounded this theory, but it seems highly questionable, at least if it is intended to have general application. If it were valid, it might hold in eastern Spain, but schematic art is found throughout the Peninsula, even in regions where Levantine art is absent. Moreover, we cannot classify all rock-shelters which lie geographically in the east, from Huesca and Lérida, through Cuenca and Teruel to Murcia and Almería, as 'Levantine': it is for example absurd to use the term for the Cueva de Doña Clotilde in Albarracín. We should also exclude many stylized figures which have been called 'Levantine' simply because they are painted near to other figures which are correctly so classified. We have to conclude that there is both naturalistic and schematic art in the eastern rock-shelters, though those of the Bronze Age have only the latter. It may be added that animals are always represented more or less naturalistically in Levantine art, and always schematically during the Bronze Age. (This for the moment leaves aside the problem of semi-naturalistic, or semi-schematic, figures.) In southern parts of eastern Spain we often find Levantine rock-shelters next to those with schematic art, as in the Barranco de los Grajos, or Cañaica del Calar. Although this is not unknown in the north (cf. Alguézar in Huesca), what is standard in this region is an addition of symbols, or entire Bronze Age friezes, without modifying the meaning of pre-existing Levantine scenes. This we find at Cogul, Val del Charco del Agua Amarga and Minateda.

The idea that schematic art arose, in Spain, by evolution from the Levantine should thus be abandoned, and replaced by the proposal that it resulted from the introduction of new ideas and a total change of outlook. Not only did this produce schematic tendencies in artistic expression, it also brought in fresh symbols (such as 'ocular' idols, or men shaped like anchors or pine trees) and abstractions, which could be expressed in simple points, rays or heavenly signs – suns and stars – or other phenomena (lines of rainfall, meanders, concentric or labyrinthine spirals), indications which remain incomprehensible to those who cannot enter into the minds of their authors. All this, however, is far removed from hunting scenes and the everyday narrative of Levantine art.

Given that these new ideas derive from the eastern and central Mediterranean, it should be possible to identify analogies which relate to particular phases within the two thousand year-currency of the Bronze Age. Occasionally we find the signs painted or engraved on the stones of dolmens; and they can also occur on pottery, pendants and bone objects. (It should be remembered that there are no dolmens in the region of Levantine art.) Influence from the earlier, native art is not entirely lacking, but where this forms a point of reference – even a model – the Bronze Age painting is unmistakably distinct, expressing radically different concepts.

Groups of schematic painting may be dated on various grounds. In shared rock-shelters, the painting over of Levantine art may provide evidence. Additionally, there is internal evidence, based on the evolution of the style. Comparison of elements with a dated series will sometimes produce an absolute figure, and the relative chronology of the supporting dolmens should be utilized. In very rare cases (cf. Porto Badisco), collapse of the shelter will provide a *terminus ante quem*.

The 'semi-naturalism' proposed by Bosch Gimpera (and also by Kühn and Anati) as a step towards schematic art is based on superimpositions in the Laguna de la Janda rock-shelters, where the older figures are fairly naturalistic while those which cover them show progressive artistic deterioration, leading to schematization. In other friezes we find figures painted fairly correctly, but already departing from classic naturalism. There are instances at Las Batuecas, in the goats of El Zarzalón and the deer of the Cerro Rabanero, Collado del Aguila, in the Sierra Morena. A further group in which forms are more rigid, lacking in movement, though with a well-drawn silhouette, comprises men with animals – sometimes asses – being held on a halter, as at Los Canforos at Peñarrubia or the Cueva de Doña Clotilde. By comparison between this last site and upper layers in the Cueva de la Cocina, semi-naturalistic art can be dated to the fifth millennium, together with scenes of initial agriculture in Levantine painting.

A more advanced phase according to Bosch would correspond to the Portuguese Valdejunco rock-shelter (Portalegre), or those at Valonsadero in Soria. A degenerate form of semi-naturalism, which did not develop into schematization, would be that found in megalithic tombs, such as the gallery-grave of Orca dos Juncais (Beira), datable between 3000 and 2700 BC. This art would be followed by the beginnings of true schematization, which developed in the eneolithic: the key date comes from the deer incised on the Los Millares pot (2345 ± 95). The same figures are also found on Beaker-type vases at Las Carolinas, Madrid, at Palmella and in the Soto dolmen, Trigueros (Huelva), where there were Beakers like those at Los Millares and schematic human figures. Finally, the last phase of schematization, in which there are human figures only, and no animals, occurs among engravings from the end of the megalithic evolution, for example in the Menga cave, the Espolla gorge, on the rock of La Torre Hércules at Coruña, and in the engravings and paintings at Peña Tú at Vidiago. Finds at Espolla include a type III maritime Beaker from the end of the third, and first centuries of the second, millennium.

Ripoll considers that schematic painting is the culmination of tendencies inherent in late Levantine art, under foreign spiritual (and no doubt religious) influence which promoted a change towards symbolism. At times, this found expression in virtual ideograms. The spread of such ideas relates to the culture of the dolmens, with its possible oriental roots and connections with metal prospectors. He accepts a date between 3000 and 2500 BC for the lassoed horse in the Abrigo de la Selva Pascuala. The archaeological finds from which absolute dates might be derived include pottery, idols such as those in the shape of anchors discussed above – especially the 'ocular' ones associated with deer figures at Los Millares – sun or zigzag signs and so on. The 'tree-of-life' originated in the Mesopotamian area, to reach the Aegean in the Early Bronze Age and pass on westwards. The double triangle sign known in the central Mediterranean until the Late Helladic, at Serraferlicchio (Agrigento), has many parallels further east. Comparisons are suggested among neolithic painting at Çatal Hüyük in Anatolia and at Levanzo in the Egadi Islands, and with circles and spirals at Hal Saflieni, Malta, the Grotta Scrita, Olmetta de Cap (Corsica) and, it may be added, at Porto Badisco, where the cave was blocked at the start of the eneolithic. The actual dates proposed were 6500–5700 BC for Çatal Hüyük, neolithic to eneolithic for Levanzo, 2000–1400 BC for the signs on Malta, and 1200–1000 BC for those at Olmetta.

The author Pilar Acosta has also sought to establish connections between schematic forms and symbols in the Peninsula and a variety of Near Eastern sites of the third and second millennia. These include early and middle Ugarit, Troy I–VIII, Tell Brak II and III, and the final chalcolithic at Mersin, and would relate to phases between the middle neolithic and Bronze II in Spain.

From all the evidence available, the following general conclusions may be inferred. Spanish schematic art is a consequence of cultural change brought about by the arrival of metal prospectors from the Near East, impinging on neolithic communities in the Peninsula. In absolute terms, the initial phase will not pre-date the fourth millennium. Rock-shelters with schematic painting lie in the south and the south-east of the Peninsula. The new art is not a continuation of the Levantine, despite independent tendencies apparent in the latter's final phase towards the simplification of figures, and schematization, which is here a purely artistic development.

The new art spread throughout the Peninsula, forming part of a movement common to much of Europe and North Africa. Evidence in Galicia and in the Canaries shows a special relationship to the Spanish. In the Peninsula, surviving pockets persisted in inland areas unknown to Levantine art, which were penetrated only late by the new metallurgy, through sporadic commercial contacts. The final phase of schematic art lasts well into the Iron Age, until the arrival of Hallstatt settlers (*Hierro I*). It dies out under cultural influences from colonizing groups, and from Iberians along the coast.

These general conclusions suffice to explain how contact arose between Levantine art and the schematic. A complete analytical study, in the light of new discoveries, of the rock-shelters listed by Breuil is however yet to be made. There are, for instance, the semi-naturalistic figures, with a highly stylized deer, in the Los Organos rock-shelter at Despeñaperros (Jaén). Two women, clothed and wearing ornaments, are painted with a body of two uneven triangles, opposed at the vertices, to indicate the waist and skirt. Lines and circles round the head denote ornaments. Thus, the figures show a slight degree of schematization, especially if compared with others nearby at La Graja de Miranda or La Graja de Jimena. There is more evidence in the Cuevas de la Sarga, Alcoy, where Levantine deer paintings cover schematic marks (pp. 64–5). However, these are earlier than works in adjacent rock-shelters which include a 'sorcerer', just remotely comparable with the one in the Cueva de las Letreros at Velez Blanco, highly schematic quadrupeds, a stylized, 'phi-shaped' human figure, and complicated, labyrinthine meanders. These last are quite distinct from linear work at El Retamoso, Despeñaperros, or at La Cimbarra, Aldeaquemada, and from the parallel curved lines of Nossa Senhora da Esperança.

The extraordinary complexity of problems which can arise is indicated further in the El Salt rock-shelter at Penáguila (Valencia). Among its extremely schematic figures, we find the representation of an anchor-shaped human, exactly in the form of eneolithic pendants found at Las Blanquizares at Lébor (Murcia) or La Barsella at Torremanzanas (Alicante), and very similar to the symbol on the dolmen at Soto, or on those at Barras at Espolla (Gerona) and Peyra Escrita in the eastern French Pyrenees. The figure is eneolithic, although, from their style, the remaining El Salt paintings are far later. In the rock-shelter of El Calvario, Onteniente (Valencia) a homogeneous collection of signs (X, or double Y, shaped and other) would appear to raise the dating to an advanced stage of the Middle, or even to the Late, Bronze Age.

All those examples we have cited (and others could be added, for example, the ocular symbols at Socovos or Nerpio in Albacete) lie in the same geographic zone as Levantine painting. Beyond, there are interesting engravings or petroglyphs in Galicia or Portugal, a result, like paintings elsewhere in the Peninsula, of cultural change, but with peculiarities probably attributable to a distinct, Atlantic, people and to a variety of further contacts which reach out into north-western Europe, especially Ireland. Even Central European comparisons, like the Carschenna site in Switzerland, or certain engravings in the Val Camonica and at Monte Bego, might also be suggested, as well as some in various regions of Africa, and the Canary Islands; all without renouncing their ultimate Mediterranean and Near Eastern inspiration.

CHAPTER NINE

Levantine art and its possible relationships

The questions of chronology and origins which determine the position of Levantine painting within the general history of art have been discussed above.

The idea of direct relationships, or contemporaneity, with palaeolithic art arose solely because Levantine art came to light shortly after the discovery of Altamira and other quaternary art sites. In fact, the Levantine work is distinctive and unique, with very few parallels. Surmised roots in palaeolithic art are vague and ill-defined and cannot be corroborated. Perhaps a statement given by the Abbé Breuil, in an interview shortly before his death with Dr Sahly, will best close this issue. His words at that time were that 'Levantine art has no direct – or, if preferred, sufficiently direct – relationship with Franco-Cantabrian paintings, except that in the general conception of its design the east Spanish work, for example in the treatment of hooves, has overall more in common with the Magdalenian than with the Perigordian. Thus it seems as though an ultimate source may lie in Perigordian art, but of a form more advanced than the Franco-Cantabrian, which had been progressively influenced by the Magdalenian or Solutré-Magdalenian of eastern Spanish regions.'

However, it is difficult to believe that Levantine art could have developed quite on its own in a secluded epi-palaeolithic area near the Mediterranean coast, without some potent initial impetus. The most fascinating of the mysteries which surround this lively painting lies in the formal perfection it achieves in its earliest phases. It would seem possible to allow some survival of palaeolithic tradition, not only because its own art had been so brilliant, but also from the way that Parpalló and other caves with palaeolithic industry (especially El Niño at Aina) lie geographically round the region of Levantine finds. If there had been a break in continuity, and similarities of convention and animal types are merely apparent, then we should have to invoke a strange and delayed reappearance of palaeolithic features, for reasons which we could not explain.

The third and fourth phases of Levantine art illustrate best its originality, especially in the treatment of the human form and in the sense of movement which emanates from all the scenes. The primary concern of the artist will have been with hunting, and the development of economic, social and religious life will have influenced the evolution of the art towards stylization and simplification. When the chase, together with gathering, ceased to be the sole source of food –

that is, when the archers of the inland sierras came under the influence of, or were absorbed by, people of the coastal zone, or when a few became subject to Almerian culture – then Levantine art would have slowly died out.

Vivacity, movement, idealism and impressionism are characteristics proper to Levantine art itself. The large, naturalistic animals, seen at rest, are a heritage from palaeolithic art which is difficult to explain, especially while the chronology remains obscure.

Connections with certain pictorial work in Africa – especially in the regions of Zimbabwe and Tanzania – also present difficulties: the animals differ in species, but in form and attitude the men are analogous, while the women wear identical skirts. There is astounding coincidence in the common, 'fossilized' art style, and we lack an easy explanation of how this came about, nor can we judge which would be the original area. In Algeria and Libya the art – respectively of Tassili and the Fezzan – during a so-called 'bovid' phase, which reflects a pastoral life, also includes certain purely formal analogues with Spain, which writers have not failed to stress. All however express extreme scepticism about a common origin, or any possibility of derivation, in either direction, between African and Peninsula art. There is a supposed pre-neolithic phase in North Africa (named by H. Lhote after the bubal antelope) which might have generated this Saharan art. But nothing relates to the coastlands, so that serious comparison with the Spanish Levant is impossible.

Analogies for more recent phases of Levantine art might be sought among hunting scenes and animal festivals found at Çatal Hüyük in Anatolia, in what James Mellaart supposed might be a sanctuary for those killed in hunting. However, a close examination of sixth millennial Anatolian friezes reveals that only after the increased stylization found at Beldibi and other sites in Anatolia and Bulgaria are there real similarities with Spanish material, and these are difficult to assess. Supposed East Mediterranean models suggested by Jordá follow those already proposed by de Morgan in 1921, and they contain little of substance. As proof of relationships, each one can be challenged: the skirts and treatment of breasts at Cogul; 'bull-fights', dance rites, files of archers, 'divinities' compared with Cretan painting, the Iazilikaja frieze, Anatolian and Syrian gods; and suggestions of animal cults, concerning the bull and deer.

The enigma remains. It will be difficult to ascribe actual similarities to direct contact while they could very well represent convergence, or a common Mediterranean inheritance, especially during neolithic phases of Levantine art. By contrast, East Mediterranean connections are apparent during the eneolithic. In our view, Levantine art was developed by an upland hunting people within a defined geographical region and began in epi-palaeolithic times. There was perhaps a component of palaeolithic tradition, but in its general aspect the art is original and local, with a novelty especially apparent in its representation of the human figure. It lasted throughout the neolithic, then, having passed through a significant evolution, it died out with the arrival of eneolithic schematic art, though slowly, and with some features surviving. To judge from present knowledge, Levantine art is unique and has no direct parallels elsewhere.

Bibliography

ABBREVIATIONS

AEArq. *Archivo Español de Arqueología,* Madrid

AIEC *Anuari de l'Institut d'Estudis Catalans,* Barcelona

AMSEAEP *Actas y Memorias de la Sociedad Española de Antropología, Etnografía y Prehistoria,* Madrid

ANTHR. *L'Anthropologie,* Paris

APL *Archivo de Prehistoria Levantina,* Valencia

ARE Juan Cabré Aguiló, *El arte rupestre en España,* Madrid, 1915

BACAEP *Butlleti de l'Associació Catalana d'Antropología, Etnología y Prehistoria,* Barcelona.

BAH *Boletín de la Real Academia de la Historia,* Madrid

BCEC *Butlletí del Centre Excursionista de Catalunya,* Barcelona

BSC *Boletín de la Sociedad Castellonense de Cultura,* Castellón de la Plana

BSEHN *Boletín de la Real Sociedad Española de Historia Natural,* Madrid

Bull. Ar. *Bulletin de la Société Préhistorique de l'Ariège,* Tarascon sur Ariège

CA *Caesaraugusta,* Saragossa

CAN *Crónica del Congreso Arqueológico Nacional.* Saragossa

CASE *Crónica del Congreso Arqueológico del Sudeste Español*

CIPP *Com. de Invest. Palaeontológicas y Prehistóricas,* Madrid

CISPP *Congrès International des Sciences Préhistoriques et Protohistoriques*

HBB *Miscelánea en homenaje al abate Henri Breuil,* Barcelona, 1964–5

IM *Informes y Memorias de la Comisaría General de Excavaciones Arqueológicas,* Madrid

IPEK *Jahrbuch für prähistorische und ethnographische Kunst,* Berlin–Leipzig

MEXC *Memorias de la Junta Superior de Excavaciones,* Madrid

NAH *Noticiario Arqueológico Hispánico,* Madrid

PAWM *Prehistoric Art of Western Mediterranean and the Sahara,* Chicago, 1965

PBA Almagro, Beltrán, Ripoll, *Prehistoria del Bajo Aragón,* I, Saragossa, 1956

PR. Sch. Henri Breuil, *Les peintures rupestres schématiques de la Péninsule Ibérique,* 1933–5

RA *Revue Archéologique,* Paris

SIMP. BARNA *Simposio Internacional de Arte Rupestre,* Barcelona, 1966 (B. 1968)

GENERAL WORKS

Acanfora, M.O. *Pittura dell'età preistorica,* Milan 1960, pp. 133–90

Almagro Basch, M. *Las pinturas rupestres levantinas,* Madrid 1954

'Arte rupestre naturalista del Levante español', *Historia de España de Menéndez Pidal,* I, 54, p. 443, and in *Ars Hispaniae,* I, Madrid 1947

'Los problemas del Epipaleolítico y Mesolítico en España' *Ampurias,* VI, 1944, p. 1

'Die Felsmalereien Ostspaniens' *Sitzungsberichte der Physikalisch-Medizinischen Societät,* LXXVIII, 1955–7, 1958

on the chronology: CISPP, Zurich 1952, p. 142; CASE, Alcoy 1951, p. 67; CISPP, 1962, p. 319; PAWM, p. 104

Almagro, M., Beltrán, A. and Ripoll, E. PBA

Anati, E. 'Quelques réflexions sur l'art rupestre d'Europe' *Bulletin de la Société Préhistorique Française,* LVII, 11–12, 1960, pp. 695–701

'Anatolia's earliest art', *Archaeology,* XXI, 1, 1968, pp. 22–35

Bandi, H.G. 'Die Vorgeschichtlichen Felsbilder der Spanischen Levante und die Frage ihrer Datierung', in *Mitteilungsblatt für Schweizerischen Gesellschaft für Urgeschichte,* 1951, pp. 156–71

'Einige Ueberlegungen zur Frage der Datierung und des Ursprungs der Levantekunst', in PAWM, p. 113

'Peintures rupestres du Levant espagnol', in *L'art dans le Monde,* Paris 1960, pp. 65–91

Bandi-Maringer. *L'art préhistorique,* 1955, pp. 114–42

Beltrán, A. 'Sobre representaciones femeninas en el arte rupestre levantino', CAN, IX, Saragossa 1966, p. 90

'Acerca de la cronología de la pintura rupestre levantina', in *Symposium International d'art préhistorique,* Val Camonica, 1970, p. 87

Arte rupestre levantino, Saragossa 1968, pp. 1–260, pls

'Arte rupestre levantino (Adiciones 1968–1978)', CA LXVII–LXVIII, Saragossa 1979, p. 5

'Las figuras naturalistas del Prado del Azogue, en Aldeaquemada, Jaén', in *Miscelánea Canellas,* Saragossa 1969, p. 97

'Die spanischen Felsmalereien der Levante und ihre chronologischen Problem', IPEK, XXIV, 1974–7, p. 32

'El arte rupestre levantino', *Historia, 16,* II, 10, Madrid Feb. 1977, p. 91

'Les animaux de l'art rupestre des chasseurs du Levant espagnol', in *Symposion de Sigriswil,* Switzerland 1979

'Problemi generali dell'arte... Mesolitico. Neolitico. Età dei Metalli', in *Enciclopedia Universale dell'Arte. Nuove conoscenze e prospettive del mondo dell'arte,* Roma 1978, pp. 5–17

'Los problemas de la investigación de las pinturas y grabados prehistóricos al aire libre. Referencia al conjunto del Tassili n'Ajjer y al del arte rupestre levantino', CA, LXXV–LXXVI, Saragossa 1978, p. 5.

Blanc, A.C. 'Sur le problème de l'Age de l'Art rupestre du Levant espagnol et les moyens à employer pour résoudre ce problème', in PAWM, p. 119

Blasco, M.C. 'La recolección en el arte rupestre levantino', in *Miscelánea Antonio Beltrán,* Saragossa 1975, p. 49

Bosch Gimpera, P. 'The Chronology of Rock Paintings in Spain and North Africa', *Art Bulletin,* XXXII, New York 1950, p. 1

'Le problème de la chronologie de l'art rupestre de l'Est de l'Espagne et l'Afrique', in *Actes du Congrès Panafricain de Préhistoire,* II, Argel 1952

'The chronology of the rock-paintings of the Spanish Levant', in PAWM, p. 125

'La chronologie de l'art rupestre seminaturaliste et schématique de la Péninsule Ibérique', in *La Préhistorie: problèmes et tendences,* Paris 1968, p. 71

'La chronologie de l'art rupestre seminaturaliste et schématique et la culture mégalithique portugaise', in *In memoriam do abate Henri Breuil,* I, Lisbon 1965, p. 113

Breuil, H. 'L'âge des cavernes et roches ornés de France et d'Espagne', RA, XIX, 1912, p. 215

'Les roches peintes leptolitiques de l'Espagne Oriental', in PAWM, p. 133

'L'occident patrie du grand art rupestre', in *Mélanges Pittard,* Brive 1957, p. 101

Breuil, H. and Lantier, R. *Les hommes de la pierre ancienne,* Paris 1951, p. 228

Cabré Aguiló, J. ARE

Del Pan, I. and Wernert, P. 'Datos para la cronología del arte rupestre del Oriente de España', BSEHN, XVI, 1916, p. 400

Interpretación de un adorno en las figuras humanas masculinas de Alpera y Cogul, Madrid 1915

Eickstedt, E.F. von. 'Menschen und Menschendarstellungen der Steinzeitlichen Höhlenkunst in Frankreich und Spanien', *Z. Morphol. Anthr.,* XLIV, 15–20, 1952, pp. 295–344

Esteve, F. 'Probable significación de unas pinturas rupestres del Maestrazgo', *Cuadernos de Prehistoria y Arqueología Castellonense,* I, 1974, p. 9

Fortea, J. 'Algunas aportaciones a los problemas del arte levantino', *Zephyrus,* XXV, 1974, p. 225

Herberts, K. *Anfänge der Malerei,* Wuppertal 1941

Hernández Pacheco, E. *Prehistoria del Solar Hispano,* Madrid 1959, pp. 341–484 and 518–531

Jordá Cerdá, F. 'Sobre posibles relaciones del arte levantino español', in HBB, p. 467

'Notas para una revisión de la Cronología del Arte rupestre levantino', *Zephyrus,* XVII, 1966, pp. 47–76

'Zur Zeitstellung der Levante-Kunst', *Madrider Mitteilungen,* VIII, 1967, p. 11

'Problemas cronológicos del arte rupestre del Levante español', *Actas del XII Congreso Internacional de Historia del Arte,* Granada 1973, I, p. 155

'Las puntas de flecha en el arte levantino', CAN, XIII, Saragossa 1975, p. 219

'Tocados de plumas en el arte levantino', *Zephyrus,* XXI–XXII, 1970–1, p. 35

'Formas de vida económica en el arte levantino' *ibid.,* XXV, 1974, p. 209

'Restos de un culto al toro en el arte levantino?', *ibid.,* XXVI–XXVII, 1976, p. 198

'La Peña del Escrito (Villar de Humo) y el culto al toro', *Cuadernos de Prehistoria y Arqueología Castellonense,* II, 1975, p. 7

'Bastones de cavar, layas y arado en el arte levantino', *Munibe,* XXIII, 1971, p. 241

'La sociedad en el arte rupestre levantino', in *III Congreso Nacional de Arqueología,* Porto 1974, p. 43; *Historia del Arte Hispánico,* ed. Alhambra, Madrid 1978, p. 133

Kühn, H. *Die Felsbilder Europas,* Stuttgart 1952

'Die Frage des Altes ostspanischen Felsbilders', IPEK, XV–XVI, 1941–2

'Das Problem der Ostspanischen Felsmalerei', in *Tagungsberichten der Deutschen Anthropologischen Gesellschaft* (offprinted, n.d.)

'Das Alterprobleme der Ostspanischen Kunst', *Kosmos,* V, 1951, pp. 200–3

Lantier, R. 'Propos sur l'art rupestre de l'Espagne Orientale', in PAWM, p. 145

Lidner, K. *La chasse préhistorique,* Paris 1950

Lothe, H. 'Le problème de la datation des peintures rupestres en Espagne et en Afrique', IPEK, XX, 1960–3, p. 62

Maluquer de Motes, J. 'Los sílex del barranco de la Valltorta', *Ampurias,* I, 1939, p. 108

Martínez Santa-Olalla, J. 'Neues über prähistorische Felsmalereien aus Frankreich, Spanien und Morokko', IPEK, XV–XVI, 1941

Mellaart, J. 'The Beginnings of mural paintings', *Archaeology,* XV, I, 1962, pp. 1–12

'Çatal-Hüyük. Une ville mésolithique du VII millenaire en Anatolie', *Archeologia,* XVII, 1967, p. 43

Çatal-Hüyük. A Neolithic Town in Anatolia, London 1967

Molinos, M.I. 'Las huellas de animales en el arte rupestre levantino', in *Miscelánea A. Beltrán,* Saragossa 1975, p. 59

Mori F. *Acacus Tadrart. Arte rupestre e culture del Sahara preistorico,* Torino 1965

Obermaier, H. 'Probleme der paläolithischen Malerei Ostspaniens'. *Quartär,* I, 1939, p. 1911

El Hombre Fósil, Madrid 1916, 2nd ed. 1925

'Nouvelles études sur l'art rupestre du Levant espagnol', ANTHR., XLVII, 1937, p. 447

'Altsteinzeitliche Justizpflege', *Paideuma,* I, 5, p. 193, Leipzig 1939

Obermaier H. and Wernert P. 'La edad cuaternaria de las pinturas rupestres del Levante español', BSEHN, XV, 1929, p. 527

Pericot Garcia, L. *La cueva de El Parpalló* (*Gandía*), Madrid 1942

Arte rupestre, Barcelona 1950

'Las pinturas rupestres del Tanganyca y el arte levantino español' CAN, III, Murcia 1947, p. 31

La España primitiva, Barcelona 1950 and in *Historia de España,* Gallach

'Sobre algunos problemas del arte rupestre del Levante español' in PAWM, p. 151

Peyrony, D. 'L'art pictural de la grotte de Lascaux et celui dit 'Levantin espagnol', *Bulletin de la Société Préhistorique Française,* XLVI, 1949, p. 117

Ripoll, E. 'Arte rupestre', in *I Symposium de Prehistoria de la Peninsula Ibérica,* Pamplona 1960, p. 23

'Para una cronologia relativa de las pinturas rupestres del Levante español', in *Festschrift fur Lothar Zotz,* Bonn, 1960, p. 457

'Para una cronologia relativa del arte levantino español', in PAWM, 1967

'Cuestiones en torno a la cronologia del arte rupestre postpaleolitico en la Peninsula Ibérica', in SIMP. BARNA, pp. 165–92

Vaufrey, R. 'L'âge de l'art rupestre naturaliste du Levant espagnol', ANTHR., LI, 1947, p. 141

Wernert, P. 'Nuevos datos etnográficos para la cronología del arte rupestre de estilo naturalista del Oriente de España' BSEHN, XVI, 1916

'La significación unitaria de las cuevas del arte paleolítico', *Investigación y Progreso,* IX, 1935

'Réflexions sur l'art rupestre naturaliste de l'Espagne orientale. Le motif de la mise-bas dans l'art paléolitique', *In memoriam do abate Breuil,* II, Lisbon 1966, p. 351

Zotz, L. 'Ein westmediterraner palaeolitischer Kunstkreis des Mittler zwischen Aquitanischer und Levantekunst', in *Homenaje Vega del Sella,* Oviedo 1956, p. 143

NEW DATING OF THE LEVANTINE NEOLITHIC

Fernández Miranda, M. 'Verdelpino, Cuenca. Nuevas fechas de Carbono 14 para el Neolitico Peninsular', *Trabajos de Prehistoria,* XXXI, p. 311

Fernández Miranda, M. and Moure, J.A. 'El abrigo de Verdelpino, Cuenca. Un nuevo yacimiento neolítico en el interior de la Península Ibérica', *Noticiario Arqueológico: Prehistoria,* III, p. 189

'Noticias de los trabajos de 1978', *Trabajos de Prehistoria,* XXXIV, 1977, p. 31

Fortea, F.J. 'La Cueva de la Cocina. Ensayo de cronología

del Epipaleolitico (facies geométrica)', in *Servicio de Investigación Prehistórica. Trabajos varios 1940*, Valencia 1971

Los complejos microlaminares y geométricos del Epipaleolítico mediterraneo español, Salamanca 1973

Lopez, P. 'La problemática cronológica del Neolitico peninsular', in *C 14 y Prehistoria en la Península Ibérica. Fundación March*, Madrid 1978, p. 45

Walker and Cuenca Paya 'Nuevas fechas de Carbono 14 para el sector de Alicante y Murcia', in *Actas de la II Reunión Nacional del grupo español de trabajos del cuaternario*, Madrid 1977, p. 309

BIBLIOGRAPHY BY SITES

1 *COLUNGO*

Beltrán, A. and Baldellou, V. 'Avance al estudio de las pinturas prehistóricas de Colungo', *Symposion Internacional de Arte Prehistórico, Madrid 1979*

Beltrán, A. 'Las pinturas rupestres de Colungo (Huesca): Problemas de extensión y relaciones entre el arte paleolítico y el arte Levantino' CA, LXIX–L, 1980

2 *OS DE BALAGUER*

Diez Coronel, L. 'Nuevas pinturas rupestres y su protección en Os de Balaguer', CAN, XIII, Saragossa 1975, p. 227

Abrigos con pinturas rupestres en Lérida', CAN XII, 1973, p. 251

Maluquer de Motes, J. 'Nuevas pinturas rupestres en Cataluña: La Bauma dels Vilars en Os de Balaguer', *Pyraene* VIII, 1972, p. 151

3 *COGUL*

Almagro, M. *El covacho con pinturas rupestres de Cogul (Lérida)*, Lérida 1952

Begouen, H. 'Une excursion aux fresques préhistoriques de Cogul, près Lerida', in *Bull. Soc. Archéologique du Midi*, 1912

Bosch Gimpera, P. and Colominas, J.M̃. 'Pintures y gravats rupestres. Pintures rupestres de la Roca dels Moros, de Cogul', AIEC, 1921–6, p. 19

Breuil, H. 'Les peintures quaternaires de la Roca de Cogul', *Butlletí del Centre Excursionista de Lleyda*, I, 1908, n. 10, p. 10

PR. Sch., IV, 1935, p. 75

Breuil, H. and Cabré, J. 'Les peintures rupestres du Bassin inférieur de l'Ebre', ANTHR., XX, 1909, pp. 8–21

Breuil, H. and Cartailhac 'Nouvelles cavernes à peintures découvertes dans l'Aragon, la Catalogne et les Cantabres', ANTHR., XIX, 1908, pp. 371–3

Cabré, J. ARE, p. 170

Gómez de Tabanera, 'Arte y magia en la Roca del Moros, de Cogul', *Revista de Ideas Estéticas*, XXXIX, 1952, pp. 313–21

Herrera y Ges, M. 'Al Cogul', BCEC, I, 1908, pp. 544–50

Huguet, R. 'De prehistoria', in *Esperanza*, Lérida 1918, p. 133

'Civilización del hombre prehistórico de Suñer y algunos pueblos de la comarca de las Garrigas', in *Congreso de Historia de la Corona de Aragón*, 1920, p. 44

Obermaier, M. 'Cogul', *Reallexicon der Vorgeschichte*, II, p. 319

Rocafort, C. 'Las pinturas rupestres de Cogul' BCEC, XVIII, 1908, p. 65

'Las exploraciones de Cogul', BCEC, XVIII, 1908, p. 212

Vidal, L.M. 'Les pintures rupestres de Cogul', AIEC, 1908, pp. 544–60

4/5 *BARRANCO DEL LLORT*

Carreras Candi, *Geografía General de Catalunya: Tarragona*, p. 768

Hübner, Ae. *Monumenta Linguae Ibericae*, Berlin 1893, XIII a, p. 148

Vilaseca, S. 'Las pinturas rupestres naturalistas y esquemáticas de Mas del Llort, en Rojals (provincia de Tarragona)', AEArq., XVII, 1944, p. 301

'Nuevas pinturas rupestres naturalistas en el Barranco del Llort (Rojals)' in *Noticiario de la Asociación Excursionista de Reus*, Dec. 1950

'Nuevo hallazgo de pinturas rupestres naturalistas en el Barranco del Llort (Rojals, provincia de Tarragona)', AEArq., XXIII, 1950, p. 371

6/11 *LOWER EBRO*

Bosch Gimpera, P. and Colominas, J.M. 'Pintures y gravats rupestres. Exploració de la sierra de Tivissa', in AIEC, 1921–6, p. 4

Hernández Pacheco, E. 'Noticia del hallazgo de pinturas rupestres en Tivissa (Tarragona)', BSEHN, XXI, 1921, p. 543

'Pinturas prehistóricas de la Font Vilella, en Tivissa (Tarragona)', *Ibérica*, 1922

Kühn, H. *Kunst und Kultur der Vorzeit Europas*, I, 1929, pl. 84

Ripoll, E. 'Una pintura de tipo paleolítico en la sierra del Montsiá (Tarragona), y su posible relación con los origenes del arte levantino', HBB II, p. 297

Beltrán, A. 'Avance al estudio de las pinturas rupestres levantinas de la provincia de Tarragona; estado de la cuestión', in *Miscelánea Sánchez Real, Boletín Arqueológico de Tarragona* 1967–8, p. 173

Vilaseca, S. and Cantarell, I. *La cova de la Mallada, de Cabra Feixet*

12 *ULLDECONA*

Miñes and Romeu y Ten. 'Noticia sobre un conjunto de arte rupestre en Ulldecona (Tarragona)', *Pyrenae* XI, Barcelona 1975, p. 145

Centro Cultural y Recreativo *L'art préhistoric d'Ulldecona*, Barcelona 1976

13/14 *BARRANCO DI CALAPATÁ*

Almagro, M. PBA, pp. 40–50

Breuil, H. and Cabré, J. 'Les peintures rupestres du bassin inférieur de l'Ebre. I. Les rochers peints de Calapatá à Cretas (Bas Aragon),' ANTHR., XX, 1909, pp. 1–21

Cabré, J. ARE, pp. 132–52

Cabré, J. and Vidiella. 'Las pinturas rupestres del término de Cretas', in *Boletín de Historia y Geografía del Bajo Aragon,* 1907

Bosch Gimpera, P. 'Les pintures del Barranco del Calapatá de Cretes (Baix Aragó)', BACAEP, II, 1924, pp. 131–46, pls. 17–20

Vallespí, E.J. 'Noticias de las pinturas rupestres del barranco dels Gascons (Calapatá, en Cretas, Teruel)', CA IX–X, p. 133

15/16 *MAZALEÓN*

Cabré, J. and Pérez Temprado, L. 'Las pinturas rupestres paleolíticas de Els Secans (Mazaleón, Teruel) y sus relaciones etnográficas con la indumentaria actual aragonesa', in *Il Congreso de Historia de la Corona de Aragón,* Huesca 1920

'Nuevos hallazgos de arte rupestre en el Bajo Aragón', BSEHN, XXI, 1921, pp. 276–86

Vallespí, E. 'Sobre las pinturas rupestres "Dels Secans" (Mazaleón, Teruel)' AEArq, XXV, 1952, p. 105

Pérez Temprado, L. and Vallespí, E. 'La caídas del Salbime, Mazaleón (Teruel), nuevo yacimiento bajoaragonés con arte rupestre', CA, IV, 1954, p. 31

17 *VAL DEL CHARCO DEL AGUA AMARGA*

Almagro, M. PBA, pp. 50–62

Cabré, J. ARE, pp. 152–70

Tomás, J. 'Del Charco del Agua Amarga', *Zephyrus* II, Salamanca 1951, p. 5

Beltrán, A. *La cueva del Charco del Agua Amarga y sus pinturas levantinas,* Saragossa 1970, pp. 1–120, pls.

18/21 *SANTOLEA*

Ortego, T. 'Nuevos hallazgos rupestres en la provincia de Teruel, la cueva del Pudial, en Ladruñan', AEArq., 1946, p. 155

Almagro, M. PBA, p. 64

Ripoll, E. *Los abrigos pintados de los alrededores de Santolea (Teruel),* Barcelona 1961, pp. 1–36, 8 pls.

22/30 *ALACÓN*

Almagro, M. PBA, pp. 66–89

Beltrán, A. 'Peintures rupestres du Levant de "El abrigo de los Recolectores" dans le ravin de "El Mortero" (Alacón, Teruel, España)', Bull. Ar., XVI–XVII, 1961–2, pp. 16–50

Beltrán, A. and Vallespí, E. 'Otro covacho con pinturas rupestres en 'El Mortero', de Alacón (Teruel), CA XV–XVI, 1960, pp. 7–18

Ortego, T. 'Nuevas estaciones de arte rupestre aragonés: "El Mortero" y "Cerro Felío", en el término de Alacón (Teruel)', AEArq., XXI, 1948, p. 3

Ripoll, E. 'La cueva Hipólito, en Alacón, *Teruel,* VI, 1951, p. 27

31 *CAÑADA DE MARCO*

Ortego, T. 'Una nueva estación de arte rupestre en el término de Alcaine (Teruel)' in SIMP. BARNA, p. 149

32/46 *ALBARRACÍN MOUNTAINS*

Almagro, M. 'Un nuevo grupo de pinturas rupestres en Albarracín: "La cueva de Doña Clotilde" ', *Teruel,* I, 2, 1949, p. 90–116

'Nuevas pinturas rupestres con una danza falica en Albarracín', in *Festschrift für Lothar Zotz*, Erlangen 1960, p. 13

'Tres nuevos covachos con pintura en la comarca de Albarracin', CAN, II, 1952, p. 112, and CA, II, 1953, p. 7

'Los problemas del Epipaleolitico y Mesolítico en España', *Ampurias,* VI, Barcelona 1944, p. 1

Breuil, H. 'Nouvelles découvertes en Espagne', ANTHR., XXII, 1910, pp. 247 and 356

Breuil, H. and Cabré, J. 'Les peintures rupestres d'Espagne. III. Los toricos de Albarracin', ANTHR., XXII, 6, 1911, p. 641

Cabré, J. ARE, p. 180

Marconell, E. 'Los toros de la Losilla', in *Miscelánea turolense,* Madrid 1892

'Pinturas rupestres arrancadas de la Cueva Remigia', BSC, XIX–XX, 1944, p. 35, reprinted NAH, I, 1–3, 1952, p. 19

Obermaier, H. and Breuil, H. 'Las pinturas rupestres de los

alrededores de Tormon (Teruel)', BAH, xc, II, 1927, p. 551

Ortego, T. 'Prospecciones arqueológicas en las Tajadas de Bezas (Teruel)', AEArq, LXXXII, 1951, p. 445

Almagro Basch, M. 'Cuatro nuevos abrigos rupestres con pinturas en Albarracín', *Teruel*, LI, 1974, p. 5

Gonzalez, F. and Merino, M.V. *Hallazgos de pinturas y grabados rupestres en la zona de Albarracín,* Teruel 1974

47/51 *VILLAR DEL HUMO*

Breuil, H. PR. Sch, 1935, p. 70

Hernández Pacheco, E. *Prehistoria del Solar Hispano. Orígenes del arte pictórico,* Madrid 1959, pp. 420–36, 18 figs

Beltrán, A. 'Sobre la pintura rupestre levantina de un caballo cazado a lazo, del abrigo de Selva Pascuala, en Villar del Humo (Cuenca)', in *Miscelánea Lacarra,* Saragossa 1968, p. 81

'Arte rupestre levantino. Adiciones 1968–69', (above).

52 *EL POLVORÍN*

Vilaseca, S. 'Las pinturas rupestres de la cueva del Polvorín (Puebla de Benifazá, provincia de Castellón)', IM, XVII, 1947

53/54 *MORELLA LA VELLA*

Hernández Pacheco, E. 'Excursión de investigación prehistórica a Morella', BSEHN, XVIII, 1917

'Estudios de Arte prehistórico. I: Prospección de las pinturas rupestres de Morella la Vella. II: Evolución de las ideas madres de la pinturas rupestres', *Revista de la R. Academia de Ciencias Exactas, Fisicas y Naturales,* XVI, Madrid 1918, republished by the CIPP

Bosch Gimpera, P. *Els problemes arqueológics de la provincia de Castelló,* Castellón 1924, pp. 8–10 (*Morella la Vella and Valltorta*).

55 *CUEVA REMIGIA*

Porcar, J., Obermaier, H. and Breuil, H. 'Excavaciones en la Cueva Remigia (Castellón)', MEXC CXXXVI, 1935, pp. 1–99, 62 pls.

Porcar, J., 'Pintures rupestres al barranco de Gasulla', BSC, XV, 1934, p. 343

'Iconografía rupestre de Gasulla y Valltorta. Danza de arqueros ante figuras humanas sacrificadas', BSC, XXI, arqueros ante figuras humanas sacrificadas', BSC, XXI, 1945, p. 145

'Escenas bélicas', BSC, XXII, 1946, p. 58

'Representación pictográfica del toro', BSC, XXIII, 1947, p. 314

'Representación de insectos', BSC, XXV, 1949, p. 169

'Impresiones sobre el arte rupestre existente en el Maestrazgo', in PAWM, p. 159

56 *CINGLE DE LA MOLA REMIGIA*

Ripoll Perelló, E. *Pinturas rupestres de la Gasulla (Castellón),* Barcelona 1963, pp. 1–59, 35 pls., republ. in *Zephyrus,* XIII, 1963, p. 91

Codina, E. 'Las pinturas rupestres del Cingle de la Mola Remigia', BSC, XXV, 1949, p. 635

Porcar, J. 'Interpretaciones y sugerencias en torno a las pinturas rupestres del abrigo X del Cingle de la Mola Remigia', BSC, XXV, 1949, p. 642

'El trazo por impresión directa y el trazo caligráfico en el arte rupestre de Ares del Maestre', BSC, XVIII, 1943, p. 262

'Sobre las pinturas rupestres de Ares del Maestre', BSC, XVIII, 1943, pp. 15–16 (on tools and hunting weapons)

57/58 *RACÓ DE MOLERO AND RACÓ DE GASPARO*

Beltrán, A. 'Nouveautés dans la peinture rupestre du Levant espagnol: El Racó de Gasparo et El Racó de Molero (Ares del Maestre, Castellón)', Bull. Ar., XX, 1965, p. 117

'Breve nota sobre un grabado rupestre en el Racó Molero, barranco de la Gasulla (Castellón de la Plana)', *Ampurias,* XXV, Barcelona 1965

Obermaier H. 'Nouvelles études sur l'art rupestre du Levant espagnol', ANTHR., XLVII, p. 488

Porcar Ripollés, J. 'Las pinturas del Racó de Molero' BSC, XLI, 1965, p. 176

'Las pinturas del Racó de Gasparo', *ibid.*

'Las damas mesolíticas de Ares del Maestre', *Atlantis,* XV, 1936–40, p. 162

Ripoll, E. *Pinturas rupestres de la Gasulla (Castellón),* Barcelona 1963, p. 47

59 *LES DOGUES*

Porcar Ripollés, J. 'Las pinturas del barranco de "Les Dogues" ', APL, IV, 1953, p. 75

'Noves pintures rupestres en el terme de Ares', BSC, XVI, 1935, pp. 30–2

Obermaier, H. 'Nouvelles études sur l'art rupestre du Levant espagnol', ANTHR., XLVII, 1937, p. 477 (defective sketch)

Ripoll, E. *Pinturas rupestres de la Gasulla (Castellón),* Barcelona 1963, p. 45

60/61 *MAS BLANC AND EL SINGLE*

Porcar, J. 'Noves pintures rupestres en el Terme de Ares', BSC, XVI, 1935, pp. 30–2 and p. 144

'Algunas pinturas del arte rupestre levantino atribuidas al periodo Eneolítico', CAN, I, Cartagena 1950, p. 53, with pl. 9

62/63 BENASAL

Gonzales Prats, A. 'El complejo rupestre del riu de Montllor', *Zephyrus,* XXV, 1974, p. 259

Chocomeli, J. 'Las pinturas naturalistas de Els Covarjos', *La labor del S.I.P. y su museo* 1935–59, p. 33

Bellot Gomez, 'Nuevas pinturas en el término de Villafranca del Cid', communication to *I° Congreso de Historia del País Valenciano,* Valencia 1971

64/71 LA VALLTORTA

Obermaier, H. and Wernert, P. 'Las pinturas rupestres del Barranco de Valltorta (Castellón)', CIPP, XXIII, 1919

Cabré Aguilo, J. 'Las pinturas rupestres de la Valltorta. Desaparición de las pinturas de una de las estaciones prehistóricas de este valle', AMSEAEP, II, 2, 2–3, 1923, p. 107

'Las pinturas rupestres de la Valltorta: Escena bélica de la Cova de Cevil', AMSEAEP, 1925, p. 201

Del Arco, L. 'Descubrimiento de pinturas rupestres en el barranco de la Valltorta (Castellón)', BAH, LXXXI, 1917, p. 5

Alcahalí, Baron de 'Frescos prehistóricos de Tirig', *Archivo de Arte Valenciano,* III, Valencia 1917, p. 3

Duran Sanpere, A. and Pallarés, M. 'Exploració arqueológica del Barranco de la Valltorta', AIEC, VI, 1915–20, p. 444

Kühn, H. 'Die Malereien der Valltorta Schlucht', IPEK, I, 1926

Eickstedt, E.F. von 'Die Sauhatz von Valltorta', *Homo,* III, 3, 1952, p. 123

Beltrán, A. 'Nota sobre el grupo de tres figuras negras del abrigo de la Saltadora, en el barranco de la Valltorta (Castellón)', *Revista da Facultade de Letras de Lisboa,* III, 9, 1965

72 LA JOQUERA

Porcar, J. 'La pintura rupestre de La Joquera', BSC, XIII, 1932, p. 228

73 GILET, ALBALAT

Las provincias, 12 Oct. 1974.

Aparicio, J. 'Pinturas rupestres esquemáticas en los alrededores de Santo Espiritu (Gilet) y Albalat de Segart (Valencia) y la cronología del arte levantino', *Saguntum,* XII, 1976, p. 31

74/77 DOS AGUAS

Jordá Cerdá, F. and Alcacer, J. *Las pinturas rupestres de Dos Aguas (Valencia),* Valencia 1951

Pla Ballester, E. 'Actividades del S.I.P. (1961–65)', APL, XI, 1966, p. 284

Fletcher, D. *Generalitat,* 1, 1962, p. 89 and NAH, VI, 1962–4, p. 380

78/82 CUEVAS DE LA ARAÑA

Hernández Pacheco, F. 'Escenas pictoricas de representación de insectos de la época paleolítica', BSEHN, L, 1921

'Las pinturas prehistóricas de las Cuevas de la Araña (Valencia). Evolución del arte rupestre en España', CIPP, XXXIV, Madrid 1924

Breuil, H. 'Vestiges de peintures préhistoriques à "La cueva del Pernil", Játiva (Valencia)', APL, I, 1928, p. 19

Beltrán, A. 'Algunas cuestiones sobre las pinturas de la cueva de La Araña', in *Trabajos dedicados a Pio Beltrán,* Valencia 1970, p. 11

Aparicio Pérez, J. 'Nuevas pinturas rupestres en la provincia de Valencia', CAN, XV, Saragossa 1979, p. 399

83/84 AYORA

Aparicio Pérez, J. *Loc. cit.*

85 QUESA

Aparicio Pérez, J. *Loc. cit.*

86 CUEVAS DE LA SARGA

Rey Pastor, A. 'Jijona (Alicante). Cuevas de la Sarga', NAH, I, 1–3, 1952, p. 25.

Visedo Molto, C. NAH, II, 1–3, 1953–5, p. 177
Alcoy. Geologia; Prehistoria, Alcoy 1959, pp. 35–7

Beltrán, A. 'Las pinturas rupestres prehistóricas de la Sarga (Alcoy), Salt (Penáguila) y El Calvari (Bocairente)', *Servicio de Investigación Prehistórica, Trabajos Varios,* XLVII, Valencia 1974 (in collaboration with V. Pascual).

87 CANTOS DE LA VISERA

Zuazo Palacios, J. *Villa de Montealegre y su Cerro de los Santos,* Madrid 1915, p. 7.

Monte Arabí, término de Yecla, Murcia, Pinturas rupestres (30 postcards, printed red, with copies by Cabré and Breuil)

Breuil, H. and Burkitt, M. 'Les peintures rupestres d'Espagne. VI: Les abris peints du Monte Arabí près Yecla (Murcia)', ANTHR., XXVI, 1915, p. 313

Cabré, J. ARE, p. 208

Breuil, H. PR. Sch., IV, 1935, p. 57

88/91 ALPERA

Sánchez, J. 'Pinturas rupestre en la sierra de Enguera', *Saitabi,* VII, 23–4, 1917, pp. 53–9

Breuil, H., Serrano Goméz, P. and Cabré Aguiló, J. 'Les peintures rupestres d'Espagne. IV. Les abris del Bosque à Alpera (Albacete)', ANTHR., XXIII, 1912, p. 529

Breuil, H. and Obermaier, H. 'Les premiers travaux de l'Institut de Paléontologie Humaine. II. Travaux sur les peintures rupestres d'Espagne. 2. Alpera (Albacete)', ANTHR., XXIII, 1912, pp. 19–23

Breuil, H. 'Nouvelles roches peintes de la Région d'Alpera (Albacete)', ANTHR., XXVI, 1915, pp. 329–31 (Fuente de la Arena, the shelters, which the author calls Carasoles del Bosque and Cueva Negra del Barranco Hondo).
Cabré, J. ARE, p. 187

92/94 MINATEDA

Breuil, H. 'Les peintures rupestres de la Péninsule Ibérique. XI. Les roches peintes de Minateda (Albacete)', ANTHR., XXX, 1920, p. 1
  'Station moustérienne et peintures préhistoriques du Canalizo del Rayo, Minateda (Albacete)', APL, I, 1928, pp. 15–17
Hernández Pacheco, E. *Prehistoria del Solar Hispano. Orígenes del arte prehistórico*, Madrid 1959, pp. 311 and 470
  'Las pinturas prehistóricas de las Cuevas de la Araña (Valencia). Evolución del arte rupestre en España', CIPP, XXXIV, Madrid 1924, p. 140

95/102 NERPIO

García Guinea, M.A. 'Los recientes descubrimientos de pinturas rupestres levantinas en Nerpio (Albacete)', *Las Ciencias*, XXXVIII, 8, p. 458 expanded 'Le nouveau foyer de peintures levantines à Nerpio (Albacete, Espagne)', Bull. Ar., XVIII, 1963, p. 17
  'Nuevos abrigos con pinturas rupestres en las proximidades de Nerpio, Albacete', in *Homenaje a Mergelina*, Murcia 1961–2, p. 397
García Guinea, M.A. and Krapovickas, P. 'Los abrigos de El Prado del Tornero', *Quartär* XI–XII, 1958–9
Sanchez Carrilero, J. 'Avance al estudio de las pinturas rupestres de Solana de las Covachas', NAH, V, 1956–61, 1962
García Guinea, M.A. and Berges Soriano, M. 'Nuevos hallazgos de pinturas esquemáticas en Nerpio (Albacete). El abrigo del castillo de Taibona', CAN, VI, 1961, p. 71
Sánchez Jiménez, J. 'Pinturas rupestres de 'Collado del Guijarral', Segura de la Sierra (Jaén)', NAH, III–IV, 1954–5, 1956, p. 5
  'Pinturas rupestres de Socovos (Albacete)', in *Homenaje a Mergelina*, Murcia 1961–2, p. 781
De Los Santos, S. and Zornoza, B. 'Nuevas aportaciones al estudio de la pintura rupestre levantina en la zona de Nerpio, Albacete', CAN, XIII, Saragossa 1975, p. 203
Vinas, R. and Alonso, A. 'L'abri de "Los Toros", Las Bojadillas, Nerpio (Albacete)', Bull. Ar., XXXIII, 1978, p. 95
  'Acerca de algunas pinturas rupestres de las Bojadillas (Nerpio, Albacete). Friso de los toros', *Speleon*, XXII, Barcelona 1974–5, p. 24

103 CUEVA DEL PELICIEGO

Fernández Avilés, A. 'Las pinturas rupestres de la Cueva del Peliciego, en término de Jumilla (Murcia)', *Boletín del Seminario de Estudios de Arte y Arqueología*, VI, Valladolid 1939–40, p. 35

104 BARRANCO DE LOS GRAJOS

NAH, VII, 1–3, 1963, p. 254 (from *ABC*, Madrid, 25 Jan. 1963)
Beltrán, A. 'Aportaciones de la cueva de los Grajos (Cieza, Murcia) al conocimiento del arte rupestre levantino español', in *Symposium International d'Art Préhistorique*, Val Camonica 1970, p. 79
  'Nuevos hallazgos de arte rupestre levantino: Las cuevas de Los Grajos (Cieza) y los abrigos de la Cañaica del Calar y de la Fuente del Sabuco (El Sabinar, Murcia)', CA, 1968

105/106 CANAICA DEL CALAR AND FUENTE DEL SABUCO

Carbonell Escobar J. 'Dos nuevos abrigos con pinturas rupestres en El Sabinar (provincia de Murcia)', in APL, XII
Beltrán, A. *Los abrigos pintados de la Cañaica del Calar y de la Fuente del Sabuco, El Sabinar, Murcia*, Saragossa 1972. cf site. 104
Beltrán Lloris, M. 'Escena bélica en el abrigo de Fuente Sabuco' CAN, XI, p. 237
Lillo Carpio, M. 'Las pinturas rupestres de la Risca', *Murcia*, XV, 1979

107–112 SOUTHERN SPAIN: NATURALISM AND SCHEMATIZATION

Breuil, H. and De Motos, F. 'Les roches à figures naturalistes de la region de Vélez Blanco (Almeria)', ANTHR., XXVI, 1915, p. 332
De Motos, F. 'Rocas y cuevas pintadas de Vélez Blanco', BAH, 1915, p. 408
Cabré Aguiló, J. 'Avance al estudio de las pinturas prehistóricas del Extremo Sur de España', CIPP, III, 1914, pl. IX
  'Las pinturas rupestres de Aldeaquemada', CIPP, XIV, 1917, pp. 6, 16 and 29
ARE, pp. 217–23
Beltrán, A. 'El problema de la cronología del arte rupestre esquemático español', CA, XXXIX–XL, Saragossa 1975–6, p. 5
Ripoll, E. '*The process of schematization in the prehistoric art of the Iberian Peninsula*, Canberra 1977

Blanc, A.C. *Dall'astrazione all'organicità,* Roma 1958

Acosta, P. *La pintura rupestre esquemática en España,* Salamanca 1968

Beltrán, A. *Las pinturas esquemáticas de Lecina,* Saragossa 1972

Pinturas esquemáticas de La Fenellosa, en Beceite (Teruel), Saragossa 1969

Las pinturas esquemáticas y abstractas del Castillo de Villafamés, Castellón, Saragossa 1969

PROBLEMS OF CONSERVATION

Soleilhavoup, P. *Les oeuvres rupestres sahariennes sont-elles menacées?,* Argel 1978

Beltrán, A. 'Los problemas de la investigación de las pinturas y grabados prehistóricos al aire libre. Referencia al conjunto del Tassili n'Ajjer y al del arte rupestre levantino', CA, LXV–LXVI,, Saragossa 1978,, p. 5

Ministère de l'Information et de la Culture *Séminaire International sur la conservation des peintures rupestres du Tassili,* Algiers 1978

Preceding page. Above: triassic land-scape with pine forest in the El Rodeno (red sandstone) region of the mountains of Albarracín (Teruel), site of the Prado del Navazo and Cocinilla del Obispo caves. *Below:* deer repainted as cattle at Las Olivanas, Tormón, in the Albarracín mountains (Teruel).

Left: Prado del Navazo, Albarracín. Naturalistic paintings in white. The bull is the dominant animal in these caves. Human figures are rare, especially in white.
Above: Cocinilla del Obispo, Albarracín. Head and forequarters of a white bull. As with the red bulls that also appear in these caves, they are very realistically portrayed but with the horns shown in *perspective tordue* (Breuil).

Left: Prado de Navazo, Albarracín (Teruel). A group of naturalistic bulls in white, painted in a variety of styles. The hindquarters of the animal on the right are covered by a thin layer of calcite.

Top: Paridera de las Tajadas, Bezas (Teruel). Pair of deer in white, length 20 cm. *Centre:* Prado de Navazo, Albarracín. White deer. *Below:* white deer and bull.

Ceja de Piezarrodilla,
Albarracín (Teruel).
Black bull painted
over a previous white
one, identical apart
from the horns, which
are modified in the
later figure. Length
0.74 m. The sole
figure in this cave.

Left: Prado de las Olivanas, Tormón (Teruel). Black deer in full colour subsequently repainted as a bull, with alteration of the forelegs and addition of horns. Length 0.34 m.

This page. Above: Cueva del Queso, Alpera (Albacete). Earlier figure, supposedly an elk, with a painting of a bull covering its hooves. *Left:* Cingle de la Cueva Remigia, Ares del Maestre (Castellón). Bull, with multiple layers of paint; somewhat patinated and poorly preserved. Length 0.49 m.

Above left: La Sarga, Alcoy (Alicante). Deer in two distinct styles, painted naturalistically over older schematic symbols.
Below left: La Sarga. Deer with an older zigzag symbol. Length 0.30 m. *Above:* Los Cantos de la Visera, Monte Arabí, Yecla (Murcia): the left section of cave II. Naturalistic deer superimposed over schematic wading-birds. The schematic quadrupeds on the right date from the Bronze Age.

Val del Charco del Agua Amarga, Alcañiz (Teruel). Scene in the central part of the cave, showing a male figure disguised in an animal pelt and with feathers in his cap, being attacked by a deer. Above him, an archer is pursuing a kid.

Below: Val del
Charco del Agua
Amarga, Alcañiz
(Teruel). Archer with
rounded head-dress
and 'gartered' legs.

Above: large-scale
head of a deer
(0.90 m) confronting
the small figure of a
hind. *Right:* tall
female figure
(0.60 m) wearing a
full skirt and cord-
like belt.

Left: Cueva de la Vieja, Alpera (Albacete). Detail of one of the central figures: a man with exaggerated profile (nose and chin) wearing a large feather head-dress. He carries arrows and stands between two bulls, repainted with deer antlers. *Above:* two women in conversation, wearing sumptuous garments and ornaments on their arms.

Far right: Cueva de la Vieja, Alpera (Albacete). Archer with triple curved bow, his arrows behind him. The painting shows gaiters (or 'gartered' legs) and the genital organ.
Above and right: hunting scenes with deer.

Cogul (Lérida). *Above:* black figure of a goat; the horns dissect those of an older, barely visible, example in red. *Below:* hind in red, belonging in a group of naturalistic animals set round the phallic dance scene.

Opposite page. Above: Cuevas de la Araña, Bicorp (Valencia). General view. *Below left:* natural holes in the rock face used to indicate hives, with painted bees flying round them. *Below right:* male figure with genitals.

Above: Minateda (Albacete). General view. *Below:* front part of a little ass, with a hunter holding a short spear. Today the figures in this cave are almost invisible.

*Above:*Cueva del Civil,
Valltorta (Castellón).
Archer, height 14 cm, now in the
Museum at Cervera (Lérida). *Below:*
Els Secans, Mazaleón (Teruel). Archer
and group of people. These figures
have now disappeared.
Following page: Cabra Feixet (Tarragona).
Scene, with detail of deer's head.

Above: Cueva Saltadora, Valltorta (Castellón). General view. *Sketch on this page:* Cueva dels Cavalls, Valltorta (Castellón). The complete hunting scene, with deer grouped in a herd.
Opposite page. Above right: deer, partially covered by water deposited calcite layer. *Lower left:* tiny warrior, with decorated cap. *Lower right:* Cingle de la Mola Remigia, Gasulla (Castellón). Stylised human figure, 5 cm high.

Cueva Remigia,
Gorge of Casulla
(Castellón). *Above:*
goat running towards
the archer who is
aiming at him. The
scene is exagger-
atedly dynamic in
style. *Below:* a
severely wounded
bull.

Cingle de la Mola Remigia, Gasulla (Castellón). Scene with tiny human figures (down to 3 cm in height). At the bottom a man is flaying a goat.

Opposite page. Above left: Cueva Remigia, Gasulla (Castellón). Spider (or beehive), with insects.
Cingle de la Mola Remigia. *Below left:* deer. *Below right:* tiny sprinting figure.
On this page. Above: Racó Gasparo. Female figure, with quadruped and fawn.
Below: general view.

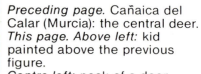

Preceding page. Cañaica del Calar (Murcia): the central deer. *This page. Above left:* kid painted above the previous figure.
Centre left: neck of a deer, showing technique of linear colouring between rough outlines. *Below left:* bear, with clearly indicated claws. *Below right:* the deer from the detail alongside, shown drinking at a water-hole represented by a cavity in the rock.

Opposite page: Solana de la Covachas, Nerpio (Albacete), general view. *Below:* the large deer, finely outlined, with partial colouring. A light red figure of a stylised human is painted below its neck. Vegetable growth obscuring the deer's body is caused by running water.

Right: Solana de las Covachas, Nerpio (Albacete). General view of the main scene in cave V, showing deer and female figures, one with prominent breasts and wearing a straight-sided skirt. In varying techniques: linear, or with colouring between definitive outlines, painted in several shades of red. *Below:* details of the deer antlers and of the tall female figure.

Solana de las Covachas, Nerpio
(Albacete). *Above left and right:*
details from cave V, showing
the technique of crude outline
strokes, without colouring.
Below left: El Prado del Tornero,
Nerpio (Albacete). Chamois.

Opposite page: Peña del Escrito, Villar del Humo (Cuenca). *Above:* Cinto de las Letras, Dos Aguas (Valencia), the central scene. *Below:* general view.

Cinto de las Letras, Dos Aguas (Valencia). *Above:* archer, in cap with ear-like projections and a pouch on his shoulder. *Below:* woman wearing a heavy skirt and carrying a digging-stick, or castanets.

Cinto de las Letras, Dos Aguas (Valencia). *Above:* woman wearing a full skirt, with sticks in her hand (an agricultural rite?). *Below:* men in flat hats and short skirts, and the upper part of a female figure with flowing hair.

Selva Pascuala, Villar del Humo (Cuenca). *Preceding page:* the central scene, with an enlargement of the naturalistic bull. *This page:* scene with lassoed horse and stylised animals. *Opposite page:* El Polvorin, La Cenia (Castellón). The large deer, and scenes with female figure and archers.

Cañada de Marco,
Alcaine (Teruel).
Far left above:
view of the cave.
Far left below:
deer.
This page: human
figure, overlying a
herd of goats with
curved horns.

Above left: Cerro Felío, Alacón (Teruel), general view, with stylised people in the cave of La Tia Mona.
Below: Riparo de Santolea (Teruel).
Above right: Els Vilás de Os, Balaguer (Lérida). Certain figures in this cave are schematic.

Cinto de la Ventana, Dos Aguas (Valencia), general view.
Opposite page: group from the final stylised phase of Levantine art, in dark paint, with schematic signs in light red dating from the Bronze Age.

Los Organos, Despeñaperros (Jaén). Schematic female figures wearing ornaments on their head and neck.

Above: Los Grajos I, Cieza (Murcia). Dance of two women with a quadruped.
Below left: Cueva de Doña Clotilde, Albarracín (Teruel). Schematic human figures, with a rarely found representation of a plant, with fruit.
Below right: Cueva de Bullón, Villar del Humo (Cuenca). Stylised women.

Schematic figures. *Above:* Covacho de la Eudoviges, Alacón (Teruel). *Below:* Riparo de Lecina (Huesca).

Opposite page: Prado del Azogue, Aldeaquemada (Jaén). Deer repainted by extending the body and changing antlers into horns.

Above: La Sarga, Alcoy (Alicante). Parallel meanders from the final schematic phase.
Opposite page: Cañaica del Calar (Murcia). Collection of signs, suns and schematised human and animal figures, from the vicinity of the Levantine caves.
Following page: view of the landscape at Alacón, showing the 'Barranco' of El Motero and Cerro Felío (photograph: E. Anati).